THINKING GLOBALLY

Writing and Reading Across the Curriculum

THINKING GLOBALLY

Writing and Reading Across the Curriculum

Andrew E. Robson, Ph.D.
Utica College of Syracuse University

The McGraw-Hill Companies, Inc.
New York • St. Louis • San Francisco • Auckland • Bogotá
Caracas • Lisbon • London • Madrid • Mexico City • Milan
Montreal • New Delhi • Paris • San Juan • Singapore • Sydney
Tokyo • Toronto

McGraw-Hill 

*A Division of The **McGraw·Hill** Companies*

THINKING GLOBALLY: Writing and Reading Across the Curriculum

Acknowledgments appear on pages 560–562 and on this page by reference.

This book is printed on acid-free paper.

1 2 3 4 5 6 7 8 9 0 FGR FGR 9 0 9 8 7 6

ISBN 0-07-053398-9

This book was set in Stemple Garamond by *The Clarinda Company.*
The editor was *Tim Julet;* the editing manager was *Peggy Rehberger,*
the production supervisor was *Annette Mayeski.*
The design manager was *Joseph A. Piliero;*
the cover was designed by *BC Graphics.*
The photo editor was *Anne Manning.*
The permissions editor was *Cheryl Besenjack.*
New figures were done by *Vantage Art, Inc.*
Project supervision was done by *Tage Publishing Service, Inc.*
Quebecor Printing/Fairfield was printer and binder.

Library of Congress Cataloging-in-Publication Data

Robson, Andrew E.
Thinking globally : writing & reading across the curriculum / Andrew E. Robson.
p. cm.
Includes bibliographical references and index.
ISBN 0-07-053398-9
1. College readers. 2. Interdisciplinary approach in education.
3. Civilization—Problems, exercises, etc. 4. English language—Rhetoric. 5. Readers—Civilization. 6. Academic writing.
I. Title.
PE1417.R586 1997
808' .0427—dc20 96-33227

http//www.mhcollege.com

ABOUT THE AUTHOR

Andrew Robson is currently Associate Professor of English at Utica College of Syracuse University, where he teaches composition, introductory literature, postcolonial literature in English, language and culture, and other courses. He received his B.A. from the University of Nottingham (1968), his P.G.C.E. from the Institute of Education at the University of London (1972), and his Ph.D. from the Australian National University (1984). He also attended Central Michigan University, taking courses for secondary school teaching certification. His career as a teacher and researcher has taken him from England to Western Samoa, Fiji, Solomon Islands, California, North Carolina, New York, Australia, New Zealand, and China. He has visited more than 70 countries.

Professor Robson has written articles on various aspects of composition, literature, TESL, education in developing countries, and history. His most recent work includes "The Use of English in Achebe's *Anthills of the Savannah*" and "The Trial of Consul Pritchard," published in the *Cla Journal* and *The Journal of Pacific History,* respectively. He is currently working on a biography of William Pritchard, who was born in Tahiti in 1829 and who became the first British Consul in Fiji. This project has involved archival research in England, Australia, New Zealand, Hawaii, and the Pacific Islands. In addition, Robson is the author of an independent study/distance education course entitled *Fundamentals of Teaching ESL,* administered by the University of North Carolina.

To Ione, Laura, and Geoffrey

CONTENTS

Unit One: *A Sense of Time*

Unit Two: A Sense of Place

Unit Three: A Sense of Modern History

PREFACE

The idea for this text emerged from my belief that freshman composition courses offer a unique opportunity to improve the academic preparedness of students while still providing effective instruction in writing. This opportunity arises because Composition, perhaps alone in the college curriculum, has little prescribed content, and even this has traditionally been secondary to the general goal of improving writing skills. "Content" has come to mean, most commonly, the writing process, and many texts combine discussion of this process with a series of readings on topics of general interest. Because writing is an essential part of most college courses, the readings in some texts have been selected to reflect the broad college curriculum, with the intention of giving the selections an added relevance to the students' work. That this across-the-curriculum approach continues to be popular is manifest in the widespread use of Behrens and Rosen's *Writing and Reading Across the Curriculum.* There have also, in recent years been a number of texts with more specific thematic content, often emphasizing cultural issues. This increasing interest in the pedagogical potential of the readings seems healthy, and I share it.

Believing that a wide variety of approaches can work, and that the selection and arrangement of readings is significant, I have devised a course that responds to a dual reality faced by many composition teachers: many of our students are not very well prepared for college work and don't read or write very proficiently, while those who *are* well-prepared usually do not see much point in having to take composition courses. I have taught at selective and non-selective colleges and have found this situation at both types of institution. Faced with this, I decided to construct a content-based composition course that would help the less-prepared students by introducing them to readings and concepts that provide useful background for other courses and that would also be of interest to the stronger students. The result is *Thinking Globally,* which, in its preliminary forms, has been well-received by students of very different academic ability and interests.

Although many composition texts have "across-the-curriculum" in their titles, *Thinking Globally* makes a conceptual leap that gives it a fundamentally different character. This consists in explicitly recognizing what is tacitly assumed in some of the more thematic texts, that composition classes can provide information as well as writing instruction, and that, if well-chosen, this information can greatly enhance the basic educational preparedness of students as well as their writing skills. Of course, this is blasphemy to some in the field, but the connection is clear: inadequate general knowledge is a major factor in producing inadequate reading proficiency at the college level; this is the basis of what reading experts call *schema theory.* In turn, inadequate reading skills are a major factor in producing inadequate writing proficiency in college assignments; if students cannot read texts effectively, then they certainly can't write informed essays based on those texts. Some writing problems can be addressed by discussing the writing process, sentence structure, and other traditional elements of the composition class, and these find an important place in *Thinking Globally.* However, deficiencies in writing skills may also be exacerbated by general educational deficiencies, and these are also addressed in this course. The best writing is not only elegant and correct; it is also *informed.* There have been many laments in recent years about the lack of knowledge that students bring to college. Professors often find themselves having to teach background information that students should already know. Students are notoriously deficient, for example, in geographical and historical information. *Thinking Globally* responds to this problem by helping students inform themselves as well as practice writing. This gives the course a special relevance and purpose, and it is this that students tend to like about it.

The range of subject matter may initially surprise both students and professors, but the text makes no undue assumptions. The topics are discussed before the readings are presented, and the latter are annotated in a convenient manner, referring to both content and writing features. For professors, the teacher's manual provides further comments, answers, and suggestions, and suggests films that offer an expert view on the subject-at-hand. I reassure my students at the outset by telling them that the purpose of the course is not to make them instant experts in astronomy, anthropology, environmental studies, and so on, but to give them a little background that they may take into courses in these areas or that they can add to their store of general knowledge. It may be worth mentioning also that the enthusiasm of a teacher for topics beyond his or her specialty can be exemplary. It encourages students to explore new directions and take pleasure in so doing.

Thinking Globally consists of nine units, each of which requires the students to address the kind of ideas and information fundamental to success at college and to an understanding of the contemporary world. Of course, it is impossible to cover everything, but the selections do cover a lot of ground. The titles of each unit are mostly self-explanatory: **A Sense of Time, A Sense of Place, A Sense of Modern History, A Sense of the World, A Sense of Number, A Sense of Nature, A Sense of Values, A Sense of Beauty,** and **A Sense of Humor.** The precise content of each of these units is outlined in the attached table of contents. Each unit provides basic information and terminology that students can take into other classes, and each one is deliberately global in reference, reflecting the increasingly interdependent world we share. At the same time, model essays (on overhead masters in the instructor's manual) and discussion of writing and language—as well as numerous informal and formal writing assignments—guarantee the distinctive character of a composition course.

In more theoretical terms, several principles are applied. First, as in more traditional composition texts, students are taught about organization, process, transitions, and other aspects of writing. They are also required to read essays that demonstrate many of the qualities discussed. These aspects of the course are presented in a way that is visually appealing and that uses a cyclical approach, pointing out details as they occur and re-occur in the essays rather than presenting a discrete chapter on each. Second, the students do a lot of writing, both informal and formal. *Thinking Globally* asks students to "think on paper" as well as to produce fully developed papers. Third, from reading theory and common sense comes the notion that students read more effectively (and are likely to write more effectively also) when they have at least a little prior knowledge to bring to the material. This *does not require that readers have expertise, only that they have a general familiarity with a topic.* This is something that is often missing when students read college-level materials, and it is something that *Thinking Globally* is designed to address. Finally, the course encourages students to enjoy learning. When the material is clearly relevant to other courses, when it is material that many students recognize they ought to know (but often don't), and when it is presented in an appealing but still challenging manner, students respond well.

I have taught draft versions of *Thinking Globally* to freshman composition and remedial classes, and it has been well-received. Many students have described *Thinking Globally* as stimulating, valuable, and different. I have found that students are often delighted to find that the subject matter provides at least some background for topics discussed in other classes; as schema theory predicts, this prior knowledge equips them to read and write more effectively. The response to this course has consistently been positive; most students—once they get over their surprise—recognize that the content is valuable, and most find almost all the material new and stimulating.

The purpose of this course, therefore, is threefold: to improve freshman students' writing, to strengthen their academic preparedness across-the-curriculum, and to enhance their awareness of the global realities that shape their world. The course attempts to strengthen student performance by linking prior knowledge, reading, and writing at a college level. The content is carefully selected, covering in an introductory way many topics that students are likely to encounter in other subject areas and that, even if they don't, will add significantly to their knowledge of the world around them. This focus on *knowing things* helps students understand references and allusions as they read, gives them subjects to write about beyond their personal experience and opinion, and encourages them to begin enjoying a more intellectual life, including an appreciation of the overlapping nature of academic disciplines. Many of the selections in the text were suggested by faculty colleagues from whom I invited suggestions for essays that they would wish all college freshmen to have read before entering their classes; this approach helped ensure that the selections were truly significant in the judgment of experts in different disciplines.

The course design is flexible and practical. It offers the inexperienced teacher a structure that is detailed and easy to follow, but it also allows plenty of scope for the teacher who wishes to adapt, omit, or add to the materials. Each of the nine units has five parts—three "sections" and two "options." Sections One, Two, and Three offer reading alternatives for the majority of students; Option One is intended to challenge stronger students; and Option Two provides discussion of a variety of language-related topics that are intended to stimulate interest in, and understanding of, how English works. Many students, even among the better-prepared, have little familiarity with grammar, etymology, and other linguistic topics, and much of the knowledge they do have comes from the study of other languages. For this reason, most students find this Option to be valuable.

Each of the sections has four parts:

1. **Prior knowledge:** An orientation to the topic, providing relevant vocabulary, discussion of issues, and thought-provoking remarks. Short **Think on paper** exercises are suggested. This section provides background that enables students to read the following selection more effectively. It also provides bits of information and general knowledge and **vocabulary webs.** Throughout the text, many opportunities are provided for students to use dictionaries and to notice the common roots of words, thereby helping themselves in both vocabulary and spelling.
2. **Annotated reading:** An article, essay, or extract, with annotations drawing attention to ideas and writing points. As noted earlier, many of these texts have been suggested by professors in different fields, and they all provide, in different ways, a valuable orientation to the kind of thinking characteristic of particular disciplines. The annotations point out noteworthy aspects of the writing, as well as the use of techniques in organization and transition that may readily be applied by the students. The readings vary in length and difficulty, and professors and/or students may choose which individual essays, or groups of essays, to read.

3. **Aspects of writing:** A discussion of a particular aspect of writing, concerning the writing process, organization, or other practical matters. Usually, such material forms a discrete section, or chapter, of composition texts, but here these discussions are part of every section. This approach gives the professor many opportunities to have frequent, but focused, discussions on writing and language. Such discussion of language is on-going throughout *Thinking Globally,* but takes on a more formal character here.
4. **Writing exercises:** A choice of writing exercises based on the reading, class discussion, and other sources, such as films, which may be used to provide additional information; relevant films for each unit are suggested in the instructor's manual. Recognizing that not all classes, or all individual students, are at the same level, this section offers the professor considerable flexibility. Some of the questions require more sophisticated responses than others. An informal written response could be required in some cases and a formal paper in others. Some questions are analytical in nature; others elicit a personal response. They are only suggestions; the professor may prefer others. The formulation of questions as a class exercise is also a good way of stimulating thinking and generating discussion; it is a way of teaching students how to make generalizations about what they have read and discussed—and of checking their ability to do so. Advice on an aspect of writing is also included. This section of Option One in each Unit is called **Writing and research** and offers suggestions on the writing of research papers as well as questions that may be used as research topics.

The final part of each unit is a **Quick Quiz,** which gives students a chance to show what they have learned in terms of general knowledge associated with the thematic and linguistic topics presented. This also gives the instructor an opportunity to review the material in an informal way and assess, orally perhaps, how effectively the students read and remember what is presented in each unit.

Thinking Globally brings a new spirit and purpose to composition teaching. It is serious but good-humored, and it makes the composition course central to the freshman experience by providing a coherent, focused, college-level content that really helps prepare students for what lies ahead.

Thanks to the following reviewers for their valuable comments and insights: Deborah Barberousse, Montgomery Community College; Robert Brannon, Johnson County Community College; Liz Buckley, East Texas State University; Kathleen Shine Cain, Merrimack College;

Jerome Cartwright, Utica College of Syracuse University; Dorothy M. Guinn, Florida Atlantic University; Lee Hammer, Culver-Stockton College; Marilyn Jody, Western Carolina University; Diana Matza, Utica College of Syracuse University; David Page, Montgomery Community College; Donna Burns Phillips, Cleveland State University; Karen Varanauskas, Central Michigan University.

Thanks also, for their suggestions and interest, to my colleagues at Utica College: Professors Frank Bergmann, Jim Caron, Jerry Cartwright, Bill Gotwald, Robert Halliday, Dave Harralson, John Johnsen, Judy McIntyre, Diane Matza, Hy Muskatt, Ted Orlin, and Bill Pfeiffer; for grant support: Thom Brown and Utica College as an institution; for library support: Kristin Strohmeyer and Julia Dickinson at Hamilton College, Liz Pattengill and Eileen Kramer at Utica College, and Deb Stannard at the Leelanau Townsend Library in Northport, Michigan; at Tage Publishing Service, thanks to Tony Caruso; for bringing my earliest drafts to the attention of the publisher, Kathy Fagin; and bringing the project to fruition, Phil Butcher and everyone else involved at McGraw-Hill and associated contractors, as listed on the copyright page; thanks especially to Tim Julet, who has been involved from the beginning.

Andrew E. Robson

THINKING GLOBALLY

Writing and Reading Across the Curriculum

SECTION ONE

PRIOR KNOWLEDGE: In the beginning. . . .

Normal human curiosity leads most people to wonder about the origin of our planet, our universe, and ourselves. We wonder how and why everything came into existence, and we also wonder *when.* All societies have thought about this, and such thoughts have led to the development of creation stories around the world. All cultures have their own creation stories, and some of these have become very closely associated with particular religions. Some of these religious stories are shared by millions of believers, and some are held in common by the great religions. The *Genesis* account of the Creation, for example, is shared by Jews, Christians, and Moslems.

To read *any* text with ease and understanding, you need to understand not just the words but also the **references,** or **allusions.** For example, on this page there are references to *Genesis,* Adam and Eve, the Bible, the great religions, and so on. Writers usually don't explain references that they consider to be so much a part of our common culture as to be familiar to everyone. They *assume* you know. This is why a good general knowledge is so important.

Using the Bible as a text, some people have tried to calculate the age of the Earth by counting back through the Biblical generations to Adam and Eve. By this method, an Irish cleric named James Ussher concluded in 1654 that the Earth was created on October 26, 4004 B.C., at 9:00 a.m. This date, like similar ones calculated by other people, corresponds roughly with the beginning of the earliest human civilizations—about 6,000 years ago, but for more than a hundred years it has been seen to be incompatible with the timescales of **geo**logy, and, more recently, of **paleo**ntology, **anthro**pology, and **astro**nomy. Creation stories are often beautiful, and they certainly have helped untold millions of people come to terms with what is perhaps the ultimate mystery, but science has given us an entirely different timescale.

Many **Latin** words and phrases—often abbreviated—have found niches in English, especially in writing, but even some of the more familiar ones are not always well understood. Here are a few examples:
A.D.—*anno Domini*—the year of the Lord (NOT "After Death," as many people think).
vide—see (as in *vide* p. 17).
i.e.—*id est*—that is.
e.g.—*exempli gratia*—for example.
viz.—*videlicet*—that is, namely.

The most widely accepted scientific version of creation is known as the **big bang.** Science does not claim to know absolute truth, and so new evidence can alter this version, but the basic story is one in which

Your dictionary should tell you that the word astronomy comes from the Greek *astron,* or *aster,* meaning "star." Now find the meanings of *geo, paleo,* and *anthro.*

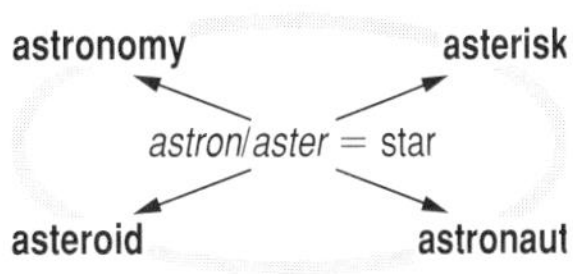

The precise date of the **big bang** is not known, but 8–20 billion years ago is the usual range. One theory predicts that, billions of years in the future, the universe will stop expanding and will go into reverse. Time will go backward and the universe will eventually be reduced once again to microscopic size. Then, perhaps, there will be another big bang, and the whole thing will start all over again.

As you read this text (or any book or newspaper), try to take note of the names of well-known people, events, books, etc. **Stephen Hawking,** for example, is one of the great mathematicians of modern times. Although Lou Gehrig's disease has left him virtually unable to move and unable to speak, he continues to investigate the mysteries of black holes and other secrets of the physical universe. He authored a best-selling book in 1990, called *A Brief History of Time.* A movie has been made about Hawking under the same title.

The Hubble space telescope and other modern instruments are designed to see deep into space, using not only light, but x-rays, radio waves, and more. In 1994, evidence from the Hubble indicated that the universe is only 8–10 billion years old. Since many stars are apparently older than this, there was clearly a lot more to be learned. In 1996, however, other researchers, also using the Hubble, claimed to have established the age of the universe at 15 billion years.

most scientists today have considerable confidence. A contemporary scientific account might open something like this:

> In the beginning, the universe was a small, dense object; all its matter was packed into a microscopically small space. About 15 billion years ago, this matter exploded. The universe started to expand at an extremely fast pace, and as it expanded it cooled. About ten billion years ago the galaxies formed, and five billion years later our solar system came into being.

This account may seem as incredible as any creation myth, but there is a lot of evidence to support it. The Earth, then, is about five billion years old, and this is confirmed by geologists, who have found rocks that are four billion years old. Cosmology gives us the ultimate timescale (of which we have any knowledge), and scientists and mathematicians such as **Stephen Hawking** talk of the big bang as the beginning of time.

The night sky is not just a collection of individual stars. Many of the "stars" are actually entire galaxies, far beyond our own Milky Way. When we look at the most distant stars, we are seeing light that has traveled for more than ten billion years. We are seeing the star as it was all that time ago. We are, in fact, looking backward in time. Modern instruments such as the **Hubble telescope** enable astronomers to see back almost to the beginning of the universe.

What is the *literal* meaning of these words?

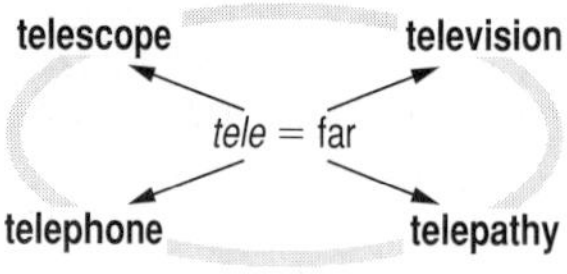

ANNOTATED READING: James S. Trefil. "The First Yesterday." *SpaceTimeInfinity.* Washington: Smithsonian Books, 1985: 10–11.

The First Yesterday

How it began, no one is quite sure. The evidence strongly suggests, however, that a tiny fraction of a second after the moment of its creation, our universe consisted of a dense, rapidly expanding collection of matter. It wasn't the familiar, homey kind of stuff that surrounds us now, sedately composed of atoms, but a swarm of strange and exotic particles with names like *gluon*, *quark*, and *boson*. Impossibly dense, impossibly hot, the universe expanded; and as it did so, it cooled. The cooling, in turn, wrought changes in the matter, something along the lines of water freezing into ice.

In the case of the universe, one such change followed another as what passed for matter cooled through the various phase changes. Before the first microsecond had elapsed, the universe had "frozen" three times, each time becoming relatively more familiar, as the exotic particles present at the beginning combined or decayed to produce matter in a more organized and potentially recognizable form.

After about 10 microseconds, the important fourth freezing occurred. Those particles we call quarks came together to form other, more familiar particles. These include the protons and neutrons that exist today in the nuclei of atoms.

But the temperature was still far too high, and the collisions of the particles too violent, for anything so complex as a nucleus to remain intact. After three minutes, the temperature had dropped to the point where nuclei of hydrogen and helium atoms swam in a sea consisting

Notice that, right from the outset, Trefil acknowledges that there is a lot we don't know about the origin of the universe. This does not mean, however, that we don't know *anything* about it. Good scientists are very careful about claiming to know the truth, because it is always possible that new discoveries will change the way we understand events. The Gould article in this unit offers more discussion on this.

"A tiny fraction of a second" here is no exaggeration. Most scientific accounts of the creation of the universe begin 10^{-43} second after the beginning. This number would be written as a zero and a point, followed by 42 zeros and a one. In words, it is a tenth of a thousandth of a millionth of a billionth of a trillionth of a trillionth of a second. Many scientists are trying to understand what happened in this fraction of a second.

"The moment of creation" is generally known as the **"big bang."**

You don't have to know the nature of these particles, but it's good to be able to recognize words such as "quark," for example.

After the big bang, the universe expanded and cooled with dramatic suddenness, and so it was the size of the present solar system before it was even one second old. The minuscule periods of time that scientists discuss in these early moments of the universe form a striking contrast with the vast periods of time that follow.

The expansion of the universe is continuing today. One of the great questions this poses concerns the fate of the universe. A concept called the **"open universe"** suggests that the universe will continue expanding forever; another concept, the **"closed universe,"** suggests that gravity will eventually stop the expansion and will put it into reverse. The universe would contract and eventually be compressed into the miniscule state in which it started. Perhaps then another big bang would occur and the whole thing would start all over again! The closed-universe idea is probably the favorite today, because there seems to be growing evidence that there is a lot of so-called "dark matter" in the universe, which would increase the overall gravitational effect and would eventually slow down and reverse the expansion of the universe.

It is important, of course, to understand the basic geography of the universe today in order to understand Trefil's account. The **universe** is everything that we know; it includes all the **galaxies** and all the space and matter between them. There are believed to be at least 100 billion galaxies in the universe, the most familiar one to us being our own **Milky Way** galaxy. The fact that the universe consists of more than one galaxy was not completely accepted until the publication in 1923 of a paper by the astronomer Edwin Hubble (after whom the space telescope is named). As you can see, our understanding of the universe has been transformed in the twentieth century. Each galaxy consists of an average of about 100 billion **stars,** the most familiar of which to us is the sun. The sun, then, is just one star among 100 billion in our galaxy! Around the sun, and probably many other stars (we don't know for sure, because planets are hard to see) are **planets.** The sun's planetary system is called the **solar system** and one of these planets is the **Earth.**

of loose electrons mixed with the hot radiation left over from the first seconds. All the building blocks of modern materials existed in their final forms. Time alone was needed for cooling until the electrons and the nuclei could come together to make atoms.

This required another half million years, during which the mixture of nuclei, electrons, and radiation continued to expand and cool. The outward pressure of radiation kept the particles spread out so that little or no clumping occurred. Once atoms were formed, however, the matter in the universe became transparent and the radiation could no longer exert as much pressure as before. From then on, the force of gravity began to dominate the behavior of the universe.

Here and there, scattered throughout the uniform distribution of atoms that filled space, we see small concentrations of matter. How they came about is still a subject of debate, but their effect is clear. Because the mass at these points was higher than normal, nearby atoms were pulled into the concentration zone by the force of gravity. The new atoms, in turn, added their contribution to the force of gravity and yet more material was attracted. In short order, the smeared-out collection of atoms that characterized the universe prior to the 500-million-year mark was transformed into a collection of large, discrete clouds of material. Inside these clouds, the same process of gravitational clumping went on, dividing the newly formed clouds into smaller clouds that would eventually become the clusters of galaxies. At the same time, the overall expansion that started with the Big Bang continued; the distances between groups of galaxies continued to increase.

Shifting our attention from the overall structure of the universe to a single protogalaxy, we see the gravitational forces continuing to segregate the gas cloud into small pieces. As these small bits of gas contracted, the pressure and temperature at their centers began to increase. It quickly became so hot that electrons were stripped from the atoms. Soon temperatures rose to the point where nuclear reactions were ignited and hydrogen fused into helium. The energy streaming out from the new fusion furnace created a pressure that balanced the inward force of gravity, and stars were born.

These early suns were made from a gas containing only the primordial atoms of hydrogen and helium that were created three minutes after the Big Bang; but the nuclear reactions that went on during the life and death of the early stars quickly produced other chemical elements. Explosions and other less dramatic star deaths dispersed metal-rich gases into the clouds of the newborn galaxies. Stars that emerged from such a polluted medium contained chemical elements heavier than helium and hydrogen. As they matured and died, these stars also manufactured new atoms of their own. In essence, they operated like the legendary alchemical crucible—transmuting one element into another. This slow process of star creation, element production, and star death went on for about 10 billion years in galaxies throughout the universe.

Then, about five billion years ago, a particular bit of enriched gas began to contract. It was located about a third of the way out in the arm of a spiral galaxy we call the Milky Way. It also began to spin faster and faster, much as ice skaters do by pulling their arms in closer to the body. The rotation became so fast that, while most of the gas in the clouds wound up in the newly forming star, some was left spread out in a thin disk. As the star was forming, this disk broke up and arranged itself (by a process whose details are poorly understood) into a series of relatively small bodies orbiting the hub. The center grew denser and hotter. When the star finally ignited, the resulting stream of outgoing particles blew the remaining gas from the system, leaving a sun with planets—nine at best count.

On the third planet, a series of rather extraordinary events started to unfold, beginning with the evolution of an atmosphere and—after a billion years—culminating with a series of simple one-celled organisms we would grace with the title "living creatures." They spread, became more complex, and, after billions of years, moved from the oceans to the land. Eventually the planet came to be dominated by huge reptiles. They, like other species before them, passed on and mammals moved to center stage, and for more than 60 million years the world teemed with their forms.

Finally, a few million years ago, the first of our lineage appeared upon the planet. The iron in their blood, the calcium in their bones, and the carbon in their tissues were all the stuff of stars. These new creatures gradually learned the use of primitive stone tools, then fire. Social groups developed agriculture and built powerful and long lasting civilizations based upon their accumulated wealth. Somewhere along the line—no one really knows when—some human being somewhere looked back up at the stars and wondered.

That's where our story begins.

Notice Trefil's account here of the birth, life, and death of stars. Our sun, too, will eventually "die," and some projections indicate that the Earth will become uninhabitable in about 1.5 billion years.

Notice Trefil's shift to the formation of the solar system, five billion years ago, and then to the story of life on Earth. One well-known way to think about the timescales of creation is to put all these events onto a 24-hour clock, beginning at midnight and ending now. If the big bang occurred at midnight, the Earth formed at 4 p.m., and the first humans walked the Earth about two seconds ago.

Rhetorical note: This essay is **informative,** but it is also a **narrative.** The organization is principally *chronological,* but Trefil also uses *spatial order.*

Astronomical distances are measured in light years. One light year is the distance traveled by light in one year, and that is 5.88 trillion miles. The sun's next-door neighbors in the Milky Way—the nearest stars—Proxima Centauri and Alpha Centauri—are "only" about 4.2 and 4.4 light years away.

ASPECTS OF WRITING: Chronological and spatial order.

When you write, you could simply put everything down on paper as it came into your head; this, however, would probably be very confusing to read. You need to organize information so that the reader can follow your meaning. The way you do this will depend on the nature of the paper you are writing, but when you are giving an account of something that happened over a period of time, **chronological order** will probably be the best choice.

If you look again at Trefil's essay, you'll see that he starts at the beginning of time—the big bang—and continues systematically through the major events in the formation of the universe until he reaches the creation of the Earth itself, five billion years ago. He then takes us briefly through the history of life on Earth, ending with humans looking up at the stars and "wondering." Trefil, then, uses strict chronological order.

Just as important as the overall organization is the way in which the writer moves from point to point. Look at Trefil's essay again and you should be able to identify transitional words and phrases that take the reader from one point in time to the next. The first of these is introductory; Trefil states, "How it began, no one is quite sure." In the next sentence he takes us to a particular moment, "a tiny fraction of a second after the moment of [the universe's] creation."

Such phrases often occur at, or near, the beginning of paragraphs, as in paragraph three, which begins, "After about 10 microseconds." In paragraph four, the transitional phrase occurs in the second sentence: "After three minutes." A slightly different situation calls for a different transition in paragraph five, where Trefil moves us through the next half-million years, "during which" various changes took place in the universe.

Notice that when you are looking for information in an essay, you look for **statements of fact,** but when analyzing how an essay is organized, you look at **structural words** and **phrases.** *Facts are important, but, in writing a coherent paper, the way you string information together matters just as much.*

Now comes a little complication. At one point Trefil's topic requires him to shift away from a simple chronology and toward a form of organization called **spatial order.** He has to move the reader's attention toward particular places, rather than particular moments in time or periods of time. He does this very clearly, using phrases that are visual and spatial in nature: "Here and there," "Shifting our attention . . . to a single protogalaxy," and so on. He also combines such transitions when necessary, as when he writes, "Then, about five billion years ago, a particular bit of enriched gas began to contract." Essay topics often require the use of more than one organizational pattern, even if only one usually predominates. The important thing is to make sure the reader can follow your line of reasoning, or your train of thought.

> Look through Trefil's essay and identify transitional phrases of each type mentioned above. Notice how effectively he leads the reader from one point to the next.

WRITING EXERCISES: Choose one of the following.

Certain qualities are always important when you write. Three to remember are listed below.
Clarity can be achieved in part by making sure you know what you want to say and by taking the time to organize your essay in a logical fashion.
Coherence can be achieved in part by using the fact that you are an expert in language; you use it every day. Read as you write, making sure that you know the meaning of words, that sentences make sense, and that paragraphs are well focused.
Precision counts on several fronts. Words have precise meanings; use them correctly. Information can be wrong; check that what you write is correct.

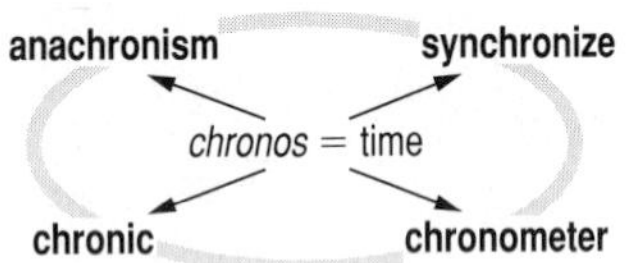

Good writing is impossible without good *thinking*.

The length of these pieces of work will be decided by you and/or your professor. Clarity is more important than length, but imagine that you are explaining the history of the universe to someone who knows nothing about it. Make it useful; make it interesting; make it comprehensible. The first essay asks you to use only the information in Trefil's essay; the second allows you to include any relevant information available to you. The third is comparative in nature.

1. Write a summary of Trefil's essay. Make sure that you refer to the author throughout the summary, so that the reader recognizes that you are summarizing someone else's work. Make sure that you put the events into chronological order.
2. In chronological order, list the most significant events leading from the big bang to the universe we have today. Include any relevant information that you already know or that is generated in class discussion, as well as information from Trefil. Write an account of the creation of the universe based on this information. Try to achieve coherence, clarity, and precision.
3. Read (or reread) one of the religious or mythological accounts of Creation (that in *Genesis,* for example). Compare this with Trefil's account of the big bang. You could start your essay something like this:

All societies have tried to explain the origins of the Earth, and today we have a scientific account as well as the traditional mythological or religious stories.

SECTION TWO

PRIOR KNOWLEDGE: Life, Time, and Us.

Compared with the approximately fifteen-billion-year timescale of the universe, geological time covers a relatively short period. As we've seen, the Earth—along with the rest of the solar system—has existed for only about five billion years. Humans have lived on Earth for a far shorter time.

Geologists have found fossil evidence of a mass extinction of species in the late Cretaceous period, about 65 million years ago. This extinction included the dinosaurs. The end of the giant dinosaurs opened the way for the so-called Age of Mammals. Other mass extinctions occurred between the Paleozoic and Mesozoic, about 225 million years ago, when 96% of all marine species became extinct, and, possibly, between the Precambrian and the Paleozoic, about 570 million years ago.

No one knows exactly how life began on Earth, but a lot of evidence suggests the sequence in which life evolved. This evidence is found in the fossil record. Stephen Jay Gould, a leading expert in this field, has noted that the evolution of life is not preordained or inevitable; there's a lot of chance involved. If the evolutionary clock could be rewound and started over again, says Gould, there is virtually no possibility that the creatures that inhabit the Earth today would exist.

The history of life on Earth is complex, and there is much that even the experts don't know, but one significant event—the development of our oxygen-rich atmosphere—is believed to have occurred about one billion years ago. This facilitated the evolution of countless species familiar to us today. Life existed before this event, however. The fossil record shows that single-cell marine organisms existed 3.4 billion years ago.

Use your Dictionary to find the precise meanings of these words

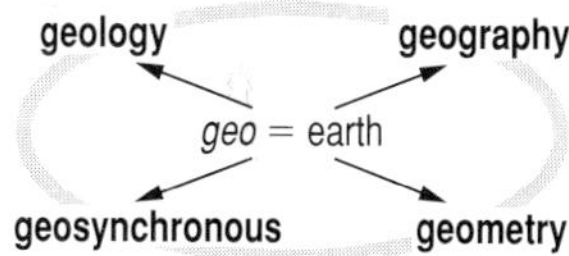

Gould and others have suggested that evolution is not a slow, steady, process of change and "improvement." Sometimes, long periods may pass with little change in the patterns of life on Earth, but then sudden change may occur, perhaps as the result of extraordinary events that alter the habitat of the Earth's creatures.

THINK ON PAPER
What kind of "extraordinary event" could affect the evolutionary process and perhaps lead to mass extinctions?

The Scales of Time chart on page 11 amalgamates the standard geological charts and information on the timescales of the big bang and life on Earth. Of course, the chart is not to scale. If you're not sure why, perhaps you'd like to redraw it to scale! It's also important to note that the dates listed are based on information presently available. New evidence is likely to change some of the numbers.

Richard Leakey and his parents, Mary and Louis Leakey, are among the important names in modern research into human origins. Most of their work has been done in East Africa, in Tanzania's Olduvai Gorge, and in Kenya, where they live.

The first thing the chart makes clear is that humans have been on Earth for a very short time. Modern humans have existed for only 40,000 to 100,000 years. Interestingly, even the experts don't agree on the identity of our ancestors. Neanderthals are believed by some experts, such as **Richard Leakey,** to have been among our immediate ancestors (so we are all part-Neanderthal, in effect), but by others to have been an evolutionary "dead end," with no modern descendants.

The fact that all the oldest hominid remains have been found in East and Southern Africa is one reason for the belief that all humans have African origins. Of course, if bones of an equal age are ever found elsewhere in the world, this theory will have to be reevaluated.

One fact is clear: all human beings on Earth today belong to the same species. At times in the past, different human types existed simultaneously, but this is not true today. All human types except ***Homo sapiens sapiens*** (us) have died out. We don't know why this is so, even for our most recent human ancestors (if that is what they were), the Neanderthals. Perhaps they were killed by modern humans, and perhaps they interbred and eventually became modern humans.

THINK ON PAPER
If Neanderthal, or some other earlier human type, lived alongside modern humans today, how do you think we would treat them? What would the relationship be?

Another controversy concerns location. Did modern humans evolve in Africa and spread from there around the world, or did we evolve in different locations around the world, in a parallel fashion? The "single-source" concept has been popular in recent years, but some evidence supports the second theory.

The most famous **hominid** remains are those of "Lucy," who lived 3.5 million years ago. In 1994, however, a hominid with some human and some chimpanzee features was found in Ethiopia by a team led by **Tim White,** an American paleoanthropologist. This presumed human ancestor—*Australopithecus ramidus*—is 4.4 million years old. The press has called it "the missing link," and it may tell us when our line diverged from the apes.

The Scales of Time

Geological Periods			Years Before Present
Cenozoic	Quaternary	Holocene	11,000
		Pleistocene	2 million
	Tertiary		63 million
Mesozoic	Cretaceous		135 million
	Jurassic		180 million
	Triassic		230 million
Paleozoic	Permian		280 million
	Carboniferous		345 million
	Devonian		405 million
	Silurian		425 million
	Ordovician		500 million
	Cambrian		600 million

Life on Earth	Years Ago
Modern humans	40,000+
Homo sapiens (Neanderthal)	100,000
Homo sapiens (archaic)	200,000
Homo erectus	1 million+
Homo habilis	2 million+
Australopithecus boisei	2 million+
Australopithecus robustus	2 million+
Australopithecus africanus	3 million
Australopithecus afarensis	3.5 million+
Australopithecus ramidus	4.4 million
Age of Mammals begins	
Age of Dinosaurs ends	64 million
First birds	
First dinosaurs	
First mammals	
First amphibians, reptiles, insects	
Age of Fishes	
First fish, land plants	

Precambrian	Years Before Present	Life on Earth
	1 billion	Earth's present atmosphere develops
	2 billion	Plants begin oxygen production
	3 billion	Oceans form
	3–4 billion	Life on Earth begins (oldest fossils)
	5 billion	Earth and solar system form
	10 billion	First galaxies form
	15(?) billion	Big bang

ANNOTATED READING: William F. Allman. "Who we were: The origins of modern humans" *U.S. News and World Report* 16 Sept. 1991: 53–60.

All people alive today are "modern humans," but our ancestry is uncertain. This article discusses some of the controversies.

In 1856, workers digging in a quarry in Germany's Neander Valley unearthed an aged skeleton. Its stooping limbs and heavy brow led anthropologists to conclude it was the remains of a diseased Mongolian Cossack who had died during the Napoleonic Wars. But subsequent discoveries of similar "diseased Mongolians" eventually revealed that in fact the skeletons belonged to a humanlike creature who had lived tens of thousands of years before. Dubbed Neanderthal, the ancient creature not only gave scientists the first clear evidence for Darwin's suggestion that humans had descended from an apelike ancestor, but its hulking form and bony forehead also etched the image of the brutish cave man indelibly in the public mind.

The "dumb caveman" stereotype is based on a paleontological error. The first Neanderthal skeleton seemed to be stooped over and bowlegged, but later analysis showed that this individual had suffered from severe arthritis, and the skeleton was, therefore, not typical. By then, however, the damage was already done; Neanderthal had entered the public imagination as a shambling, dim-witted creature.

More than a century later, new findings about this still mysterious creature continue to redefine humanity's sense of itself. Research has revealed that far from being dumb brutes, Neanderthals were intelligent creatures who were superbly adapted to their Ice Age environment. Even more important, studies of the Neanderthals are providing fresh clues to one of the hottest, most contentious questions in anthropology: Where did our kind, *Homo Sapiens*, come from? The public's imagination about human origins has long been captivated by spectacular finds of fossils millions of years old, but recent research suggests that these ancient ancestors were in fact far from being "almost human." There is now a growing consensus that it was only with the comparatively recent emergence of "anatomically modern" people that the human lineage took the gigantic leap into truly human behavior. These ancient humans—who wouldn't warrant a second look on a subway car today—appear to have been the first to make complex tools, use sophisticated hunting techniques, stage elaborate burials of the dead, use body ornamentation and create works of art. "The earliest fossils get all the attention," says paleontologist Matthew Nitecki of the Field Museum of Natural History in Chicago. "But the real question is, *who are we*?"

The last **ice age** ended only about 11,000 years ago. It has long been believed that, at about this time, Asian people began to move into North America across the Bering Straits; however, considerable evidence now exists that this migration began much earlier.

The debate over the origins of anatomically modern humans has undergone a sea change over the past several years. Nearly all anthropologists agree that the human lineage began some 2.5 million years ago with a creature known as *Homo habilis*, a hominid that walked upright, had a brain larger than that of any ape and was the first to use stone tools. About 1.6 million years ago, this primitive human

Here, Allman summarizes two theories about the origin of modern humans. The fossil record is still incomplete, and the debate continues. Newspapers often carry articles describing new discoveries that influence this debate. Look out for them!

species gave rise to a brainier human ancestor, *Homo erectus*, which spread out of Africa into much of the Near East, Europe and Asia. Researchers have long believed that these various populations of H. *erectus* that existed throughout the Old World simultaneously evolved into modern humans—*Homo Sapiens*. In this "multiregional" scenario, Neanderthals are thought to have been among the transitional hominids that led to modern Europeans.

But now some researchers have begun to argue that only a few of H. *erectus*'s descendants went on to become modern humans. These researchers believe that *Homo sapiens* arose as a small population some 200,000 to 100,000 years ago, then quickly swept through the world, replacing all other humanlike creatures who lived at the time—including Neanderthals. Recently revised dates of anatomically modern human fossils seem to suggest an African origin: The oldest modern human fossils, dating from more than 100,000 years ago, have been uncovered in Africa, and another fossil found close by in what is now Israel has been recently dated at about 100,000 years old.

In 1994, a revised dating of hominid fossils found in Java indicated that our ancestors left Africa much earlier than had hitherto been assumed. This suggests that modern humans may have evolved separately, but at about the same time, in different parts of the world, but this issue is by no means settled.

If correct, this "Out of Africa model" has profound implications for the human species. The theory implies, for instance, that all humans are very recent descendants of African stock and that the various races today reflect only superficial physical differences. Even more important, the Out of Africa model suggests that modern human beings are not an inevitable product of evolution but rather the sole survivor among many different kinds of brainy, bipedal primates that have peopled the earth for the past 3 million years—and that they in fact may have contributed to some of those other creatures' demise.

Allman makes an interesting reference here to two ramifications of the "out-of-Africa" hypothesis. This is a good example of how you, too, can make your essays interesting; comment on the significance of what you write.

As in most such accounts, Allman's dates are approximations. You may remember that "Lucy," one of the "bipedal primates" referred to here, is about 3.5 million years old.

By an accident of history, Europe is a crucial testing ground for theories about modern human origins. Not only is the continent teeming with professional anthropologists; climatic and geological conditions there are ideal for preserving fossils. So despite the fact that most researchers consider Europe an evolutionary cul-de-sac compared with Africa and Asia in the grand story of the development of humans, it nevertheless is one of the places where the details of early humans' lives are best preserved.

This summer, researchers in Europe provided a major boost to the Out of Africa model. Physicist Norbert Mercier of the Center of Low-Level Radioactivity in France and his colleagues showed that for perhaps several thousand years, Neanderthals lived side by side with anatomically modern humans in Western Europe.

The Neanderthals and the Cro-Magnons coexisted in Europe about 36,000 years ago. The Neanderthals had broader faces, with heavier brow ridges; their relatively thick bones also suggest that they were significantly stronger than modern humans. The tools made by Neanderthals were more sophisticated than those of their ancestors, but their scrapers and spearpoints were crude compared with the sophisticated technology of the Cro-Magnons.

Evolution's Dead End. By dating bits of flint that had been discovered along with a Neanderthal skeleton, the researchers found that the Neanderthal lived as recently as 36,000 years ago—at least several thousand years after modern humans are thought to have arrived in Europe. The dating of this "last" Neanderthal suggests that Nean-

Although the Cro-Magnons were much weaker physically than Neanderthals, their technological advances more than made up for this deficiency. They (one is tempted to say "we") used reindeer antlers and materials such as ivory to make spear points, jewelry, fishhooks, harpoons, and needles for stitching clothes. Their stone tools also showed greater variety and greater sophistication of workmanship than those of earlier human types.

Notice that brain *size* was not the crucial factor in determining which human type survived to the present day.

derthals could not possibly be ancestors of modern Europeans, says anthropologist Christopher Stringer of the Natural History Museum in London, one of the leading proponents of the Out of Africa model. Instead, he says, Neanderthals were an evolutionary "dead end" that disappeared with the arrival in Europe of *Homo sapiens*—whom anthropologists call "Cro-Magnons" after the French site where their fossils were first discovered.

In many ways, the Neanderthal and Cro-Magnon were very much alike; most researchers, in fact, classify them as closely related "subspecies" of *Homo Sapiens*. Both were two-legged creatures who made tools, used fire and buried their dead, though earlier claims that Neanderthals ceremoniously decorated graves with flowers or bones are now disputed. Neanderthals appear to have been mentally sophisticated. Indeed, their brains are estimated to have been slightly larger than those of today's humans. Studies of Neanderthal skulls by Columbia University's Ralph Holloway and others reveal that Neanderthal brains also display the same kinds of overall structure as those of modern humans, indicating that Neanderthals probably used at least some kind of rudimentary language and were predominantly right-handed.

Notice how Allman refers to a number of experts in the course of this essay. These people are "expert witnesses" who contribute their ideas and research to the debate. *Notice, however, that the "witnesses" and their evidence are selected by the author, who integrates these ideas into his essay.* Even though Allman makes liberal use of such experts, there is never any doubt that this is *his* essay; all the quotes and paraphrases are introduced in support of topics Allman is discussing, but he does not allow them to take over. His essay is a good example of the kind of balance between author and sources that you should try to achieve in documented papers.

Fit for Survival. Recent studies suggest, however, that while Neanderthals were by no means the dumb cave dwellers they were portrayed to be at the turn of the century, neither were they merely a minor variant of modern humans. According to Erik Trinkaus of the University of New Mexico, the thick, sturdy leg and arm bones of the Neanderthals reveal that they were far more powerfully built and could lift perhaps twice as much as Cro-Magnon people. The Neanderthals' apparent strength, says Trinkaus, is evidence that they relied more on their bodies than their wits for survival.

Neanderthals also were shorter than modern humans and had shorter arm and leg bones. Some researchers believe that may have been an evolutionary adaptation to cold weather. Shorter limbs mean that the body radiates less heat. Neanderthals are thought to have existed in Europe for more than 100,000 years, during which time the landscape was frequently covered by glaciers. In contrast, Cro-Magnon people appear to have been long and lanky—an easy-to-cool body type that is better suited to the tropics of Africa. The marked physical differences between modern humans and Neanderthals have led some researchers to conclude there was little likelihood of interbreeding between the two.

Allman always tells us who his sources are and indicates their credentials by telling us where they work. This gives the reader some confidence that these people are worth listening to; they may not agree (and notice that Allman makes no attempt at all to hide these disagreements), but they all have genuine expertise. When you write papers of this sort, you should follow this kind of model.

Some anthropologists are uncomfortable with the Out of Africa model because it suggests that modern humans must have committed widespread genocide to replace the other hominids in their path. Yet the newly revised dates of the "last" Neanderthal indicate that, despite being at a distinct technological disadvantage vis-à-vis the Cro-Magnons, the Neanderthals managed to hang on in Europe for thousands of years. They "went out with a whimper," Stringer contends, "not a bang."

The Cro-Magnons need not have been physically overpowering to displace the Neanderthals. According to research by Ezra Zubrow of the State University of New York at Buffalo, even if the Cro-Magnons caused as little as a 2 percent decrease in the Neanderthals' overall population growth through indirect competition for food, shelter or other resources, the Neanderthals would have died out in as few as 30 generations, or about 1,000 years. What's more, Cro-Magnons had longer life spans: Bone studies by Trinkaus suggest that Neanderthals barely lived into their 40s, whereas Cro-Magnons appear to have lived well into their 50s. In a time when there was no written word, says Trinkaus, having elders who remembered and passed on vital information about how to deal with severe climate, for instance, may have been crucial to survival.

Having discussed several factors that possibly contributed to the success of Cro-Magnons, Allman uses a nice transition to introduce what may be the most important factor: "But the ultimate factor. . . ." This is a good example of another kind of logical organization—**emphatic order,** in which the most significant element is kept until last, and is emphasized in the fashion used here.

But the ultimate factor in the Cro-Magnons' success may have been how they kept warm. According to Arthur Jelinek of the University of Arizona, the discovery of needles made of bone and evidence of closely fitting clothes in Cro-Magnon graves indicates that the modern humans were able to stave off the cold with well-made clothes of animal hides. Archaeologists also have found that Cro-Magnons built more substantial shelters than the Neanderthals and that their hearths were more efficient—using dug-out-channels that allowed better airflow to the flame, for instance. The superior insulation and heating technology, says Jelinek, meant that the Cro-Magnons did not have to expend as much energy as the Neanderthals did to stay warm during the Ice Age winters. Needing fewer calories to survive, a greater number of Cro-Magnons could live off the same resources. Indeed, surveys of various ancient sites around Europe indicate that an area of a given size supported five times as many Cro-Magnons as Neanderthals.

This is an interesting example of the benefits of a superior technology. It was an ability to create furnaces able to sustain high temperatures that was one of the crucial factors in the transition from stoneworking to metalworking among our ancestors.

Research by University of Hawaii geneticist Rebecca Cann suggests that the newcomers' germs may also have played a decisive role as modern humans swept into Europe and around the world. Just as European colonists of the 15th century are thought to have killed off more American natives with smallpox and measles than with warfare, Cann believes that an influx of new diseases came with the arrival of the Cro-Magnons, contributing to the demise of the Neanderthals.

Eve's Genes. The most important—and most controversial—support for the Out of Africa model comes from genetic evidence that all humans are descended from a woman who lived in Africa some 200,000 years ago. For their "Eve" hypothesis, Cann, Mark Stoneking of

Pennsylvania State University and the late Allan Wilson of the University of California at Berkeley examined a particular type of genetic material, called mitochondrial DNA, that exists in all human cells. While ordinary DNA from both parents is mixed and remixed every time a human is conceived—which is why children tend to resemble both their parents—mitochondrial DNA passes directly from a mother to all her offspring. Thus a woman's mitochondrial DNA passes intact to her daughters, granddaughters and so on.

DNA? Make sure that you know what it is and why it's so important.

But occasionally, random mutations can produce slight differences in the mitochondrial DNA from one generation to the next. So, while the mitochondrial DNA of a woman and her daughter might differ only slightly, the differences between the mitochondrial DNA of the woman and her great-great-great-granddaughter would be more numerous, because more time has elapsed in which mutations can occur.

The genetic research described here by Allman has been severely criticized and is now rejected by many experts. It is still widely referred to, however, and you should know what it is all about.

Using the same principle and comparing samples of the mitochondrial DNA from people around the world, Cann and her colleagues found that the mitochondrial DNA of humans today is remarkably similar—so much so, they believe, that all humans must have derived from a common ancestor only about 150,000 to 250,000 years ago. This does not mean that the hypothetical "Eve" gave rise to all humans on earth who ever lived, says Cann. Rather, "Eve" is the only woman to have had at least one daughter in every generation up to the present. Just as in some cultures a family's last name will disappear if there are no males in a generation to carry it on, so too have other strands of mitochondrial DNA died out as no female offspring appeared in a particular generation.

Critical to the Out of Africa model is the geneticist's finding that the samples of human mitochondrial DNA form a family tree that has two main branches: one that gives rise exclusively to African mitochondrial DNA and another that contains not only African mitochondrial DNA but that found in all other peoples around the world as well. The best interpretation of such a tree, say the researchers, is that the original population of anatomically modern humans arose in Africa, then split when some people left to populate the rest of the world, taking their African based genes with them. The African samples of mitochondrial DNA are also the most variable of all the populations studied, meaning that the DNA had undergone the most changes and hence was the oldest. But researchers found no genetic evidence that modern humans interbred with Neanderthals.

Remember that although no evidence of breeding between Neanderthals and Cro-Magnons has been found, the fact that they coexisted for a long time suggests that it *may* have occurred. Some experts remain convinced that this happened.

The genetic research is hotly contested by many researchers, including some prominent geneticists. But a new, more comprehensive study to be published this fall in the journal *Science* has produced nearly identical findings. Examining almost 150 samples from people around the world today, Stoneking, Wilson, Linda Vigilant of Pennsylvania State University and their colleagues confirm the earlier finding

The importance of **summary** is clear here. Allman does not depend on direct quotation: he summarizes and paraphrases the writings of the researchers he cites. In doing this, he is demonstrating his understanding of the material and is often "translating" the original articles from more technical to less technical language. You will often have to use summary in this way in your research papers.

that Africa appears to be the ultimate source of all modern human mitochondrial DNA. Further, they calculate that there is only about a 1 in 16,000 chance that such a result could appear by chance.

Despite the dramatic findings of the genetic studies, the Out of Africa model is not yet accepted by all anthropologists. One of its most vocal critics is Milford Wolpoff of the University of Michigan, who is perhaps the biggest champion of the multiregional model. Wolpoff bases his objections on his interpretation of the fossil record, which he says shows signs of H. *erectus*'s evolving gradually into modern humans, especially in Asia. As for the supposed "tropical" body type of Cro-Magnon, Wolpoff points to the Pygmies in Africa and contends that Cro-Magnon's lanky legs were adapted for walking, not heat. Wolpoff does not fundamentally disagree with the conclusions of geneticists that all humans are ultimately descendants of Africa. He simply feels the "molecular clock" geneticists use to measure the time that has passed between genetic mutations is not valid. To Wolpoff, the genetic similarity among mitochondrial DNA in humans today simply reflects the original migration of H. *erectus* out of Africa roughly a million years ago.

Rhetorical note: Allman is not arguing for any position in this debate. He has the attitude of **an interested observer,** reporting and summarizing the current state of our knowledge about human origins. This is a good model for such an essay. Remember that much (although certainly not all) of the writing you do at college will be of this type; **it is an exercise in *synthesis* rather than *argument.*** When he describes questions over which the experts disagree, Allman never allows himself to express his opinion; he's not as qualified as the experts and it's not his role to decide these matters. His job is to describe the experts' views evenhandedly and pull them all together (synthesize) in language that the lay reader can clearly understand. It's for you to judge whether or not he succeeds in this.

Other researchers, such as Trinkaus of the University of New Mexico, endorse a more complex model of human origins that combines elements of both theories. Modern humans may have indeed originated in Africa, they say, but they interbred with some humanlike creatures and replaced others as they moved throughout the world. They concede that the fossil record is still too sketchy to sort out precisely what happened to whom.

Sophisticated Tools. New genetic studies—on Neanderthals—may someday clarify the controversy. The tools of genetics are becoming so sophisticated that it may be possible to extract DNA from a Neanderthal fossil, says Cann. Researchers have already shown that DNA can be gathered from 7,500-year-old human remains, and scientists recently retrieved DNA from a 16-million-year-old leaf that was preserved in rock. If researchers can find a pocket of preserved DNA in a Neanderthal fossil, there is a possibility that the genetic relation of the ancient creatures to modern humans can be determined once and for all.

But even finding Neanderthal DNA may not explain perhaps the most puzzling question in the human story—the "cultural explosion" that seems to have occurred with the appearance of the Cro-Magnon in Europe. It is a phenomenon that lacks concrete theories, yet an answer is crucial to understanding why we are who we are.

As mentioned earlier in this unit, ancient humans produced great works of art that have survived on the walls and ceilings of caves to the present day. The most famous may be those at Lascaux, in southern France. More cave paintings—possibly 20,000 years old—were found in southwest France in 1995.

The puzzle centers on the fact that while fossils of anatomically modern humans date back more than 100,000 years, it wasn't until some 40,000 years ago that a sudden explosion of new kinds of stone

This may signal the beginning of what seems to us to be the ever-quickening pace of change, especially technological change. Allman refers here to two types of change—anatomical and behavioral—in terms of evolution. It's interesting that the evolution of "modern behavior" is seen here in terms of the development of technology.

Another feature of Allman's essay worthy of note is the **diversity of evidence** he has gathered. How many experts does he cite, and how many different kinds of evidence—genetic, for example, being one—does he describe? This is a genuine **research** paper; Allman pulls together a great deal of information from a variety of sources.

and bone tools, artwork, elaborate burials and a host of other quintessentially human behaviors appears to have occurred. Indeed, says Richard Klein of the University of Chicago, the tools left by the earliest modern humans are virtually indistinguishable from those of Neanderthals.

This sudden transformation of "anatomically modern" humans to "behaviorally modern" people appears to have taken place in Africa, Asia and Europe simultaneously, says Klein, and was perhaps the most dramatic change in behavior in the evolution of humans since some ancient ancestor rose up on two legs. While the tools used by more ancient humans remained the same for literally tens of thousands of years throughout the world, the technology of modern humans after about 40,000 years ago appears to have differed from valley to valley and rapidly evolved in sophistication. "There was more change in the first five minutes of the cultural explosion than in all the human evolution before it," says archaeologist Randall White of New York University.

Just what precipitated the change in behavior is open to speculation; Klein suggests that there was a mutation in the brains of modern humans that led to increased language skills and the rise of culture. But other researchers, including White, argue that the tremendous change in the way people behaved was in principle no different from the birth of agriculture some 30,000 years later. In both instances, increases in population and dwindling food supplies compelled humans around the world to abandon one way of life for another, precipitating radical changes in technology and lifestyle along the way.

Perhaps the most intriguing clue in the puzzle of the human cultural explosion comes from the site where the "last" Neanderthal was found. The skeleton was found along with a peculiar type of tool that, unlike those typically associated with the Neanderthal, actually looks like slightly cruder versions of the kinds of implements made by Cro-Magnon.

The Neanderthals' seemingly abrupt leap in technological sophistication may have come as they suddenly found themselves under pressure to compete with the Cro-Magnons. One insight into this leap comes perhaps from the Yerkes Primate Center in Georgia, where Indiana University archaeologist Nick Toth recently taught a chimp named Kanzi to make simple stone tools that crudely resembled those of the early human ancestor H. *habilis*. Toth's research provides evidence that chimps have the mental capability to make complex stone tools—even though they never do so in the wild. Similarly, the sudden appearance of new kinds of tools among the Neanderthals indicates that these creatures might all along have been mentally capable of producing tools similar to those of modern humans. But apparently they lacked some other fundamentally human attribute that made such tools an important factor in their lives until the very end.

A Social Species. That crucial element, argue some researchers, may be the human species' extreme sociability, which created an environment where sophisticated tools, language and artwork became a vital part of existence. Evidence of the extensive social relations among Cro-Magnons is everywhere: They left behind the remains of huge campsites, suggesting that they occasionally gathered in large groups for ceremonial purposes. Studies by Klein and others establish that hunting techniques took an enormous leap in sophistication, revealing intense cooperation among group members. Discoveries of shells, bone and flint that are hundreds of miles from their original sources indicate that modern humans had vast networks for exchanging goods among groups. The elaborate burials of some Cro-Magnons suggest a structured society where leaders held a special status, and even artwork appears to have arisen in part because of its crucial role in social relations.

Though the overall picture of the origins of modern humans has become far more clear, the debate over where to place Neanderthals in the story remains as contentious as when the first Neanderthal fossils were discovered more than a century ago. If the Out of Africa model proves even partially correct, however, it will fundamentally change our view of who we are. It suggests that in the end, all humans are in essence Africans and far more closely related than we might imagine. Indeed, the gene research reveals that there is more genetic variability among the members of any one race than there is between different races as a whole, says geneticist Cann. A Caucasian, for instance, might be genetically more similar to an Asian or African than to another Caucasian.

Most important, the Out of Africa model indicates that the human species—and the radical changes it has brought about on land, sea and air—is in fact a very recent phenomenon in the saga of life on earth. Latecomers to the planet, humans are an evolutionary "work in progress," whose final outcome is yet to be determined.

THE LOCKHORNS by Bunny Hoest & John Reiner
"I'M HOPING THAT ONE DAY LEROY WILL EVOLVE INTO A HIGHER LIFE-FORM."

ASPECTS OF WRITING: Developing a thesis.

A **thesis** is not simply a statement of the main idea in an essay, although this is certainly an important part of what it is. The thesis has three functions:

1. **To state the main idea in the essay.** This is a service to the reader, by means of which you, the writer, orient the reader to the topic. It also serves as a check for you; you should refer back to your thesis as you write, to make sure that you're still writing about the same thing you promised at the beginning! You won't normally write something like "I'm going to write about human evolution." This gives a **topic,** but it isn't a thesis. **A thesis must say something *about* the topic.** For example, you might write, *"In the story of life on Earth, humans have put in only a very recent appearance."*
2. **To *suggest* the organization of the essay.** Note the use of "suggest" here. You won't say, "I'm going to write about the history of life on Earth and then about the place of humans in that history." The sentence in italics above says the same thing, but in a less direct and less personal way. It suggests that the essay will probably have two parts, one dealing with the wider story of life on Earth, the other dealing with the human story, emphasizing, at least in part, the relative brevity of human existence as a species.
3. **To *suggest* the attitude of the writer.** If appropriate, you may state your position in an argument, but not all essays require this. Many do not require you to state any personal position or belief, requiring, instead, that you be objective, describing or reporting events (in history, in anthropology) or issues (in philosophy, in sociology) analytically, without any overt intrusion of personal belief or preference. This does not mean that you can't express opinions; it simply means that attitudes will emerge more subtly than they would in a statement beginning, "I think that. . . ."

   What is the attitude of the writer of the italicized thesis already discussed? Clearly, this writer is intending to make a point, but the point being made is probably indisputable, and so we might say that the attitude is objective. If the thesis had stated, *"In the story of life on Earth, humans have played a totally insignificant part,"* you might observe that the writer has made a more controversial statement. This is a perfectly good thesis, but you should note that it suggests a different essay, reflecting a definite point of view on the writer's part.

Apparently minor changes in word choice can affect the reader's perception of the writer's attitude. Look at the following:

a. Humans have had an enormous impact on the planet.
b. Humans have had a disastrous impact on the planet.

The first of these statements is objective, the second is subjective. You may be more used to writing in a subjective manner; academic writing often requires objectivity.

Note that the thesis often spells out in some detail how the essay will be organized. For example, if you wrote, *"The large-scale human impact on the environment began in agricultural societies, and has become even more profound since industrialization,"* you would be suggesting to the reader your intention to write a two-part essay, the first dealing with the impact of agricultural practices, even in the distant past, and the second dealing with the impact of industrialization. This would be a good thesis; it states the main idea, it suggests the organization of the paper, and it suggests the attitude of the writer.

WRITING EXERCISES: Choose one of the following.

1. Allman's essay tells the story of human origins. Tell this story in your own words, being careful to distinguish between what seems fairly certain and what remains conjecture.
2. a. Write down two different possibilities for main ideas that emerge from the reading and discussion in this section. You may get at least one idea from the discussion on the thesis on the previous page.

   b. Compare your ideas with others in your class and choose the main idea that you would like to write about. Write a *statement* (not a question) based on this idea. This will be your thesis; make sure it meets the requirements discussed in the *Aspects of writing* section.

   c. Complete an essay based on the thesis you have developed. Make sure that you stick to the point and follow the organization indicated in the thesis.

> One possibility for this essay would involve a discussion of the controversy over whether Neanderthals were a "dead end" in evolutionary terms, or whether they are among our human ancestors.

When you write, you should know what you want to say. You need a *main idea,* and this comes from your reading and thinking about a topic. You may also get ideas from other people. Think about what you want to say and try to stick to the point.

You may have had the experience of finding, when you get to the end of an essay, that you have changed the subject or the **focus** as you've gone along. This can be avoided by continually rereading as you write, and this, in turn, can also help you achieve coherence. Always be asking, "Does this sound right?", "Does this make sense?", "Is this relevant?" If you already do this, you know how valuable such **editing as you go** can be.

Your thesis is really a generalization, and the ability to make generalizations about what you have read is a higher-level reading skill. In exercises of this sort, therefore, high-quality reading is just as important as high-quality writing.

SECTION THREE

PRIOR KNOWLEDGE: Time, culture, and the calendar.

Early centers of civilization include Mesopotamia (from 4000 B.C.), Egypt (from 3500 B.C.), and Northern India (from 3000 B.C.). China has had writing for 3000 years, and the Benin culture of West Africa created exquisite bronze castings from about 1000 B.C. You may also be interested in early American cultures, such as the Mayan.

Some cultures have survived into the 20th century with essentially Stone Age technology. A large population of such people was encountered by the outside world in Papua New Guinea in the 1920s and 1930s. Today, however, most such societies are rapidly acquiring modern technologies.

THINK ON PAPER
Technology is part of culture. What other cultural developments suggest change and progress in the prehistoric era?

Look for the Root—the common origin of words

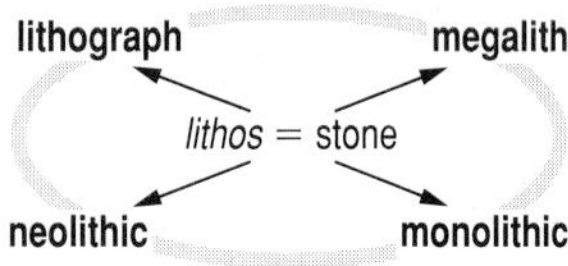

Most of the dates in the chart in Section Two are subject to correction as new evidence is discovered, but it is clear that humans have been on Earth for only a tiny fraction of the existence of the planet. From our vantage point, however, this brief period may seem like a very long time indeed, encompassing as it does the whole story of human life on Earth.

This story can be divided into two parts: history and prehistory. The former is that period since the creation of written records, which happened at different times in different societies. Anything before that is prehistoric. This prehistoric period can be divided up in a familiar way, as follows:

Period	Thousands of Years Ago
Paleolithic (Old Stone Age)	c. 750–15
Mesolithic (Middle Stone Age)	c. 15–6
Neolithic (New Stone Age)	c. 6–3
Bronze Age	c. 3
Iron Age	c. 0.8

Notice the **c.** This stands for *circa,* a Latin word meaning 'about' or 'approximately.'

These dates are approximations. Different cultures around the world achieved new levels of technology at different times; the whole world did not change overnight. Nevertheless, they provide a rough guide to the development of human societies, with a special focus on the technology that had been developed. Today, we speak of the "Computer Age" in much the same way.

In the prehistoric periods, the sophistication and variety of stone tools, and then the development of metallurgy, indicate technological

Think about the words **million, billion,** and **trillion.** It takes about 11.5 days for a million seconds to pass, 32 years for a billion seconds, and 32,000 years for a trillion seconds.

advances. The pace of change seems to have quickened as time went on in the ancient past, and many people have said the same thing about the modern world.

As noted earlier, the formal distinction between history and prehistory concerns the existence of written records. The Sumerians had developed a **cuneiform alphabet** by about 3000 B.C., and some of the clay tablets from this period have survived. The Egyptians, as is well known, were also among the innovators, making papyrus, and the Chinese invented paper in the early second century. Today, the documentation of events has increased in scope to the point where recent American presidents have each created an entire library to store four or eight years' worth of presidential papers.

Written records are not, however, our only window on the past. Archaeologists find material evidence of what life was like in ancient times when they dig and discover artefacts, the foundations of buildings, and so on. Even in caves there are discoveries to be made. In one famous discovery in what is now Iraq, a Neanderthal grave, in which flowers had been lain, suggested to researchers that these human ancestors had developed ritual and perhaps a belief in an afterlife. In what is now Algeria, on the Tassili Plateau in the Sahara, cave paintings dating back as far as 6000 years suggest that what is now desert was then grassland, with elephants, giraffes, sheep, and other animals that were herded and hunted by the human population. Extraordinary cave art in France and elsewhere also testifies to the development of an aesthetic awareness, a sense of beauty, in the prehistoric people of the time.

Many great civilizations have contributed to the making of the modern world. One example of this is in the development of our modern calendar, which is the subject of your next reading.

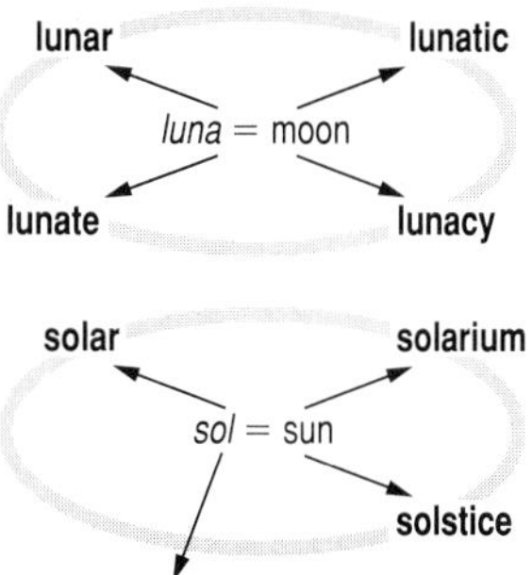

Be careful! Not all words containing *sol* come from this root. Some, for example, come from *solus* = alone, single. Check your dictionary.

Different cultures treat time differently. In the United States, time is taken very seriously, and "every second counts," but not all cultures value time in this way. Cross-cultural research (and perhaps your own experience) shows that there are differences in the way different cultures view punctuality, for example. If you are invited to dinner by a family in the United States, what is the "correct" time to show up? Exactly on time, a little early, or a little late? How late, or early, can you be without giving offense? Elsewhere in the world, the social conventions may be different.

Have you ever wondered why Easter occurs on a different date each year? It is defined, in part, according to the phases of the moon. It is part of the ecclesiastical calendar, which is *lunisolar,* beginning on Advent Sunday each year. Our January–December calendar is called the **Gregorian calendar.** The Hindu and Jewish or Hebrew calendars are also lunisolar. Many calendars begin the modern era from a day of religious significance; for example, the Jewish numbering of years begins in the year of creation 3761 B.C. (in Gregorian terms), while the Moslem year is calculated from A.D. 622 (in Gregorian terms). This was the year of the Hegira—are you using your dictionary?

ANNOTATED READING: Daniel J. Boorstin. "The Temptations of the Moon." *The Discoverers.* New York: Random House, 1983: 4–12.

The Temptations of the Moon

If you know where Greenland and Patagonia are located, you'll realize that Boorstin has chosen locations at opposite ends of the Earth in order to demonstrate the significance of the moon in ritual and language throughout the world.

Tacitus was a Roman historian and orator.

From far-northwest Greenland to the southernmost tip of Patagonia, people hail the new moon—a time for singing and praying, eating and drinking. Eskimos spread a feast, their sorcerers perform, they extinguish lamps and exchange women. African Bushmen chant a prayer: "Young Moon! . . . Hail, hail, Young Moon!" In the light of the moon everyone wants to dance. And the moon has other virtues. The ancient German communities, Tacitus reported nearly two thousand years ago, held their meetings at new or full moon, "the seasons most auspicious for beginning business."

Everywhere we find relies of mythic, mystic, romantic meanings—in "moonstruck" and "lunatic" (Latin *luna* means moon), in "moonshine," and in the moonlight setting of lovers' meetings. Even deeper is the primeval connection of the moon with measuring. The word "moon" in English and its cognate in other languages are rooted in the base *me* meaning measure (as in Greek *metron*, and in the English *meter* and *measure*), reminding us of the moon's primitive service as the first universal measurer of time.

Notice the first suggestion here that the phases of the moon may not be ideal as a measure of time. The phrase *a trap for naïve mankind* is the indicator.

Despite or because of its easy use as a measure of time, the moon proved to be a trap for naïve mankind. For while the phases of the moon were convenient worldwide cycles which anybody could see, they were an attractive dead end. What hunters and farmers most needed was a calendar of the seasons—a way to predict the coming of rain or snow, of heat and cold. How long until planting time? When to expect the first frost? The heavy rains?

Boorstin provides roots and definitions. Notice how *sidereal month* is defined within his text.

The vernal and autumnal equinox and summer and winter solstice mark the "official" change of the seasons. They occur 3 months apart, with the winter solstice (in the Northern Hemisphere) occurring on Dec. 21 or 22 each year, when the sun reaches its furthest position south, relative to the Earth. This, then, is the shortest day of the year for Americans and others north of the equator. For those south of the equator, this is the summer solstice—the longest day of the year.

For these needs the moon gave little help. True, the cycles of the moon had an uncanny correspondence with the menstrual cycle of women, because a sidereal month, or the time required for the moon to return to the same position in the sky, was a little less than 28 days, and a pregnant woman could expect her child after ten of these moon-months. But a solar year—the proper measure of days between returning seasons—measures 365 1/4 days. The cycles of the moon are caused by the moon's movement around the earth at the same time that the earth is moving around the sun. The moon's orbit is elliptical, and departs by an angle of about five degrees from the earth's orbit about the sun. This explains why eclipses of the sun do not occur every month.

The discomfiting fact that the cycles of the moon and the cycles of the sun are incommensurate would stimulate thinking. Had it been possible to calculate the year, the round of seasons, simply by multiplying the cycles of the moon, mankind would have been saved a lot of trouble. But we might also have lacked the incentive to study the heavens and to become mathematicians.

The seasons of the year, as we now know, are governed by the movements of the earth around the sun. Each round of the seasons marks the return of the earth to the same place in its circuit, a movement from one equinox (or solstice) to the next. Man needed a calendar to find his bearings in the seasons. How to begin?

The ancient Babylonians started with the lunar calendar and stayed with it. Their obstinacy in sticking with moon cycles for their calendar-making had important consequences. In search of a way to measure the cycle of the seasons in multiples of moon cycles, they eventually discovered, probably around 432 B.C., the so-called Metonic cycle (after an astronomer Meton) of nineteen years. They found that if they used a nineteen-year cycle, assigned to seven of the years thirteen months, and assigned to the other twelve years only twelve months, they could continue to use the conveniently visible phases of the moon as the basis of their calendar. Their "intercalation," or insertion of extra months, avoided the inconvenience of a "wandering" year in which the seasons wandered gradually through the lunar months, so that there was no easy way of knowing which month would bring the new season. This Metonic calendar with its nineteen-year clusters was too complicated for everyday use.

The Greek historian Herodotus, writing in the fifth century B.C., illustrated these complications in a famous passage when he reported how the wise Solon answered the rich and irascible Croesus, who asked him who was the happiest of mortals. To impress on Croesus the vast unpredictability of fortune, he calculated according to the Greek calendar then in use the number of days in the seventy years which he regarded as the limit of the life of man. "In these seventy years," he observed, "are contained, without reckoning intercalary months, 25,200 days. Add an intercalary month to every other year, that the seasons may come round at the right time, and there will be, besides the seventy years, thirty-five such months, making an addition of 1,050 days. The whole number of the days contained in the seventy years will thus be 26,250, whereof not one but will produce events unlike the rest. Hence man is wholly accident. For yourself, Croesus, I see that you are wonderfully rich, and the lord of many nations; but with respect to your question, I have no answer to give, until I hear that you have closed your life happily."

Have you heard the expression "As rich as Croesus"? You can find the story of Croesus, and many other names from Greek and Roman mythology and literature in a **classical dictionary**—check in the library or bookstore.

The Egyptians somehow escaped the temptations of the moon. So far as we know, they were the first to discover the length of the solar year and to define it in a useful, practical fashion. As with many other cru-

Boorstin tells the history of the calendar in chronological order, although there is some overlapping.

cial human achievements, we know the *what*, but remain puzzled still about the *why*, the *how*, and even the *when*. The first puzzle is why it was the Egyptians. They had no astronomical instruments not already well known to the ancient world. They showed no special genius for mathematics. Their astronomy remained crude compared with that of the Greeks and others in the Mediterranean and was dominated by religious ritual. But it seems that by about 2500 B.C. they had figured out how to predict when the rising or setting sun would gild the tip of any particular obelisk, which helped them add a glow to their ceremonies and anniversaries.

Acknowledging that we don't know something is not a sign of weakness; in fact, it suggests the exciting truth that there are many things left to be discovered about our human past. Notice Boorstin's careful phrasing: "But it seems that by about 2500 B.C. . . ."

The Babylonian scheme, which kept the lunar cycles and tried to adjust them to the seasonal or solar year by "intercalation," was inconvenient. Local whims prevailed. In Greece, fragmented by mountains and bays and fertile in landscape loyalties, each city-state made its own calendar, arbitrarily "intercalating" the extra month to mark a local festival or to suit political needs. The result was to defeat the very purpose of a calendar—a time scheme to hold people together, to ease the making of common plans, such as agreements on the planting of crops and the delivery of goods.

Boorstin tells us why the development of the calendar was so important. It's a useful reminder of the value of something that we take completely for granted.

The Egyptians, even without the Greek yen for mathematics, solved the practical problem. They invented a calendar that served everyday needs throughout their land. As early as 3200 B.C., the whole Nile Valley was united with the Nile Delta into a single kingdom which lasted for three thousand years, until the Age of Cleopatra. Political unity was reinforced by nature. Like the heavenly bodies themselves, the Nile displayed a regular but more melodramatic natural rhythm. The longest river in Africa, the Nile stretches four thousand miles from its remote headstream, gathering the rainfall and snowmelt of the Ethiopian highlands and all the northeastern continent into a single grand channel to the Mediterranean. The pharaoh's realm was aptly called the Empire of the Nile. The ancients, taking Herodotus' cue, called Egypt "the gift of the Nile." The search for the sources of the Nile, like the search for the Holy Grail, had mystic overtones, which stirred death-defying explorers into the nineteenth century.

Your dictionary contains historical and religious references, as well as definitions. Check the historical **Cleopatra.**

Similarly, you can find the origin of the phrase "the Holy Grail," which is commonly used today to mean "the ultimate goal," or "the very best outcome."

The Nile made possible the crops, the commerce, and the architecture of Egypt. Highway of commerce, the Nile was also a freightway for the materials of colossal temples and pyramids. A granite obelisk of three thousand tons could be quarried at Aswan and then floated two hundred miles down the river to Thebes. The Nile fed the cities that clustered along its banks. No wonder that the Egyptians called the Nile "the sea" and in the Bible it is "the river."

The rhythm of the Nile was the rhythm of Egyptian life. The annual rising of its waters set the calendar of sowing and reaping with its three seasons: inundation, growth, and harvest. The flooding of the Nile from the end of June till late October brought down rich silt, in

You want your essay to be as interesting as possible, but sometimes it's hard to think of ways of expanding the discussion. Here, Boorstin focuses on the significance of the Nile in Egyptian life and then leads us back to the main topic: "The rhythm of the Nile was the rhythm of Egyptian life." Clearly, the connection between the river, everyday life, and the development of the calendar is suggested in this sentence.

which crops were planted and grew from late October to late February, to be harvested from late February till the end of June. The rising of the Nile, as regular and as essential to life as the rising of the sun, marked the Nile year. The primitive Egyptian calendar, naturally enough, was a "nilometer"—a simple vertical scale on which the flood level was yearly marked. Even a few years' reckoning of the Nile year showed that it did not keep in step with the phases of the moon. But very early the Egyptians found that twelve months of thirty days each could provide a useful calendar of the seasons if another five days were added at the end, to make a year of 365 days. This was the "civil" year, or the "Nile year," that the Egyptians began to use as early as 4241 B.C.

This date, 4241 B.C., is considered to be the first year in history to be precisely dated. It marks, in a sense, the beginning of history, as distinct from prehistory.

Avoiding the seductively convenient cycle of the moon, the Egyptians had found another sign to mark their year: Sirius, the Dog Star, the brightest star in the heavens. Once a year Sirius rose in the morning in direct line with the rising sun. This "heliacal rising" of Sirius, which occurred every year in the midst of the Nile's flood season, became the beginning of the Egyptian year. It was marked by a festival, the five "epagomenal days" (days outside the months), celebrating in turn the birthday of Osiris, of his son Horus, of his Satanic enemy, Set, of his sister and wife, Isis, and of Nephthys, the wife of Set.

The **Julian calendar,** which was based on the Egyptian year, was introduced in 46 B.C. Its great innovation was the leap year.

Since the solar year, of course, is not precisely 365 days, the Egyptian year of 365 days would, over the centuries, become a "wandering year" with each named month gradually occurring in a different season. The discrepancy was so small that it took many years, far longer than any one person's lifetime, for the error to disturb daily life. Each month moved through all the seasons in fourteen hundred and sixty years. Still, this Egyptian calendar served so much better than any other known at the time that it was adopted by Julius Caesar to make his Julian calendar. It survived the Middle Ages and was still used by Copernicus in his planetary tables in the sixteenth century.

Words and phrases are sometimes so familiar that readers never think about what they mean. For example, what are the **Middle Ages,** just mentioned by Boorstin? For that matter, what are the **Dark Ages?** When the Roman Empire collapsed in the fifth century, there ensued a period of disorder in Europe, with no "superpower" (as we would say today) able to achieve supremacy. These were the "Dark Ages"; this name is a little misleading, because the continent was by no means entirely sunk in barbarism. The Middle Ages brought this period to an end, with the emergence of feudalism with its social order, its castles, and its organization of what would become nation states.

While the Egyptians for their everyday calendar succeeded in declaring their independence of the moon, the moon retained a primeval fascination. Many peoples, including the Egyptians themselves, kept the lunar cycle to guide religious festivals and mystic anniversaries. Even today people dominated by their religion let themselves be governed by the cycles of the moon. The daily inconvenience of living by a lunar calendar becomes a daily witness to religious faith.

The Jews, for example, preserve their lunar calendar, and each Jewish month still begins with the appearance of a new moon. To keep their lunar calendar in step with the seasonal year the Jews have added an extra month for each leap year, and the Jewish calendar has become a focus of esoteric rabbinical learning. The Jewish year was made to comprise twelve months, each of 29 or 30 days, totaling some 354 days. In order to fill out the solar year, Jewish leap years—following the Metonic cycle of Babylonia—add an extra month in the third, sixth, eighth, eleventh, fourteenth, seventeenth, and nineteenth year of every nineteen-year period. Other adjustments are required occasionally to make festivals occur in their proper seasons—for example, to ensure that Passover, the spring festival, will come after the vernal equinox. In the Bible most of the months retain their Babylonian, rather than the Hebrew, names.

Once again, Boorstin shows how everyday life was intertwined with the calendar, sometimes in unexpected ways. Even today, as he observes, the lunar cycles have a special significance in some aspects of life.

Christianity, following Judaism for most religious anniversaries, has kept its tie to the lunar calendar. "Movable feasts" in the Church were moved around in the solar calendar because of the effort to keep festivals in step with the cycles of the moon. They still remind us of the primeval charm of the most conspicuous light in the night sky. The most important of these Christian, moon-fixed festivals is, of course, Easter, which celebrates the resurrection of Jesus. "Easter-Day," prescribes the English Book of Common Prayer, "is always the first Sunday after the Full Moon which happens upon, or next after the Twenty-first day of March; and if the Full Moon happens upon a Sunday, Easter-Day is the Sunday after." At least a dozen other Church festivals are fixed by reference to Easter and its lunar date, with the result that Easter controls about seventeen weeks in the ecclesiastical calendar. The fixing of the date of Easter—in other words, the calendar—became a great issue and a symbol. Since the New Testament recounted that Jesus was crucified on the Passover, the anniversary of the Easter resurrection would obviously be tied to the Jewish calendar. The inevitable result was that the date of Easter would depend on the complicated lunar calculations by which the highest Jewish council, the Sanhedrin, defined the Passover.

Boorstin has moved us along to recent times, connecting the religious practices of the ancient Egyptians with those of today. He doesn't maintain strict chronological order here, but these comments on the continuing use made of the lunar cycles fit right in thematically with his discussion.

Many of the early Christians, following their own literal interpretation of the Bible, fixed the death of Jesus on a Friday, and the Easter resurrection on the following Sunday. But if the anniversary of the festival was to follow the Jewish lunar calendar, there was no assurance that Easter would occur on a Sunday. The bitter quarrel over the calendar led to one of the earliest schisms between the Eastern Orthodox Church and the Church of Rome. The Eastern Christians, holding to the lunar calendar, continued to observe Easter on the fourteenth day of the lunar month, regardless of the day of the week. At the very first ecumenical (worldwide) council of the Christian Church, held at Nicaea in Asia Minor in 325, one of the world-unifying questions to be decided was the date of Easter. A uniform date was fixed in such a way as both to stay with the traditional lunar calendar and to assure that Easter would always be observed on Sunday.

The politics of calendar making were clearly as complex and rancorous as international affairs today!

But this did not quite settle the matter. For community planning someone still had to predict the phases of the moon and locate them on a solar calendar. The Council of Nicaea had left this task to the bishop of Alexandria. In that ancient center of astronomy he was to forecast the phases of the moon for all future years. Disagreement over how to predict those specified cycles led to a division in the Church, with the result that different parts of the world continued to observe Easter on different Sundays.

Now we get to our present calendar—the **Gregorian calendar.** Notice that the 11 minute error in the Julian calendar accumulated over the years and eventually created a problem that needed to be corrected.

The reform of the calendar by Pope Gregory XIII was needed because the year that Julius Caesar had borrowed from the Egyptians, and which had ruled Western civilization since then, was not a precise enough measure of the solar cycle. The actual solar year—the time required for the earth to complete an orbit around the sun—is 365 days, 5 hours, 48 minutes, and 46 seconds. This was some 11 minutes and 14 seconds less than the 365 1/4 days in the Egyptian year. As a result, dates on the calendar gradually lost their intended relation to solar events and to the seasons. The crucial date, the vernal equinox, from which Easter was calculated, had been fixed by the First Council of Nicaea at March 21. But the accumulating inaccuracy of the Julian calendar meant that by 1582 the vernal equinox was actually occurring on March 11.

Pope Gregory XIII, though notorious now for his public Thanksgiving for the brutal massacre of Protestants in Paris on Saint Bartholomew's Day (1572), was in some matters an energetic reformer. He determined to set the calendar straight. Climaxing a movement for calendar reform which had been developing for at least a century, in 1582 Pope Gregory ordained that October 4 was to be followed by October 15. This meant, too, that in the next year the vernal equinox would occur, as the solar calendar of seasons required, on March 21. In this way the seasonal year was restored to what it had been in 325. The leap years of the old Julian calendar were readjusted. To prevent the accumulation of another 11-minute-a-year discrepancy, the Gregorian calendar omitted the leap day from years ending in hundreds, unless they were divisible by 400. This produced the modern calendar by which the West still lives.

Simply because the reform had come from Rome, Protestant England and the Protestant American colonies obstinately refused to go along. Not until 1752 were they persuaded to make the change. The Old Style calendar year that governed them till then had begun on March 25, but the New Style year began on January 1. When the necessary eleven days were added, George Washington's birthday, which fell on February 11, 1751, Old Style, became February 22, 1752, New Style.

Once again, Boorstin shows how the calendar—or changes in the calendar—made a difference in the lives of ordinary people. Repeated references to related themes may give you ideas for research topics or essays. A good thesis might read: "From the beginning, the calendar was an important tool, helping societies organize their activities more efficiently."

Back in 1582, when Pope Gregory took ten days out of the calendar, there had been grumbling and confusion. Servants demanded their usual full monthly pay for the abridged month; employers refused. People objected to having their lives shortened by papal decree. But when Britain and the American colonies finally got around to making

The Gregorian calendar is widely used today, even in countries which also use a different calendar.

the change, Benjamin Franklin, aged forty-six when he lost the ten days of his life, with his usual cheery ingenuity gave readers of his *Poor Richard's Almanack* something to be thankful for:

> Be not astonished, nor look with scorn, dear reader, at such a deduction of days, nor regret as for the loss of so much time, but take this for your consolation, that your expenses will appear lighter and your mind be more at ease. And what an indulgence is here, for those who love their pillow to lie down in peace on the second of this month and not perhaps awake till the morning of the fourteenth.

The world never entirely accepted the Gregorian reform. The Eastern Orthodox Church, wary of subjecting itself to any Romish rule, has kept the Julian calendar for its own calculation of Easter. And so the Christian world, supposedly held together by a Prophet of Peace, has not been able to agree even on the date to celebrate the resurrection of their Savior.

Still, for everyday secular affairs, the whole Christian world has shared a solar calendar which serves the convenience of the farmer and the merchant. But Islam, insisting on literal obedience to the words of the prophet Muhammad and to the dictates of the holy Koran, continues to live by the cycles of the moon.

The significance of the crescent moon as a symbol of Islam is noted by Boorstin. In Islamic countries the Red Cross organization is known as the Red Crescent.

The crescent, the sign of the new moon, appears on the flag of Muslim nations. Despite scholarly dispute about the origin of the crescent symbol, there can be no doubt of its appropriateness for the peoples who have obediently submitted the schedule of their lives to the divinely commanded measure of the moon. And it is doubly significant as a conspicuous exception to the Muslim ban on representing natural objects. At least as early as the thirteenth century, the crescent became the military and religious symbol of the Ottoman Turks. There is reason to believe that its adoption and its survival as a sign of Islam came from the dominance of the new moon, which not only is a signal of the beginning and end of the month-long Muslim season of fasting, but is the regular punctuation for the whole calendar.

The Ottoman Empire lasted until the end of World War I. Like Germany, Turkey lost her empire at that time.

The new moons, declares the Koran, "are fixed times for the people and for the pilgrimage." The Muslim world, with orthodox scrupulosity, has tried to live by the moon. Just as Caesar had decisively committed his world to the convenience of the solar year, with the months serving as indices of the seasons, so Muhammad committed his everyday world to the cycles of the moon. These lunar cycles would guide the faithful to the divinely ordained dates for the prime religious duties—the pilgrimage to Mecca and the Ramadan month of fasting. The Muslim year consists of twelve lunar months, of alternately 29 and 30 days. The fractional correction to keep the months in

Rhetorical note: Boorstin's essay is partly **narrative**—telling the story of the calendar—and partly **exposition**—informing the reader about the topic. He uses chronological order, and he also uses definition, as necessary. Note how his discussion/definition on this page of the use of the crescent in Islamic countries, and of Easter earlier in the essay, add a lot of interesting detail to the essay.

step with the moon was secured by varying the length of the twelfth month in the year. A cycle of thirty Muslim years was defined, in nineteen of which the final month had 29 days, with 30 days in the others.

Since the Muslim calendar contains only 354 or 355 days, the months have no regular relation to the seasons. Ramadan, the ninth month—the month of fasting, the observance which marks the true Muslim—and Dhu'l-Hijja, the twelfth month, during the first two weeks of which the faithful are to make their pilgrimage to Mecca, may occur in summer or in winter. In each year the festival of Ramadan and the Pilgrimage occur ten or eleven days earlier than in the previous year. The everyday inconveniences of this kind of calendar are simply another reminder of the good Muslim's surrender to the will of Allah. The calendar itself, for others a mere schedule of worldly affairs, the Muslim makes an affirmation of faith.

Boorstin draws our attention to *Ramadan* and the pilgrimage to Mecca, two of the most important events in the Islamic year.

The Muslim's literal submission to the moon cycle has had some interesting consequences. To live by the God-given visible phases of the moon (and not by some human calculation of when the new moon is expected) has meant, of course, that celebration of a festival must await the actual sight of the moon. Most Muslims hold to this view, following a traditionally accepted utterance of the prophet Muhammad, "Do not fast until you see the new moon, and do not break the fast until you see it; but when it is hidden from you [by cloud or mist] give it its full measure." If clouds or mist prevent the new moon from being seen in certain villages, those villages will observe the beginning and the end of Ramadan at different times from their neighbors.

One of the most hotly debated issues in Islam is whether it is permissible to define the beginning and end of festivals not by observation but "by resorting to calculation." The members of the Ismaili sect, who separated themselves in this way, failed to persuade most of their fellow Muslims, who still stand by the need to *observe*, that is, actually to see the new moon. Strict adherence to the lunar calendar has become a touchstone of loyalty to traditional Islam. "Resort to calculation"—the appeal to the sophisticated mathematics of a solar year rather than to the simple, visible dictates of the lunar cycle—has marked the modern revolts against tradition. In 1926, when Kemal Atatürk (Mustapha Kemal) proclaimed the end of the sultanate in Turkey and "modernized" the nation by adopting a new code of laws, by making civil marriage compulsory, and by abolishing the fez for men and the veil for women, he also abandoned the lunar calendar of Islam and adopted the solar calendar of the West.

Atatürk is a lesser-known figure than some great leaders, and so Boorstin tells us something about him.

While for many in the West the calendar may seem nothing more than a system of chronological bookkeeping, it has proved to be one of the most rigid of human institutions. That rigidity comes partly from the potent mystic aura of sun and moon, partly from the fixed

The French Revolution, which overthrew the monarchy, occurred in 1789. Napoleon Bonaparte was Emperor of France, 1804–1815.

boundaries of the seasons. Revolutionaries have frequently tried to remake the calendar, but their success has been short-lived. The National Convention of the French Revolution set up a committee on calendar reform—made up of mathematicians, an educator, a poet, and the great astronomer Laplace—which produced a new calendar of charming rational symmetry. In 1792 their decimal calendar replaced the 7-day week by a 10-day week called a *décade*, each day of which was given a Latin numerical name, three of which comprised a month. The day was divided into ten hours, each consisting of 100 minutes, each minute of 100 seconds. In addition to the 360 days of these twelve months, the extra 5 or 6 days were given edifying names: Les Vertus, Le Génie, Le Travail, L'Opinion, Les Récompenses, with a leap day called Sans-culottide dedicated to holidays and sports. This calendar, designed to loosen the grip of the Church on daily life and thought, lasted uneasily for only thirteen years. When Napoleon became ruler of France, he restored the Gregorian calendar with its traditional saint's days and holidays, for which he received the Pope's blessing.

Elsewhere in *The Discoverers*, Boorstin tells us that the first mechanical clocks (as distinct from sundials, sandglasses, and water clocks) were made in the 14th century and were intended to remind monks of when they were supposed to be at prayer. The hour didn't become a precise unit until about 1330, and the minute and second weren't familiar notions to most people until the 16th and 17th centuries.

In China the Revolution of 1911 brought a reform, which introduced the calendar of the West, alongside the traditional Chinese calendar.

In 1929 the Soviet Union, aiming to dissolve the Christian year, replaced the Gregorian with a Revolutionary calendar. The week was to have 5 days, 4 for work, the fifth free, and each month would consist of six weeks. The extra days needed to make up each year's complement of 365 or 366 would be holidays. The Gregorian names of the months were kept, but the days of the week were simply numbered. By 1940 the Soviet Union had returned to the familiar Gregorian calendar.

ASPECTS OF WRITING: Chronological order and transitions.

You have already seen how Trefil uses certain structural words and phrases to connect, in a logical way, the chronological events of the big bang and the evolution of life on Earth. These words and phrases enable the writer to make smooth **transitions** from one idea to the next. This, in turn, contributes to the coherence of the essay, and helps the reader follow the discussion.

Structural words like these may be called **transition words,** and there are many such words and phrases that help us show time relationships. Notice the specific time relationships indicated by such words: *then, next, first, second,* and *following this* all suggest a conventional chronology from beginning to end. *Before that, prior to,* and *going further back in time* all suggest a reverse chronological order. *In the meantime, at that moment,* and *while* can be used to connect simultaneous events. You can probably think of other examples.

This is an easy concept, but some writers fail to realize how the use of such words can improve the coherence of their work. For example, if we write a paragraph describing a series of events, but devoid of transition words, we might come up with something like the following:

> The prehistoric hunters awoke. The sun rose. They picked up their weapons. They left the cave. They walked toward a river. They saw a mammoth. The mammoth saw them. They surrounded the beast. The mammoth charged.

You probably noticed that this paragraph sounds very simplistic. To improve it you need to add transitions and combine some of the sentences. When combining sentences, you will also see a need to make more effective use of pronouns; some may be added, but others should be deleted. All those sentences beginning with "they" make a bad paragraph!

> As an informal assignment in class, rewrite the bad paragraph ("The prehistoric hunters . . ."), adding transitions, combining sentences, and generally improving it. Then compare your paragraph with what others in your class have written. You will probably find some differences in the sequence of events, as well as in the way different people combine sentences. **Your choice of transitions and other structural words makes a difference.**

Chronological order is one of our most commonly used ways of organizing information. We tend to think in a linear or chronological way about events, "how to" manuals are always written in chronological order (imagine the uselessness of a manual that wasn't!), and it seems natural to present a lot of information in this fashion. For example, historical questions (How did the United States get involved in Vietnam? Who are the three most recent presidents?), criminal investigations (Where were you between noon and three o'clock yesterday?), and the résumés we write for job applications all call for the use of a strict chronology.

WRITING EXERCISES: Choose one of the following.

1. Write a summary of Boorstin's essay. To prepare for this, first think about what Boorstin has written. Make a general observation that effectively summarizes or characterizes his essay. This will become the thesis of your summary. Remember that the focus throughout must be on what Boorstin says. Next, analyze the essay and break it up into sections. This will give your summary a structure similar to (although not necessarily identical with) the original. When you write the summary, make sure that you use effective transitions.

   Paying attention to transition words is important in reading questions, too! Note the words "first" and "next" in the above instructions.

   The length of your summary should be determined in advance. Writing within a word limit requires a certain discipline.
2. Compare the origins and organization of two different types of calendar (lunar and solar, for example), making reference to Boorstin's essay. Make sure that anything you take directly from Boorstin's writing is put inside quotation marks. Limit such quotation to significant words and observations.
3. Describe the ways in which your life (or "our lives") is governed by the calendar and the clock. If you have any knowledge of a culture that pays less attention to time, you can opt to compare this culture with our own.

Sample thesis: The sun still rises and sets, and the tides go in and out, but most people today don't organize their lives according to the rhythms of Nature; they are ruled by the clock.

You will have noticed that one option in some of these early writing assignments is a **summary.** The reason is that a great deal of the writing you do at college involves summarizing information you have read and/or heard in lectures. It is a very important writing activity.

An effective summary depends on effective reading and listening. You have to understand the original.

The structure of the original often becomes clear when you look for the major transition words and phrases—as pointed out in the annotations on Boorstin's essay. When you see how the original essay is organized—and so understand its logic—you will understand it better and will be better able to imitate it in your summary.

OPTION ONE

PRIOR KNOWLEDGE: Science, religion, and truth.

Some people are troubled by apparent conflict between their religious beliefs and scientific accounts of evolution and the "big bang." Over the years, there has been continuing debate over such things as the teaching of "creationism" in schools, with some people insisting that religious versions of creation should be included in school science textbooks. Such debates have a long history; one of the most famous trials in American history was the so-called "Scopes trial" or "monkey trial" of 1925, in which a teacher was put on trial in Tennessee for teaching evolution in school. He lost the case. A fine movie, *Inherit the Wind*, tells the story of this case and the famous people involved in it.

Of course, people committed to a literal understanding of religious texts which describe a divinely inspired and virtually simultaneous creation of the Earth and humans are unlikely to have much willingness to consider the discoveries of science concerning the age of the Earth, its origin, the place of humans in evolutionary history, and so on. However, it is also true that many religious people find room in their minds for both religious faith and an acceptance of the revelations of science. Many churches, Roman Catholic and Protestant, have long accepted the big bang. They assert, however, that this event had a divine origin. This kind of thinking seems to appeal to many people, and, following several dramatic discoveries which tend to confirm aspects of the big bang theory, a number of books have been published that are based on the premise that as scientists get closer to the beginning of time, the distinction between science and religion is becoming blurred. In part, this has been sparked by a remark by Stephen Hawking, in *A Brief History of Time*, about scientists getting close to "knowing the mind of God." If you're interested in such ideas, browse in a bookstore or library and look under "cosmology" and "space."

Words have specific meanings and should be used as precisely as possible. Making frequent use of your dictionary and making a habit of looking up the roots of words will help you achieve this precision.

Not all words come from ancient roots; some are derived from the names of people. The study of evolution is, of course, associated with Charles Darwin, the author of *On the Origin of Species* (1859). Words such as *Darwinism* and *Social Darwinism* come from this source, directly or indirectly. Other examples include Karl Marx *(Marxism)*, Samuel Goldwyn *(Goldwyinism)*, and Winston Churchill *(Churchillian)*. Check the meaning of these words. Can you think of others?

On another level, however, the debate over "creationism" and science cannot be so readily swept under the carpet, and in the following essay Stephen Jay Gould confronts the issue directly. While we must always be concerned to defend the right of people to hold their own beliefs, we should not pretend that one version of events is just as good as any other. This idea suggests that no one knows the truth, and so no one is justified in saying that one "theory" is correct while another is wrong. Gould clarifies the terminology here, focusing on the meaning of "fact" and "theory" and making it clear that all such versions of events are *not* equal.

READING: Stephen Jay Gould. "Evolution as Fact and Theory." *Hen's Teeth and Horse's Toes.* New York: Norton, 1984: 253–262.

Evolution as Fact and Theory*

Kirtley Mather, who died last year at age ninety, was a pillar of both science and Christian religion in America and one of my dearest friends. The difference of a half-century in our ages evaporated before our common interests. The most curious thing we shared was a battle we each fought at the same age. For Kirtley had gone to Tennessee with Clarence Darrow to testify for evolution at the Scopes trial of 1925. When I think that we are enmeshed again in the same struggle for one of the best documented, most compelling and exciting concepts in all of science, I don't know whether to laugh or cry.

According to idealized principles of scientific discourse, the arousal of dormant issues should reflect fresh data that give renewed life to abandoned notions. Those outside the current debate may therefore be excused for suspecting that creationists have come up with something new, or that evolutionists have generated some serious internal trouble. But nothing has changed; the creationists have presented not a single new fact or argument. Darrow and Bryan were at least more entertaining than we lesser antagonists today. The rise of creationism is politics, pure and simple; it represents one issue (and by no means the major concern) of the resurgent evangelical right. Arguments that seemed kooky just a decade ago have reentered the mainstream.

The basic attack of modern creationists falls apart on two general counts before we even reach the supposed factual details of their assault against evolution. First, they play upon a vernacular misunderstanding of the word "theory" to convey the false impression that we evolutionists are covering up the rotten core of our edifice. Second, they misuse a popular philosophy of science to argue that they are behaving scientifically in attacking evolution. Yet the same philosophy demonstrates that their own belief is not science, and that "scientific creationism" is a meaningless and self-contradictory phrase, an example of what Orwell called "newspeak."

In the American vernacular, "theory" often means "imperfect fact"—part of a hierarchy of confidence running downhill from fact to theory to hypothesis to guess. Thus, creationists can (and do) argue: evolution is "only" a theory, and intense debate now rages about many

*First appeared in *Discover Magazine*. May 1981.

As you read, think about what Gould is trying to do in this essay. It's a good idea to note down, as you read, what seem to you to be significant statements. At the very least, you should take a mental note of what seem to be key ideas and observations. These might include statements of purpose and any definitional statements.

In reading any essay, it's important that you, the reader, "catch on" to the context of the discussion, and the author's purpose, as quckly as possible. Gould helps establish the context right away with his reference to **the Scopes trial.** *It's clear that Gould expects his readers to know what this trial was about.* You have already read something about this case in the *Prior knowledge* section, above, and this should be enough to orient you to his discussion. Note the importance of this "prior knowledge," even if it isn't very detailed.

Clarence Darrow and **William Jennings Bryan** were opposing attorneys in the Scopes trial. Bryan, who was a famous orator and who had twice run for president as the Democratic nominee, prosecuted the case, and Darrow defended Scopes, the teacher. Any encyclopedia will give you an account of this famous trial.

Gould is scathing in his introduction. Notice the key observation that "The rise of creationism is politics, pure and simple." He is drawing a clear line between what is science and what is not.

Notice the *structural words* in Gould's third paragraph on this page. He clearly sets up this part of his discussion.

Gould now begins to **define** the key terms in this debate. This is essential, because one of his main points is that people use the word "theory" without understanding what it means in the scientific context.

This essay contains references to several major figures in science and literature. Make sure you know who they are.

Don't miss this key reference to Darwin's "two great and separate accomplishments." Make sure you understand what these are, and why Gould stresses that these are *separate*—they aren't the same thing.

The readings in each of the Option One sections are annotated only at the beginning, if at all. There are no more annotations in this essay.

aspects of the theory. If evolution is less than a fact, and scientists can't even make up their minds about the theory, then what confidence can we have in it? Indeed, President Reagan echoed this argument before an evangelical group in Dallas when he said (in what I devoutly hope was campaign rhetoric): "Well, it is a theory. It is a scientific theory only, and it has in recent years been challenged in the world of science—that is, not believed in the scientific community to be as infallible as it once was."

Well, evolution *is* a theory. It is also a fact. And facts and theories are different things, not rungs in a hierarchy of increasing certainty. Facts are the world's data. Theories are structures of ideas that explain and interpret facts. Facts do not go away while scientists debate rival theories for explaining them. Einstein's theory of gravitation replaced Newton's, but apples did not suspend themselves in mid-air pending the outcome. And human beings evolved from apelike ancestors whether they did so by Darwin's proposed mechanism or by some other, yet to be discovered.

Moreover, "fact" does not mean "absolute certainty." The final proofs of logic and mathematics flow deductively from stated premises and achieve certainty only because they are *not* about the empirical world. Evolutionists make no claim for perpetual truth, though creationists often do (and then attack us for a style of argument that they themselves favor). In science, "fact" can only mean "confirmed to such a degree that it would be perverse to withhold provisional assent." I suppose that apples might start to rise tomorrow, but the possibility does not merit equal time in physics classrooms.

Evolutionists have been clear about this distinction between fact and theory from the very beginning, if only because we have always acknowledged how far we are from completely understanding the mechanisms (theory) by which evolution (fact) occurred. Darwin continually emphasized the difference between his two great and separate accomplishments: establishing the fact of evolution, and proposing a theory—natural selection—to explain the mechanism of evolution. He wrote in *The Descent of Man*: "I had two distinct objects in view; firstly, to show that species had not been separately created, and secondly, that natural selection had been the chief agent of change . . . Hence if I have erred in . . . having exaggerated its [natural selection's] power . . . I have at least, as I hope, done good service in aiding to overthrow the dogma of separate creations."

Thus Darwin acknowledged the provisional nature of natural selection while affirming the fact of evolution. The fruitful theoretical debate that Darwin initiated has never ceased. From the 1940s through the 1960s, Darwin's own theory of natural selection did achieve a temporary hegemony that it never enjoyed in his lifetime. But renewed debate characterizes our decade, and, while no biologist questions the importance of natural selection, many now doubt its ubiquity. In particular, many evolutionists argue that substantial amounts of genetic change may not be subject to natural selection and may spread through populations at random. Others are challenging Darwin's linking of natural selection with gradual, imperceptible change through all intermediary degrees; they are arguing that most evolutionary events may occur far more rapidly than Darwin envisioned.

Scientists regard debates on fundamental issues of theory as a sign of intellectual health and a source of excitement. Science is—and how else can I say it?—most fun when it plays with interesting ideas, examines their implications, and recognizes that old information may be explained in surprisingly new ways. Evolutionary theory is now enjoying this uncommon vigor. Yet amidst all this turmoil no biologist has been led to doubt the fact that evolution occurred; we are debating *how* it happened. We are all trying to explain the same thing: the tree of evolutionary descent linking all organisms by ties of genealogy. Creationists pervert and caricature this debate by conveniently neglecting the common conviction that underlies it, and by falsely suggesting that we now doubt the very phenomenon we are struggling to understand.

Secondly, creationists claim that "the dogma of separate creations," as Darwin characterized it a century ago, is a scientific theory meriting equal time with evolution in high school biology curricula. But a popular viewpoint among philosophers of science belies this creationist argument. Philosopher Karl Popper has argued for decades that the primary criterion of science is the falsifiability of its theories. We can never prove absolutely, but we can falsify. A set of ideas that cannot, in principle, be falsified is not science.

The entire creationist program includes little more than a rhetorical attempt to falsify evolution by presenting supposed contradictions among its supporters. Their brand of creationism, they claim, is "scientific" because it follows the Popperian model in trying to demolish evolution. Yet Popper's argument must apply in both directions. One does not become a scientist by the simple act of trying to falsify a rival and truly scientific system; one has to present an alternative system that also meets Popper's criterion—it too must be falsifiable in principle.

"Scientific creationism" is a self-contradictory, nonsense phrase precisely because it cannot be falsified. I can envision observations and experiments that would disprove any evolutionary theory I know, but I cannot imagine what potential data could lead creationists to abandon their beliefs. Unbeatable systems are dogma, not science. Lest I seem harsh or rhetorical, I quote creationism's leading intellectual, Duane Gish, Ph.D., from his recent (1978) book, *Evolution? The Fos-*

sils Say No! "By creation we mean the bringing into being by a supernatural Creator of the basic kinds of plants and animals by the process of sudden, or fiat, creation. We do not know how the Creator created, what processes He used, *for He used processes which are not now operating anywhere in the natural universe* [Gish's italics]. This is why we refer to creation as special creation. We cannot discover by scientific investigations anything about the creative processes used by the Creator." Pray tell, Dr. Gish, in the light of your last sentence, what then is "scientific" creationism?

Our confidence that evolution occurred centers upon three general arguments. First, we have abundant, direct, observational evidence of evolution in action, from both field and laboratory. This evidence ranges from countless experiments on change in nearly everything about fruit flies subjected to artificial selection in the laboratory to the famous populations of British moths that became black when industrial soot darkened the trees upon which the moths rest. (Moths gain protection from sharp-sighted bird predators by blending into the background.) Creationists do not deny these observations; how could they? Creationists have tightened their act. They now argue that God only created "basic kinds," and allowed for limited evolutionary meandering within them. Thus toy poodles and Great Danes come from the dog kind and moths can change color, but nature cannot convert a dog to a cat or a monkey to a man.

The second and third arguments for evolution—the case for major changes—do not involve direct observation of evolution in action. They rest upon inference, but are no less secure for that reason. Major evolutionary change requires too much time for direct observation on the scale of recorded human history. All historical sciences rest upon inference, and evolution is no different from geology, cosmology, or human history in this respect. In principle, we cannot observe processes that operated in the past. We must infer them from results that still surround us: living and fossil organisms for evolution, documents and artifacts for human history, strata and topography for geology.

The second argument—that the imperfection of nature reveals evolution—strikes many people as ironic, for they feel that evolution should be most elegantly displayed in the nearly perfect adaptation expressed by some organisms—the camber of a gull's wing, or butterflies that cannot be seen in ground litter because they mimic leaves so precisely. But perfection could be imposed by a wise creator or evolved by natural selection. Perfection covers the tracks of past history. And past history—the evidence of descent—is the mark of evolution.

Evolution lies exposed in the *imperfections* that record a history of descent. Why should a rat run, a bat fly, a porpoise swim, and I type this essay with structures built of the same bones unless we all inherited them from a common ancestor? An engineer, starting from scratch, could design better limbs in each case. Why should all the large native mammals of Australia be marsupials, unless they descended from a common ancestor isolated on this island continent? Marsupials are not "better," or ideally suited for Australia; many have been wiped out by placental mammals imported by man from other continents. This principle of imperfection extends to all historical sciences. When we recognize the etymology of September, October, November, and December (seventh, eighth, ninth, and tenth), we know that the year once started in March, or that two additional months must have been added to an original calendar of ten months.

The third argument is more direct: transitions are often found in the fossil record. Preserved transitions are not common—and should not be, according to our understanding of evolution (see next section)—but they are not entirely wanting, as creationists often claim. The lower jaw of reptiles contains several bones, that of mammals only one. The non-mammalian jawbones are reduced, step by step, in mammalian ancestors until they become tiny nubbins located at the back of the jaw. The "hammer" and "anvil" bones of the mammalian ear are descendants of these nubbins. How could such a transition be accomplished? the creationists ask. Surely a bone is either entirely in the jaw or in the ear. Yet paleontologists have discovered two transitional lineages of therapsids (the so-called mammal-like reptiles) with a double jaw joint—one composed of the old quadrate and articular bones (soon to become the hammer and anvil), the other of the squamosal and dentary bones (as in modern mammals). For that matter, what better transitional form could we expect to find than the oldest human, *Australopithecus afarensis*, with its apelike palate, its human upright stance, and a cranial capacity larger than any ape's of the same body size but a full 1,000 cubic centimeters below ours? If God made each of the half-dozen human species discovered in ancient rocks, why did he create in an unbroken temporal sequence of progressively more modern features—increasing cranial capacity, reduced face and teeth, larger body size? Did he create to mimic evolution and test our faith thereby?

Faced with these facts of evolution and the philosophical bankruptcy of their own position, creationists rely upon distortion and innuendo to buttress their rhetorical claim. If I sound sharp or bitter, indeed I am—for I have become a major target of these practices.

I count myself among the evolutionists who argue for a jerky, or episodic, rather than a smoothly gradual, pace of change. In 1972 my colleague Niles Eldredge and I developed the theory of punctuated equilibrium. We argued that two outstanding facts of the fossil record—geologically "sudden" origin of new species and failure to change thereafter (stasis)—reflect the predictions of evolutionary theory, not the imperfections of the fossil record. In most theories, small isolated populations are the source of new species, and the process of speciation takes thousands or tens of thousands of years. This amount of time, so long when measured against our lives, is a geological microsecond. It represents much less than 1 per cent of the average lifespan for a fossil invertebrate species—more than ten million years. Large, widespread, and well established species, on the other hand, are not expected to change very much. We believe that the inertia of large populations explains the stasis of most fossil species over millions of years.

We proposed the theory of punctuated equilibrium largely to provide a different explanation for pervasive trends in the fossil record. Trends, we argued, cannot be attributed to gradual transformation within lineages, but must arise from the differential success of certain kinds of species. A trend, we argued, is more like climbing a flight of stairs (punctuations and stasis) than rolling up an inclined plane.

Since we proposed punctuated equilibria to explain trends, it is infuriating to be quoted again and again by creationists—whether through design or stupidity, I do not know—as admitting that the fossil record includes no transitional forms. Transitional forms are generally lacking at the species level, but they are abundant between larger groups. Yet a pamphlet entitled "Harvard Scientists Agree Evolution Is a Hoax" states: "The facts of punctuated equilibrium which Gould and Eldredge . . . are forcing Darwinists to swallow fit the picture that Bryan insisted on, and which God has revealed to us in the Bible."

Continuing the distortion, several creationists have equated the theory of punctuated equilibrium with a caricature of the beliefs of Richard Goldschmidt, a great early geneticist. Goldschmidt argued, in a famous book published in 1940, that new groups can arise all at once through major mutations. He referred to these suddenly transformed creatures as "hopeful monsters." (I am attracted to some aspects of the non-caricatured version, but Goldschmidt's theory still has nothing to do with punctuated equilibrium—see essays in section 3 and my explicit essay on Goldschmidt in *The Panda's Thumb*.) Creationist Luther Sunderland talks of the "punctuated equilibrium hopeful monster theory" and tells his hopeful readers that "it amounts to tacit admission that anti-evolutionists are correct in asserting there is no fossil evidence supporting the theory that all life is connected to a common ancestor." Duane Gish writes, "According to Goldschmidt, and now apparently according to Gould, a reptile laid an egg from which the first bird, feathers and all, was produced." Any evolutionist who believed such nonsense would rightly be laughed off the intellectual stage; yet the only theory that could ever envision such a scenario for the origin of birds is creationism—with God acting in the egg.

I am both angry at and amused by the creationists; but mostly I am deeply sad. Sad for many reasons. Sad because so many people who respond to creationist appeals are troubled for the right reason, but venting their anger at the wrong target. It is true that scientists have often been dogmatic and elitist. It is true that we have often allowed the white-coated, advertising image to represent us—"Scientists say that Brand X cures bunions ten times faster than . . ." We have not fought it adequately because we derive benefits from appearing as a new priesthood. It is also true that faceless and bureaucratic state power intrudes more and more into our lives and removes choices that should belong to individuals and communities. I can understand that school curricula, imposed from above and without local input, might be seen as one more insult on all these grounds. But the culprit is not, and cannot be, evolution or any other fact of the natural world. Identify and fight your legitimate enemies by all means, but we are not among them.

I am sad because the practical result of this brouhaha will not be expanded coverage to include creationism (that would also make me sad), but the reduction or excision of evolution from high school curricula. Evolution is one of the half dozen "great ideas" developed by science. It speaks to the profound issues of genealogy that fascinate all of us—the "roots" phenomenon writ large. Where did we come from? Where did life arise? How did it develop? How are organisms related? It forces us to think, ponder, and wonder. Shall we deprive millions of this knowledge and once again teach biology as a set of dull and unconnected facts, without the thread that weaves diverse material into a supple unity?

But most of all I am saddened by a trend I am just beginning to discern among my colleagues. I sense that some now wish to mute the healthy debate about theory that has brought new life to evolutionary biology. It provides grist for creationist mills, they say, even if only by distortion. Perhaps we should lie low and rally round the flag of strict Darwinism, at least for the moment—a kind of old-time religion on our part.

But we should borrow another metaphor and recognize that we too have to tread a straight and narrow path, surrounded by roads to perdition. For if we ever begin to suppress our search to understand nature, to quench our own intellectual excitement in a misguided effort to present a united front where it does not and should not exist, then we are truly lost.

Arguments may be flawed by fallacious reasoning. Among the most common **fallacies** are these:

ad hominem Literally, from the Latin, this means "to the man." It occurs when the argument focuses on the person rather than the point under discussion, as when someone might say, "I'm sure the book is no good; the author is a horrible person."

non sequitur Occurs when one statement isn't logically connected to the other. In other words, **"It doesn't follow."** For example, "She has worked on that paper for days; she'll probably get an 'A'."

either-or Occurs when options are reduced to two extremes, ignoring any middle ground or alternative possibilities. Bumper-sticker philosophers are especially fond of this fallacy: "If you're not part of the solution, you're part of the problem"; "America, love her or leave her."

If elections are usually won by the person with the most money, is this democracy at its best?

In Australian democracy, voting is compulsory. Is this system more democratic than ours?

If only 20% of voters actually cast ballots (as is common in local elections), is this democracy at its best?

Many European democracies use various forms of *proportional representation.* Do you know how such systems work? Is it a good idea?

ASPECTS OF WRITING: Definition and argument; fallacies.

Many discussions lead nowhere because people are too loose in their definition of terms. Gould's discussion of fact and theory draws our attention to such problems. In discussing the results of scientific inquiry, it is necessary also to understand the nature of **the scientific method.** Science is strikingly modest in its claims; even things that are widely accepted laws of physics are subjected to scrutiny and testing. If such testing produces an outcome contrary to that predicted by the "law," then the law has to be reconsidered, revised, or even scrapped.

Disputes in other fields are also sometimes based on differences in definition. Many of the most fundamental terms in politics, for example, are widely used without much regard for specific definition. What is "democracy"? The German Democratic Republic (East Germany) was a communist state. How could the word "democratic" be justified there? What about us? How do we define "democracy," and do we meet our own definition? The word is derived from the Greek **demos,** meaning "common people." In our tradition, democracy has come to mean "government by the people, who freely elect political representatives," but this definition is still open to interpretation. There are many versions of democracy in the world.

THINK ON PAPER
Respond to one of the questions in the boxes opposite.

WRITING AND RESEARCH: Answer one of the following.

1. The argument taken up by Gould—between creationists and evolutionists—has a long history. Use your library to find other commentaries on this theme and write an essay in which you discuss some of the views and arguments expressed. Of course, you may include Gould in your discussion.

More fallacies:

post hoc From the Latin, *post hoc, ergo propter hoc,* meaning "after this, therefore because of this." It's sometimes hard to resist this fallacy, as when we say, "Of course it will rain; I don't have my umbrella with me." Just because this happened in the past doesn't mean that the one thing *caused* the other.

One hint in writing research-based papers is to be **"led by the literature."** This means that you should do plenty of reading before you commit yourself to a thesis or main idea. When you've done some reading, you may be able to identify several possible directions for a paper. Your job then is to choose one of these possibilities and narrow your focus accordingly.

2. Having read Gould's essay carefully, create a thesis that expresses your response. Write a critique in which you summarize *and discuss* the main points made by Gould. Notice that this is more than a summary. The word "critique" does not suggest negative criticism. It suggests a thoughtful analysis and response. Such a response may reflect agreement, disagreement, or a combination of the two. One way to approach this would be to think about why Gould's essay is important.

association fallacy Very common in advertising, this fallacy links an idea or a product with a widely recognized symbol. The use of a sports star to endorse a product for advertising purposes says nothing about the product, but consumers may buy it because they admire the athlete. Other associations may be negative, as in some political propaganda.

Think about the *logic* of what you write.

OPTION TWO

TALKING ABOUT LANGUAGE: Language and time.

Clocks and watches have existed for about 500 years, and their technology has led us to refer to the time ever more precisely. We still use traditional references to the sun, the tides, and other natural phenomena in our lives, but most of our activities and routines seem to be determined by the calendar and the clock.

In the United States most people are very conscious of time. This consciousness is learned as part of our general culture; it isn't something we are born with. Some babies are fed according to a rigid schedule from birth, but by the age of six or seven virtually all children are learning to run their lives according to the clock. They have to be at school on time; lunch is eaten at a particular time; almost everything has its own time and place. Not all cultures are organized this way, but in the United States even our language is full of references to the importance of time:

Benjamin Franklin is usually credited with coining the phrase "Time is money." "Procrastination is the thief of time" comes from Mr. Micawber in Charles Dickens' *David Copperfield.*

Time is money.
She's got time on her hands.
Procrastination is the thief of time.
Don't waste time!

Other common **key words and phrases** include *yesterday, at the moment, soon, while, next, before that, occasionally, sometimes, never, every so often. . . .*

There are many more!

You have already used one kind of logical sequencing—**chronological order.**

English contains many references to the importance of time and is constructed in ways that help us be **precise** when we are indicating when events happened, not only in terms of year, or the time of day, but also in terms of the sequence of events. This is done by means of **tenses, key words** that indicate when something happened, and **logical sequences.**

On the next page you'll find information on tenses, but first think about how key words and phrases determine what you say. For example, which of the following sentences are possible in standard English?

a. Tomorrow, I went home.
b. Tomorrow, I'll go home.
c. Tomorrow, I'll be going home.
d. Tomorrow, I have gone home.

Clearly, (a) and (d) are not possible sentences because the key word—*Tomorrow*—is incompatible with the tense used.

It's important to recognize that language has its own logic, and precision is necessary if you wish to use your language effectively. This means **using the right word, constructing coherent sentences,** and **organizing your thoughts** in a recognizably logical way. If you can do these things, the chances are that you will communicate effectively in writing. It helps if you know something about the language you use every day, and so Option Two provides some basic information about tenses, as well as other aspects of language and time.

The word *tense* comes from the Middle English word *tens,* which in turn came from the Latin word *tempus,* meaning *time.* This may be written as follows: [ME *tens* > Lat. *tempus*]. Check how your dictionary gives this etymology. Then look up the meaning and derivation of "etymology."

ASPECTS OF WRITING: The tense system.

The verb in the chart opposite is **TO PLAY.** This "to" form of the verb is called *the name of the verb,* or the **infinitive.** All verbs have a "to" form: *to be, to go, to study . . . .*

Different languages express time relationships in different ways, but most English tenses can be simply presented in a grid that indicates a general timeframe—**past, present,** and **future**—and a four-part system of tenses—**simple, continuous, perfect,** and **perfect continuous.** The example in the accompanying chart uses the **third person singular** forms of the verb **to play.**

Third person singular means the form of the verb that goes with *he, she, it,* or *one.* In the verb *to play,* this would be *he/she* **plays.** Note that the *-s* ending here does *not* indicate plurality; it marks the third person singular form of the verb.

	PAST	PRESENT	FUTURE
SIMPLE	played	plays	will play
CONTINUOUS	was playing	is playing	will be playing
PERFECT	had played	has played	will have played
PERFECT-CONTINUOUS	had been playing	has been playing	will have been playing

If you think about these tenses, you can see that each form is used to show a particular time relationship. For example,

She plays tennis [every weekend].

She is playing [right now].

She has played [already] .

She has been playing [for an hour].

Notice in these examples that both kinds of continuous tense (sometimes called progressive tense) suggest that the action is still taking place as the statement is made. Notice also that the simple present tense does *not* indicate current action; it indicates habitual events, or something that is always true.

Thinking about how tenses are used is one way of appreciating the precision of language. The comments on this page will also help you to avoid common errors in the use of verbs, and they will give you some useful terms to help you talk about your writing.

The perfect tenses use **participles.** In regular verbs, the participle is the same as the simple past form *I **studied**—I have **studied**),* but in irregular verbs it is *not.* Two examples are **to go** *(I **went**—I have **gone**)* and **to swim** *(She **swam**—She has **swum**).* Can you think of others?

THINK ON PAPER

Many verbs, such as **to play,** are conjugated in the same way. This means that their various forms follow a particular pattern. These are called **regular verbs.** Another example is **to work.** Using **to play** as a model (see the example opposite), fill in the correct form of the verb **to work** in a grid showing the 12 tenses.

Many verbs in English do *not* follow the pattern of **to play** and **to work;** these are **irregular verbs.** The most commonly used irregular verb is **to be;** we say *I am, you are, he/she is, we are, you are, they are* [not "I be," "You be," etc.]. Other verbs that are irregular in some of their forms include **to go** ("I went"), **to eat** ("they ate"), and **to have** ("we had"). Can you think of others? There are plenty!

Quick Quiz

What is the derivation of the word etymology?

A. Check your sense of time in terms of content and language.

1. How old is the universe?
2. How old is the Earth?
3. When did dinosaurs become extinct?
4. How long have modern humans been on Earth?
5. What is the event called that marks the beginning of the universe, according to most cosmogonists?
6. How do scientists know anything about life millions of years ago?
7. What does a paleontologist study?
8. What does A.D. stand for?
9. Who is "Lucy"?
10. What is the zoological name for modern humans?
11. What is our calendar called?

B. Roots

Create a vocabulary web for the following roots, following the models in this unit. Use your dictionary.

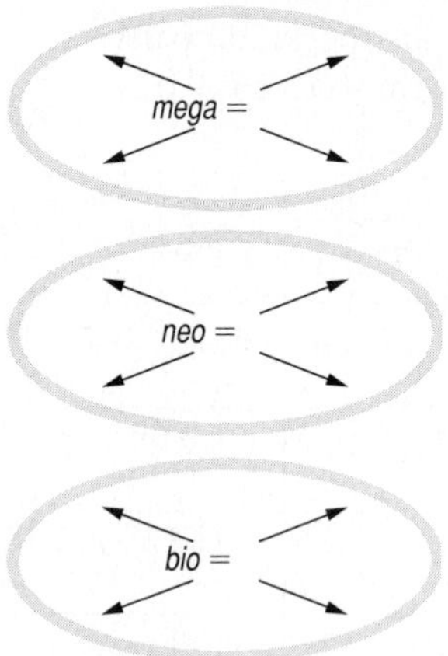

C. Which pronouns are used to conjugate verbs in the following forms?

First person singular
Second person singular
Third person singular
First person plural
Second person plural
Third person plural

How many different forms of the verb **to work** are possible in the following examples?

1. She _____ on the roof at the moment.
2. I _____ when you came home.
3. That librarian only _____ on Tuesdays.

It is likely that there will be disagreement in class about whether a particular form is possible in these sentences. This doesn't matter; the point is to **think** about the language we use.

Calvin and Hobbes **by Bill Watterson**

SECTION ONE

PRIOR KNOWLEDGE: The physical world.

There are many contexts in which we can see ourselves and our world. In the largest context—that of the universe itself—we seem very small. The Earth is one of nine planets orbiting an ordinary star located on an outer arm of a spiral galaxy called the Milky Way. This galaxy, which contains at least 100 billion other stars, is just one of at least 100 billion galaxies in the universe. After the sun, our nearest stellar neighbor within the Milky Way is more than four light-years away; our nearest galactic neighbors, including Andromeda, are about *two million* light-years away. These distances are so great that the possibility of thoroughly exploring even our own galaxy seems remote.

The nine planets of the solar system, in order of their mean distance from the sun, have the initial letters M, V, E, M, J, S, U, N, and P. One way to remember such lists is to make up a sentence in which the beginning letters follow this same pattern. Can you invent one? Memory helpers like this are called **mnemonics.**

The Earth herself, however, has been quite thoroughly explored, except for the deep oceans. We know the Earth's basic structure, from its metallic core to its dynamic crust, which is broken into a system of slowly moving plates. The study of **plate tectonics** has allowed us to understand that the "fit" between western Africa and eastern South America is not just coincidence; the continents were once all connected in a supercontinent called Pangaea, which broke up as the continents slowly drifted over the face of the globe. Some, such as South America and Africa, drifted apart; others collided, as happened when India moved north and bumped into Eurasia. This collision, which continues today, led to the creation of the Himalayas. The way the world is today is not the way it always was, or always will be.

The distribution of animals today and in prehistoric times reflects, in part, the movement of the Earth's plates. Think about the worldwide distribution of dinosaur fossils and the uniqueness of Australia's animals, for example.

California will eventually drift into the Pacific, East Africa will drift into the Indian Ocean, and Africa will collide with Europe, eliminating the Mediterranean Sea, but more immediate effects of plate tectonics occur in the form of earthquakes and volcanoes. The "ring of fire," which marks the boundaries between the Pacific plate and its neighbors, gives the inhabitants of the **Pacific Rim countries** frequent earthquakes and volcanic eruptions. California, New Zealand, Japan, Alaska, and other countries around the Pacific are part of the "ring of fire."

The phrase "Pacific Rim countries" is becoming widely used, especially in an economic context, as this region contains many of the world's most vigorous economies, such as South Korea and Taiwan.

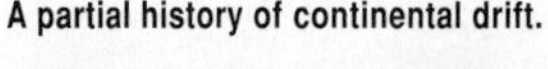

A partial history of continental drift.

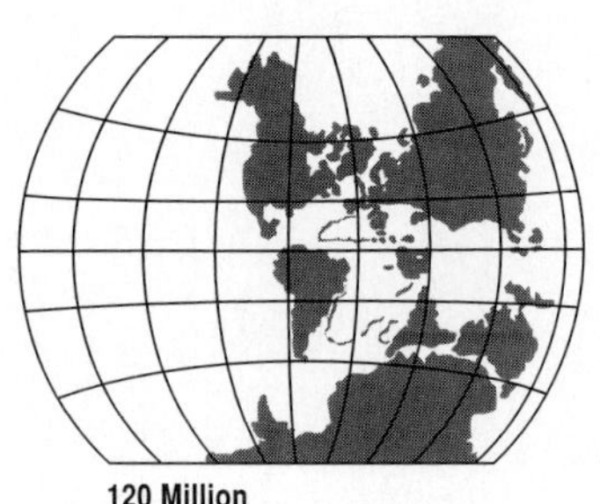

120 Million

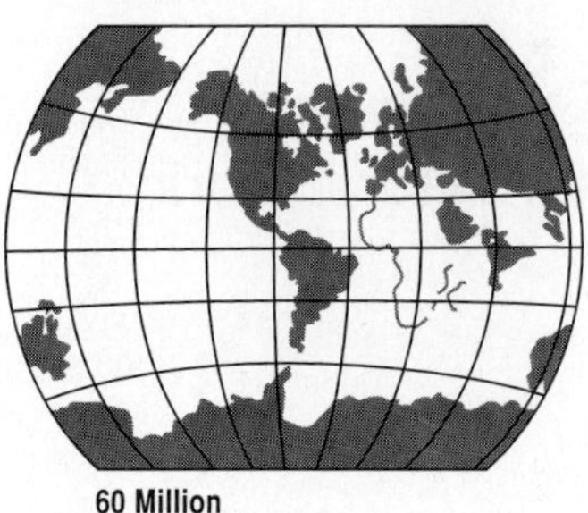

60 Million

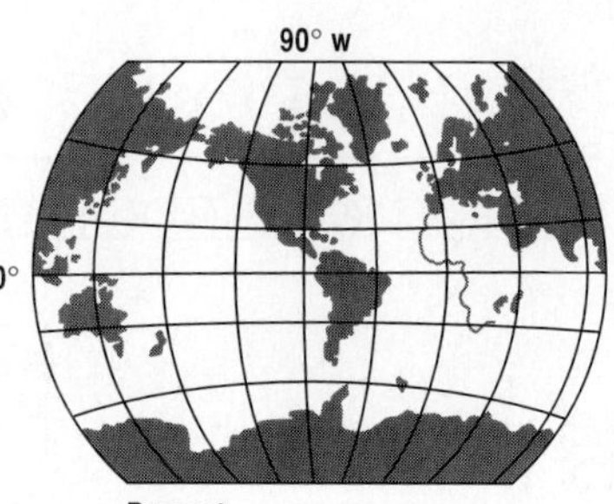

Present

Time shown in millions of years before present.

(From: *Earth's Dynamic Crust* (map), National Geographic Society, August, 1985.)

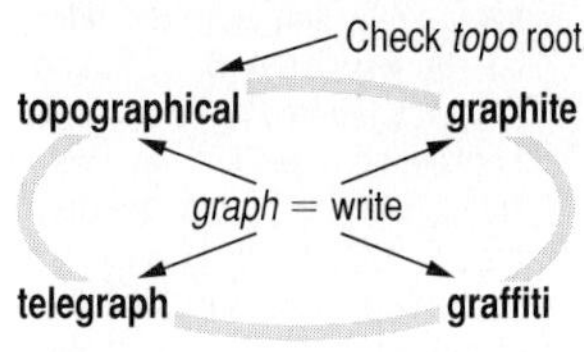

Other people's daily lives may be more affected by other phenomena. Whether you live in the mountains, on the prairie, in a river valley, on an island, in the desert, or by an ocean, your life, and perhaps your sense of who you are, is affected. Even the latitude at which we live is likely to have a crucial impact on the way we live, for the climate affects almost everything.

Like other fields, geography has many specialties. For example, a **physical geographer** looks at topography; a **human geographer** looks at people within their **environment;** a **demographer** studies population; and a **meteorologist** studies climate and weather.

The importance of our immediate environment is obvious, but we often ignore the familiar. If you live near a river, do you know where that river rises and where it flows to? Can you describe the physical environment around you, or in your country, or in your continent, or in your world?

Topographical maps reveal the physical features of a continent, country, or region in ways that other maps don't, and they can help us visualize what different parts of the world are like. Each continent has a few major features that enable us to draw a thumbnail sketch—either literally or in words. **Almanacs** and **atlases** provide this kind of information about particular countries as well as about whole continents.

THINK ON PAPER
Briefly describe where you live from a topographical point of view. You might start by pooling everything the class knows about your region of the country.

If you don't own an almanac, think about getting one. They only cost a few dollars and provide an enormous amount of factual information.

ANNOTATED READING: Kenneth C. Davis. Selections from *Don't Know Much About Geography.* New York: Avon, 1992: 81–85, 118–122.

WERE THE CONTINENTS ACTUALLY ATTACHED AT ONE TIME?

What *was* that? Did you hear a bump in the night? Perhaps it was California rubbing shoulders with the Pacific Ocean.

One of the most perplexing theories about our so-called "solid Earth" is the notion that all of the land on Earth isn't sitting still but sloshing around like toy boats in a wash tub on which small boys are banging hammers!

This notion is technically known as *global plate tectonics*, an almost universally accepted theory. Although the idea that pieces of the Earth are in constant motion and that the continents had once been attached to each other goes back hundreds of years, it was formally put forward first by Alfred Wegener in his 1915 book, *The Origin of the Continents and Oceans*. A German meteorologist and naturalist, Wegener was interested in the seeming alignments of the continents. Like a jigsaw puzzle waiting to be put together, the Atlantic coastlines of South America and Africa looked like they could be snapped together into a fairly neat arrangement. When Wegener learned of the discovery of fossils in Brazil that were similar to those found in Africa, it added fuel to his notion that the two places were once connected. Based on these and other bits of physical evidence, Wegener proposed the idea that the continents had once been a single mass, which later split. He even christened his theoretical giant landmass Pangaea ("All Land") and surrounded it by an all-encompassing sea, Panthalassa ("All Seas").

Like so many other new ideas in science, Wegener's theory of "continental drift" was largely dismissed in his day, principally because he was unable to explain the forces that could propel such enormous landmasses. Wegener thought that tidal pull might have something to do with the process. A visionary and hero of science, Wegener died in 1930 in Greenland as he attempted to establish a mid-ice observatory. For decades to come, his ideas were simply dismissed as the left-field notions of a crackpot.

But somewhere in science heaven, Wegener is having the last laugh. A large body of evidence collected since the 1960s has shown that Wegener was indeed on the right path. British geologist S. Keith Runcorn was one of the first champions of the revised notions of continents being connected. Wegener's theory of continental drift has

Davis' book, like his earlier *Don't Know Much About History* is both light-hearted and serious. He jokes about widespread "geographical illiteracy," but his book is intended to help remedy the situation. Listeners to "oldies" radio stations may recognize the titles of his books as coming from an old hit song.

In Unit One you were urged to make sure that you know the **references** and **allusions** to people and events in what you read. It is just as important that you know the **places** you come across in your reading. In Boorstin's article on the calendar, for example, he refers to many places that are still on the map—including Egypt, Greece, and China—and some that aren't—such as Babylon. Do you know where these places are? If you don't, *get a map and look them up.* For Babylon, a dictionary should help you.

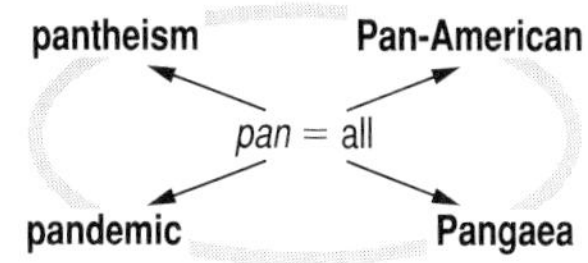

The movement of the plates is usually slow, and it isn't constant, but in some places the ocean floors have spread apart by up to eight inches per year. The mid-Atlantic ridge is one area where such spreading is taking place: the Atlantic is still getting wider.

evolved into what is now called "plate tectonics theory." Continental drift is out because it is now known that more than just the continents are on the move. The Earth's crust is divided into mobile sections called *plates*. Some of these plates contain continents, or large parts of them; others carry the sea floor. The plates—Canadian geophysicist J. T. Wilson first used the term *plates* in 1965—move over the Earth's superheated, molten core, pushed and pulled by convection currents in the molten material generated by the heat of the Earth's core. The study of the movements of these large plates is called *tectonics* (from the Greek word *tekton*, "to build"). Think of cooking tapioca pudding. You get it to boiling and you can see bubbles move up to the top. If you put something that could float on top of the pudding into the top, it would start bucking and jostling around the cooking pot. The inside of the Earth is like a big vat of bubbling tapioca, except that the pudding is magma, the liquefied matter within the Earth's core that gets blasted out in volcanoes. Floating on top of the magma are the pieces of Earth's crust called the plates.

Definition of words is often necessary, especially when using technical vocabulary. This can be done in a number of ways, one of which is demonstrated here by Davis, who provides a parenthetical note on the etymology of the word *tectonics.* This kind of **in-text definition** allows you to use the right words without raising the level of technicality beyond the understanding of the reader.

The plates average from thirty to fifty miles in thickness and move at rates as great as a few inches per year. They may be as large as a few thousand miles across—the North American plate stretches for six thousand miles from the Pacific coast to the mid-Atlantic—or as little as a few hundred miles across. People tend to associate rock with the idea of solidity. It is hard to imagine such massive pieces of rock cruising around the planet's surface. The key to their movement is the flexibility of the upper part of Earth's mantle—the layer beneath the crust—which is partly molten. As the plates "float" on this elastic, moving mantle, they play a planetary game of hockey—jostling each other for position, rubbing each other the wrong way, pushing one another down or occasionally banging straight into each other with dramatic and sometimes catastrophic effects. And they are not fin-

You're probably familiar with valleys cut in the earth by rivers and glaciers, but a **rift valley** is different; it is formed by land movements between parallel faults, or breaks in the Earth's crust.

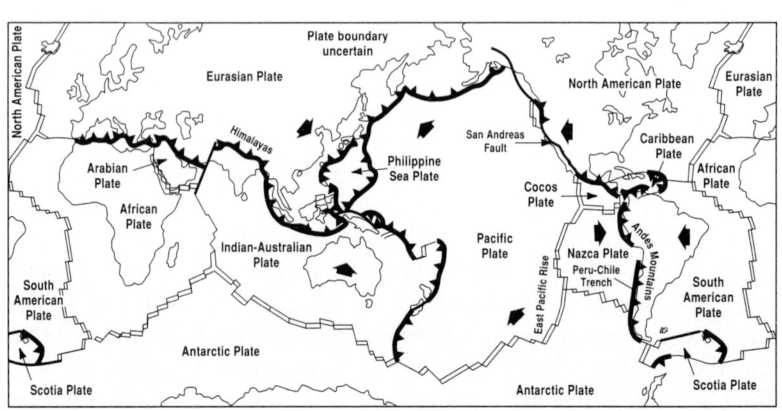

ished yet. The world we recognize today will be quite different in, say, 50 million years. (Again, this is a blink of the eye in the geological time frame.) For instance, a good-sized portion of East Africa will probably break off. You can see where it will happen if you stand in the Great Rift Valley, which extends from Syria to Mozambique. And Baja California will have detached itself from the Mexican mainland.

The Great Rift Valley is one of the world's most spectacular natural features. Its best-known sections are in East Africa, especially in Kenya. Check the location of Syria and Mozambique, so that you know where the Rift Valley is located.

THE MAJOR CRUSTAL PLATES AND WHERE THEY ARE GOING

African plate: heading southwest, away from Europe

Arabian plate: moving north toward Eurasia

Eurasian plate: moving toward the southeast

Australian plate: heading due north

Pacific plate: moving generally to the northwest

North American plate: sliding west toward the Pacific and edging south

South American plate: heading west

Davis seems to be in error here. Most experts believe that Africa is moving north, as indicated in the map on page 52.

Back to Wegener's Pangaea, or supercontinent. The best thinking goes that all the Earth's land masses were concentrated in one great mass some 220 million years ago. As the plates moved apart, Pangaea was split into two huge continental masses. Laurasia, in the northern hemisphere, was made up of what became North America, Europe, Greenland, and Asia. In the southern hemisphere, the second supercontinent was Gondwanaland, made up of the future Africa, South America, Antarctica, and Australia. Other scientists suggest that the process may have started out with the two smaller masses crashing together around 300 million years ago to form Pangaea, which then later reseparated. But either way, by 100 million years ago, the current continents were taking shape. Europe broke off from North America to join with Asia, and South America was breaking off from Africa. Then, 65 million years ago, India broke off from Africa and moved north on a collision course with Asia. Australia, severed from Antarctica, moved to its present position.

Here, Davis takes us efficiently around the primordial world with a combination of spatial and chronological order. Notice the transitional phrases, such as "In the southern hemisphere."

As India moves north, the Himalayas are being pushed a little higher every year. This range already includes the highest mountains in the world, including **Mt. Everest,** the highest point on Earth, which reaches 29,028 feet above sea level. Some measurements of Everest suggest it may be even higher, but experts are divided on this. How do we measure the height of mountains?

IS AMERICA ONE CONTINENT OR TWO?

If a continent is a large unbroken land mass completely surrounded by water, why call North and South America different continents? They are clearly connected to each other. Central America—comprised of the seven independent republics of Belize, Costa Rica, El Salvador, Guatemala, Honduras, Nicaragua, and Panama—creates a land bridge

Many dictionaries include notes on word **usage** as well as definitions, etymology, and so on. Discussions of usage usually focus on words that are widely misused or for which the usage is changing. Experts often disagree, in the latter case, whether or not a particular word usage is acceptable. Davis' use of *comprised of* is a good example of this. Look it up in your dictionary and see if there is a usage note discussing *comprise* and *composed of.*

between North and South America. And even though this thin strip was often flooded in the past, logically speaking, the two continents are one. But political and historical considerations—especially the fact that the history of Canada and the United States were dominated by the British, while Spain retained its control of Mexico and almost everything south of it save Brazil—often override geographical facts. And no one ever said that geography is a perfectly logical science anyway!

Americans may be poor on the facts about Canada and Mexico, their nearest neighbors, but they are utterly desperate when it comes to South America. For instance, most Americans would be surprised to learn that virtually the whole continent of South America lies east of Savannah, Georgia. With an area of 6,883,000 square miles (c. 18 million square km), South America is the world's fourth-largest continent, with almost 12 percent of the Earth's land surface. South America's 302 million people live in twelve independent republics and one colonial-era holdover (French Guiana). And even though it seems that the population density is comparatively low, South America is intensely urban, because much of the continent is either inaccessible or can't be farmed because of the its two most prominent geographical features, the Andes Mountains and the Amazon rain forest.

The **colonial history** of the Americas—mostly Spanish and Portuguese in Central and South America, mostly British and French in North America (although these lines are not clear-cut)—also explains some of the cultural differences, including language, political traditions, and religion. In an ever-changing world, these distinctions are blurring, but, as we'll see again in Unit Three, the colonial inheritance has done much to shape the modern world.

The Andes Mountains run for approximately 4,500 miles along almost the entire western, or Pacific, coast of South America, more than three times the length of the American Rockies. Passing through seven of South America's 12 republics—Argentina, Chile, Bolivia, Peru, Ecuador, Colombia, and Venezuela—the Andes are second only to the Himalayas in terms of average height. (The other South American republics are Brazil, Guyana, Paraguay, Suriname, and Uruguay; French Guiana is the last remaining European possession on the continent.) Cerro Aconcagua, the western hemisphere's tallest peak at 22,834 feet (6,960 meters), is in the Andes near Argentina's northwest border with Chile. In Chile, a slender thread of country 1,800 miles long, the Andes Mountains cover one third of the land, making much of the country unfarmable. Chile is home to a large, mineral-rich desert, the Atacama, and also claims the world's southernmost city, Punta Arenas.

The Atacama Desert is the driest place on Earth. In some parts, rain has never been recorded. Check your almanac!

Hidden in the Peruvian Andes for almost five hundred years was the mystery of Machu Picchu, once a great Incan city. Lords of an extensive and highly centralized empire, the Inca (also the title of the empire's ruler) held territory that extended 3,000 miles from north to south along a 250-mile-wide corridor from the Pacific coastal plain to the high Andes. Although they lacked the wheel or writing, the Inca were master builders, with an elaborate system of roads and cable suspension bridges that allowed messengers to travel as much as 150 miles per day. The Inca system of terraced farms not only produced ample

The Inca, Mayan, and other great civilizations of South and Central America went into decline, but a large part of the present population of countries such as Peru is of Indian descent.

food but controlled erosion of the soil on the steep mountainside farmlands—techniques that are being reintroduced after centuries of colonial neglect and governmental mismanagement. Inca architects raised fine buildings in the capital city of Cuzco, which meant "navel" in the Quechua language of the Incas, another example of the omphalos syndrome . . . Goldsmiths fashioned beautiful objects that immediately caught the attention of the Spaniards who arrived in 1532. Weakened by internal wars, the Incas fell easy prey to the conquistadors, who brought smallpox, far more devastating than any weapon.

The Andes are one of the great natural features of South America that Davis chooses to describe. Notice that his account includes references not only to the **physical geography** of the region, but also to its **political geography** (countries), **human geography** (people and culture), and **economic geography** (wealth, resources, industry). These references allow him to include details that expand and inform his essay.

The details make the essay interesting; think about this in your own writing!

But their greatest building feat may have been Machu Picchu. Perched high up in the Andes, on a mountainous crag that drops steeply on every side, Machu Picchu went undiscovered until the American Hiram Bingham reached it in 1911. In the city, steep stairways lead to granite shrines, marvelously carved stone temples and houses, terraced walls built without mortar, and huge ceremonial stones. Streets, stairways, and plazas were all laid out in perfect harmony with the contours of the mountaintop. With windows placed in temples to permit observation of the midwinter solstice, Machu Picchu was most likely a sacred city where the Inca lords and Virgins of the Sun went to worship. Even though the Spanish had destroyed almost every other vestige of Incan society, Machu Picchu was found almost intact. But its origins and the reasons for its apparent abandonment remain a mystery.

Located on the northwest coast, Peru is today the third-largest South American republic. Once the principal source of Spain's gold and silver in South America, Peru was largely stripped of its wealth and today its economy struggles. Because of the Andes, only 3 percent of the land is arable, and communication and transportation are also made difficult by the terrain, a perfect example of the negative interaction between geography and a nation's economy. Although commercial fishing is a significant part of the Peruvian economy, overfishing of its coastal waters has caused a steep decline in the catch.

The other great geographical region described by Davis is the **Amazon.** The River Amazon is 4,000 miles long, and it drains one of the greatest river basins in the world. It is also, of course, the centerpiece of the Amazon rainforest, which has received so much attention in recent years because of controversy over logging, settlement, development, and the rights of indigenous people.

South America's other most extraordinary feature is Brazil's Amazon rain forest and its river. Nearly half of South America is covered by Brazil, and its heavily-wooded Amazon basin covers half the country. The largest country in South America and the fifth-largest in the world, Brazil is larger than the contiguous forty-eight American states. But the vast Amazon river basin holds only a tiny population. Ten percent of Brazil's 140 million people live in two cities, São Paulo and Rio de Janeiro, and almost half the population lives in the south-central region, which produces 80 percent of the nation's industrial output and 75 percent of its farm products. One of the world's leading debtor nations, Brazil is in the midst of a major economic makeover that is attempting to break decades of unimaginable inflation rates.

Like most places in the world, Brazil is becoming increasingly urban. **Rio de Janeiro** and **Sao Paolo** are the two largest cities, but the capital is **Brasilia,** a new city built in the interior of the country.

A simplified geography of South America might include the two regions described by Davis—the Andes and the Amazon—and also the **pampas,** the great grasslands of Argentina and Uruguay stretching from the Andes to the Atlantic, and **Patagonia,** the barren far south of the continent.

The Sears Tower is no longer the world's tallest building.

Rhetorical note: Davis's essay is informative, but its most interesting rhetorical feature is probably the lightness and informality of his **tone.**

THINK ON PAPER
How does Davis achieve his informal tone? Find examples in his essay.

Among its other geographical wonders, South America is also home of the world's highest waterfall, Angel Falls (Salto Angel), in southeast Venezuela (which means "Little Venice," a name given by Amerigo Vespucci, who was struck by native huts perched above the coastal waters). Hidden in Venezuela's remote forests, the falls drop 3,212 feet from the side of a twenty-mile-long flat-topped mountain, or *mesa,* known as Auyán-tepuí (Devil Mountain). That is thirteen times higher than Niagara Falls and more than double the size of the Sears Tower in Chicago, the world's tallest building (1,454 feet; 443 meters). Almost totally inaccessible, Angel Falls can be seen fully only from the air. Which is how it was first seen and then got its name. It would be logical to think that the waterfall, unlike the nearby mountain named for the devil, is named for celestial messengers. The image certainly applies, as the white water sails through the air from such great heights. But the falls are actually named for an American flier and prospector, Jimmy Angel, who discovered them in 1935 and crashed his plane nearby in 1937. The falls were not reached by foot and accurately surveyed until 1949, when an American team confirmed their height.

ASPECTS OF WRITING: Spatial order.

Just as chronological order gives us a logical way of describing events by using time sequences, so **spatial order** allows us to describe the physical world in orderly fashion by moving systematically from one location to another. Sometimes, as we saw in Trefil's essay in Unit One, it's helpful to use both of these methods of organization in the same essay.

Some kinds of spatial order are obvious. When describing the planets of the solar system, for example, it makes sense to start with the one nearest the sun, Mercury, and move outward from there. Virtually all lists of the planets use this pattern. A little less predictable is the spatial order used in a national weather report. The starting point for this may be determined by meteorological events, rather than location. In the following example, although the description moves generally from West to East, several major areas are not mentioned; an accompanying map provides details of weather conditions in places not mentioned in the written account:

> Tropical moisture streaming east from Hawaii will interact with a powerful jet stream disturbance approaching northern California, fueling a major storm. Heavy rain will arrive at the coast, with rainfalls of four inches possible in some areas, especially along west-facing slopes of the Coastal Range. . . .
>
> The influx of relatively mild, humid air will cause snow levels to rise in the northern Sierra and the Siskiyous. Heavy snow is likely.
>
> Farther north, windswept rain will buffet western Oregon and Washington, with snow in the Cascades. . . . Snow will spread to the Bitterroots of Idaho later today. Along the Front Range of the Rockies, gusty winds will at times exceed 50 miles an hour from eastern Colorado across Wyoming to western Montana.
>
> Strengthening onshore winds along the southeast coast of Florida will combine with a jet stream disturbance approaching from the Gulf of Mexico to raise the risk of locally moderate to heavy rain later today and tonight.
>
> Light snow will fall early today in northern New England as a low-pressure system pivots towards the Canadian Maritimes. As the system departs, sunny skies, seasonable temperatures and gusty winds from the northwest will prevail on the northern Middle Atlantic and southern New England Seaboards.
>
> (*New York Times,* February 16, 1994: B13)

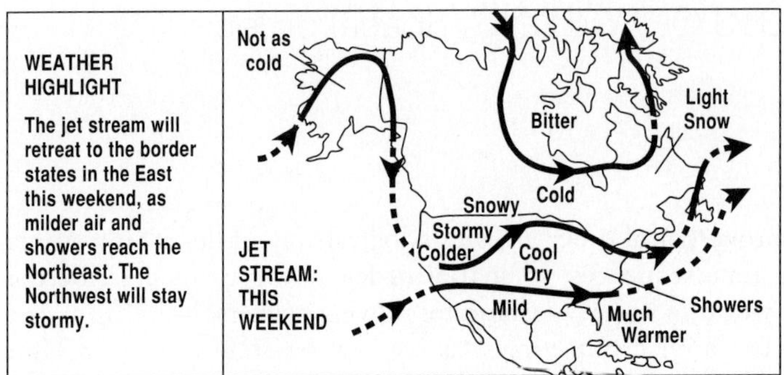

Notice how this weather forecast takes the reader from place to place by providing directions ("farther north") and by referring to specific states (Hawaii, Wyoming, etc.), physical features (the Rockies), and regions (New England, the Canadian Maritimes). It's up to you to know where these places are! Can you identify them on the map that accompanies this weather report?

Like the above weather forecast, any geographical description of a country would require the writer to make an arbitrary decision about where to start. The weather report, for example, could have started in Florida rather than in the Pacific Ocean. Where would you start a description of the physical geography of the United States? First, you would probably look at a map, or sketch your own, and decide which

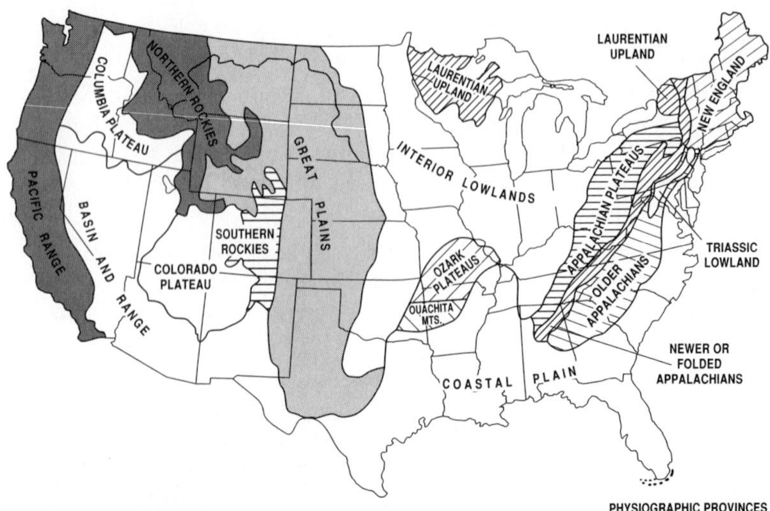

(From: *The National Atlas of the USA.* Washington, DC: U.S. Department of the Interior, Geological Survey, 1970.)

major features you would include. Any list would include the major mountain ranges of the East and the West, the Appalachians and the Rockies, respectively, and other major regions such as the coastal plains, the deserts of the Southwest, the Great Lakes, the Mississippi-Missouri river system, the prairies, and the Great Central Lowlands. But where would you start? You might follow the pioneers and move from East to West, or you might choose to use familiar regional terms: the East, the South, the Midwest, and the West. Sometimes we refer to smaller areas within these regions; if we're discussing Native American cultures, for example, important geographical and cultural distinctions would include the High Plains (Montana, Wyoming) and the Pacific Northwest. Making an orderly sequence is important, but it is also quite a challenge.

Of course, an interesting account of the physical geography of a country would include **details** and **description,** not just a simple list of features. An almanac will provide you with all sorts of information about land areas, high points (Mt. McKinley), low points (Death Valley), the dimensions of the Grand Canyon, and much more. Use such details, and any personal knowledge you have, to make your account informative. Simple things you can include would be the direction of flow for major rivers, the location of the continental divide, and the north-south orientation of the major mountain ranges.

Keep in mind that you are **systematically** covering an area, and that you need to take your reader with you. Good transitions help make your description coherent.

One of the instructions in this and other assignments is to make your writing *interesting.* This may seem difficult to achieve, but if you take opportunities to add *details,* then you should find that your writing comes alive. Of course, a lot depends on your willingness to look for information when you don't know very much about a topic. In these units, a lot of information is supplied in the text, class discussion is encouraged, and films may be available, but you may still find it valuable to find additional information. Two of the principles that inspire this course are that

knowing things is more fun than not knowing things

and that

knowing how to find information is just as important as what you know already.

If you agree with these sentiments, then you'll probably find it easier to make your papers interesting.

WRITING EXERCISES: Answer one of the following.

1. Write a description of where you live, starting with your immediate environment and moving on progressively to your state, country, continent, hemisphere, world, solar system, galaxy, and universe. If you can think of any variations on this idea, by all means use them. The key is to be systematic, coherent, and interesting. One variation would be to reverse the sequence; another would be to imagine an alien finding our galaxy (even our universe?) and reporting his/her/its discoveries. Use your imagination, but remember that *you must use spatial order,* even if it is in combination with chronological order or some other logical sequence.
2. Describe, systematically and clearly, the physical geography of the contiguous United States (the lower 48) or another country or continent. Concentrate on *the most important features*—that is to say, those features with which everyone should have at least some familiarity. A successful account will include details and comments that make the description interesting. For example, if you describe the Grand Canyon, you should certainly mention the river that runs through it, the dimensions of the canyon, and possibly the fact that it is a major international tourist attraction and a national park.

Sample thesis: The United States has a wealth of natural features, even if we focus only on the lower 48 states and leave out the spectacular sights of Alaska and Hawaii. Each region has its different attractions: the East has the Appalachians, the Southeast has the Everglades, the central areas of the country have the Great Lakes and the Great Plains, the West has the Rockies, and the Southwest has its deserts.

(You may choose to divide the country differently and mention different or additional features, but this gives the idea. Add Hawaii and Alaska, too, if you wish.)

SECTION TWO

PRIOR KNOWLEDGE: The world according to maps.

There are many kinds of maps: road maps, campus maps, world maps, geological maps, topographical maps, weather maps, population maps, and many more. These all have specific uses; we all use road maps to help us find our way, gardeners use maps showing climatic zones to know when to start planting, road engineers use topographical maps to find the best route for a new highway.

Familiarity with the world map allows us to follow news stories and to read articles and books much more effectively. Many people, however, have very limited knowledge of this type. Despite all the events of recent years, for example, how many people in your class can locate **Iran** and **Iraq** on the map—or even countries as important as **Japan?** Or **Vietnam?** We put ourselves in a position of weakness, both personally and nationally, if we know nothing about countries with whom we trade, compete, and sometimes even go to war.

As the world becomes more interdependent, it is in our own self-interest to inform ourselves about events outside our borders. To keep yourself informed, to enrich your understanding of the world around you, you should read a newspaper (a *good* one!); this will also help your reading and writing. Read the editorials and feature articles as well as the news; at their best, they can be excellent models for thoughtful, articulate writing on important issues.

This kind of knowledge—knowing your way around the world—is especially important today because of the dramatic changes that are occurring. It is a cliché, but it is also true, that the world is "shrinking." Many terms are used to describe this phenomenon, including *interdependence, globalization, the global economy, the global village,* and so on. New communications technology is only one aspect of this; it also involves the increasingly international nature of trade, banking, stock market and currency transactions, insurance, manufacturing, entertainment, and sports. It has become impossible for any modern nation to isolate itself from the world and sustain an acceptable standard of living for its citizens.

The United States has the world's largest economy; Japan's is second. Japan has about 124 million people; what's the population of the United States?

The five most populous countries in the world are China, India, the United States, Indonesia, and Russia. Where's Indonesia?

People who know nothing outside their own town or country may be described as being *parochial* in outlook.

Whenever you read about a country, make sure you know where it is.

An **almanac** contains all sorts of wonderful information between its covers: the highest point on Earth? the lowest point on Earth (on land and in the oceans)? the longest river? the wettest and driest places on Earth? Browse through it—it's a gold mine. The biggest gold mine in the world?

Many people believe that developing a global outlook is a necessary response to the new realities. The idea of the *Earth* being home to us all is dramatically and beautifully illustrated by NASA photographs of the Earth floating in space. This image is now widely used by environmentalists, advertisers, and others, as illustrated here.

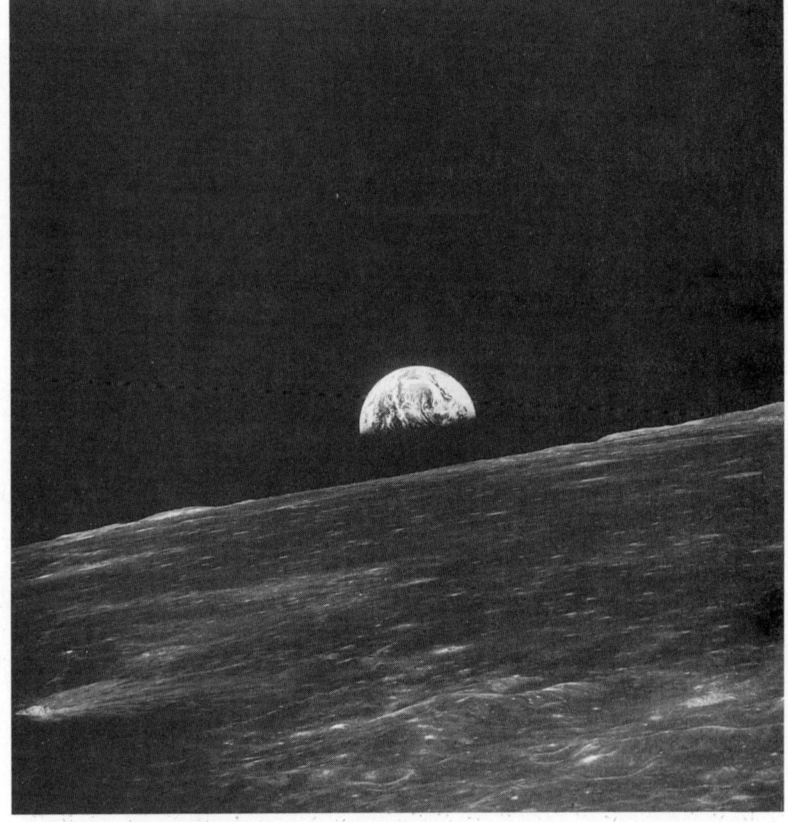

(UPI/Corbis-Bettmann)

Cars are a good example of how the **global economy** works. Is a U.S.-made Honda a Japanese car? Is a Plymouth Voyager with a Japanese engine and a Canadian body an American car? What about the Ford Escort described in the accompanying diagram? It is assembled in Britain and Germany from parts produced in *fifteen* different countries.

The global economy is not just an abstraction; whenever an American company moves a factory to another country, or whenever a foreign company moves into the United States, we see the global economy in action. When the Tokyo, Hong Kong, London, Sydney, and New York stock markets react to good or bad news, and to each other's ups and downs, this also is the global economy at work. On a political level, when military bases in the United States and Europe close down after the collapse of the Soviet Union and the end of the Cold War, we see how events in one country can affect, in a direct way, families and communities in another country.

If it's impossible to understand the modern world without having a sense of the global dimensions of trade, jobs, politics, and related matters, then, surely, it's necessary to know something about the world beyond one's own town, state, and country. To be a modern person, it might be said that one needs to be able to **think globally!**

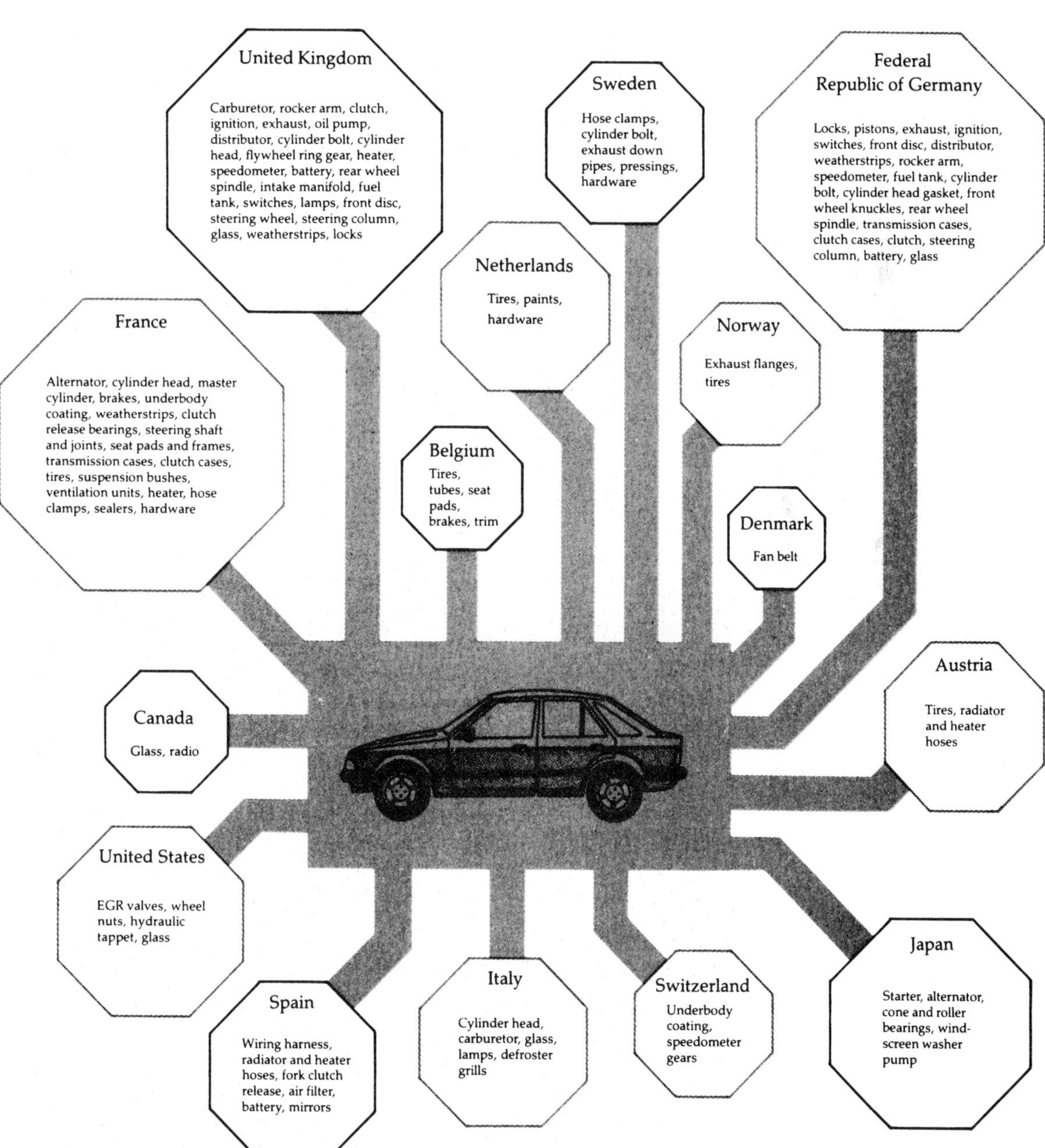
United Kingdom
Carburetor, rocker arm, clutch, ignition, exhaust, oil pump, distributor, cylinder bolt, cylinder head, flywheel ring gear, heater, speedometer, battery, rear wheel spindle, intake manifold, fuel tank, switches, lamps, front disc, steering wheel, steering column, glass, weatherstrips, locks
Sweden
Hose clamps, cylinder bolt, exhaust down pipes, pressings, hardware
Federal Republic of Germany
Locks, pistons, exhaust, ignition, switches, front disc, distributor, weatherstrips, rocker arm, speedometer, fuel tank, cylinder bolt, cylinder head gasket, front wheel knuckles, rear wheel spindle, transmission cases, clutch cases, clutch, steering column, battery, glass
Netherlands
Tires, paints, hardware
France
Alternator, cylinder head, master cylinder, brakes, underbody coating, weatherstrips, clutch release bearings, steering shaft and joints, seat pads and frames, transmission cases, clutch cases, tires, suspension bushes, ventilation units, heater, hose clamps, sealers, hardware
Norway
Exhaust flanges, tires
Belgium
Tires, tubes, seat pads, brakes, trim
Denmark
Fan belt
Austria
Tires, radiator and heater hoses
Canada
Glass, radio
United States
EGR valves, wheel nuts, hydraulic tappet, glass
Japan
Starter, alternator, cone and roller bearings, windscreen washer pump
Spain
Wiring harness, radiator and heater hoses, fork clutch release, air filter, battery, mirrors
Italy
Cylinder head, carburetor, glass, lamps, defroster grills
Switzerland
Underbody coating, speedometer gears

(From: World Development Report 1987. Washington, D.C.: World Bank.)

The **Babylonians** were mentioned by Boorstin in Unit One for their contributions to the development of the calendar. Babylon is part of Mesopotamia on the maps of the ancient world. **The Hanging Gardens of Babylon** were one of the wonders of the world.

Maps shape the way we think of the world. American world maps typically show the Americas in the middle, with Africa and Europe on one side and East Asia on the other. European and African maps usually show those continents in the middle, with the Americas off to the west and Asia off to the east. Australian and Chinese maps, no surprise, give those countries center stage. Seeing oneself as the center of the world seems to be a universal human weakness! This is a form of the **omphalos syndrome** mentioned by Kenneth Davis; the phrase comes from the Greek word for *navel*.

Rhetorical note: Makower provides a good example of expository writing, providing a brief history of cartography. Of particular interest later in his essay are examples of different ways of showing the world in maps; these open up nice possibilities for a **comparison and contrast** essay.

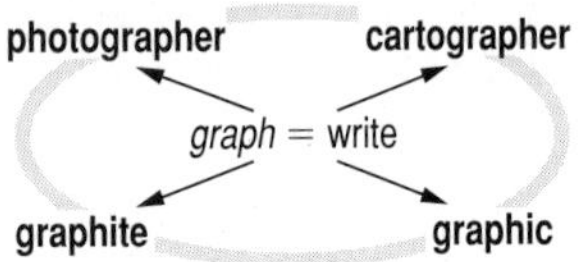

The etymology above shows two words with more than one useful root: photo = light, carte = map.

ANNOTATED READING: Joel Makower. "The Map Unfolds." *The Map Catalog.* New York: Vintage, 1986: 10–13.

The history of the map dates back to man's first realization that a picture truly is worth a thousand words. Archaeologists and other social scientists have often marveled at early man's almost instinctive ability to produce rough but amazingly accurate sketches of his surroundings. Throughout the world's civilizations—from African tribesmen to Arctic Eskimos—there are examples of these early maps, drawn in the earth or on stones or animal skins, showing the relative positions and distances of landmarks and localities. The Babylonians, more than two thousand years before Christ, surveyed individual land holdings on clay tablets. Known as cadastral maps, they represent one of the earliest forms of graphic expression. Those ancient surveys later became the basis for map making in Europe during the Middle Ages and, four millennia later, for land plats produced by the U.S. government.

The modern-day craft of making maps can be traced to western Europe in the 13th century. The regional and local maps of the day represented radical changes from the drawings that preceded them: rather than being derived from literary sources and mythology, they were based on observation and measurements, the first maps intended for practical use by travelers on land or sea. The second half of the thirteenth century produced the earliest surviving nautical charts and post-Roman road maps.

It was in the waters of the Mediterranean and the Black Sea that map making made great strides. The development of the mariner's compass permitted angular measurement, enabling a level of accuracy in nautical charts that wouldn't be seen in land maps for several hundred years. Among those first efforts were the Italian portolan charts, which were sets of sailing instructions created on parchment around 1250 by a community of Italian draftsmen just becoming familiar with mathematics and measurement. Many of the early European cartographers were recruited from the ranks of painters, miniaturists, and other artists, whose introduction to the profession consisted largely of copying and decorating existing maps. Later, they were able to compile their own. Italy, and especially Florence, was a center of cartographic activity for several centuries. Here, a succession of explorers, artists, and mathematicians created new pictures that expressed an expanding world view.

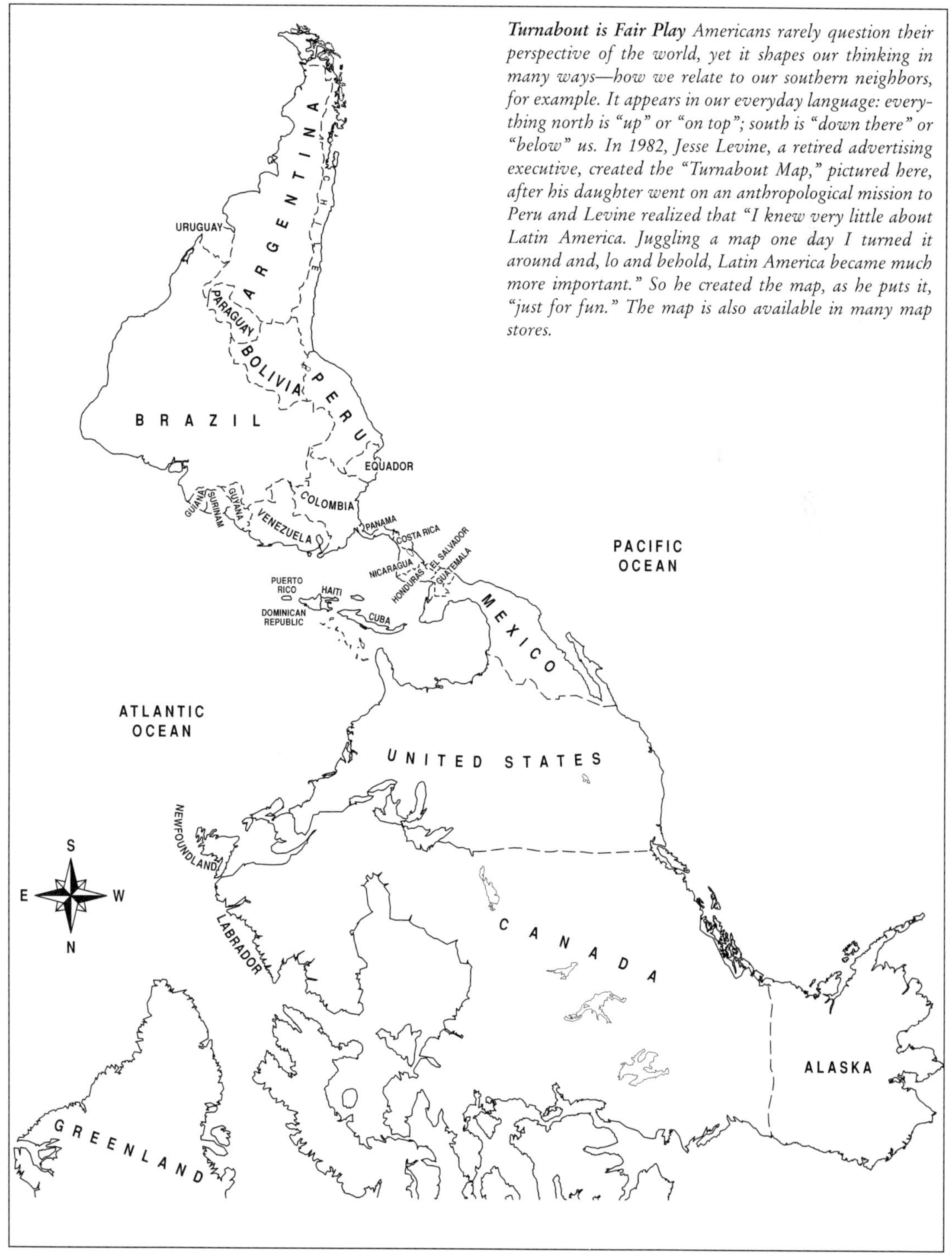

Turnabout is Fair Play *Americans rarely question their perspective of the world, yet it shapes our thinking in many ways—how we relate to our southern neighbors, for example. It appears in our everyday language: everything north is "up" or "on top"; south is "down there" or "below" us. In 1982, Jesse Levine, a retired advertising executive, created the "Turnabout Map," pictured here, after his daughter went on an anthropological mission to Peru and Levine realized that "I knew very little about Latin America. Juggling a map one day I turned it around and, lo and behold, Latin America became much more important." So he created the map, as he puts it, "just for fun." The map is also available in many map stores.*

A New World View

For centuries, map makers have grappled with the problem of how to depict a round world on a flat surface. Despite advancements in geometry and the creation of complex mathematical models, there has been little agreement on the optimum method of producing maps of the world without distorting one or more sections of the Earth's surface.

For more than 400 years, the traditional view of the world was based on models produced by Gerhardus Mercator, considered the leading cartographer of the sixteenth century. His grid system of cartography—revealed in his 1569 map of the world—became the classic expression of cartography and has dictated our geographical world concept ever since. His map was revolutionary; among other things, the spherical nature of the globe, proved by Ferdinand Magellan's circumnavigation of the world, was clearly expressed in it.

But Mercator's perspective reflected the "Europeanization" of the world. For one thing, the map placed the Equator deep in the bottom half of the map, giving about two thirds of the map's surface to the Northern Hemisphere. This allowed Germany (Mercator's chosen domicile after being exiled from his Flemish homeland by religious persecutors) to appear in the center of the map, although it actually lies in the northernmost quarter of the globe. Moreover, the white colonist nations appeared relatively larger on the map than they actually were; the colonies, inhabited primarily by people of color, appeared smaller than in reality. Thus, say critics, Mercator's map reinforced the European sense of superiority.

The results of such distortions are astonishing. Compare Europe and South America on the following maps, for example. In Mercator's world, the two continents appear to be of relatively equal size, even though South America actually has nearly twice the land mass of Europe. Similarly, Africa appears smaller than North America, although it is really about 50 percent larger.

Only recently has a new perspective emerged. A map created in 1974 by German historian Arno Peters attempts to correct Mercator's distortions in world geographic perception. The Peters map, say its proponents, shows all countries, continents, and oceans according to their actual size, making accurate comparisons possible. On Peters' map, for example, South America is twice as large as Europe, and Africa appears half again as large as North America.

Peters' innovative notions, while not generally accepted by geographers and cartographers, are intriguing. Among others, they have caught the fancy of the United Nations, which helped fund the development of a detailed 51" × 35" color world map based on the "Peters Projection." Copies are available from Friendship Press. P.O. Box 37844, Cincinnati, OH 45222-0844: 513-948-8733. For a more detailed interpretation of Arno Peters' work, see *The New Cartography* (New York: Friendship Press, 1983; $20).

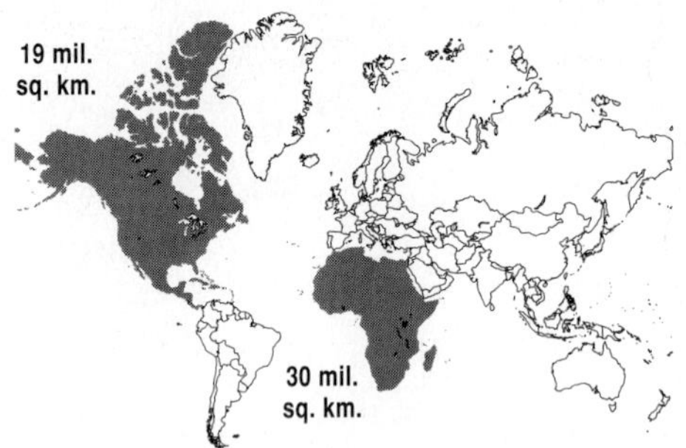

The traditional Mercator projection map (above) distorts the shape of continents to overemphasize Caucasian countries in temperate regions. Below, the Peters projection, designed to provide a more accurate view. Note that in the Mercator map, North America (19 million square kilometers) appears almost twice the size of Africa (30 million square kilometers). The Peters version draws the continents in more realistic proportions.

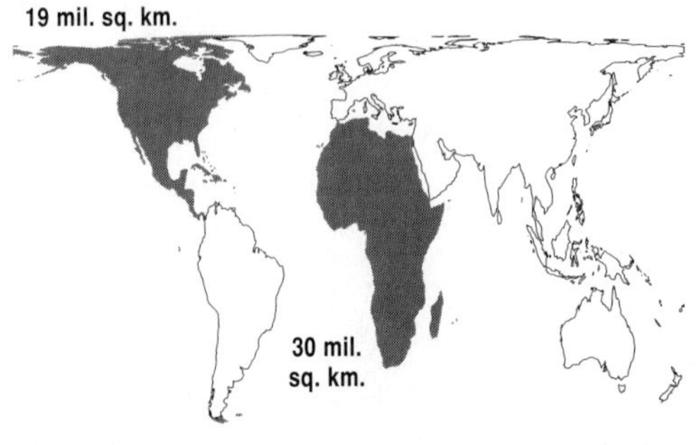

The era of Christopher Columbus was another time of great map-making advances. The year 1492, in fact, saw creation of the first modern terrestial globe, the work of Germans Martin Behaim, a cosmographer, and Georg Holzschuher, a miniaturist. The 20-inch-wide globe showed the Equator, the two tropics, and the Arctic and Antarctic circles; the Equator was divided into 360 degrees. Another key innovation was the copperplate, which proved a far more effective medium for map reproduction than the woodcut and helped launch a booming map trade throughout Europe. By the early 1600s, the governments of Spain, Portugal, and England were among those recognizing the importance of maps, using them for property assessment, taxation, military planning, and to inventory national resources.

1492? If there's a date that *everyone* knows, could this be it?

Various technological advances contributed to the development of map making, and, as map making became more sophisticated, new uses for maps were identified.

Mapping underwent radical changes in seventeenth-century France, due largely to an unquenchable thirst for maps and nautical charts. Such innovations as the telescope, the pendulum clock, and logarithm tables permitted accurate astronomical observations and the measurement of arcs on the earth's surface. Both contributed to major advances in cartography. New standards of precision, in turn, led to other advancements, such as the creation of the bubble level, the aneroid barometer, and the theodolite, all of which resulted in great leaps forward in plotting topographic measurements and absolute altitudes. The eighteenth century brought advancements in printing, not the least of which was the introduction of chromolithography—the ability to print several colors at once—which enabled map makers to enhance their works with color detail. All of these things aided the creation of such early cartographic masterpieces as Jacques Cassini's remarkable *Description geometrique de la France.* Published in 1783, this volume consisted of 182 engraved maps showing an entire nation in unprecedented detail—everything from canyons to channels to churches.

The tropics of Cancer and Capricorn, the Antarctic and Arctic Circles, the Equator, and **the lines of longitude and latitude** are all shown on most world maps. Finding a way for sailors to keep track of longitude was particularly vexing. In 1714, stirred by the loss of a fleet off the southwest coast, the British government offered a £20,000 prize (pretty good money today, but an enormous amount of money in those days) for the first person to solve this problem. In 1761, John Harrison succeeded in making a clock that gave the sailors—and the government—what they wanted. The full story is in Boorstin's *The Discoverers* and in *Longitude: The True Story of a Lone Genius Who Solved the Greatest Scientific Problem of His Time,* by Dava Sobel, 1995.

Meanwhile, in the newly formed United States of America, efforts were being made to take inventory of the burgeoning nation. As early as 1777 George Washington appointed a geographer and surveyor to the Continental Army to "take sketches of the country." This marked the first time that the U.S. government became involved in cartography. The first official large-scale U.S. surveying and mapping program was proposed by Thomas Jefferson and his congressional Committee on Public Land in 1784. This led to creation of the General Land Office, which produced a mountain of township plats and accompanying field notes. As President, Jefferson was deeply concerned with the lack of geographical information available about the newly acquired land west of the Mississippi River. During the War of 1812, his concerns led to the creation by the War Department of an elite Bureau of Topographical Engineers, later the Army Corps of Engineers, which played a vital role in surveying and documenting the nation's

THINK ON PAPER
Can you describe where you live in terms of latitude and longitude?

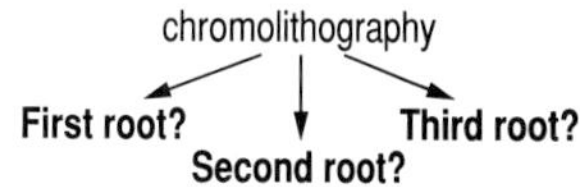

Mercator's projection, shown earlier, is still widely used, but projections like Peters' are increasingly used by international organizations and geographical societies. Note, however, that Mercator's projection has not been discredited. As you've seen already, we design maps that suit how we wish to see the world, and Mercator's has done that for a very long time.

In approximate figures, here are some land areas that will help you see the apparent distortions made by Mercator and the "corrections" made by Peters. The numbers are *in millions of square miles.*

South America	5.9
North America	9.4
Alaska	0.6
Mexico	0.7
Africa	11.6
Greenland	0.8
India	1.3
Scandinavia	0.4
Europe	3.8

The great explorers have often seen map making as a critical part of their function. Lewis and Clark, the American explorers, mapped the territory west of the Mississippi between 1804 and 1806. This territory later became part of the United States with the Louisiana Purchase. Perhaps the greatest sea captain/navigator/map maker was Captain James Cook, who undertook scientific, exploring, and chart-making expeditions for the British government in North America and the South Seas, including three voyages around the world in the 1760s and 1770s.

When was the Civil War? World War II? Notice, as has been said before, that the author assumes you know.

lands and waters. Jefferson is further credited with the creation of the Survey of the Coast, later called the Coast and Geodetic Survey.

During the nineteenth century, while General Land Office surveyors measured and subdivided regions that were relatively well known, the War Department sent exploring parties into largely unmapped territory. Many of the documents that emerged were vital in building the roads, canals, and railroads needed to accommodate a prospering populace. The topographic surveying and mapping programs conducted by the U.S. Geological Survey (USGS) from its inception in 1879 were based on a complex system set up by the Coast and Geodetic Survey, the leading scientific agency in the federal government during that century.

Prior to the Civil War, government surveys were limited to the vast hinterland of the Midwest. The westward migration that followed the war created an urgent need for detailed information about the resources and natural features of the western United States. By the beginning of the twentieth century, the USGS was undertaking a twenty-year program to map nearly every inch of the nation in rigorous scientific detail.

Map making reached new heights during World War I, when many USGS topographers were commissioned for duty with the Army Corps of Engineers. Some topographers played key roles in developing aerial photography techniques used for military intelligence. Returning to USGS after the war, these topographers applied their new aerial photography skills to cartography. Throughout the 1920s, experimenting with the new science of photogrammetry—the ability to take measurements from photographs—they succeeded in making maps from aerial photos. This development would change map making forever.

A great surge in the application of photogrammetry came with the establishment in 1933 of the Tennessee Valley Authority. One of TVA's first needs was map coverage of the entire valley. Working with USGS, surveyors prepared planimetric maps of the area using state-of-the-art, five-lens aerial photographs and innovative radial-line plotting techniques. Their efforts began a revolutionary swing away from field methods as the basis of map making, establishing aerial photos as the basis for all the maps that would follow.

After World War II, map-making innovations were rampant. Combining a variety of sophisticated measuring instruments with emerging computer systems, cartographers produced a treasure trove of new map types and products. The advent of space imagery and electronic imaging, along with the digitization of map data in computers, produced yet another revolution in map making. And there would be more revolutions to come.

ASPECTS OF WRITING: Comparison and contrast, outlines.

At college, you are often asked to **compare and contrast.** This involves showing similarities and differences between situations, cultures, places, theories, and any of an almost unlimited number of other possibilities. This kind of essay requires careful organization, and it lends itself to a demonstration of the usefulness of **outlining** your paper before you start.

Joel Makower gives us a good subject for comparison in his account of the Mercator and Peters projections, but if you were to undertake such an essay, you would need first to decide upon the principle of organization. Do you want to look at the world continent-by-continent, or do you want to select particular countries and continents that best illustrate the differences? Do you want to discuss similarities first, and then differences? If you wished to do the latter, your emphasis would almost certainly be on the differences, and so emphatic order would suggest that you mention similarities first and then move on to the more important matter of the differences between the projections.

This form of organization could be outlined under the headings

A. Similarities

B. Differences

but a more sophisticated way of achieving the same thing would be to discuss the similarities in an introductory paragraph or two, and then move on to the differences. This would still be a short essay, and you would probably wish to elaborate it somewhat, but how? One possibility would be to think about the impact of the new projection, and how it changes one's perception of the world. This, in turn, could give you the idea for a thesis: *Maps affect the way we think about the world.* A thesis that conveyed this idea—not necessarily in exactly these words—would then allow you to introduce the Mercator and Peters projections as examples, and your comparison and contrast could commence with a solid thesis, including an indication of the structure of the essay, clearly stated for the reader.

The opening to such a paper would probably discuss maps in general, including how they reflect and shape our perception of the world around us. You might point out that both Mercator and Peters, being Europeans, put Europe in the middle—another example of the omphalos syndrome. The main discussion, however, will be on the differences, and Makower points out several features that you could

A little defense of Mercator might also be in order. To accuse him of deliberately distorting the world map to show the superiority of Europeans over the colonial peoples seems far-fetched. Neither Belgium nor Germany even existed as a political state at that time. The most "distorted" area in Europe is Scandinavia, which wasn't a colonial power; the rest of Europe still looks pretty small, even on Mercator's map. North America is also highly distorted, but these were "colonial" territories—or would soon be. Mercator's achievement should not be dismissed simply because, after 400 years, we find that we prefer another way of looking at the world. It should also be noted that Mercator achieved greater accuracy in shape than Peters. Mercator's map was designed in part as a navigational tool, whereas Peters' was designed to show relative size.

use, such as the placement of the equator on the maps and the apparent size of the land masses, depending on where they are located in the projection.

You could end with a discussion of the **impact** of these differences. What difference does it make how we perceive the world?

WRITING EXERCISES: Answer one of the following.

1. Compare and contrast the world maps designed by Mercator and Peters. In the course of your paper, make sure that you say something about these demographers (dates, nationality, and so on), and make sure that you refer to the world view that each could be said to represent.
2. Identify three different kinds of map (your library should be able to help you find some to look at), then describe what they show, and how they might be used.

Sample thesis: There are many different kinds of map, each with its distinctive purpose and function. Different maps make us look at the world in different ways, as can be illustrated by the contrast between X, Y, and Z.

[Fill in the blanks. One suggestion here is to look at a topographical map of the ocean floor; it may change the way you imagine the world to be.]

Outlines help you to plan your essays. This is an essential stage in the writing of a research paper, but it may also be useful in the writing of shorter essays. Outlines may be formal or informal, but even the most informal should help you organize your ideas and help you write a coherent paper.

There are a number of different formats for organizing an outline, but they all do the same thing, and they all have one important thing in common: within each section, they move from the more general to the more specific, as indicated below.

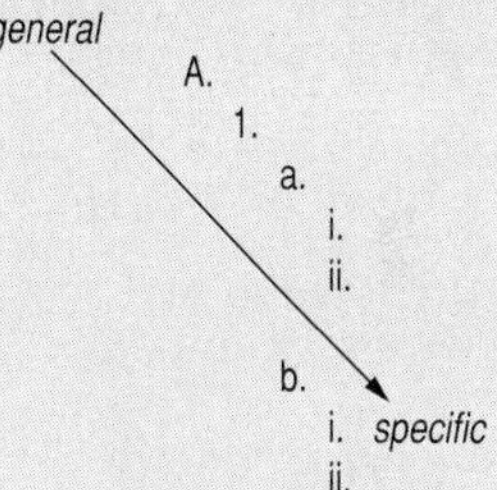

In this diagram, the most general level of discussion is indicated by **A** (and you'll probably have a **B** and so on), while the most specific details or examples are indicated by **i** and **ii**.

In the case of Mercator and Peters, this might become the following:

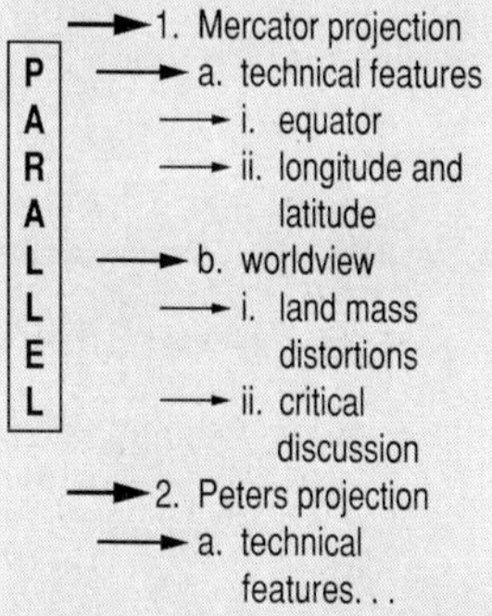

PARALLEL
1. Mercator projection
a. technical features
i. equator
ii. longitude and latitude
b. worldview
i. land mass distortions
ii. critical discussion
2. Peters projection
a. technical features. . .

In this example, each part is identical or at least perfectly parallel in form and level of generality. You should try to achieve this in your outlines.

SECTION THREE

PRIOR KNOWLEDGE: Different people in different places.

Sociolinguistics is the study of language as it is used within different cultures and in particular situations. Cultures differ not only in the languages people use, but also in the loudness or softness of their speaking, the distance apart they stand when having a conversation, and the gestures they use in nonverbal communication. People in some cultures simply *talk more* than people in others, and all cultures have conventions governing how people in different social categories (child-adult, male-female, and so on) talk to each other. This kind of information is also covered in cross-cultural communication classes.

Where we're born and live has much to do with the kind of life we live, the beliefs we have, the work we do, and the nature of our daily concerns and responsibilities. Of course, our own efforts and talents also may play some part in all of these things, but it's hard to avoid the fact that who we are is to a considerable extent determined by the **physical, political, and cultural geography** of where we live. Many things can affect the way we live—location, climate, political system, language, and religion being just a few.

Culture is **learned;** other human characteristics are **inherited** through our genes. This **genetic** side includes our physical characteristics and could possibly include psychological and behavioral characteristics that are affected by our body chemistry and other **somatic** influences.

No matter where we are born, we are raised within a particular **culture.** Cultural information is *learned;* for example, we learn a particular language, we learn how to behave in different situations, we learn what kind of clothes to wear, we learn to eat in a certain way and to cook and enjoy certain kinds of food. At home and at school we are taught certain values and certain beliefs about ourselves and our country. When you think this way, it's easy to see that, despite individual differences, the people of every country create a culture of which each person is a part and within which we usually feel comfortable. When we visit another culture, we have a sense of being in unfamiliar territory, where people speak differently, behave differently, and have different expectations. In a multicultural society (increasingly the norm around the world), it is, of course, possible to have this experience without going to a foreign country. The United States is a multicultural society, but there is also a describable American culture. Some of the features often ascribed to American culture are individualism, competitiveness, future orientation, rationality, and majority rule.

THINK ON PAPER
Why are so many countries becoming increasingly multicultural? Think about why people move from one country to another. This trend is especially apparent in the United States, Canada, Western Europe, Australia, and New Zealand. It is even beginning to affect Japan, which is generally thought of as a very **homogeneous** country.

Depending on how you wish to look at it, cultures can be described as being very similar or very different. On the most general level, all

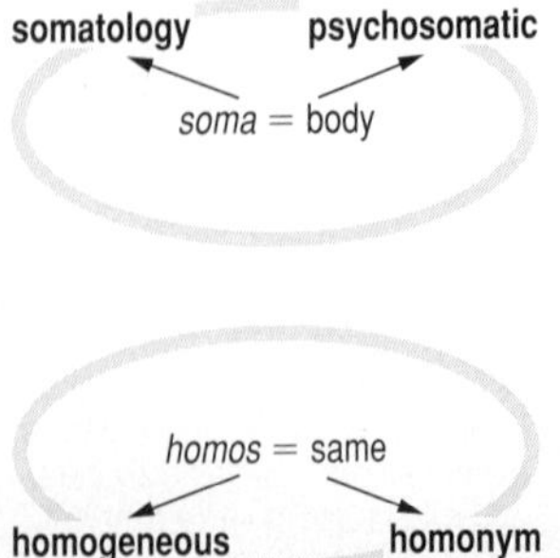

cultures have the same systems: these include **family systems** involving marriage and the care of children; **educational systems,** both informal (within the family and community) and formal (within schools); **economic systems,** including money and the production, ownership and disposal of goods and property; and **social systems,** including the status and relationships of different groups of people within the culture. When we look more closely at different cultures, however, it soon becomes clear that the details, or the actual practice, of these systems is often very different. Marriage is a universal cultural feature, but some societies allow polygamy while others are monogamous; some are **patrilocal,** requiring the couple to live in the husband's village, while others are **matrilocal;** still others, like many **Western societies,** have no such rule, with couples being expected to make their own lives, independent of and separate from parents. The rights and responsibilities of husbands and wives also vary considerably from culture to culture.

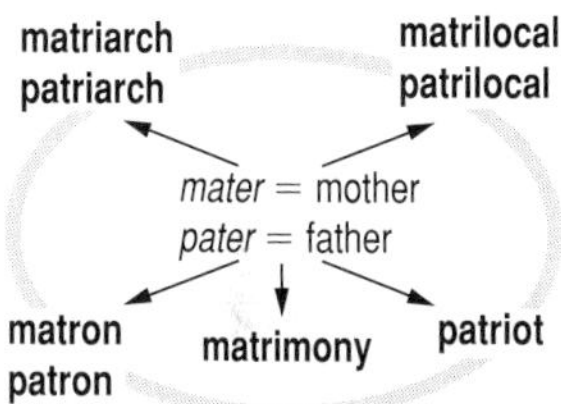

Westerners often think of themselves as being very individualistic, autonomous, and "free." When we think about how we are shaped by our culture, however, we may see ourselves as less individualistic than we usually assume. Most people spend much of their lives in groups—at home, school, work, and play—and groups function according to cultural conventions and rules. Even the thoughts in our head, and our beliefs and assumptions about our lives, relationships, and the world, may be said to be in large part culturally determined.

Several references have been made here to **the West**, or *Westerners, Western countries,* or *the Western world.* These terms refer to countries (or their people) sharing, in a very broad sense, a common cultural legacy. These countries include the United States, Canada, Australia, New Zealand, and the countries of Western Europe. Of course, within the United States, the term "Westerner" also has a particular geographical meaning.

One cultural pattern that is unfamiliar to most Americans is the *arranged marriage.* In traditional Hindu families in India, for example, the newlyweds often don't know each other; they may have never met before the marriage ceremony. This custom is less prevalent among less traditional segments of Indian society. In the past, marriages in Western cultures were also often arranged, but this is very rare today. The notion of an arranged marriage is strange to most Westerners, but some experts claim that the success rate of arranged marriages is at least as good as that for "love" marriages.

THINK ON PAPER

List the principal influences shaping the ideas and world view of young people in the United States today.

ANNOTATED READING: Roland-Pierre Paringaux. "A Day in the Life of Catherine Bana." *The Guardian Weekly* (*Le Monde* section) 20 Aug. 1989: 14.

You'll see the source of these "rankings" of the richest and poorest countries in Unit Five. The figure used here—gross domestic product per capita—is the value of all the goods and services produced in the country in a year, divided by the population. GDP per capita is a standard measure of the wealth of countries. **Burkina Faso** (formerly known as Upper Volta) has a GDP per capita of £100 per annum, which is equivalent to about $150.

BALKOUI—Catherine Bana is a farmer's wife in Balkoui, a village in Burkina-Faso, one of the poorest countries in the world (it comes 136th in the rankings, just ahead of Ethiopia).

Expressed in terms of gross domestic product per capita, her "wealth" is a bare £100 a year, or 100 times less than that of an average inhabitant of an industrialized nation. But no such sum ever actually passes through her hands. In her case, as for millions of other Africans who still do not enjoy such basic services as water, health care and education, statistics tell only half the story.

I visited Balkoui, one of Burkina-Faso's 7,500 villages, one stormy day in June. To find out what life was like there, I picked out Catherine Bana at random from a group of women who were pounding red millet. She lives, like most of her compatriots, light-years away from such concepts as the affluent society and the welfare state. Burkina-Faso is a destitute, landlocked nation in the Sahel. Its eight million peasants scrape a meagre living from agriculture, livestock rearing and crafts, and are helped to some degree by foreign aid.

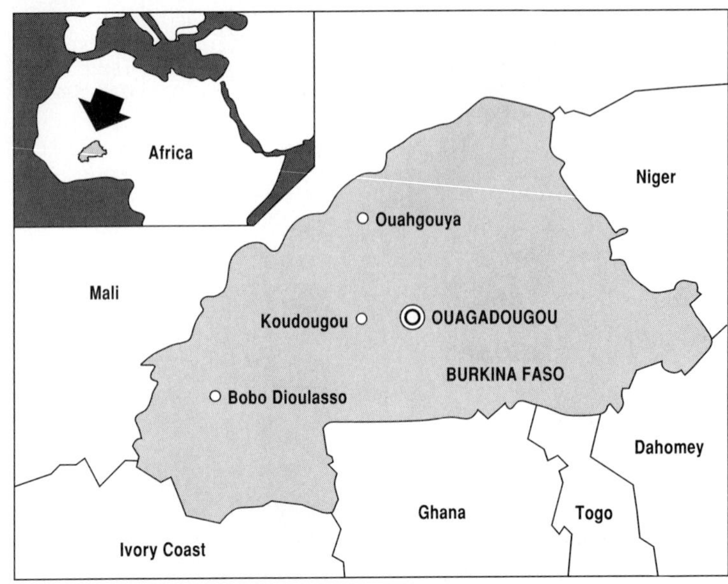

Balkoui, which is located on an arid plain near Burkina-Faso's modest capital, Ouagadougou, consists of a group of "concessions" (clusters of round huts surrounded by a wall), each of which is occupied by an extended family. It is a Mossi village (centuries ago, the Mossi founded a number of powerful kingdoms in the region). Its 69-year-old traditional chief, Johnson Sibiri Tapsoba, an amiable retired civil servant, holds audience under a thatched roof.

(£100 is a hundred **pounds**—the British currency (the article is printed in the French section of an English newspaper). Other important international currency symbols include ¥—the Japanese **yen, DM** —the **deutschemark** or German **mark,** and **F**—the French **franc.**

In Balkoui, where a minority of Christians live side by side with a population that is mainly animist and polygamous, it is the women and children who are most in evidence. This is hardly surprising: chief Tapsoba has six wives and 21 children, and regards four wives as a fair average for any man who believes in traditional values. There is a shortage of labour on the farms, and, as he puts it, "the more women and children you have, the bigger the field gets."

The Sahel is a geographical region, not a country. It is the arid region along the southern edges of the Sahara Desert.

Tapsoba remembers the village always being poor. Like the rest of Burkina-Faso, it subsists on small mixed farming, a few livestock, bartering and crafts. Famine as such is rare, but during the rainy season, when the grain runs out, malnutrition is widespread.

In Balkoui as in the rest of the country, "once the October harvest is over, the menfolk have nothing to do for six months," says chief Tapsoba. Nothing, that is, except indulge in their favourite tipple, *dolo*, which is made from fermented millet, and produce children. Fortunately for them, they have their wives to help out.

In many traditional, rural societies, children represent wealth and security. They are essential to work the land and to care for the elderly when they can no longer work for themselves. When combined with the high death rate of infants, this often means that the birth rate is higher than it would otherwise be.

At the age of 27, Catherine Bana looks already worn out by hard work and a succession of pregnancies. She has one husband, six children and a life expectancy of 45 years. Her latest-born clings to a breast that has been withered by years of voracious feeding. "God willing", she says, she will have even more children.

Like her animist neighbours, Catherine, who is a Christian, uses no contraceptive methods. Under the twin pressures of the labour shortage and infant mortality, even men with only one wife have lots of children. As Tapsoba puts it, "to end up with six children you need to produce at least ten."

Sisyphean is an allusion to a Greek myth. King Sisyphus of Corinth was a cruel man, and his punishment in Hades (Hell) was to forever push a boulder up a hill; every time he got it near the top, it would roll down again. Catherine Bana's work is similarly endless and repetitive, according to Paringaux.

Catherine and her family share a concession with two other peasant families, as well as a few chickens, sheep and dogs. Their huts, utensils, furniture and standards of hygiene are all pretty rudimentary. They are poor, but not destitute. There is a tradition of helping one another. The womenfolk share the cooking, the household chores and the carrying of loads.

In much of the Sahel, as well as in some other parts of **Sub-Saharan Africa,** different religions coexist. Two are mentioned in this article: Christianity and animism (traditional African religions); the other is Islam.

For Catherine Bana, an ordinary day begins at about 4 a.m., when, according to an unchanging ritual, she embarks on the first of a long succession of Sisyphean tasks. After doing the housework and feeding the children, chickens and animals, she fetches water and wood, and washes clothes. Then she has to prepare the household's staple food (a kind of porridge) and red millet for making *dolo*. She must also remember to grind some grain by hand or else take some to the mill.

Africa has more than forty countries and hundreds of different cultural groups with different languages and traditions. However, writers often find it convenient to divide Africa into two parts: **North Africa** and **Sub-Saharan Africa.** North Africa includes countries such as Egypt, Libya, Algeria, and Morocco and is principally Arab, Islamic, and Arabic speaking. Sub-Saharan Africa includes all the countries south of the Sahara, and is principally Black (the term "Black Africa" is synonymous with "sub-Saharan Africa"), Christian or animist, and linguistically diverse.

The morning has already got very hot by the time Catherine begins her second work fatigue of the day—in the fields. Setting off with her youngest child strapped to her back, a *daba* (a kind of hoe) in one hand, a bowl of *tô* in the other, a jug of water on her head and nothing to protect her feet from the hot ground, she is the archetype of the African woman.

At the age of 27 Catherine Bana looks already worn out by hard work and a succession of pregnancies. She has one husband, six children and a life expectancy of 45 years.

The climate, the soil, and the crops help shape the lives of the villagers, just as they do in rural areas around the world. Conditions in the Sahel, however, are distinctive and difficult.

Groundnuts are peanuts.

Walking for miles in each direction to collect potable **water** is a daily chore for millions of women in Africa and some other parts of the world. Many international development agencies believe that the world is already facing a water crisis, and that the situation is rapidly getting worse. The installation of even a single well within easy reach of a village would make the lives of many women much easier. Experts tell us that the water crisis is not limited to poor countries; even in the United States many people see signs of serious trouble ahead as we deplete water resources. Here's a good research topic for someone!

Paringaux presents a detailed picture of this more traditional aspect of the daily life of Catherine Bana. Clearly, he is very sympathetic, portraying her life as hard. As with the men, however, there does seem to be a social aspect to her life; even the long walk to fetch water is probably undertaken in the company of other women.

Whether it is sunny or raining, she spends the whole afternoon in the fields tending the crops (millet, sorghum or groundnut, depending on the time of year), walking considerable distances to fetch water and tirelessly scratching the parched soil. She stops only briefly to rest or eat a little food. Catherine returns home well before nightfall to do various odd jobs. Later she makes dinner, washes, tidies up, puts the children to bed and prepares the next day's meals. Then at last she can go to sleep, except when she is required to satisfy her husband's sexual appetite or sit up looking after a sick child. She works a good 16 hours on the trot every day of the week.

Twice a week, trips to market break the monotony of Catherine Bana's life. Like other women in her village, she goes to market to barter or sell the jugs and pots she somehow finds time to make so as to be able to afford one or two little luxuries, pay the healer or buy some medicine. Sometimes she goes all the way to Ouagadougou, 15 kilometers away. About twice a year she buys cheap second-hand clothes for the family.

On market day the menfolk get a chance to meet for protracted discussions well lubricated by *dolo*. "There's no better way of forgetting one's problems and whiling the time away," says chief Tapsoba. True, but some husbands, when they run out of drink money, make serious inroads into their wives' meagre savings. "If we refuse, they beat us", says Catherine with an embarrassed smile.

When all goes well, market day is a pretext for people to enjoy themselves and have a bit of a feast. This can involve jazzing up the universal diet of *tô* with pieces of meat and chicken. Such a luxury is rare in the Bana family: "My husband doesn't work," says Catherine. "I don't ask for that sort of thing so as not to embarrass him."

From time to time—"when he's in a good mood"—her husband kills one of the chickens she has reared. If they find they are short of money (because of an illness in the family, or some unexpected purchase), they sell one of the sheep or goats which the children look after.

Catherine's husband needed to sell only two animals to be able to buy a luxury contraption that distinguishes him from other villagers: a second-hand bicycle. Otherwise heads of families live from day to day without really knowing how much they earn. They just leave it to God—or rather to their womenfolk.

Poverty is rife in Balkoui. Yet the village is gradually emerging from centuries of underdevelopment, which 60 years of colonization (by the French) and 30 years of independence (interspersed by a succession of military coups) changed in almost no way despite its being so close to the capital.

In the last few years, the government has at last begun to do something about modernizing Balkoui. The villagers had almost given up hope when they suddenly got, in quick succession, water (five pumps and a small dam), a school with three teachers, a maternity clinic and even a grainmilling machine donated by the United Nations Children's Fund (UNICEF).

Vaccination "commandos" were sent in, and 50 or so women, including Catherine Bana, managed to find time to attend reading and writing lessons. Lastly, the only manifestation of the central government's presence in the area, a compulsory flat-rate tax, has been abolished.

True, the dam often dries up. Only a minority of children go to school, even though there are 100 pupils to each class. The maternity clinic, which was built ten years ago, got a professional midwife only last year and is still waiting for running water.

But when one listens to chief Tapsoba and old Ma Tenga, a matronly woman with tattooed cheeks, talking about how things used to be, and when one looks at national and international socioeconomic indicators, it is easy to gauge the extent of the changes that have been made and to see that Balkoui does not come absolutely bottom on the poverty scale.

Three of her children are already going to school, and she herself has learned to read. The maternity clinic is round the corner, and there is water more or less on her doorstep.

Not so long ago, the village was regularly ravaged by fatal outbreaks of measles and whooping cough. Women had to walk kilome-

The man is head of the household, but Paringaux seems as unsympathetic to the men as he is sympathetic to the women. He is an outsider—a Frenchman—and he sees the village realities from a Western point of view.

The poverty of Balkoui is nothing new, but the arrival of international development aid is. The best-known parts of the United Nations are the General Assembly and the Security Council, which are based in New York City, but the UN also has important agencies that do a lot of work in poorer countries around the world. These include the United Nations Children's Fund (UNICEF), mentioned in the article, which is based in Paris, the Food and Agricultural Organization (FAO), which is based in Rome, and the United Nations Educational, Scientific and Cultural Organization (UNESCO), which is also based in Paris.

Here, Paringaux gives a relatively optimistic account of development programs promoting literacy, children's health, and so on. Many experts claim that the single most significant development project in places like Balkoui is the education of women. When you read what Catherine Bana and her fellow women do—raising the crops as well as the children—this is not surprising. The fact that Catherine Bana attends the literacy class is, therefore, very significant.

Paringaux—or the editors at *Le Monde*—clearly see the article as being divided into two parts. This is signified in the selection of two extracts that are highlighted in the text; the first, earlier in the article, focused attention on the hardships of Catherine Bana's life: the second, at the top of this page, focuses attention on the recent changes and the optimism that these changes encourage.

Balkoui, it turns out, is now one of the more fortunate villages in the area; others have not received the same level of attention and aid from the national government in Burkina Faso and from the international aid agencies. Nevertheless, the level of development is still very low by international standards.

The statistics Paringaux provides—infant and maternal mortality, literacy rates, and so on—are among the standard measurements by means of which the economic and social development of countries can be compared. As noted earlier, you'll be looking at this more closely in Unit Five.

Rhetorical note: Paringaux gives us a **description** that moves from the economic situation to the physical geography, and then to the development program. The question of *objectivity* and *subjectivity* is important here; a different person might have chosen to describe different realities. An element of subjectivity is inevitable in such writing (as in most kinds of writing, perhaps).

ters to have their babies, to draw water ("Over there, towards the hills"), to get vaccinated or be treated by a doctor. Only the chief knew how to read and owned a radio set.

That recent past, which is fast becoming no more than a memory in Balkoui, is still quite common in Burkina-Faso: in the neighbouring village of Kossovo, "there's almost nothing—no school, no maternity clinic, just two water pumps," says Ma Tenga. Elsewhere the situation is often even worse.

In Burkina-Faso, the international standards of what passes for development are still virtually impossible to achieve in almost all areas: infant mortality and the number of mothers who die in childbirth are among the highest in the world; half the population has no access at all to health care; a third of all children suffer from malnutrition; only a third go to primary school; the adult literacy rate is under 20 per cent; average life expectancy is about 40 years; per capita income is one of the lowest in the world.

The fact that some people are even worse off than Catherine Bana does not really make life any easier for her. But after giving birth to six children, at least she is still alive, as are her children. Three of them are already going to school, and she herself has learned to read. The maternity clinic is round the corner, and there is water more or less on her doorstep.

So if, on top of that, the rains are good, if foreign generosity does not let up (20 per cent of Burkina-Faso's budget comes from development aid), and if the latest military government succeeds in turning its revolutionary promises into genuine progress for people like Catherine Bana and her fellow villagers, there are surely grounds for hope.

ASPECTS OF WRITING: Description; adding details; subjectivity and objectivity.

An **analogy** is a kind of comparison in which you try to explain the unfamiliar in terms of the familiar. A **false analogy** is a comparison of this kind, but one that fails because of important differences between the things or situations being compared.

Essays without details are like the skeletons in your biology lab; you can tell what they are, but they all look pretty much alike and they're clearly all dead. Before this rather grim **analogy** gets out of control, let's say that an essay needs **details** to bring it to life, to make it interesting. In a philosophical essay, the details may involve definition, or discussion of the implications of a certain proposition; in a geographical essay, details of how humans interact with their environment may be appropriate. In other words, the kinds of details you put into an essay will depend on the subject and on what you know. This is why in school you were probably encouraged to write from *personal experience,* which gives us something familiar to write about and requires no special information that has to be read or researched. At college, however, most of the essays you write require some knowledge beyond personal experience. This is the crucial point; you have to approach a wide range of subject matter with an **intellectual curiosity** powerful enough to gather up information, understand it, think about it, challenge it, add to it, agree with it, dissect it, relate it to other things you know, summarize it, interpret it, elaborate it, and so on and on.

This can be fun. The more you know, the more you realize that everything is related to everything else in one way or another. Shooting a basket is an exercise in physics as well as physical coordination, and it may become art in the form of a poster on a teenager's wall. A Robert Frost poem about a flower, a moth, and a spider is really a discussion of life, death, and fate, and is quoted in Stephen Jay Gould's *Wonderful Life* in a discussion of mass extinctions and evolution.

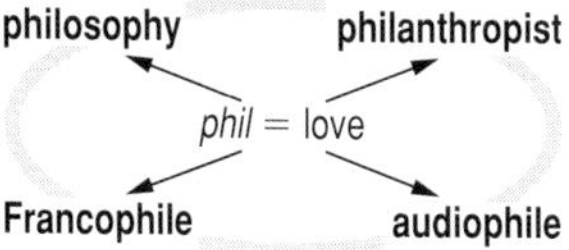

How many roots can you see here? And what do they all mean?

When you write from a personal point of view, you are being **subjective;** when you write without reference to personal opinion you are being **objective.** In many kinds of writing, the use of the first person is perfectly acceptable, but in others it is unnecessary.

Consider the following example: *I think that geography is making a comeback in schools today.*

Now delete the first three words: *Geography is making a comeback in schools today.*

The deleted words added nothing of any significance to the sentence; in fact, the more objective second sentence is much better; **the focus is on the statement, not on the writer.** When you want to sound more objective, but find yourself using "I," or "In my opinion," or similar words and phrases, try this technique for eliminating them.

Information is only useful, interesting, or entertaining if you make it so. Making your essays more objective doesn't make them less "yours."

WRITING EXERCISES: Choose one of the following.

Just in case you've forgotten what **person** and **number** are. . . .

PERSON	NUMBER: *singular*	*plural*
First:	**I**	**we**
Second:	**you**	**you**
Third:	**he/she/it/one**	**they**

You may be more familiar with *conjugating verbs* if you are studying a foreign language. Just as in other languages, English verbs take particular forms depending on the subject. This is called **subject-verb agreement.**

Sometimes, subject-verb agreement can be tricky. In the following examples, the **subject** is in bold and the *verb* is in italics. Where the subject is a phrase, the critical word is also **underlined.**

1. **Everyone** *is* here.
2. **Each of the horses** *is* ready to run.
3. **One of my friends** *is* a jockey.
4. **Nobody among the thousands of people in the bleachers** *knows* who will win.

1. Discuss Paringaux's article from Burkina Faso. What do you learn from it, and what do his intentions appear to be?

This kind of question requires a systematic response. To focus on the first part, for example, you might decide that you learned something about the geography of the Sahel, about male and female roles in this society, and about the impact of international development. These would then give you a structure upon which to build this part of your essay.

2. Describe how the environment affects how people live. Use at least two contrasting examples. You may, if you wish, use information from Paringaux's article and from your own experience (check with your professor as to whether you should use the first person). Work out a formal outline first, making sure that you achieve *parallel structure*—or at least get as close as you can, as described in Section Two.

The wording of the question often suggests possibilities for **opening your essay.** Here, for example, question 2 asks you to "describe how the environment affects how people live." Picking up on this, you could begin as follows: *The way people live is largely determined by their environment.* Then go on to introduce the examples you intend to use.

Don't forget the details!

OPTION ONE

PRIOR KNOWLEDGE: Knowing the world; Made in USA?

This "shrinking" of the Earth has been effected by modern technology, especially in transportation and communication. It's true that many people in the world don't know very much about anything beyond their own village, town, or country, but it's also true that this lack of knowledge puts people at a great disadvantage when they come into contact with the rest of the world, as they almost inevitably do, eventually. This is true for everyone, from Colombia to California, from Mozambique to Manhattan.

The disappearance of geography from the curriculum of many colleges over the last 20 years is a paradoxical phenomenon, because it has coincided with the dramatic "shrinking" of the Earth that has made knowledge of our world so important and such a distinguishing feature of the modern person.

The significance of this awareness of the world can be illustrated by reference to the clothes on your back and the merchandise in your room. When you buy something, do you look to see where it was made? If you don't, you *should,* because it's an education in itself. The frequency with which you see "Made in China," or Indonesia, or Malaysia, or Mexico, or the USA, or Japan, or Germany, and so on, tells you a lot about the world you live in today.

THINK ON PAPER
Identify companies or industries in your area that are involved in international trade, or are foreign owned, or that own interests overseas.

Of course, knowing where things are made is more significant if you know where the country is located, and it's even more significant if you know something about the country and its place in the global economy. Almost any professional career today may have an international dimension.

One American in 20 now works for a foreign-owned company.

One likely reason that geography fell out of favor is that its focus was a little blurred; it often overlapped with other disciplines. Today, however, the need for greater geographical awareness is widely acknowledged. In one way or another, we're all geographers. At home, at work, at the store, on vacation, and in our cars, trains, and planes we're participating in life in a particular place and environment. **We affect the Earth and are affected by it; this is geography.**

Foreign languages, of course, and skills in cross-cultural communication are also helpful in the modern world. In many countries it's expected that educated people be bilingual. The international use of English takes some pressure off Americans and other English-speaking people, but we should not use this as an excuse to know nothing about the rest of the world.

Darrell A. Norris, a geographer at the State University of New York at Geneseo, asks his students to produce an inventory of their personal effects and identify their place of manufacture. He reports the students' surprise when they discover that "Brian's wallet turns out to be Uruguayan, his shorts Egyptian, his radio Malaysian . . . and Brenda's wardrobe includes a Bangladeshi shirt and Romanian boots" (Norris, "Global Interdependence: Learning from Personal Effects." *Social Education* October 1991: 371–373). Look at the accompanying table and check the figures for the United States, Japan, China, and the smaller Pacific Rim countries.

As you probably know, international trade laws require that the place of manufacture be identified on every item. English is the conventional language for this—along with French—and so items made anywhere in the world are marked MADE IN ________.

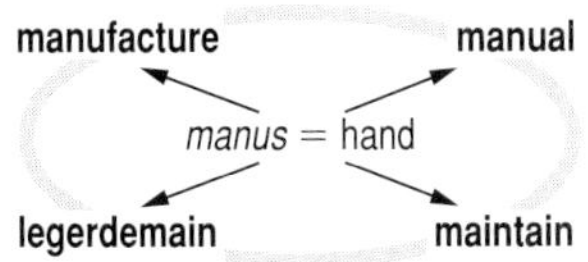

The personal effects categories are fairly self-explanatory: "Equipment" includes radios, computers, and all other battery-powered or plug-in items.

There are surprises here. These students own more items from China than from Japan, and the Chinese items are more likely to be classified as "equipment" than as "clothing."

THINK ON PAPER
Based on these figures, what generalization(s) can you make about the world economy today?

Inventoried Personal Effects: Geneseo Students Surveys, 1989–1990

	Total Items		*Personal Effects Categories (percent, row sum)*		
ORIGIN	NO.	PERCENT	CLOTHING	EQUIPMENT	OTHER
South and East Asia					
Japan	593	7.9	10	70	20
Taiwan	613	8.2	31	46	22
South Korea	482	6.4	38	22	40
Hong Kong	368	4.9	49	32	19
China	689	9.2	32	44	24
Singapore	180	2.4	36	53	11
Indonesia	80	1.1	70	16	14
India	217	2.9	83	5	12
Philippines	99	1.3	53	30	17
Other East Asian origins	164	2.2	54	28	18
Other South Asian origins	45	.6	80	16	4
Europe					
Germany	78	1.0	13	24	62
United Kingdom	96	1.3	36	16	48
Italy	141	1.9	57	11	31
France	117	1.6	27	16	56
Rest of Western Europe	171	2.3	42	17	41
Eastern Europe	71	.9	41	21	38
Turkey	49	.7	94	-	6
USSR	10	.1	20	30	50
Western Hemisphere					
United States	2592	34.7	35	21	45
Canada	124	1.7	31	18	51
Mexico	146	2.0	43	16	41
Brazil	120	1.6	69	7	24
Central America	30	.4	83	3	13
Caribbean	43	.6	70	2	28
Other origins	64	.9	59	5	36
Near East	27	.4	56	15	30
Africa	42	.6	50	10	40
Oceania					
Australia	28	.4	39	11	50
Total	7479	100.2	38	29	33

Source: Surveys completed in GEO 102 (Human Geography), SUNY Geneseo, fall 1989, spring 1990, and fall 1990 semesters. Compilation by Robert Wells, work-study assistant, Department of Geography. Analysis by the author.

READING: Yi-Fu Tuan. "A View of Geography." *The Geographical Review.* Vol. 81, No. 1, Jan. 1991: 99–107.

Abstract. What is the intellectual character and core of geography? An answer, from a broadly humanist viewpoint, that may satisfy the genuinely curious and literate public lies in the definition of the field as the study of the earth as the home of people. Home is the key, unifying word for all the principal subdivisions of geography, because home, in the large sense, is physical, economic, psychological, and moral; it is the whole physical earth and a specific neighborhood; it is constraint and freedom—place, location, and space.

An **abstract** is a very brief summary of an article. It is extremely helpful when you are doing research, because it gives you an almost immediate indication of whether or not the article is relevant to your topic. People who write articles and give conference presentations often have to write abstracts, like this one, of less than 100 words.

Colleagues in other disciplines have asked me, out of genuine curiosity, What is geography? and, specifically, How do you consider what you do geography? It may be that other geographers have been so questioned, although I suspect that those of us who work at the extreme human end of the field are especially likely to be approached. My reply naturally reflects my own line of work. I have tried, however, to embed what I have called "a view of geography" in the broadest possible context so that it can be of interest not only to geographers but also to scholars in other disciplines and, more generally, to the literate public. What I state here makes no appeal to geography's usefulness to society in the narrow sense: everyone by now knows or should know that "places and their products" are an integral part of every modern citizen's education. I wish to satisfy well-read and thoughtful persons who, having already accepted the field's practical value, would like to be better acquainted with its intellectual core.

Notice Tuan's reference to the "peoples and their products" aspect of geography; he describes this as "an integral part of every modern citizen's education."

I start with a definition popular during the late 1940s and early 1950s: geography is the study of the earth as the home of people. I like this definition for a number of reasons, one of which is that it makes immediately clear that geography, for all the technical sophistication of its specialized subfields, is not remote or esoteric knowledge but rather a basic human concern. Humans everywhere seek to understand the nature of their home. When this understanding is

DR. TUAN is the John K. Wright professor of geography and a Vilas Research Professor at the University of Wisconsin, Madison, Wisconsin 53706.

Every writer needs to have a clear sense of his/her **audience.** Ask yourself, *For whom am I writing?* This will affect the level of technicality in a paper, how much you have to explain, and what you want to say. In the last sentence of the first paragraph, Tuan defines his audience very precisely.

articulated in words or as sketches and maps, however primitive, it constitutes geography. So long as humans exist, there will always be such understanding—such geographies (Sauer 1956).

EARTH

Consider three key words in the definition. The first is earth. Geography is the study of the earth as a human home. What is the earth like? What are its physical characteristics? No human group can survive unless it makes sense of its environs—its Airs, Waters, and Places, as Hippocrates put it. Physical geographers have built on this basic curiosity and need. They have tried to understand the earth as the physical or natural entity on which humans live. Physical geography can be a pure physical science that scarcely mentions people and their works (Leighly 1955). Yet, for all its rightful claim to being a physical science, it remains a science tied, at a fundamental level, to the human scale (Hartshorne 1959, 41–47). Thus, whereas physical geographers may study the earth as a whole or its parts, the parts they study rarely, if ever, reach the microscale of, say, the molecular structure of minerals or the turbulences of air over leaves of different shape. Physical geographers examine the surface and the upper crust of the earth but almost never its core, which is too remote from ordinary human interest. They study landforms, climates, and biological organisms of the last two million years, but rarely those of more distant geological times. They restrict themselves to the Quaternary period, with special emphasis on the Holocene (Knox 1985), because it is then that the earth has become the home of the human species.

In making the point that geographers of all sorts focus on topics of "ordinary human interest," Tuan is helping to define where geography ends and geology, or paleontology, for example, begins. Clearly, there's considerable overlap, as there may be with anthropology also.

Because the Quaternary is also the period of humans and their ancestors, there is a tendency for physical geography to dovetail with prehistoric human geography. The livelihoods of remote forebears cannot be understood without a detailed knowledge of the environments of the past (Holliday 1988). A geographer of prehistoric migrations must also be a competent physical geographer to postulate open corridors in the ice sheets or available coastal routes on elevated marine terraces (Sauer 1944).

HUMANS

Tuan provides the **sources of information,** even when he does not quote them directly. In your documented papers, you should do the same. Different documentation styles are required by different journals—and different professors—but they all achieve the same end.

Now that I have introduced humans onto the scene, let me explore their importance, because they constitute the third key term in the definition. Early in the twentieth century geographers, especially ones trained in geology, tended to view humans largely as geological agents: their significance, it was argued, lies in their ability to transform the surface of the earth. Later, people were considered as cultural or sociopolitical beings and, still later, as psychological beings and even as individuals capable of wisdom or folly (Vale 1988). As geographical conceptualization of humans gained complexity, they themselves moved closer to the center stage of interest. To the extent that such a move has occurred, geographers enter the ranks of humanists. True humanist geographers explore the earth less for its own sake than for what it can tell of its human residents and their character. Without doubt much of human character is revealed in the innumerable ways that people traffic with external reality. To geographers it is revealed, above all, in the synergies of land and life.

Tuan uses the first person in his essay. This is justifiable here because the essay is in many ways a personal statement about the nature of geography.

Let me give an example. A chief theme in geographical scholarship is the role of humans in changing the face of the earth (Thomas 1956; Goudie 1990). Traditionally, attention is directed to the earth that has been altered. Even when geographers turn to humans rather than to wind and water as agents of change, the focus remains the earth: geography therefore remains an earth science. But suppose the focus is shifted. The study of transformed nature then becomes one of the routes toward a better understanding of people and society. To the question, What is such a people like? a geographer may reply that they are the sort that foul their own nest (environmental pollution), or the sort that show remarkable ingenuity and energy in creating ridged fields in tropical wetlands (Parsons and Denevan 1967). In the measure any scholar pursues the question, Why do people act toward nature the way they do? the thinking is that of a humanist geographer, and the discoveries that are a consequence of geography's distinctive perspective are a contribution to the humanist enterprise.

Let me take the idea a step further. I have noted that geographers now show an interest in the human being's psychological dimension. One way for geographers to explore this dimension is to study how humans have playfully transformed nature: for example, water in fountains is forced to jump, and wilderness is miniaturized into bonsai. In the careful examination of these activities, human distortion of plants and animals as well as the pleasure in and affection for them is evident, with a vividness beyond the capability of abstract cogitation. Pleasure in the great gardens of the world can so command the foreground of consciousness that their admirers quite forget their source in the playful, that is, willful or arbitrary exercise of power (Tuan 1984).

HOME

Of the three key terms in the definition of geography, home occupies the central position, and it can perhaps be argued that to the degree that geographers move from the idea of home, they shift from the core of their field. This notion appears to have the backing of intuition and common sense. Physical geographers may be described as earth scientists who happen to be drawn to those layers of the earth—from the lithographic mantle to the stratosphere—that are closest to human needs; intuitively, they have confined their research to upper and lower limits that still fall within a commonsensical notion of the earth as home.

Home is a very broad, elastic concept. The field of study that seeks to comprehend its totality must therefore also be broad and elastic. Home obviously has a physical component. At one end of the spectrum, the planet earth is a physical or natural entity. At the other end, the house is a material structure. Between them, the bounded spaces of the humanized world, from fenced fields to political states protected by radar screens, are all tangible realities. What are the material characteristics of this home? People must know if a unit of space is to offer the familiarity and material support of home; they must know the layout of home, its spatial character, how one part differs from another. They must know its resources and their location, and how to maintain its material integrity. The skill of an applied geographer is, in essence, the skill of every person who has a home and the responsibility to manage it. The difference is one of scale and of sophistication. For instance, with regard to the quantity and quality of information needed to manage a home, a householder's simple plan and inventory of the property become, at the scale of region and country, an elaborate land use survey (Stamp 1951) and a contemporary geographer's computerized geographic information system.

Home obviously means much more than a natural or physical setting. Especially, the term cannot be limited to a built place. A useful point of departure for understanding home may be not its material manifestation, but rather a concept: home is a unit of space organized mentally and materially to satisfy a people's real and perceived basic biosocial needs and, beyond that, their higher aesthetic-political aspirations.

Home is created symbolically as well as materially. The most powerful and precise symbol system of humans is language. Words or speech calls homes into being. An example will make the point. Forager-hunters who barely make a dent on their natural environment nevertheless live in home space. A thoroughly humanized world is created through naming natural features, classifying them in some manner, and telling stories about them. The naming and the taxonomy are a sort of inventory of economic resources. Language, in this sense, is a practical instrument of survival. But it may be that more objects are named than are strictly necessary for survival. A home is created larger than bodily needs require; its enlargement through verbal means may be presumed to satisfy the mind. Moreover, although most words in human language carry an emotional tone that provides an automatic bond between things out there and self, some words are more emotionally charged than are others, and these may be applied to features of special importance, for instance, a prominent tree or rock.

What is briefly sketched here for forager-hunters becomes enormously more complex with large literate societies. In them, cultivated fields and settlements now hit the eye, but it should be remembered that in the settling of North America and Australia by Europeans, long before axes fell on trees to prepare the making of farms, extensive stretches of land were already appropriated through the familiarizing rites of the survey, the naming of natural features, the drawing of maps, and the writing of epics of exploration. Without these steps that symbolically transform space into home or world, material changes can hardly proceed other than haphazardly and at small scale (Carter 1988). Moreover, these symbolic procedures have to be continued and renovated if the created world is not to lose meanings that motivate people to maintain their material environment. An example of renovation, or a shift of symbolic procedure, is the making of beautiful atlases that cover total space rather than survey maps of a linear-directional thrust, and the writing of local or national histories and geographies rather than diaries, journals, and epics of exploration. And, of course, the materially altered landscape itself immediately acquires symbolic resonance: for if objects in nature, through the human magic of storytelling or dance, can vibrate with meaning, then all the more so can artifacts and humanly created environments (Langer 1967, 87, 241). Words such as home, neighborhood, ghetto, slum, town, city, farm, countryside, region, province, and nation-state are hardly neutral in meaning, hardly descriptive only of physical characteristics. They appear not as labels but as proper nouns or minipoems that evoke and enhance—render in some sense more vivid and real—the personality of places (Ward 1989).

CONSTRAINT AND FREEDOM

Humans transform environments into worlds, nature into homes. Humans are actors and agents, but they also suffer from all degrees of passivity. People everywhere are very much aware of the impingements of external forces—floods and droughts and human enemies—on their lives. Indeed, the uncertainty of life in premodern societies and times was such that people seldom saw themselves as agents or creators. Thus a landscape of fields and crops is essentially "nature" to simple agriculturalists as well as to sophisticated premodern Europeans; it is without history, even though almost everything in it has been humanly altered extensively and progressively in the course of time (Yen 1982; Tuan 1989). Again, in Europe and China, garden is "nature," although it can be a work of the utmost artifice and sophistication. Only the city is manifestly the result of human agency. It has been viewed ambivalently as at once a proud achievement in stable human order set against nature's vicissitudes and an overweening impiety that may call upon it the anger of the gods.

Most of the constraints that circumscribe lives are unknown to humans. They are unaware of these constraints because they do not intrude as unexpected events. For instance, structures of space, time, and resources put certain limits on the action of any human group, but they may not be seen as such. Unless the group has the opportunity to compare itself with other groups, the structures that underlie its livelihood are likely to function not as constraints but as the unexamined points of departure for cultural ways of doing things. With greater awareness, humans may come to see how the sense of agency and of control promised by cultural practices is often an illusion. Thus Labrador Indians use scapulimancy to predict good hunting areas. They may think that a solemn practice enables them to control their food supply. In fact, the solemnity has little to do with locating the next area of abundant game successfully. The practice is successful because it happens to randomize the sites selected for hunting (Moore 1957).

Consider another example. Cities and towns on gently rolling plains such as the Middle West may show a hierarchical locational pattern. The pattern displayed by the location of urban centers of different size suggests overall design, but it is no more that, in the sense of emerging from a planner's mind, than is the polygonal perfection of a snowflake. Humans are not as much in control as they would like to think they are, and their frailty is exposed not only by threat of chaos but also in the existence of orderly processes and patterns that are not part of human intention. Geographers writing in a positivist vein have been of great value to humanist geography by showing the limitations of human awareness, by teaching modern men and women to see, with a precision and range unknown to tragedians of the past, the subtle and ubiquitous operations of fate.

Humans act to achieve a goal, and it may turn out that the goal attained is not the result of intentional action but rather of larger forces of which there is no prior knowledge. Again, when humans act to achieve a goal, it may happen that the one attained, for all its temporary or local advantages, has long-range, bad consequences that cannot be predicted. One's own culture is not only a pair of glasses that enable persons to see but also glasses that are inevitably tinted and thus bias the viewing in some way. The mind makes it possible for humans to transcend the limitations of culture, but humans have come to recognize increasingly the mind's own limitations, operating as it does in the binary mode or in some other genetically determined mode that future scientists will discover.

Freedom, paradoxically, depends on the recognition of limits—of constraint. A major effort in liberal education is to teach how "unfree" humans are. It is human to impose boundaries, material and conceptual, around self and worlds. Home, neighborhood, and nation-state are all delimited spaces, and culture itself frees humans to the extent that it confines and channels their energies. Basic humanity is nurtured in the confined spaces of home and neighborhood, family and community. Even when a people feel threatened at home and escape boldly across an ocean or a continent to freedom, their purpose is still to reestablish a bounded world in which they can pursue a familiar way of life (Ostergren 1988).

During the last century, such bounded worlds have come under a new threat, in addition to the disasters of nature and sociopolitical violence long familiar to humankind. I refer to the disruptive yet potentially liberating openness of modern life and its socioeconomic order. Modern openness is good to the extent that it forces people to examine traditional places and institutions unsentimentally, but bad if it destroys the concept of boundedness—of limitation—altogether. Without that concept people would lose not only a sense of piety that makes them human but also the very power of transcending whatever bounded condition they happen to be in. Home, for the modern person, is a point of departure rather than the locus of permanent loyalty. This idea of home as a mere stopping point, which has roots in a religion or philosophy of a universalist and ascetic bent, is by now almost totally secular and hence without transcendental purpose or support. A great challenge for the contemporary geographer is to see how the forces of modernity, which include not only technical power but also critical intelligence exercised responsibly or cynically, transform a premodern world of circumscribed and rooted places into shifting patterns that, if they show any directional thrust at all, tend toward a disorienting world of local variety and global uniformity (Sack 1988).

HOME AND MORALITY

Home, insofar as it is an intimately lived-in place, is imbued with moral meaning. Moral codes apply first of all to humans. Indeed, in folk and traditional communities, they apply foremost to the local group: outsiders, who cannot be expected to behave properly, do not enjoy the full courtesies. However, as the concept of home expands, so also expands the population for whom the moral codes are operative. In the course of time, people everywhere are seen to inhabit the same moral universe. Universal religions and philosophies subscribe to this viewpoint; in the case of Buddhism, even plants and lowly animals come under codes of behavior inspired by an overarching sense of compassion.

In a number of premodern hunting cultures, certain animals are treated with respect, even as they are killed, and among premodern agriculturalists with a world view tinged by fear, certain plants and animals are regarded as taboo. But this attitude to nonhuman living things is not the same as attributing rights and obligations to them, or as seeing them as falling under the aegis of a suprapersonal conception of justice (Kay 1985). Even today, such conceptions tend to be applied only to the human species. For instance, when geographers talk about justice they almost always have in mind social justice in a world of human strangers. Redwoods and whales are not included (Nash 1989). But what if the entire planet is taken as the human home, and we realize that there are no strangers, human or nonhuman? And what if this realization comes at a time when the religious underpinnings of morality that make deep sacrifices possible have been weakened not only by material affluence but also by rational secularist thought?

THE CULTURE OF GEOGRAPHY

I have tried to show that geography, for all the distinctive character of its specialties, is a coherent field of study, but I would be dishonest if I do not confess that this is not the whole picture. Geography holds together for ultralogical reasons as well, namely, that it is a tradition and a culture, a world view and even a temperament that some persons happen to have. As a tradition and an academic culture, geography has its roots in Greek thought. It has flourished at certain times more than at others, in certain parts of the world more than in others. I would say that for the culture of geography to flourish, an intimate awareness of one's own locality based on a knowledge of how places and peoples could differ profoundly, often within short distances, is combined with a more abstract appreciation of the earth as a whole. Europe, from the mid-nineteenth century onward, appears to have fulfilled this condition; not so the United States, however, where a powerful cultural-political ideology that favored a conception of America as space and scene overwhelmed the experience and awareness of local differences and attachments (Lowenthal 1968; Jackson 1972). And yet, ironically, is not this abstract sense of earth and place precisely the phenomenon that contemporary geographers must seek to understand in order to comprehend the modern world?

I now turn to world view. Here I again emphasize the three key words: earth, home, and people. These words, and specifically the central term home, give geographers a unique perspective on reality. They are unified by this perspective, which is not so much a conscious program as a temperament or natural disposition. Thus physical geographers, if they leave geomorphology or climatology, almost always shift to human geography rather than to geology or upper-atmospheric science. For their part, human geographers, however deeply immersed they are in human reality, are inevitably attuned to the sirens of nature: they retain a curiosity as to how their colleagues in the physical branch approach the natural world, and in human geographers' own work, even if it concerns cities, there hovers in the background the pale New England sky or the merciless Florida sun.

A final observation. No matter how reductive and abstract may be an individual's line of research, geographers are never comfortable with the single vision of Newton or an economist. The reason is simple: if in every instance geographers insist on precision and quantifiability at the expense of a roundedness of view and resonance, they can never hope to understand the earth as home.

REFERENCES

Carter, P. 1988. Road to Botany Bay: An exploration of landscape and history. New York: Alfred A. Knopf.

Goudie, A. 1990. Human impact on the natural environment. Cambridge, Mass.: MIT Press.

Hartshorne, R. 1959. Perspective on the nature of geography. Chicago: Rand McNally.

Holliday, V. T. 1988. Genesis of a late-Holocene soil chronosequence at the Lubbock Lake archaeological site, Texas. *Annals, Association of American Geographers* 78:594–610.

Jackson, J. B. 1972. American space: The centennial years 1865–1876. New York: Norton.

Kay, J. 1985. Native Americans in the fur trade and wildlife depletion. *Environmental Review* 9:118–130.

Knox, J. C. 1985. Responses of floods to Holocene climatic change in the upper Mississippi valley. *Quaternary Research* 23:287–300.

Langer, S. K. 1967. Mind: An essay on human feeling. Baltimore: Johns Hopkins Press.

Leighly, J. B. 1955. What has happened to physical geography? *Annals, Association of American Geographers* 45:309–315.

Lowenthal, D. 1968. American scene. *Geographical Review* 58:61–88.

Moore, O. K. 1957. Divination, a new perspective. *American Anthropologist* 59:69–74.

Nash, R. 1989. Rights of nature: A history of environmental ethics. Madison: University of Wisconsin Press.

Ostergren, R. C. 1988. Community transplanted: The transatlantic experience of a Swedish immigrant settlement in the upper Middle West, 1835–1915. Madison: University of Wisconsin Press.

Parsons, J. J., and W. M. Denevan. 1967. Pre-Columbian ridged fields. *Scientific American* 219:92–101.

Sack, R. D. 1988. Consumer's world: Place as context. *Annals, Association of American Geographers* 78:642–664.

Sauer, C. O. 1944. Geographic sketch of early man in America. *Geographical Review* 34:529–573.

______ 1956. Education of a geographer. *Annals, Association of American Geographers* 46:287–299.

Stamp, L. D. 1951. Applied geography. London essays in geography, eds. L. D. Stamp and S. W. Wooldridge, 1–18. London: Longmans.

Thomas, W. L., ed. 1956. Man's role in changing the face of the earth. Chicago: University of Chicago Press.

Tuan, Y.-F. 1984. Dominance and affection: The making of pets. New Haven: Yale University Press.

______ 1989. Morality and imagination: Paradoxes of progress. Madison: University of Wisconsin Press.

Vale, T. R. 1988. Clearcut logging, vegetation dynamics, and human wisdom. *Geographical Review* 78:375–386.

Ward, D. 1989. Poverty, ethnicity, and the American city: Changing conceptions of the slum and the ghetto, 1840–1925. New York: Cambridge University Press.

Yen, D. E. 1982. Tikopia: The prehistory and ecology of a Polynesian outlier. Honolulu: Bishop Museum Press.

ASPECTS OF WRITING: Documentation.

Tuan's essay is a documented paper, which means that he **cites** various sources and tells the reader where these sources can be found. This is very important in academic publications and also in student **research papers.**

There are many different documentation styles, but they all do the same thing: they tell the reader where certain information came from and provide the bibliographic information so that the reader may find the source if he or she wishes to do so. Documentation is, then, both a courtesy to the writer of the article or book being cited and a help to the reader who may wish to read more from the same source.

You may have noticed that Tuan does not use footnotes to document his sources; he uses **in-text citation.** In the humanities, perhaps the most widely used documentation style is that of the Modern Language Association **(MLA),** which also uses in-text citation but which differs from the American Psychological Association **(APA)** style used by Tuan in certain respects. For example, whereas Tuan provides the author's name and the year of publication in his **parenthetical references** (an alternative phrase to intext citations), the MLA requires the author's name and the page number. Thus, a typical entry may look like this:

Direct quotations *and* paraphrases must be cited. In MLA, the page reference must be given for both, but in APA page numbers are provided only for direct quotes, although Tuan varies this somewhat. See Unit Eight, Option One, for more on documentation.

> One expert notes that there has never been a greater need for the teaching of geography than there is today (Smith 97).

The most serious academic crime is **plagiarism,** which is the stealing of other people's writing and ideas. You may *use* other people's words, but you must *acknowledge* their work.

Notice that the parenthetical reference includes only a name and a page number; notice also the punctuation.

If the source of the above paraphrase had been given by the writer, the MLA does not require the name to be repeated, and the entry would look like this:

> According to Jane Smith, there has never been a greater need for the teaching of geography than there is today (97).

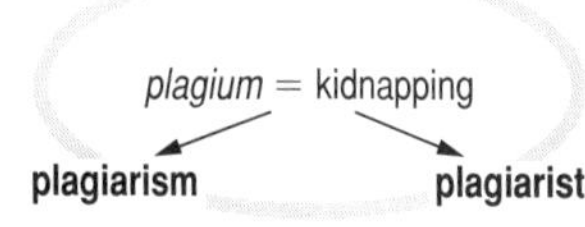

An unexpected but appropriate root.

No matter where the name of the source occurs, it refers the reader to the bibliography, which MLA calls **Works Cited;** this appears, as in Tuan's essay, at the end of the article. The Works Cited is restricted to **works actually mentioned in your paper;** it excludes other items, even if you read them. The Works Cited is presented in alphabetical order, and MLA provides a detailed description of how to present and punctuate all sorts of different sources—a book with one author, for example, and an article from a monthly publication, and an article from a daily newspaper. A typical MLA list, therefore, *may* look like this:

WORKS CITED

Anderson, John. *The Search for Atlantis.* New York: McGraw-Hill, 1987.

Smith, Jane. "Geography Today." *Harper's* Dec. 1976: 91–103.

Thomas, L. "Renaissance Map Discovered." *New York Times* 21 Nov. 1991: A:4.

WRITING AND RESEARCH: Answer one of the following questions.

1. Complete an inventory of your belongings (better still, make this a class project), categorize them (you may use Norris's system if you wish to), and write a report describing your findings. You may wish also to compare your result with Norris's and discuss the implications of your results.

> If you make this a group project, or if you wish to compare your findings with Norris's, try to ensure that your methods and categories are consistent.

2. Tuan appears to assume a need to define and justify geography as a discipline. Discuss (or critique) this assumption, noting the widespread belief that Americans are in general weak in their knowledge of the world and that this weakness needs to be remedied. You may use your own experience to comment on the teaching of geography in schools. Make some reference to Tuan's essay and perhaps to other sources you find in the library, as appropriate.

When you comment on and discuss an essay, you are writing a **critique.** An element of summary is required because, in most cases, you cannot assume that the reader has read the work under discussion. Notice that the word "critique" does *not* infer a negative commentary; it may be entirely favorable. The word merely suggests that you will discuss the ideas in the essay—and possibly the writing style as well, if you consider it to be worthy of notice in one way or another.

Naturally, the most interesting critiques are written by people who know something about the subject under discussion. An **informed discussion** is always better than an uninformed one. Be careful, therefore, if you ever have to critique something on a topic you don't know much about. Try to limit your comments to aspects of the essay about which you think you have something worthwhile to say. For example, in response to Tuan's essay, you might comment on the need for geography teaching in schools and/or your response to his essay. Is it important? How?

OPTION TWO

TALKING ABOUT LANGUAGE: Language and place.

Some countries have many language groups within them, and the choosing of a national language can present a problem. The **national language** is the official language of a country, and it is used in schools, government, courts, public notices, and all other official business. Some countries avoid trouble by naming several official languages, and many countries make extensive use of the language of their former colonial rulers, even if it isn't a native language of the country. For example, India, Pakistan, Nigeria, and many other countries have given English official status. French serves the same function in most former French colonies. In some countries, the colonial language has become the dominant language of the people, as in Brazil (Portuguese), most of the rest of Latin America (Spanish), Canada (English and French), and Australia, the United States, and New Zealand (English). In the Caribbean, either English, Spanish, or French predominates, depending on which colonial power ruled any particular country.

Language can be very dangerous. Not only can you get into trouble because of the things you say, but the language itself can sometimes be the problem. In most cases, language is probably the single most important indicator of culture, and so it can arouse tremendous nationalistic and political controversy. Language riots have occurred in countries as different as Belgium—where there are Flemings and Walloons—and India—where there are many different language groups. The troubles that erupted in Soweto, South Africa, in 1976, and which contributed to the eventual end of apartheid in that country, were sparked off by a change in policy requiring the students to use Afrikaans, the language of the politically dominant Afrikaners, in school. Even the United States is not immune from language controversies; the question of whether we should make English our official language—and limit the use of other languages for official business—is vigorously, often angrily, debated.

On another level, we may tell listeners quite a lot about ourselves every time we speak. Our accent tells people where we are from geographically, not only in terms of country, but also in terms of regions within countries. In England, accent is also traditionally associated with class status. The "upper crust" speak in a manner that is instantly identifiable to people living within that culture, and other social classes are similarly "marked." In the United States the class system is based on economic rather than social status, and accent does not reveal a person's class, but the way we speak may tell a listener about our level of education and even our character.

Not only accent, but also vocabulary can differ from country to country and region to region. The "hood" of a car in the United States is the "bonnet" in England, and the "trunk" is the "boot." A "flashlight" is a "torch," and a "wrench" is a "spanner." This last example means that in one country when something goes wrong with a plan we say, "That throws a wrench in the works," while in the other country we say, "That throws a spanner in the works."

THINK ON PAPER

Identify some words and expressions that are unique to your region of the country, or to another place you know.

ASPECTS OF WRITING: The right word; standard and nonstandard English.

In slang, using the "right" word marks the speaker as a member of a particular group, or even of a particular generation. The words of the 1960's—*groovy, fab,* and so on—sound very dated today, just as the words of today will sound very dated tomorrow. If you care about being "in," however, you probably use currently popular words and expressions. If you have people of different generations in class, you might swap examples.

Standard usage of English words also changes over time, but not as quickly as with slang. The same rule applies, however: if you care about being identified as a member of a large and influential club called "educated people," you need to pay attention to the words you use. Some usages (*ain't,* for example) clearly aren't (not *ain't*) "standard English." Similarly, nonstandard participles (She has *went* already, for example) can create a bad impression. The choice of other kinds of wrong word can also trip people up: "Runs good" (talking about a car) is a common example of choosing an adjective *(good)* instead of the correct adverb *(well).*

Words have precise meanings, as you've seen in the vocabulary webs in this text. Knowing the correct word, and using it, can make a very good impression. Dictionaries and similar reference books are necessary tools for anyone who wishes to use the language well; that is why you are so frequently urged to look things up in this course. Look up the roots, meanings, and usage of words; it will enrich your vocabulary, improve your spelling, and generally enhance your academic performance.

Puns play on the fact that many words have more than one meaning.

Dialect is distinctive, and it is often associated with stereotypes. Perhaps you can describe stereotypes associated with accent and manner of speech from these places:

the Deep South
New York City
the Midwest
California.

Of course, you may be able to distinguish dialects *within* your own region as well. Remember, too, that the people whom you can describe in stereotypical terms also probably have a stereotypical view of *you.*

The Oxford English Dictionary (the OED) is probably the most famous dictionary in English. It's a prodigious work of scholarship, for it traces the history of words as they've changed in meaning over the centuries. It is especially useful if you're studying literature or any other writing from the past, because it gives you the meaning of words as they were used at that particular time.

Fond used to mean *foolish* (and still does in some English dialects).
Appall used to mean *to grow pale* or *white.*
A *deer* used to be *any animal,* not just the particular animal we know today.

Quick Quiz

Note: You may have to consult your almanac for some of the answers.

A. Either on your own, or as a class, identify ten countries that are currently in the news or that are important for one reason or another. Japan, for example, is an economic superpower, and South Africa, Russia, and Israel are frequently in the news. When you have made your list, identify these countries on the map below.

B. Working alone or as a group, match the following, and identify the countries on the map.

C. 1. Which **two** hemispheres is North America in?
2. What was *Pangaea?*
3. What, and where, is the *continental divide?*
4. What's a *cartographer?*
5. Name two countries in North Africa and two in Sub-Saharan Africa.
6. Who was Mercator?
7. Is there more land in the Northern or the Southern Hemisphere?
8. Who was Alfred Wegener?
9. What are the *Western countries?*
10. What is the *Sahel?*

1. Africa's most populous country	a. Brazil
2. European economic power, reunified in 1989	b. Norway
3. African country once notorious for apartheid	c. Vatican City
4. Oil-rich and Scandinavian	d. Mexico
5. A Sahel country	e. Germany
6. South America's largest country	f. Australia
7. The economic superpower of Asia	g. Nigeria
8. The island continent	h. Burkina Faso
9. Country with the western hemisphere's most populous city	i. South Africa
10. Smallest country in the world	j. Japan

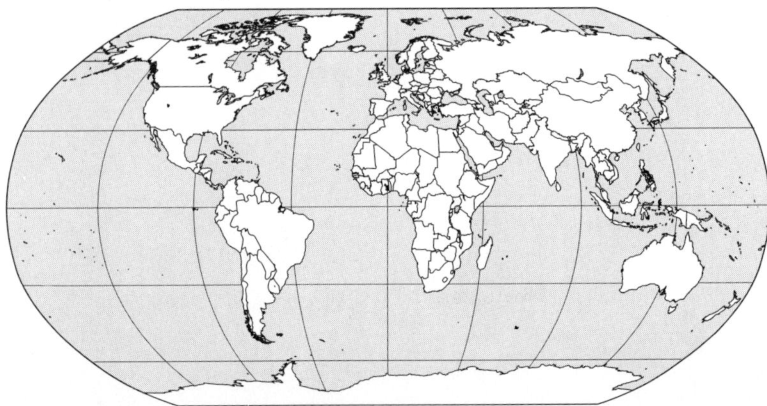

(*The Development Data Book. Teaching Guide.* Washington: The World Bank, 1995.)

SECTION ONE

PRIOR KNOWLEDGE: What's history? What's modern?

History is more or less bunk.
—Henry Ford

We cannot escape history.
—Abraham Lincoln

History is little else than a picture of crimes and misfortunes.
—Voltaire

The study of history has been derided as foolish and irrelevant as often as it has been advocated as vital to an understanding of the world around us. For some, history has no lessons to teach us, for as the world changes the past becomes irrelevant; for others, human nature and the human experience remain pretty much the same, despite technological changes, and so the past has a lot to teach us. Many well-known people have offered their views on this subject, as indicated opposite.

To some people, history means monarchs, presidents, wars, and memorizing dates; to others, it means understanding what life was like for ordinary people in the past. But how do we know the past? Studies of prehistoric life depend on archaeological and other excavations, which may produce bones or artifacts which can be studied. Studies of life in historical times can use **written records.** Today, of course, these written records are so voluminous that in the United States it has become traditional to build an entire library to house the presidential papers of each administration.

Whether written records are scarce or abundant, historians must still interpret and select. Different people see the past differently, just as you and your neighbor may have different views of the state of the country or the world today. If historians don't agree about the past, does this mean that history is bunk? Not unless you claim that anything upon which experts disagree is also bunk, and this would include every subject in the world.

People can have honest disagreements over interpretation of documents, and documents are often contradictory. Just as you may disagree with a friend over the interpretation of a work of literature or a

What are the dates of these historical events?

World War I
World War II
The Russian Revolution
The French Revolution
The Industrial Revolution
The American Revolution
The Great Depression
The American Civil War
Reunification of Germany

In general, it may be said that events before the development of writing are **prehistoric.** Of course, **oral history** may be passed down the generations without any written record.

A recent example of disagreement among historians and others concerns the Vietnam War. Was American intervention justified because we were committed to the defense of South Vietnam against communist aggression? Or was it an unjustifiable act of aggression on our part in intervening in an internal Vietnamese conflict?

Each country, of course, emphasizes its own history and shapes it to suit itself. What appears in the history books, and what doesn't appear, is often a reflection of nationalistic or political sentiment. History books play an important role in shaping the ideas of students at all levels. In a spectacular example, all history books used in the schools of the former Soviet Union were withdrawn when Soviet ideology was discredited; examinations in the subject were suspended until new texts were written.

THINK ON PAPER
In the history books you studied in school, which aspects of American history were emphasized and which were skimmed over or even ignored? (If you attended school in a different country, you will be able to add some interesting variations on this theme.)

or

THINK ON PAPER
How important is it, do you think, to give students a generally positive view of their nation's history?

movie, so people also come to different conclusions about historical events and personalities. Imagine what impression a future historian might form of *you* if all documents about you and written by you were to come into his or her possession. The complexity and challenge of the historian's task—and the biographer's task—is clear.

The second question in this section is "What's modern?" For some, anything that occurred before their own birth is "ancient history" and of little interest—a spectacularly self-centered view! For others, many different answers make sense. The end of World War II, the beginning of the twentieth century, the Industrial Revolution—all these and others may sensibly be claimed to mark the beginning of the modern era.

In selecting an event to mark the beginning of modern history, this course has made an unusual choice. The event, however, is truly global in its significance, has affected in a direct way most people in the world in the twentieth century, and has had political, social, cultural, and economic repercussions that are still visible today. The event is the **Berlin Conference** of 1872, in which the European powers decided not to fight each other over the colonization of Africa, but to divide up the continent peacefully among themselves. This choice emphasizes the place of **colonialism** and its aftermath in the twentieth century experience.

The **Berlin Conference** can be seen as a symbol of the worldwide domination achieved by the 19th-century industrial powers. At the beginning of the 20th century, the European powers, the United States, and Japan dominated the world economically and politically. Britain and France held worldwide empires, Holland held what is now Indonesia, Germany held territory in Africa and the Pacific, Belgium was a power in Africa, the United States was the colonial power in the Philippines and parts of the Caribbean, and Japan occupied Taiwan and was soon to annex Korea and move into China.

ANNOTATED READING: Glenn Frankel. "How Europeans Sliced Up Africa." *Washington Post* 6 Jan. 1985: C5.

Politically, Africa consists of more than forty countries. In discussing the continent, experts often distinguish between **North Africa** (the principally Arab, Arabic-speaking, Moslem countries of the Mediterranean and Saharan regions) and **Sub-Saharan Africa** (the rest of Africa, south of the Sahara, also sometimes known as "Black Africa"). These are terms of convenience; there are many geographical, political, economic, and cultural contrasts within each of these regions.

Harare, Zimbabwe—Africa is quietly marking an important centennial between November and February, but it is not an occasion for trumpets, speeches or champagne.

It is the 100th anniversary of the Berlin Conference, an extraordinary conclave of European diplomats that divided Africa into spheres of influence and ushered in an era of colonial rule whose effects still can be seen across the continent.

Note Frankel's **thesis** in the second paragraph: *the effects of colonialism can still be seen across the continent.* This idea is repeated in different words in the last sentence of the third paragraph. As you read on, you should be able to identify the specific effects noted by Frankel; the annotations will suggest some others.

At a time when African famine is again on the front page and when the West is viewing the continent and its daunting problems with a mixture of sympathy, horror and disdain, it is instructive to recall those days when Europe carved up Africa like a Christmas turkey, with each participant fighting for his favorite piece. Many of the problems that haunt Africa today have their origins at that diplomatic table.

The conference was a brief breathing spell in what became known as the "scramble for Africa." After nibbling at the edges of the conti-

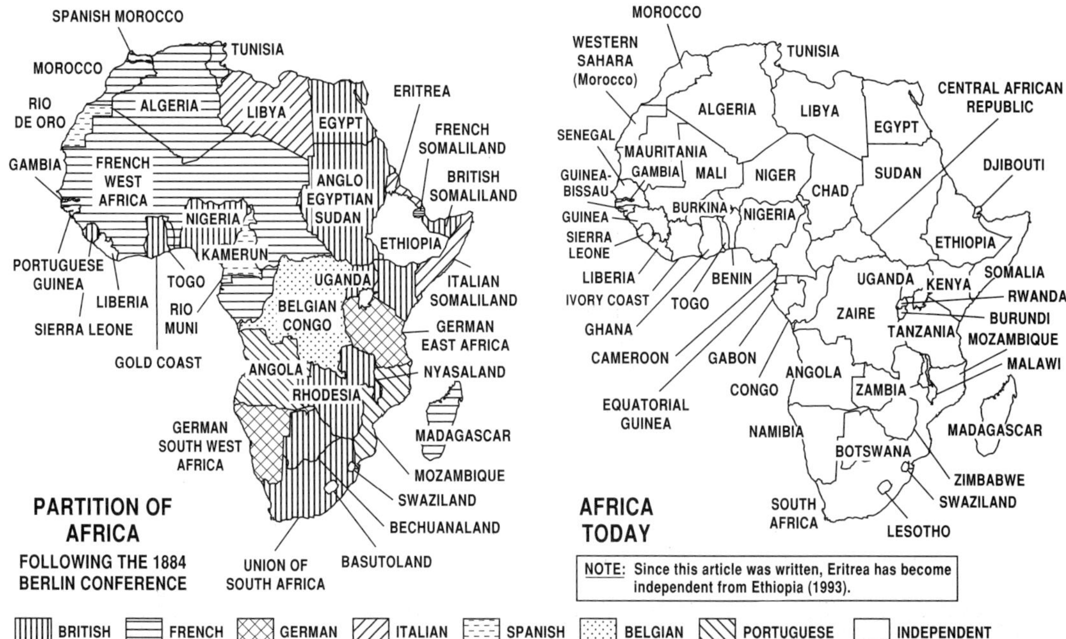

Frankel is clearly focusing on the problems faced by African countries and is showing how some of these problems can be traced back to the Berlin Conference. It should also be noted, however, that other, perhaps more benign, consequences of colonial rule have persisted as well. The languages of the colonial powers, especially French and English, have become the predominant languages of government, schools, and business in many countries. Educated Kenyans and Nigerians, for example, are virtually all bilingual in their native language and English, and educated people from Chad and Cameroon are bilingual in their native language and French. In **language, business, sports, schools, religion, television and pop culture,** and often in **government and legal institutions,** the influence of the former colonial powers may still be seen.

More specifically:

Languages: English, French, Portuguese.

Business: Presence of companies from former colonial power; special trading status.

Sports: Cricket, soccer, field hockey, etc.

Religion: Christianity.

Political and military: Close ties with former colonial power.

Schools: Often use European models.

nent for several centuries, the Europeans in the 1870s began a mad rush into the interior. Armed with superior weapons, Bibles and makeshift treaties, imperial agents laid claim to more than 10 million square miles of territory and 100 million people in the space of a decade.

It was a haphazard, chaotic process and one that threatened several times to plunge the European powers into war. German Chancellor Otto von Bismarck, who abhorred chaos and wanted to ensure Germany a piece of the spoils, decided it was time to lay down some ground rules. His French and British counterparts, who were the main competitors in Africa, agreed.

Fourteen western nations attended the three-month session. Conspicuous by their absence were those who had the most at stake—the Africans. But there was little hypocrisy: no one pretended the lines were drawn for any interests other than those of the countries at the table. The interests of Africans were never a factor.

"The Europeans came and assumed command of African history," wrote British historian Basil Davidson, "and the solutions they found were solutions for themselves, not for Africans."

The Africa of a century ago consisted of several hundred independent states, some large and powerful and well advanced, others smaller, weaker and more primitive. When the Europeans finished drawing their lines, these states had been condensed into about 40 pieces of territory.

It was not an easy or neat process. Ethnic groups were cleaved into fragments—the Ovambo were split in half by the boundary line that divided Portuguese Angola from German South-West Africa.

Others were combined with disparate neighbors. The Ibos and Yorubas of the West African coast found themselves thrown together with the Moslem Hausas and Fulanis of the north into a country that became British-ruled Nigeria, where their rivalries helped trigger the Biafra war and continue to echo to the present.

The Germans were given title to what became Tanganyika not because they had claimed it, but because the British thought it best

Many academic and other articles include references to major names in particular fields, such as **Basil Davidson,** mentioned here, in the field of African history.

Note Frankel's emphasis on tribal identities. Later, he talks about the weakness of the concept of nationhood in some African countries. You may be able to think of related problems in other parts of the world.

to placate Bismarck. Similarly, Portugal was given reign over territory 22 times larger than itself mostly because Lisbon's British allies used the Portuguese as a tool to deny African land to their principal competitors in Paris. Belgium's King Leopold won the grand prize: the mineral-rich lease to what became the Belgian Congo.

Bismarck united Germany under Prussian leadership in 1871, after going to war with France in 1870. He remained Chancellor of the new Germany until 1890. He made Germany an economic and military power, but this was achieved with a certain ruthlessness. In a famous phrase, he once said that "the great questions of the day will not be settled by speeches and majority decisions . . . but by blood and iron."

Cities are often named after famous people; **Bismarck, North Dakota,** is one.

At first, Africans paid little attention to the new lines, which seemed to have everything to do with European rivalries and little to do with them. But gradually the paper lines on the map became real borders, not only to the Europeans but to the Africans themselves. Africa's acquiescence became part of its general acceptance of the standards, mores and ideas of the Europeans who sought to rule it.

One of the great issues for African intellectuals during the independence movement following World War II was whether to accede to those borders, draw new ones or have none at all. The movement for a United States of Africa had strong intellectual and emotional force behind it.

But that idealism was undermined and ultimately overruled by the stronger reality of power politics and the ambitions of those who inherited governments from the Europeans. In the end, the Organization of African Unity, designed to bring Africans together, became a tragicomic monument to their enduring separation.

The Organization of African Unity **(OAU)** has its headquarters in Addis Ababa, Ethiopia.

But borders alone do not make nations, and this has been one of the cruelest lessons recent history has taught Africa. In countries such as Angola, Uganda, Burundi, Nigeria and even South Africa, the concept of nationhood is at best only marginally understood. Most of these countries lack a George Washington—someone from the political or cultural past whom everyone can admire and who provides the glue to hold diverse groups together.

Lacking that glue, Africa has become atomized into smaller, conflicting groups. People identify themselves by tribe, ideology, profession, religion or economic class, seldom by nation.

THINK ON PAPER

Frankel suggests that a national "father figure" is important in the development of a sense of nationhood. Do you agree? Does George Washington "provide the glue" that holds the United States together?

Thus it is not too surprising that in the 27 years since Ghana became the first colonial state to gain independence, Africa has suffered through a dozen wars, 70 military coups and the assassination of 13 heads of state. It has 5 million refugees—more than any other continent—and they, too, are part of the harvest of maladjusted borders and nations that exist mostly on paper.

Note Frankel's conclusion. How is it connected to his thesis?

In analyzing Africa's woes, Africans themselves tend to blame their problems on European colonialism. Westerners, on the other hand, tend to treat the continent as a blank slate whose real history only began at independence and whose problems can be laid at the feet of corrupt African leaders and misplaced priorities.

Both, of course, are right, and both are wrong, but the Westerners who during the last three decades have been so free with their advice

Rhetorical note: Frankel links an historical account of the Berlin Conference with an analysis of Africa's current problems. The organizational principle he employs is **cause-and-effect,** but note that his conclusion avoids oversimplifying this relationship.

and criticism of the new Africa should not forget that it was their ancestors who designed, constructed and launched the continent's modern history 100 years ago in Berlin.

Glenn Frankel covers Africa for *The Washington Post*.

ASPECTS OF WRITING: Cause and effect; conclusions.

Why is the world the way it is today? In order to answer such a question, one is inevitably driven to look both at the present (What *is* the world like today?) and into the past. Here we are talking about **causes** and **effects,** and much of history (and other subjects) is concerned with such matters.

Frankel's essay is a good example of a **cause-and-effect analysis.** His focus is principally on the political condition of African countries since independence. He describes this condition in bleak terms, mentioning the many wars, coups, and assassinations of the past 30 years, and he attributes much of this history to the impact of the Berlin Conference of 1884–85. Undoubtedly he is correct in emphasizing the importance of this event and the effect that the borders drawn at that time have had on Africa, but are there other things to be said?

The first consideration must be whether the chaotic political and social circumstances described in the essay are a fair account of the reality, and it's hard to avoid the unhappy conclusion that they are. However, it would be relevant also to note the success of some African countries in maintaining a relatively stable political life over this period. One example is Botswana, which has remained not only stable but also democratic since independence in 1966. When describing the present situation, therefore, we should try to present as accurate a picture as possible.

The second consideration, if we wished to think slightly beyond the scope of Frankel's essay, would be whether the Berlin Conference, and the colonial rule that followed, had other effects not noted in the article. As you have seen, the effects have been very widespread, and some have been happier than the political impacts described by Frankel. The fact that great writers such as Chinua Achebe and Wole Soyinka, both of Nigeria, write in English widens their audience and enriches the lives of millions around the world.

In discussing the causes and effects of colonialism in Africa, therefore, it may be helpful to categorize. The effects may be seen as **political, economic,** and **cultural.** Frankel concentrates on the first of these, although he does mention Europeans coming "armed with . . . Bibles" as well as with "superior weapons," which clearly suggests a significant cultural impact.

This kind of approach, in which you read attentively and thoughtfully, feeling free to add well-informed discussion and being able to think conceptually about a topic, will help you write well.

The relationship between **thesis** and **conclusion** is sometimes misunderstood. Notice that *Frankel does not merely repeat his thesis in his conclusion* but adds a final thought on his topic. This final thought adds significantly to the discussion. Although he repeats the idea that the Berlin Conference and the events that followed it help to explain the political problems experienced by so many African countries in the postcolonial world, he also introduces the idea that Africans bear some responsibility for what has happened. Notice how carefully balanced his final thoughts are, but also how his essay ends with a reminder of his thesis.

WRITING EXERCISES: Choose one of the following.

1. Beginning with a brief discussion of how a knowledge of the past can help us understand the realities of the present, discuss Frankel's essay commemorating the 100th anniversary of the Berlin Conference. Frankel focuses on political realities, but, if you wish, you may expand the essay to include some of the economic and social effects, as mentioned in the earlier discussion.

A model thesis might go something like this (you can fill in the blanks): *On the 100th anniversary of the Berlin Conference, Glenn Frankel discusses. . . . The impact of colonial rule can still be seen in the political, economic, and cultural life of the countries of Africa.*

2. Describe another situation that interests you (perhaps one of the stories currently in the news), in which an understanding of the present requires a knowledge of the past. It may be helpful to generate some ideas in a group to answer this question; pool your knowledge.

If your idea has several parts to it (for example, if you write about political, economic, and cultural effects) this structure should appear in your introduction and should then provide the structure of your essay. *If you usually just repeat your thesis in your conclusion, do more this time: follow Frankel's example and offer some final thoughts on your topic.*

Many people who think they are poor spellers simply make the same few mistakes over and over again. This creates a bad impression but is easy to fix. For example, this section has been about causes and effects—but what is the difference between **effect** and **affect?**

Effect is usually a noun (an effect, the effect, this effect) and *affect* is usually a verb (to affect).

For example, you might say, "The weather affects my mood," and you might also say, "The effect of this lecture was dramatic." Consult your dictionary for other uses of these words.

If you have spelling problems, one tip is to make sure you pay attention to words as you read them, and use the readings as a quick reference for spelling, just as you might if you needed to write Bismarck's name, for example.

SECTION TWO

PRIOR KNOWLEDGE: Characterizing the twentieth century.

THINK ON PAPER
What do you know about the lives of your ancestors of 100 years ago. Where and how did they live? Where did they work? How did they entertain themselves? What did they own? Were they happy? Various aspects of life may be relevant here: location, transportation, utilities, domestic technology and tools, jobs, home life, education, family size, cultural expectations, legal limitations, and so on.

An almanac will give you a thumbnail sketch of the **political** and **military** history of most countries on Earth. The **social** and **technological** changes, however, are also very important.

THINK ON PAPER
The two world wars produced the greatest loss of life and material devastation in the history of warfare, but many smaller wars take place without the majority of people in the world taking much notice. As a group or individually, can you make a list of conflicts that are going on in the world today?

One type of change is political, and maps can show us this. The map of Africa in Section One of this unit showed dramatic changes from colonial status to independence during this century. The map of Europe has also changed. Look at the four accompanying maps and notice not only what has disappeared but also what has reappeared. For some countries, especially those in the **Balkans** and the **Baltic,** the 1990s have seen the rebirth of countries that haven't existed as such for most of the century.

When a century—not to mention a millennium—comes to its end, it's natural to look back and think about the changes, triumphs, and tragedies that have occurred. What was the world, the country, your home town, your family like 100 years ago, 50 years ago, 25 years ago? Have we learned anything from the experiences of this period? How can we sum up the world's experience of the last hundred years?

Different people may answer each of these questions differently, but is there any common ground? Can we make a statement that would be just as true of the American experience as of the Ethiopian or Chinese experience? Obviously, such a statement, or characterization, would have to be very general in nature, but two things seem true of virtually every society on Earth: there has been a lot of **change,** and there has been a lot of **violence.** Every society has changed, even those of previously isolated tribes in the Amazon, New Guinea, and elsewhere, and all countries, even the few not directly involved in warfare, have certainly witnessed and been affected by the conflicts of the century.

Change and violence are not new. Few places in the world have steered clear of warfare or other violence for any long period of history, and many periods have produced impressive social, scientific, and technological advances. The twentieth century, however, has seen change and conflict on a scale unprecedented in history, and so these words may give us the characterization we are looking for.

Geography and history frequently overlap, helping island nations such as Britain and Japan, for example, to remain relatively insulated from foreign aggression and other influences. Japan was able to maintain her self-imposed isolation from the rest of the world until the U.S. Navy, represented by Commodore Perry, sailed into Tokyo Bay in 1858. Britain was able to resist Napoleon and Hitler in part because of her geographical separation from the European mainland.

Other countries have had the opposite experience. Poland, situated between Germany and Russia, has sometimes disappeared from the map, only to reappear when political circumstances altered. The accompanying maps vividly reflect the dynamics of history.

Where are the Balkans and the Baltic?

EUROPE IN THE TWENTIETH CENTURY

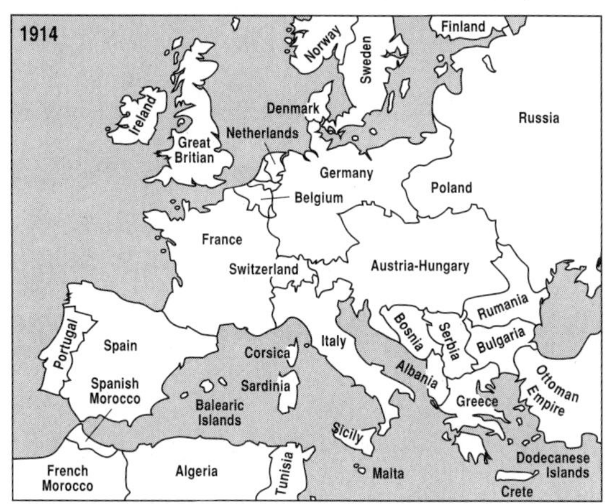

Reading between the lines, what **inferences** do you pick up in the first paragraph? Two related ideas seem especially important: "mankind's steps had at last been guided unerringly up the right path" and "progress was gradual but inevitable, ordained by natural law." Having read this paragraph, do you expect the rest of the essay to show how these ideas were vindicated by later events, or how they were exposed as naive and simplistically optimistic? Or something else?

From 1750–1900, the **industrial revolution** spread from England to other countries. Japan committed herself to industrialization after 1868 and was a world economic and military power only 30 years later. Since 1900, industrialization has spread to a greater or lesser extent to most regions of the world.

Change is here identified as a key characteristic of 20th-century life (note the article's subheading), but it is noted that "progress" has had a dark side. Gray uses strong terms here, saying that our century has seen "a massive regression toward savagery." Can you add examples of this?

Rhetorical note: Gray gives us a thesis statement in his title, and his essay is essentially a **description** and **analysis** of the technological, medical, and cultural changes of the 20th century.

THINK ON PAPER

The tone of an essay like this is influenced by the examples the author chooses (and vice versa). What tone does Gray establish early in this essay?

ANNOTATED READING: Paul Gray. "The Astonishing 20th Century." *Time* (Special Issue), "Beyond the Year 2000." Fall 1992:27–29.

For Good and Ill, People of Our Time Have Witnessed More Change Than Anyone Who Ever Lived

The 20th century began slowly, to the ticking of grandfather clocks and the stately rhythms of progress established by high Victorian seriousness. Thanks to science, industry and moral philosophy, mankind's steps had at last been guided unerringly up the right path. The century of steam was about to give way to the century of oil and electricity, new and transforming sources of power and light. Charles Darwin's theory of evolution, only 41 years old in 1900, proposed a scientific basis for the notion that progress was gradual but inevitable, ordained by natural law.

And everything argued that such development would continue in the small, incremental steps that had marked the progress of much of the 19th century. Inventions like the railroad or the telegraph or the typewriter had enabled people to get on with their ordinary lives a little more conveniently. The news, in 1901, that an Italian physicist named Guglielmo Marconi had received wireless telegraphic messages sent from Cornwall to Newfoundland was hailed as a triumph, but few discerned its full meaning: the birth of a communications revolution. Rather, it was another welcome convenience.

No one could have guessed then that, in the century just dawning, new ideas would burst upon the world with a force and frequency that would turn this stately march of progress into a long-distance, free-for-all sprint. Thrust into this race, the children of the 20th century would witness more change in their daily existence and environment than anyone else who had ever walked the planet.

This high-velocity onslaught of new ideas and technologies seemed to ratify older dreams of a perfectible life on earth, of an existence in which the shocks of nature had been tamed. But the unleashing of unparalleled progress was also accompanied by something quite different: a massive regression toward savagery. If technology endowed humans with Promethean aspirations and powers, it also gave them the means to exterminate one another.

Those means did not for long remain unemployed. Assassinations in Sarajevo in 1914 lit a spark that set off an unprecedented explosion of destruction and death. The Great War did more than devastate a generation of Europeans. It set the tone—the political, moral and intellectual temper—for much that followed. Once the carnage (more than 8.5 million military deaths alone) had ended, the tectonic aftershocks began to reverberate around the world.

The assassination of the Archduke Ferdinand of Austria-Hungary while visiting the Bosnian city of Sarajevo is usually seen as the event that led to the outbreak of World War I, known at the time as the Great War.

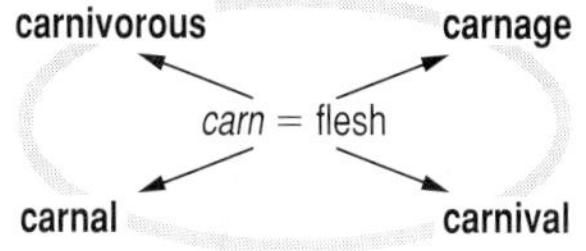

The war hastened the already simmering Russian Revolution and the founding of the Soviet Union and, hence, that protracted standoff between vast swatches of the planet that came to be called the cold war. It foretold the beginning of the end of European overseas expansion. And the U.S., against many of its instincts, became a superpower.

Before long, the Great War received a new name: World War I. The roaring 1920s and the Depression years of the 1930s proved to be merely a lull in the fighting, a prelude to World War II. Largely hidden during that war was an awful truth that called into question progress and the notion of human nature itself. Even now, the Holocaust—an industry set up for the purpose of slaughtering human beings—remains incomprehensible.

But civilization was not crushed by the two great wars, and the rubble provided the impetus to build a way of life again—and this time to try to build it better. To a degree previously unheard of and perhaps unimaginable, the citizens of the 20th century felt free, or even fated, to reinvent themselves. In that task they were assisted by two profound but unsettling developments, both of them conceived, oddly enough, before the Great War began. A Viennese physician named Sigmund Freud altered the way people would come to see themselves, their emotions, desires and dreams. And a gentle German-born patent examiner named Albert Einstein thought up an entirely new shape for reality itself—and opened the door to the Bomb.

Notice the enormousness of the events Gray lists among the outcomes of World War I. These changes were so significant that many people consider World War I to mark the "real" beginning of the 20th century.

At the beginning of the century, people had inherited a world in which household electricity was a luxury, an automobile an object of curiosity, recreation a trip to a concert or vaudeville show. As the century progressed, these same people witnessed unparalleled explosions of technical advances. Recorded music began to proliferate. Silent films acquired plots and, later, became talkies. Radio took off in the 1920s and led to television, which transformed the American family's idea of leisure and entertainment. Cars ran off the assembly line by the tens of thousands, launching the great American love affair with the auto. It took scarcely 30 years from the Wright brothers' first powered flight at Kitty Hawk, North Carolina, to the launching of the first large airliner for civilian traffic, and less than that until jet aircraft had made much of the globe less than a day away from most airports. The power

Gray covers a lot of ground here, but notice that each paragraph has its own distinct focus. This quality is called **paragraph unity.** Notice the transitions at the beginning of each paragraph. Some refer back to the previous paragraph *(Those means . . . , The war hastened . . .)*, while others tend to take us more directly in a new direction *(At the beginning of the century . . .)*.

Gray organizes his discussion on a broader level, also, showing that technological progress has produced devastating weapons as well as medical and other forms of progress.

and sophistication of computers enabled people to work and think in previously unexplored ways. And then there was space travel, interplanetary probes, geosynchronous communication satellites.

Relief from disease, the fearsome companion of centuries, arrived with the application of chemical research to healing and preventive medicine. The most impressive, far-reaching book of the 20th century is its pharmacopoeia, the list of wonder drugs that have changed the tenor of human existence. During the span of a single lifetime, science learned to cure or prevent through vaccination a staggering list of plagues, ranging from syphilis and gonorrhea to typhoid and polio.

Constant innovations and culture shocks had startling effects on the 20th century consciousness. The belief—or faith—that science can meet all challenges was coupled with the sense that science also creates plenty of problems. Constant change, for example, has had a deracinating effect. Traditional loyalties and ties have all been challenged or superceded by the allure of the new. As technology's blessings have spread, so have anxieties, the sense that some vital control over individual destiny has been ceded to impersonal forces.

Gray refers to "wonder drugs," and rightly so, but there is often a gap between the ideal and the real. New strains of some of the old plagues, such as tuberculosis, have recently come back to haunt us, and, of course, vaccines can work only if people have access to them and actually receive them.

THINK ON PAPER
Some paragraphs or sections of a piece of writing seem to represent the spirit of the whole. Is Gray's paragraph beginning "Constant innovations . . . " one such paragraph? Read it carefully and respond.

Gray's conclusion raises an age-old question about the purpose of life, but he does so with specific reference to the decisions we're making today.

The art of the 20th century, particularly in its first five decades, impressively reflected and helped shape the sensibilities of an age that saw itself as distinct, cut off from its past. "These fragments I have shored against my ruins," wrote T.S. Eliot in *The Waste Land* (1922), the poem that most typifies its age. A similar attitude prevailed among a number of revolutionary artists: Picasso in art, Stravinsky in music, Joyce in literature, Balanchine in ballet and Mies Van Der Rohe in architecture. Each of these men mastered the techniques of his trade and then saw fit to wrench old forms into previously unheard-of shapes.

In the wake of this movement, which came to be known as Modernism, an entirely different tendency arose. The Modernists had been élitist, scornful of mass values and tastes. Now their worst nightmares came true. Postwar culture after 1945 began to drown Modernism in a torrent of mass entertainment, facilitated by film, TV, records and a host of allied electronic innovations. At the same time, during the '50s and '60s, a form of institutionalized rebellion took hold among the world's youth as a cultural norm. The old, normal urge to flout authority was greatly magnified and aided by the ubiquity of mass culture.

As this flood of sensory stimuli grew, the very notion of "high" art began to be questioned. The new cultural icons, including pioneers like Elvis and the Beatles, were immediately accessible and understandable. Even while it splintered into different subgenres, rock music spread around the world, dominating record sales and the airwaves.

Pop culture's frenzied quest for the new and the shocking continued to make traditionalists blanch, but the beat and the noise went on.

In one respect, at least, the century provided a complete, old-fashioned story, one with a beginning, a middle and an end. The collapse of the Soviet Union in late 1991 settled the cold war, that long, Manichaean, superpower struggle between two opposing philosophies of governance. The suppression of individual liberties in the service of a common good stood exposed as hollow, inefficient and, most damning of all, corrupt.

But the moral of this story remains untold. With their adamantine enemy suddenly broken, liberal democracies found themselves groping after the certainties that their peers of 100 years ago had taken for granted. The tools for engineering longer, more comfortable lives have increased exponentially, but the ends for which such improvements are intended are still unclear. More shopping malls? Ever greater material abundance ripped from a depleted earth? All of this has sharpened and brought into higher focus a question as old as the dawn of philosophy: What is life for and why are we here to lead it? Thanks to this amazing age, more people than ever before have the freedom to ask the question for themselves.

The following words and phrases appear in Gray's essay. Your understanding of the essay will be enriched if you know what they mean:

Promethean
tectonic aftershocks
Manichaean
adamantine

Make a habit of looking words up; it will make a difference.

ASPECTS OF WRITING: Forming concepts; referring back to the thesis.

Each of the essays you read is the product of an idea. Paul Gray, for example, was probably asked to write an article characterizing the twentieth century, and so the basic idea was someone else's—perhaps that of an editor at *Time* magazine. Having been given a topic, the author had to gather information and think about the major events and trends over the past hundred years. Clearly, such an essay must be based on information, and the information must be correct and it must be relevant. To be included in such an essay, the events and individuals mentioned must have had a major impact. Gray's essay could be faulted for focusing too much on America, when an account of the 20th-century experience clearly should be global in reference and relevance. Fortunately, though, the word that Gray finds to characterize the century is "change," and change has been characteristic of every country's experience. For example, as was discussed in Section One of this unit, for a great many countries in the world the dominant reality of the century was a transition from colonial rule in the first half of the century to independence in the second half.

If you switch away from Gray's essay and think about writing your own on this topic, you may remember the suggestion that the twentieth century has been violent, with two world wars and innumerable smaller conflicts taking or damaging untold millions of lives. The concept that you come up with is, therefore, that **change** and **violence** have been the most characteristic features of this century.

Once you have gone this far, the essay starts to take shape; you have your thesis, and what you have to do next is outline the kind of details that would best illustrate your thesis. "Change" may be of different kinds: political, social, economic, cultural, and technological, among others. You may find that some of these can conveniently be combined: sociocultural or socioeconomic, for example. These categories then give you the points of focus for this part of your discussion. "Violence" may be similarly treated. You may break it up into war, crime, terrorism (remember that World War I began with an act of terrorism in Sarajevo), and so on. Again, these categories can provide the focus for this part of your paper.

Throughout the essay, you should not let the reader forget its point. If you refer back to Gray's essay, you'll notice that it is divided into three major sections, each referring back to the basic concept, which is a characterization of the twentieth century. The essay opens with the observation that "*The twentieth century began slowly . . .* "; the second section opens with, "*At the beginning of the century . . .* "; and the last opens with, "*The art of the twentieth century . . .* " Reminders of this sort help give the essay coherence and thereby help ensure that the reader can follow the discussion. It's the responsibility of the reader to read attentively, but it's the responsibility of the writer to write clearly.

WRITING EXERCISES: Answer one of the following questions.

1. Identify a period of history that interests you—it may be the twentieth century, or the last 20 years, or any other appropriate span of time—and, in a group, pool your ideas about how you might characterize that period. Think of examples and write them down. Then organize these examples into categories, in the way described in the *Aspects of Writing* section, and write your essay.
2. Discuss Paul Gray's essay, explaining his characterization of the twentieth century and commenting on it. Point out the strengths and any weaknesses in his discussion.
3. Refer to Gray's essay, and then develop the idea that *change* continues to be the most characteristic—and possibly bewildering—feature of the present. If another feature of current experience seems to you to be more characteristic of today, substitute this for "change."

In one of these questions, you've been asked to pool ideas. This, of course, is **brainstorming.** Whether you generate ideas on your own or in a group, this is an important part of writing. You're providing possible answers to the question, "What is there to say?" or "What do I know about this?" Once you've generated a few ideas, more are likely to come. Then the task is to select the ideas that seem useful for your immediate purpose and organize them in a logical and coherent way.

Referring to another person's writing is one way to begin your own. (Note the different verbs that you may use to describe what an author is doing—there are, of course, many others too.)

Paul Gray, in his essay "The Astonishing Twentieth Century,"

notes
argues
suggests
maintains
contends
says

that . . .

What you have read can in this way provide you with a starting point for your own essay. Having summarized what Gray has written (in whole or in part), you would probably offer a response to Gray or introduce some further point for discussion. This will be the germ of your own essay.

SECTION THREE

PRIOR KNOWLEDGE: The ups and downs of superpowers.

One lesson of history is that no political power lasts forever. We have been reminded of that in very recent times with the disintegration of the Soviet Union. The empires of the distant past—those of Persia in the fifth century B.C., of Macedonia, by which Alexander the Great established the supremacy of Greek culture from Western Europe to northern India, and of Rome, which ruled most of Western Europe, the Middle East, and North Africa until about the fifth century—all came to an end. In Asia, Asoka united most of India in the third century B.C., and in China various dynasties, going back to at least 1500 B.C., held sway, as did the Khmer in Cambodia from about A.D. 1000. In the Americas, the Mayans developed their civilization after the fifth century B.C., while in Africa there were not only the great Pharaohs of Egypt, but also the kingdoms of Benin, Congo, Buganda, and Zimbabwe, among others. In the South Pacific, Polynesian voyagers spread throughout the Pacific islands beginning around 1500 B.C.

In "Ozymandias," composed in 1818, the poet Shelley alludes to the transience of power. In the following extract, a traveler reads an inscription on the pedestal of a statue of a great and ancient king (the pharaoh Rameses II) he found while traveling through the desert in "an antique land":

"My name is Ozymandias, King of Kings
Look on my works, ye Mighty, and despair!"
Nothing beside remains. Round the decay
Of that colossal wreck, boundless and bare
The lone and level sands stretch far away.

In the 16th century, the Spanish and Portuguese colonized what is now known as Latin America, and their legacy includes the **predominant** languages of that region today. The Dutch extended their power to what is now Indonesia, the Turks (Ottomans) dominated parts of central and southern Europe, and the French and British ruled vast areas of the world well into the 20th century.

Don't confuse the different forms of words—the *parts of speech:*
predominant (adjective)
predominantly (adverb)
predominate (verb)

What are the other parts of speech?

All of these countries and peoples have had a significant impact either regionally or globally, but, since World War II, the preeminent powers have been the United States and the U.S.S.R. Now, without the U.S.S.R., many people see only one superpower, but others already see signs of further change. If the 19th century was the British century, and the 20th century was **the American century,** who will most influence the world in the 21st century? Some people anticipate a "Pacific century," others a "European."

THINK ON PAPER
What does the phrase "the American century" mean?

In the following article, Yale historian Paul Kennedy puts American power into perspective and suggests that the way the country responds to the realities of **"relative decline"**—the reality that economic and political power in the world will have to be shared with other wealthy and ambitious nations—will determine the future status of the country. He looks at the causes of the decline of earlier superpowers and suggests that the United States should learn the lessons of history.

"Relative decline" differs from **"absolute decline."** The former suggests that, although the American economy continues to grow, other countries have been growing more quickly (they may even have overtaken us in some areas). The latter term suggests an actual decline in the wealth of the country—a very different matter.

In his article, Kennedy anticipates five nations or regions sharing most of the wealth and power in the 21st century. Before you read the article, can you guess who these nations/regions may be?

Look up the following words to check their ***literal*** meaning.

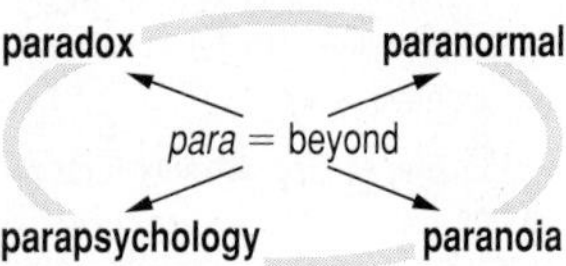

You have an advantage over Kennedy, in that you can read his article knowing what has happened in the world since 1987, when he wrote his influential book, *The Rise and Fall of the Great Powers,* upon which the following article is based. You can substitute "Russia" for "the Soviet Union" and think about the various policies that have been enacted since the end of the Cold War. You may be able to judge whether or not the country has heeded Kennedy's warning.

One issue that emerges from the article involves the difference between **military, economic,** and **political power,** and it is here, perhaps, where the **paradox** of the American situation is most apparent. At a time when the United States is the only truly global military power, she is being challenged by rivals for economic and political power. International trade may be the battleground of the next century, determining where the jobs are, where the money is, and where the political power and influence will flow.

ANNOTATED READING: Paul Kennedy. Selections from "The (Relative) Decline of America." *The Atlantic Monthly* Aug. 1987: 29–38.

In 1945 the United States commanded a 40 percent share of the world economy; today its share is half that, and yet our military commitments have grown dramatically. This imbalance, which conforms to a classic historical pattern, threatens our security, both military and economic.

The Erosion of U.S. Grand Strategy

In February of 1941, when Henry Luce's *Life* magazine announced that this was the "American century," the claim accorded well with the economic realities of power. Even before the United States entered the Second World War, it produced about a third of the world's manufactures, which was more than twice the production of Nazi Germany and almost ten times that of Japan. By 1945, with the Fascist states defeated and America's wartime allies economically exhausted, the U.S. share of world manufacturing output was closer to half—a proportion never before or since attained by a single nation. More than any of the great world empires—Rome, Imperial Spain, or Victorian Britain—the United States appeared destined to dominate international politics for decades, if not centuries, to come.

Notice the nice transition opening the second paragraph: **"In such circumstances"** refers back to what has just been said and takes the reader on to the next stage of the discussion.

In such circumstances it seemed to American decision-makers natural (if occasionally awkward) to extend U.S. military protection to those countries pleading for help in the turbulent years after 1945. First came involvement in Greece and Turkey; and then, from 1949 onward, the extraordinarily wide-ranging commitment to NATO; the special relationship with Israel and, often contrarily, with Saudi Arabia, Jordan, Egypt, and lesser Arab states; and obligations to the partners in such regional defense organizations as SEATO, CENTO, and ANZUS. Closer to home, there was the Rio Pact and the special hemispheric defense arrangements with Canada. By early 1970, as Ronald Steel has pointed out, the United States "had more than 1,000,000 soldiers in 30 countries, was a member of 4 regional defense alliances and an active participant in a fifth, had mutual defense treaties with 42 nations, was a member of 53 international organizations, and was

NATO North Atlantic Treaty Organization—a military alliance linking most of the countries of Western Europe with the United States and Canada.
SEATO included much of Southeast Asia.
CENTO (Central Treaty Organization) included Iran, Pakistan, and Turkey.
ANZUS includes Australia and New Zealand.

SEATO existed from 1954–1977
CENTO existed from 1959–1979.

The Vietnam War ended when the North Vietnamese entered Saigon (now Ho Chi Minh City) in 1975.

Kennedy is making the apparently paradoxical point that the U.S. share of the world's wealth has declined since the years following World War II, but that the United States is still richer than it was at that time. The country's share of the pie (the world economy) is smaller now, but the pie itself is much bigger.

Notice the structure of this section of Kennedy's essay. He introduces the idea that "the economic foundations of America's power" have eroded in several ways. Then he proceeds to discuss this erosion in the areas of **manufacturing, agriculture,** and **finance.**

Kennedy discusses the advantage low-wage Third World countries have when competing with the United States, but competition is also fierce with other high-wage countries in Western Europe and Japan. Compared with some of these countries, average American wages and benefits are relatively modest. In fact, some European companies have opened factories in the United States in order to take advantage of lower wages and other costs here.

furnishing military or economic aid to nearly 100 nations across the face of the globe." Although the end of the Vietnam War significantly reduced the number of American troops overseas, the global array of U.S. obligations that remained would have astonished the Founding Fathers.

Yet while America's commitments steadily increased after 1945, its share of world manufacturing and of world gross national product began to decline, at first rather slowly, and than with increasing speed. In one sense, it could be argued, such a decline is irrelevant: this country is nowadays far richer, absolutely, than it was in 1945 or 1950, and most of its citizens are much better off *in absolute terms*. In another sense, however, the shrinking of America's share of world production is alarming because of the implications for American grand strategy—which is measured not by military forces alone but by their integration with all those other elements (economic, social, political, and diplomatic) that contribute toward a successful long-term national policy.

The gradual erosion of the economic foundations of America's power has been of several kinds. In the first place, there is the country's industrial decline relative to overall world production, not only in older manufactures, such as textiles, iron and steel, shipbuilding, and basic chemicals, but also—though it is harder to judge the final outcome at this stage of industrial-technological combat—in robotics, aerospace technology, automobiles, machine tools, and computers. Both areas pose immense problems: in traditional and basic manufacturing the gap in wage scales between the United States and newly industrializing countries is probably such that no efficiency measures will close it; but to lose out in the competition in future technologies, if that indeed should occur, would be even more disastrous.

The second, and in many ways less expected, sector of decline is agriculture. Only a decade ago experts were predicting a frightening global imbalance between food requirements and farming output. But the scenarios of famine and disaster stimulated two powerful responses: the first was a tremendous investment in American farming from the 1970s onward, fueled by the prospect of ever larger overseas food sales: the second was a large-scale investigation, funded by the West, into scientific means of increasing Third World crop outputs. These have been so successful as to turn growing numbers of Third World countries into food exporters, and thus competitors of the United States. At the same time, the European Economic Community has become a major producer of agricultural surpluses, owing to its price-support system. In consequence, experts now refer to a "world awash in food," and this state of affairs in turn has led to sharp declines in agricultural prices and in American food exports—and has driven many farmers out of business.

Like mid-Victorian Britons, Americans after 1945 favored free trade and open competition, not just because they held that global commerce and prosperity would be advanced in the process but also because they knew that they were most likely to benefit from a lack of protectionism. Forty years later, with that confidence ebbing, there is a predictable shift of opinion in favor of protecting the domestic market and the domestic producer. And, just as in Edwardian Britain, defenders of the existing system point out that higher tariffs not only might make domestic products *less* competitive internationally but also might have other undesirable repercussions—a global tariff war, blows against American exports, the undermining of the currencies of certain newly industrializing countries, and an economic crisis like that of the 1930s.

Kennedy makes an interesting point here. The long argument over the merits of **free trade** and **protectionism** continues, and he puts it into some historical perspective. The European Union (EU) and the North American Free Trade Association (NAFTA) are large free-trade areas, and the World Trade Organization (WTO) is devoted to creating increased trade through the lowering of tariffs.

Along with these difficulties affecting American manufacturing and agriculture has come great turbulence in the nation's finances. The uncompetitiveness of U.S. industrial products abroad and the declining sales of agricultural exports have together produced staggering deficits in visible trade—$160 billion in the twelve months ending with April of 1986—but what is more alarming is that such a gap can no longer be covered by American earnings on "invisibles," which are the traditional recourse of a mature economy. On the contrary, the United States has been able to pay its way in the world only by importing ever larger amounts of capital. This has, of course, transformed it from the world's largest creditor to the world's largest debtor nation in the space of a few years.

Kennedy assumes that you know the basic terminology of trade and economics:
exports goods sold to buyers in another country
imports goods purchased from companies in another country
tariff a tax on imported goods
trade gap the difference between the value of goods exported and goods imported, producing a **trade deficit** or a **trade surplus.**
Interest on the national debt the payments the government has to make to its creditors. This money comes out of the country's yearly budget; in 1993, interest payments took about 14% of the Federal budget.
GNP gross national product. The total value of all the economy of a country in a given year.

Compounding this problem—in the view of many critics, causing this problem—have been the budgetary policies of the U.S. government itself.

Federal Deficit, Debt, and Interest (in billions)

	Deficit	Debt	Interest on Debt
1980	$59.6	$914.3	$52.5
1983	$195.4	$1,381.9	$87.8
1985	$202.8	$1,823.1	$129.0

In 1994 the U.S. national debt was about $4 trillion and the annual interest payments were about $300 billion.

A continuation of this trend, alarmed voices have pointed out, would push the U.S. national debt to around $13 *trillion* by the year 2000 (fourteen times the debt in 1980) and the interest payments on the debt to $1.5 *trillion* (twenty-nine times the 1980 payments). In fact a lowering of interest rates could make those estimates too high, but the overall trend is still very unhealthy. Even if federal deficits could be reduced to a "mere" $100 billion annually, the compounding of national debt and interest payments by the early twenty-first century would still cause unprecedented sums of money to be diverted in that direction. The only historical examples that come to mind of Great Powers so increasing their indebtedness *in peacetime* are France in the 1780s, where the fiscal crisis finally led to revolution, and Russia early in this century.

Kennedy moves systematically to his main point, that the United States has been following the same path trodden by other world powers, in which military commitments are maintained past the time when they are economically sustainable. This, he says, is the path of decline, and he calls it **"imperial overstretch."**

Indeed, it is difficult to imagine how the American economy could have got by without the inflow of foreign funds in the early 1980s, even if that had the awkward consequence of inflating the dollar and thereby further hurting U.S. agricultural and manufacturing exports. But, one wonders, what might happen if those funds are pulled out of the dollar, causing its value to drop precipitously?

IMPERIAL OVERSTRETCH

THINK ON PAPER

Since this article was written, in 1987, the world has changed dramatically, most notably with the end of the Cold War and the demise of the U.S.S.R. In response to these changes, has the United States changed its military posture? Have defense budgets been cut? Are the budget deficits and national debt increasing or decreasing? How is the country doing in the global marketplace? There is a lot of room for discussion here, but you may find it helpful to pool your knowledge of these matters.

This brings us, inevitably, to the delicate relationship between slow economic growth and high defense spending. The debate over the economics of defense spending is a heated one and—bearing in mind the size and variety of the American economy, the stimulus that can come from large government contracts, and the technological spin-offs from weapons research—the evidence does not point simply in one direction. But what is significant for our purposes is the comparative dimension. Although (as is often pointed out) defense expenditures amounted to ten percent of GNP under President Eisenhower and nine percent under President Kennedy, America's shares of global production and wealth were at that time around twice what they are today, and, more particularly, the American economy was not then facing challenges to either its traditional or its high-technology manufactures. The United States now devotes about seven percent of its GNP to defense spending, while its major economic rivals, especially Japan, allocate a far smaller proportion. If this situation continues, then America's rivals will have more funds free for civilian investment. If the United States continues to direct a huge proportion of its research and development activities toward military-related production while the Japanese and West Germans concentrate on commercial research and development, and if the Pentagon drains off the ablest of the country's scientists and engineers from the design and production of goods for the world market, while similar personnel in other countries are bringing out better consumer products, then it seems inevitable that the American share of world manufacturing will decline steadily, and likely that American economic growth rates will be slower than those of countries dedicated to the marketplace and less eager to channel resources into defense.

Rhetorical note: Kennedy is presenting an **argument,** backed up by detailed historical and economic evidence and analysis. His argument depends in part on an **analogy:** he claims that American policies since she achieved superpower status have been similar to those followed by the great powers of the past, and that the result may also be the same.

It is almost superfluous to say that these tendencies place the United States on the horns of a most acute, if long-term, dilemma. Simply because it is *the* global superpower, with military commitments far more extensive than those of a regional power like Japan or West

Germany, it requires much larger defense forces. Furthermore, since the USSR is seen to be the major military threat to American interests around the globe, and is clearly devoting a far greater proportion of its GNP to defense, American decision-makers are inevitably worried about "losing" the arms race with Russia. Yet the more sensible among the decision-makers can also perceive that the burden of armaments is debilitating the Soviet economy, and that if the two superpowers continue to allocate ever larger shares of their national wealth to the unproductive field of armaments, the critical question might soon be, Whose economy will decline *fastest*, relative to the economies of such expanding states as Japan, China, and so forth? A small investment in armaments may leave a globally overstretched power like the United States feeling vulnerable everywhere, but a very heavy investment in them, while bringing greater security in the short term, may so erode the commercial competitiveness of the American economy that the nation will be less secure in the long term.

The arms race was, of course, partly **technological** in nature, but note Kennedy's observation that it was also partly **economic.** Some commentators believe that, in the end, the arms race was principally economic; David Stockman, Budget Director in the first Reagan administration, has remarked that the arms race was a race to see which side's economy collapsed first, and that "we won—just."

Here, too, the historical precedents are not encouraging. Past experience shows that even as the relative economic strength of number-one countries has ebbed, the growing foreign challenges to their position have compelled them to allocate more and more of their resources to the military sector, which in turn has squeezed out productive investment and, over time, led to a downward spiral of slower growth, heavier taxes, deepening domestic splits over spending priorities, and a weakening capacity to bear the burdens of defense. If this, indeed, is the pattern of history, one is tempted to paraphrase Shaw's deadly serious quip and say: "Rome fell. Babylon fell. Scarsdale's turn will come."

Kennedy asks and answers the basic question of whether the United States can avoid the decline that eventually overtook all other great powers with a definite "No," but he doesn't leave the discussion with this simple answer. What is the rest of his article concerned with?

MANAGING RELATIVE DECLINE

Ultimately, the only answer to whether the United States can preserve its position is *no*—for it simply has not been given to any one society to remain permanently ahead of all the others, freezing the patterns of different growth rates, technological advance, and military development that have existed since time immemorial. But historical precedents do not imply that the United States is destined to shrink to the relative obscurity of former leading powers like Spain and the Netherlands, or to disintegrate like the Roman and Austro-Hungarian empires; it is too large to do the former, and probably too homogeneous to do the latter. Even the British analogy, much favored in the current political-science literature, is not a good one if it ignores the differences in scale. The geographic size, population, and natural resources of Great Britain suggest that it ought to possess roughly three or four percent of the world's wealth and power, all other things being equal. But precisely because all other things are never equal, a

As you read on to the end, think about how, overall, you would characterize Kennedy's article. For example, some people might find it very pessimistic, but others may not agree. What do you think Kennedy would say?

Kennedy's **"multipolar world"** is one in which economic and political power is shared more or less equally among the leading societies of the 21st century. He thinks that these will be the **United States, Japan, Europe, China,** and **Russia** (he actually said the U.S.S.R., not knowing that that country would now no longer exist). It could be said that, after World War II, we lived in a **bipolar world,** dominated by Washington and Moscow; after the collapse of communism in Europe, we lived in a **unipolar world** dominated by the United States. Kennedy suggests, however, that the world is rapidly becoming multipolar, with no single power in a dominant position; some historians have observed that this end-of-century multipolar world is similar in some respects to the situation at the beginning of the century, before World War I.

peculiar set of historical and technological circumstances permitted Great Britain to possess, say, 25 percent of the world's wealth and power in its prime. Since those favorable circumstances have disappeared, all that it has been doing is returning to its more "natural" size. In the same way, it may be argued, the geographic extent, population, and natural resources of the United States suggest that it ought to possess 16 or 18 percent of the world's wealth and power. But because of historical and technological circumstances favorable to it, that share rose to 40 percent or more by 1945, and what we are witnessing today is the ebbing away from that extraordinarily high figure to a more natural share. That decline is being masked by the country's enormous military capability at present, and also by its success in internationalizing American capitalism and culture. Yet even when it has declined to the position of occupying no more than its natural share of the world's wealth and power, a long time into the future, the United States will still be a very significant power in a multipolar world, simply because of its size.

Just how well can the American system adjust to a state of relative decline? Already, a growing awareness of the gap between U.S. obligations and U.S. power has led to questions by gloomier critics about the overall political culture in which Washington decision-makers have to operate. It has been suggested with increasing frequency that a country needing to reformulate its grand strategy in the light of the larger, uncontrollable changes taking place in world affairs may be ill served by an electoral system that seems to paralyze foreign-policy decision-making every two years. Foreign policy may be undercut by the extraordinary pressures applied by lobbyists, political-action committees, and other interest groups, all of whom, by definition, are prejudiced in favor of this or that policy change, and by the simplification of vital but complex international and strategic issues, inherent to mass media whose time and space for such things are limited and whose raison d'être is chiefly to make money and only secondarily to inform. It may also be undercut by the still powerful escapist urges in the American social culture, which are perhaps understandable in terms of the nation's frontier past but hinder its coming to terms with today's complex, integrated world and with other cultures and ideologies. Finally, the country may not always be helped by the division of decision-making powers that was deliberately created when it was geographically and strategically isolated from the rest of the world, two centuries ago, and had time to find a consensus on the few issues that actually concerned foreign policy. This division may be less serviceable now that the United States is a global superpower, often called upon to make swift decisions vis-à-vis countries that enjoy far fewer constraints. No one of these obstacles prevents the execution of a coherent, long-term American grand strategy. However, their cumulative effect is to make it difficult to carry out policy changes that seem to hurt special interests and occur in an election year. It may therefore be here, in the cultural and political realms, that the evolution of an overall American policy to meet the twenty-first century will be subjected to the greatest test.

Nevertheless, given the considerable array of strengths still possessed by the United States, it ought not in theory to be beyond the talents of successive Administrations to orchestrate this readjustment so as, in Walter Lippmann's classic phrase, to bring "into balance . . . the nation's commitments and the nation's power." Although there is no single state obviously preparing to take over America's global burdens, in the way that the United States assumed Britain's role in the 1940s, the country has fewer problems than had Imperial Spain, besieged by enemies on all fronts, or the Netherlands, squeezed between France and England, or the British Empire, facing numerous challengers. The tests before the United States as it heads toward the twenty-first century are certainly daunting, perhaps especially in the economic sphere; but the nation's resources remain considerable, *if* they can be properly utilized and *if* there is a judicious recognition of both the limitations and the opportunities of American power.

ASPECTS OF WRITING: Critical reading and critique; fallacies and selective evidence.

Whenever we argue something, whether in speech or writing, and whenever we read such writing, we should be on the lookout for logical fallacies. These are flawed arguments; they may be honest errors or they may be tricks, intended to mislead the unwary. Two of the best-known types of fallacy are the **non sequitur** and the **ad hominem** argument.

The Latin phrase "*non sequitur*" means that something "doesn't follow" from an earlier statement.

> **Example:** College X has the bigger football team; they're bound to win.

Even when the sport involved is football, or another in which size may be a significant factor, it's obvious that size isn't everything. Other factors may also influence the result, and so the statement doesn't follow.

Debates on social issues seem to invite non sequiturs:

> **Example:** If people would get jobs, they wouldn't need welfare.

Many people work in jobs that pay wages too low to take them above the poverty line. This statement also assumes that appropriate jobs are available; this may be a case of **begging the question.**

Another kind of fallacy is the ad hominem argument, literally "to the man," in which irrelevant personal attacks take the place of reasoned argument.

> **Example:** That artist was a very unpleasant person; I don't like his pictures.

Obviously, the character of an artist is not a good basis for appreciating his or her art; if it were, a lot of famous artists would never be seen, read, or heard! The same can be said of people in other fields. It must be admitted, however, that it's sometimes hard to avoid being influenced by what we know about a person's private life, even if that information is entirely irrelevant to the issue at hand.

It's important that we pick up on logical flaws in what we read, and it's important also that we recognize when writers are presenting only those parts of situation that suit their argument; this is called using **selective evidence.** Of course, it will be difficult to recognize selective evidence if you don't know anything about the topic under discussion, and so, in such cases, you may be easily led by the writer.

A critique, unlike a summary, allows you to comment on and discuss the work you have read, and in your response you should also try to avoid fallacious arguments. For example, Kennedy's article is scholarly and his analysis challenging, but if you bristle when he writes about the inevitability of American decline, it's incumbent on you to find errors in his analysis; **it's not enough simply to reject what he says because you don't like what he says.** Did he ignore any aspect, or is he misleading in any way? Are his facts right? Does the notion of history repeating itself apply in this case? If not, why not? These and other questions might help you consider a response to this essay.

A careful reading of the essay would also show that Kennedy does not give an absolutely pessimistic account of America's future. He emphasizes that the decline is relative, not absolute; he suggests that the size, natural resources, and wealth of America guarantee her a continuing place among the world's leading nations; and he suggests that the adjustment to more manageable international commitments can be achieved. All of these points could be the subject of discussion in a critique.

WRITING EXERCISES: Answer one of the following.

When responding to an essay, either to summarize it or to critique it, you will almost certainly find it useful to quote key ideas from the original. When you do this, make sure that you **integrate the quote into your sentence** in an effective way, as in this example:

Kennedy's article describes in detail the reasons for what he sees as "the gradual erosion of the economic foundations of America's power."

Identifying key ideas and phrases is vital when discussing essays like Kennedy's. Key concepts here include "relative decline" and "imperial overstretch"; if you understand these concepts, then you are in a good position to talk about the essay.

1. Write a critique of Kennedy's article. This will involve summarizing what he says, identifying his principal ideas and phrases (or some of them), and commenting on each. Remember that "critique" does not necessarily suggest a negative assessment; it's rather like a movie review, which may be favorable, unfavorable, or a mixture of the two.

Of course, you have an advantage over Kennedy in that you have seen what has happened since he wrote his article, especially the end of the Cold War and the collapse of the Soviet Union. In the United States, concerns over budget matters dominate the political debate, and America's role in the world has ________________ [strengthened/weakened?]. Have Kennedy's warnings been heeded? Was he right?

2. What do *you* think the future holds in store for the United States? You could begin by noting that the whole world is changing in many ways—politically, culturally, and so on—and then focus on one of these aspects. A group or class discussion could generate ideas for this.

OPTION ONE

PRIOR KNOWLEDGE: "The war to end all wars"; visiting the past.

In 1914 a conflict known as "The Great War" began. At the time, it was talked about as "the war to end all wars," but 25 years later another war began and the Great War was renamed World War I. When the surviving soldiers returned to their countries, even the victors were exhausted, disillusioned, and determined that their governments should not restore the class-bound social order of the prewar period. Change was in the air, politically, socially, and culturally. Inspired by the idealism of the Russian Revolution (1917), many turned to socialist parties, especially in Europe; society became more democratic; women won the vote in many countries and increasingly took their place in politics and the workforce; new technologies began to transform everyday life; the arts flourished. To many historians, 1914 was the real beginning of the 20th century.

The Great War was not, however, simply a transforming moment in history; it was a shattering personal experience of such savagery and pain as to be the stuff of nightmares. Just as the American Civil War, especially in the South, has its place in the collective memory, so, especially in Europe, the images of World War I have been passed down from generation to generation: trench warfare, armies bogged down in mud and slaughter, thousands dying in efforts to win a few yards of ground, poison gas, no man's land, going "over the top," shell shock, the Somme, Passchendaele, Verdun, the first use in warfare of submarines, tanks, and aircraft. More than eight million soldiers died, and millions more civilians; twenty million more, worldwide, died in the influenza epidemic that followed. To many, despite the changes it precipitated, the Great War remains the ultimate symbol of futility on the battlefield and incompetence among politicians and generals.

The memory of some events and places becomes embedded in the national memory. Such memories are passed from generation to generation through books, including textbooks; through movies; through national days of commemoration; through public memorials such as the Vietnam War memorial in Washington; through organizations whose members are anxious that certain things should not be forgotten; through the preservation and protection of historic sites, which are open to the public; and through ordinary people who remember not only their personal experiences but also the experiences of their forebears, and who talk about these things with their families and friends.

Many historians see the aftermath of World War I leading directly to World War II. This is partly because the allies, especially the Europeans, wanted to punish Germany by making them pay large financial reparations. It is often said that this weakened the German economy and helped create conditions which were exploited by Hitler to win support for his ultranationalist and racist Nazis. Books on World War I and World War II continue to be published in large numbers, as you'll see if you browse in any library or book store.

In his article, Beatty makes several references to poets and other writers. **Wilfred Owen,** one of the poets he mentions, is perhaps the best known of the World War I poets. Owen died in battle one week before the armistice, and legend has it that his parents received the news of his death as the bells of victory were ringing in their village. Some of Owen's poems form the text of Benjamin Britten's choral masterwork, the *War Requiem.* Poetry and music here combine in another way to record, celebrate, lament, and otherwise remember the past.

The widespread interest in **genealogy**—tracing family history—inevitably takes people into the past. History is not simply a record of great events and famous people; it's also the story of ordinary people. Millions of people spend time researching their own families; historical research is their hobby. Such research often takes people back to the great events of the past—wars and migrations, for example—and so personal and public histories overlap. We all, in one way or another, represent the times in which we live.

As always, check your dictionary for any word you don't know.

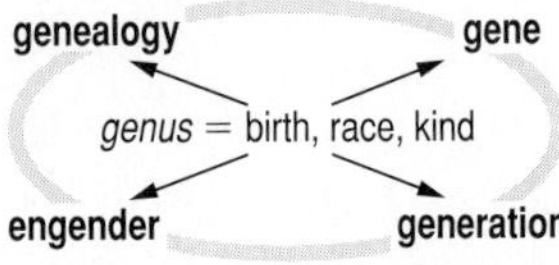

The end of World War I saw the end of the Austro-Hungarian, Ottoman, and German Empires. The **Treaty of Versailles** (1919), where the United States was represented by President Wilson, made Poland and Czechoslovakia independent states, and, as mentioned earlier, treated Germany in ways that some historians believe undermined the postwar German state and led to the rise of the fascist dictatorship under Hitler. This can be contrasted with the treatment of Germany and Japan after World War II, when these countries were helped economically and politically. Perhaps this is a real example of learning from history.

There are many sites in the United States of great historical interest, and visiting them can be a powerful experience, both intellectually and emotionally. Some sites commemorate events of national importance, and some have a more local significance. All, however, tell a story; you may have visited such sites.

The following essay recounts the journey of an American family to the battlefields of World War I, and the writer evokes powerful images of an event that continues to haunt the imagination. The essay speaks to us about why this war changed so many things. It reminds us of the experience of the many nations involved in this conflict, and it allows us to share the thoughts of the writer about the many faces of war. Above all, his message is that the world changed profoundly in 1914–18, and it's worth knowing why.

READING: Jack Beatty. "Along the Western Front." *Atlantic Monthly* Nov. 1986: 108–117.

A visit to the shrines and battlefields of the war that ended on the eleventh hour of the eleventh day of the eleventh month

Along the Western Front

The Western Front of the 1914–1918 war stretched 466 miles, from the North Sea to the Swiss frontier, forming a scar across the face of Europe. On summer vacation, with my wife and young son, I toured the front. It proved a strange vacation: an excursion across a death-scape.

The war on the Western Front began and ended as a war of motion, with the two great German offensives of late summer, 1914, and spring, 1918. In the years between, it was a static war, with only little mockeries of movement here and there along the whole expanse. Imagine a giant S inscribed across the top of France, its tail grazing a corner of Belgium: the Germans held the north and east side of this curving line, in places just yards away from the Belgian, British, and French troops facing them on its south and west. The line had no strategic significance whatsoever; it was simply where the million-man armies had wound up after Germany's failure to destroy the Allies in the quick war-opening battle of annihilation that its General Staff had been planning for years. A complicated series of actions beginning on September 5, 1914, known to history as the Battle of the Marne, had checked the German drive just short of Paris. Thereafter the armies had tried to outflank each other in a weeks-long "race to the sea." At the Belgian coast they ran out of room to maneuver and, exhausted, dug in. The Western Front was born of their digging.

The first section of the front lay in Flanders, and there, in the tidy Flemish city of Ypres, we began our tour.

Ypres was not the actual start of the front; that distinction belongs to Nieuport, a city on the North Sea twenty-odd miles down the river Yser from Ypres. Belgian troops held the line of the Yser between the sea and Ypres, where the British sector began. Ypres is pronounced

By Jack Beatty

Eep, but in the doggerel the British Tommies wrote about it they dubbed it "Wipers":

Far, far from Wipers I long to be,
Where German snipers can't snipe at me.
Damp is my dug-out.
Cold are my feet.
Waiting for the whizz-bangs
To send me to sleep.

Whizz-bangs were a species of shell that came in on a flat trajectory and made no sound warning of their approach.

The British position at Ypres was an exposed one: it lay in a salient, or bulge, of the front that was enclosed on three sides by German troops, who, to make matters worse, occupied the high ground. Despite its precariousness the British held fast to the salient for the duration. They did so for political reasons. In a treaty signed in the nineteenth century the British had pledged themselves to defend Belgian neutrality, and they had declared war on Germany because, by invading Belgium, it had violated that neutrality. Thus Belgium furnished the British with their *casus belli* in the First World War. That is why they were reluctant to quit the small slice of the country they held for more defensible positions just across the border, in France. It was a matter of British honor. You can see what it cost in the fifty-odd cemeteries around Ypres, as well as at the single most affecting monument we saw on our trip, the Menin Gate.

We arrived in Ypres (a four-hour drive from Paris) at dusk. After checking into an inn we had dinner in a restaurant on the town square. We were almost finished when we noticed a stirring among the diners at the other tables. To judge by their accents, they were British tourists, and they were on their way to the Menin Gate. We paid our bill and followed them.

The Menin Gate is a massive arch that spans the road leading out of the town center. Built by the British in the late twenties, it is inscribed with the names, ranks, and regiments of more than 50,000 British servicemen who, in the words of the dedication, "fell in the Ypres salient in the 1914–1918 war and who have no known grave." As my son and I climbed the stairs leading to the park above the monument, the sounds of British accents filled our ears. "Look, Tom, isn't that Da's lot?" an elderly woman asked her husband as she pointed to a list of the Manchester dead. "Da," it turned out, had belonged to a different unit.

It was almost eight o'clock when the little knot of people in the park started to file down to the sidewalk beneath the gate. A last car drove by. Then two Belgian policemen appeared at either end of the gate and held up their hands. All traffic stopped. A man (we later learned that he was a town fireman) detached himself from the crowd, walked into the middle of the road, and raised a bugle to his lips. Mothers shushed their children, a couple in front of me clasped hands, an old man doffed his cap and held it to his breast. Silence. Then, under the echoing arch, the bugler commenced to play.

The tune was "The Last Post," the British version of taps, and it went on and on, filling the gate with a keening sound that stretched our emotions taut until, at last, it quavered and broke. For long seconds no one moved. Then, with the men turned away from their families to hide their tears, the little crowd of military pilgrims slowly dispersed.

The ceremony at the Menin Gate is a gesture of perpetual remembrance from the Belgian people to the British, New Zealand, Australian, Indian, Maori, Canadian, and South African troops who fought and died here to make good on Britain's promise to Belgium. From 1940 to 1944 Ypres was occupied by the Germans, who forbade any show of piety toward their British enemy. But at eight o'clock on the evening of the day the Germans left. "The Last Post" was played at the Menin Gate, and it has been played every evening since.

In a book kept in a kind of tabernacle inside the gate, visitors are invited to leave their names and nationalities and to comment on the ceremony. Not all of the visitors are British, and indeed I saw some German names, but most of them are. A Graham Vincent, of Edinburgh, wrote this: "Let us remember not so much those who gave their lives here as those whose lives were *taken* from them, and from that learn a lesson for the future." Many visitors found that Kipling summed up their feelings: "Lest We Forget" appeared regularly in the comments column. But the mood of Menin was perhaps best caught by a woman who wrote, "Words are few, thoughts are deep."

There are no trenches around Ypres, but shell craters pock the wooded hills, and at intervals on the low Flanders plain, pillboxes loom up like so many cement haystacks. The Salient War Museum is on the town square, in the Cloth Hall, which was built between 1260 and 1304, destroyed by German artillery between 1914 and 1918, and rebuilt with German reparations, mostly between the wars. There the visitor can obtain maps showing him what to see in the Ypres area. He can also buy a copy of *Before Endeavors Fade*, by Rose E. B. Coombs, M.B.E., an invaluable guidebook not only to Ypres but also to many other battlefields on the Western Front. We tried to follow Coombs's detailed itineraries ("To return to the Ramparts and the moat; just beyond the cemetery, the walks meander over the corner bastion known as the Lion Tower which like the Lille Gate . . . ") but, frustrated, failed. Thereafter we confined ourselves to visiting the places where the soldiers fell—Polygon Wood, Messines Ridge, Mount Kemmel, Pilkem Ridge, and New Irish Farm, where "a number of Chinese Labour Corps are buried beneath the chestnut trees," according to Rose Coombs. The British lost 908,371 men in the Great War, and most of them are buried in these Flanders cemeteries. By far the largest is Tyne Cot, a twenty-minute drive northeast of Ypres, near a village called Passchendaele.

Passchendaele "has come to be . . . a synonym for military failure—a name black-bordered in the records of the British Army," Basil Liddell Hart wrote of the British offensive fought between July 31 and November 4, 1917, and named for the village where, "in a porridge of mud," it stalled. The motives behind the offensive give it a patina of plausibility. The French Army was near mutiny, having been pounded for nearly a year at Verdun and then decimated in a foolhardy April attack across the Chemin des Dames, far down the front from Flanders. A British drive out of the Ypres salient would lift enemy pressure on the French, giving them time to save their army before it melted away. Also, it would give the British the chance to seize the Belgian ports of Ostend and Zeebrugge, where there were large German submarine bases. Since the previous February the Germans had been conducting unrestricted submarine warfare from these bases—sinking one of every four ships leaving England—and the Admiralty feared that Britain might not be able to hold out through 1918 unless, somehow, the submarines were stopped.

Initially the British met with success. The longer the battle lasted, however, the more thoroughly did their artillery destroy the dikes and drainage systems of the tenuously reclaimed fields over which their infantry would have to attack. Worse, fall is the wet season in Flanders, and the sky poured rain. Under such aquatic conditions the offensive slowed to a crawl and then stopped altogether. Seven miles of mud had been taken, at a cost of 300,000 casualties. "Good God, did we really send men to fight in that?" a British general exclaimed upon seeing the swamplike condition of the battlefield. Liddell Hart's lapidary judgment on that comment applies equally to many other generals of the Great War: "If the exclamation was a credit to his heart it revealed on what a foundation of delusion and inexcusable ignorance" the British plan had been based.

"They died in Hell, they called it Passchendaele," Siegfried Sassoon wrote. Tyne Cot, once a suburb of this hell, is today a garden of death. Red and pink roses, lavender hydrangea, livid monkshood, exuberant daisies, orange gaillardia—each of the 12,000 gravestones is flanked by these or other flowers. Behind the cemetery is a wheat field, across from it the first of many farms extending over the plain to the horizon, and the spire of Ypres Cathedral poking over the last hill. We got there in the late evening of a rain-washed day and watched as the westering sky turned a tortured red, with bruises of black and flashes of yellow showing through. To stand amid those flowers in that perfumed air and watch the slow guttering of the daylight made one feel as if Nature were in a conspiracy with Man to deny what had once gone on here. The loveliness of Tyne Cot is a sort of reaction formation against the memory of hell. That is the aesthetic principle behind these British War Graves Commission cemeteries, or so I came to conclude. They are transfigurations of the terrible. They serve to remind us that the civilization said to have been destroyed by the Great War, that "old bitch gone in the teeth" of Ezra Pound's bitter postwar poem, still remembers how to mask death with beauty.

That is one face of our civilization; the back wall of the Tyne Cot cemetery recalls another. It is a big wall, and it is inscribed with the names of thousands of soldiers to whom, in the words of the dedication, "the fortunes of war denied the known and honored burial given to their comrades in death." That stately language is another mask. Those men have no individual graves because they were killed by means that obliterated them. What Wilfred Owen called "the monstrous anger of the guns" claimed far more victims than did bullets in the Great War. At the start of the Passchendaele offensive, for example, the British fired 4,500,000 artillery shells, and the German guns replied with a comparable prodigality. Men were dismembered, cut in half, punched into the earth by shells they often could not hear coming, fired by gunners they could not see. It was a spectacle of mass technological death, and it made courage as meaningless as mercy. The memory of this impersonal, inconceivably destructive violence is one of the Great War's legacies—a permanent shudder in history.

In the visitor's book at Tyne Cot someone has written, "If ye break faith with us who die/We shall not sleep, though poppies grow/In Flanders Fields." But how, after all this time, can we keep faith with them? John McCrae's poem, from which those lines are taken, also bids its readers, "Take up our quarrel with the foe:/To you from failing hands we throw/The torch. . . ." That appeal meant something while the war still raged, but not now. What foe should we take up arms against? And what are we to do with the torch?

We came to Europe to see "the trenches"; I even had the droll notion of spending a day walking a length of them. That, I discovered, is not possible. Seventy years of farming in the meticulous French manner, of road-building and town-extending and city-reconstructing, have combined with the destruction wrought by the tank battles and the aerial bombings of the Second World War to expunge the trench system of the Great War. Still, in a few places bits of the trenches have been restored—at Vimy Ridge, for instance.

Vimy Ridge is a spectacular and, for parents traveling with a small child, frightening battlefield to visit. It lies perhaps thirty miles down the front from Ypres, just north of Arras, in the department of Artois. To quote Rose Coombs, Vimy Ridge is today "preserved and owned in perpetuity by Canada," for it was Canadian troops who, on April 9, 1917, stormed and seized it.

Vimy Ridge nicely illustrates the strategic problem faced by the Allies from November of 1914 to March of 1918, when the Germans stood on the defensive and the Allies mounted attack after attack—at Ypres, Loos, the Somme, Lens, Arras, La Bassée, Neuve Chapelle—against a trench barrier that daily grew thicker, as more and yet more trenches were dug behind the front line. During an Allied bombardment the Germans would withdraw from the front trenches by means of communications trenches and scuttle to the comparative security of the rear trenches, or they would burrow into dugouts thirty feet deep and wait out the shelling in safety. The shelling over, they would clamber up from the dugouts or race down the communication trenches and be ready to machine-gun the advancing waves of British infantry. Thus the pattern of stalemate—and slaughter.

Winston Churchill summed up the Allied dilemma in a war memorandum: "We must, therefore, either find another theatre or another method." That is, either the Allies had to go around the trench barrier or they had to devise a way to break through it. Churchill's Dardanelles expedition was an attempt to find another theater: it failed. So did the new method of poison gas. Introduced by the Germans at Ypres in 1915, it was quickly copied by the British and as quickly neutralized by their enemy. The method that finally broke the trench barrier was, of course, the armored tank. But that deliverance was not fully matured until 1918. Meanwhile, other methods were tried.

At Vimy Ridge the Canadians had miners dig up to the German front trench, place heavy explosives beneath it, and then blow it up at the moment of attack. The mining worked: the Canadians achieved a complete tactical victory (which they were unable to exploit into a strategic breakthrough, however). Today two enormous mine craters, perhaps fifty feet deep and a hundred feet wide, testify to the success of this new method. My son and I scrambled up and down those craters for what seemed like hours one hot August afternoon. From then on, for the rest of the trip, at the most inconvenient times, he would demand to see another "craber," until, exasperated, I gave in.

Vimy Ridge can also be recommended for its opposing rows of restored trenches, so close that you could hear your enemy sigh, and for the Canadian Memorial on the flank of the ridge opposite the trenches, an easy ten-minute walk away through the intervening Memorial Park. To keep the grass in the park clipped, the Canadians allow goats to roam free behind a wire fence. Do not try to feed the goats—the fence is electrified. "It's raining," my son said as he felt the mild charge of the wire against his flesh. We didn't know what he was talking about until we brushed against it ourselves.

But that is the least of the dangers in the park: the woods are liberally strewn with unexploded gas and artillery shells, and red signs phrased in the imperative mood of several languages warn visitors to stay on the road. "To you . . . we throw/The torch"—but who would have guessed that the flame would still be burning so many years later?

The Canadian Memorial is a huge, grandiloquent sculpture. Part abstract design, part figurative rendering, it shows the Spirit of Canada weeping for her dead sons. Placed at the crest of a bare, steep ridge, the memorial commands panoramic views of the Scarpe Valley, the Douai Plain, and the coalfields and slag heaps around Lens. It is girdled by an ample meadow pocked with shell holes—and is out of bounds because of unexploded shells.

One of Kipling's "Epitaphs of the War" is a memorial to Canada:

From little towns in a far land we came,
To save our honour and a world aflame.
By little towns in a far land we sleep;
And trust that world we won for you to keep!

Again that familiar note: *We* must give meaning to *their* sacrifice.

Canada lost 66,655 men in the Great War. Kipling lost his son.

The Canadian Memorial at Vimy Ridge, France: the spirit of Canada weeps for her fallen sons. (*Veteran's Affairs, Canada*)

The Canadian dead were in our thoughts as we drove away from Vimy Ridge, and so were those Germans blown out of an April morning by the Canadian mines. Earlier we had visited the German cemetery at Neuville St. Vaast and looked out over 37,000 graves, rows of black metal crosses with many Stars of David breaking the symmetry. Less than a half mile away was a British cemetery; beyond it a billowing tricolor marked the location of a French cemetery. Divided in life, united in death—you couldn't help thinking in such Family of Man clichés; you couldn't help being moved, either.

In the visitor's book at the German cemetery someone had written: "When you are visiting your dead hero's grave/Remember too the German soldiers/Who were loyal and brave."

Indeed they were. Germany had staked everything on the one big war-opening battle. When that failed, its chances of winning disappeared. It could not hope to prevail in a prolonged two-front war (Russia was a combatant right up until 1918), for the Allied blockade would slowly cut the muscles of the German war effort. Yet the soldiers held on, serving with a loyalty that their leaders, the criminally stupid Kaiser, and Ludendorff the Nazi-to-be, did not deserve. Germany lost 1,800,000 men in the Great War.

In F. Scott Fitzgerald's *Tender Is the Night*, Dick Diver and some of his friends take time out from their strenuous dissipations in Paris to drive to a Great War battlefield far to the northeast of the city. Caught up in the mood of the still-ravaged land (the time is the 1920s), Diver delivers himself of this remarkable speech:

> See that little stream—we could walk to it in two minutes. It took the British a month to walk to it—a whole empire walking very slowly, dying in front and pushing forward behind. And another empire walked very slowly backward a few inches a day, leaving the dead like a million bloody rugs. No Europeans will ever do that again in this generation. . . . This western-front business couldn't be done again, not for a long time. The young men think they could do it but they couldn't. They could fight the first Marne again but not this. This took religion and years of plenty and tremendous sureties and the exact relation that existed between the classes. The Russians and Italians weren't any good on this front. You had to have a whole-souled sentimental equipment going back further than you could remember. You had to remember Christmas, and postcards of the Crown Prince and his fiancée, and little cafés in Valence and beer gardens in Unter den Linden and weddings at the mairie, and going to the Derby, and your grandfather's whiskers. . . . This was a love battle—there was a century of middle-class love spent here. . . . All my beautiful lovely safe world blew itself up here with a great gust of high explosive love.

Notice the distinction Diver makes between "first Marne" and "this western-front business." The former belonged to the brief weeks of the war of motion, the latter to the four years of the war of stalemate. In Diver's mind the essence of the Great War lies in the classic Western Front battle fought in the place that he and his friends have driven to visit. It began on July 1, 1916, and though its official designation is the Battle of Albert, to almost everybody by now it is known as the Somme, after the river that flows nearby.

Dick Diver lays a rare stress on the affective psychology of the soldiers who fought in the Somme, on their capacity to be linked by memory to love. He is on to something big here, another legacy of the Great War. Students of mass conformity, of fascism and totalitarianism, of nationalism and patriotism, could profitably confront the Somme with a disturbing question: What made them do it?

"It" was to march, in an orderly way, rank by rank, column by column, to their death. That is what 20,000 British soldiers did on July 1, most of them falling between 7:30 and 8:30 A.M., the taste of tea and bacon still fresh on their lips. They got out of their trenches and marched to their death, or to some form of mutilation—total casualties for July 1 came to 60,000. They had been told that the German trenches facing them, uphill, in the hard clay ground of Picardy would be cleared of the enemy. At worst they would be lined with dazed and dying soldiers, victims of the tremendous, days-long British artillery barrage. Instead the trenches were full of machine gunners, who had sat out the barrage in deep "bomb proofs." Methodically these gunners raked the British formations. Methodically new formations set out, were shot down in no-man's-land, were replaced by other formations, and so on, turn and turn about, through the long day.

North of Albert, near the village of Beaumont-Hamel, is the Newfoundland Memorial Park. You can stand in the restored British trenches there, look 500 yards across to the German trenches, and ask yourself if you could do what the 752 members of the Newfoundland regiment did on July 1—attack across that piece of ground. Private F. H. Cameron, of the 1st King's Own Scottish Borderers, who had been wounded in an earlier assault on the German position, lay in no-man's-land watching the regiment attack. "On came the Newfoundlanders, a great body of men, but the fire intensified and they were wiped out in front of my eyes. I cursed the generals for their useless slaughter." The attack lasted forty minutes, and fully 91 percent of the Newfoundlanders were shot down in it.

"You had to have a whole-souled sentimental equipment"—that or be mad. I thought, as my son and I scuttled across no-man's-land at the Newfoundland Park one afternoon. We got halfway, climbing up and down the gulleys and shell holes and swales where the Tommies had tried to hide from the killing fire, and then started back, my son waving to my wife, who sat on the parapet of the German trenches, waving back. We mix love and obedience in our children's psyches, making them susceptible to authority—fearing it, identifying with it, wanting its approval. So it's no use putting all the blame for a slaughter like the Somme on the State; we soften our children up for the kill by weakening their will to rebel with mithridatic doses of guilt. Obedience to authority is a liability of our natures, and the Newfoundland Memorial is one of its monuments.

We drove away in low spirits. Next stop, Château-Thierry.

To get to the American sector of the war from the Somme battlefields you drive east and then south, down the valley of the Marne. The drive east, from Albert to Péronne, is very beautiful. The road runs along the high ground and offers generous views of the French countryside. Every few miles you pass a British cemetery. The introductions to the registers of these cemeteries, it is useful to know, contain brief histories of the fighting in the area. Some of the funerary monuments are impressive, others "hideous, but done in good faith," as one visitor wrote of the Thiepval Monument.

From Péronne you drive through St. Quentin, with its monuments commemorating the American assault on the Hindenburg Line; past Laon, where you can still see the emplacement of the great German gun that lobbed shells over fifty air miles into Paris; and then through Soissons and on into Château-Thierry. Here, in June of 1918, in front of this provincial city nestled in a bend of the Marne, the raw American Army and Marines stopped Ludendorff's lunge for Paris. Of 310,000 U.S. soldiers engaged, 67,000 became casualties. A rather fascistic white monument, but done in good faith, honors the American dead. Set on a bluff overlooking the Marne Valley and the Champagne country beyond, it includes a relief map depicting where the fighting took place. The names of the battles—Crimpetes Wood, Vaux, Fismes, Missy-aux-Bois—were all unfamiliar to me, except one.

The Bois de Belleau—Belleau Wood—ranks with Gettysburg and Omaha Beach as one of the great place-names in American military history. Lying perhaps a dozen miles outside of Château-Thierry, deep in the country, Belleau Wood is today the site of a surpassingly lovely cemetery, its large white crosses and Stars of David arrayed in graceful curving lines, its grass rich and well cared for, its stands of roses huge and, against that white and bright green background, passionately vermillion. Behind the cemetery one can walk in the Bois, which contains numerous guns and plaques recording acts, usually fatal, of Marine valor. Altogether, the cemetery makes one proud to belong to a country that can afford to honor its dead with such tasteful munificence.

Just down the hill is the hamlet of Belleau, and there, on the lawn of a tiny park across from the *mairie,* we had a picnic. The scene was beckoningly pastoral. Five or six dun-colored stucco farmhouses, with red tiled roofs and green shutters, filled the foreground. Behind us was an apple orchard, in the middle distance a hill speckled with black and white cows. It was as if we had stepped out of history and into art—a painting by Cézanne, say.

By the side of the road was a rustic water pump, the sort of humble prop that lends pathos and authenticity to French landscape paintings. Close inspection revealed it to be a gift to Belleau from a Pennsylvania regiment. So much for escaping from history.

North from Château-Thierry, on Route 380, the views are delightful, the tiny *villes* so many brief and charming anecdotes. On one side for much of the trip is the valley of the Marne, steep and serpentine; on the other are the lush wheat fields and arching arbors of the Champagne country. On a high point of the road just beyond Bligny sits a rare sight on the Western Front—an Italian cemetery. Buried there are 5,000 Italian soldiers who, in the words of a nearby monument, died "*pour la France* 1914–1918." The main pathway through the cemetery, paved with round white pebbles and bordered with tall cedar bushes, might be an old Roman road. The setting is deeply Italian in feeling. Across Route 380 are more graves and another novel sight. Walking through this cemetery annex, I noticed the familiar shell welts scalloping the surrounding ground. A vagrant impulse led me to leap the wall and make my way to an adjacent copse. There I was startled to find an old rusting cannon: "1916 Fried, Krupp," it said on the breech. The barrel was grotesquely bent back, the way gun barrels are in cartoons. Had a shell hit it head on, or had it been spiked by the Germans to keep it from falling into enemy hands?

In Reims there is the cathedral to see, the champagne cellars to tour (no samples), and the military museum at Fort Pompenelle to visit. West of Reims is the battlefield of the Chemin des Dames, scene of epic butcheries; east of it the Argonne Forest and Verdun. We took the road east.

The shock of the Ludendorff offensive in the spring of 1918 caused the Allies to reform their command structure. A generalissimo of all the armies was appointed to coordinate the Allied counteroffensive. He was Marshal Foch, and it fell to him to give orders to the British and American generals under his command. John J. Pershing among them. The relationship of these two commanders did not go smoothly.

Pershing wanted to command an independent American army in the field, Foch to parcel out the American divisions to fill the gaps in the French ranks. Foch's motivation, historians speculate, was as much political as military. In the summer of 1918, with Germany's defeat now only a question of time, the French feared that an American army crowned with triumphs might enhance President Woodrow Wilson's bargaining position at the inevitable peace conference—might even give him the leverage to write his too-generous Fourteen Points into a treaty with the hated Boche. In the event, Pershing won the argument with Foch, but only after agreeing to attack with his independent army at a site of Foch's choosing. This was the Argonne Forest, where Pershing's army came to grief.

Driving into the Argonne off the A-4, which runs between Reims and Verdun, you can glimpse something of Pershing's problem. Here is no *bois* but a teeming fecundity of tall trees and dense undergrowth. The Allies had never dared to attack through the Argonne, leaving the Germans four unharassed years to construct defenses twelve miles deep. It is no wonder that the cemetery at Romagne-sous-Montfaucon, deep in the Argonne, is the largest American military cemetery in Europe, containing the remains of 14,246 soldiers.

Opened on September 26, 1918, Pershing's attack soon stalled. His troops, most of whom had been drafted just two months before, were so green that old-timers were charging as much as five dollars to show them how to load their rifles. In the dark woods, following Pershing's order to push ahead "without regard of losses and without regard to the exposed conditions of the flanks," units quickly became cut off from each other. One, the 1st Battalion of the 308th Infantry, was lost for five days. After word leaked to the press, "The Lost Battalion" became front-page news in America, as well as an embarrassment to Pershing. Subject to ferocious German counterattacks—spearheaded by flamethrowers—the battalion held its ground,

Military cemetery, Argonne. *(UPI/Corbis-Bettmann)*

encircled and depleted but game. Through a captured doughboy the Germans demanded the battalion's surrender. Its commander, Major Charles Whittlesey, refused. Immediately he did so, a shout went up from the American foxholes: "You Heinie bastards, come and get us!" Which they did. However, thanks to the flight of its only remaining carrier pigeon, Cher Ami, the lost battalion had at last been found, and relief was quick in coming.

Cher Ami became a national hero; after his death, a year later, he was stuffed, and today he is on exhibit at the Smithsonian Institution. Major Whittlesey was awarded a Medal of Honor, but that was not enough to heal his scars. In November of 1921 he jumped off a ship headed for Cuba. One of his business associates later told reporters, "He was a victim engulfed in a sea of woe. He would go to two or three funerals every week, and visit the wounded in the hospitals, and try to comfort the relatives of the dead."

Not all went badly for the Americans in the Argonne, and closer to the Meuse River you can see plaques and monuments to their victories; the roads secured, bridges taken, villages liberated—Varennes-en-Argonne, for example. A tank attack led by the young George Patton freed this village in September, 1918. Varennes now boasts a first-rate military museum, featuring photographs of the Argonne fighting and, in a cabinet of curios, a snapshot of Captain Harry Truman, who commanded an artillery battery here. Outside the museum is a bosky park leading to a modest yet majestic plaza, through which we had to walk to get to our car. Children rode their bicycles in circles on the plaza while their parents and grandparents sat on its walls talking and laughing—and our hearts swelled when we saw a plaque saying that the plaza was a gift from the Commonwealth of Pennsylvania. Surely these Ardennois, happy and free, are what men like Major Whittlesey were fighting for. If only he could come back today to see what their suffering had made possible—the tranquil life of this forest village—the demons of his memory might be stilled, allowing him, a very old man, to die at peace with himself. Peace: Varennes-en-Argonne reminds us that sometimes it must be won.

We picnicked in the town forest of Verdun, in a little clearing between the road and the woods. My son had no appetite for lunch. He preferred to climb up the bank leading to the woods. I ran after him—and shivered at what I saw. Beneath the thick overhang of branch and bush the ground was gouged with deep holes, like the face of a leper under his beard. The holes were filled halfway up with stagnant water, and trees grew out of them at grotesque angles. Seventy years ago this forest was cruelly punished in a ferocious battle from which neither it nor the French nation has fully recovered.

I make a poor guide to Verdun. The place depressed me. You have to be French to know how to respond to it. Or so I concluded as I watched the French tourists who swarmed over its monuments and crowded its museums.

They seem awestruck, as if Verdun were a kind of Lourdes without the miracles. In the hallways of Fort Douaumont, windowless and lit by yellow light, they shuffle by with the stricken air of mourners at the funeral of someone very dear. They mourn the death not so much of heroes as of heroism. Brave men fought and died here, *pour la France*. From the observation tower on Fort Douaumont you can look down on the forested hills to where the noble Colonel Driant held out to the last against the Germans' savage opening attack. For generations after the battle every French schoolboy honored his name. To the west lie the ruins of Fort Vaux, where Commandant Raynal and his few-score men fought for days against thousands of storm troopers. Raynal, too, is a national hero. Perhaps because the commanding general at Verdun was Henri Pétain, who dishonored his fame by collaborating with the Nazis during the Second World War, Verdun is remembered not for its commander but for the valor and more: the stoicism in adversity of its ordinary soldiers. Yet the cult of Driant, Raynal, and the others like them serves less to reveal what life was like for the *poilu*, the common French fighting man, than to mask the reality of Verdun. More than Passchendaele, more than the Somme, Verdun shows the essential irrelevance of the martial ideal in the world of industrial warfare. It was shell against flesh here, and the bodies lay thick upon the ground. In his splendid book *The Price of Glory: Verdun 1916*, Alistair Horne wrote: "The compressed area of the battlefield became an open cemetery in which every square foot contained some decomposed piece of flesh." A nation can't raise its sons to courage on such images. Hence the necessity of men like Driant and Raynal. If they did not exist, France would have had to invent them.

An infernal strategic logic lay behind the carnage of Verdun. In December of 1915 Erich von Falkenhayn, the German commander on the Western Front, submitted a memorandum to the Kaiser sketching out a plan of victory. Germany would lure the French Army into defending a position "for the retention of which the French General Staff would be compelled to throw in every man they have. If they do so the forces of France will bleed to death. . . ." Since France was "England's best sword," a defeat of France would compel England to capitulate. Alistair Horne wrote: "Falkenhayn's memorandum made military history. Never through the ages had any great commander or strategist proposed to vanquish an enemy by gradually bleeding him to death." The old fortified city of Verdun was picked for this macabre experiment because it lay in a salient all but surrounded by German forces. Also, because its forts were thought to be impregnable, French morale would be irretrievably dashed if Verdun should fall.

Falkenhayn's strategy nearly worked. The French rotated seven tenths of their army through the meat grinder of Verdun. A colonel's order to his regiment gives the death-heavy flavor of the battle: "You have a mission of sacrifice. . . . On the day they want to, they will massacre you to the last man, and it is your duty to fall." The losses on both sides were appalling—perhaps a million and a quarter casualties in all. (The *ossuaire* at Verdun is full of the bones of the 150,000 unidentified and unburied corpses.) In short, Verdun was a demographic catastrophe for France. Yet, following Pétain's famous order "*Ils ne passeront pas!*" the French Army held Verdun for the ten months of the battle—an epic of courage and endurance but not of victory. The standoff of Verdun, in the words of Alistair Horne, "was the indecisive battle in an indecisive war; the unnecessary battle in an unnecessary war; the battle that had no victors in a war that had no victors."

We traveled beyond Verdun, down into the plains of Lorraine, which, in the summer of 1914, were carpeted with the corpses of French soldiers; following the doctrine of "*offensive à outrance*," they had charged the hungry German machine guns with their bayonets fixed, their scarlet pantaloons billowing in the breeze of their rush. We had thought to drive on, through the high Vosges, where French chasseurs and German Alpine troops had fought a mountain war, and then down the valley of the Moselle, past the strong points of Epinal and Belfort, which Falkenhayn had considered attacking instead of Verdun, to Besançon and the end of the front at the Swiss border. That was our plan. But time pressed, the skies poured rain, and the grim spell of Verdun failed to release us from its grip. We cut short our trip and returned to Paris. Before we left France, I wanted to tour Versailles, where the Allies wrote the script for the Second World War, the vilest legacy of a Great War so ripe with evils.

We share a kinship of hazard with the soldiers of the trenches, living as we do under what President John F. Kennedy called a "nuclear sword of Damocles," which may fall on us at any moment as the shells fell on them. Their helplessness before their fate prefigures ours, or so we brood when we despair of ever making the world safe not for democracy but, this time, for life itself.

"On or about December 1910 human nature changed." The date is off by four years. Still, Virginia Woolf's pensée captures the sense of one world dying in the years of the Great War and another being born—one crueler and without security. Only a year into the war a Belgian poet, speaking of himself in the third person, dedicated a book on the invasion of his country with these words: "With emotion, to the man he used to be." He changed, we changed, somewhere along the Western Front.

ASPECTS OF WRITING: The personal essay.

Everything we write—unless we're simply copying—has our personal stamp on it. Even a summary is based on our own reading of a text and involves a certain selectivity. On the other hand, it might also be said that an essay like Jack Beatty's, which is very much a personal memoir, draws on many sources. Beatty achieves a wonderful blend of these two elements; he informs the reader not only about the past, but, perhaps indirectly, also about himself. He admits at the beginning that this was "a strange vacation: an excursion across a deathscape," and he proceeds to take us along on his tour of the battlefields of World War I and their monuments. Along the way, we hear what other tourists are saying, and what poets, soldiers, and historians have said about the events described. It's a personal essay, but it's also informed and informative. When Beatty quotes someone, it is a reflection of his own sensibilities as well as those of the person quoted.

You might have visited historical sites—perhaps an old fort, or Ellis Island, or a famous person's birthplace. You may also know a place that holds some special interest for you, because of its history, perhaps tied in with your own family's history. You might have asked older people to talk about their lives. No matter what the situation, when we are confronted by the past, as when we visit places where significant events happened, two elements are present: the historical place or account, and ourselves in that place or listening to that account. These aspects are interwoven in personal essays such as Beatty's.

One key to the success of Beatty's essay may be its honesty. He does not pretend to know everything, or to understand everything, but he is a sensitive, interested, and interesting observer, as he shows when he arrives at Verdun:

> I make a poor guide to Verdun. The place depressed me. You have to be French to know how to respond to it. Or so I concluded as I watched the French tourists who swarmed over its monuments and crowded its museums.
>
> They seem awestruck. . . . They mourn the death not so much of heroes as of heroism. . . . More than Passchendaele, more than the Somme, Verdun shows the essential irrelevance of the martial ideal in the world of industrial warfare. It was shell against flesh here, and the bodies lay thick upon the ground.

The Vietnam Memorial, in Washington, D.C., evokes a similarly powerful response in visitors, whether they have had any direct experience of that conflict or not. It's an emotional place, where visitors trace with their fingers the inscribed names of their friends and loved ones, or take rubbings of the names, or leave flowers, letters, or other mementos in front of the wall. It's a public memorial, but it's also one of the world's most intensely personal places.

The second key to the success of Beatty's essay lies in the personal and informed nature of his discussion. When he writes, "An *infernal* strategic logic lay behind the carnage at Verdun," a single word lets us know what he thinks about the military planners at the battle. His writing also benefits from the fact that he has read enough history and poetry, among other things, to be able to allude to people in these fields and enrich his own writing in so doing. You can enrich your own writing by picking up on literary, political, geographical, and other references as you read.

WRITING AND RESEARCH: Answer one of the following.

Objectivity is difficult to achieve on topics dear to nationalistic or patriotic sensibilities. As discussed earlier, parents, teachers, the media, and governments all influence our attitudes. When writing, however, you may want your understanding and human sympathy to shine through rather than the prejudices you may have acquired over the years. Reading widely, being able to distinguish between propaganda and reality, avoiding overgeneralizations and oversimplistic conclusions can all help achieve a thoughtful, humane assessment. These qualities seem apparent in Beatty's essay.

1. Write an account of a visit you have made to an historic site. You may try to imitate Beatty's combination of the historical and the personal. To do this, you should do some research on the place you have chosen.
2. As an alternative to writing about an actual site, you might write a personal response to watching or reading about one of the great events of history. For example, you might write about a documentary account of the Civil War, Women's Suffrage, the Civil Rights Movement, World War II, or the Vietnam War. Another option would be to write a response to Beatty's essay about World War I.
3. Discuss the concept of "collective memory." How do certain things become part of the collective memory of a whole population? Give examples and describe the significance—for good or evil—of such transgenerational memories. This could also include reference to some further reading.

OPTION TWO

TALKING ABOUT LANGUAGE: Language and history.

In this text you have seen many vocabulary webs, showing the relationships between words that have grown from the same root. But what are these roots? Where do they come from? The answer is given in the etymology of each word, as found in most dictionaries. The etymology is the history of the word.

The original home of English was, unsurprisingly, England, but the original inhabitants of England were not English-speakers. Fifteen hundred years ago, the superpower of the day, Rome, was in decline, and [think of Paul Kennedy's notion of "imperial overstretch"] began to withdraw her forces from distant occupied lands like Britain, which they left early in the 5th century. The inhabitants of Britain at this time were Celtic-speakers, and some, after 400 years of Roman occupation, were culturally influenced by Rome and were Latin-speakers. The Romans left what today we would call a power vacuum, and this was filled by Germanic tribes from across the English Channel. These people—including Saxons, Jutes, Angles, and Friesians—came into southern Britain in waves over the next few hundred years, steadily pushing the Britons westward and northward. The descendants of these Britons today include the Welsh, Cornish, and other Celtic or Gaelic people, some of whom speak modern versions of the old tongue. Two of the Germanic tribes—the Angles and the Saxons—give us the familiar term "Anglo-Saxon," which describes people of English ancestry.

The real **King Arthur** was probably a Celtic leader who resisted the Anglo-Saxon invaders in the fifth century. The later stories of Arthur and the Round Table are medieval in origin.

Following the Germanic tribes, starting at the end of the eighth century, came the Vikings, who brought with them their north Germanic language, which we know as **ON,** or **Old Norse.** These Germanic tongues eventually merged, bringing change to the Anglo-Saxon language, which is referred to in dictionaries as **OE,** or **Old English.**

In 1066 another invasion took place, and this was the last successful invasion of Britain; it is sometimes known as the Norman Conquest and was led by William the Conqueror. Although of Viking origin, the Normans were by this time speakers of Norman French, a dialect of what dictionaries refer to as **OF,** or **Old French.** The Normans brought enormous cultural changes to Britain, not the least of which was a whole new language, which eventually merged with Old English to become something new: **ME,** or **Middle English.**

Words have entered English from all over the world: *catamaran* (India), *zero* (Arabia), *taboo* (Polynesia), *ranch* (Mexico/Spain), *tycoon* (China) Of course, a similar process has also taken many English words into other languages.

No further invasions were successful, but the language continued to change, and, around 1500 it achieved a form that is recognizable as **Modern English.** Of course, the language has continued to change; many words came from the British colonies and, later, from the Americas. The coincidence that the dominant world powers of the 19th and 20th centuries—Britain and the United States—are predominantly English speaking has made English the most widely spoken language in history.

ASPECTS OF WRITING: Roots and your dictionary.

Many of the most commonly used words in English are of Anglo-Saxon origin. These include *you, is, I, the, dog, work,* and *and.*

If you get in the habit of always looking at the etymology when you use your dictionary, you'll build up a very useful store of roots and connections that will help you use words accurately and increase your vocabulary. You may also find yourself getting interested in language itself, with its history, changing meanings, precision, and beauty.

Many words beginning with *sk* are of Norse origin, as in *ski, skin,* and *skirt.*
Check the dictionary.

Check to see if your dictionary provides etymological information. A typical entry might look like this, from the *American Heritage Dictionary:*

manufacture . . . [old French *manufacture,* a making by hand, handiwork, from Late Latin *manufactus,* handmade: Latin *manu,* by hand, from *manus,* hand.]

This etymology shows a word that entered English after the Norman conquest of 1066. The original meaning—"making by hand"—has now broadened to include modern, automated, industrial techniques. You can probably think of other words that come to us from the Latin *manus,* hand. If you know any French, you'll also note that the modern French word for the hand *(le main)* comes from the same Latin root.

Latin and **Greek** words and roots started to come into English on a significant scale with the gradual conversion of the people of Britain to Christianity following the arrival of St. Augustine in 597. This influx was then augmented on a massive scale with the arrival of Norman French after 1066.

faith [Middle English *feith, feth,* from Old French *feid, feit,* from Latin *fides.*]

Much of the vocabulary of law and politics came into English via French—as in *attorney, perjury, parliament, president, democracy,* and *election.* Check the literal meaning of *parliament*—it comes, appropriately, from *parler,* to talk, which, in turn, gives us the colloquial "Let's parley."

The most famous works of literature in Old English and Middle English are *Beowulf* and Chaucer's *The Canterbury Tales,* respectively. The language of Shakespeare (1564–1616) is Modern English.

Knowing the roots of words can also help improve **spelling.** For example, if you know the roots *bene, syn,* and *chron,* you'll probably recognize them in words like "benefactor" and "synchronize."

Quick Quiz

The mongrel nature of English has made it tremendously rich in **synonyms.** To take just one example, look at the many synonyms of **brave:** *courageous, heroic, reckless, audacious, valiant, doughty, gritty, plucky, dauntless, fearless, intrepid, bold, daring, gallant, valorous, game, mettlesome, lionhearted.* Just like the synonyms in a **thesaurus,** many of these words have subtly different meanings, but they're also partly synonymous.

Check the etymology of the words "etymology" and "synonymous."

A **prefix** is also a type of root: can you match these from the following list? *after, across, before, around, against*

ante-
anti-
post-
trans-
peri-

Can you think of five others?

A. Check your sense of modern history—and etymology.
1. Name two major artists, two major writers, and two major scientists who worked in the 20th century.
2. When did the World Wars take place, and who were the leading combatants in each case?
3. What was "The Great War"?
4. Which 25-year period is most associated with the coming of independence for the colonized "Third World" countries?
5. The 20th century has seen the demise of several empires; name two that ended after World War I and two that ended (or mostly ended) after World War II.
6. Who were FDR, Churchill, Stalin, and Mao Zedong?
7. What was the "Cold War," and when did it end?
8. Name five major technological advances in the 20th century.
9. Name five major social/political advances in the 20th century.
10. What does "multipolar world" mean?
11. Create a four-word vocabulary web from the following roots. Be careful; words are sometimes derived from similar-looking, but different, roots.

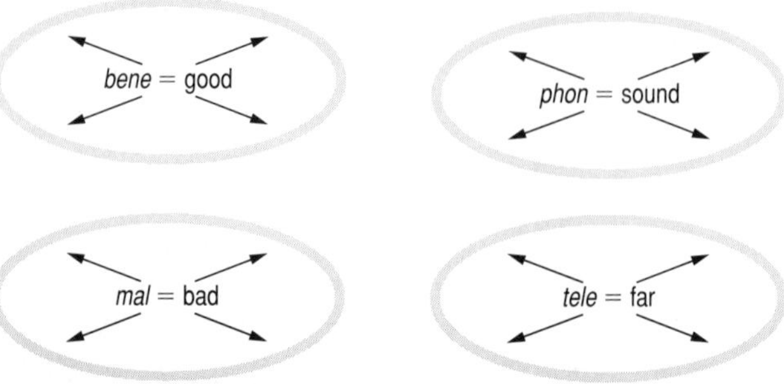

SECTION ONE

PRIOR KNOWLEDGE: Classifying the world's countries.

When things have similar characteristics, we tend to group them together and say that they are alike in some important respects; biologists call this **taxonomy**, but the more familiar word is **classification.** It is often more efficient to talk about groups of things rather than about a large number of individual cases. This is true of the world's countries just as much as it is of the world's animals and plants. There are some 200 countries in the world, and it is useful for geographers, political scientists, economists, and others to be able to put them into groups.

In biology, **taxonomy** identifies all living things according to kingdom, division, class, subclass, order, family, genus, species, and variety. Some living things are hard to classify, and their classification may be changed as new studies are undertaken. One famous dispute involved the classification of the duckbill platypus, an egg-laying mammal found in Australia. Some countries are also hard to classify, as you'll see in this unit.

Since 1945, the most important classification has probably been that which identified countries as **East** or **West.** This classification was the product of World War II, reflecting the new superpower status of two of the victors in the war against Germany: the United States and the U.S.S.R. Europe was divided between Eastern Europe, which quickly became a Soviet **sphere of influence,** and Western Europe, which allied itself with the United States. For almost 50 years the rivalry of East and West, struggling for influence all over the world and threatening each other with thousands of nuclear weapons and vast armies, seemed intractable, and the world seemed destined to live forever under the threat of nuclear annihilation. With the end of the Cold War and the collapse of the Soviet Union in 1991, however, the situation changed utterly, and the East-West classification became **obsolete.**

In Europe and North America, the East-West confrontation was political and military in nature. The Soviet Union led an alliance known as the **Warsaw Pact,** which was dissolved in 1993, and the United States led an alliance known as the North Atlantic Treaty Organization **(NATO),** which still exists.

Soon after the end of World War II, India, Pakistan, and Burma became independent from Britain, and, in a steady stream, virtually all the colonies became independent over the next 25 years, and a new classification emerged: **Third World.** The **First World** included the wealthy, industrialized, democratic countries, including the United States, Canada, the countries of Western Europe, Japan, Australia, and New Zealand. The **Second World** included the industrialized, communist countries of Eastern Europe and the Soviet Union. The **Third World** included everyone else—the less industrialized, poorer countries.

The **basis of classification** for the First World and Second World was **economic, political, and military.** It divided the industrialized countries into democratic and communist camps.

The basis of classification for the **Third World** countries is **economic.** These are the poorer countries, regardless of their politics.

North-South is also an **economic** classification. It focuses on the overwhelming dominance of the northern countries and their corporations in manufacturing, patents, banking, new technology, trade, and investment. The South, with far more people, has relatively little wealth and power, and some people conclude that this huge economic imbalance represents a basic and dangerous injustice. A former West German Chancellor, **Willy Brandt**, was the leading advocate of this position as chairman of an international commission that published *North-South, A Program for Survival,* in 1980.

demographic **demographer** **democracy** **democratic**

demos = people

This classification is now also partly obsolete, because the Second World no longer exists in its old definition and some Third World countries have modern and prosperous economies. In response to this, some people use a **Fourth World** classification for the very poorest countries.

As the above classifications have become unsatisfactory or obsolete, a new system—**North-South**—has been introduced, which puts the richer countries of the First and Second Worlds into the "North" category and the poorer nations into the "South" category. This way of seeing the world seems to avoid some problems associated with other classifications, although both "North" and "South" include a very wide range of countries and wealth.

These classifications all reflect political and economic realities, but we have seen that these realities can change. The change from East-West to North-South perspectives involves a shift from an **ideological** confrontation to an **economic** and **demographic** one. It's a new world.

ANNOTATED READING: Charles Lane. "Let's Abolish the Third World." *Newsweek* 27 April, 1992: 43.

Let's Abolish the Third World

It never made much sense, and it doesn't exist in practice. So why not get rid of it in theory?

Sometimes language lags history. Take the Third World. Did we ever have another name for the poor, unstable nations of the south? In fact, the Third World is a 1950s coinage, invented in Paris by French intellectuals looking for a way to lump together the newly independent former European colonies in Asia and Africa. They defined *le tiers monde* by what it wasn't: neither the First World (the West) nor the Second (the Soviet bloc). But now the cold war is over, and we are learning a new political lexicon, free of old standbys like "Soviet Union" that no longer refer to anything. It's a good time to get rid of the Third World, too.

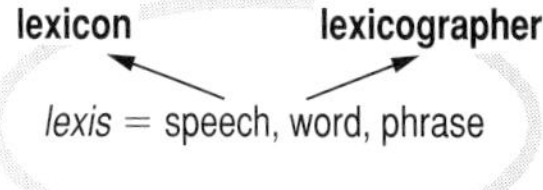

The Third World should have been abolished long ago. From the very beginning, the concept swept vast differences of culture, religion and ethnicity under the rug. How much did El Salvador and Senegal really have in common? And what did either share with Bangladesh? One of the bloodiest wars since Vietnam took place between two Third World brothers, Iran and Iraq. Many former colonies remained closer to erstwhile European metropoles than to their fellow "new nations."

El Salvador? Senegal? Bangladesh? If you don't know where these countries are, look at a map. Build up your sense of what the world looks like.

In the second paragraph, Lane uses **rhetorical questions,** or questions that he assumes need no answer. When he asks what El Salvador and Senegal have in common, he is really saying that they have nothing in common. This is a perfectly legitimate tactic in argument, but it is sometimes risky. What if the reader doesn't accept your premise? For example, you might argue that Senegal and El Salvador, although very different culturally, *do* have things in common. When you read, be aware of rhetorical devices like this, and don't automatically accept the writer's assumptions.

Nevertheless, the Third World grew. Intellectuals and politicians added a socioeconomic connotation to its original geopolitical meaning. It came to include all those exploited countries that could meet the unhappy standard set by Prime Minister Lee Kuan Yew of Singapore in 1969: "poor, strife-ridden, chaotic." (That was how Latin America got into the club.) There's a tendency now to repackage the Third World as the "South" in a global North-South, rich-poor division. To be sure, in this sense the Third World does refer to something real: vast social problems—disease, hunger, bad housing—matched by a chronic inability to solve them. And relative deprivation does give poor nations some common interests: freer access to Western markets, for example.

Here, Lane acknowledges that the term "Third World" "does refer to something real." The conditions he describes here apply to El Salvador and Senegal and many other countries. They have similar problems.

But there are moral hazards in defining people by what they cannot do or what they do not have. If being Third World meant being poor, and if being poor meant being a perennial victim of the First and Second Worlds, why take responsibility for your own fate? From Cuba to Burma, Third Worldism became the refuge of scoundrels, the "progressive" finery in which despots draped their repression and economic mismanagement. Remember "African socialism" in Julius Nyerere's Tanzania? It left the country's economy a shambles. A good many Western intellectuals hailed it as a "homegrown" Third World ideology.

Lane reveals his prejudices here. He coins the phrase "Third Worldism" and suggests that this means seeing oneself as a victim and not taking responsibility for one's own actions. His examples, however, can be challenged; Nyerere in Tanzania, despised by some, is respected by others. If his policies failed (some did, others didn't—especially in education and health care), does this make him a "scoundrel"? The world has its share of "scoundrels"—and worse—who have looted their country's wealth and behaved in barbarous ways; not many people would put Nyerere, or even Castro, high on such a list.

This is an example of **critical reading.** Of course, you may decide that Lane is correct in his assertions, but to be convincing, you should be able to produce evidence to justify such a conclusion.

Paternalism is one characteristic Western response to a "victimized" Third World. Racism is another. To nativists such as France's Jean-Marie Le Pen or Patrick Buchanan, "Third World" is a code phrase for what they see as the inherent inferiority of tropical societies made up of darkskinned people. Either way, the phrase Third World, so suggestive of some alien planet, abets stereotyping. "The Third World is a form of bloodless universality that robs individuals and societies of their particularity," wrote the late Trinidad-born novelist Shiva Naipaul. "To blandly subsume, say, Ethiopia, India, and Brazil under the one banner of Third Worldhood is as absurd and as denigrating as the old assertion that all Chinese look alike."

Today, two new forces are finishing off the tattered Third World idea. The first is the West's victory in the cold war. There are no longer two competing "worlds" with which to contrast a "third." Leaders can't play one superpower off the other, or advertise their misguided policies as alternatives to "equally inappropriate" communism and capitalism. The second is rapid growth in many once poor countries. The World Bank says developing countries will grow twice as fast in the 90s as the industrialized G 7. So much for the alleged immutability of "Third World" poverty—and for the notion that development must await a massive transfer of resources from north to south. No one would call the Singapore of Lee Kuan Yew poor, strife-ridden or chaotic: per capita GNP is more than $10,000, and its 1990 growth rate

The generally negative connotations of the phrase "Third World" do seem a reason to question its usefulness, and Lane goes on to give other reasons, notably the rapid growth of some Third World nations, especially in the **Pacific Rim** of East Asia, which are rapidly becoming wealthy. Singapore and Hong Kong are already ranked among the wealthiest countries in the world (although Hong Kong is not an independent country), and the people of Hong Kong have a longer average life expectancy than the people of the United States. It does, as Lane suggests, seem absurd to continue to classify such countries as "Third World" or even "developing."

G 7 = Group of Seven, the largest First World economies. Their leaders meet every year to try to coordinate economic strategy.

Lane makes some interesting observations here. He notes that some Third World economies are among the most dynamic in the world today, that some of the First and Second World countries have regions that seem Third World in some respects, and that some Third World countries have a good quality of life for some or even most of their population. More on this later in this unit.

was 8 percent. South Korea, Taiwan and Hong Kong also have robust economies, and Thailand and Malaysia are moving up fast.

American steelmakers have recently lodged "dumping" complaints against half a dozen Asian and Latin American countries. Cheap wages explains much of these foreign steelmakers' success, but the U.S. industry's cry is still a backhanded compliment. "A nation without a manufacturing base is a nation heading toward Third World status," wrote presidential candidate Paul Tsongas. But Tsongas was using obsolete imagery to make his point: soon, bustling basic industries may be the *hallmark* of a "Third World" nation.

Patina of modernity: Nor can the Third World idea withstand revelations about what life was really like in the former "Second World." It was assumed that, whatever the U.S.S.R.'s political deformities, that country was at least modern enough to give the West a run for its money in science and technology. In fact, below a patina of modernity lay gross industrial inefficiency, environmental decay and ethnic strife. Nowadays, it's more common to hear conditions in the former Soviet Union itself described as "Third World," and Russia seeks aid from South Korea. Elsewhere in Europe, Yugoslavia's interethnic war is as bad as anything in Asia or Africa. The United States itself is pocked with "Third World" enclaves: groups with Bangladeshi life expectancies and Latin American infant-mortality rates.

THINK ON PAPER
What is Lane referring to when he says that "the United States itself is pocked with 'Third World' enclaves"?

A concept invoked to explain so many things probably can't explain very much at all. The ills that have come to be associated with the Third World are not confined to the southern half of this planet. Nor are democracy and prosperity the exclusive prerogatives of the North. Unfair as international relations may be, over time, economic development and political stability come to countries that work, save and organize to achieve them. Decline and political disorder come to those who neglect education, public health—and freedom. The rules apply regardless of race, ethnicity, religion or climate. There's only one world.

Lane's conclusion is interesting, but perhaps simplistic. Can cultural and economic differences be dismissed so easily? Is Lane simply saying, "Be like us, and everything will be OK?" For another perspective on the relationship between the poorer countries and the richer ones, see Deepa Ollapally's essay in Section Two of this unit.

Rhetorical note: Lane's essay, part **definition** and part **argument,** is interesting in part because of its **tone,** which tends to be rather combative. This can help stir up the reader, but may also leave the writer exposed to criticism, as suggested in some of the annotations above.

ASPECTS OF WRITING: Definition; classification and division; stereotyping.

Classification of the world's countries can take many forms, depending on the type of information we are dealing with. Some specialists find it useful to divide the world up into climatic zones; others prefer to think about the world's countries continent by continent. Linguists sometimes divide the world up into language groups, showing how different languages are related to each other. No matter how things are classified, or divided, it's important that there be a clear basis for the classification, and this involves defining terms.

English belongs to the **Indo-European** group of languages, which includes most European languages and about one-third of all languages.

For example, if we were to use a climatic basis for classification, we would have to define "arid," temperate," and the other terms used. Similarly for other bases of classification. This can be harder than it sounds. Consider the apparently simple task of defining the continents; where does Asia end and Europe begin? How would you classify the Eastern Mediterranean countries, such as Israel, Jordan, Lebanon, and Syria? The problem can become just as vexing in the political and economic spheres. Is China Second World or Third World in the old classification? Some commentators say the former, because China has a communist government; the Chinese, however, have consistently identified themselves as third world, feeling a greater affinity with the poorer countries in general than with the (former) Soviet Union, the dominant nation in the Second World classification. What about South Africa? She is in many ways a wealthy country, and many of her people live a First World life, but even more live a Third World life.

THINK ON PAPER
In how many ways can you define the country (or region) in which you live? For example, how would you classify it climatically, politically, or geographically? Can you think of other possibilities?

Some phrases that have traditionally been capitalized are now sometimes written in lower case. First World, first world; Third World, third world. Similar changes have affected organizations such as UNESCO, now frequently written Unesco.

Such problems can be overcome by careful definition of terms. If the basis for a classification is **political** in nature, one confronts problems in choosing which categories to use and in defining terms such as "democratic," "totalitarian," "military," and "one-party."

THINK ON PAPER
What categories would you use if you were to make a political classification of the world's countries?

If the basis for the classification is **economic,** similar problems abound. What is a "free market"? Does any country actually have such an economy? What about "centrally organized economy" such as that in the communist states? Can China be defined this way when her special economic zones, where private enterprise flourishes, are so important? Another way to define countries economically is to use wealth as the basis for the classification, but how best to measure a country's wealth? **The World Bank** uses GNP per capita, but many economists have noted the unreliability of such data, especially when coming from each individual government.

How would you define "free market," or "capitalist," "socialist," "communist," or "democratic"? These words are very widely used as catchwords or slogans, and to different people they have different **connotations**—positive and negative. What connotations does each have for you? What are the **denotations** of each word—what do they actually mean?

Difficult though it may be, it's essential to define terms carefully if classifications are to be meaningful and useful. Understanding the terms we use can also help us avoid stereotyping groups of countries in ways that limit our appreciation of differences both within and among them. Many people have a **stereotyped** view of the Third World as full of starving people living in miserable conditions. Such situations can certainly be found at some times in some places, but it's also true that many people in poor countries live healthy and pleasant lives, enjoying many of the amenities familiar to people in the West. Such realities rarely make it into the news; it is the emergency that gets into our media, and this distorts our image of the poorer countries just as TV and movie images of America present distorted images for overseas audiences.

People are likely not only to hold stereotypical views but also to be the object of the same. What is the stereotypical view, in America, of different nationalities, and what view of Americans is held by people of those nationalities? Interesting perspectives may be offered by people of different national origins in your class.

As noted in Lane's article, most countries have both wealth and poverty within their borders. The difference between "poverty" and "Third World poverty" may lie in the availability of basic amenities such as running water and sewage systems, and access to health care and universal education. This **stereotypical** image of the Third World, however, must be balanced by acknowledgment of improved—or even good—living conditions in many countries that are usually classified as "poor."

WRITING EXERCISES: Answer one of the following questions.

Precision and **clarity** are related, and both are qualities of good writing, whether we discuss the word, the sentence, the paragraph, or the essay as a whole.
Words should mean what you think they mean. Misused words damage your writing.
Sentences should be clearly stated. The key is not whether the writer knows what is meant, but whether the reader does.
Paragraphs should be well focused, avoiding sudden changes in topic or other confusing sequences. This well-focused quality is called *paragraph unity.*
Essays should also be well focused. Lane's essay on abolishing the "Third World" classification certainly has this quality. The entire essay attempts to justify the call he makes in the title.

1. As the world changes, political and economic classifications may become obsolete. Carefully defining your terms, explain three ways in which the world's countries have been classified since the end of World War II. Show how each reflected the world as it was at a particular time.
2. Discuss the usefulness of classification in general. To answer this, you don't have to restrict your discussion to the classification of countries. Think of other ways in which we use classification.
3. Define "stereotype," give examples, and discuss how stereotypes affect the way people think.

Question 1 provides an **organizing principle** you should use—that classifications change as the world changes—but questions 2 and 3 leave it up to you to come up with such a concept. In some ways, these two questions may seem easier than the first one, but they require more of you—the writer—in terms of *forming a concept.*

An introduction to question 1 could go as follows (although this is not the only way to start, and the classifications alluded to here are also not the only possibilities for your discussion):

As the world changes, political and economic classifications may become obsolete. This can be demonstrated by looking at the changes in the world since the end of World War II. The Cold War gave us the East-West classification; the need to recognize the place of the poorer countries as they became independent led to the First, Second, and Third World classification; and the obsolescence of some of these categories has encouraged the present widespread use of the North-South classification.

SECTION TWO

PRIOR KNOWLEDGE: All change! After the Cold War . . . .

The initial euphoric response of most people in the West to the collapse of the Soviet Union and the end of the Cold War in the early 1990s was understandable, but it is probably fair to say that it has not lasted. Of course, this is only natural; one cannot live in a state of euphoria for ever. The normal routines of daily life still have to be followed, and new problems and challenges soon take the place of the old ones. Of course, most people take satisfaction in the lessened threat of nuclear war and the democratic reshaping of many countries, but what is the West doing with its victory?

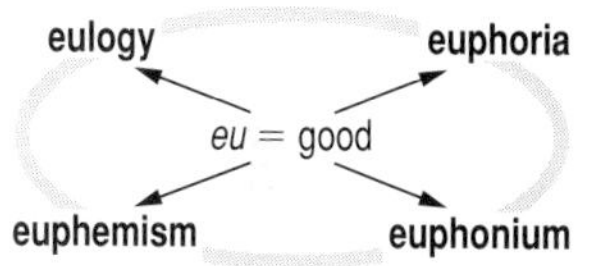

In the essay that follows, Deepa Ollapally observes that "Unlike the Western world, the developing world would seem to have little to celebrate with the ending of the cold war." The behavior of winners is sometimes more important than the behavior of losers, and the rest of the world will judge the outcome on the basis of how their lives are affected by the triumph of the West.

Readers have their own attitudes, beliefs, and prejudices, which affect their response to what they read. Your reading of Ollapally's article may be influenced by your attitude toward foreign countries (and people), toward poor countries (and people), and toward foreign aid programs; it may also be influenced by your own nationality and national point of view. Ollapally's article is clearly written from a point of view not often heard in the West; it may provoke a good discussion in your class.

In Central and Eastern Europe, the transition to democracy and a market economy has been bumpy, and in Russia it has led to enormous social, political, and economic crises. The offensive police state aspect of the old order has disappeared, but, for many people, the security and employment of the past has been replaced by insecurity and joblessness. Helping these countries succeed in their transition to a more Western political and economic model has become a high priority for the United States and her wealthy partners, and billions of dollars of private and public funds have been loaned and invested, but what about the rest of the world? Using terms discussed in Section One of this unit, Ollapally suggests that the end of the East-West confrontation has led to a realignment, with the West focusing on the new democracies of Europe and turning away from the Third World. The East-West struggle has been replaced by a North-South struggle.

What has really changed, says Ollapally, is that the West no longer has to worry about the Soviet Union in its attempts to influence events in the Third World. Looked at another way, the poor countries now have no one else to look to for help, and so they have lost the leverage they may once have had when dealing with the rich nations. Instead of receiving aid from the West simply because they were anticommunist, or from the Soviet Union because they were anti-Western, countries now are subject to much more difficult tests. The West increasingly has made economic and political reforms the price for aid. This means

THINK ON PAPER
Briefly explain the idea, which you'll find in Ollapally's paper, that the end of the Cold War has made it more difficult for some Third World countries to win aid and attention from the United States.

that countries must follow the economic policies recommended by Western governments and Western-dominated international organizations even when such policies may cause social unrest. For example, many poor countries subsidize basic foods, such as bread, but Western countries have sometimes made the ending of such subsidies part of the price for receiving economic aid. In some cases, the ending of subsidies has led to rioting.

Should we expect the whole world to follow a single economic and political model? Even in the West, experts disagree about economic policy, and different countries take different paths. Free to demand reforms or withhold aid, the West is in a new position **vis-à-vis** the poor countries. It is this position that Ollapally discusses.

Many words and phrases have come unaltered into the English language; **vis-à-vis** is one of these. The literal meaning, from the French, is "face to face"; in English it means "compared with" or "in relation to."

Different languages are sometimes associated with particular fields. French, for example, gives us many words and phrases in the areas of politics and food; Italian gives us much of our musical terminology. Discuss in class the meanings of the following examples, and check your dictionary:

coup d'état	élite
omelette	hors d'oeuvres
cuisine	fricassée
sauté	virtuoso
maestro	forte
soprano	prima donna

ANNOTATED READING: Deepa Ollapally. "The South Looks North: The Third World in the New World Order." *Current History* April 1993: 175–179. (Selections).

The South Looks North: The Third World in the New World Order

The end of the cold war has produced an anomalous situation for the world's developing countries. Although superpower competition was played out most often and most virulently in the developing world, the West's euphoria over the collapse of Soviet power has not been matched in third world nations.[1] While the implications of the new international system clearly are not uniform among the developing countries, there is reason to be skeptical about third world prospects generally.

anomalous
not | even, same ⟶ unusual, abnormal

Deepa Ollapally, an assistant professor of political science at Swarthmore College, is the author of Confronting Conflict: Domestic Factors and U.S. Foreign Policy in the Third World *(Westport, Conn.: Greenwood Press, 1993).*

Such skepticism is found among third world leaders as diverse as Robert Mugabe of socialist Zimbabwe and Malaysia's Mohamad Mahathir, who has steered his country's economy with capitalist strategies for growth. What these two had to say at the meeting of the nonaligned nations in Caracas on November 27, 1991, is instructive. Mahathir declared, "Lamentably these changes do not augur well for the countries of the developing South. . . . Indeed, the new unipolar world is fraught with dangers of a return to the old dominance of the powerful over the weak. . . . A new world order is propounded seemingly to legitimize interference in the affairs of independent nations. . . ."

> Ollapally's thesis is stated clearly at the end of the first paragraph: "there is reason to be skeptical about third world prospects generally."

> President Mugabe and Prime Minister Mahathir both worry about the possibility that the West, and the United States in particular, with its new, unrivaled position in the world, will simply bully the rest of the world in order to serve its own interests, and this seems to be Ollapally's point when she notes how "the players involved are so unequal."

[1]Although the term "third world" may be questioned, it retains conceptual meaning and is used interchangeably with "developing countries" in this article.

One good tactic when writing about a controversial topic is to **anticipate criticism,** as Ollapally does in the second and third paragraphs. The third world contains a wide variety of countries, with vastly different political, cultural, and economic situations. Anticipating the criticism that it is impossible to say anything useful about "third world prospects generally," Ollapally supports her theme with quotes from two important, but quite different, Third World leaders.

At the same meeting, Mugabe charged—as his colleagues have long been contending in one form or another, especially since the 1974 United Nations-based demand for a New International Economic Order—"The current . . . order continues to accentuate poverty in the developing countries. . . . Developed countries are continually manipulating international systems to their benefit yet purporting to be democratic." These comments raise the question whether the former axis of conflict between the United States and the Soviet Union is being replaced by the North-South divide between rich and poor countries.

The thinking in the North—particularly the United States—increasingly locates security threats in the third world. The United States Joint Chiefs of Staff noted in a 1991 report that "major portions of the world lag in the continuing struggle to improve the human condition. This lag, coupled with heightened expectations born of the ever-widening span of knowledge of progress in other areas of the world, are giving rise to insurgencies, terrorism, drug trafficking, and nationalist fervor." This reorientation in the developed world's perception of where danger might lie is bound to cause concern in third world capitals, since the players involved are so unequal.

Ollapally notes that despite seismic political changes in the world—in Russia and Eastern Europe, in South Africa, the Middle East, and elsewhere—the Third World's position seems much the same. Of course, a critic might note that many Third World countries, including Mahathir's Malaysia, have achieved enormous economic growth. Zimbabwe, too, is widely considered to be a Third World success story.

The Joint Chiefs of Staff report alludes to the link between instability and dire economic conditions—a connection third world analysts are accustomed to treating as a foregone conclusion. Thus an important issue for this era after the cold war will be whether the conditions of underdevelopment can be overcome.

INTO THE FIRE?

Notice how Ollapally opens the essay. She starts by introducing her main theme—that Third World countries are worried about their position in the post-Cold War period. She then gives a Western perspective (from the U.S. Joint Chiefs of Staff) that "is bound to cause concern in third world capitals." This leads into the second section of the essay, which opens with a nice **transition:** "From the South's perspective. . . ."

From the South's perspective, the new international environment does not necessarily portend more favorable prospects for their primary concern: improving material conditions at home. Now as during the cold war, the third world is in a generally weak position in the international political economy; change at that level has been lacking, amid the other momentous shifts of a world in transition.

THINK ON PAPER
Define "aid fatigue" and think about whether Ollapally is correct in saying that this is a "key problem."

One key problem is that the developing countries' growing need for aid is being met with "aid fatigue" in the North. Without superpower competition, what was under cold war logic the most compelling reason for the advanced industrial nations to assist developing countries has evaporated. Indeed, in its place has arisen a plethora of new demands from the erstwhile second world for aid and investment capital. Given the political importance of keeping these former Communist states on the path toward liberalization and preventing backsliding, the West has pledged financial help and will almost certainly provide more, diverting resources that might have gone to the South. So after remaining essentially stagnant during the 1980s, official development assistance to the third world dropped 2 percent in 1989 from the year before, according to the Organization for Economic Cooperation and Development, and continued to decline in 1990.

Simultaneously, the political economies of the developed countries appear to be turning inward, which at the very least leads to benign neglect of international needs and at worst could spell economic nationalism. The trend emerged in the late 1970s, when Northern countries, having decided that fighting inflation was their number one economic priority, proceeded to introduce recessionary macroeconomic policy that relied heavily on monetary instruments. This resulted in a significant slowdown in the North and a downturn in demand for Southern commodities—a downturn not seen since the 1930s; at the same time, interest rates rose to unprecedented heights, with the untenable consequence that developing countries paid more and more to service their foreign debt while receiving less and less for their exports. In effect, the third world has ended up absorbing a good part of the costs of the North's attempt to curb inflation.

Ollapally makes several references to **international organizations** such as the World Bank and the International Monetary Fund, which are essentially the bankers to the world's poorer countries, and GATT (General Agreement on Tariffs and Trade), which has now been replaced by the World Trade Organization. Other references include those to the OECD (Organization for Economic Cooperation and Development), the European Community (now the European Union), and NAFTA (North American Free Trade Agreement). Understanding the politics and economics of the modern world requires a knowledge not only of countries but also of international organizations and agencies.

Although the recovery in the developed economies began in 1983, compared to past recoveries this one has been singularly unimpressive. The critical point for the South is that there has been no noticeable improvement in external economic conditions for most of the developing countries. The debt crises that began with Mexico in 1982 triggered a sharp reduction in international lending by commercial banks so that repayments of principal and interest charges exceeded loans from 1983 onward; thus the usual North-to-South debt-related financial flows were reversed. Direct foreign investment also fell dramatically in real terms in the early 1980s, and while it picked up by 1986, most of the benefits were concentrated in the newly industrializing countries of Asia. Indeed, the 1980s has come to be regarded as a "lost decade" for development. While internal factors contributed to the development crises in many third world countries, it is impossible to discount the impact of the inhospitable broader economic environment.

The situation has persisted into the 1990s. With the failure of the Communist experiment in the Soviet Union and eastern Europe, the virtues of the market model have been accepted as fact with renewed vigor in Western policy circles, as well as at the World Bank and the International Monetary Fund (IMF). Whether the lessons drawn from what was the second world may be extrapolated is not at all clear; as opposed to eastern Europe's experience, for most developing countries it has been their association with capitalism that has failed to produce growth and development.

Rhetorical note: This is an **expository** essay, analyzing the state of the post-Cold War world from a Third World point of view (or the point of view of the South). Notice also, however, that there is a strong element of **narration,** as on this page, where Ollapally tells the story of what happened in the 1980's.

The newly industrializing nations of Asia, whose economic success is by now legendary, are the one group in the third world exempt from the generally dismal picture. But in practically all cases, government

Looking at recent history from the point-of-view of the South—the Third World countries—reminds us that the decisions made in the North by the richest countries affect everyone, not just themselves. A recession in the North means that demand declines for raw materials such as copper and tin, which are the principal export items of some Third World countries. Many poorer countries are very dependent on only one or two products, which they trade around the world; when commodity prices fall, the income of such countries can fall dramatically.

Another challenge to conventional thinking appears in Ollapally's statement that although "the virtues of the market model have been accepted as fact with renewed vigor in Western policy circles," the experience of developing countries does not necessarily support this position. This idea is continued over the page, where it is pointed out that some Asian countries have enjoyed spectacular economic growth without following Western models of either democracy or the free market system.

intervention in the economy in one form or other was pervasive; pure market principles were not adhered to. Almost all the countries were under authoritarian regimes with repressive social policies, especially when it came to labor. And these Asian states were lucky because at the critical stage of their export-led strategy the international economic climate was highly receptive, unlike at present.

THE NEW PROTECTIONISM

From the point of view of aspiring industrializers, post-cold war conditions have, if anything, worsened their prospects. The growing protectionism in the West has tended to be directed against items of special importance to the South, such as textiles, petrochemicals, steel, processed agricultural products, automotive parts, and electronics. The so-called "new protectionism" based on nontariff barriers such as voluntary export restraints and "orderly marketing arrangements" has had the pernicious effect of blocking entry to the market for even the most efficient producers.

There is no evidence that this trend will be reversed. The United States is confronted by an increasing number of domestic constituencies demanding protection from international competition, and this is clearly eroding earlier government commitment to global integration and free trade. As the cold war recedes, critics from across the political spectrum argue against keeping markets open for erstwhile allies and partners practicing protectionism in the name of a defunct pact against communism. Taiwan and South Korea reaped enormous benefits thanks to their strategic importance, with the United States tolerating their restrictive market practices, but developing countries today cannot count on anything similar.

One fundamental area of disagreement is intellectual property rights, which has brought what may be termed the most "assertive industrializers," including Brazil and India, into the fray. Third world countries tend to have much less restrictive patent protection than the developed countries, and sometimes none at all; significantly, patents are granted for processes rather than products. This more permissive approach is geared toward encouraging technological gains and adaptations that developing countries believe essential if they are to overcome their technology deficit. The South sees the North's efforts to construct a more restrictive system as simply increasing the monopolistic power of the multinationals.

Another emerging point of contention is America's insistence on including services such as banking, insurance, and telecommunications in GATT negotiations. Doing this would open these sectors in the developing world to highly competitive American corporations, with huge benefits for them. Again, the developing world, led by the assertive industrializers, is resisting, since this is certain to stymie growth in nascent service sectors as well as invite foreign control over key parts of the national economy.

Responding to its deteriorating global position, the United States has designed new mechanisms to shore up its economy. Provisions of the 1988 Omnibus Trade and Competitiveness Act specifically empower the executive to retaliate against countries deemed to have "unfairly" discouraged American exports. By 1990 more than half the 32 cases being investigated under the provisions involved developing countries. Two of those singled out as the "worst violators" were Brazil and India—as coincidence would have it, the leading spokesmen for the third world at the Uruguay Round.

THINK ON PAPER
What is Ollapally suggesting in the paragraph beginning, "Responding to her deteriorating global position . . . "?

The drive by the advanced industrial nations to maintain and even improve their economic status relative to the developing world is crystallizing in the formation of regional trade blocs, exemplified by moves in the European Community, by the North American Free Trade Agreement, and in Japan's evolving ties with the Association of Southeast Asian Nations. As cold war alliance politics disappears and economic competition among the first world countries gives rise to the tactics of bloc politics, the impact on the developing world is mixed. African, Middle Eastern, and South Asian countries will have a more difficult time insinuating themselves into these schemes. And as for those third world nations in the blocs, one wonders whether they will continue to serve as the weak periphery—providing, for example, cheap labor and a poorly protected environment that richer countries can pollute. On the whole, the economic sovereignty of developing countries may be more fragile now than under the "old world order." . . .

Ollapally sees huge trade blocs in Europe, North America, and Asia becoming the means for the rich countries to protect their wealth. This is not a view Westerners would generally welcome, and so it is interesting to think about. How convincing is Ollapally's argument?

Unlike the Western world, the developing world would seem to have little to celebrate with the ending of the cold war. Whether in the areas of political economy, security, or ideology, the space on the global agenda for third world concerns has shrunk. The developing countries' bargaining power and leverage, never great, have steadily eroded since the onset of the debt crises in the early 1980s. With the cold war over, developing countries matter even less for the North.

You have read an extract from Ollapally's article, but the conclusion is added below. Note how the author does not merely repeat the ideas already discussed. She offers some final thoughts that put the whole discussion into an appropriately challenging context.

But with three-quarters of humankind living in the third world and the gap between rich countries and poor continuing to widen, the potential for instability in the international system—ranging from the movement of refugees to the North to social upheavals in the South—is high. Unless the West is fully cognizant of such pressures and the need to address them, the benefits that were expected to come from the more beneficent climate of the post-cold war period are likely to be short-lived for all.

ASPECTS OF WRITING: Point of view.

It's well known that when two people look at the same thing, they don't necessarily *see* the same thing. This is literally true in everyday life; you might ask two people to describe a person or an object in front of them; the answers will probably differ in significant ways. An old saying holds that "Beauty is in the eye of the beholder," and you can probably think of occasions when you've noticed the truth of that assertion.

Everyone's way of seeing the world is shaped by their own experience, and the German word *Weltanschauung* ("world view") is often used in this context. Priding ourselves on our individuality, we often like to think that all our ideas are our own, shaped and developed by us, but, within any culture, there is a striking commonality of world view, despite individual differences. Americans are often said, for example, to be characteristically **future oriented,** in ways that many other cultures are not. Another characteristic is **rationality,** meaning that Americans tend to believe that everything can, at least in principle, be explained by physical laws. This may be contrasted with cultures in which magic and other supernatural forces are said to influence events. Growing up within a particular culture, we develop a certain point of view, which influences what we think of each other (men—women—children—the elderly, for example), how we behave, what we value, and so on. This point of view develops as we become acculturated in our society, but we acquire it subtly and may not even be aware of it.

Within our own culture, we may be more likely to see the differences between people, thinking that there is little common ground, but if we travel, or in some other way come into contact with people who were brought up in a different culture, with a different point of view, we soon realize that people within our own culture share far more in common than they usually acknowledge.

In Ollapally's article it is clear that the author, although she lives in America, is seeing the world from a non-Western point of view, in which the rich countries' behavior is seen as being much less generous and more self-serving than we are accustomed to hearing. It is, of course, important to hear such views, because if we assume that everyone is just like us—a kind of moral solipsism—we stand no chance of understanding the rest of the world.

In writing, we can express our point of view in a variety of ways. When we say "I think . . . ," we are asserting a view, but so are we when we merely make statements. Notice that Ollapally never uses the personal pronoun "I". It's not necessary, and its omission in no way weakens the strength, or even the personal nature, of the point of view expressed. Think about this in your own writing. The use of "I" is, of course, perfectly legitimate in most contexts, but it may not be very appropriate in academic writing, because it tends to emphasize the personal nature of the views expressed rather than their merit. If you are used to writing in the first person, try simply deleting such words and phrases; in most cases, it will make no difference whatever to the meaning of your sentence, and, at the very least, it will make your writing more concise. Here's a very simple example:

I think Ollapally presents a Third World point of view.

Ollapally presents a Third World point of view.

WRITING EXERCISES: Answer one of the following questions.

At the end of her essay, Ollapally writes a short conclusion that introduces something new to the essay—the idea that because three-quarters of the world's people live in the so-called Third World, the results will be disastrous for everyone if the gap in wealth between the rich and the poor countries continues to grow wider. She sees mass migration of people from the South to the North, and other social upheavals. You can follow this example; don't waste your conclusion by simply repeating what you've already said.

1. Identify one or more example of the Third World point of view described by Ollapally, and show how it differs from the familiar Western point of view.
2. In class, see whether you can identify different attitudes that are characteristic of different cultures, either within the United States or overseas. Such different views may involve attitudes toward family, authority, education, particular world crises, or just about anything else. Describe and discuss these differences. This could be approached from an academic or a more personal point of view.
3. Reference was made in the *Aspects of writing* section to two features often considered to be part of the American world view. Discuss the idea that Americans, just like people elsewhere in the world, have a describable common culture and world view. [You could adapt this last sentence to give you a starting point for your essay.]

Chappatte/La Tribune de Genève/Geneva

SECTION THREE

PRIOR KNOWLEDGE: Classifying and describing the physical world.

The world can be classified in politicoeconomic terms, such as East-West and North-South, but there are other ways of looking at the world as well. The Earth has a great diversity of landforms and climates that, taken together, profoundly affect the way different people live.

In his book and television series, *The Living Planet,* subtitled "A Portrait of the Earth," David Attenborough describes the world in terms of the physical and botanical/zoological character of different regions. These include the polar regions, the northern forests, the tropical rainforests (or "the jungle," as he calls it), the savannahs ("seas of grass"), the deserts, the sky, the oceans, and so on. As a naturalist, he is especially interested in the life forms characteristic of each region. These show great diversity, each being adapted to the particular conditions of its environment, whether that be the newly discovered world of the deep ocean vents or the familiar world of wherever you live.

The chapter presented in this unit concerns the volcanic regions of the world, and these, of course, coincide with the tectonic-plate structure of the Earth itself, as was discussed in Unit Two. When plates collide, the Earth can buckle, and mountains can be formed. The Himalayas, for example, are still being forced upward by the pressure of the Indian plate moving north. When plates get caught against each other, and then suddenly are freed, earthquakes occur, sometimes with devastating results, as when the movement of the Pacific and North American plates causes the ground to shake in California. At the perimeter of each plate there is likely to be an area of volcanic activity, as all around the Pacific, in the so-called "Ring of Fire," and in the Mediterranean region, where the African plate is gradually pushing north into Europe.

The fundamental structure of the planet, therefore, produces some of the Earth's most spectacular physical displays and some of the most extraordinary forms of life. In recent years, technology has allowed more and more research to be undertaken in the deep oceans, where the dynamics of plate tectonics and the life forms of a previously unknown environment are now being explored. Attenborough explains and describes these interactions and takes us on a worldwide tour of what he calls "The Furnaces of the Earth."

A simple climatic classification system would divide the world up into bands going around the world. Starting at the equator, the basic pattern would be the same in both the northerly and southerly directions, as shown in this visual:

polar regions
temperate regions
tropical regions
equatorial regions
tropical regions
temperate regions
polar regions

Of course, different topographical conditions produce different environments, and so Mt. Kilimanjaro, in equatorial East Africa, has snow at its highest elevations. The volcanic activity that Attenborough describes is worldwide in distribution.

THINK ON PAPER
Look at a map and list all the places around the "Ring of Fire" where you know earthquakes and volcanic activity occur.

Given the above roots, can you guess the meaning of "toponym"? You might also check the dictionary for two meanings of "toponymy."

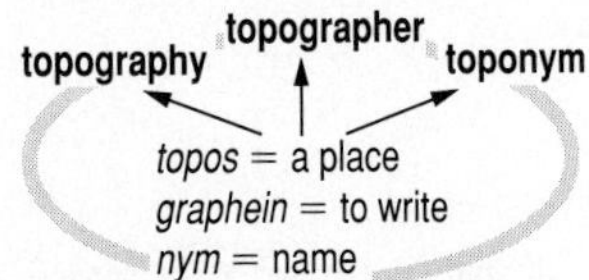

Descriptions of natural scenes are not easy to write. They require acute observation and a very precise use of language in order to be convincing.

As you read Attenborough's essay, you may find it useful to have a map handy, so that you can know where you are on his tour. Best, perhaps, would be a physical map, showing the **topographical** features of the world, including the mid-Atlantic and other oceanic ridges. Seeing the mountains and depths of the oceans can give one a new perspective concerning the physical nature of the Earth.

To describe such a dramatic environment, you might expect Attenborough to use evocative language, and you'll see that he does. Pay attention not only to what he says but to how he says it, and pick up on any vocabulary that is new to you. To capture such scenes, very precise language is needed, and you'll notice that he calls on all our senses as he describes the sights, sounds, smells, and feel of the fiery places in our world.

ANNOTATED READING: David Attenborough. "The Furnaces of the Earth." *The Living Planet.* Boston: Little, Brown, 1984: 21–38.

The Furnaces of the Earth

The titanic forces that built the Himalayas and all the other mountains on earth proceed so slowly that they are normally invisible to our eyes. But occasionally they burst into the most dramatic displays of force that the world can show. The earth begins to shake and the land explodes.

The drama of **vulcanism** (or **volcanism**)—volcanic activity—is captured in Attenborough's introduction. As a writer, he is able to let us see what he has seen, in all its vividness, and to feel what he has felt, as grit and blasts of heat hit his face.

If the lava that erupts from the ground is basalt, black and heavy, then the area may have been continuously active for many centuries. Iceland is just such a place. Almost every year there is volcanic activity of some kind. Molten rock spills out from huge cracks that run right across the island. Often it is an ugly tide of hot basalt boulders that advances over the land in a creeping unstoppable flood. It creaks as the rocks cool and crack. It rattles as lumps tumble from its front edge. Sometimes the basalt is more liquid. Then a fountain of fire, orange red at the sides, piercing yellow at its centre, may spout 50 metres into the air with a sustained roar, like a gigantic jet engine. Molten basalt splashes around the vent. Lava froth is thrown high above the main plume where the howling wind catches it, cools it and blows it away to coat distant rocks with layers of grey prickly grit. If you approach upwind, much of the heat as well as the ash is blown away from you, so that you can stand within 50 metres of the vent without scorching your face, though when the wind veers, ash will begin to fall around you and large red-hot lumps land with a thud and a sizzle in the snow nearby. You must then either keep a sharp eye out for flying boulders or run for it.

The word "volcano" is derived from the Latin *Volcanus,* the Roman name for the god **Vulcan** (hence "vulcanism" or "volcanism"). Vulcan was the god of fire and craftsmanship—especially metalworking, in which furnaces are usually used. Attenborough's title reflects this etymology and suggests that volcanic forces helped shape the Earth.

Flows of cooling black lava stretch all round the vent. Walking over the corded, blistered surface, you can see in the cracks that, only a few inches beneath, it is still red hot. Here and there, gas within the lava has formed an immense bubble, the roof of which is so thin that it can easily collapse beneath your boot with a splintering crash. If, as well as such alarms, you also find yourself fighting for breath because of unseen, unsmelt poisonous gas, you will be wise to go no further. But you may now be close enough to see the most awesome sight of all—a lava river. The liquid rock surges up from the vent with such force that it forms a trembling dome. From there it gushes in a torrent, 20 metres across maybe, and streams down the slope at an astonishing speed, sometimes as much as 100 kilometres an hour. As night falls, this extraordinary scarlet river illuminates everything around it a baleful red. Its incandescent surface spurts bubbles of gas and the air above it trembles with the heat. Within a few hundred yards of its source, the edges of the flow have cooled sufficiently to solidify, so now the scarlet river runs between banks of black rock. Farther down still, the surface of the flow begins to skin over. But beneath this solid roof the lava surges on and will continue to do so for several miles more, for not only does basaltic lava remain liquid at comparatively low temperatures, but the walls and ceiling of solid rock that now surround it act as insulators, keeping in the heat. When, after days or weeks, the supply of lava from the vent stops, the river continues to flow downwards until the tunnel is drained, leaving behind it a great winding cavern. These lava tubes, as they are called, may be as high as 10 metres and run for several kilometres up the core of a lava flow.

Iceland is one of a chain of volcanic islands that runs right down the centre of the Atlantic Ocean. Northwards lies Jan Mayen; to the south, the Azores, Ascension, St Helena and Tristan da Cunha. The chain is more continuous than most maps show, for other volcanoes are erupting below the surface of the sea. All of them lie on one great ridge of volcanic rocks that runs roughly midway between Europe and Africa to the east, and the Americas to the west. Samples taken from the ocean floor on either side of the ridge show that, beneath the layers of ooze, the rock is basalt, like that erupting from the volcanoes. Basalt can be dated by chemical analysis and we now know that the farther away from the mid-ocean ridge a sample is taken, the older it is. The ridge volcanoes, in fact, are creating the ocean floor which is slowly growing away from them, on either side of the ridge.

The Mid-Atlantic Ridge, and similar features in other oceans, can be seen on topographical maps. Most atlases show this feature. Attenborough is describing some of the mechanics of plate tectonics, the mechanisms of continental drift.

The mechanism that produces this movement lies deep within the earth. Two hundred kilometres down, the rocks are so hot that they are plastic. Below them, the metallic core of the earth is hotter still and this causes slow, churning currents in the layers above, which rise up along the line of the ridge and then flow out on either side, dragging the basaltic ocean floor with them like solid skin on custard. Such moving segments of the earth's crust are known as plates. And most of these plates carry on them, like lumps of scum, continents.

One hundred and twenty million years ago, Africa and South America were joined together, as you might guess from the jigsaw similarity of their coastlines and as is demonstrated by the likeness of the rocks on opposite sides of the ocean. Then, about 60 million years ago, a current welling up beneath this supercontinent created a line of volcanoes. A fracture developed across the supercontinent and the two halves slowly moved apart. The line of the split is today marked by the Mid-Atlantic Ridge. Africa and South America are still moving

Most people think of the continents as stable and permanent features, but tectonic forces are continuing to change the face of the Earth.

away from one another and the Atlantic is getting wider by several centimetres each year.

Another similar ridge, extending from California southwards, was responsible for creating the floor of the eastern Pacific. A third, running from Arabia southeast towards the South Pole, produced the Indian Ocean. It was the plate on the eastern side of this ridge that dragged India away from the flank of Africa and carried it towards Asia.

The convection currents that flow up at the ridges must clearly descend again. The lines along which they do so are where a plate meets that of a neighbouring system. It is here that continents collide. As India approached Asia, sediments on the sea floor between the two continents were crumpled and piled high to form the Himalayas, so the plate junction here is concealed beneath a mountain range. But farther along the same junction line, to the southeast, a continental mass exists on the Asian side only. The line of crustal weakness, therefore, is much more exposed and is marked by a chain of volcanoes that runs down from Sumatra through Java to New Guinea.

The descending convection current sucks down the ocean floor, creating a long deep trench. This runs along the southern coast of the Indonesian chain. As the edge of the basaltic plate descends, it takes with it water and much of the sediment that was eroded from the Indonesian land mass and had been lying on the ocean floor. This introduces a new ingredient into the melt deep in the crust, so that the lava that wells up into the Indonesian volcanoes is crucially different from the basalt issuing from a mid-ocean ridge. It is much more viscous. In consequence, it does not pour out of cracks or flow like a river, but congeals in the throat of the volcanoes. The effect is like screwing down the safety valve of a boiler.

It was one of the Indonesian volcanoes that produced the most catastrophic explosion yet recorded. In 1883, a small island named Krakatau, 7 kilometres long by 5 kilometres wide, lying in the straits between Sumatra and Java, began to emit clouds of smoke. The eruptions continued with increasing severity day after day. Ships sailing nearby had to make their way through immense rafts of pumice that floated on the surface of the sea. Ash rained down on their decks and electric flames played along their rigging. Day after day, enormous quantities of ash, pumice and lava blocks were thrown out from the crater, accompanied by deafening explosions. But the subterranean chamber from which all this material was coming was slowly emptying. At 10 a.m. on 28 August, the rock roof of the chamber, insufficiently supported by lava beneath, could bear the weight of the ocean and its floor no longer. It collapsed. Millions of tons of water fell on to the molten lava in the chamber and two-thirds of the island tumbled on top of it. The result was an explosion of such magnitude that it

Krakatau is often spelled **Krakatoa.**

Attenborough refers to many different places and situations in his essay, and it is important that he doesn't lose or confuse his reader. His writing is a good model, not only for its precision and descriptiveness but also for the unity of its paragraphs.

THINK ON PAPER
Look at the paragraphs on this page and see how easy it is to tell, in just a few words, what each is about. Your writing should have this quality of clarity, and you can achieve it, in part, by making sure that your paragraphs have a clear focus, or point.

produced the loudest noise ever to echo round the world in recorded history. It was heard quite distinctly over 3000 kilometres away in Australia. Five thousand kilometres away, on the small island of Rodriguez, the commander of the British garrison thought it was the sound of distant gunfire and put out to sea. A tempest of wind swept away from the site and circled the earth seven times before it finally died away. Most catastrophic of all, the explosion produced an immense wave in the sea. As it travelled towards the coast of Java, it became a wall of water as high as a four-story house. It picked up a naval gunboat, carried it bodily nearly 2 kilometres inland and dumped it on top of a hill. It overwhelmed village after village along the thickly populated coast. Over 36,000 people died.

The biggest explosion of recent years occurred on the other side of the Pacific, where the eastern edge of the Pacific plate grinds along the western coast of North America. Once again, there is continental cover on only one side of the junction, so the line of contact is not deeply buried. But because continents are made of rocks that are lighter than basalt, they override the downwards-plunging oceanic plate and the line of volcanoes breaks through some 200 kilometres inland from the coast. And once again, the lava that rises up in them carries the sedimentary ingredient that makes them catastrophically explosive.

Until 1980, Mount St. Helens was famous for the beautiful symmetrical shape of its cone. It rose nearly 3000 metres high and was crowned with snow the year round. In March that year, warning rumbles began to come from it. A plume of steam and smoke rose from its peak, dusting its snow cap with streaks of grey. All through April, the column of smoke grew. Most ominous of all, the northern flank of the mountain, about 1000 metres below the summit, began to bulge outwards. The swelling grew at a rate of about 2 metres a day. Thousands of tons of rock were being pushed upwards and outwards. Every day there were fresh spouts of ash and smoke from the crater above. Then, at half past eight on the morning of 18 May, the mountain exploded.

The northwest face, about a cubic kilometre of it, simply blew out. The pine, fir and hemlock trees that had clothed the lower slopes of the mountain, over an area of 200 square kilometres, were laid flat, as though they were matches. An immense burgeoning black cloud rose above the mountain, towering 20 kilometres into the sky. Few people lived close to the volcano and there had been a lot of warning, but even so sixty people were killed. Geologists estimated that the force of the explosion was 2500 times as powerful as the nuclear blast that destroyed the city of Hiroshima.

Nothing can live on a volcano immediately after its eruption. If there has been an explosion, steam, smoke and poisonous gas will continue to billow up from the wreckage of rocks in the crater for weeks. Nor can any organism survive the heat of the basalt flows that issue from the volcanoes of the mid-ocean ridge. If any parts of the earth are sterile and lifeless, it must be sites such as these. But if the convection currents deep beneath the surface shift slightly, the ferocity of the volcanic furnaces begins to wane. In these later stages, a dying volcano often produces eruptions not of lava but of scalding water and steam. Part of this water existed in the magma, and part is from the natural water table of the earth's crust. It carries, dissolved in it, a great variety of chemical substances. Some will have come from the same deep source as the lava, others have been dissolved from the rocks through which the hot water passed on its way to the surface. Among them are compounds of nitrogen and of sulphur, often in such concentrations that the water can serve as food for very simple living organisms. Indeed, it is possible that the very first forms of life to appear on earth originated in just such circumstances, some 3000 million years ago.

Rhetorical note: This essay is clearly descriptive in nature. It also uses spatial order, moving from one region of the world to another.

At that unimaginably distant time, the earth had not yet acquired its oxygen-rich atmosphere and the position of the continents bore no relation to their present distribution. Volcanoes were not only very much larger than those of today, but were very much more numerous. The seas, which had condensed from clouds of steam that surrounded this new planet, were still hot and water was still gushing into them from volcanic sources deep in the crust. In these chemically rich waters, complex molecules were forming. Eventually, after an immense span of time, tiny microscopic specks of living matter appeared. They had little internal structure, but they were able to convert the chemical substances in the water into their own tissues, and to reproduce themselves. These were bacteria.

The origins of life on Earth continue to challenge researchers, but many now believe that the first life forms emerged in the volcanic conditions described here.

Bacteria today are of many different kinds, and practise a great variety of chemical processes to maintain themselves. And they are found throughout the land, the sea and the sky. Some even still flourish in volcanic environments which may well parallel the circumstances in which they first arose.

In 1977, an American deep-sea research ship was investigating underwater volcanoes erupting from a ridge south of the Galapagos Islands. Three kilometres below the surface of the ocean they found vents on the sea floor that were spouting hot, chemically rich water into the sea. In these jets, and in the crevices of the rocks around the vents, the scientists discovered great concentrations of bacteria consuming the chemicals. The bacteria, in turn, were being fed upon by immense worms, up to 3.5 metres long and 10 centimetres in circumference. They were unlike any other worms so far encountered by science, for they had neither mouth nor gut and they fed by absorbing the bacteria through the thin skin of feathery tentacles, rich in blood

The dramatic discovery of life in the deep oceans, flourishing in conditions under which other forms of life on Earth could never survive, changed the way we think about life and the history of life on Earth.

vessels, that sprouted from their tip. Since these organisms live in the black depths of the ocean, they are unable to tap directly the energy of sunlight. Nor can the worms obtain it second-hand from the falling fragments of dead animals drifting down from above, since they have no mouths. Their food comes entirely from the bacteria which in turn derive their sustenance from the volcanic waters. Indeed, the worms may well be the only large animals anywhere that draw their energy entirely from volcanoes.

Alongside the worms lie huge clams 30 centimetres long which also feed on the bacteria. The rising jets of hot water create other currents which flow towards the vents across the sea floor, bringing with them organic fragments which are eaten by other organisms—strange, hitherto unknown fish and blind white crabs—clustering around the clams and the worms. So in these submarine volcanic springs, a dense and varied colony of creatures flourishes in the darkness.

Hot springs also bubble up on land. The water they produce, which originates partly from sources far below and partly from rainwater that has permeated deep into the ground, has been heated by the lava chamber and so forced up again through cracks in the rocks, like water up the spout of a boiling kettle. Sometimes, because of the particular geometry of these conduits, the upward progress is spasmodic. Water accumulates in small subterranean chambers and becomes superheated under pressure until finally it flashes into steam and a column of water spouts to the surface as a geyser. In other cases the upward flow is more regular and then the water forms a deep, perpetually brimming pool. It may be so scaldingly hot that the surface steams, but even at these temperatures bacteria flourish. Growing with them here are slightly more advanced organisms—blue-green algae. These are scarcely more complex in their internal structure than the bacteria but they do contain chlorophyll, the remarkable substance that enables them to use the energy of the sun to convert chemical substances into living tissue.

Such organisms are found in the hot springs of Yellowstone in North America. There the algae and bacteria grow together to form slimy green or brown mats that cover the bottom of the pools.

Nothing else can survive in the hottest parts of the springs occupied by these mats, but where the pool spills over to form a stream, the water cools slightly and so allows occupation by other creatures. The algal mats here are so thick that they break the surface. This living dam diverts the main flow to another freer part. As the water slowly trickles through, it cools further and above it assemble clouds of brine flies. If parts of the algae are cooler than 40°C, the flies settle and begin to graze voraciously. Some of them mate and lay their eggs on the algae and soon there are grubs feeding alongside their parents. But they are working towards their own destruction or that of their descendants, for as they chew away at the mat, so they weaken it. Eventually, it breaks up, the channel clears and much hotter water from the pool gushes down it, sweeping away the remains of the algae and killing all the grubs that were feeding on it. But enough will have hatched for the flies to survive this setback and to start the process all over again in another part of the spring.

In colder parts of the world, the dwindling heat of a volcano may represent not a hazard but a haven. The line of volcanoes that built the Andes along the junction of the South American and eastern Pacific plates continues south and east into the southern ocean to form several small arcs of volcanic islands. Bellinghausen is one of a group called the South Sandwich Islands. The ferocious Antarctic seas have cut into its base, creating, on one side, a cliff which displays, with textbook clarity, alternating layers of ash and lava, cut through with zig-zag lines of lava-filled pipes. Ice floes rim it like a tattered white skirt and sheets of snow drape its slopes. Battalions of Adelie penguins march all over this white parade ground. If you climb up through their ranks to the top of the volcano, you find a vast gaping pit, half a kilometre across. Its floor is filled with snow, icicles hang from the jutting rocks in its throat and snow petrels, elegant pure-white birds, nest in the crags just beneath the crater's lip. But its volcanic fires have not been totally extinguished. In one or two places around the rim, steam and gas still spurt from cracks, filling the air with the stench of hydrogen sulphide and coating the boulders with brilliant yellow encrustations of sulphur. The ground around the vent is warm to the touch so, as the polar gales bite into you, it is a pleasant place to crouch, in spite of the smell. And on the rocks at your feet, surrounded by snow, there are lush cushions of mosses and liverworts.

"In colder parts of the world, the dwindling heat of a volcano may represent not a hazard but a haven." With this nice transition, Attenborough captures the extraordinary ways in which life adapts to its environment.

These few small patches are the only places in the entire island where it is warm enough for plants to grow. The islands are as isolated as any in the world. The Antarctic continent and the tip of South America are both some 2000 kilometres away. Yet the spores of these simple plants are so widely dispersed by winds throughout the atmosphere of the world that even these tiny isolated sites in this hostile island are colonised just as soon as they become habitable.

It is not only in the bitterly cold parts of the world that organisms take advantage of volcanic heat. Even tropical creatures have learned how to exploit it. The megapodes are a group of birds living from Indonesia to the western Pacific which have developed extremely ingenious methods of incubating their eggs. Typical of them is the mallee fowl of Australia. When this remarkable bird nests, it first digs an enormous pit that may be 4 metres across, fills it with decaying leaves and then piles sand on top of it. Into this great heap, the female excavates a tunnel and there she lays her eggs. Then she fills

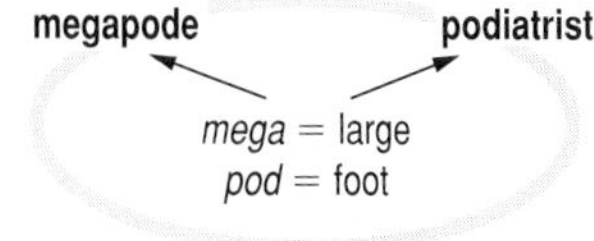

the tunnel with sand and relies on the heat produced by the rotting vegetation to keep her eggs warm. But she does not abandon them. On the contrary. Several times a day, she returns to the mound and pokes her beak into the sand. Her tongue is so sensitive that she can detect a change in heat of one-tenth of a degree. If she considers that the sand is too cool for her eggs, she will pile on more; if too hot, she will scrape it away. Eventually, after an unusually long incubation, the young mallee fowl chicks dig their way up to the surface of the mound, emerge fully-feathered and scamper away.

The mallee fowl, however, has a relative in the Indonesian island of Sulawesi called the maleo. This creature buries its eggs in black volcanic sand at the head of beaches. Being black, this sand absorbs the heat and gets quite hot enough in the sunshine to incubate the eggs. Other maleo have left the coast and colonised the slopes of a volcano inland. There they have discovered large areas of ground that are permanently heated by volcanic steam; and there a whole colony regularly lays its eggs. A dying volcano has become an artificial incubator.

Eventually, as the plates of the earth's crust move and the currents beneath shift, volcanoes do become completely extinct. The ground cools and animals and plants from the surrounding countryside move in to colonise the new, sterile rocks and the devastated land. Basalt flows present considerable problems to the colonists. Their shiny blistered surface is so smooth that water runs off it and there are few crevices into which seedlings can insinuate their young roots. Some flows may remain totally bare for centuries. The species of flowering plant that makes the first pioneering invasion differs from one part of the world to another. In the Galapagos, where the flora is derived primarily from South America, it is often a cactus which gains the first roothold. Specially adapted to conserve every particle of moisture and living normally in deserts, it manages to survive the roasting temperatures out on the black lava. In Hawaii, the pioneer is a less obvious conserver of water, the ohia lehua tree. Its roots manage to penetrate deep into the lava flow to gather moisture. Often, they find a way down into the empty cavern, the lava tube, that runs down the centre of most of these flows. Down there, the roots hang from the ceiling like huge brown bell-ropes. Rain water, running from the lava surface, trickles down the cracks and over the roots and drips on to the floor. Away from the evaporating rays of the sun, it lingers in pools making the air in the cave dank and humid.

The Galapagos Islands, which are part of Ecuador, are famous for their wildlife and for being the site of some of Darwin's most celebrated research.

A lava tube is an eerie place to explore. Since neither rain storms nor frost can reach it, nothing erodes the surface of its walls or floor. It looks exactly as it must have done when the last trickle of lava was draining away and its floor was still hot enough to incinerate anything that touched it. Congealed drips of lava hang from the ceiling like stalactites. The floor is covered by a stream of lava like solidified por-

The fact that Nature has such regenerative power, and that fire has an important function in many environments, causes differences in opinion over whether fires should be put out in the national forests and parks of America, Canada, Australia, and elsewhere. Some fires look disastrous but may be beneficial in the long run.

ridge. In some places, where it swept over a barrier of some kind, it has left behind a solidified cascade. As a sudden surge swept through it, the lava river rose temporarily, cooled particularly quickly and so left a smooth tide mark along the wall.

Several kinds of creatures have taken up permanent residence in these strange places. In the tiny hairs that cover the hanging roots, and feeding on them, are several kinds of insects including crickets, springtails and beetles. And preying on them are spiders. But these creatures are not exactly the same as their close relatives that live in the open air elsewhere on the island. Many of them have lost their eyes and wings. It seems that once a part of an animal's anatomy loses its function, its development is a waste of bodily energy. Individuals that do not squander their resources in this way, therefore, have an advantage over those that continue to do so. So, over generations, there is a tendency for useless organs to be reduced in size and finally to disappear. On the other hand, it is a positive advantage in the blackness of the cave to have long antennae and legs so that a creature can detect obstacles or food around it. And these lava-tube creatures do indeed have unusually long legs and antennae.

The wastelands produced by continental eruptions seem to be easier to colonise than smooth basaltic flows, for it is not difficult for plants to get a root-hold on ash or rubbly lava. The great desert that was created when Mount St. Helens blew off its side is already being reclaimed by plants. In the corners of the mud banks and beneath boulders, you can find small accumulations of fluffy airborne seeds. Many belong to willow-herb, a waist-high plant which produces a spike of handsome purple flowers. Its seeds are so light and fluffy that they float on the wind for hundreds of miles. In Europe, during the last World War, willow-herb appeared on bombed sites within weeks, cloaking the broken masonry with colour. In North America, the plant is known as fire-weed, for it is one of the first to appear among the blackened stumps in the wake of a forest fire. And it is an equally enterprising colonist of the sites devastated by a volcanic eruption.

Even so, it may be several years before it succeeds in covering the naked slopes of Mount St. Helens. This is not so much because the volcanic ash lacks sustenance, but because the muds and gravels are so loosely compacted that a rainstorm or a strong wind quickly shifts the surface and uproots any seedlings. But even though there are few plants growing on it yet, there are animals to be found. The same winds that transport the willow-herb seeds also carry up moths, flies and even dragonflies. These strays, transported here by accident, are doomed to an early death, for there is virtually nothing for them to eat except one another. But they will, nevertheless, provide a basis for more permanent colonisation. When they die, the fragments of their bodies are blown with the seeds into crevices and corners. There they

Attenborough notes the great paradox of volcanoes. Like fire in the forests, they seem to be violent and destructive, but they are also "the great creators."

decay and the nutrients from their tiny corpses are absorbed into the ash beneath them, so that when the seeds germinate, they find a nutritious element immediately beneath them in the otherwise sterile, unweathered volcanic dust.

Krakatau shows how complete a recovery can be. Fifty years after the catastrophe, a small vent spouting fire arose from the sea. The people called it Anak—the child—of Krakatau. Already it has thickets of casuarina and wild sugar cane growing on its flanks. A remnant of the old island, now called Rakata, lies a mile or so away across the sea. The slopes that a century ago were bare are now covered by a dense tropical forest. Some of the seeds from which it sprang must have floated here across the sea. Others were carried by the wind or brought on the feet or in the stomachs of birds. In this forest live many winged creatures—birds, butterflies and other insects—that clearly had little difficulty in reaching the island from the mainland a mere 40 kilometres away. Pythons, monitor lizards and rats have also arrived here, perhaps on floating rafts of vegetation that frequently get swept down tropical rivers. But evidence of the newness of the forest, and the cataclysm that preceded it, is easy to find. The tree roots cover the surface of the ground with a lattice that clasps the earth together, but here and there, a stream has undermined them, and a tree has toppled to reveal the still loose and powdery volcanic dust beneath. Once the plant cover has been broken in this way, the loose ash is easily eroded by the stream and a narrow gorge, 6 or 7 metres deep, appears beneath a roof of interlaced roots. But these breaks are the exception. The tropical forest has, within a century, reclaimed Krakatau. Without much doubt, the coniferous forest, in another century, will have reclaimed Mount St. Helens.

So the wounds inflicted on the land by volcanoes eventually heal. Although volcanoes may seem, on the short scale by which man experiences time, the most terrifyingly destructive aspect of the natural world, in the longer view they are the great creators. They have constructed new islands, like Iceland, Hawaii and the Galapagos, and built mountains like Mount St. Helens and the Andes. And it is the great shifts in the continents of the earth, with which they are associated, that set in train the long sequence of environmental changes and, over millennia, provide animals and plants with new opportunities to build their communities.

ASPECTS OF WRITING: Summary, synthesis, and crossing borders.

Our sense of the world is shaped by what we know, and what we know is shaped by our life experience and by our curiosity. If we're curious—interested in understanding the world around us—then we are likely to take advantage of the information that is available to us, and we enrich our lives by doing so. Not everyone can travel the world in the style of David Attenborough, but through his television films and books we can share his adventures and learn what he has learned.

THINK ON PAPER
Look through Attenborough's essay and identify the essay structure just described. Where does he shift from one focus to the next? What transitional phrases or sentences does he use?

No one could write a piece like "The Furnaces of the Earth" without having an insatiable curiosity about the world and without having a sense of wonder at its magnificence. Attenborough talks about volcanoes, the spreading of the ocean floor, tube worms, megapodes, plate tectonics, evolution, and many other things, and he ties it all together into a coherent whole. In explaining each individual feature, he often **summarizes** what is known about the topic; in pulling it all together, he is **synthesizing** information. Another kind of synthesis occurs when you write a research paper and draw on different sources of information, but the principle is the same, as is the challenge—to finish up with a clear and coherent piece of writing.

If you analyze the essay you've just read, you'll see that there is a clear logic to its organization. The author starts with a vivid description of volcanic activity of the kind that most people have seen, at least on film, except that he gives an up-close view. Next, he turns to the mechanisms that produce these displays, and then to the connection between volcanic activity and the appearance of the first life on Earth. This leads to a discussion of the varied relationships established between living things and their volcanic environments, and he ends with an observation about the dual nature of vulcanism—its destructive and creative force.

Attenborough crosses many borders in his travels, but, like several other writers represented in this text, he also crosses intellectual borders. His writing is a model of clarity, and the range of his interests and observations may also serve as a model. He touches on biology, chemistry, geology, zoology, and many other things in his essay, and he uses writing and film to bring all of these together. Seeing the connections between disciplines improves our understanding, even within our own field of expertise.

WRITING EXERCISES: Answer one of the following questions.

To approach any question, we first need to understand what is required and then to form a concept that responds appropriately. For example, in response to question 1, you might respond by deciding that religion would be the basis for the classification. This would be your **concept.** Then you would have to make sure that you were sufficiently informed to provide the **details** of the classification. You might already be able to do this, based on your existing knowledge of the subject, but you might have to look things up and provide yourself with adequate information. You would have to decide what **categories** you would use. If you were interested in the topic, but lacked information, you would have to find some sources of information, and you should first try some general reference works, such as encyclopedias and almanacs. Here you would find plenty of information about categories, number of adherents, and the nature of the different beliefs. You will probably find too much information, and some **further refinement of your concept** might be necessary, perhaps by focusing only on the largest religious groups. If you were to write a more elaborate paper, you would then go beyond the reference books to more specialized books and articles. This is a basic approach to any kind of paper requiring research.

1. a. The world can be described in terms of countries, continents, economic and political systems, cultures, topography, climate, language groups, religions, and many more. Using a basis of classification of your choice, write an essay in which you divide the world up into different areas. Be as descriptive and informative as you can.

   b. As above, but limit your classification to a single state, country or continent.

North Carolina, for example, could be described in terms of three regions: the coastal area, the Piedmont, and the western mountains.

2. Describe a place of natural beauty or interest that you have visited or that you know something about from reading or other sources. Include in your description some reference to the physical geography or geology of the area.

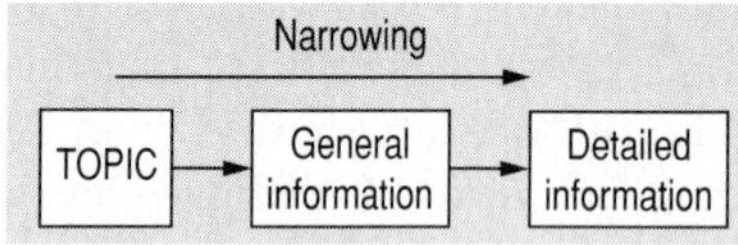

OPTION ONE

PRIOR KNOWLEDGE: The world today—and tomorrow.

Fiction gives us many different pictures of the future. Some, of course, were written long enough ago for us to judge how prescient their authors were. Jules Verne wrote *A Trip to the Moon* in 1865, and H. G. Wells wrote *The Time Machine* in 1895. Some writers of science fiction have seen their ideas realized in their own lifetimes, one example being Arthur C. Clarke, the author of *Childhood's End* and collaborator on *2001,* who first suggested that satellites could be placed in orbit in such a way that they would stay stationary relative to the Earth; this is known as a geosynchronous orbit. Other writers have had a social and political—as well as technological—orientation to the future, like George Orwell in *Nineteen Eighty-four* and Aldous Huxley in *Brave New World.* The point seems to be that the future, like the past, is not just about technology; people have to live in the brave new world, too.

Classifying the countries of the world, as you have seen, is not a particularly easy task, but at least it's possible to test the classification against the historical reality. For example, the East-West classification system worked for the bipolar world of the Cold War era but did not describe the world before World War II or after the collapse of the Soviet Union. If you wish to look into the future, however, you have no way of testing your analysis; you just have to wait and see whether you were correct.

In the following essay, Alan Ryan looks into the future and sees a tripolar world dominated by the United States, Japan, and Europe. In some ways, of course, he's on safe ground, because these are the great economic and political powers of today, and there seems to be no rival ready to join this club. In looking at the new situation, many people make reference to the "certainties" of the old Cold War days, when things were more predictable, but it should be noted that no one predicted the sudden collapse of the Soviet Union or the peaceful transition of Eastern Europe to Western-style political and economic systems. Ryan seems to ask an interesting question: How well do we know our own world, even our own country? Who can describe the new realities and provide a basis for anticipating the future?

Ryan sees the collapse of communism in Europe as the product of moral weaknesses. The system produced a state run by people who had no stake in truth telling. Corruption, bribery, and mistrust were universal, and no economy can flourish under such circumstances.

Economists, Ryan says, are held in high regard in the United States, and their analyses attract attention, but social scientists seem to be less well regarded. However, the interests of the social scientist overlap those of the economist. What really matters most in any economy, in any nation, are the people, and people are what social scientists study. One role of education, for example, is to qualify people for jobs, which, in turn, give social status and other rewards. Education, however, is also of great interest to economists, for improved education leads to increased productivity, which has a great impact on the national economy. The question of how well our schools are doing quickly takes on enormous significance in the global rivalry for wealth, influence, and power, and Ryan offers some interesting observations on the importance of both grade-school and college education.

Ryan's comments on the collapse of communism have relevance to Western countries too. He stresses the role of government, saying that "reasonably effective political arrangements" are essential to the satisfactory operation of capitalism, too.

Other factors of interest to social scientists also may influence the future. Health care, the distribution of wealth, and the workings of a multicultural society are all important, and Ryan provides statistics and discussion that are often surprising. He challenges us to think about our own society, as well as others around the world, and to face up to realities and comparisons that are not always very comforting.

Ryan suggests the possibility that our deficiencies in education, health care, and other areas may soon begin to have a very great economic impact. To thrive, we need a sophisticated population and workforce, top to bottom, not one divided between the few who have the knowledge and skills to understand the world around them and the many who don't. Ryan is not America bashing; he points to strengths in higher education and in dealing with the complexities of the multicultural society, to give just two examples. However, he suggests that social scientists get more involved in shaping our understanding of the way the world is, and the way we are, to help us, as a nation and as individuals, equip ourselves for life in a competitive world.

THINK ON PAPER
Ryan seems to suggest that a reasonably equitable distribution of wealth in a country is better than a situation in which most of the wealth belongs to relatively few people. Why do you think he thinks this? Do you agree? This question is further discussed in Unit Five.

READING: Alan Ryan. "Twenty-First Century Limited." *The New York Review* 19 Nov. 1992: 20–24.

Twenty-First Century Limited

The popularity of the idea that we have arrived at the "End of History" coincides strangely with the popularity of its direct opposite—the view that a wholly new and unsettling era has opened. For forty-five years many Europeans felt geographically, culturally, militarily, and economically trapped between the two competing superpowers. Now we seem to have a tripolar world, anchored on the US, Japan, and the European Community. This is a world whose history is about to begin, and whose future is entirely unpredictable, at any rate by contemporary social science.

Ryan orients the reader to his discussion by alluding to Francis Fukuyama's much-discussed idea that the end of the Cold War meant "the end of history." Ryan asserts, to the contrary, that while the old world order may have finished, history is just beginning for the post-Cold War world, and that this history is "entirely unpredictable."

"Tripolarity" can be a slogan that spares us thought in much the same way as "the end of history," however, and never more dangerously than if it suggests that the main parties to the new historical order understand their future roles, and are ready to play them. Recent events in fact suggest that our three leading actors are in considerable disarray. The US and Japan are just too engrossed with domestic problems to attend to anything else. But Europe is in disarray along several dimensions simultaneously; the European Economic Community has thirteen members, and this is visibly both too many and too few—Britain, Italy, Greece, and Portugal can't keep up with the economic policies demanded by their membership of the common monetary system, while the struggling ex-*comecon* countries such as Hungary, Poland, Czechoslovakia, Rumania, and Bulgaria, which are infinitely less capable of full membership, nonetheless have to be brought into some association with the Community if they are ever to catch up. Every one of these relationships has its own complications, and while the problems of the pound and the lira are hardly in the same league as the social and political disintegration of the former Soviet bloc, British and Italian politicians might be forgiven for feeling that if the EC can't cope with the former, it is unlikely to do better with the latter.

In Unit Three, reference was made to the **bipolar world** dominated by the United States and the Soviet Union between 1945 and 1991. Since the collapse of the U.S.S.R. some people think we have had a **unipolar** world, with the United States as the sole superpower. Many believe the future will be a **multipolar** world, which is the same as Ryan's **tripolar** world, plus China and Russia.

One of Ryan's references needs to be updated. The European Community is now the **European Union,** and its membership increased to 15 with the entry of Sweden, Finland, and Austria in 1995.

There are innumerable European institutions besides the EC; indeed, Europe has an "alphabet soup" of overlapping and competing organizations. The Council of Europe has existed since 1948 to promote democracy and human rights throughout Europe and it already embraces many more countries than the Economic Community—

Note the many references in his essay to famous names and international institutions. On the first page, note the reference to the economist **John Maynard Keynes,** for example, and the "alphabet soup" of organizations.

Poland, Hungary, Czechoslovakia are members, and Russia and Ukraine will probably join soon. On the security front, the Western European Union is as old as NATO; the Conference on Security and Cooperation in Europe is another umbrella that has now been opened to take in the former Soviet dependencies. But none of these organizations has been any use in meeting the military challenge of the civil wars in Bosnia and Croatia; none offers much prospect for doing better in Moldavia or Armenia, and none has helped to concentrate European efforts to relieve starvation in Somalia. They may do more for the political and legal education of the former Soviet dependencies, but whether in time to stem the disintegrating effects of economic and political disillusionment is another matter.

The concept of tripolarity is indeed more hope and expectation than description, a gesture toward the thought that Japan, the EC, and the US must take the economic, cultural, and strategic lead in their respective geographical regions, that economic growth in the developed world, and the sponsoring of growth—along with peace, democracy, and a respect for human rights—in the less developed world must depend on their efforts and their cooperation.

Not, to be sure, on their cooperation alone. These are capitalist economies whose health depends on the energy—what Keynes aptly labeled "animal spirits"—that they bring to the familiar tasks of inventing new products and stimulating a demand for them. They are competitors as well as cooperators. Contrary to Lester Thurow's view in his recent book, *Head to Head*, this is generally all to the good. Just as a competitive market economy that keeps individual firms on their toes is the best way we know for generating resources for public purposes, international competition that keeps the major economies on their toes is as good a way as we can imagine of producing the resources for international public purposes—whether these are peace-keeping forces under a UN banner, global public works schemes to save the environment, or modest educational efforts to teach the elements of economic efficiency and political accountability to societies that have spent the postwar years neglecting them in the name of Marxist or nationalist fundamentalism. Just as competition in a single national economy constantly educates firms and consumers about products, techniques, costs, and markets, so it should internationally.

But here is the rub. We know that capitalism is vastly productive only when it is controlled by reasonably effective political arrangements. We know that governments are staffed by people whose conceptions of public policy, along with their willingness to govern uncorruptly and efficiently, are sustained by all sorts of local cultural and legal conditions. What we don't know is what we need to know if we are to borrow intelligently from one another's institutions and pass the knowledge on to the rest of the world. We don't know whether one set of political and cultural arrangements is uniquely effective or how easily they can be transplanted—whether parliamentary systems work better than an American "separation of powers" system for instance, or whether it would be worth investing in an Ecole nationale d'administration in Washington, or indeed whether foreign revisions of such institutions can be successfully erected.

The evidence of the postwar years is that very different arrangements can work equally well, but also that they may work well for a while but then eventually stagnate unpredictably—Sweden, for instance, combined high growth rates, low unemployment, and an elaborate and expensive welfare state for many years, and now seems to have lost the knack of it, while the occasional heretical voice has already been heard to suggest that the Japanese economy is not merely faltering but may face deeper trouble. If the leaders of the tripolar world have something to teach everyone else—other than that communism, militarism, and the cruder sorts of nationalism are bad for your health, welfare, and human rights—what is it? How much do we know about what mixtures of culture, politics, and economics will prosper in the new world?

It's easy to see what is at stake—what we would like the social sciences to tell us—by considering the way Americans so widely believe that in the near to medium term they face economic disaster because of the inadequacies of American education. Anyone working in the educational field in the contemporary US is aware that all is not well and that American public high schools, for example, produce on the whole a badly educated group of eighteen year olds. Even good schools are exceedingly bad at teaching foreign languages; even the best schools teach history and geography very poorly, and give little real understanding of the literature and culture of other societies. In mathematics, the best 5 percent of American high-school students learn calculus; but calculus is taught to the best 75 percent of Japanese students. The worst schools are simply nightmarish. Ought we not to spend whatever it takes to remedy this at once?

For all the gloom, the rottenness of American education seems (at any rate so far) to be less damaging than one might expect. Part of the reason seems to be that America's universities are much better than its high schools, partly that Japanese universities do not make the same efforts as Japanese high schools, so that by the time the American young are twenty-five, those who have been through an advanced graduate education are formally better educated than their peers anywhere in the world, save for the traditional American deficiency in language and general cultural knowledge. The fact that over 40 percent of Ph.D.s in mathematics and engineering and around 30 percent of Ph.D.s in computer science and physical science are awarded to nonresident aliens suggests where the American advantage lies. And the proportion of Americans who go to colleges and universities is still unrivaled elsewhere.[1]

Other possibilities might be considered. Perhaps the ill effects of poor secondary education have just been slow to show up; perhaps American college education has been so effective in encouraging the inventiveness of entrepreneurs that the educational deficiencies of much of the work force has to some degree been offset. Perhaps the American economy is elaborately divided internally, with a sophisticated, highly paid, intellectually demanding information-processing sector and a poorly paid, intellectually undemanding manual and service sector—the view that Robert B. Reich's *The Work of Nations* puts forward. Whichever view we accept, the deficiencies of American education might not matter very much—in gross.

As a matter of distributive justice, they remain intolerable. The defects of public high-school education would matter very much to the manual working class no matter what their effect on the overall efficiency of the economy, because they would determine that in the global economy the most sophisticated production jobs will tend to go to Japan and Germany—while what British managers once called "low value-added metal bashing" would be carried on in the US and Britain, and otherwise in the third world. But the badness of the worst education would not necessarily matter to the economy overall, and particularly not to the better off. Nor would the traditional defects of the best American education. The deficiency in linguistic skills and general culture of managers, public servants, and political leaders might make for a rather coarse ruling elite, but it would be economically irrelevant.

This view is morally ugly, if only because it takes for granted an increasingly wide income and welfare gap between better and worse off. Its moral ugliness alone would not be enough to discredit it, however. More significantly, it seems unlikely that the US can allow itself the luxury of running that sort of economy very much longer, and that the deficiencies of both the best and the worst American education

---

[1]American higher education statistics are summarized in the *Annual Statistical Abstract of the United States*; other countries publish similar annual abstracts. Institutional differences make detailed comparison very difficult, and comparisons of quality almost impossible; but a crude indicator is that in 1989 there were some 15 million students in higher education and 800,000 college and university teachers of the rank of lecturer and above in the US—many of both categories parttime—and nowhere else comes close on a per capita basis. It is open to anyone to retort that much or even most of what goes on is not really "higher" education, to wish that more of it was German apprenticeship training, or that more of it took place in high school. These are my own views; still the sheer size and availability of the higher education system remain astonishing.

will matter increasingly. It is a commonplace that what makes modern economies tick is their "human capital"—a point made long ago by both J. S. Mill and Marx, but now coming increasingly to the fore. Human capital—the qualities of commitment, skill, adaptability, and so on that make one work force more productive than another—is very much man-made, or, to put it more elaborately, culturally produced. The tripolar world can only promote global economic sophistication if we can understand better than we do now how to foster the cultural capacities that support it. I do not mean that only one kind of culture can support a sophisticated economy—that is plainly false for we know that different cultures will do it differently. But some combinations of cultural characteristics will be possible and fruitful, some impossible, some possible and destructive, and it is increasingly important to know which is which. The importance of the influence of the political, legal, and social culture on the economy emerges particularly vividly when one considers the negative example of the baleful influence of a Leninist political culture on the economies of the former Communist bloc.

The lesson of the collapse of the Soviet bloc is not just that the one-party regime and the command economy can't deliver the goods—as economists say, they gave the USSR the most impressive nineteenth-century industrial infrastructure in the world, seventy-five years too late—but it is at least that; and understanding why the disaster was so comprehensive is of more than intellectual interest. Whatever the case in pure economic theory, command economies really did suffer from the inability to secure and process information that writers like Friedrich von Hayek and Ludwig von Mises claimed was the Achilles heel of socialism. But an even more important feature of such systems was the moral rot that they engendered. The distortion of information was as extreme and as damaging as it was because too many people had perverse incentives to present misleading and inaccurate data, and too many had perverse incentives to pretend to believe what they knew to be entirely false.

In his book *East European Alternatives*, written just as communism was collapsing in his native Hungary, the social scientist Elemér Hankiss gave a deeply depressing and deeply convincing account of the way in which the corruption of a regime that claimed to "mobilize" resources had produced what Hankiss called "the demobilized society." In the demobilized society corruption flourished; everyone was forced to make deals with employers and officials to achieve the least result; and distrust of anyone other than friends and family was rampant. The impact on economic modernization and growth hardly needs describing.

The alternative to the degeneration caused by the vain pursuit of the wholly managed society, in which innovation and inspiration is supposed to be provided by a cadre of Party enthusiasts, is not schematic laissez-faire capitalism. One of the innumerable problems in post-Communist Eastern Europe has been the inadequacy of the local understanding of the enormous role that the state must play even in a laissez-faire economy, as well as the limited initial understanding of such matters by Western economists who have gallantly been offering help.

The immense prestige in which economics is held in the American academy, together with the current contempt for sociology, has diverted the cleverest students of the social sciences away from institutional economics and into the theoretical analysis of elaborate financial matters where their mathematical skills have the freest play. Only when they encounter a really barren landscape in former Communist countries do they appreciate the extent to which they have taken for granted the existence of an efficient legal regime with the abilities to define and enforce property rights and contracts and also to supply individuals and enterprises with the legal means to create new transferable interests in the goods and services they propose to produce.

That is merely one part of a vast problem; imagine running an industry with managers who are entirely unfamiliar with the concept of depreciation, or who find it hard to understand how checkbooks work in a banking system. The Eastern European hope that "civil society" would emerge from beneath the stifling blanket of one-party politics is understandable—there was a wonderful uncrushed vitality in the opposition to communism—but it does leave many observers wondering how a state that has lost so much of its authority will be able to create the legal institutions on which the new world is to depend. The moral of the situation in the former Communist bloc is one that applies to the three partners in the new tripolar world system. There is a creative role for the state in the economy of the twenty-first century, but that role is both circumscribed by culture and facilitated by culture in ways that we find hard to describe, let alone to measure with any exactness. Three examples—concerning American industry, education, and health care—point the same moral about our need for social understanding that is sensitive to the interplay of culture and institutions.

The degree to which American industry currently is competitive or uncompetitive remains debatable. American automobiles are unloved by American consumers, but American airplanes still dominate the world market. The mass production of computer chips now lies largely in the hands of NEC Toshiba and Hitachi, but it is widely believed that the American firm Intel will wipe the floor with them during the next decade. American television manufacturing is a thing of the past, but Japanese television producers apparently also lose money on sales of television sets, and they remain in the business for the sake of the next generation of "high-definition TV" and the like. American industry is very good at turning out astonishingly cheap but simple products that never get onto a world market, partly because of transport costs, partly because consumer tastes preclude their doing so. American washing machines, for instance, are cheaper than anyone else's, but are huge and clumsy, and not plausible items of export. The US can be a paradise for consumers with standard tastes, but it is not so clear that it is a paradise for producers of exportable products that will make money during the next century.

If it is hard to tell whether American commercial and industrial culture promotes efficiency better or worse than other cultures do, it is at any rate clear that American commercial and industrial culture is very different from that of Germany or Japan. I hesitate to say it is unlike that of the EC as a whole, because Britain is (though not in the ways that led General de Gaulle to pronounce his successive "nons" back in the 1960s) something of a halfway case, right down to the features of its present recession. In contrast to the practice of many Japanese companies, American industry is run on nonconsensual principles in which the "us" and "them" line of demarcation between management and the work force is clear, and the conflict of interest between managers seeking returns for shareholders and workers seeking secure and well-paid employment is a simple fact of life. By the same token, the pay differentials between American managers and blue-collar workers are wider than anywhere else in the world, as are the levels of remuneration that CEOs feel entitled to. Donald Trump described some of the more spectacular buildings he owned as "trophies," and one imagines that when the head of Coca-Cola takes home $86 million, that is similarly a "trophy" salary. It would certainly be hard to claim that it was a nicely calculated reflection of the value he adds to Coca-Cola's business.

Paradoxically, American pay differentials are as wide as they are even though American industry supports more managers than its competitors. I do not know precisely how the figures are calculated, but it has been estimated that there are three times as many managers in proportion to the work force as in Japan and four times as many as in Finland.[2] Nor do the differentials reflect the fact that the American workers work short hours and at a low intensity. American working hours per year are only slightly lower than in Japan and a good deal higher than in Germany.

It is generally known that the U.S. employs, or at any rate supports, far more lawyers than any other country on earth; on a per capita basis, the US supports one lawyer to 250 people, Japan, one lawyer to

---

[2]Andrew Shapiro, *We're Number One* (Vintage, 1992), p. 99, pp. 134–136.

7,500 people. Even if these estimates are exaggerated, the differences between the two cultures in this matter are clear. The interesting question is: what follows, if anything? One ought always to consider that perhaps nothing follows at all. There are many ways of doing business, many ways of handling relations between firms, between firms and customers or clients, between firms and governments, and so on; perhaps there is no reason to believe that any particular way is functionally more effective than any other.

This seems implausible, however, if only because the American public has been notably discontented with the behavior of the American political system and economy during the past several years. Even at the height of the Reagan boom, dissident voices pointed out that the benefits of prosperity were inequitably distributed; that financial services were promoted more than productive industry; that already rich persons in a good position to manipulate company finances for their own personal gain were creaming off resources that often were not, when taken, used for productive purposes. The incapacity of the economy to absorb all those who needed steady, reasonably well-paid employment was much commented on, as was rising crime, and the deteriorating condition of the schools. Where there was growth, it was chaotic and where there was not, as in the rustbelt, the results were appalling. Running an old-fashioned version of capitalism left much to be desired; even if it did not threaten immediate disaster.

The solutions proposed for this state of affairs vary widely. Some of the people who engineered the situation complained of think it was a great success, and all its costs were necessary costs. Even if we suppose that the economic policies of the Reagan years were on balance a success—a moral and political judgment on which it would be impossible to secure agreement—the question would remain whether they could have been carried out at lower cost. It would be impossible to get an agreement on this question as well, not because it requires a moral or political judgment, but because we do not know whether there are cultural, political, and other social obstacles to the institutional and behavioral changes that might have produced better results. Could American investment bankers have been imaginative in conceiving new forms of financing without engaging in the excesses of the kind that sent Michael Milken to jail? Could the management of General Motors have been so imbued with an unselfish devotion to the corporation that its executives might have accepted lower salaries, imagined ways of restructuring the business that would result in fewer job losses, and conducted relations with stockholders that kept them loyal while the firm rebuilt itself instead of trying to prop up the share price on a short-term basis?

Closely related questions can be raised about education. It is not a simple task to transplant other societies' working practices and executive culture; nor is it absolutely impossible. But any discussion of the question should recognize that schools, universities, and particularly graduate professional schools do much to inculcate goals and standards of success, the images of a flourishing personal life and community that guide people's actions.

One of the interesting, but faintly absurd, features of the present discontent with American education and the widespread hope that we might borrow what we need from Japan or Europe is that many of the educational methods applied in Asian elementary and junior schools were advocated in 1899 in John Dewey's most famous book, *The School and Society*. But Dewey was usually, and inaccurately, accused by his critics of having corrupted American education by his advocacy of a secular, practical, child-centered education, thus slighting eternal religious values, high culture, and the virtues of hierarchy. His admirers have equally overstated his impact on American practice, but naturally think it was all for the best. Dewey himself thought that teacher training institutions often paid lip service to his ideas, but that he had made very little difference to the practice of elementary schools. He denied that his views were "child-centered"; the progressive educators' view of a "child-centered" education, he thought, sometimes suggested that there was no need for teachers at all, and this he thought quite mad.

What his views really were, he insisted, were practice-based; learning was both an activity in its own right and sprang most naturally out of practical activities. At its simplest, this amounted to an appeal to teach chemistry by first letting young children learn to cook, and to teach geometry by first letting them build boxes to hold their pens and pencils. As it got increasingly complicated, it meant that teachers should always stress applications rather than rote-learned principles. Since practice was essentially social, learning ought always to be a group activity; instead of holding children to assessment by individual examinations that set child against child, schools should encourage them to engage in collective projects where each had to contribute something to the group's achievements where knowledge was pooled, and a variety of skills was drawn on to get a project accomplished. Such anecdotal evidence as there is suggests that one reason why Asian students in American universities do strikingly better in difficult mathematics courses than most Caucasian or African American students is that they work together on problems, pooling skills and working their way from easier to harder problems with much less strain on the individual student than occurs when students study alone.

What is curious is this. Dewey is widely thought to be the archetypical American thinker, commentators on his work commonly suggest that his philosophy is, so to speak, the American heartland thinking aloud. He did not really think that, though he did think that his ideas were implicit in the consciousness of any "modern" society, and that the US was in some ways the archetypical modern society. Yet any claim that one could easily make Dewey's ideas the working theory of American elementary and subsequent education would simply be false. In spite of the lip service paid to them for the past sixty years, they do not inform current practice. Presumably there is something about American culture that explains why not—though no one has plausibly suggested what it is. It is not enough to talk hopefully of "individualism." Were individualism a sufficiently precise concept, it might be argued that the characteristic American vice is to think of the individual knower, not of knowledge, as a collective resource; to fixate on individual creativity as the intellectual ideal, to think of the classroom as the individual teacher's property, not as one more place in which children grow up. Yet none of these things is entirely true, and to an English observer, America often seems astonishingly group-minded, and the local school culture can be deeply unsympathetic to the child who is out of step. It is, after all, the country in which the concept of "other-directedness" took hold.

Similar issues arise in the current debates over health care. In several respects, the US runs a welfare state like almost any other welfare state. This is especially true for the old-age pensions that consume most of welfare state spending that is not for health; Americans have the same sort of not-quite-contributory old-age insurance schemes that one finds in Britain and most European countries. Where the US is odd is in health care for the non-elderly. No other developed country leaves such a large proportion of its young and working-age population without adequate health insurance.

No other country, moreover, wastes so much money on providing unnecessary health care; and no other country wastes so much money on administrative costs. (Those are the costs that are counted; in view of the way the American system requires the patient, who does not charge for his or her time, to fill out endless forms, the true cost of the administrative overhead is even greater than appears in the accounts.) For a far higher expenditure in absolute terms, and a greater proportionate share of GNP than any other country in the world, the US provides very poor health care or none at all to about 15 percent of its population; at the other end of the spectrum, a well-to-do person over fifty-five can expect better care than any comparable person in the world. The inefficiency of the system is astonishing. To give poor medical care to mothers before and during the birth of children, as too often happens, is a terrible failure of investment in human capital. One of the absurdities of health insurance run for profit is that job mobility decreases as people are reluctant to work for companies that don't provide benefits; and pervasive anxiety about health care and its cost is a great source of unhappiness.

Americans do not like their health care system. When polled, they say they much prefer the Canadian national health service. Yet it is extraordinarily difficult to change over to anything resembling the Canadian system. Is this a matter of American culture, or is it simply that the beneficiaries of the present system are well placed to block change? The Princeton health economist Uwe Reinhardt insists that the professions and industries that benefit from the current system are the problem. On this matter Americans and Canadians tend to think identically, he argues, but the Canadian political system offers fewer opportunities for veto groups such as doctors and large corporations to prevent dramatic changes in the system from occurring, and Canadian politicians are not dependent on PAC money in the way American politicians are. Most Canadian experts think this is only a small part of the answer; it is not negligible, but it makes as large a difference as it does only because the American political and economic culture has less social solidarity than the Canadian culture, and puts more emphasis on making contracts for services, and is less imbued with an image of the "caring state."

In spite of the vast amount of research on political culture that has gone on since World War II it is astonishingly difficult to test any of these hypotheses empirically. There are good reasons why it is difficult—the popular view that social scientists are chronically idle and not very intelligent is not one. In the first place it is almost impossible to identify attitudes that one might think of as intrinsic to "being American" as opposed to being Japanese or Canadian or European—that is attitudes that are durable and constrain institutional change as distinguished from those that are simply responses to the local institutions. Many attitudes change quite swiftly when institutions change and many do not; few social scientists are such rationalists that they think most of our attitudes can be instantly changed, or such antirationalists that they think we are stuck with whatever social and cultural attitudes we have been socialized into by the age of twenty-five. But until we have a much surer grasp of cross-cultural political psychology than we currently do, it is impossible to say anything very reliable about how far each view is correct.

What might social scientists do? On my reading of the matter, they ought to promote what I would want to call multiculturalism if it weren't that the term has been stolen for other purposes. That is, they ought to be readier than most of us usually are to try to answer large, messy questions about the interaction of cultural, political, and economic phenomena, globally as well as locally. The odds are that they will be wrong much of the time, but they will at any rate not be wholly irrelevant to the emerging world that their children will inhabit.

The three components of the tripolar world system each have strengths and weaknesses of a distinctive kind in fostering this kind of work. The US has a mass higher education system that reaches out to a higher percentage of the population than most other countries dream of. On the other hand its students are poorly educated, and American academic culture is in general insular—even though popular culture is multifaceted, vivid, and at the level of McDonald's and Madonna highly exportable. Japan and Europe devote much more effort to the sort of linguistic and cultural formation that is needed, but the European universities currently have a small part in the political lives of their societies—they have not been central to the current debate over the future shape of Europe, for example—and the elite universities in Japan train only a small proportion of the appropriate age group. Again, the cultural and ethnic solidarity that has made it easier for Germany to develop the social market economy comes at a high price—German citizenship is largely a matter of blood not allegiance, and Japanese social cohesion appears to exact an equally high price.

Here the US has a real advantage; for all the horrors of racial inequality in this country the US has had two centuries of not unsuccessful practice in the art of combining ethnic diversity with political unity; it continues to absorb a remarkable mixture of immigrants and even its failures imply ambitions that few other societies have ever entertained. How much of this experience can be passed on to the Balkans, East Germany, or the fringes of the former Soviet Union is anybody's guess. Even when it comes to shared intellectual assumptions, tripolar cooperation may be harder to achieve than the obvious coincidence of interests between the US, the EC, and Japan suggests it should be. Still, unless we aspire, as the great sociologists and anthropologists of the nineteenth century did, to the understanding of our brave new world that all this demands, we shall no more be masters of our fates in the next half century than we have been in the past half century.

ASPECTS OF WRITING: Synthesis and the essay of ideas.

How is it possible to describe the state of the world, or of a country? First, you have to know what aspects you're interested in—is your picture going to be economic in nature? Political? Cultural? Demographic? Then you have to gather information, but, again, what information? Reading widely will help you put together your picture; it will be composed of information and impressions from a variety of sources, as well as your own experience. The pulling together of all these disparate sources is the **synthesis.**

In the foregoing essay Alan Ryan is looking ahead, trying to see what the world will be like as we move into the next century, and his focus appears to be principally economic. It soon becomes clear, however, that to weigh the strengths and weaknesses of each economic giant in a **tripolar world**—Japan, the United States, and Europe—Ryan finds himself looking at education, health care, decision making, multicultural societies, and more. He sees a vital place for the social scientist, not just the economist, in this analysis.

Ryan includes some fascinating information in his essay—that 75% of Japanese high school students study calculus, compared with only 5% of American students; and that American universities are so highly regarded that more than 40% of Ph.D.'s in mathematics and engineering, and approximately 30% of Ph.D.'s in computer science and physics, are won by nonresident aliens—foreign students. By finding and using interesting information, Ryan makes his essay interesting in its **details** as well as in its overall thesis. You should try to do this, too.

Looking into the future is a speculative activity. No one knows whether the factors they are measuring are the significant ones or not. The sudden and dramatic collapse of the Soviet Union, and the consequent end of the Cold War, took everyone by surprise; no one predicted it. It's good, therefore, to be cautious and to avoid extravagant claims, but this doesn't preclude you from playing with ideas. Ryan introduces many paragraphs on a cautionary note:

> The degree to which American industry currently is competitive or uncompetitive remains debatable.
>
> It is hard to tell whether American commercial and industrial culture is very different from that of Germany or Japan.

but he is constantly providing data and discussing ideas. The tone is important.

There is a lesson here. If the evidence is inconclusive, or if there really isn't any way to be sure about something, then admit it. In fact, Ryan's concluding remarks are a call to social scientists and anthropologists to do more to understand the new realities in the world. If we can't understand ourselves and others better, "We shall no more be masters of our fates in the next half century than we have been in the past half century." Notice how this concluding thought follows from the thesis in the opening paragraph: "This is a world whose history is about to begin, and whose future is entirely unpredictable, at any rate by contemporary social science."

Essays of ideas are supposed to make us think, and Ryan's essay does this. He has many things to say that challenge common notions about the United States as well as about other countries. Perhaps you would like to explore one of these themes further in the *Writing and research* section that follows.

WRITING AND RESEARCH: Answer one of these questions.

1. Supplementing your general knowledge with information from the *Annual Statistical Abstract of the United States*, or similar reference works, describe one aspect of life in the United States. Naturally, you should choose something that lends itself to statistical description. You may choose something discussed in Ryan's essay.
2. Looking into the future, what do you see for the United States and/or the world? Your essay may be as analytical or as imaginative as you like, and it should focus on one or two particular aspects.
3. Identify one or two issues discussed by Ryan and respond to his remarks. Add, however, reference to other writers on the topic you choose.

In this text you have been urged on occasion to refer to your almanacs. A lot of basic statistical information can be found in such publications, and they have the important merit of being up-to-date, assuming that you refer to the latest annual edition. Ryan refers in a footnote to another major resource, the *Annual Statistical Abstract of the United States*, and he notes that other countries produce similar texts. Further resources include the World Bank's annual *World Development Report* and the United Nations Development Program's annual *Human Development Report* (both used in Unit Five of this text). Check your libraries for all these publications. If you know about them, you'll probably use them in some of your courses.

One topic Ryan discusses is *American education*, and this is something you already know a lot about. You, or others in your class, may also know something about the education systems and standards of other countries. Make sure, first, that you understand what Ryan is saying on this topic, and then you might look in the library for further information to support a discussion arising from Ryan's essay. There are a lot of different possibilities here; you wouldn't have to focus on international comparisons.

OPTION TWO

TALKING ABOUT LANGUAGE: Language and politics.

Language is important, and nowhere more so than in politics, where it's possible to imagine a situation in which a few careless words could have disastrous consequences for the entire world. On this level there is a whole language of code words that diplomats use to describe their discussions. For example, if an ambassador emerges from a conference and says that the meetings were "frank," it's safe to assume that tempers were flaring inside. Some code words have rather grim connotations: *ground zero* is the place where a nuclear blast actually occurred; an *incursion* can be a full-scale invasion; a *cold,* given as the reason for a political absence, can signal political pneumonia.

There may sometimes be good reasons for saying less than the truth; creating panic does not usually help anyone. There are also occasions when personal or ideological interests may be at stake. When this occurs, it may be that the rhetoric has left the world of diplomatic niceties and has entered the world of propaganda and sloganeering. Not all propaganda is untrue, of course, but it is designed to push or support a cause, be it a war, a social reform, or a political cause.

Military propaganda has a long history. Domestically, it is usually intended to demonize the enemy and whip up popular enthusiasm for the war. On the foreign front, it may be designed to influence the population against their government and undermine morale among the people and the troops.

Political propaganda of another kind is most evident at election times, when efforts to embarrass the rival candidate and extol one's own virtues take over the airwaves and the press.

THINK ON PAPER
As a class, make a list of political phrases and code words familiar to you.

Propaganda often uses language that is intended to persuade or frighten. If the listener doesn't know any better, he or she may be easily deceived. The former communist regimes were fond of referring to Western countries as "the imperialists," and they fed their own people a propaganda diet that emphasized the problems of unemployment, crime, homelessness, and racism in the West. Our images of life in the East were often no more balanced.

Certain words have acquired strong connotations, favorable or unfavorable. *Third World,* for many people, conjures up images of destitution and misery, even though life in many Third World countries can be as pleasant as anywhere else. *Socialism* and *capitalism* may have positive or negative connotations, depending on the values and political persuasion of the person. In recent years, phrases and words such as *welfare queen* and *handout* have developed certain connotations. Some code words have a long history, as does *Munich,* which stands for political appeasement, or trying to buy off an aggressor nation by giving in to its immediate demands in return for a promise to end its aggression. The slogan *No More Vietnams* makes reference to the quagmire of U.S. "intervention" (another political word) in the Vietnam War between c. 1965–1975.

ASPECTS OF WRITING: The power of language.

Literature gives us some of our most memorable observations.

"Beauty is truth, truth beauty,"—that is all
Ye know on earth, and all ye need to know.
—Keats, *Ode on a Grecian Urn*

The mass of men lead lives of quiet desperation.
—Thoreau, *Walden*

Patriotism is the last refuge of a scoundrel.
—Dr. Johnson (in Boswell, *Life of Johnson*)

Life's but a walking shadow, a poor player
That struts and frets his hour upon the stage
And then is heard no more; it is a tale
Told by an idiot, full of sound and fury,
Signifying nothing.
—Shakespeare, *Macbeth*

Language can be powerful, dangerous, empty, persuasive, beautiful, profound, ridiculous. It can be illogical or logical. An orator can stir emotions and arouse great enthusiasm or anger; a writer can change the way people think and can help people understand their own lives and the human condition. We all use language, and we all hear and read, and most jobs depend in part on our ability to do these things well.

We have seen that propagandists often use **loaded words**—that is to say, words whose impact is **emotional** rather than **rational.** Many arguments depend heavily on the emotional impact of a single phrase—especially in these days of debate by soundbite. In business, a marketing strategy called "competitive pricing" by some may be an "unfair trading practice" to others. A huge salary or pay demand may be seen by sympathizers as "a fair return" and by others as "greed."

In advertising and politics, repetition is seen as a powerful weapon, based on the belief that "If you say something often enough, people will start believing it." In politics, this tactic is sometimes called "The Big Lie."

You may not be a propagandist, but **your words also convey messages and attitudes and should be carefully considered.** Using the right word gives your writing a precise and sophisticated quality.

The frequent use of vocabulary webs in this text is intended to encourage a high level of interest in words, so that you will want to use them as precisely as possible. This precision will help you **avoid simply misusing and misspelling words,** it will help you strike **an appropriate tone,** and it will help you **say exactly what you mean.**

If you want to improve your vocabulary and spelling, one practical thing you can do is **read as much and as widely as possible.** Cultivate your ability to distinguish between the imprecise and the precise, between the dull and the beautiful, and develop an interest in the meanings of words.

Quick Quiz

A. Check your "sense of the world."
   1. Name the six continents and the oceans.
   2. Approximately how many countries are there in the world?
   3. What do "East" and "West" mean in Cold War history?
   4. What are plate tectonics?
   5. Is the Atlantic Ocean getting wider or narrower each year?
   6. In which direction are Africa and India moving?
   7. What is "taxonomy"?
   8. What do "North" and "South" mean as ways of classifying countries today?
   9. Where are the world's great rainforests, deserts, and grasslands?
   10. Where are these mountain ranges: the Rockies, the Himalayas, the Alps, the Urals, and the Andes?
   11. Name five countries that could be described in the following terms: First World, wealthy, democratic, part of the free world, Northern.
   12. Name five countries that could be described in the following terms: Third World, poor, developing, Southern.
   13. What is meant by "bipolar world," "unipolar world," "tripolar world," and "multipolar world"?

B. As you read in this unit, the Roman god **Vulcan** is the source of our word "vulcanism" or "volcanism," and "volcano." The connection is that Vulcan is the **god of fire** and metallurgy. What is the connection between these other classical deities/characters and modern English words?

Mars—martial

Aphrodite—aphrodisiac

Narcissus—narcissism

Janus—January

Bacchus—bacchanal

Hercules—herculean

Ceres—cereal

Sisyphus—sisyphean

Draco—draconian

Check the stories of these characters in a **classical dictionary;** they are often highly entertaining.

SECTION ONE

PRIOR KNOWLEDGE: Statistical pictures; measuring wealth, health, education. . . .

Public opinion pollsters and social science researchers frequently provide us with statistical snapshots of American life, telling us about ourselves. It's healthy to be a little skeptical of statistical pictures, for they can be distorted, but they can also provide information of great interest. When looking at the following data from around the world, the same problems exist—on an even greater scale—but the numbers offer the most objective basis for comparison that is now available.

In this section you'll be looking at statistical tables that enable us to compare economic, health, educational and other conditions around the world, and you'll be thinking about what the numbers mean in human terms.

The statistics presented here come from the **World Bank,** which, with its cousin, the **International Monetary Fund (IMF),** is the most important provider of development assistance funds to poorer countries. Both are international organizations based in Washington, D.C. Unlike other banks, the World Bank is owned by governments and can loan money only to governments. It funds projects in many countries and so is interested in measuring the progress that countries make in both economic and human terms; reflecting these two realms, the statistical tables are called **economic indicators** and **social indicators.**

This information is published every year in the *World Development Report,* and the statistics collected there enable us to make comparisons between countries and identify trends.

Two key words in statistics (and testing of any kind) are **validity** and **reliability.** *Validity* is a measure of whether the question is actually asking what the questioner thinks is being asked, and *reliability* measures whether or not the same question would consistently elicit the same answer from the same person.

There are three kinds of lies—lies, damn lies, and statistics.
Benjamin Disraeli,
as reported by Mark Twain

You might prove anything by figures.
Thomas Carlyle

If you take courses in international studies or Third World studies—or read a major newspaper—you'll probably find many references to **international organizations** and agencies. Most writers assume that you know the abbreviations for these organizations. Here's a list of some of the best-known **United Nations (U.N.) agencies,** with their headquarters:

- **UNICEF**—United Nations Children's Fund (New York)
- **UNESCO**—United Nations Educational, Scientific, and Cultural Organization (Paris)
- **FAO**—Food and Agricultural Organization (Rome)
- **WHO**—World Health Organization (Geneva)
- **ILO**—International Labor Organization (Geneva)

Other organizations involved in international development or relief programs either are associated with governments, such as the U.S. government's Agency for International Development (AID), or are nongovernmental organizations (NGO's), such as Oxfam, the International Committee of the Red Cross, or Médecins sans Frontières. Many governments and organizations from around the world are involved. Japan gives more money than any other country in international aid; the Scandinavian countries are the most generous on a per-capita basis.

Many newspapers show **exchange rates** every day; they are extremely important in business, especially as the world's economies become more interdependent and competition for trade becomes more fierce. The exchange rate affects the price of all goods sold in the global marketplace. If the dollar loses value against other currencies, for example, America's exports can be sold more cheaply overseas, but America's imports become more expensive. In the mid-1980s the U.S. dollar was worth about 250 Japanese yen; ten years later the dollar was worth about 85 yen. Most newspapers will show you today's exchange rate.

Collecting such information is a daunting task, and making the numbers truly comparable is a challenge. For example, all the financial data in these tables are expressed in U.S. dollars; this involves converting other currencies into dollars, but **currency exchange rates** change every day. The World Bank explains how it deals with such statistical problems in the "Technical Notes" section of each *World Development Report.*

Other problems also exist. The way different countries keep accounts and report statistics varies, and some are notoriously unreliable. Also, there are questions of interpretation. The World Bank ranks countries by a measure of wealth called **Gross National Product per capita,** but national wealth does not always indicate social or even economic development—much depends on where the wealth comes from, how widely it is distributed, and how governments spend their revenue. This is why you should look at several tables in order to form a more rounded picture of each country's performance.

The selected World Bank tables that follow focus mainly on economic status, health, population, education, and gender differences. Most information is presented in **percentage** or **per capita** terms; this is important, for it enables comparisons to be made between countries of different sizes. More babies are born in China every year than in Nigeria, for example, but China is a much more populous country, and the raw numbers do not allow any realistic comparison. Demographers are more interested not in the *number of births* but in the *population growth rate,* which shows that Nigeria's population is growing much faster than China's.

In Unit Four certain countries were identified as having "outgrown" their "Third World" classification. **GNP per capita** is the standard way to measure this kind of economic development.

GNP per capita is the value of a country's output of goods and services in a given year, divided by the country's population. The *per capita* (per-head, or per-person) value makes it possible to compare countries of all sizes.

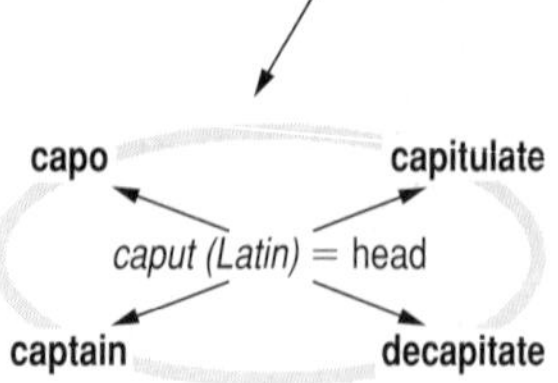

ANNOTATED READING: World Bank. "Overview" (extracts) and "What Do We Know about the Poor?" (extracts). *World Development Report, 1990.* New York: Oxford UP, 1990. World Bank Tables (selections). *World Development Report 1994.* New York: Oxford UP, 1994.

OVERVIEW

During the past three decades the developing world has made enormous economic progress. This can be seen most clearly in the rising trend for incomes and consumption: between 1965 and 1985 consumption per capita in the developing world went up by almost 70 percent. Broader measures of well-being confirm this picture—life expectancy, child mortality, and educational attainment have all improved markedly. Viewed from either perspective—income and consumption on the one hand, broad social indicators on the other—the developing countries are advancing much faster than today's developed countries did at a comparable stage.

This discussion is a good demonstration of how life expectancy, child mortality rates, and other statistical information can be used for comparative purposes. It's important also to understand exactly what these figures tell us in human terms.

Against that background of achievement, it is all the more staggering—and all the more shameful—that more than one billion people in the developing world are living in poverty. *World Development Report 1990* estimates that this is the number of people who are struggling to survive on less than $370 a year. Progress in raising average incomes, however welcome, must not distract attention from this massive and continuing burden of poverty.

The same is true of the broader measures of well-being. Life expectancy in Sub-Saharan Africa is just 50 years; in Japan it is almost 80. Mortality among children under 5 in South Asia exceeds 170 deaths per thousand; in Sweden it is fewer than 10. More than 110 million children in the developing world lack access even to primary education; in the industrial countries anything less than universal enrollment would rightly be regarded as unacceptable. The starkness of these contrasts attests to the continuing toll of human deprivation.

This Report is about poverty in the developing world—in other words, it is concerned with the poorest of the world's poor. It seeks first to measure poverty, qualitatively as well as quantitatively. It then tries to draw lessons for policy from the experience of countries that have succeeded in reducing poverty. It ends with a question that is also a challenge: what might be achieved if governments in rich and poor countries alike made it their goal to attack poverty in this closing decade of the twentieth century?

Poverty Today

In the countries that have participated in the overall economic progress that has taken place since the 1960s, poverty has declined and the incomes even of those remaining in poverty have increased. In some cases this change has been dramatic. Indonesia, for example, took less than a generation in the 1970s and 1980s to reduce the incidence of poverty from almost 60 percent of the population to less than 20 percent. On a variety of social indicators, some developing countries are now approaching the standards of the developed world. In China, which accounts for a quarter of the developing world's people, life expectancy reached 69 in 1985. But in many countries economic performance was weaker, and the number in poverty fell more slowly. Where rapid population growth was an important additional factor, as in much of Sub-Saharan Africa, consumption per head stagnated and the number in poverty rose.

THINK ON PAPER
Which regions and countries have developed most rapidly in recent years, and which are lagging?

The 1980s—often called a "lost decade" for the poor—did not, in fact, reverse the overall trend of progress. The incomes of most of the world's poor went on rising, and under 5 mortality, primary school enrollment ratios, and other social indicators also continued to improve. The setbacks of the 1980s fell heavily on particular regions. For many in Sub-Saharan Africa and Latin America incomes fell during the decade, and the incidence of poverty increased—although the social indicators, at least in Latin America, proved somewhat more resilient.

The burden of poverty is spread unevenly—among the regions of the developing world, among countries within those regions, and among localities within those countries. Nearly half of the world's poor live in South Asia, a region that accounts for roughly 30 percent of the world's population. Sub-Saharan Africa accounts for a smaller, but still highly disproportionate, share of global poverty. Within regions and countries, the poor are often concentrated in certain places: in rural areas with high population densities, such as the Gangetic Plain of India and the island of Java, Indonesia, or in resource-poor areas such as the Andean highlands and the Sahel. Often the problems of poverty, population, and the environment are intertwined: earlier patterns of development and the pressure of rapidly expanding populations mean that many of the poor live in areas of acute environmental degradation.

Notice that the authors assume that you know your way around the world:

- **Sub-Saharan Africa** (Africa south of the Sahara or "Black Africa")
- **the Gangetic Plain** (River Ganges, India)
- **Java** (Indonesia)
- **the Andean Highlands** (South America)
- **the Sahel** (arid region on southern fringes of the Sahara)

HAVE A MAP HANDY.

The weight of poverty falls most heavily on certain groups. Women in general are disadvantaged. In poor households they often shoulder more of the workload than men, are less educated, and have less access to remunerative activities. Children, too, suffer disproportionately, and the future quality of their lives is compromised by inadequate nutrition, health care, and education. This is especially true for girls: their primary enrollment rates are less than 50 percent in many African countries. The incidence of poverty is often high among ethnic groups and minorities such as the indigenous peoples in Bolivia, Ecuador, Guatemala, Mexico, and Peru and the scheduled castes in India.

"A Day in the Life of Catherine Bana" (Unit 2, Section 3) gives an account of the kind of situation faced by many women in the world, as described at the end of the "Overview" extract.

In many but not all cases low incomes go hand in hand with other forms of deprivation. In Mexico, for example, life expectancy for the poorest 10 percent of the population is twenty years less than for the richest 10 percent. In Côte d'Ivoire the primary enrollment rate of the poorest fifth is half that of the richest. National and regional averages, often bad enough in themselves, mask appallingly low life expectancy and educational attainment among the poorest members of society.

WHAT DO WE KNOW ABOUT THE POOR?

Reducing poverty is the fundamental objective of economic development. It is estimated that in 1985 more than one billion people in the developing world lived in absolute poverty. Clearly, economic development has a long way to go. Knowledge about the poor is essential if governments are to adopt sound development strategies and more effective policies for attacking poverty. How many poor are there? Where do they live? What are their precise economic circumstances? Answering these questions is the first step toward understanding the impact of economic policies on the poor. This chapter draws on a number of detailed household surveys done over the past ten years or so, including some conducted by the World Bank, to estimate the number of poor people and to establish what is known about them.

Three Poor Families

We begin by focusing on the people this Report is intended to help—by telling the stories of three poor families living in three different countries. These families have much in common. For them, the difference between a tolerable quality of life and mere survival depends on their capacity to work and on their opportunities to work. Lack of education, landlessness, and acute vulnerability to illness and seasonal hard times affect all of them to varying degrees. Problems such as these are at the core of poverty.

Rhetorical note: This essay is **descriptive** and **analytical** and also has sections on which the reader could base a *comparison and contrast*—as here, where three poor families, from different parts of the world, are described.

A Poor Subsistence Farmer's Household in Ghana

In Ghana's Savannah region a typical family of seven lives in three one-room huts made from mud bricks, with earthen floors. They have little furniture and no toilet, electricity, or running water. Water is obtained from a stream a fifteen-minute walk away. The family has few possessions, apart from three acres of unirrigated land and one cow, and virtually no savings.

The family raises sorghum, vegetables, and groundnuts on its land. The work is seasonal and physically demanding. At peak periods of tilling, sowing, and harvesting, all family members are involved, including the husband's parents, who are sixty and seventy years old. The soil is very low in quality, but the family lacks access to fertilizer and other modern inputs. Moreover, the region is susceptible to drought; the rains fail two years out of every five. In addition to her farm work, the wife has to fetch water, collect firewood, and feed the family. The market town where the husband sells their meager cash crops and buys essentials is five miles away and is reached by dirt tracks and an unsealed road that is washed away every time the rains come.

None of the older family members ever attended school, but the eight-year-old son is now in the first grade. The family hopes that he will be able to stay in school, although there is pressure to keep him at home to help with the farm in the busy periods. He and his two younger sisters have never had any vaccinations and have never seen a doctor.

A Poor Urban Household in Peru

The Peruvian family is part of a worldwide pattern of internal migration from rural to urban areas that is contributing to the rapid expansion of Third World cities.

In a shantytown on the outskirts of Lima a shack made of scraps of wood, iron, and cardboard houses a family of six. Inside there is a bed, a table, a radio, and two benches. The kitchen consists of a small kerosene stove and some tins in one corner. There is no toilet or electricity. The shantytown is provided with some public services, but these tend to be intermittent. Garbage is collected twice a week. Water is delivered to those who have a cement tank, but this family has been unable to save enough for the cement. In the meantime, the mother and eldest daughter fill buckets at the public standpipe 500 yards away.

Husband and wife are Indians from the same mountain village in the Sierra. Neither completed primary school. They came to Lima with two children almost four years ago, hoping to find work and schools. Although they have jobs, the economic recession of the past few years has hit them hard. Better-off neighbors who arrived in Lima three to six years before they did say that it was easier to get ahead then. Still, husband and wife are hopeful that they will soon be able to rebuild their house with bricks and cement and, in time, install electricity, running water, and a toilet like their neighbors. They now have four children, after losing one infant, and the two oldest attend the local community school, recently built with funds and assistance from a nongovernmental organization (NGO). All the children were given polio and diphtheria-pertussis-tetanus (DPT) inoculations when a mobile clinic came to the shantytown. Community solidarity is strong, and a community center is active in the shantytown.

The father works in construction as a casual laborer. The work is uncertain, and there are periods when he must take any odd job he can find. When he is hired on a construction site, however, it is frequently for a month or so. His wife worries that he will be injured on the job like some of his fellow workers, who can no longer work and yet receive no compensation. She earns some income doing laundry at a wealthy person's house twice a week. To get there she must take a long bus ride, but the job does enable her to look after her one- and three-year-old children. She is also in charge of all domestic chores at home. When she is away from the house for long periods, the two oldest children take morning and afternoon turns at school so as not to leave the house unattended. There have been many burglaries in the neighborhood recently, and although the family has few possessions, radios and kerosene stoves are much in demand. The family lives on rice, bread, and vegetable oil (all subsidized by the government), supplemented with vegetables and, occasionally, some fish.

A Poor Landless Laborer's Household in Bangladesh

In a rural community in a drought-prone region of Bangladesh a landless laborer and his family attempt to get through another lean season.

THINK ON PAPER
These sketches of three families provide a useful model for comparison and contrast essays. Look at each and identify any consistent (or reasonably consistent) pattern in how each family is described.

Their house consists of a packed mud floor and a straw roof held up by bamboo poles from which dry palm leaves are tied to serve as walls. Inside there is straw to sleep on and burlap bags for warmth. The laborer and his wife, three children, and niece do not own the land on which the shack is built. They are lucky, however, to have a kindly neighbor who has indefinitely lent them the plot and a little extra on which they are able to grow turmeric and ginger and have planted a jackfruit tree.

The father is an agricultural day laborer and tends to be underemployed most of the year. During slow agricultural periods in the past he could sometimes find nonagricultural wage labor—for example, in construction in a nearby town—but he lost the strength to do much strenuous work after a bout of paratyphoid. He therefore engages in petty services around the village for very low pay.

(*Text continues on page* 224.)

All countries with more than 1 million population are listed, starting with the poorest country and ending with the richest, as measured by GNP per capita.

The third and fourth columns give basic economic information. The gross national product (GNP) per capita (defined earlier in this section) is the most widely used measure of a country's wealth. The average annual growth rate indicates whether each country is getting richer or poorer. Mozambique's GNP per capita, for example, fell by an average of 3.6% each year between 1980 and 1992.

Life expectancy at birth (1992) is the average age babies born in 1992 can expect to achieve.

TABLE 1 *Basic Indicators*

	Population (millions) mid-1992	Area (thousands of sq. km)	GNP per capita[a] Dollars 1992	GNP per capita[a] Avg. ann growth (%) 1980–92	Avg. annual rate of inflation (%) 1970–80	Avg. annual rate of inflation (%) 1980–92	Life expect. at birth (years) 1992	Adult illiteracy (%) Female 1990	Adult illiteracy (%) Total 1990
Low-income economies	**3,191.3 *t***	**38,929 *t***	**390 *w***	**3.9 *w***	**••**	**12.2 *w***	**62 *w***	**52 *w***	**40 *w***
Excluding China & India	**1,145.6 *t***	**26,080 *t***	**370 *w***	**1.2 *w***	**15.7 *w***	**22.1 *w***	**56 *w***	**56 *w***	**45 *w***
1 Mozambique	16.5	802	60	−3.6	•	38.0	44	79	67
2 Ethiopia	54.8	1,222	110	−1.9	4.3	2.8	49	••	••
3 Tanzania[a]	25.9	945	110	0.0	14.1	25.3	51	••	••
4 Sierra Leone	4.4	72	160	−1.4	12.5	60.8	43	89	79
5 Nepal	19.9	141	170	2.0	8.5	9.2	54	87	74
6 Uganda	17.5	236	170	••	••	••	43	65	52
7 Bhutan	1.5	47	180	6.3	••	8.7	48	75	62
8 Burundi	5.8	28	210	1.3	10.7	4.5	48	60	50
9 Malawi	9.1	118	210	−0.1	8.8	15.1	44	••	••
10 Bangladesh	114.4	144	220	1.8	20.8	9.1	55	78	65
11 Chad	6.0	1,284	220	3.4	7.7	0.9	47	82	70
12 Guinea-Bissau	1.0	36	220	1.6	5.7	59.3	39	76	64
13 Madagascar	12.4	587	230	−2.4	9.9	16.4	51	27	20
14 Lao PDR	4.4	237	250	••	••	••	51	••	••
15 Rwanda	7.3	26	250	−0.6	15.1	3.6	46	63	50
16 Niger	8.2	1,267	280	−4.3	10.9	1.7	46	83	72
17 Burkina Faso	9.5	274	300	1.0	8.6	3.5	48	91	82
18 India	883.6	3,288	310	3.1	8.4	8.5	61	66	52
19 Kenya	25.7	580	310	0.2	10.1	9.3	59	42	31
20 Mali	9.0	1,240	310	−2.7	9.7	3.7	48	76	68
21 Nigeria	101.9	924	320	−0.4	15.2	19.4	52	61	49
22 Nicaragua	3.9	130	340	−5.3	12.8	656.2	67	••	••
23 Togo	3.9	57	390	−1.8	8.9	4.2	55	69	57
24 Benin	5.0	113	410	−0.7	10.3	1.7	51	84	77
25 Central African Republic	3.2	623	410	−1.5	12.1	4.6	47	75	62
26 Pakistan	119.3	796	420	3.1	13.4	7.1	59	79	65
27 Ghana	15.8	239	450	−0.1	35.2	38.7	56	49	40
28 China	1,162.2	9,561	470	7.6	••	6.5	69	38	27
29 Tajikistan[b]	5.6	143	490	••	••	••	69	••	••
30 Guinea	6.1	246	510	••	••	••	44	87	76
31 Mauritania	2.1	1,026	530	−0.8	9.9	8.3	48	79	66
32 Sri Lanka	17.4	66	540	2.6	12.3	11.0	72	17	12
33 Zimbabwe	10.4	391	570	−0.9	9.4	14.4	60	40	33
34 Honduras	5.4	112	580	−0.3	8.1	7.6	66	29	27
35 Lesotho	1.9	30	590	−0.5	9.7	13.2	60	••	••
36 Egypt, Arab Rep.	54.7	1,001	640	1.8	9.6	13.2	62	66	52
37 Indonesia	184.3	1,905	670	4.0	21.5	8.4	60	32	23
38 *Myanmar*	43.7	677	••	••	11.4	14.8	60	28	19
39 *Somalia*	8.3	638	••	••	15.2	49.7	49	86	76
40 *Sudan*	26.5	2,506	••	••	14.5	42.8	52	88	73
41 *Yemen, Rep.*	13.0	528	••	••	••	••	53	74	62
42 *Zambia*	8.3	753	••	••	7.6	48.4	48	35	27
Middle-income economies	**1,418.7 *t***	**62,740 *t***	**2,490 *w***	**−0.1 *w***	**31.0 *w***	**105.2 *w***	**68 *w***	**••**	**••**
Lower-middle-income	**941.0 *t***	**40,903 *t***	**••**	**••**	**23.8 *w***	**40.7 *w***	**67 *w***	**••**	**••**
43 Côte d'Ivoire	12.9	322	670[c]	−4.7	13.0	1.9	56	60	46
44 Bolivia	7.5	1,099	680	−1.5	21.0	220.9	60	29	23
45 Azerbaijan[b]	7.4	87	740	••	••	••	71	••	••
46 Philippines	64.3	300	770	−1.0	13.3	14.1	65	11	10
47 Armenia[b]	3.7	30	780	••	••	••	70	••	••
48 Senegal	7.8	197	780	0.1	8.5	5.2	49	75	62
49 Cameroon	12.2	475	820	−1.5	9.8	3.5	56	57	46
50 Kyrgyz Republic[b]	4.5	199	820	••	••	••	66	••	••
51 Georgia[b]	5.5	70	850	••	••	••	72	••	••
52 Uzbekistan[b]	21.5	447	850	••	••	••	69	••	••
53 Papua New Guinea	4.1	463	950	0.0	9.1	5.1	56	62	48
54 Peru	22.4	1,285	950	−2.8	30.1	311.7	65	21	15
55 Guatemala	9.7	109	980	−1.5	10.5	16.5	65	53	45
56 Congo	2.4	342	1,030	−0.8	8.4	0.5	51	56	43
57 Morocco	26.2	447	1,030	1.4	8.3	6.9	63	62	51
58 Dominican Republic	7.3	49	1,050	−0.5	9.1	25.2	68	18	17
59 Ecuador	11.0	284	1,070	−0.3	13.8	39.5	67	16	14
60 Jordan[d]	3.9	89	1,120	*−5.4*	••	*5.4*	70	30	20
61 Romania	22.7	238	1,130	−1.1	••	13.1	70	••	••
62 El Salvador	5.4	21	1,170	0.0	10.7	17.2	66	30	27
63 Turkmenistan[b]	3.9	488	1,230	••	••	••	66	••	••
64 Moldova[b]	4.4	34	1,300	••	••	••	68	••	••
65 Lithuania[b]	3.8	65	1,310	−1.0	••	20.7	71	••	••
66 Bulgaria	8.5	111	1,330	1.2	••	11.7	71	••	••
67 Colombia	33.4	1,139	1,330	1.4	22.3	25.0	69	14	13
68 Jamaica	2.4	11	1,340	0.2	17.3	21.5	74	1	2
69 Paraguay	4.5	407	1,380	−0.7	12.7	25.2	67	12	10
70 Namibia	1.5	824	1,610	−1.0	••	12.3	59	••	••
71 Kazakhstan[b]	17.0	2,717	1,680	••	••	••	68	••	••
72 Tunisia	8.4	164	1,720	1.3	8.7	7.2	68	44	35

Note: For other economies see Table 1a. For data comparability and coverage, see the Key and the technical notes. Figures in italics are for years other than those specified.

	Population (millions) mid-1992	Area (thousands of sq. km)	GNP per capita[a] Dollars 1992	GNP per capita[a] Avg. ann growth (%) 1980–92	Avg. annual rate of inflation (%) 1970–80	Avg. annual rate of inflation (%) 1980–92	Life expect. at birth (years) 1992	Adult illiteracy (%) Female 1990	Adult illiteracy (%) Total 1990
73 Ukraine[b]	52.1	604	1,820	••	••	••	70	••	••
74 Algeria	26.3	2,382	1,840	−0.5	14.5	11.4	67	55	43
75 Thailand	58.0	513	1,840	6.0	9.2	4.2	69	10	7
76 Poland	38.4	313	1,910	0.1	••	67.9	70	••	••
77 Latvia[b]	2.6	65	1,930	0.2	••	15.3	69	••	••
78 Slovak Republic	5.3	49	1,930	••	••	••	71	••	••
79 Costa Rica	3.2	51	1,960	0.8	15.3	22.5	76	7	7
80 Turkey	58.5	779	1,980	2.9	29.4	46.3	67	29	19
81 Iran, Islamic Rep.	59.6	1,648	2,200	−1.4	••	16.2	65	57	46
82 Panama	2.5	77	2,420	−1.2	7.7	2.1	73	12	12
83 Czech Republic	10.3	79	2,450	••	••	••	72	••	••
84 Russian Federation[b]	149.0	17,075	2,510	••	••	••	69	••	••
85 Chile	13.6	757	2,730[c]	3.7	187.1	20.5	72	7	7
86 *Albania*	3.4	29	••	••	••	••	73	••	••
87 *Mongolia*	2.3	1,567	••	••	••	••	64	••	••
88 *Syrian Arab Rep.*	13.0	185	••	••	11.8	15.5	67	49	36
Upper-middle-income	**477.7 *t***	**21,837 *t***	**4,020 *w***	**0.8 *w***	**34.5 *w***	**154.8 *w***	**69 *w***	**18 *w***	**15 *w***
89 South Africa	39.8	1,221	2,670[c]	0.1	13.0	14.3	63	••	••
90 Mauritius	1.1	2	2,700	5.6	15.3	8.6	70	••	••
91 Estonia[b]	1.6	45	2,760	−2.3	••	20.2	70	••	••
92 Brazil	153.9	8,512	2,770	0.4	38.6	370.2	66	20	19
93 Botswana	1.4	582	2,790	6.1	11.6	12.6	68	35	26
94 Malaysia	18.6	330	2,790	3.2	7.3	2.0	71	30	22
95 Venezuela	20.2	912	2,910	−0.8	14.0	22.7	70	17	8
96 Belarus[b]	10.3	208	2,930	••	••	••	71	••	••
97 Hungary	10.3	93	2,970	0.2	2.8	11.7	69	••	••
98 Uruguay	3.1	177	3,340	−1.0	63.9	66.2	72	4	4
99 Mexico	85.0	1,958	3,470	−0.2	18.1	62.4	70	15	13
100 Trinidad and Tobago	1.3	5	3,940	−2.6	18.5	3.9	71	••	••
101 Gabon	1.2	268	4,450	−3.7	17.5	2.3	54	52	39
102 Argentina	33.1	2,767	6,050	−0.9	134.2	402.3	71	5	5
103 Oman	1.6	212	6,480	4.1	28.0	−2.5	70	••	••
104 Slovenia	2.0	20	6,540	••	••	••	73	••	••
105 Puerto Rico	3.6	9	6,590	0.9	6.5	3.3	74	••	••
106 Korea, Rep.	43.7	99	6,790	8.5	20.1	5.9	71	7	4
107 Greece	10.3	132	7,290	1.0	14.5	17.7	77	11	7
108 Portugal	9.8	92	7,450	3.1	16.7	17.4	74	19	15
109 Saudi Arabia	16.8	2,150	7,510	−3.3	24.9	−1.9	69	52	38
Low- and middle-income	**4,610.1 *t***	**101,669 *t***	**1,040 *w***	**0.9 *w***	**26.2 *w***	**75.7 *w***	**64 *w***	**46 *w***	**36 *w***
Sub-Saharan Africa	**543.0 *t***	**24,274 *t***	**530 *w***	**−0.8 *w***	**13.6 *w***	**15.6 *w***	**52 *w***	**62 *w***	**50 *w***
East Asia & Pacific	**1,688.8 *t***	**16,368 *t***	**760 *w***	**6.1 *w***	**16.6 *w***	**6.7 *w***	**68 *w***	**34 *w***	**24 *w***
South Asia	**1,177.9 *t***	**5,133 *t***	**310 *w***	**3.0 *w***	**9.7 *w***	**8.5 *w***	**60 *w***	**69 *w***	**55 *w***
Europe and Central Asia	**494.5 *t***	**24,370 *t***	**2,080 *w***	**••**	**18.7 *w***	**47.5 *w***	**70 *w***	**••**	**••**
Middle East & N. Africa	**252.6 *t***	**11,015 *t***	**1,950 *w***	**−2.3 *w***	**17.0 *w***	**10.1 *w***	**64 *w***	**57 *w***	**45 *w***
Latin America & Caribbean	**453.2 *t***	**20,507 *t***	**2,690 *w***	**−0.2 *w***	**46.7 *w***	**229.5 *w***	**68 *w***	**18 *w***	**15 *w***
Severely indebted	**504.6 *t***	**22,483 *t***	**2,470 *w***	**−1.0 *w***	**42.1 *w***	**208.0 *w***	**67 *w***	**28 *w***	**23 *w***
High-income economies	**828.1 *t***	**31,709 *t***	**22,160 *w***	**2.3 *w***	**9.1 *w***	**4.3 *w***	**77 *w***	**••**	**••**
110 Ireland	3.5	70	12,210	3.4	14.2	5.3	75	••	••
111 New Zealand	3.4	271	12,300	0.6	12.5	9.4	76	e	e
112 †Israel	5.1	21	13,220	1.9	39.6	78.9	76	••	••
113 Spain	39.1	505	13,970	2.9	16.1	8.7	77	7	5
114 †Hong Kong	5.8	1	15,360[f]	5.5	9.2	7.8	78	••	••
115 †Singapore	2.8	1	15,730	5.3	5.9	2.0	75	••	••
116 Australia	17.5	7,713	17,260	1.6	11.8	6.4	77	e	e
117 United Kingdom	57.8	245	17,790	2.4	14.5	5.7	76	e	e
118 Italy	57.8	301	20,460	2.2	15.6	9.1	77	e	e
119 Netherlands	15.2	37	20,480	1.7	7.9	1.7	77	e	e
120 Canada	27.4	9,976	20,710	1.8	8.7	4.1	78	e	e
121 Belgium	10.0	31	20,880	2.0	7.8	4.1	76	e	e
122 Finland	5.0	338	21,970	2.0	12.3	6.0	75	e	e
123 †United Arab Emirates	1.7	84	22,020	−4.3	••	0.8	72	e	e
124 France	57.4	552	22,260	1.7	10.2	5.4	77	e	e
125 Austria	7.9	84	22,380	2.0	6.5	3.6	77	e	e
126 Germany	80.6	357	23,030	2.4[g]	5.1[g]	2.7[g]	76	e	e
127 United States	255.4	9,373	23,240	1.7	7.5	3.9	77	e	e
128 Norway	4.3	324	25,820	2.2	8.4	4.9	77	e	e
129 Denmark	5.2	43	26,000	2.1	10.1	4.9	75	e	e
130 Sweden	8.7	450	27,010	1.5	10.0	7.2	78	e	e
131 Japan	124.5	378	28,190	3.6	8.5	1.5	79	e	e
132 Switzerland	6.9	41	36,080	1.4	5.0	3.8	78	e	e
World	**5,438.2 *t***	**133,378 *t***	**4,280 *w***	**1.2 *w***	**11.6 *w***	**17.2 *w***	**66 *w***	**45 *w***	**35 *w***

†Economies classified by the United Nations or otherwise regarded by their authorities as developing. a. In all tables GDP and GNP data cover mainland Tanzania only. b. Estimates for economies of the former Soviet Union are subject to more than usual range of uncertainty and should be regarded as very preliminary. c. Data reflect recent revision of 1992 GNP per capita: from $700 to $670 for Côte d'Ivoire, from $2,510 to $2,730 for Chile, and from $2,700 to $2,670 for South Africa. d. In all tables, data for Jordan cover the East Bank only. e. According to UNESCO, illiteracy is less than 5 percent. f. Data refer to GDP. g. Data refer to the Federal Republic of Germany before unification.

Reports of a "world population crisis" reflect concern over figures like these in Table 25. Look, for example, at Nigeria (#21), whose population is expected to more than double between 1992 and 2025.

Average annual growth rates of more than 3% are very high. Compare the annual growth rates of the poorest countries with those of the richest countries.

TABLE 25 *Population and Labor Force*

	Population[a]								Labor force[a]			
	Total (millions)			Hypothetical stationary pop. (millions)	Average annual growth (%)			Age 15–64 (millions)	Total (millions)	Average annual growth (%)		
	1992	2000	2025		1970–80	1980–92	1992–2000	1992	1992	1970–80	1980–92	1992–2000
Low-income economics	**3,191** *t*	**3,654** t	**5,062** *t*	**7,600** t	**2.2** *w*	**2.0** w	**1.7** *w*	**1,934** t	**1,475** *t*	**2.2** w	**2.2** *w*	**1.7** w
Excluding China & India	**1,146** *t*	**1,382** t	**2,220** *t*	**4,032** t	**2.6** *w*	**2.6** w	**2.3** *w*	**631** t	**441** *t*	**2.3** w	**2.5** *w*	**2.5** w
1 Mozambique	17	20	40	100	2.5	2.6	2.6	9	9	3.8	2.0	2.0
2 Ethiopia	55[b]	67	141	370	2.6	3.1	2.6	26	22	2.0	1.9	2.2
3 Tanzania	26	33	59	117	2.9	3.0	3.0	13	13	2.8	2.9	3.0
4 Sierra Leone	4	5	10	23	2.1	2.4	2.6	2	1	1.0	1.2	1.5
5 Nepal	20	24	38	65	2.5	2.6	2.4	11	8	1.8	2.3	2.2
6 Uganda	17	22	45	121	2.7	2.6	3.0	9	9	2.6	2.8	3.0
7 Bhutan	1[b]	2	3	6	1.8	2.1	2.4	1	1	1.8	1.9	1.9
8 Burundi	6	7	14	31	1.6	2.8	2.7	3	3	1.3	2.2	2.5
9 Malawi	9	11	21	51	3.1	3.2	2.5	5	4	2.2	2.6	2.6
10 Bangladesh	114	132	182	263	2.6	2.3	1.8	63	36	2.0	2.9	2.9
11 Chad	6	7	14	29	2.0	2.4	2.6	3	2	1.7	1.9	2.1
12 Guinea-Bissau	1	1	2	4	4.3	1.9	2.0	1	0	3.8	1.3	1.6
13 Madagascar	12	16	26	49	2.6	2.9	2.8	6	5	2.2	2.1	2.3
14 Lao PDR	4	6	10	20	1.7	2.6	2.8	2	2	1.3	2.0	2.1
15 Rwanda	7	9	13	22	3.3	2.9	2.1	4	4	3.1	2.8	2.9
16 Niger	8	11	24	71	2.9	3.3	3.3	4	4	1.9	2.4	2.6
17 Burkina Faso	10	12	24	56	2.1	2.6	3.0	5	4	1.7	2.0	2.2
18 India	884	1,016	1,370	1,888	2.3	2.1	1.7	527	336	1.7	2.0	1.7
19 Kenya	26	31	47	75	3.7	3.6	2.5	13	11	3.6	3.5	3.6
20 Mali	9	12	24	57	2.1	2.6	3.2	4	3	1.7	2.6	2.7
21 Nigeria	102	128	217	382	2.9	3.0	2.8	52	44	3.1	2.7	2.9
22 Nicaragua	4[b]	5	8	12	3.1	2.7	2.7	2	1	2.9	3.8	3.8
23 Togo	4	5	10	20	2.6	3.3	3.1	2	1	2.0	2.3	2.5
24 Benin	5	6	11	20	2.7	3.1	2.8	3	2	2.0	2.2	2.5
25 Central African Republic	3	4	7	18	2.2	2.6	2.5	2	1	1.2	1.5	1.8
26 Pakistan	119[b]	148	243	400	3.1	3.1	2.7	63	36	2.7	2.9	2.9
27 Ghana	16	20	36	68	2.2	3.2	3.0	8	6	2.4	2.7	3.0
28 China	1,162	1,255	1,471	1,680	1.8	1.4	1.0	780	699	2.4	2.0	1.1
29 Tajikistan	6	7	11	18	••	2.8	2.5	3	••	••	••	••
30 Guinea	6[b]	8	15	33	1.5	2.6	2.8	3	3	1.8	1.7	1.9
31 Mauritania	2	3	5	11	2.4	2.4	2.8	1	1	1.8	2.8	3.1
32 Sri Lanka	17	19	24	29	1.6	1.4	1.1	11	7	2.3	1.6	1.6
33 Zimbabwe	10	12	18	28	2.9	3.3	2.1	5	4	2.8	2.8	3.0
34 Honduras	5	7	11	18	3.3	3.3	2.8	3	2	3.1	3.8	3.7
35 Lesotho	2	2	3	6	2.3	2.7	2.3	1	1	2.0	2.0	2.1
36 Egypt, Arab Rep.	55	63	86	121	2.1	2.4	1.7	31	15	2.1	2.6	2.7
37 Indonesia	184	206	265	355	2.3	1.8	1.4	111	75	2.1	2.4	2.0
38 *Myanmar*	44[b]	52	73	109	2.2	2.1	2.1	25	19	2.2	1.9	1.7
39 *Somalia*	8[b]	10	21	47	2.9	3.1	2.9	4	2	3.7	1.7	1.9
40 *Sudan*	27[b]	33	57	108	2.9	2.7	2.7	14	9	2.6	2.9	3.1
41 *Yemen, Rep.*	13	17	36	88	2.6	3.8	3.3	6	3	1.1	3.0	3.4
42 *Zambia*	8	10	17	35	3.0	3.2	2.8	4	3	2.7	3.3	3.5
Middle-income economies	**1,419** *t*	**1,595** t	**2,139** *t*	**2,976** t	**3.1** *w*	**1.8** w	**1.5** *w*	**873** t	**433** *t*	**2.5** w	**2.2** *w*	**2.8** w
Lower-middle-income	**941** *t*	**1,055** t	**1,422** *t*	**2,011** t	**3.5** *w*	**1.8** w	**1.4** *w*	**578** t	**257** *t*	**2.3** w	**2.2** *w*	**3.3** w
43 Côte d'Ivoire	13	17	34	74	4.0	3.8	3.5	6	5	2.5	2.6	2.5
44 Bolivia	8	9	14	22	2.5	2.5	2.4	4	2	2.1	2.7	2.6
45 Azerbaijan	7	8	11	13	••	1.5	1.2	5	••	••	••	••
46 Philippines	64	77	115	172	2.5	2.4	2.3	37	24	2.4	2.5	2.3
47 Armenia	4	4	5	6	••	1.4	1.1	2	••	••	••	••
48 Senegal	8	10	16	30	2.9	2.9	2.6	4	3	3.2	1.9	2.1
49 Cameroon	12	16	28	54	2.9	2.8	3.0	6	5	1.5	1.9	2.3
50 Kyrgyz Republic	4	5	7	10	••	1.8	1.2	3	••	••	••	••
51 Georgia	5	5	6	7	••	0.6	0.0	4	••	••	••	••
52 Uzbekistan	21	26	39	57	••	2.5	2.2	12	••	••	••	••
53 Papua New Guinea	4	5	7	12	2.4	2.3	2.3	2	2	1.9	1.5	1.0
54 Peru	22[b]	26	36	48	2.7	2.1	1.8	13	8	3.3	2.8	2.7
55 Guatemala	10	12	20	33	2.8	2.9	2.8	5	3	2.1	3.0	3.3
56 Congo	2[b]	3	6	15	2.8	3.1	3.2	1	1	2.1	2.0	2.4
57 Morocco	26[b]	30	43	61	2.4	2.5	1.8	15	8	3.4	3.2	2.9
58 Dominican Republic	7[b]	8	11	14	2.5	2.1	1.5	4	2	3.1	3.3	2.7
59 Ecuador	11	13	18	25	2.9	2.5	2.0	6	3	2.6	3.0	2.7
60 Jordan	4	5	9	14	3.7	4.9	3.4	2	1	1.0	4.3	4.0
61 Romania	23	23	23	23	0.9	0.2	0.0	15	12	0.0	0.7	0.7
62 El Salvador	5	6	9	13	2.3	1.4	1.7	3	2	2.9	3.1	3.1
63 Turkmenistan	4	5	7	10	••	2.5	2.1	2	••	••	••	••
64 Moldova	4	4	5	6	••	0.7	0.2	3	••	••	••	••
65 Lithuania	4	4	4	4	••	0.7	0.0	2	2	••	••	••
66 Bulgaria	9	8	8	7	0.4	−0.3	−0.4	6	4	0.1	0.0	0.3
67 Colombia	33	37	49	62	2.2	1.9	1.4	20	11	2.5	2.6	2.2
68 Jamaica	2	3	3	4	1.3	1.0	0.6	1	1	2.9	2.7	2.2
69 Paraguay	5	6	10	17	2.9	3.0	2.8	3	1	3.5	3.0	2.7
70 Namibia	2	2	3	5	2.7	3.0	2.6	1	1	1.8	2.4	2.7
71 Kazakhstan	17	18	22	28	••	1.1	0.7	11	••	••	••	••
72 Tunisia	8	10	14	20	2.2	2.3	2.2	5	3	3.6	3.0	2.6

Note: For data comparability and coverage, see the Key and the technical notes. Figures in italics are for years other than those specified.

	Population[a]								Labor force[a]			
	Total (millions)			Hypothetical stationary pop. (millions)	Average annual growth (%)			Age 15–64 (millions)	Total (millions)	Average annual growth (%)		
	1992	2000	2025		1970–80	1980–92	1992–2000	1992	1992	1970–80	1980–92	1992–2000
73 Ukraine	52	52	53	56	••	0.3	0.0	34	••	••	••	••
74 Algeria	26	31	47	67	3.1	2.8	2.2	14	6	3.2	3.7	3.6
75 Thailand	58	65	81	104	2.7	1.8	1.3	37	31	2.8	2.2	1.5
76 Poland	38	39	42	46	0.9	0.6	0.2	25	20	0.7	0.6	0.8
77 Latvia	3	3	3	3	••	0.3	−0.4	2	1	••	−0.1	••
78 Slovak Republic	5	6	6	7	0.9	0.5	0.6	3	2	••	••	••
79 Costa Rica	3[b]	4	5	6	2.8	2.8	1.9	2	1	3.8	2.7	2.3
80 Turkey	59	68	92	122	2.3	2.3	1.9	35	25	1.7	2.1	1.9
81 Iran, Islamic Rep.	60	75	126	204	3.2	3.5	2.8	30	16	3.1	3.2	3.1
82 Panama	3	3	4	5	2.4	2.1	1.7	2	1	2.4	2.8	2.3
83 Czech Republic	10	11	11	12	0.5	0.1	0.2	7	••	••	••	••
84 Russian Federation	149	150	153	160	0.6	0.6	0.1	99	••	••	••	••
85 Chile	14	15	19	23	1.6	1.7	1.3	9	5	2.4	2.2	1.5
86 *Albania*	3	4	5	6	2.2	1.9	1.5	2	2	3.0	2.7	2.2
87 *Mongolia*	2	3	4	7	2.8	2.7	2.6	1	1	2.8	2.9	2.7
88 *Syrian Arab Rep.*	13	17	34	66	3.3	3.3	3.3	6	3	3.4	3.6	4.0
Upper-middle-income	**478 *t***	**540 *t***	**717 *t***	**965 *t***	**2.5 *w***	**1.8 *w***	**1.5 *w***	**295 *t***	**176 *t***	**2.9 *w***	**2.3 *w***	**2.1 *w***
89 South Africa	40	47	69	103	2.7	2.5	2.2	23	13	1.3	2.8	2.7
90 Mauritius	1	1	1	2	1.5	1.1	1.0	1	0	2.5	2.7	1.9
91 Estonia	2	2	2	2	0.8	0.4	−0.3	1	1	••	−0.5	••
92 Brazil	154	172	224	285	2.4	2.0	1.4	95	58	3.4	2.2	2.1
93 Botswana	1	2	3	4	3.7	3.4	2.8	1	0	3.0	3.3	3.3
94 Malaysia	19	22	30	41	2.4	2.5	2.0	11	7	3.7	2.8	2.5
95 Venezuela	20	24	34	45	3.4	2.6	2.2	12	7	4.8	3.2	2.8
96 Belarus	10	10	11	12	••	0.5	0.2	7	••	••	••	••
97 Hungary	10	10	9	10	0.4	−0.3	−0.4	7	5	−0.5	0.2	0.3
98 Uruguay	3	3	4	4	0.4	0.6	0.5	2	1	0.2	0.7	1.0
99 Mexico	85	99	136	182	2.9	2.0	1.9	50	32	4.3	3.1	2.7
100 Trinidad and Tobago	1	1	2	2	1.1	1.3	0.9	1	1	2.2	2.3	2.0
101 Gabon	1[b]	2	3	7	4.6	3.4	2.9	1	1	0.8	0.7	1.1
102 Argentina	33	36	43	53	1.6	1.3	1.0	20	12	1.0	1.2	1.6
103 Oman	2	2	5	12	4.1	4.3	4.1	1	0	4.5	3.5	2.8
104 Slovenia	2	2	2	2	0.9	0.5	0.1	1	••	••	••	••
105 Puerto Rico	4	4	4	5	1.7	0.9	0.7	2	1	2.3	2.1	1.6
106 Korea, Rep.	44	47	53	56	1.8	1.1	0.8	31	19	2.6	2.3	1.8
107 Greece	10	11	11	9	0.9	0.5	0.5	7	4	0.7	0.4	0.2
108 Portugal	10	10	10	9	0.8	0.1	0.0	7	5	2.5	0.9	0.8
109 Saudi Arabia	17	22	43	85	4.9	4.9	3.3	9	4	5.5	3.9	3.2
Low- and middle-income	**4,610 *t***	**5,248 *t***	**7,201 *t***	**10,576 *t***	**2.5 *w***	**1.9 *w***	**1.6 *w***	**2,807 *t***	**1,908 *t***	**2.3 *w***	**2.2 *w***	**1.9 *w***
Sub-Saharan Africa	**543 *t***	**681 *t***	**1,229 *t***	**2,565 *t***	**2.8 *w***	**3.0 *w***	**2.8 *w***	**287 *t***	**222 *t***	**2.4 *w***	**2.5 *w***	**2.7 *w***
East Asia & Pacific	**1,689 *t***	**1,858 *t***	**2,280 *t***	**2,792 *t***	**1.9 *w***	**1.6 *w***	**1.2 *w***	**1,101 *t***	**928 *t***	**2.4 *w***	**2.1 *w***	**1.8 *w***
South Asia	**1,178 *t***	**1,369 *t***	**1,913 *t***	**2,778 *t***	**2.4 *w***	**2.2 *w***	**1.9 *w***	**682 *t***	**429 *t***	**1.8 *w***	**2.1 *w***	**1.9 *w***
Europe and Central Asia	**495 *t***	**516 *t***	**581 *t***	**672 *t***	**4.3 *w***	**1.0 *w***	**0.5 *w***	**326 *t***	**94 *t***	**1.4 *w***	**1.1 *w***	**0.2 *w***
Middle East & N. Africa	**253 *t***	**309 *t***	**509 *t***	**856 *t***	**2.8 *w***	**3.1 *w***	**2.5 *w***	**135 *t***	**69 *t***	**3.0 *w***	**3.2 *w***	**3.2 *w***
Latin America & Caribbean	**453 *t***	**515 *t***	**690 *t***	**913 *t***	**2.4 *w***	**2.0 *w***	**1.6 *w***	**276 *t***	**166 *t***	**3.1 *w***	**2.5 *w***	**2.3 *w***
Severely indebted	**505 *t***	**579 *t***	**815 *t***	**1,191 *t***	**2.3 *w***	**2.0 *w***	**1.7 *w***	**302 *t***	**187 *t***	**2.7 *w***	**2.3 *w***	**2.2 *w***
High-income economies	**828 *t***	**865 *t***	**922 *t***	**903 *t***	**0.8 *w***	**0.7 *w***	**0.5 *w***	**555 *t***	**380 *t***	**1.3 *w***	**0.6 *w***	**0.4 *w***
110 Ireland	4	4	4	5	1.4	0.4	0.6	2	2	1.1	1.6	1.5
111 New Zealand	3	4	4	5	1.0	0.8	0.8	2	2	1.9	1.5	1.0
112 †Israel	5	6	8	9	2.7	2.3	2.2	3	2	2.8	2.2	1.9
113 Spain	39	39	38	32	1.0	0.4	0.0	26	15	0.8	1.1	0.7
114 †Hong Kong	6	6	6	5	2.5	1.2	0.6	4	3	4.3	2.0	1.2
115 †Singapore	3	3	4	4	2.0	1.8	1.4	2	1	4.3	1.4	0.6
116 Australia	17	19	23	24	1.6	1.4	1.2	12	8	2.3	1.6	1.2
117 United Kingdom	58	59	61	60	0.1	0.2	0.2	38	28	0.5	0.3	0.1
118 Italy	58	58	54	43	0.5	0.2	0.0	40	23	0.5	0.5	−0.1
119 Netherlands	15	16	16	15	0.8	0.6	0.5	10	6	1.5	1.1	0.2
120 Canada	27	30	34	35	1.2	1.1	0.9	18	14	3.1	1.1	0.8
121 Belgium	10	10	10	9	0.2	0.2	0.1	7	4	0.9	0.4	0.0
122 Finland	5	5	5	5	0.4	0.5	0.3	3	3	0.8	0.6	0.2
123 †United Arab Emirates	2[b]	2	3	4	15.6	4.0	2.0	1	1	17.2	3.6	1.8
124 France	57	59	63	62	0.6	0.5	0.4	38	26	0.9	0.7	0.4
125 Austria	8	8	8	7	0.2	0.4	0.4	5	4	0.8	0.5	0.0
126 Germany	81	81	75	62	0.1	0.2	0.1	55	39	0.6	−1.5	−0.5
127 United States	255	276	323	348	1.1	1.0	1.0	168	124	2.3	1.0	0.8
128 Norway	4	4	5	5	0.5	0.4	0.4	3	2	2.0	0.8	0.5
129 Denmark	5	5	5	5	0.4	0.1	0.2	4	3	1.3	0.5	0.0
130 Sweden	9	9	9	10	0.3	0.4	0.4	6	4	1.1	0.4	0.2
131 Japan	124	127	124	108	1.1	0.5	0.2	86	63	0.7	0.8	0.3
132 Switzerland	7	7	7	7	0.1	0.7	0.6	5	3	0.3	0.4	−0.2
World	**5,438 *t***	**6,113 *t***	**8,122 *t***	**11,479 *t***	**2.2 *w***	**1.7 *w***	**1.5 *w***	**3,361 *t***	**2,288 *t***	**2.1 *w***	**1.9 *w***	**1.7 *w***

a. For the assumptions used in the projections, see the technical notes. b. Based on census data or a demographic estimate 5 years or older; timing is only one element of data quality. See the Key for the latest census year.

Infant mortality rate is one of the most widely used measures of the quality of a country's health care services. It measures the deaths before the age of one year per 1,000 live births. The child death rate does the same thing for children under the age of five years. The U.S. figure (#127) is low by world standards but high compared with that of other rich countries. One problem is uneven access to health care; the infant mortality rate in some rural and inner city areas of the United States is higher than the rate in many Third World countries.

TABLE 27 *Health and Nutrition*

	Population per				Low birthweight babies (%)	Infant mortality rate (per 1,000 live births)		Prevalence of malnutrition (under 5)	Under-5 mortality rate 1992 (per 1,000 live births)	
	Physician		Nursing person							
	1970	1990	1970	1990	1990	1970	1992	1987–92	Female	Male
Low-income economies	**8,860 *w***	**••**	**5,580 *w***	**••**		**114 *w***	**73 *w***		**102 *w***	**114 *w***
Excluding China & India	**22,380 *w***	**11,190 *w***	**11,580 *w***	**2,690 *w***		**139 *w***	**91 *w***		**137 *w***	**154 *w***
1 Mozambique	18,860	••	*4,280*	••	20	156	162[a]	••	269	283
2 Ethiopia	86,120	*32,500*	••	••	16	158	122	••	194	216
3 Tanzania	22,600	*24,970*	*3,310*	*5,490*	14	132	92	25.2	139	158
4 Sierra Leone	17,830	••	2,700	••	17	197	143[a]	••	229	253
5 Nepal	51,360	*16,830*	*17,700*	*2,760*	••	157	99[a]	••	145	139
6 Uganda	9,210	••	••	••	••	109	122	23.3	194	216
7 Bhutan	••	13,110	••	••	••	182	129	••	195	187
8 Burundi	58,570	••	*6,870*	••	••	138	106[a]	31.0	165	185
9 Malawi	76,580	*45,740*	*5,330*	*1,800*	20	193	134	••	215	238
10 Bangladesh	8,450	••	*65,780*	••	50	140	91	66.5	132	127
11 Chad	61,900	*30,030*	*8,010*	••	••	171	122[a]	••	194	216
12 Guinea-Bissau	17,500	••	*2,820*	••	20	185	140[a]	••	224	248
13 Madagascar	10,110	8,120	*240*	••	10	181	93	••	141	160
14 Lao PDR	15,160	*4,380*	*1,390*	*490*	18	146	97	••	149	168
15 Rwanda	59,600	40,610	5,610	2,330	17	142	117[a]	••	185	206
16 Niger	60,090	*34,850*	*5,610*	*650*	16	170	123	••	196	218
17 Burkina Faso	97,120	57,310	••	*1,680*	21	178	132[a]	45.5	186	205
18 India	4,890	*2,460*	*3,710*	••	33	137	79	63.0	108	104
19 Kenya	8,000	10,150	*2,520*	••	16	102	66	18.0	95	110
20 Mali	44,090	*19,450*	*2,590*	*1,890*	17	204	130[a]	25.1	189	212
21 Nigeria	19,830	••	*4,240*	••	15	139	84	35.7	174	192
22 Nicaragua	2,150	1,460	••	••	15	106	56[a]	••	68	75
23 Togo	28,860	••	*1,590*	••	20	134	85	24.4	127	145
24 Benin	28,570	••	*2,600*	••	••	155	110[a]	35.0	172	193
25 Central African Republic	44,020	25,890	*2,450*	••	15	139	105[a]	••	163	183
26 Pakistan	4,310	*2,940*	*6,600*	*5,040*	25	142	95	40.4	129	142
27 Ghana	12,910	22,970	*690*	*1,670*	17	111	81	27.1	120	138
28 China	1,500	••	*2,500*	••	9	69	31	21.3	32	43
29 Tajikistan	••	*350*	••	••	••	••	49	••	57	70
30 Guinea	50,010	••	*3,720*	••	21	181	133[a]	••	213	237
31 Mauritania	17,960	••	*3,740*	••	11	165	117[a]	30.0	186	207
32 Sri Lanka	5,900	••	*1,280*	••	25	53	18	36.6	19	24
33 Zimbabwe	6,300	*7,110*	*640*	*990*	••	96	47	10.0	53	66
34 Honduras	3,770	3,090	*1,470*	••	9	110	49	20.6	57	70
35 Lesotho	30,400	••	*3,860*	••	11	134	46	••	61	73
36 Egypt, Arab Rep.	1,900	*1,320*	*2,320*	*490*	10	158	57	10.4	80	93
37 Indonesia	26,820	7,030	*4,810*	••	14	118	66	39.9	82	98
38 *Myanmar*	8,820	*12,900*	*3,060*	*1,240*	16	121	72[a]	32.4	91	108
39 *Somalia*	32,660	••	••	••	16	158	132[a]	••	186	205
40 *Sudan*	14,520	••	990	••	15	149	99	••	152	171
41 *Yemen, Rep.*	34,790	••	••	••	19	175	106	30.0	144	162
42 *Zambia*	13,640	*10,920*	*1,730*	*580*	13	106	107	25.1	167	187
Middle-income economies	**3,800 *w***	**2,020 *w***	**1,720 *w***	**••**		**••**	**43 *w***		**51 *w***	**61 *w***
Lower-middle-income	**••**	**2,230 *w***	**••**	**••**		**••**	**45 *w***		**54 *w***	**64 *w***
43 Côte d'Ivoire	15,520	••	*1,930*	••	14	135	91[a]	12.4	121	138
44 Bolivia	2,020	••	*3,070*	••	12	153	82	11.4	106	115
45 Azerbaijan	••	*250*	••	••	••	••	32	••	33	44
46 Philippines	9,270	8,120	*2,690*	••	15	66	40	33.5	44	56
47 Armenia	••	*260*	••	••	••	••	21	••	21	29
48 Senegal	15,810	17,650	*1,670*	••	11	135	68	••	98	113
49 Cameroon	28,920	*12,190*	*2,560*	*1,690*	13	126	61	13.6	109	124
50 Kyrgyz Republic	••	*280*	••	••	••	••	37	••	40	52
51 Georgia	••	170	••	••	••	••	19	••	19	27
52 Uzbekistan	••	*290*	••	••	••	••	42	••	47	59
53 Papua New Guinea	11,640	*12,870*	*1,710*	*1,180*	23	112	54[a]	••	64	78
54 Peru	1,920	960	••	••	11	108	52	10.8	61	75
55 Guatemala	3,660	••	••	••	14	100	62[a]	28.5	76	84
56 Congo	9,940	••	*810*	••	16	126	114[a]	23.5	157	175
57 Morocco	13,090	*4,840*	••	*1,050*	9	128	57	11.8	69	84
58 Dominican Republic	••	••	*1,400*	••	16	90	41	10.4	49	54
59 Ecuador	2,910	*980*	*2,680*	*620*	11	100	45	16.5	51	64
60 Jordan	2,480	*770*	*870*	*500*	*7*	••	28	6.4	32	41
61 Romania	840	*560*	*430*	••	*7*	49	23	••	24	32
62 El Salvador	4,100	••	*890*	••	11	103	40	15.5	47	52
63 Turkmenistan	••	*290*	••	••	••	••	54	••	64	78
64 Moldova	••	*250*	••	••	••	••	23	••	23	32
65 Lithuania	••	*220*	••	••	••	••	16	••	16	23
66 Bulgaria	540	320	*240*	••	6	27	16	••	17	22
67 Colombia	2,260	••	••	••	10	74	21	10.1	21	29
68 Jamaica	2,630	••	*530*	••	11	43	14	7.2	15	19
69 Paraguay	2,300	*1,250*	*2,210*	••	8	57	36	3.7	38	49
70 Namibia	••	*4,610*	••	••	12	118	57	••	79	92
71 Kazakhstan	••	*250*	••	••	••	••	31	••	32	43
72 Tunisia	5,930	*1,870*	*940*	*300*	8	121	48	7.8	51	63

Note: For data comparability and coverage, see the Key and the technical notes. Figures in italics are for years other than those specified.

	Population per				Low birthweight babies (%)	Infant mortality rate (per 1,000 live births)		Prevalence of malnutrition (under 5)	Under-5 mortality rate 1992 (per 1,000 live births)	
	Physician		Nursing person							
	1970	1990	1970	1990	1990	1970	1992	1987–92	Female	Male
73 Ukraine	••	230	••	••	••	••	18	••	17	25
74 Algeria	8,100	2,330	••	*330*	9	139	55	9.2	66	80
75 Thailand	8,290	4,360	*1,170*	960	13	73	26	13.0	26	36
76 Poland	700	*490*	*250*	••	••	33	14	••	14	20
77 Latvia	••	200	••	••	••	23	17	••	17	25
78 Slovak Republic	••	280	••	••	••	25	13	••	13	18
79 Costa Rica	1,620	*1,030*	*460*	••	6	62	14	••	15	19
80 Turkey	2,230	*1,260*	*1,010*	••	8	147	54	••	66	72
81 Iran, Islamic Rep.	3,270	*3,140*	*1,780*	*1,150*	9	131	65	••	81	88
82 Panama	1,660	*840*	*1,560*	••	10	47	21[a]	••	23	28
83 Czech Republic	••	••	••	••	••	21	10	••	10	14
84 Russian Federation	••	*210*	••	••	••	••	20	••	20	28
85 Chile	2,160	*2,150*	*460*	*340*	7	78	17	••	18	24
86 *Albania*	1,070	••	*230*	••	7	66	32	••	37	42
87 *Mongolia*	580	380	*250*	••	10	102	60	••	73	88
88 *Syrian Arab Rep.*	3,860	1,160	*1,790*	*870*	11	96	36	••	38	50
Upper-middle-income	**1,910 w**	**1,140 w**	**2,090 w**	••		**70 w**	**40 w**		**46 w**	**55 w**
89 South Africa	••	*1,750*	*300*	••	••	79	53[a]	••	63	77
90 Mauritius	4,190	1,180	*610*	••	9	60	18	••	20	25
91 Estonia	••	*210*	••	••	••	20	13	••	13	18
92 Brazil	2,030	••	*4,140*	••	11	95	57[a]	7.1	70	76
93 Botswana	15,220	5,150	*1,900*	••	8	101	35	15.0	37	49
94 Malaysia	4,310	*2,590*	*1,270*	*380*	10	45	14	••	14	20
95 Venezuela	1,120	590	*440*	350	9	53	33	5.9	35	43
96 Belarus	••	*250*	••	••	••	••	15	••	15	21
97 Hungary	510	340	*210*	••	9	36	15	••	15	21
98 Uruguay	910	••	••	••	8	46	20	7.4	20	28
99 Mexico	1,480	••	1,610	••	12	72	35[a]	13.9	37	49
100 Trinidad and Tobago	2,250	••	*190*	••	10	52	15	5.9	15	21
101 Gabon	5,250	••	*570*	••	••	138	94[a]	25.0	143	162
102 Argentina	530	••	*960*	••	8	52	29	••	33	38
103 Oman	8,380	1,060	*3,420*	*400*	10	119	20	••	20	28
104 Slovenia	••	••	••	••	••	••	8	••	9	12
105 Puerto Rico	••	••	••	••	••	29	13	••	14	18
106 Korea, Rep.	2,220	1,070	*1,190*	510	9	51	13	••	13	18
107 Greece	620	*580*	*990*	••	6	30	8	••	9	12
108 Portugal	1,110	*490*	*820*	••	5	56	9	••	10	13
109 Saudi Arabia	7,460	*700*	*2,070*	*450*	7	119	28	••	29	38
Low- and middle-income	**7,630 w**	**4,810 w**	**4,700 w**	••		••	**65 w**		**99 w**	**88 w**
Sub-Saharan Africa	**31,720 w**	**19,690 w**	**3,160 w**	••		**142 w**	**99 w**		**160 w**	**179 w**
East Asia & Pacific	**5,090 w**	••	**2,720 w**	••		**84 w**	**39 w**		**43 w**	**55 w**
South Asia	**6,120 w**	**2,930 w**	**10,150 w**	••		**138 w**	**85 w**		**111 w**	**122 w**
Europe and Central Asia	••	**410 w**	••	••		••	**30 w**		**34 w**	**41 w**
Middle East & N. Africa	**6,410 w**	**2,240 w**	**1,940 w**	**670 w**		**139 w**	**58 w**		**72 w**	**84 w**
Latin America & Caribbean	**2,020 w**	••	**2,640 w**	••		**85 w**	**44 w**		**52 w**	**61 w**
Severely indebted	**3,460 w**	**2,250 w**	**2,340 w**	••		**86 w**	**52 w**		**65 w**	**76 w**
High-income economies	*710 w*	**420 w**	*220 w*	••		**20 w**	**7 w**		**8 w**	**11 w**
110 Ireland	980	*630*	*160*	••	4	20	5	••	6	7
111 New Zealand	870	••	*150*	••	6	17	7	••	8	11
112 †Israel	410	••	••	••	7	25	9	••	10	13
113 Spain	750	*280*	••	••	4	28	8	••	9	11
114 †Hong Kong	1,510	••	*560*	••	8	19	6	••	7	9
115 †Singapore	1,370	*820*	*250*	••	7	20	5	••	6	7
116 Australia	830	••	••	••	6	18	7	••	8	10
117 United Kingdom	810	••	*240*	••	7	19	7	••	8	10
118 Italy	550	210	••	••	5	30	8	••	9	12
119 Netherlands	800	410	*300*	••	••	13	6	••	7	9
120 Canada	680	*450*	*140*	••	6	19	7	••	8	10
121 Belgium	650	*310*	••	••	6	21	9	••	10	13
122 Finland	960	410	*130*	••	4	13	6	••	7	9
123 †United Arab Emirates	1,100	*1,040*	••	*550*	6	87	20[a]	••	22	27
124 France	750	*350*	*270*	••	5	18	7	••	8	11
125 Austria	540	*230*	*300*	••	6	26	7	••	9	11
126 Germany	580[b]	*370*[b]	••	••	••	23	6	••	7	9
127 United States	630	*420*	*160*	••	7	20	9	••	9	12
128 Norway	720	••	*160*	••	4	13	6	••	7	9
129 Denmark	690	*390*	••	••	6	14	7	••	7	9
130 Sweden	730	*370*	*140*	••	5	11	5	••	6	8
131 Japan	890	*610*	*310*	••	6	13	5	••	5	7
132 Switzerland	700	*630*	••	••	5	15	6	••	7	9
World	**6,180 w**	**3,850 w**	**3,980 w**	••		**97 w**	**60 w**		**81 w**	**92 w**

a. Based on a demographic estimate 5 years or older; timing is only one element of data quality. See the Key for the latest year. b. Data refer to the Federal Republic of Germany before unification.

Gender comparisons show that women, on average, live longer than men almost everywhere, but that female access to education and paid employment is limited in many countries.

Considerable progress is evident in many countries in expanding access to education, especially at the primary (elementary) level.

TABLE 29 *Gender Comparisons*

	Health					Education									Employment	
	Life expectancy at birth (years)				Maternal mortality per 100,000 live births, 1988	% of cohort persisting to grade 4				Females per 100 males					Female share of labor force (%)	
	Female		Male			Female		Male		Primary		Secondary[a]				
	1970	1992	1970	1992		1970	1987	1970	1987	1970	1991	1970	1991		1970	1992
Low-income economies	**54 *w***	**63 *w***	**53 *w***	**61 *w***	••	••	••	••	••	••	**78 *w***	••	**65 *w***		**36 *w***	**35 *w***
Excluding China & India	**47 *w***	**57 *w***	**46 *w***	**55 *w***	••	**65 *w***	**66 *w***	**74 *w***	**69 *w***	**61 *w***	**77 *w***	**44 *w***	**66 *w***		**32 *w***	**31 *w***
1 Mozambique	42	45	36	43	••	••	••	••	••	••	70	••	61		50	47
2 Ethiopia	44	50	43	47	••	57	56	56	56	46	64	32	67		40	37
3 Tanzania	47	52	44	49	*342*	82	90	88	89	65	98	38	72		51	47
4 Sierra Leone	36	45	33	41	••	••	••	••	••	67	70	40	56		36	32
5 Nepal	42	53	43	54	*833*	••	••	••	••	18	47	16	••		35	33
6 Uganda	51	44	49	43	*550*	••	••	••	••	65	••	31	••		43	41
7 Bhutan	41	49	39	48	*1,305*	••	••	••	••	5	59	3	41		35	32
8 Burundi	45	50	42	46	••	47	84	45	84	49	84	17	59		50	47
9 Malawi	41	45	40	44	*350*	55	67	60	72	59	82	36	53		45	41
10 Bangladesh	44	56	46	55	*600*	••	43	••	43	47	81	••	49		5	8
11 Chad	40	49	37	46	••	••	77	••	81	34	44	9	22		23	21
12 Guinea-Bissau	36	39	35	38	••	••	••	••	••	43	56	62	53		43	40
13 Madagascar	47	53	44	50	*333*	65	••	63	••	86	97	70	99		42	39
14 Lao PDR	42	53	39	50	*561*	••	••	••	••	59	77	36	66		46	44
15 Rwanda	46	48	43	45	*300*	63	75	65	75	79	99	44	56		50	47
16 Niger	40	48	37	44	••	75	93	74	78	53	57	35	42		49	46
17 Burkina Faso	42	50	39	47	*810*	71	86	68	84	57	62	33	50		48	46
18 India	49	62	50	61	••	42	••	45	••	60	71	39	55		30	25
19 Kenya	52	61	48	57	••	84	78	84	76	71	95	42	78		42	39
20 Mali	39	50	36	47	*2,325*	52	68	89	75	55	58	29	50		17	16
21 Nigeria	43	54	40	50	800	64	••	66	••	59	76	49	74		37	34
22 Nicaragua	55	69	52	65	*300*	48	62	45	59	101	104	89	138		20	26
23 Togo	46	57	43	53	••	85	78	88	86	45	65	26	34		39	36
24 Benin	45	52	43	49	*161*	71	••	75	••	45	51	44	37		48	47
25 Central African Republic	45	49	40	45	••	67	81	67	85	49	63	20	38		49	45
26 Pakistan	47	59	49	59	270	56	44	60	53	36	52	25	41		9	13
27 Ghana	51	58	48	54	*1,000*	77	••	82	••	75	82	35	63		42	40
28 China	63	71	61	68	*115*	••	76	••	81	••	86	••	72		42	43
29 Tajikistan	••	72	••	67	*39*	••	••	••	••	••	••	••	••		••	••
30 Guinea	37	44	36	44	*1,247*	••	77	••	86	46	46	26	31		42	39
31 Mauritania	41	50	38	46	*800*	••	83	••	83	39	73	13	45		22	23
32 Sri Lanka	66	74	64	70	*80*	94	97	73	99	89	93	101	105		25	27
33 Zimbabwe	52	61	49	58	*77*	74	81	80	81	79	99	63	88		38	34
34 Honduras	55	68	51	64	*221*	••	••	••	••	99	98	79	••		14	20
35 Lesotho	52	63	48	58	*220*	87	87	70	76	150	121	111	149		48	43
36 Egypt, Arab Rep.	52	63	50	60	••	85	••	93	••	61	80	48	76		7	10
37 Indonesia	49	62	46	59	*450*	67	81	89	99	84	93	59	82		30	31
38 *Myanmar*	53	62	50	58	••	39	••	58	••	89	••	65	••		39	37
39 *Somalia*	42	50	39	47	••	46	••	51	••	33	••	27	••		41	38
40 *Sudan*	43	53	41	51	••	••	••	••	••	61	75	40	80		20	22
41 *Yemen, Rep.*	42	53	41	52	*330*	••	••	••	••	10	31	3	18		8	14
42 *Zambia*	48	49	45	46	••	••	••	••	••	80	91	49	59		28	30
Middle-income economies	**62 *w***	**71 *w***	**58 *w***	**65 *w***	••	**77 *w***	**86 *w***	**76 *w***	**90 *w***	**86 *w***	**91 *w***	**92 *w***	**106 *w***		**30 *w***	**32 *w***
Lower-middle-income	••	**71 *w***	••	**64 *w***	••	••	••	••	••	••	••	••	••		••	••
43 Côte d'Ivoire	46	59	43	53	••	77	83	83	88	57	71	27	47		38	34
44 Bolivia	48	62	44	58	*371*	••	••	••	••	69	90	64	••		21	26
45 Azerbaijan	••	75	••	67	29	••	••	••	••	••	••	••	••		••	••
46 Philippines	59	67	56	63	*74*	••	85	••	84	••	94	••	99		33	31
47 Armenia	••	73	••	67	*35*	••	••	••	••	••	••	••	••		••	••
48 Senegal	44	50	42	48	••	••	90	••	94	63	72	39	51		41	39
49 Cameroon	46	58	43	54	••	59	85	58	86	74	85	36	71		37	33
50 Kyrgyz Republic	••	70	••	62	*43*	••	••	••	••	••	••	••	••		••	••
51 Georgia	••	76	••	69	*55*	••	••	••	••	••	••	••	••		••	••
52 Uzbekistan	••	72	••	66	*43*	••	••	••	••	••	••	••	••		••	••
53 Papua New Guinea	47	57	47	55	*700*	76	••	84	••	57	80	37	62		29	35
54 Peru	56	67	52	63	*165*	••	••	••	••	85	••	74	••		20	24
55 Guatemala	54	67	51	62	••	33	••	73	••	79	••	65	••		13	17
56 Congo	49	54	43	49	••	86	88	89	71	78	87	43	72		40	39
57 Morocco	53	65	50	62	••	78	80	83	81	51	66	40	69		14	21
58 Dominican Republic	61	70	57	65	*300*	55	52	13	70	99	98	••	••		11	16
59 Ecuador	60	69	57	65	156	69	••	70	••	93	••	76	••		16	19
60 Jordan	••	72	••	68	••	90	97	92	99	78	94	53	105		6	11
61 Romania	71	73	67	67	••	90	••	89	••	97	106	151	174		44	47
62 El Salvador	60	69	56	64	*148*	61	••	62	••	92	98	77	95		20	25
63 Turkmenistan	••	70	••	63	*55*	••	••	••	••	••	••	••	••		••	••
64 Moldova	••	72	••	65	*34*	••	••	••	••	••	••	••	••		••	••
65 Lithuania	75	76	67	66	*29*	••	••	••	••	••	••	••	••		••	••
66 Bulgaria	74	75	69	68	••	91	91	100	93	94	93	••	198		44	46
67 Colombia	63	72	59	66	*200*	57	74	51	72	101	98	73	100		21	22
68 Jamaica	70	76	66	71	*115*	••	100	••	98	100	99	103	••		42	46
69 Paraguay	67	70	63	65	*300*	70	77	71	77	89	93	91	102		21	21
70 Namibia	49	60	47	58	••	••	••	••	••	••	108	••	127		24	24
71 Kazakhstan	••	73	••	64	*53*	••	••	••	••	••	••	••	••		••	••
72 Tunisia	55	69	54	67	*127*	••	91	••	94	64	85	38	77		12	25

Note: For data comparability and coverage, see the Key and the technical notes. Figures in italics are for years other than those specified.

	Health					Education								Employment	
	Life expectancy at birth (years)				Maternal mortality per 100,000 live births, 1988	% of cohort persisting to grade 4				Females per 100 males				Female share of labor force (%)	
	Female		Male			Female		Male		Primary		Secondary[a]			
	1970	1992	1970	1992		1970	1987	1970	1987	1970	1991	1970	1991	1970	1992
73 Ukraine	74	75	67	66	*33*	••	••	••	••	96	••	127	••	••	••
74 Algeria	54	68	52	67	••	90	95	95	97	60	81	40	79	6	10
75 Thailand	61	72	56	67	*37*	71	••	69	••	88	95	69	97	47	44
76 Poland	74	75	67	66	••	99	••	97	••	93	95	251	266	45	46
77 Latvia	••	75	••	64	*57*	••	••	••	••	••	••	••	••	••	••
78 Slovak Republic	••	75	••	67	••	••	••	••	••	••	••	••	••	••	43
79 Costa Rica	69	79	65	74	18	93	91	91	90	96	94	111	103	18	22
80 Turkey	59	70	55	65	*146*	76	98	81	98	73	89	37	63	38	34
81 Iran, Islamic Rep.	54	66	55	65	*120*	75	92	74	93	55	86	49	74	13	19
82 Panama	67	75	64	71	60	97	88	97	85	92	93	99	103	25	28
83 Czech Republic	••	76	••	69	••	••	••	••	••	••	••	••	••	••	••
84 Russian Federation	••	75	••	64	*49*	••	••	••	••	••	••	••	••	••	••
85 Chile	66	76	59	69	40	86	••	83	••	98	95	130	115	22	29
86 *Albania*	69	75	66	70	••	••	••	••	••	90	93	92	124	40	41
87 *Mongolia*	54	65	52	62	*140*	••	••	••	••	••	100	••	••	45	46
88 *Syrian Arab Rep.*	57	69	54	65	*143*	92	93	95	95	57	87	36	71	12	18
Upper-middle-income	**64 w**	**72 w**	**59 w**	**66 w**	••	**75 w**	••	**70 w**	••	**94 w**	**95 w**	**100 w**	**112 w**	**25 w**	**30 w**
89 South Africa	56	66	50	60	••	••	••	••	••	98	••	95	••	33	36
90 Mauritius	65	73	60	67	*99*	97	99	97	99	94	98	66	100	20	27
91 Estonia	74	75	66	65	*41*	••	••	••	••	••	••	••	••	••	••
92 Brazil	61	69	57	64	*140*	56	••	54	••	99	••	99	••	22	28
93 Botswana	51	70	48	66	••	97	96	90	97	113	107	88	114	44	35
94 Malaysia	63	73	60	69	26	••	••	••	••	88	95	69	104	31	35
95 Venezuela	68	73	63	67	55	84	91	61	81	99	99	102	137	21	28
96 Belarus	76	76	68	67	25	••	••	••	••	••	••	••	••	••	••
97 Hungary	73	74	67	65	••	90	97	99	97	93	95	202	198	40	45
98 Uruguay	72	76	66	69	*36*	••	98	••	96	91	95	129	••	26	31
99 Mexico	64	74	60	67	*200*	••	73	••	94	92	94	••	92	18	27
100 Trinidad and Tobago	68	74	63	69	*89*	78	••	74	••	97	97	113	102	30	30
101 Gabon	46	56	43	52	••	*73*	*80*	78	78	91	••	43	••	40	37
102 Argentina	70	75	64	68	*140*	92	••	69	••	98	*103*	156	*176*	25	28
103 Oman	49	72	46	68	••	••	*97*	••	*100*	16	89	0	82	6	9
104 Slovenia	••	77	••	69	••	••	••	••	••	••	••	••	••	••	••
105 Puerto Rico	75	78	69	71	*21*	••	••	••	••	••	••	••	••	••	••
106 Korea, Rep.	62	75	58	67	*26*	96	100	96	100	92	94	65	87	32	34
107 Greece	74	80	70	75	••	97	99	96	99	92	94	98	103	26	27
108 Portugal	71	78	64	70	••	92	••	92	••	95	91	98	116	25	37
109 Saudi Arabia	54	71	51	68	••	93	••	91	••	46	84	16	79	5	8
Low- and middle-income	**56 w**	**66 w**	**54 w**	**62 w**	••	**61 w**	••	**64 w**	••	**69 w**	**81 w**	**59 w**	**74 w**	**35 w**	**35 w**
Sub-Saharan Africa	**46 w**	**53 w**	**43 w**	**50 w**	••	**66 w**	••	**69 w**	••	**63 w**	**77 w**	**44 w**	**67 w**	**40 w**	**37 w**
East Asia & Pacific	**60 w**	**69 w**	**58 w**	**66 w**	••	••	••	••	••	••	**88 w**	••	**76 w**	**41 w**	**42 w**
South Asia	**48 w**	**61 w**	**50 w**	**60 w**	••	**45 w**	••	**48 w**	••	**55 w**	**69 w**	**38 w**	**54 w**	**26 w**	**22 w**
Europe and Central Asia	**69 w**	**74 w**	**64 w**	**66 w**	••	••	••	••	••	••	••	••	••	••	••
Middle East & N. Africa	**54 w**	**66 w**	**52 w**	**63 w**	••	**83 w**	**90 w**	**87 w**	**92 w**	**54 w**	**79 w**	**41 w**	**72 w**	**10 w**	**16 w**
Latin America & Caribbean	**63 w**	**71 w**	**58 w**	**65 w**	••	**66 w**	••	**60 w**	••	**96 w**	**97 w**	**101 w**	**114 w**	**22 w**	**27 w**
Severely indebted	**62 w**	**70 w**	**58 w**	**64 w**	••	**75 w**	••	**73 w**	••	**87 w**	**89 w**	**107 w**	**121 w**	**26 w**	**29 w**
High-income economies	**75 w**	**80 w**	**68 w**	**74 w**	••	**95 w**	**98 w**	**93 w**	**97 w**	**96 w**	**95 w**	**95 w**	**98 w**	**36 w**	**38 w**
110 Ireland	73	78	69	73	••	••	98	••	97	96	95	124	100	26	29
111 New Zealand	75	79	69	73	••	••	98	••	98	94	94	94	98	••	••
112 †Israel	73	78	70	75	••	96	97	96	97	92	98	131	116	30	34
113 Spain	75	81	70	73	••	76	98	76	97	99	93	84	102	19	24
114 †Hong Kong	73	81	67	75	*4*	94	••	92	••	90	••	74	••	••	••
115 †Singapore	70	77	65	72	10	99	*100*	99	*100*	88	*90*	103	*100*	26	32
116 Australia	75	80	68	74	••	76	97	74	94	94	95	91	99	31	38
117 United Kingdom	75	79	69	73	••	••	••	••	••	95	96	94	96	36	39
118 Italy	75	81	69	74	••	••	••	••	••	94	95	86	97	29	32
119 Netherlands	77	81	71	74	••	99	••	96	••	96	99	91	109	26	31
120 Canada	76	81	69	75	••	95	97	92	93	95	93	95	96	32	40
121 Belgium	75	79	68	72	••	••	87	••	85	94	97	87	••	30	34
122 Finland	74	80	66	72	••	••	98	••	98	90	95	112	111	44	47
123 †United Arab Emirates	63	74	59	70	••	97	98	93	98	61	93	23	103	4	7
124 France	76	81	68	73	••	97	••	90	••	95	94	107	106	36	40
125 Austria	74	80	67	73	••	95	99	92	98	95	95	95	94	39	40
126 Germany	74	79	67	73	••	97[b]	99[b]	96[b]	97[b]	96[b]	96[b]	93[b]	98[b]	40	39
127 United States	75	80	67	73	••	••	••	••	••	95	95	••	95	37	41
128 Norway	77	80	71	74	••	99	••	98	••	105	95	97	105	29	41
129 Denmark	76	78	71	72	••	98	100	96	100	97	96	102	106	36	45
130 Sweden	77	81	72	75	••	98	••	96	••	96	95	92	109	36	45
131 Japan	75	82	69	76	••	100	100	100	100	96	95	101	99	39	38
132 Switzerland	76	82	70	75	••	94	••	93	••	98	96	93	100	33	36
World	**60 w**	**68 w**	**57 w**	**64 w**	••	**67 w**	••	**69 w**	••	**77 w**	**84 w**	**67 w**	**78 w**	**35 w**	**35 w**

a. See the technical notes. b. Data refer to the Federal Republic of Germany before unification.

Infrastructure is an indicator of the development of a country. You would probably expect a wealthy, economically developed country to have plenty of roads, power stations, telephones, and so on. Although many countries don't provide all the data, the comparison between rich countries and poor is as clear insofar as infrastructure is concerned as it is with all the other tables preented here. Modern technology is, however, allowing people in many countries access to fax machines and other modern communication systems.

TABLE 32 *Infrastructure*

	Power		Telecommunications		Paved roads		Water		Railways	
	Households with electricity (% of total) 1984	System losses (% of total output) 1990	Telephone mainlines (per 1,000 persons) 1990	Faults (per 100 mainlines per year) 1990	Road density (km per million persons) 1988	Roads in good cond. (% of paved roads) 1988	Population with access to safe water (% of total) 1990	Losses (% of total water provision) 1986	Rail traffic (km per million $ GDP) 1990	Diesels in use (% of diesel inventory) 1990
Low-income economies Excluding China & India										
1 Mozambique	4	26	3	••	343	12	22	••	••	••
2 Ethiopia	••	••	2	116	84	48	18	46	••	••
3 Tanzania	6	20	3	••	156	25	52	••	••	••
4 Sierra Leone	••	36	6	••	194	62	39	••	••	••
5 Nepal	30	27	3	16	139	40	48	45	••	••
6 Uganda	••	40	2	••	118	10	33	••	••	49
7 Bhutan	••	••	••	••	••	••	34	••	••	••
8 Burundi	1	19	2	71	195	58	45	46	••	••
9 Malawi	16	19	3	••	278	56	51	••	43	77
10 Bangladesh	••	30	2	••	59	15	78	47	41	73
11 Chad	••	••	1	149	56	••	57	••	••	••
12 Guinea-Bissau	4	••	••	••	••	••	25	••	••	••
13 Madagascar	••	17	3	78	475	56	21	••	••	••
14 Lao PDR	••	17	••	12	••	••	28	••	••	••
15 Rwanda	••	15	1	38	149	41	69	••	••	••
16 Niger	••	••	1	88	383	60	53	••	••	••
17 Burkina Faso	••	10	••	••	21	24	70	••	••	••
18 India	54	19	6	••	893	20	73	••	593	90
19 Kenya	••	16	8	••	278	32	49	18	120	52
20 Mali	••	18	1	••	308	63	11	••	106	44
21 Nigeria	81	51	3	••	376	67	42	••	17	20
22 Nicaragua	41	20	13	••	••	••	55	20	••	••
23 Togo	10	26	3	25	444	40	70	••	••	••
24 Benin	••	20	3	••	233	26	55	••	••	••
25 Central African Rep.	••	32	2	••	155	30	24	••	••	••
26 Pakistan	31	24	8	120	229	18	55	40	168	79
27 Ghana	••	20	3	••	430	28	••	47	••	••
28 China	••	15	••	••	••	••	72	••	••	••
29 Tajikistan	••	••	••	••	••	••	a	••	••	••
30 Guinea	••	37	3	••	240	27	52	••	••	••
31 Mauritania	••	••	3	193	804	58	66	••	••	••
32 Sri Lanka	15	18	7	••	536	10	60	••	••	••
33 Zimbabwe	9	10	13	217	1,389	27	84	••	505	54
34 Honduras	25	24	17	66	335	50	64	••	••	••
35 Lesotho	••	••	7	••	359	53	47	••	••	••
36 Egypt, Arab Rep.	46	14	33	5	302	39	90	••	394	93
37 Indonesia	14	21	6	5	160	30	51	29	••	74
38 *Myanmar*	••	36	••	••	210	••	74	••	••	72
39 *Somalia*	••	••	2	••	375	52	36	33	••	••
40 *Sudan*	26	19	2	••	98	27	34	••	27	29
41 *Yemen, Rep.*	••	15	11	20	951	39	36	45	••	••
42 *Zambia*	28	9	8	69	751	40	59	••	294	44
Middle-income economies Lower-middle-income										
43 Côte d'Ivoire	40	••	5	••	357	75	69	16	35	58
44 Bolivia	33	16	26	••	198	21	53	••	81	60
45 Azerbaijan	••	••	••	••	••	••	a	••	••	••
46 Philippines	46	19	10	7	242	31	81	53	••	••
47 Armenia	••	••	••	••	••	••	a	••	••	••
48 Senegal	96	10	6	••	542	28	44	••	78	62
49 Cameroon	6	••	3	••	299	38	44	••	84	72
50 Kyrgyz Republic	••	••	••	••	••	••	a	••	••	••
51 Georgia	••	••	••	39	••	••	a	••	••	••
52 Uzbekistan	••	••	••	••	••	••	a	••	••	••
53 Papua New Guinea	56	••	8	••	196	34	33	••	••	••
54 Peru	90	18	26	••	347	24	53	••	22	••
55 Guatemala	37	17	21	52	350	7	62	••	••	••
56 Congo	9	19	7	••	584	50	38	••	170	56
57 Morocco	37	14	16	101	618	20	56	5	141	88
58 Dominican Republic	37	33	48	••	364	52	68	••	••	••
59 Ecuador	47	19	47	••	336	53	54	47	••	••
60 Jordan	77	16	75	100	••	••	99	41	62	60
61 Romania	49	9	102	102	1593	30	95	28	••	52
62 El Salvador	34	15	24	••	••	••	47	••	••	••
63 Turkmenistan	••	••	••	61	••	••	a	••	••	••
64 Moldova	••	••	••	43	••	••	a	••	••	••
65 Lithuania	••	••	••	46	••	••	a	••	••	••
66 Bulgaria	••	21	••	50	••	••	99	••	••	••
67 Colombia	79	22	75	6	309	42	86	38	5	35
68 Jamaica	49	19	45	7	1,881	10	72	31	••	••
69 Paraguay	••	16	26	••	••	••	79	••	••	••
70 Namibia	••	••	••	••	••	••	47	••	••	••
71 Kazakhstan	••	••	••	••	••	••	a	••	••	••
72 Tunisia	63	12	38	130	1,177	55	70	30	123	50

Note: For data comparability and coverage, see the Key and the technical notes. Figures in italics are for years other than those specified.

	Power		Telecommunications		Paved roads		Water		Railways	
	Households with electricity (% of total) 1984	System losses (% of total output) 1990	Telephone mainlines (per 1,000 persons) 1990	Faults (per 100 mainlines per year) 1990	Road density (km per million persons) 1988	Roads in good cond. (% of paved roads) 1988	Population with access to safe water (% of total) 1990	Losses (% of total water provision) 1986	Rail traffic (km per million $ GDP) 1990	Diesels in use (% of diesel inventory) 1990
73 Ukraine	••	••	••	••	••	••	a	••	••	••
74 Algeria	49	14	32	••	1,366	40	••	••	85	99
75 Thailand	43	11	24	2	513	50	77	48	76	72
76 Poland	96	15	86	••	617	69	89	••	••	72
77 Latvia	••	••	••	••	••	••	a	••	••	••
78 Slovak Republic	••	••	••	••	••	••	••	••	••	••
79 Costa Rica	97	10	93	••	1,059	22	92	••	••	••
80 Turkey	57	15	123	1	••	••	84	44	69	73
81 Iran, Islamic Rep.	48	12	40	••	••	••	89	••	••	57
82 Panama	66	24	89	10	1,332	36	84	••	••	••
83 Czech Republic	••	••	••	••	••	••	••	••	••	••
84 Russian Federation	••	••	••	••	••	••	a	••	••	••
85 Chile	85	19	65	97	753	42	87	••	48	57
86 *Albania*	••	••	••	27	••	••	97	••	••	••
87 *Mongolia*	48	••	••	57	••	••	80	••	••	••
88 *Syrian Arab Rep.*	42	••	41	66	••	••	79	34	49	52
Upper-middle-income										
89 South Africa	••	••	87	••	••	••	a	••	987	88
90 Mauritius	93	14	56	••	1,579	95	95	••	••	••
91 Estonia	••	••	••	••	••	••	a	••	••	••
92 Brazil	79	14	63	4	704	30	86	30	60	62
93 Botswana	••	6	21	53	1,977	94	90	25	••	••
94 Malaysia	64	16	89	7	••	••	78	29	37	76
95 Venezuela	89	18	77	6	10,269	40	92	••	••	••
96 Belarus	••	••	••	••	••	••	a	••	••	••
97 Hungary	96	11	96	55	5804	••	98	••	••	82
98 Uruguay	81	22	134	••	2,106	26	95	••	15	56
99 Mexico	75	13	66	••	820	85	81	••	90	64
100 Trinidad and Tobago	83	9	141	6	1,724	72	96	••	••	••
101 Gabon	50	••	18	••	650	30	66	22	55	94
102 Argentina	87	20	96	78	858	35	64	••	161	49
103 Oman	••	••	68	2	2,322	66	46	••	••	••
104 Slovenia	••	••	••	••	••	••	••	••	••	••
105 Puerto Rico	97	••	••	5	••	••	••	••	••	••
106 Korea, Rep.	100	6	310	••	236	70	93	••	••	89
107 Greece	89	••	391	••	••	••	98	••	39	59
108 Portugal	78	11	241	••	1,740	50	92	••	105	89
109 Saudi Arabia	••	13	78	2	••	••	93	••	••	••
Low- and middle-income										
Sub-Saharan Africa										
East Asia & Pacific										
South Asia										
Europe and Central Asia										
Middle East & N. Africa										
Latin America & Caribbean										
Severely indebted										
High-income economies										
110 Ireland	95	9	281	40	••	••	100	••	57	71
111 New Zealand	••	10	437	••	••	••	97	••	61	••
112 †Israel	97	4	350	••	••	••	100	••	30	••
113 Spain	95	9	323	10	••	••	100	••	70	89
114 †Hong Kong	••	11	434	••	••	••	100	••	••	••
115 †Singapore	98	3	385	••	••	••	100	8	••	••
116 Australia	98	7	456	••	25,695	b	100	••	62	••
117 United Kingdom	••	8	442	16	6,174	b	100	••	66	••
118 Italy	99	8	388	21	5,254	b	100	••	90	80
119 Netherlands	95	4	464	4	6,875	b	100	••	73	83
120 Canada	100	7	577	••	••	••	100	••	210	••
121 Belgium	100	5	393	8	12,440	b	100	••	110	77
122 Finland	96	5	535	12	••	••	96	••	165	87
123 †United Arab Emirates	••	••	••	3	••	••	100	••	••	••
124 France	99	6	495	10	14,406	b	100	••	146	93
125 Austria	••	6	418	35	14,101	b	100	••	209	90
126 Germany[c]	100	5	483	••	••	••	100	••	117	••
127 United States	100	9	545	••	14,172	b	••	333	••	••
128 Norway	••	6	503	21	••	••	100	••	••	••
129 Denmark	100	6	566	••	13,775	b	100	••	93	••
130 Sweden	96	6	683	12	••	••	100	••	198	••
131 Japan	••	4	441	2	6,007	b	96	••	144	87
132 Switzerland	••	7	587	45	10,817	b	100	••	••	••
World										

a. For range estimates, see map on access to safe water in the introduction. b. 85 percent or more of roads are in good condition; see the technical notes. c. Data refer to the Federal Republic of Germany before unification.

The wife typically spends her day cooking, caring for the children, husking rice, and fetching water from the well. She is helped in these tasks by her thirteen-year-old niece, whose parents died in a cholera epidemic some years ago. The woman and her niece are always on the lookout for ways to earn a little extra. Such work as husking rice, weeding fields, and chopping wood is sometimes available from better-off neighbors. The nine-year-old son attends school a few mornings a week in a town an hour's walk away. The rest of the day he and his seven-year-old sister gather fuel and edible roots and weeds. The sister also looks after the baby when her mother or cousin cannot.

The household spends about 85 percent of its meager income on food—predominantly rice. Family members are used to having only two meals a day. They hope to struggle through to the rice harvest without having to cut down and sell their jackfruit tree or the bamboo poles supporting their roof.

ASPECTS OF WRITING: Interpreting data. What do the numbers mean?

Having said already that you should be careful when interpreting statistical data, it should also be said that numbers can inject an element of **objectivity** into a discussion. This is what we ask for when we ask for the *bottom line* or when we ask, "What are the numbers?" If we disagree about whether a certain climate is pleasant or not, our differences are **subjective,** but if we produce *data* on daily temperatures, humidity, and so on, there can be no argument over these objective facts, only over the subjective matter of whether such conditions are to our liking.

Numbers are sometimes used simply to try to influence debate. If we use data that tend to support our own ideas (or those of the people who are paying for the poll) and ignore other data that contradict these views, then this is self-serving and deceptive. Similarly, if the questions are framed so as to increase the possibility of eliciting a certain answer, then this might also be seen as *loaded* and deceptive.

Would the following questions produce similar answers?

a. Should murderers be executed?

b. Would you support life imprisonment without parole as an alternative to execution?

Interpreting data can also be unexpectedly difficult. For example, if one school graduates 95% of its seniors, and another graduates 80%, does this mean that the first school is better? Similarly, if one hospital has 90% of its pneumonia patients recover, while another has only 70% recover, does this mean that the former is the better hospital? In both cases, the answer may be "Yes," but a close study may also indicate significant differences between the schools or the hospitals. What if many of the weaker students at the first school dropped out before the senior year? What if graduation requirements were significantly different? In the case of the hospitals, what if the second one served a lot of elderly people, while the first one served a younger community?

Clearly, it's possible to be misled by statistical information, and it's usually a good idea to read any technical information provided, including the size and makeup of the sample. Many statistics, however, provide information that enables us to make useful comparisons. For example, having numbers to cite gives us a much more vivid sense of what it means to be in a rich country or a poor one—compare the GNP per capita of Mozambique and Switzerland, for example. Similarly, infant mortality and life expectancy figures are widely used as measures of the overall quality of health care in a country. Figures on education can suggest the place of women in a society and the priority given to education by different governments.

In general, a country with a high GNP per capita and a benevolent government interested in improving the lives of the country's citizens will have a lot of investment in things that improve the quality of life. A rich country with economic growth more rapid than its rate of population growth will also continue to grow richer; the opposite situation will produce the opposite result. The figures show that the gap between the richest and poorest countries is growing, but that many countries in-between are making substantial economic and social progress.

When discussing these numbers, ask yourself not only what they mean, but also what they don't mean.

WRITING EXERCISES. Answer one of the following questions.

1. Discuss what the World Bank tables show in terms of the differences between the wealthiest and poorest countries. To do this, you could follow the model in the reading, which describes poor families in three different countries. Decide which countries and which aspects you would like to discuss—GNP per capita, health, education, gender differences, etc.—and look at the numbers. You can present the data and offer some commentary on why there is such a large gap and whether it is growing larger or smaller.
2. Choose three countries that represent different levels of income—low, middle, and high—and illustrate how wealth seems to correlate with levels of health and education. In explaining this, you should remember that, in most countries, education and health services are provided by the government. The government's income, therefore, affects what can be done in terms of services. It is interesting to note, however, that the correlation is not perfect; government priorities are another factor. For example, China and Sri Lanka are poor countries, but their health statistics suggest that they give health services substantial resources and attention.

Statistical information invites **comparison and contrast.** As also illustrated in Section Two, such essays can have a nicely symmetrical outline:

1. Country X
   a. GNP per capita
      i. population growth rate
      ii. trend in GNP per capita
   b. Health statistics
      i. doctors and nurses
      ii. infant mortality
      iii. life expectancy
      iv. trends
   c. Education statistics
      i. access to schools
      ii. gender differences
      iii. trends
2. Country Y
   a. GNP per capita
      i.
      ii.
   b. Health statistics
      i.
      ii.
      iii.
   c. Education
      i.
      ii.
      iii.
3. Discussion

An essay such as this can do more than simply present numbers. Class discussion and individual insight should produce some significant generalizations suggested by the statistical pictures.

SECTION TWO

PRIOR KNOWLEDGE: The scene from on the ground in Africa.

The 1994 World Bank figures (see Section One in this unit) show that 44 countries had negative growth in GNP per capita between 1980 and 1992. In regional terms, Sub-Saharan Africa lost an average of 0.8% GNP per capita every year during this period; the Middle East and North Africa lost 2.3%; Latin America and the Caribbean lost 0.2%. The other regions of the world showed growth over this period, with East Asia and the Pacific growing an average of 6.1% every year. Some of the declines can be explained in terms of the drop in commodity prices, especially oil.

Poor families often have larger families because children are potential workers, because children represent some security for the parents in old age in countries where there is no national pension or social security plan, and because, when infant mortality is high, additional children provide a guarantee that at least some will survive. Wealthier families generally benefit from more secure incomes, better education, and better access to health care.

When experts talk about "international development," they are looking at social and economic trends of the kind presented in World Bank statistics (see Section One of this unit). The poorest nations, however, show little—or even negative—per capita economic growth, and this tends to stunt social development also. Many experts refer to the 1980s as a "lost decade" for many of the poorest nations, especially in Africa, and the following reading discusses the situation on the ground in that continent.

Two Americans, one a foreign correspondent (Mort Rosenblum) and the other an environmental scientist (Doug Williamson), both old "Africa hands" (i.e., people with long experience in Africa), describe and discuss what they see there. Many of the numbers they cite are from the World Bank, and their writing offers at least one model for integrating statistics into a discussion.

Why have the poorest countries in Africa made so little headway in recent years? Some people point out that population growth has outpaced economic growth, making it very difficult to keep up with the demand for new schools, health services, jobs, and so on. The answer, these people say, is to reduce population growth, which in Africa as a whole is very high. Others say that economic growth will eventually lead to lower population growth rates, because wealthier people tend to protect their resources by having fewer children.

Education is another factor. Not only is an educated workforce more productive, according to economists, but educated parents—especially educated women—tend to have smaller families. Education, therefore, has an impact on economic growth and population growth. Many development experts see the education of women as the single most important factor in bringing about economic and social advances in poor countries.

Just as not everyone in a wealthy country is rich, not everyone in a poor country is impoverished. One statistic that economists generate shows the **distribution of income and wealth.** A country may be statistically quite wealthy, but if most of the wealth is in the hands of only a few people, then social development is likely to be limited and social unrest may be threatened. A widely quoted example is Brazil, where the 1994 World Bank figures show that the top 10% of households took 51.3% of income and consumption, and the top 20% took 67.5%. The figures for the United States were 25% and 41.9%, respectively.

Many things can affect the economic and social development of a country. War can devastate the economy, the infrastructure, and human lives, as seen in Mozambique, Angola, Chad, Liberia, Sierra Leone, Sudan, and many other countries. Drought and other natural disasters pose problems, too, as in the Sahel (the arid region on the southern fringes of the Sahara), Ethiopia, Zimbabwe, and elsewhere. Bad government or the collapse of central authority of any kind can devastate even a potentially prosperous country, as happened in Uganda under Idi Amin, and as seen in Zaire, Liberia, and Somalia.

Idi Amin was president of Uganda from 1971–1979. His regime became notorious for its expulsion of residents of Indian descent and for its brutality. Amin was overthrown by Tanzanian forces and Ugandan exiles. Uganda is now more settled, and development has resumed. If Amin's Uganda became a symbol of Africa's problems, Botswana may represent the continent's successes in achieving political stability within a democratic system and economic and social progress.

It's important not to oversimplify or overgeneralize. All the countries of Africa are not the same; some are rich in natural resources, some have plenty of arable land, some have stable and democratic governments. The 1990s have seen devastation in parts of West and Central Africa but have seen encouraging trends toward peace (in Mozambique and Angola, for example) and democracy (in Zambia, South Africa, Namibia, and Malawi, for example) in southern Africa.

The end of apartheid in South Africa and the introduction of democracy there may help other countries. South Africa's economy is larger than all the other economies of Sub-Saharan Africa combined, and she could become an engine of growth for the continent.

Look at a map, so that you can see where Rosenblum and Williamson are taking you on their tour of the continent.

ANNOTATED READING: Mort Rosenblum and Doug Williamson. "People: Women and Children First." *Squandering Eden: Africa at the Edge.* San Diego: Harcourt Brace Jovanovich, 1987: 250–261.

People

Women and Children First

Some counsel calm in the face of Africa's population growth rate of more than 3 percent. If it is the world's highest, Africa also has the lowest population density. According to FAO figures, a lot of land is left. But that misses the point. Rwandans looking for land do not settle in northern Mali. Population is not a critical problem everywhere in Africa, but it will be.

As is the case elsewhere in this text, the authors assume the reader's familiarity with international development and aid organizations such as the FAO (the Food and Agricultural Organization—an agency of the United Nations based in Rome).

The question, once again, is balance.

A World Bank study released in 1986 began, "The population of sub-Saharan Africa, currently about 470 million, will exceed 700 million by 2000. At no time in history has any group of nations faced the challenge of development in a situation of such rapid population growth."

The 1994 World Bank figures give a total population for Sub-Saharan Africa of 543 million in 1992 and projections of 681 million in 2000 and 1.229 billion in 2025. Projections are based on various factors, including current trends. These projections are, therefore, always subject to change.

That is on top of everything else. At a time when food production per capita continues to fall, when most Africans' real buying power is less now than it was at independence, population growth rates are climbing. In the 1970s, it was 2.8 percent. In 1985, it was 3.1 percent. And trends suggest it is going up. Everywhere else in the world, rates are dropping.

Ethiopia is struggling to feed its 42 million people on fast disappearing land. By the turn of the century, if famine can be staved off, there will be 65 million. If an Ethiopian infant saved in 1984 lives to age sixty-five, he may have to share his land with 170 million people.

Nigeria has 100 million inhabitants, in a country the size of Texas and New Mexico. By 2050, according to World Bank projections, there could be twice as many Nigerians in the world as there are Americans today.

Nigeria (#21 in the 1994 World Bank tables) is the most populous country in Africa. It is also a potentially wealthy country, with oil and other natural resources. It has, however, suffered from political instability.

Overall, the bank projects a sub-Saharan African population of 730 million for 2000. At a constant rate, that will grow to nearly 1.8 billion in 2050. If fertility is slowed, the figure might be 1.3 billion. But if it follows an upward trend, it could reach 2.2 billion. That is twice the current population of China.

> China's annual population growth rate was 1.4% between 1980 and 1992, and the World Bank (1994) estimates only 1% growth each year from 1992–2000.

In human terms, it is good news. In the past in Africa, nature arranged what a scientist friend coolly refers to as "massive mammal die-offs." Famine and disease wiped out populations whenever they got too large. If Africans survived their childhood, a hit-or-miss prospect, they were middle-aged in their teens.

Now we can alleviate famine and head off pandemics, just as we can fight disease and help mothers rear healthier children. What we have not done is to show mothers they need no longer be constantly pregnant, playing child roulette in hopes of ending up with enough surviving sons.

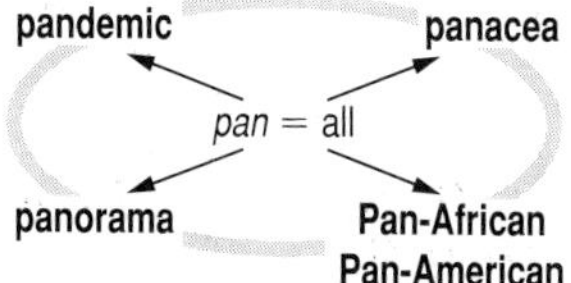

The problem is not too many people. It is too little economic growth to sustain them. In theory, there should be no reason to declare Africa more overpopulated than, say, Japan. Tokyo can afford not to grow its own food; in fact, grain producers around the world are anxious for Tokyo's business. But unless sudden massive strides are made in development, burgeoning populations in Africa translate to human misery—and disaster for the land, which will be called upon to be increasingly more productive.

> Improved health services, cleaner water supplies, and other benefits can lead to a drop in infant and child mortality, and this is good news in human terms, as the authors say. It also can lead to increased population growth, until parents feel secure about the likelihood of their children surviving and begin to limit the number of children they have.

Today, Africa is desperately short of jobs. Underemployment may be as high as 60 percent. Within thirty years, there are likely to be three times as many people in the labor force. By the same projections, Africa's cities will grow five times larger.

Birth-control programs might win some time. But more important is basic education. Educated women decide for themselves how many children to have. And they work out how best to teach their families old values and new methods.

In Kenya, every study on Africa reports, the average mother has 8.5 children. Kenya's population growth rate, over 4 percent, is perhaps the highest in the world.

Evelyn Muindi is a Kenyan mother. "I have two kids, and I don't want any more," she told me. "These days we don't want too many, maybe two or three." Mrs. Muindi, if one stretches it, is a rural Kenyan yuppie. She is twenty-eight, married, and has a modest job operating the radio on a sprawling farm near Thika. Her family has 10 acres of maize, beans, pumpkins, seven cows, twenty-two goats.

She finished a girls' high school and then studied typing and shorthand. She learned a little French. In short, she decided she could use her head for more than just a balancing pad for water pots and bales of firewood. That was her decision, not a family planner's.

But she is still in the minority. Kenyan President Daniel arap Moi presses hard to control the birthrate, against tremendous resistance. When he had free milk delivered to schools, some children scrambled

> The suggestion that education produces different attitudes has been supported by research. Inkeles and Holsinger, in *Education and Individual Modernity in Developing Countries* (Leiden, 1974), note that
>
> > Those who had been in school longer were not only better informed and verbally more fluent. They had a different sense of time, and a stronger sense of personal and social efficacy; participated more actively in communal affairs; were more open to new ideas. . . ; showed more concern for subordinates and minorities. They valued science more, accepted change more readily, and were more prepared to limit the number of children they would have. In short, by virtue of having had more formal schooling, their personal character was decidedly more modern.

out of windows rather than drink it. Their parents had warned them against being poisoned by antifertility drugs. A Kenyan brewery had to destroy 10,000 bottles after someone spread a rumor that the beer would cause impotency.

At the London School of Hygiene and Tropical Medicine, William Brass is working with Kenyan demographers to assess the situation. "We see no evidence of any significant drop," he reported. Later, I questioned a senior Kenyan cabinet minister about birth control. He was not fond of the subject. Finally, he dismissed further talk with a hearty guffaw: "Well, we're not going to sterilize the men."

Rosenblum and Williamson use effective **topic sentences** that immediately characterize the paragraph being introduced. Note, for example, the opening of each paragraph in the section beginning "African leaders on occasion express suspicion. . . ." If you just read the first sentence of each paragraph, you would get quite a good sense of the authors' theme and the logical progression of their essay, although you would miss their discussion and analysis.

African leaders on occasion express suspicion of Western efforts to curb their population. France, for example, pays Frenchwomen to produce children and urges Africans to use contraception. Western societies argue that their populations are dropping, while Africa's increases twentyfold in a century. A reasonable reply might be that this is a racist argument.

Rural farmers resist efforts to limit families. They cannot control their markets or their weather. All they control is their labor supply.

But rapid population growth is a serious concern. Africa is stretching its resources far too thinly, in too many places.

One notion often applied to African demography is flatly wrong. European populations once grew as fast as contemporary Africa, it is believed; they stabilized by emigration and education. In fact, between 1751 and 1939, the population of England and Wales seldom grew faster than just over one percent a year, with a doubling time of sixty-five years. At its highest levels, emigration did not reduce the population growth by more than 10 percent. Kenya's population doubling time is seventeen years, and emigration is no option. The United States, despite all of its immigrants, has grown at an average of 2 percent a year since independence.

Most of Europe showed similar patterns, still irrelevant to Africa's condition. But consider an analysis of Ireland by British demographer N. L. Tranter. From 1753 to 1845, it grew at rates up to 2.1 percent per year. The result was catastrophic destitution, leading to famine. Causes cited were lack of natural resources, no investment, absentee landlordism, tariffs, competition from foreign manufacturers, religious divisiveness, vast inequality between rich and poor, the communal nature of Irish agriculture, and a preference for leisure over working to accumulate material wealth.

The authors' allusion is to the **Rev. Thomas Malthus** (1766–1834), an English economist best remembered for his warning that human population growth would outpace the growth of agricultural production. Malthus is still widely quoted and is discussed further in Section Three of this unit.

Africa suffers from each of those problems, with dwindling resources at the head of the list. Economist Julian Simon argues that human ingenuity makes resources infinitely expandable. Such reasoning may refute Malthus on a grander scale, but it does little for an African herder out of grass. Technically, it is possible to restore much of the Sahel the way engineers can make a golf course of southern Arizona desert. But not even the tiniest fraction of the funds needed are available to do it.

Alternative fuel and building supplies could reduce the pressure on Africa's shrinking forests. Unless those alternatives are available, however, Africans will not stop cutting wood.

Unspoiled ecosystems and wildlife are disappearing fast under the spread of human populations. Some economists argue that such concerns are needless. One remarked to Doug that the concept of respect for the earth was "utterly inane." Anyone who sees the world in such purely economic terms has a tragically narrow view of its potential. Deprived of an ability to appreciate natural wealth, such a man is hardly in a position to call an African poor. Cold, mechanical calculation of profit and loss has already squandered far too much of Africa.

The authors' views on the population question emerge gradually, but their view of the environmental degradation that is accompanying the rapid growth of human populations is stated at the outset: "Anyone who sees the world in . . . purely economic terms has a tragically narrow view of its potential." Perhaps this reflects the nature of the two authors, who don't disguise their affection for the African landscape and its people and animals. The writing is very personal here.

But some economists cling tightly to a one-dimensional view of the world. Simon writes, "Some people even impute feelings to trees or to animals, and they aim to prevent pain to these feelings." We have some wildebeest we would like to introduce to him. His human ingenuity may increase yields on depleted rangeland. But it will never replace a Bushman out after spring hare in the Kalahari sunrise.

To convince the bloodless, the argument goes beyond the question of natural resource.

The **Kalahari Desert** is in southern Africa, and the **Bushmen** (the Khoi) are the original inhabitants of the region.

African states now struggle to offer the most basic of education and health services to their current populations. How will they deal with greater numbers? It is clear that Africa must develop management skills, communications, civil services, industries, and practical sciences. While literacy stagnates in Africa, Japan turns out 71,000 new engineers a year.

Frederick T. Sai, a Ghanaian doctor and senior population adviser to the World Bank, remarked dryly: "We haven't got time on our side."

The point of development is to improve individuals' lives and equip their societies to compete in a modern world. Africa is falling behind on both counts.

Doug's friend Sam Modisane illustrates, as clearly as anyone, the loss to Africa's potential. Doug hired Sam to do some building on a farm he managed in Botswana. Sam soon revealed himself as an expert at everything: thatching, fixing motors, shoeing horses, welding gates, and playing the guitar. He was an African Zorba the Greek, down to the taste for working four days and getting blind drunk for three. Sam was paid by the job. Doug got his money's worth, and they became good friends.

Rhetorical note: The concerns and attitudes of the authors are very clear, and the tone is quite informal ("Doug's friend . . ."). The essay is full of **anecdotes** that support a certain point of view; this is a more journalistic way of writing about serious issues than you have seen in some of the other essays, but it is no less effective for that.

Sam had spent two years at a mission school learning to read and write, but his father yanked him out to come back to work. He herded cattle and goats for a while and then ran away to the northern Trans-

The authors move on to the real focus of their essay, which concerns the use and waste of human potential. Individual stories illustrate their general point.

vaal. An Afrikaner family paid him fifty cents a month, plus food and lodging, to look after the kids. He loved the children but decided he had to move on.

After rough jobs with hard men, Sam found work with a kindly building contractor. The man broke South African law to train him in skills reserved then for whites. After a few years, Sam got into a drunken brawl and returned to Botswana, a step ahead of the police. At home, where his skills were badly needed, he had more work than he could handle.

His gifts were remarkable. "You know, Douglas," he said once, with no hint of a boast, "I understand things very quickly." He knew four-wheel drives intimately but preferred his donkey cart. "When I get drunk," he explained, "I fall into the back of the cart, and the donkeys take me home, no matter where I am."

Sam read perfectly in spite of his brief schooling. Given the education and the chance, he could have accomplished just about anything Botswana needed done. Africa cannot afford to waste its Sam Modisanes.

Like Sam Nodisane, many people from countries bordering South Africa went there to work, despite the apartheid laws. The Transvaal is a South African province; the Afrikaners are South African whites of Dutch descent. The apartheid state, which imposed racial segregation and reserved political power for the white population in South Africa, has now been abandoned.

As much as its children, Africa wastes its women. "In our society, the woman is a beast of burden," Captain Thomas Sankara, of Burkina Faso, once remarked. "She is exploited like a cow which produces offspring, gives milk and has the force to work and offer pleasure. When she is old and tired, she is replaced by another cow."

Hotel employees in Gaborone once ejected a Ugandan guest for bringing too many women to his room. The man was indignant. "How can they prevent me from having women?" he demanded. "I must have a random sampling wherever I go."

As has been noted elsewhere in this section, the place of women in society is widely seen as critical, not only as a matter of basic human rights and decency, but also in terms of economic and social development.

African men, by and large, are cool to the idea of their women getting uppity. With the exception of some cabinet ministers—often tokens—there have been no women leaders of African governments. Far fewer women than men can read or write. But they carry 90 percent of the water and firewood, and they plant 80 percent of the food. An average woman's workday runs to eighteen hours—rearing children, pounding grain, cooking, farming, and hauling produce to market.

Because of a crippling lack of draft animals, it is the women who haul and pull. René Dumont calculated that to carry thirty tons of fertilizer to fields two miles away, women must carry fifty pounds for 4,000 miles.

THINK ON PAPER

What do Rosenblum and Williamson say here that suggests the vital place of women in their countries' economies, and why is women's education so important?

Women, often illiterate, dominate West African markets and much of the commerce. Elsewhere in Africa, they run small businesses and amass substantial fortunes. When wronged, they face police and soldiers with surprising courage. But few stand up to their husbands.

Women live in fear that their husbands will throw them out. If they scrape together any cash, they buy jewelry and gold. It is their only security. Baule women in the Ivory Coast have a little ditty they sometimes sing on the job: "If I'd have known how hard it is to be a woman, I'd have been a man."

In neighboring Mali, Monique Munz of CARE told me, "The men have the power, and they won't give it up. Everything waits until the men gather. By the age of eight, a girl's thumbs are deformed from pounding millets. By womanhood, she has large splayed hands. Her clitoris is removed. In villages, you see only boys hanging around, or studying. The girls are working. Is that going to change? Come on, you're a man. How is that going to change?"

A new generation is showing some change. Desiré Ecaré, an Ivorian filmmaker, expressed an evolving attitude: "We must fix it so we don't have a twentieth-century man living with a woman of the Middle Ages."

West Africa, despite its problems, has a significant film industry, especially in former French colonies such as Burkina Faso and Ivory Coast.

Women are offering examples in every field. In Liberia, President Samuel Doe's greatest threat is from Ellen Johnson-Sirleaf, a former finance minister, who formed an opposition party when he would not let her leave the country. In exile, she directs international attention to Doe's excesses.

The brutal Samuel Doe was overthrown and killed in 1990. Since 1989, Liberia has been devastated by continuous civil war.

The problem is critical in rural areas where most Africans live, and where Sankara's description is distressingly apt. Men clear the land, tend cash crops and animals. If there is game, they hunt. But mainly they are in charge of customs and wisdom, and of spending the family money. Women do the rest.

Because of skewed divisions of labor, women run short of time for planting food. Often, crops are limited not by available land and seed, but, rather, by the efforts village women can muster. When there are surpluses, it is women who haul them to the nearest crossroads and sell them in the market. Despite their leading role, women seldom receive the training, tools, or credits provided to men. They rarely share in the decisions on subsistence farms.

That especially peeves Josephine Ouedraogo, Sankara's minister for family development. "Agricultural modernization always passes through the hands of men while it is the women who form the pillar of family food production," she told a visiting reporter. "When a farmer decides to devote two-thirds of his land to cash crops, he is counting mainly on feminine labor, but the women never take part in the decision that creates a terrible load on their work schedule."

Money for investment is very limited in many poor countries, as is suggested here by a member of Burkina Faso's government. Wealthier countries can be important in such situations, but **foreign aid** is unpopular in difficult economic times in some donor countries. The international community has set a target of 0.7% of gross national product (GNP) for industrial countries to give in aid each year; UNICEF reported in 1995 that the United States was second to Japan in the dollar amount of aid given, but that this was only 0.15% of the country's GNP, placing it last in generosity among the 21 industrial nations by this measurement.

But Minister Ouedraogo, thirty-six and energetic, has few illusions about how much she can change. "The means of my ministry?" she reflected. "Zero, or almost. I've got the smallest budget in the government."

In every country of Africa, women have shown they can increase productivity, run flourishing enterprises, and devise new ways to increase the family income. But first they must break free of traditional constraints.

"Look, it is easy," said Fanta Babacissé Diallo, with a merry laugh. She waved her arm toward a legion of liberated housewives happily beavering away on an irrigation project in the ancient city of Djenné, in Mali. She is president and head motivator of a cooperative of several hundred Djenné women. Most are married and have children and a full range of wifely duties to perform, but they have broken their bonds.

Mrs. Diallo was showing off a self-help cooperative to grow rice and vegetables along the Bani River. The government supplied a gasoline-powered pump. Men and women, working together, did the rest. Later she took her visitors downtown. To drums and chanting, women performed Songhai and Bambara dances that, for lack of time to dance them, had been slipping toward oblivion.

Then we went to the craft shop. In the good old days, women on the river wore their riches above the shoulders: great gold earrings, necklaces of golden spheres the size of softballs, chunks of amber. Too poor for that any more, the women found a way to save their traditional dress. They carve gourds in the shape of the old jewelry and paint them in brilliant yellow. Only a banker or a killjoy would note the difference.

But Mrs. Diallo's real joy is the oven campaign. She worked out a pattern for a one-burner mud dome that consumes a fraction of the wood of an open fire. She knows to the oven how many are in service around Djenné, and there are more than a thousand.

Mrs. Diallo is thirty-three. Her first husband died, leaving her with three children. She married a lawyer who lives in Bamako, the Malian capital, but she preferred to stay and work with the women of Djenné. She will likely go far. But she is happy enough to be the mother of the improved mud oven.

The "Eve" hypothesis alluded to here is discussed in Unit One, Section Two, of this text.

If you can believe Professor Allan Wilson, of the University of California at Berkeley, all of us descended from a single Eve who lived in Eden, somewhere in Africa, 140,000 to 280,000 years ago. Wilson, a biochemist, bases his theory on the estimated rate of mutation of DNA in human cells. He concludes that preceding species in Indonesia, China, or Greece may have died out or been swept aside by the progeny of the African mother.

Maybe. But it is beyond dispute that African women form a class apart. Harvard physiologist Norman C. Heglund has determined that a 130-pound African woman can walk with a twenty-six-pound weight on her head and burn up no more energy than if she were carrying nothing. She can carry seventy-five pounds on her head with far less strain than an army recruit can hump a backpack.

That comes as no surprise to anyone who has visited Africa. I have seen a Nigerian woman glide smoothly through crowded streets with two king-size mattresses balanced on her head, and, in Zaire, a village woman similarly carrying a stack of folded textiles nearly as tall as she was. Heglund speculates that African women start carrying loads early enough so their bodies make the necessary adjustments. They learn balance and a smooth gait. My own theory is that they have no choice: How else would they get their work done?

Improving women's lot must start with health and nutrition. In much of Africa, a woman is forty-five times more likely to die during childbirth than a woman her age in Sweden or Denmark. Her children are fifteen times more likely to die before age five.

From the outside, it would seem that Africa lives in mass terror of the acquired immune deficiency syndrome that seems to have spread from the continent's tropical center. But concern over AIDS is growing slowly. Africans have more immediate killers to worry about—like the common cold. A million children a year die of whooping cough, measles, and tetanus. Polio, diphtheria, and leprosy still flourish, but ordinary diarrhea is still the biggest killer.

Since Rosenblum and Williamson wrote this, the AIDS situation in many African countries has reached crisis proportions.

The common killers mentioned here are all preventable, but resources for vaccinations, clean water, and other preventive measures are limited.

Soon enough, health officials warn, AIDS will worry Africans a great deal. World Health Organization specialists said in early 1987 that as many as five million Africans are believed to carry the AIDS virus, and a million of them may die. In isolated parts of Uganda, whole villages are threatened. But the disease is widely reported elsewhere.

At first, some African health authorities underplayed AIDS, fearing discrimination and a loss of tourism. When scientists began tracing the disease to Africa, some governments said they were victims of racism. Although most have admitted the problem and are helping Western doctors with research, more familiar health problems still take priority.

By 1987, health authorities in West Africa acknowledged that the virus was spreading from Central Africa. In Abidjan, the fast-paced capital of Ivory Coast, the government issued firm warnings. Reaction was mixed. A French reporter saw crowds of children running after a prostitute, stoning her and chanting: "AIDS, AIDS!" But a more common response came from a young woman in a waterfront bar: "Each week, boatloads of sailors come for sex here and no one has ever complained. Who has seen AIDS? Nobody. Not even on TV. A disease you can't see, with no treatment, does not exist."

Basic hygiene education can save a lot of lives. Private volunteer agencies often concentrate on mother-child nutrition care. A simple dime bag of oral rehydration salts can restore essential liquids to a child stricken with severe diarrhea. But most endangered African children suffer the same crippling deficiency: lack of food. Even in Zimbabwe when crops are good, nearly 36,000 children die each year from malnutrition. UNICEF estimates 30 to 48 percent of Zimbabwean children under five are malnourished. Among the worst off are farm workers' children. The problem is poverty.

Throughout this chapter of their book, the authors make liberal use of quotations from people they interview. These illustrate the points they are making and lend further credibility to what they are saying. Here, for example, the head of UNICEF comments on the disastrous impact of poor nutrition on young children. In **research papers,** you will usually find your sources in the library, but your quotes and paraphrases will serve the same function. More on this in the *Aspects of writing* and *Writing exercises* parts of this unit.

James P. Grant, executive director of UNICEF, calls the annual death of 4 million African children "the silent emergency." The cost of malnutrition is incalculable, he notes, since 90 percent of the growth of the human brain, and much of the body, takes place in the first five years. And the World Bank has even found an argument for the cold-blooded: "Better health and nutrition are not only humanitarian imperatives . . . they are also basic requirements for sustained economic growth."

This last point is no small one. Africa cannot possibly develop effectively with so much of its energy sapped by disease. The commonly known ailments and malnutrition are bad enough. But there is more.

Africa suffers from virulent, endemic diseases most Westerners cannot even pronounce: onchocerciasis and schistosomiasis, among others. The first is river blindness, spread by black flies along swift-moving rivers, which starts with a painful swelling and ends often in total blindness. The second is an invasion of microscopic parasites that bore into the body to debilitate and kill.

Malaria attacks and recurs all over Africa. "We used to call malaria 'weeks' because when you got it, you knew that's how long you would be in bed," Djibril Diallo remembers. "People in Europe and America sometimes think Africans grow immune to malaria. Hardly."

In the first wave of development aid, donors built hospitals and clinics. The idea was to reduce the number of miles the average African had to travel to a health facility. But not enough thought was given to what happened when he got there.

Bamako is the capital city of Mali.

An hour up a paved road from Bamako, is the provincial town of Segou. For centuries, Segou has been a major Sahelian crossroads and river port. In 1986, I stopped at the central clinic and found Dr. Mbayi Babambiba. She was twenty-six years old, tending a long line of people stoically waiting their turn. "We are out of aspirin, malaria tablets, and antibiotics," she told me. "We are supposed to be supplied every three months, but the ministry has nothing."

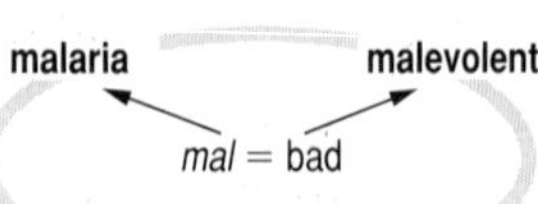

The name "malaria" originated in the belief that the disease was caused by "bad air"; now, we know that it is carried by the anopheles mosquito.

At least, the clinic had a doctor. At the time, a number of Malian doctors were out of work because the government had no money to pay them. In some countries, young doctors back from medical school abroad refuse to leave the capital cities. They worked hard to escape the bush, many felt, and they were anxious to reap the rewards.

At Diré, an Italian doctor sweated in the heat. He was hard at work learning to deal with challenges he never faced in Italy. "The Malian doctors," he said, "they just don't have the experience." A European aid official with me muttered under his breath: "And how are they going to get it?" Mali, he felt, needed fewer foreign doctors and more wherewithal to equip its own.

As a general rule for Africa, in almost all fields, it was not a bad thought.

THINK ON PAPER
What is the "general rule" referred to in the last sentence, and how could it be applied to medical and other fields?

ASPECTS OF WRITING: Finding good quotes.

THINK ON PAPER
Rosenblum and Williamson write about several aspects of the situation in Africa as they see it, including population growth, environmental degradation, the roles and status of women, birth control, and health issues. **Choose one of these and identify several quotes that you think represent the authors' views.** You will have an opportunity to use these quotes in one of the essay choices that follow.

When you **take notes,** make sure that you write the quotation accurately and put it in quotation marks. Notes are often a mixture of quote and paraphrase, and you must make it clear to yourself which is which. It's also important, especially in a research paper, to write down the page number from which the quote or paraphrase comes, so that you can cite it and also so that you can find it again easily if you need to.

As mentioned in the annotations accompanying the above reading, Rosenblum and Williamson quote people they encounter in the course of their work and travels in Africa, and you can do the same in your academic writing, except that most of your sources will be found in the library. In research papers, of course, you will be required to use a number of different sources.

Choosing quotes that add something significant to your paper requires a good understanding of the topic you are reading and writing about. You need to be able to pick out only those words, phrases, or sentences that, when said by an acknowledged expert, or by someone who represents a certain attitude toward your topic, will illustrate **the point you are making.** The key word here is "you," because research papers are not supposed to be mere summaries of what other people say, or collections of other people's observations.

Your quotes should not, therefore, be so lengthy that you give the impression of relying on your sources to say everything for you. Neither should the quotes be so ill chosen that they don't add anything to the discussion.

The relationship between quote and essay is suggested by the fact that **no paragraph or even sentence consists entirely of quotation.** The quotes and other sourced material are important, but they don't dominate. Rosenblum and Williamson are like court attorneys calling up expert witnesses to testify. The attorneys make the case, but they get expert help on particular points. You can establish a similar relationship with the sources in your writing.

WRITING EXERCISES: Answer one of the following questions.

1. Following up on the exercise suggested on the previous page, identify one aspect of Rosenblum and Williamson's essay that you find interesting and create a thesis that characterizes their view. Describe and discuss what they say, making use of several direct quotes and paraphrases.
2. The authors clearly indicate that the waste of human potential—especially involving women but including the undereducation of many men also—is a major problem in many African countries. They advocate giving top priority to the health and education of women and children (boys and girls, of course) as the best way forward. To what extent do you think that your own country should adopt a similar strategy?
3. Mention was made earlier in this section of evidence that formal schooling tends to influence and change the attitudes of people in traditional societies. Does the same apply in countries like the United States? What impact does (or should) schooling have on children? To answer this, it may help to refer to the quote from Inkeles and Holsinger in the annotations to Rosenblum and Williamson's essay. Your personal experience of school would also be relevant here.

Acceptable and unacceptable ways of using quotations:

Unspoiled ecosystems and wildlife are disappearing fast under the spread of human populations.
Comments: Completely unacceptable; plagiarism. The writer has stolen Rosenblum and Williamson's words, copied them, and given no credit to the real authors.

Rosenblum and Williamson note that unspoiled ecosystems and wildlife are disappearing fast under the spread of human populations.
Comments: Completely unacceptable; plagiarism, even though the source is given. Copied directly from the original with no quotation marks.

"Unspoiled ecosystems and wildlife are disappearing fast under the spread of human populations" (Rosenblum and Williamson 254).
Comments: Not acceptable, despite being accurately quoted from the original. Quote is not introduced. The sentence is 100% quotation. The writer has let the source speak for him/her.

Rosenblum and Williamson note that "Unspoiled ecosystems and wildlife are disappearing fast under the spread of human populations" (254).
Comments: Good. Quote is introduced and correctly cited.

Expressing their alarm at the environmental degradation underway in Africa, Rosenblum and Williamson note that natural habitats and the animals that inhabit them "are disappearing fast under the spread of human populations" (254).
Comments: Good. The sentence combines commentary, paraphrase, and direct quote. Quote is well integrated into the sentence. Correctly cited.

SECTION THREE

Prior knowledge: Measuring quality of life.

Both the World Bank and UNDP group countries into three categories:

World Bank (1994)	**UNDP** (1994)
high income	high human development
middle income	medium human development
low income	low human development

The number of countries in each category can change significantly each year. The following is the distribution in the 1994 reports of these organizations (UNDP includes more countries):

high income (23)	high human development (53)
middle income (66)	medium human development (65)
low income (42)	low human development (55)

The World Bank tables list only those countries with more than one million people. Another 75 "other economies" are listed separately; not all of these are independent countries.

In Section One of this unit, the World Bank tables ranked nations according to their GNP per capita. Nation #1, Mozambique, was by this measure the world's poorest country, and #132, Switzerland, was the world's richest. As one might expect from a bank, the principal basis for determining rank is wealth, but some critics have observed that wealth alone does not tell us much about the **quality of life** in different countries. The World Bank offers social indicators as well as economic ones, but no ranking is offered on any basis but GNP per capita.

This gap has been filled by another United Nations agency, the United Nations Development Programme (UNPD), which publishes a *Human Development Report* each year. This provides a "Human Development Index," which in 1994 ranked 173 countries by a combination of economic, health, and educational factors. In addition, the UNDP shows how these rankings are affected by the addition of other variables, such as **gender disparity** and **income distribution.** Additional tables are also provided that give a statistical picture of things that affect quality of life, such as crime, drug use, and unemployment.

Subjective factors may influence one's choice of "best country to live in"—climate, for example, or cultural factors—but the UNDP offers an interesting alternative to the World Bank's way of ranking countries.

It might be argued that such rankings fail to recognize that the quality of life within any country varies considerably, but the income-distribution and gender-disparity adjustments help to compensate for this. Quality-of-life indicators help to identify those countries that spend the resources available to them in ways most advantageous to the majority of their people. The 1993 *Human Development Report,* for example, notes that, despite the end of the Cold War and a general reduction in world military expenditures since 1987, "for many poor countries, the ratio of military spending to social spending remains far too high."

THINK ON PAPER
Which factors would you consider most significant in comparing the quality of life in different countries?

Japan is ranked first in the Human Development Index for 1993, but when this is adjusted for **gender disparity** she falls to 17th.

Income, the tables show, does not necessarily indicate human development. Demonstrating this, the 1993 report notes that Chile, China, Colombia, Costa Rica, Sri Lanka (despite an ongoing civil war), Tanzania, and Uruguay had human development rankings far ahead of their GNP per capita rank. On the other hand, some countries had higher GNP per capita than human development rankings; these included Algeria, Angola, Gabon, Guinea, Namibia, Saudi Arabia, Senegal, South Africa, and the United Arab Emirates. The United States was tenth in GNP per capita rank and sixth in human development rank, as is shown in the tables that follow.

Life in relatively poor countries can be very pleasant, and vice versa. Many Americans choose to live in Costa Rica and Mexico, for example, even as some people from those countries choose to move to the United States. The tables perhaps say more about government priorities than about individual experience, but they offer rich data. Among the wealthy countries, they suggest a broadly similar quality of life, with some countries revealing startling differences in particular areas, as in the high rate of drug crimes in Australia and of homicides and imprisonment in the United States.

Asiaweek, of Hong Kong, has calculated that worldwide military spending fell about 8% between 1981–1991, but that many developing countries were going in the opposite direction. The following nations spent the largest percentages of their 1991 budgets on military projects. Note that two of these countries no longer exist.

Saudi Arabia	60.6%
Syria	60.3%
[Former] Yugoslavia	55.0%
Ethiopia	52.1%
United Arab Emirates	44.0%
[Former] Soviet Union	43.1%
Vietnam	40.0%
Oman	35.5%
Poland	32.9%
Taiwan	32.4%

(from *World Press Review,* May 1995)

The quality of life in some countries may be unfavorably affected by **human rights considerations,** such as freedom of speech and political participation. Objective measurement of political factors is difficult, but they are discussed in the commentary sections of the UNDP reports.

In many poor countries, the quality of life is sustained in part by domestic food production (producing what the anthropologist Raymond Firth called "subsistence affluence" in the South Pacific islands) and remittances—cash payments—from relatives in other countries.

ANNOTATED READING: United Nations Development Programme (UNDP). "Assessing Human Development." *Human Development Report 1993*. New York: Oxford U.P., 1993: 10–18.

Assessing Human Development

The first *Human Development Report*, in introducing the concept of human development, argued that the real purpose of development should be to enlarge people's choices. Subsequent Reports have developed the basic concept, looking in particular at how human development could be financed and at its international dimensions—through trade, official development assistance and international migration flows. Each Report has also presented balance sheets for human development, for both industrial and developing countries (see boxes 1.2 and 1.3 for this year's balance sheets).

To quantify and clarify the process of human development, the 1990 Report also introduced a new yardstick of human progress: the human development index (HDI). By combining indicators of real purchasing power, education and health, the HDI offers a measure of development much more comprehensive than GNP alone.

The second Report, in 1991, took up the question of financing human development—and the role of governments. It looked at the potential for restructuring national budgets away from wasteful expenditure on the military and on loss-making public enterprises, for example—and towards more relevant priorities, such as basic education and primary health care.

There is a growing feeling among some rich countries ("donor countries") that aid should be tied to higher spending in health, education, and other **human development priorities** rather than in the military and related areas.

The analysis used four ratios to highlight government spending priorities. These showed that developing countries spend more than 25% of their GNP through the budget, yet devote less than one-tenth of this to human development priorities. The 1991 Report also discovered similar imbalances in international aid: less than 7% of total aid is spent on human priority areas. It concluded that the world had an enormous opportunity to increase investments in human development—even with existing resources.

The 1992 Report extended the analysis by adding an international dimension. It focused specifically on global markets and on how they meet—or fail to meet—human needs. The Report discovered that global markets make developing countries lose economic opportunities worth around $500 billion annually—ten times what they receive in foreign assistance. No wonder that the global income disparity

Box 1.2 *Balance Sheet of Human Development—Developing Countries*

PROGRESS	DEPRIVATION
Life Expectancy	
• Average life expectancy increased by over one-third during the past three decades; 23 countries have achieved a life expectancy of 70 years and more.	• Of the 300 million above the age of 60, only 20% have any form of income security.
Health and Sanitation	
• In the developing world, more than 70% of the population has access to health services. • Nearly 60% of the population has access to sanitation.	• About 17 million people die every year from infectious and parasitic diseases, such as diarrhoea, malaria and tuberculosis. • More than 80% of the 12–13 million HIV-infected people are in the developing world, and the cumulative direct and indirect cost of AIDS during the past decade was around $30 billion.
Food and Nutrition	
• Between 1965 and 1990, the number of countries that met their daily per capita calorie requirements doubled—from about 25 to 50.	• Some 800 million people still do not get enough food.
Education	
• Primary school enrollment increased in the past two decades—from less than 70% to well over 80%. In the same period, secondary enrollment almost doubled—from less than 25% to 40%.	• Nearly one billion people—35% of the adult population—are still illiterate, and the drop-out rate at the primary level is still as high as 30%.
Income and Poverty	
• In South and East Asia, where two-thirds of the developing world's population live, the GNP growth averaged more than 7% a year during the 1980s.	• Almost one-third of the total population, or 1.3 billion people, are in absolute poverty.
Children	
• During the past 30 years, infant and under-five mortality rates were more than halved.	• Each day, 34,000 young children still die from malnutrition and disease.
Women	
• The secondary enrollment ratio for girls increased from around 17% in 1970 to 36% in 1990.	• Two-thirds of illiterates are women.
Human Security	
• With the end of the cold war, developing countries no longer have to serve as proxies for superpower rivalry, and in 1990, about 380,000 refugees returned to their homelands in Asia, Africa and Latin America.	• Internal conflicts afflict some 60 countries, and about 35 million people are refugees or internally displaced.
Environment	
• The percentage of rural families with access to safe water has increased from less than 10% to almost 60% during the past two decades.	• More than 850 million people live in areas that are in various stages of desertification. • The rate of tropical forest destruction is about the equivalent of one soccer field per second.

BOX 1.3 *Balance Sheet of Human Development—Industrial Countries*

PROGRESS	DEPRIVATION
LIFE EXPECTANCY AND HEALTH	
• In 1960, life expectancy was more than 70 years in only 12 countries. Now, it is more than 70 years in all industrial countries.	• Nearly two million people are HIV-infected, and the direct and indirect cost during the 1980s was $210 billion.
EDUCATION	
• The tertiary enrollment ratio more than doubled between 1965 and 1990.	• More than one-third of the adults lack any upper-secondary or higher education.
INCOME AND EMPLOYMENT	
• The per capita GNP grew at an annual rate of 2.4% between 1965 and 1990.	• The average unemployment rate is about 7%, and a quarter of the more than 30 million unemployed have been out of work for more than two years.
SOCIAL SECURITY	
• Social security expenditures now account for just under 15% of GDP.	• About 100 million people live below the poverty line.
WOMEN	
• Women now account for more than 40% of total employment.	• Women hold fewer than 10% of parliamentary seats.
SOCIAL FABRIC	
• There are now five library books and more than one radio for every person, and more than one telephone and one TV set for every two people. One in three people reads a newspaper.	• There are more than 15 suicides, more than 100 drug crimes and more than 15 deaths from road accidents per 100,000 people. • The number of divorces is now one-third the number of marriages contracted, and well over 5% of households are single-parent homes.
POPULATION AND ENVIRONMENT	
• Energy requirements per unit of GDP fell by 40% between 1965 and 1990.	• People in industrial countries make up about one-fifth of world population but consume ten times more commercial energy than people in developing countries, and they account for 71% of the world's carbon monoxide emissions and 68% of the world's industrial waste.

has doubled during the past three decades: the richest 20% of the world's people now receive more than 150 times the income of the poorest 20%.

That Report suggested two priority areas for future action. First, developing countries should invest massively in their people to sharpen their competitive edge in international markets. Second, there should be a radical dismantling of trade barriers and a major reform of international institutions, including the United Nations and the Bretton Woods institutions, to establish a new vision of global cooperation for the 21st century.

The HDI has attracted much attention from the academic community and from policy-makers. Technical note 1 explains its construction, and our intention is to continue to refine the methodology of the HDI in the light of comments and to steadily improve the database. Technical note 2 presents a detailed discussion of the HDI's methodology, the criticisms received, the refinements contemplated and the methodological options for dealing with some of the issues raised [these technical notes are not included here]. We include this note to elicit further comments so that a much improved methodology can be devised for the 1994 Report. This Report introduces no changes in the method of HDI measurement, enabling a comparison of country rankings with the 1992 Report.

This brief review of the history of the HDI suggests the process by which agencies attempt to refine and improve a new concept.

This year's country rankings show that Japan has displaced Canada at the top because of its significant increase (23%) in real GDP per capita during 1989–90 (table 1.1). For the countries with the lowest levels of human development, there has not been much change in ranking (table 1.2 and figure 1.4).

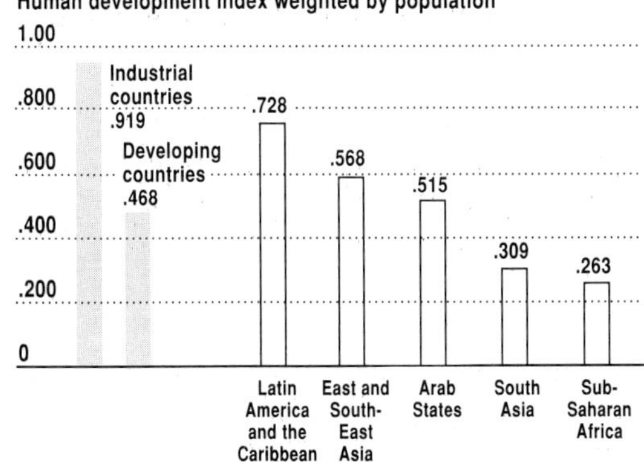

Figure 1.4. Human development varies by region

TABLE 1.1 ***HDI Ranking for Industrial Countries [1993]***

COUNTRY	HDI VALUE	HDI RANK	GNP PER CAPITA RANK	GNP PER CAPITA RANK MINUS HDI RANK[a]
Japan	0.983	1	3	2
Canada	0.982	2	11	9
Norway	0.978	3	6	3
Switzerland	0.978	4	1	–3
Sweden	0.977	5	5	0
USA	0.976	6	10	4
Australia	0.972	7	20	13
France	0.971	8	13	5
Netherlands	0.970	9	17	8
United Kingdom	0.964	10	21	11
Iceland	0.960	11	9	–2
Germany	0.957	12	8	–4
Denmark	0.955	13	7	–6
Finland	0.954	14	4	–10
Austria	0.952	15	14	–1
Belgium	0.952	16	16	0
New Zealand	0.947	17	23	6
Luxembourg	0.943	18	2	–16
Israel	0.938	19	27	8
Ireland	0.925	21	29	8
Italy	0.924	22	18	–4
Spain	0.923	23	28	5
Greece	0.902	25	35	10
Czechoslovakia	0.892	26	49	23
Hungary	0.887	28	52	24
Malta	0.855	39	33	–6
Bulgaria	0.854	40	67	27
Portugal	0.853	41	38	–3
Poland	0.831	48	80	32
Romania	0.709	77	84	7
Albania	0.699	78	90	12
Other countries				
Lithuania	0.881	29	51	22
Estonia	0.872	34	42	8
Latvia	0.868	35	43	8
Russian Fed.	0.862	37	47	10
Belarus	0.861	38	50	12
Ukraine	0.844	45	58	13
Armenia	0.831	47	63	16
Georgia	0.829	49	72	23
Kazakhstan	0.802	54	55	1
Azerbaijan	0.770	62	82	20
Moldova, Rep.	0.758	64	61	–3
Turkmenistan	0.746	66	81	15
Uzbekistan	0.695	80	92	12
Kyrgyzstan	0.689	83	85	2
Tajikistan	0.657	88	94	6

a. A positive figure shows that the HDI rank is higher than the GNP rank, a negative the opposite.

TABLE 1.2 ***HDI Ranking for Developing Countries***

Country	HDI Value	HDI Rank	GNP Rank	Country	HDI Value	HDI Rank	GNP Rank	Country	HDI Value	HDI Rank	GNP Rank
Barbados	0.928	20	34	Ecuador	0.646	89	108	Ghana	0.311	131	140
Hong Kong	0.913	24	24	Paraguay	0.641	90	97	Pakistan	0.311	132	136
Cyprus	0.890	27	30	Korea, Dem. Rep.	0.640	91	103	Cameroon	0.310	133	107
Uruguay	0.881	30	54	Philippines	0.603	92	114	India	0.309	134	146
Trinidad and Tobago	0.877	31	46	Tunisia	0.600	93	88	Namibia	0.289	135	98
Bahamas	0.875	32	25	Oman	0.598	94	36	Côte d'Ivoire	0.286	136	113
Korea, Rep. of	0.872	33	37	Peru	0.592	95	95	Haiti	0.275	137	143
Chile	0.864	36	75	Iraq	0.589	96	73	Tanzania, U. Rep. of	0.270	138	172
Costa Rica	0.852	42	76	Dominican Rep.	0.586	97	112	Comoros	0.269	139	129
Singapore	0.849	43	26	Samoa	0.586	98	109	Zaire	0.262	140	158
Brunei Darussalam	0.847	44	19	Jordan	0.582	99	91	Lao People's Dem. Rep.	0.246	141	161
Argentina	0.832	46	62	Mongolia	0.578	100	104	Nigeria	0.246	142	153
Venezuela	0.824	50	56	China	0.566	101	142	Yemen	0.233	143	124
Dominica	0.819	51	70	Lebanon	0.565	102	87	Liberia	0.222	144	127
Kuwait	0.815	52	15	Iran, Islamic Rep.	0.557	103	59	Togo	0.218	145	135
Mexico	0.805	53	60	Botswana	0.552	104	69	Uganda	0.194	146	167
Qatar	0.802	55	22	Guyana	0.541	105	141	Bangladesh	0.189	147	159
Mauritius	0.794	56	68	Vanuatu	0.533	106	96	Cambodia	0.186	148	168
Malaysia	0.790	57	66	Algeria	0.528	107	65	Rwanda	0.186	149	151
Bahrain	0.790	58	32	Indonesia	0.515	108	122	Senegal	0.182	150	115
Grenada	0.787	59	71	Gabon	0.503	109	44	Ethiopia	0.172	151	170
Antigua and Barbuda	0.785	60	41	El Salvador	0.503	110	102	Nepal	0.170	152	166
Colombia	0.770	61	93	Nicaragua	0.500	111	133	Malawi	0.168	153	162
Seychelles	0.761	63	39	Maldives	0.497	112	131	Burundi	0.167	154	160
Suriname	0.751	65	48	Guatemala	0.489	113	110	Equatorial Guinea	0.164	155	147
United Arab Emirates	0.738	67	12	Cape Verde	0.479	114	116	Central African Rep.	0.159	156	139
Panama	0.738	68	77	Viet Nam	0.472	115	156	Mozambique	0.154	157	173
Jamaica	0.736	69	86	Honduras	0.472	116	118	Sudan	0.152	158	138
Brazil	0.730	70	53	Swaziland	0.458	117	99	Bhutan	0.150	159	163
Fiji	0.730	71	78	Solomon Islands	0.439	118	121	Angola	0.143	160	126
Saint Lucia	0.720	72	64	Morocco	0.433	119	106	Mauritania	0.140	161	128
Turkey	0.717	73	83	Lesotho	0.431	120	123	Benin	0.113	162	145
Thailand	0.715	74	89	Zimbabwe	0.398	121	117	Djibouti	0.104	163	125
Cuba	0.711	75	101	Bolivia	0.398	122	119	Guinea-Bissau	0.090	164	165
Saint Vincent	0.709	76	79	Myanmar	0.390	123	152	Chad	0.088	165	164
Saint Kitts and Nevis	0.697	79	45	Egypt	0.389	124	120	Somalia	0.087	166	171
Syrian Arab Rep.	0.694	81	105	Sáo Tomé and Principe	0.374	125	137	Gambia	0.086	167	148
Belize	0.689	82	74	Congo	0.372	126	100	Mali	0.082	168	154
Saudi Arabia	0.688	84	31	Kenya	0.369	127	144	Niger	0.080	169	150
South Africa	0.673	85	57	Madagascar	0.327	128	157	Burkina Faso	0.074	170	149
								Afghanistan	0.066	171	169
Sri Lanka	0.663	86	130	Papua New Guinea	0.318	129	111	Sierra Leone	0.065	172	155
Libyan Arab Jamahiriya	0.658	87	40	Zambia	0.314	130	134	Guinea	0.045	173	132

An analysis of the HDI country rankings brings out some interesting policy conclusions:

1. **There is no automatic link between income and human development** Several countries—such as Chile, China, Colombia, Costa Rica, Madagascar, Sri Lanka, Tanzania and Uruguay—have done well in translating their income into the lives of their people: Their human development rank is way ahead of their per capita income rank (figure 1.5). Other societies—such as Algeria, Angola, Gabon, Guinea, Namibia, Saudi Arabia, Senegal, South Africa and United Arab Emirates—have income ranks far above their human development rank, showing their enormous potential for improving the lives of their people.

   Several countries enjoying similar incomes per capita have very divergent human development experiences. Five countries with a GNP per capita of around $380 in 1990 had human accomplishments that could not be more dissimilar: Guyana, Kenya, Ghana, Pakistan and Haiti. Of this group, Guyana has the highest HDI value (0.541, rank 105), Haiti the lowest (0.275, rank 137). Ghana's average life expectancy is ten years shorter than Guyana's, and Pakistan's infant mortality rate is twice as high as Guyana's—and its illiteracy rate 16 times higher. Income alone is obviously a poor indicator of human development.

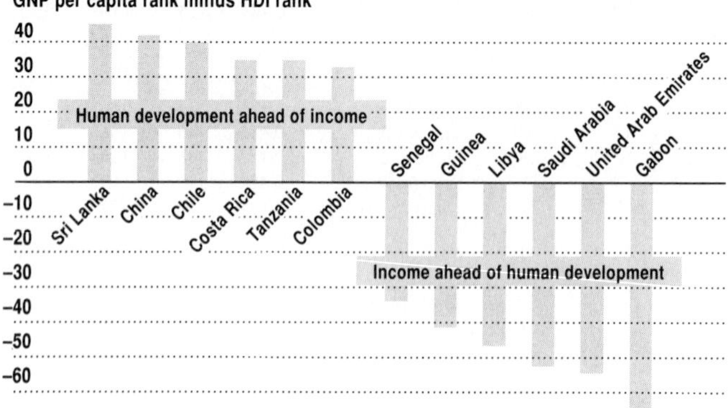

Figure 1.5. There is no automatic link between income and human development

2. **The change in human development is as significant as its level** Many countries started at a low level of human development three decades ago but have since made very rapid progress, particularly the Gulf States, whose real economic prosperity came in the mid-1970s after the steep increase in oil prices (figure 1.6). It clearly took time to invest the new income in people, but during the past 20 years, the Gulf States have made much faster progress than the average

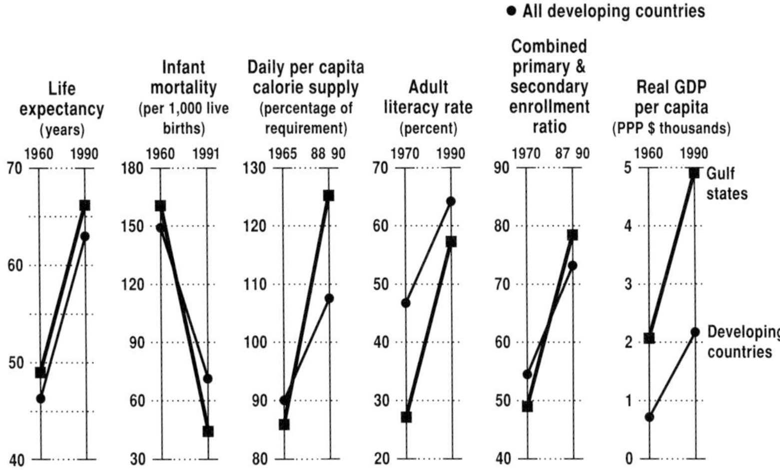

Figure 1.6. Human development progress in the Gulf States

developing country. Saudi Arabia had the greatest change in its HDI value—from 0.386 in 1970 to 0.688 in 1990.

Several countries with similar HDIs in 1970 have since had dissimilar experiences. Myanmar and Saudi Arabia, for example, started with similar HDIs in 1970, as did Zaire and Morocco. For Myanmar and Zaire, the world has stood still in terms of human development—a factor which no doubt has contributed to the countries' present problems. But Saudi Arabia has since nearly doubled its HDI, and Morocco has raised its HDI by 60% (figure 1.7).

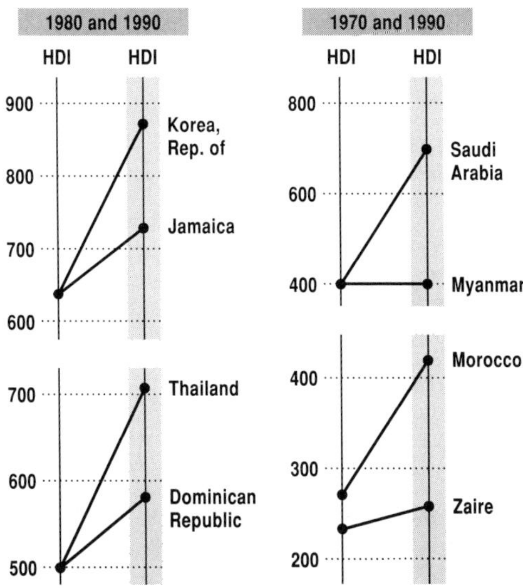

Figure 1.7. HDIs have diverged for countries with similar starting points

For comparative purposes, the 1994 HDI for industrial countries is given below. The changes in rankings, which seem remarkable for only a one-year time period, may be largely explained by *changes in the way UNDP calculates the index.* In this regard, it should always be remembered that the method of calculation, and the factors chosen for inclusion, will always affect the outcome. The fact that all the wealthy industrial countries share a very similar standard of living may also explain why relatively small changes can affect the HDI rankings. In 1995, when further technical changes were made, the rankings changed again, with the United States jumping to second place, behind Canada.

HDI ranking for industrial countries [1994]

	HDI VALUE	HDI RANK	GNP PER CAPITA RANK	GNP PER CAPITA RANK MINUS HDI RANK[a]
Canada	0.932	1	11	10
Switzerland	0.931	2	1	-1
Japan	0.929	3	3	0
Sweden	0.928	4	4	0
Norway	0.928	5	5	0
France	0.927	6	13	7
Australia	0.926	7	18	11
USA	0.925	8	9	1
Netherlands	0.923	9	16	7
United Kingdom	0.919	10	19	9
Germany	0.918	11	12	1
Austria	0.917	12	14	2
Belgium	0.916	13	15	2
Iceland	0.914	14	8	-6
Denmark	0.912	15	7	-8
Finland	0.911	16	6	-10
Luxembourg	0.908	17	2	-15
New Zealand	0.907	18	24	6
Israel	0.900	19	25	6
Ireland	0.892	21	27	6
Italy	0.891	22	17	-5
Spain	0.888	23	23	0
Greece	0.874	25	35	10
Czechoslovakia	0.872	27	56	29
Hungary	0.863	31	55	24
Malta	0.843	41	32	-9
Portugal	0.838	42	38	-4
Bulgaria	0.815	48	76	28
Poland	0.815	49	79	30
Romania	0.729	72	89	17
Albania	0.714	76	86	10
Successor states of the former Soviet Union				
Lithuania	0.868	28	63	35
Estonia	0.867	29	43	14
Latvia	0.865	30	47	17
Russian Fed.	0.858	34	48	14
Belarus	0.847	40	49	9
Ukraine	0.823	45	68	23
Armenia	0.801	53	73	20
Kazakhstan	0.774	61	71	10
Georgia	0.747	66	80	14
Azerbaijan	0.730	71	92	21
Moldova, Rep. of	0.714	75	81	6
Turkmenistan	0.697	80	88	8
Kyrgyzstan	0.689	82	95	13
Uzbekistan	0.664	91	104	13
Tajikistan	0.629	97	116	19

[a] A positive figure shows that the HDI rank is better than the GNP per capita rank, a negative the opposite.

3. **The economies in transition have very high levels of human development** Two-thirds of the 15 newly independent states of the former Soviet Union fall into the category of high human development, the other third into the medium. The formerly socialist countries have already made major investments in the education and health of their people—and thus have considerable human capital available for the transition ahead. The average life expectancy for these economies is 70 years, and the population per doctor is around 300, compared with 63 years and 5,000 respectively for developing countries.
4. **When the HDI is adjusted for gender disparity, no country improves its HDI value** The meaning: no country treats its women as well as it treats its men, a disappointing result after so many years of debate on gender equality, so many struggles by women and so many changes in national laws (table 1.3 and figures 1.8 and 1.9). But some countries do better than others, so adjusting for gender disparity makes a big difference to the rankings: Japan falls from number 1 to 17, Canada from number 2 to 11 and Switzerland from number 4 to 14. By contrast, Sweden improves its rank from number 5 to 1, Denmark from number 12 to 4 and New Zealand from number 16 to 7.

   In industrial countries, gender discrimination (measured by the HDI) is mainly in employment and wages, with women often getting less than two-thirds of the employment opportunities and about half the earnings of men.

Another example of how rankings can change when different factors are considered is provided here. When factors that measure female participation in education, health, and other areas are taken into consideration, the rankings change dramatically, with the Scandinavian countries and France doing particularly well.

The 1995 *Human Development Report* takes gender equality (or lack of it) as its principal theme.

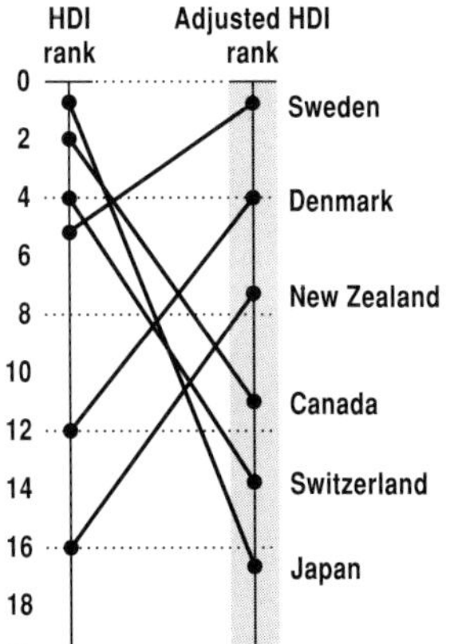

Figure 1.8. Changes in rank with a gender-disparity-adjusted HDI

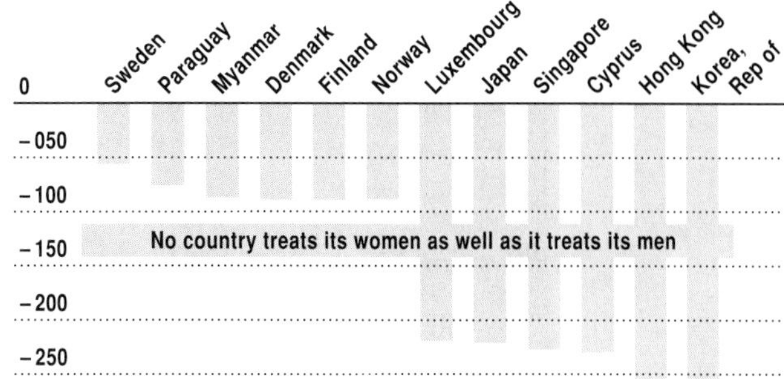

Figure 1.9. Difference between HDI and gender-disparity-adjusted HDI

TABLE 1.3 *Gender-Disparity-Adjusted HDI*

Country	HDI Value	Gender-Disparity-Adjusted HDI	Difference between HDI and Gender-Disparity-Adjusted Ranks
Sweden	0.977	0.921	4
Norway	0.978	0.881	1
France	0.971	0.864	5
Denmark	0.955	0.860	8
Finland	0.954	0.859	8
Australia	0.972	0.852	1
New Zealand	0.947	0.844	9
Netherlands	0.970	0.826	1
USA	0.976	0.824	–3
United Kingdom	0.964	0.818	0
Canada	0.982	0.816	–9
Belgium	0.952	0.808	3
Austria	0.952	0.782	1
Switzerland	0.978	0.768	–10
Germany	0.957	0.768	–4
Italy	0.924	0.764	3
Japan	0.983	0.763	–16
Czechoslovakia	0.892	0.754	4
Ireland	0.925	0.720	–1
Luxembourg	0.943	0.713	–3
Greece	0.902	0.691	0
Portugal	0.853	0.672	3
Cyprus	0.890	0.656	0
Costa Rica	0.852	0.632	2
Hong Kong	0.913	0.618	–5
Singapore	0.849	0.585	1
Korea, Rep. of	0.872	0.555	–3
Paraguay	0.641	0.546	1
Sri Lanka	0.663	0.499	–1
Philippines	0.603	0.451	0
Swaziland	0.458	0.344	0
Myanmar	0.390	0.297	0
Kenya	0.369	0.241	0

A positive difference shows that the gender-disparity-adjusted HDI rank is higher than the unadjusted HDI rank, a negative the opposite.

In developing countries, the great disparities, besides those in the job market, are in health care, nutritional support and education. For instance, women make up two-thirds of the illiterate population. And South and East Asia, defying the normal biological result that women live longer than men, have more men than women. The reasons: high maternal mortality and infanticide and nutritional neglect of the girl-child. According to one estimate, some 100 million women are "missing."

5. **The poor distribution of income has a major impact on human development** Income disparities are wide in many countries, particularly in the developing world. Brazil has one of the most unequal distributions of income—the richest 20% of the population receives 26 times the income of the poorest 20%. When the income component of its HDI is reduced to reflect this maldistribution, its HDI falls by 14% (figure 1.10). The same correction also causes a major drop in the HDI of many other countries, including Jamaica, Malaysia, Mexico, Panama and Turkey (figure 1.11). Table 1.4 gives the income-distribution-adjusted HDI for 52 countries having data. Among the industrial countries, the largest adjustments downwards are for Portugal, New Zealand, Australia, Canada, France, Italy and the United States.

A severely lopsided distribution of income has long been considered typical of many poorer countries, in which a few wealthy families own most of the land and income. Brazil is often thought of as a typical example. Some wealthy countries, however, are showing increasingly unequal income distributions. The United States, which traditionally has been seen as a highly egalitarian country, now has the most unequal distribution of income among the rich countries. Reporting a new study by Edward N. Wolff, *The New York Times* (April 17, 1995) states that "the wealthiest 1% of American households—with net worth of at least $2.3 million each—owns nearly 40% of the nation's wealth."

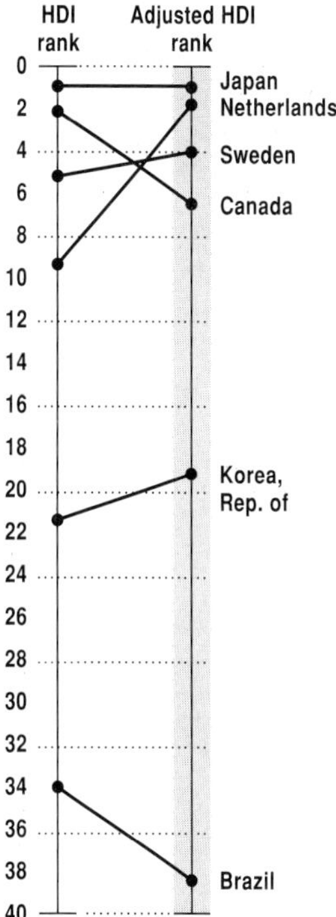

Figure 1.10. Changes in rank with an income-distribution-adjusted HDI

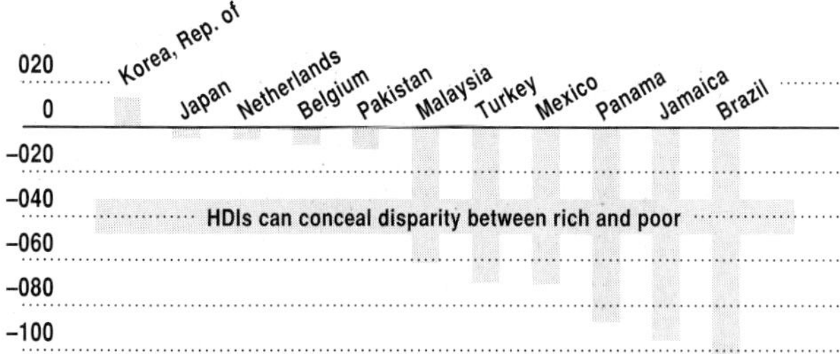

Figure 1.11. Difference between HDI and income-distribution-adjusted HDI

TABLE 1.4 ***Income-Distribution-Adjusted HDI***

Country	HDI Value	Income-Distribution-Adjusted HDI Value	Difference Between HDI and Income-Distribution-Adjusted Ranks
Japan	0.983	0.981	0
Netherlands	0.970	0.966	7
Switzerland	0.978	0.958	1
Sweden	0.977	0.958	1
Norway	0.978	0.956	–2
Canada	0.982	0.947	–4
Belgium	0.952	0.946	6
United Kingdom	0.964	0.945	2
USA	0.976	0.943	–3
France	0.971	0.938	–2
Australia	0.972	0.934	–4
Finland	0.954	0.932	0
Denmark	0.955	0.925	–2
Israel	0.938	0.912	1
New Zealand	0.947	0.909	–1
Ireland	0.925	0.908	0
Spain	0.923	0.898	1
Italy	0.924	0.892	–1
Korea, Rep. of	0.872	0.885	2
Hungary	0.887	0.873	0
Hong Kong	0.913	0.871	–2
Singapore	0.849	0.836	3
Costa Rica	0.852	0.829	1
Chile	0.864	0.818	–2
Portugal	0.853	0.802	–2
Argentina	0.832	0.791	0
Venezuela	0.824	0.771	0
Mauritius	0.794	0.745	1
Mexico	0.805	0.737	–1
Colombia	0.770	0.734	1
Malaysia	0.790	0.732	–1
Thailand	0.715	0.672	4
Panama	0.738	0.654	–1
Turkey	0.717	0.650	1
Syrian Arab Rep.	0.694	0.644	2
Jamaica	0.736	0.643	–3
Sri Lanka	0.663	0.634	1
Brazil	0.730	0.627	–4
Tunisia	0.600	0.583	1
Philippines	0.603	0.575	–1
Iran, Islamic Rep.	0.557	0.519	0
Indonesia	0.515	0.519	0
El Salvador	0.503	0.488	0
Honduras	0.472	0.419	0
Egypt	0.389	0.377	0
Kenya	0.369	0.344	0
Pakistan	0.311	0.303	1
Zambia	0.314	0.291	–1
India	0.309	0.289	0
Côte d'Ivoire	0.286	0.246	0
Bangladesh	0.189	0.172	0
Nepal	0.170	0.138	0

A positive difference shows that the income-distribution-adjusted HDI rank is higher than the unadjusted HDI rank, a negative the opposite.

6. **When the HDI is disaggregated by calculating the specific HDI for groups or regions in a country, there can be startling divergences from the national average** Disaggregating HDIs provides a group-specific or region-specific human development measure, whereas the gender-adjusted and income-distribution-adjusted HDIs are still national averages incorporating the extent of inequality. Five countries that have readily available data to undertake such a disaggregation: the United States, India, Mexico, Turkey and Swaziland. More countries should launch efforts to gather such data.

In the United States, with the HDIs of white, black and hispanic populations separated, whites rank number 1 in the world (ahead of Japan), blacks rank number 31 (next to Trinidad and Tobago) and hispanics rank number 35 (next to Estonia). This, even despite the fact that income levels are considerably discounted in the HDI calculations. So, full equality is a distant prospect in the United States (figures 1.12 and 1.13).

Similar disparities are obvious elsewhere. In India, the HDI in Uttar Pradesh is a third lower than the national average and 60% lower than that in Kerala. In Mexico, the state of Oaxaca has an HDI 20% lower than the national average. In Turkey, the HDI for rural females is 25% lower than that for rural males. By contrast, Swaziland, with a smaller population of less than one million, is a more homogeneous society.

The UNDP's use of these **disaggregated indicators**—the separation out of different groups within a country in order to see contrasts within a society—reinforces what has been said earlier in this unit, that "wealthy countries" don't have uniformly affluent citizens and that income distribution can be very unequal. Of course, it should also be remembered that a "disaggregated" statistical picture of "white Americans," "black Americans," and so on, would show substantial differences in income and quality of life within these smaller groups also.

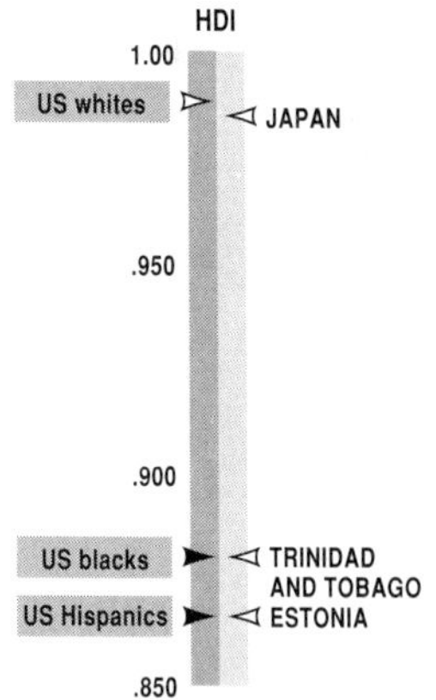

Figure 1.12. HDIs are higher for whites than for blacks and hispanics in the United States

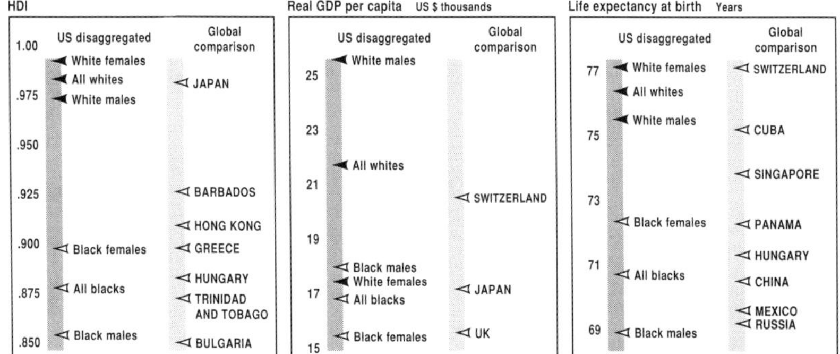

Figure 1.13. Disaggregated human development indicators for the United States

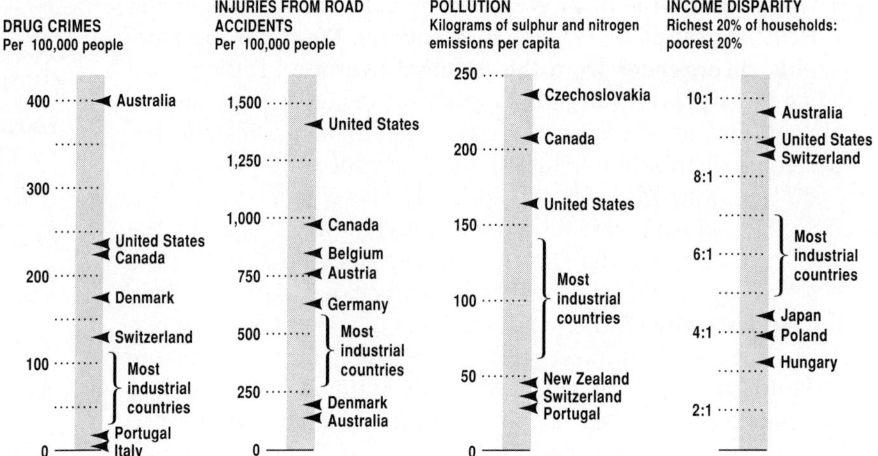

Visuals showing comparative figures for murder and reported rapes appear in Unit Seven, Section Two, of this text.

With so many inequalities in multiethnic and otherwise divided societies, a disaggregated HDI profile is essential to eventually understanding the underlying sources of tension and potential causes of future trouble.

The HDI is thus a useful and informative tool for analysing and assessing development. But it probably is still too early to use the HDI to evaluate a country's performance, or to allocate aid funds. That kind of application must await further improvements to the HDI.

Weakening Social Fabric: Industrial Countries

HDI Rank	Prisoners (per 100,000 people) 1980–86	Juveniles (as % of total prisoners) 1980–86	Intentional homicides by men (per 100,000) 1985–90	Reported rapes (per100,000 women ages 15_59) 1987–89	Drug crimes (per 100,000 people) 1980–86	Asylum applications received (thousands) 1983–92	Divorces (as % of marriages contracted) 1987–91	Births outside marriage (%) 1985–92	Single-female-parent homes (%) 1985–91	Suicides by men (per 100,000) 1989–91
1 Canada	94	••	2.7	23	225	236	43	23	••	20
2 Switzerland	54	••	1.1	18	129	181	33	6	4	34
3 Japan	••	••	0.9	5	31	4	22	1	5	21
4 Sweden	••	••	1.7	43	••	252	48	52	6	27
5 Norway	••	••	1.6	20	116	37	45	34	••	23
6 France	40	1	1.4	17	••	318	39	32	7	30
7 Australia	60	6	2.5	44	403	24	35	16	••	21
8 USA	426	••	12.4	118	234	508	48	27	8	20
9 Netherlands	27	3	1.2	26	38	111	30	12	5	12
10 United Kingdom	77	5	1.6	••	••	139	42	31	10	12
11 Germany	77	12	1.2	26	••	1,498	33	15	8	28
12 Austria	87	••	1.4	27	77	144	36	22	••	35
13 Belgium	27	14	2.3	••	40	85	32	12	7	32
14 Iceland	••	••	0.6	••	••	••	19	••	6	22
15 Denmark	47	••	1.4	35	176	59	49	47	6	30
16 Finland	75	8	4.1	19	••	9	58	••	10	49
17 Luxembourg	••	••	1.6	••	••	2	39	13	3	25
18 New Zealand	60	••	2.6	••	••	••	38	25	8	23
19 Israel	••	32	0.5	4	25	••	19	1	••	11
21 Ireland	••	3	1.2	••	••	••	••	18	••	14
22 Italy	60	13	2.5	4	6	65	8	7	2	11
23 Spain	49	20	1.7	12	15	43	11	10	3	12
25 Greece	24	12	1.2	••	••	36	14	3	••	6
27 Czechoslovakia	••	••	1.3	12	••	3	32	••	••	30
31 Hungary	142	7	3.5	31	••	57	37	9	••	58
41 Malta	••	••	0.6	2	••	••	••	1	••	6
42 Portugal	58	12	2.3	5	13	4	13	16	6	15
48 Bulgaria	160	2	4.0	21	••	(.)	20	12	••	23
49 Poland	204	11	2.5	19	••	3	17	5	••	24
72 Romania	••	••	••	••	••	1	20	••	••	13
76 Albania	••	••	••	••	••	••	10	••	••	••
Aggregates										
Industrial	••	••	5.4	48	••	3,820T	34	17	••	21
Developing	••	••	••	••	••	••	••	••	••	••
World	••	••	••	••	••	••	••	••	••	••
OECD	201	••	5.0	51	••	3,760T	34	20	7	20
Eastern Europe and former Soviet Union	••	••	6.9	••	••	••	34	13	••	••
Eastern Europe only	186	••	2.6	19	••	64T	22	7	••	26
European Community	59	••	1.6	17	••	2,360T	28	19	6	19
Nordic	••	••	2.1	32	••	360T	50	46	7	32
Southern Europe	53	••	2.1	7	••	150T	10	9	3	11
Non-Europe	370	••	7.9	74	178	770T	39	19	7	20
North America	393	••	11.5	109	233	740T	48	27	8	20
Successor states of the former Soviet Union										
28 Lithuania	••	••	••	••	••	••	36	7	••	••
29 Estonia	••	••	••	••	••	••	47	25	••	••
30 Latvia	••	••	••	••	••	••	46	16	••	••
34 Russian Federation	••	••	9.0[a]	••	••	••	42	14	••	35[a]
40 Belarus	••	••	••	••	••	••	35	8	••	••
45 Ukraine	••	••	••	••	••	••	40	11	••	••
53 Armenia	••	••	••	••	••	••	••	••	••	••
61 Kazakhstan	••	••	••	••	••	••	••	••	••	••
66 Georgia	••	••	••	••	••	••	••	••	••	••
71 Azerbaijan	••	••	••	••	••	••	••	••	••	••
75 Moldova, Rep. of	••	••	••	••	••	••	31	10	••	••
80 Turkmenistan	••	••	••	••	••	••	••	••	••	••
82 Kyrgyzstan	••	••	••	••	••	••	••	••	••	••
91 Uzbekistan	••	••	••	••	••	••	••	••	••	••
97 Tajikistan	••	••	••	••	••	••	••	••	••	••

a Data for former Soviet Union.
(.) Less than half the unit shown.

The information on this page comes from the *Human Development Report 1994.* It focuses on problems familiar to anyone who reads a newspaper or who follows the news, but it does so in a fashion that enables us to compare our problems with those in other wealthy countries.

ASPECTS OF WRITING: Assessing the data.

People often make comparisons between countries that are based more on prejudice, patriotism, and ignorance than fact. Citizens of one country may have so little information about the rest of the world that they are easily persuaded to believe stereotypical or selective evidence presented to them in the media. What did most Americans and Soviet citizens really know about each other during the Cold War, when such strong opinions were presented on both sides? In political terms, such a question may be irrelevant, for public opinion can be manipulated by those in power, but in other ways it is significant, because it asks us to question things that we may strongly believe only because we have been told them so often.

A good example is the ongoing debate over the American health care system. Time and again, politicians on both sides preface their speeches with the statement that "America has the best health care system in the world. . . ." But is this true? How can such a claim be substantiated? The figures provided by the World Bank, UNDP, and other organizations offer the best evidence we have on which to make or dispute such claims. The standard measurements for the effectiveness of health care in any country include infant mortality rate, child mortality rate, and life expectancy. By these measurements, the United States does not have "the best health care system in the world." In fact, it ranks quite modestly compared with the other rich countries. Why, then, do politicians and others repeat the old refrain about being "the best"? Perhaps it has less to do with health care than with an ideological aversion to what Americans have long referred to as "socialized medicine." If this is so, what about the uncomfortable fact that every other rich country has some form of "socialized medicine" and that most have better health care statistics—at lower cost—than we do? The propaganda has usurped the statistics, and many people find it difficult to accept that other countries do very well with a philosophy that makes universal access to health care a right of citizenship, just like schooling. It is very hard to find people in Europe, Canada, or other wealthy countries who would wish to swap their national health system for ours.

Evaluating national performance in health, education, and other important areas necessitates being willing to decide on objective bases for comparison. This is what the United Nations agencies try to provide. If you wish, for example, to compare national performances with regard to the status of women, the World Bank, UNDP, and UNESCO tables provide a basis for such research. The status of children could be investigated in the same way.

Users of statistics must always, however, make sure that they understand what the numbers mean and that the same definitions are being used in different countries. The U.N. agencies try to make sure that the figures are comparable, but they acknowledge that in some cases this is difficult to guarantee.

WRITING EXERCISES: Answer one of the following.

Some people find it difficult to start essays. The international organizations whose data are presented in this unit begin their annual reports with statements that are remarkably similar in tone and purpose:

> Infrastructure services—including power, transport, telecommunications, provision of water and sanitation, and safe disposal of wastes—are central to the activities of households and to economic production.
>
> *World Development Report 1994,* The World Bank

> The 1980's were, in many ways, a decade of the people. All over the world, people had an impatient urge to guide their political, economic and social destinies.
>
> *Human Development Report 1993,* UNDP

In both cases, the topic to be discussed is immediately introduced and its importance emphasized. This is a useful model for many kinds of essay. For example, you could start exercise 2, opposite, with a statement about the difficulty of comparing quality of life in different countries. You could observe that money is only one of a number of factors that can be considered.

1. Briefly explain the following terms and explain why each is widely used by international organizations as a basic statistical measurement. Integrate examples from the tables into your discussion.
   a. GNP per capita
   b. infant mortality rate
   c. illiteracy rate
   d. life expectancy
2. Describe how you would compare the quality of life in different countries. You don't need to restrict yourself to the data provided in this unit, but include some. Climate and cultural factors may also be factors. On this basis, compare two (or more) countries that interest you. An element of subjectivity will be hard to avoid, but try to be as objective as possible and give evidence to support any comparative statements you make.
3. Find one or two recent public opinion polls and discuss what they mean. What technical data are provided? Was the question loaded? What conclusions does the newspaper draw (try the editorial column, perhaps), and what conclusion do you draw? If you can find polls from different polling organizations about the same topic, this may provide interesting raw material for your discussion.

OPTION ONE

PRIOR KNOWLEDGE: People, people everywhere . . . .

Among all the many changes that have transformed the Earth over the last 200 years, one of the most dramatic has been the increase in the world's human population. Population growth was slow through most of human history but increased dramatically after the industrial revolution, beginning in about 1750. Since World War II the world's population has exploded—an image made famous by Paul Ehrlich in his book *The Population Bomb* (1968).

Population expansion has seen only temporary interruptions. Bubonic plague (the Black Death) killed about half of Europe's population between 1348 and 1350, and the combination of World War I (8 million deaths) and the influenza epidemic that followed it (about 20 million deaths) shows up on world population graphs. Approximately 45 million people died in World War II.

The worldwide HIV/AIDS outbreak is a reminder that we remain vulnerable to medical—as well as military—crises, but the population trend is inexorably and ever more rapidly upward. It took all of human existence until about 1830 to reach the first billion; the second billion took 100 years; the third billion took 30 years; the fourth took 10 years. Just as important is the fact that population growth is distributed very unevenly, with most of the growth today occurring in the poorest countries. This difference in population growth rates is one factor in the widening economic gap between the richest Northern and the poorest Southern countries. Today, about 100 million people are added to the world's population every year—one every three seconds.

A large percentage of the world's population is concentrated in a few countries, nine of which currently have populations over 100 million. This select club will soon be getting some new members, however; demographers project that Mexico and Pakistan will reach 100 million each by about the year 2000, and the tables in Section One of this unit reveal dramatic figures for population growth in many other developing countries.

Such numbers pose enormous challenges. Can the world feed 10 billion people, or 15 billion? Can poor countries build schools, houses, and hospitals for their rapidly growing populations? Can jobs be found for all these people? What happens if hundreds of millions of people in poorer countries decide that life is hopeless in their own countries? How should rich countries respond to such pressures? Can

Perhaps the most famous pessimist in the area of population studies is the **Rev. Thomas Malthus,** a 19th-century English economist, and author of "An Essay on the Principle of Population." The subtitle suggests a lot about the content: "Or a View of Its Past and Present Effects on Human Happiness with an Inquiry into the Prospects Respecting the Future Removal or Mitigation of the Evils Which It Occasions." Malthus wrote that "population, when unchecked, goes on doubling itself every twenty-five years, or increases in a geometrical ratio. . . . But the food to support the increase . . . will by no means be obtained with the same facility."

The World Health Organization estimates that more than 13 million people worldwide were HIV positive in 1994 and that about 6,000 people become infected every day.

Largest population by country (in millions)

China	1,162
India	884
United States	255
Indonesia	184
Brazil	154
Russia	149
Japan	125
Pakistan	119
Bangladesh	114
Nigeria	102

World Bank, 1994

Short of a global catastrophe, population growth is virtually certain to continue at a very high rate well into the 21st century. This can be confidently predicted because, in many poor countries, a very high percentage of the population is very young. Even if these young people limit the size of their families, there will be a large population increase. In wealthy countries the population is aging, and population growth rates tend to be low.

the North fence itself in and keep the South out? How good an investment does well-spent foreign aid seem when put into this context?

Many people believe that world population growth is the gravest threat now facing the planet, threatening starvation, homelessness, disease, environmental destruction, pollution, depletion of natural resources, and numerous other ills. Others think the world will manage, mainly by the application of technological ingenuity.

Population policies arouse controversy, for attitudes toward birth control, women, men, sexual mores, government planning, national sovereignty, economic development, health, global survival, and more are all involved.

READING: Charles C. Mann. "How Many Is Too Many?" *Atlantic Monthly* Feb. 1993: 47–56. (Original article, 47–67).

Biologists have argued for a century that an ever-growing population will bring the apocalypse. Economists argue that man and markets will cope—so far none of the predicted apocalypses have arrived. The near-term questions, though, are political, and they are overlooked in the fierce battles

How Many Is Too Many?

In 1980, when I was living in New York City, it came to my attention that the federal government was trying to count every inhabitant of the United States. In my building—subject, like many in New York, to incredibly complicated rent-control laws—a surprising number of apartments were occupied by illegal subtenants. Many went to elaborate lengths to conceal the fact of their existence. They put the legal tenant's name on the doorbell. They received their mail at a post-office box. They had unlisted telephone numbers. The most paranoid refused to reveal their names to strangers. How, I wondered, was the Census Bureau going to count these people?

Mann uses a first-person anecdote to start his essay, and it works well to illustrate that counting heads is more difficult than most people imagine.

I decided to find out. I answered an advertisement and attended a course. In a surprisingly short time I became an official enumerator. My job was to visit apartments that had not mailed back their census forms. As identification, I was given a black plastic briefcase with a big red, white, and blue sticker that said U.S. CENSUS. I am a gangling, six-foot-four-inch Caucasian; the government sent me to Chinatown.

Strangely enough, I was a failure. Some people took one look and slammed the door. One elderly woman burst into tears at the sight of me. I was twice offered money to go away. Few residents had time to fill out a long form.

Eventually I met an old census hand. "Why don't you just curbstone it?" he asked. "Curbstoning," I learned, was enumerator jargon for sitting on the curbstone and filling out forms with made-up information. I felt qualms about taking taxpayers' money to cheat. Instead, I asked to be assigned to another area.

As usual, the Option One reading is not annotated. As you read, take note of interesting words and allusions: "the dismal science," Cassandra, and so on.

Wall Street is not customarily thought of as residential, but people live there anyway. Some live in luxury, some in squalor. None were glad to see me, even though I had given away the damning U.S. CENSUS briefcase to my four-year-old stepson. The turning point came when I approached two small buildings. One was ruined and empty. The other, though scarcely in better condition, was obviously full of people, but not one of them would answer the bell. In a fit of zealotry I climbed through the ruin next door. Coated with grime and grit, I emerged on the roof and leaped onto the roof of my target. A man was living on it, in a big, dilapidated shack.

He flung open his door. Inside I dimly perceived several apparently naked people lying on gurneys. "Go away!" the man screamed. He was wearing a white coat. "I'm giving my wife a cancer treatment!"

My enthusiasm waned. I jumped back to the other roof. On the street I sat on the curbstone and filled out a dozen forms. When I was through, fifty men, women, and children had been added to the populace of New York City.

Professional demographers are not amused by this sort of story. This is not because they are stuffy but because they've heard it all before. Finding out how many people live in any particular place is strikingly difficult, no matter what the place is. In the countryside people are scattered through miles of real estate; in the city they occupy nooks and crannies often missed by official scrutiny. No accurate census has ever been taken in some parts of Africa, but even in the United States, the director of the Census Bureau has said, the last official count, in 1990, missed more than five million people—enough to fill Chicago twice over. If my experience means anything, that number is low.

It's too bad, because How many are we? is an interesting question. Indeed, to many people it is an alarming question. For them, thinking about population means thinking about *over*population—which is to say, thinking about poverty, hunger, despair, and social unrest. For me, the subject evokes the vague unease I felt toting around *The Population Bomb*, which I read in school. ("It's Still Not Too Late to Make the Choice," the cover proclaimed. "Population Control or Race to Oblivion.") In other people it evokes the desire to put fences on our borders and stop the most wretched from breeding.

The Population Bomb appeared twenty-five years ago, in 1968. Written by the biologist Paul Ehrlich, of Stanford University, it was a gloomy book for a gloomy time. India was still undergoing a dreadful famine, Latin American exports of grain and meat had dropped to pre-war levels, and global food production was lagging behind births. More than half the world's people were malnourished. Nobel laureates were telling Congress that unless population growth stopped, a new Dark Age would cloud the world and "men will have to kill and eat one another." A well-regarded book, *Famine* 1975!, predicted that hunger would begin to wipe out the Third World that year. (Fortunately, the book pointed out, there was a bright side: the United States could increase its influence by playing triage among the victims.) In 1972 a group of researchers at MIT would issue *The Limits to Growth*, which used advanced computer models to project that the world would run out of gold in 1981, oil in 1992, and arable land in 2000. Civilization itself would collapse by 2070.

The projections failed to materialize. Birth rates dropped; food production soared; the real price of oil sank to a record low. Demographers were not surprised. Few had given much credence to the projections in the first place. Nonetheless, a certain disarray appeared in the work of what Ansley Coale, of Princeton's Office of Population Research, calls the "scribbling classes." Doubts emerged about the wisdom and effectiveness of the billion-dollar population-control schemes established by the United Nations and others in the 1960s. Right-wingers attacked them as bureaucratic intrusions into private life. Critics on the left observed that once again rich whites were trying to order around poor people of color. Less ideological commentators pointed out that the intellectual justification for spending billions on international family-planning programs was shaky—it tacitly depended on the notion that couples in the Third World are somehow too stupid to know that having lots of babies is bad. Ehrlich dismissed the carpers as "imbeciles."

Population has become the subject of a furious intellectual battle, complete with mutually contradictory charts, graphs, and statistics. The cloud of facts and factoids often seems impenetrable, but after peering through it for a time I came to suspect that the fighters had become distracted. Locked in conflict, they had barely begun to address the real nature of the challenge posed by population growth. *Homo sapiens* will keep growing in number, as everyone agrees, and that growth may have disagreeable consequences. But those consequences seem less likely to stem from the environmental collapse the apocalyptists predict than from the human race's perennial inability to run its political affairs wisely. The distinction is important, and dismaying.

CASSANDRAS AND POLLYANNAS

How many people is too many? Over time, the debate has spread between two poles. On one side, according to Garrett Hardin, an ecologist at the University of California at Santa Barbara, are the Cassandras, who believe that continued population growth at the current rate will inevitably lead to catastrophe. On the other are the Pollyannas, who believe that humanity faces problems but has a good shot at coming out okay in the end. Cassandras, who tend to be biologists, look at each new birth as the arrival on the planet of another hungry mouth. Pollyannas, who tend to be economists, point out that along with each new mouth comes a pair of hands. Biologist or economist—is either one right? It is hard to think of a question more fundamental to our crowded world.

Cassandras and Pollyannas have spoken up throughout history. Philosophers in ancient China fretted about the need to shift the masses to underpopulated areas; meanwhile, in the Mideast, the Bible urged humanity to be fruitful and multiply. Plato said that cities with more than 5,040 landholders were too large; Martin Luther believed that it was impossible to breed too much, because God would always provide. And so on.

Early economists tended to be Pollyannas. People, they thought, are a resource—"the chiefest, most fundamental, and precious commodity" on earth, as William Petyt put it in 1680. Without a healthy population base, societies cannot afford to have their members specialize. In small villages almost everyone is involved with producing food; only as numbers grow can communities afford luxuries like surgeons, scientists, and stand-up comedians. The same increase lowers the cost of labor, and hence the cost of production—a notion that led at least one Enlightenment-era writer, J. F. Melon, to endorse slavery as an excellent source of a cheap work force.

As proof of their theory, seventeenth-century Pollyannas pointed to the Netherlands, which was strong, prosperous, and thickly settled, and claimed that only such a populous place could be so rich. In contrast, the poor, sparsely inhabited British colonies in the New World were begging immigrants to come and swell the work force. One of the chief duties of a ruler, these savants thought, was to ensure population growth. A high birth rate, the scholar Bernard Mandeville wrote in 1732, is "the never-failing Nursery of Fleets and Armies."

Mandeville wrote when the Industrial Revolution was beginning to foster widespread urban unemployment and European cities swarmed with beggars. Hit by one bad harvest after another, Britain tottered through a series of economic crises, which led to food shortages and poverty on a frightful scale. By 1803 local parishes were handing out relief to about one out of every seven people in England and Wales. In such a climate it is unsurprising that the most famous Cassandra of them all should appear: the Reverend Thomas Robert Malthus.

"Right from the publication of the *Essay on Population* to this day," the great economic historian Joseph Schumpeter wrote in 1954, "Malthus has had the good fortune—for this *is* good fortune—to be the subject of equally unreasonable, contradictory appraisals." John Maynard Keynes regarded Malthus as the "beginning of systematic economic thinking." Percy Bysshe Shelley, on the other hand, derided him as "a eunuch and a tyrant." John Stuart Mill viewed Malthus as a great thinker. To Karl Marx he was a "plagiarist" and a "shameless sycophant of the ruling classes." "He was a benefactor of humanity," Schumpeter wrote. "He was a fiend. He was a profound thinker. He was a dunce."

The subject of the controversy was a shy, kindly fellow with a slight harelip. He was also the first person to hold a university position in economics—that is, the first professional economist—in Britain, and probably the world. Married late, he had few children, and he was never overburdened with money. He was impelled to write his treatise on population by a disagreement with his father, a well-heeled eccentric in the English style. The argument was over whether the human race could transform the world into a paradise. Malthus thought not, and said so at length—55,000 words, published as an unsigned broadside in 1798. Several longer, signed versions followed, as Malthus became more confident.

"The power of population," Malthus proclaimed, "is indefinitely greater than the power in the earth to produce subsistence for man." In modern textbooks this notion is often explained with a graph. One line on the graph represents the land's capacity to produce food; it slowly rises from left to right as people clear more land and learn to farm more efficiently. Another line starts out low, quickly climbs to meet the first, and then soars above it; that line represents human population. Eventually the gap between the two lines cannot be bridged and the Horsemen of the Apocalypse pay a call. Others had anticipated this idea. Giovanni Botero, an Italian scholar, described the basic relationship of population and resources in 1589, two centuries before Malthus. But few read Malthus's predecessors, and nobody today seems inclined to replace the term "Malthusian" with "Boterian."

The *Essay* was a jolt. Simple and remorselessly logical, blessed with a perverse emotional appeal, it seemed to overturn centuries of Pollyanna-dom at a stroke. Forget Utopia, Malthus said. Humanity is doomed to exist, now and forever, at the edge of starvation. Forget charity, too: helping the poor only leads to more babies, which in turn produces increased hardship down the road. Little wonder that the essayist Thomas Carlyle found this theory so gloomy that he coined the phrase "dismal science" to describe it. Others were more vituperative, especially those who thought that the *Essay* implied that God would not provide for His children. "Is there no law in this kingdom for punishing a man for publishing a libel against the Almighty himself?" demanded one anonymous feuilleton. In all the tumult hardly anyone took the trouble to note that logical counter-arguments were available.

"Overpopulation" is hard to define exactly. Part of the reason is that attempts to isolate specific social or environmental consequences of rapid population growth tend to sink into ideological quicksand.

The most important derived from the work of Marie-Jean-Antoine-Nicolas Caritat, Marquis de Condorcet, a French *philosophe* who is best known for his worship of Reason. Four years before Malthus, Condorcet observed that France was finite, the potential supply of French infinite. Unlike Malthus, though, Condorcet believed that technology could solve the problem. When hunger threatens, he wrote, "new instruments, machines, and looms" will continue to appear, and "a very small amount of ground will be able to produce a great quantity of supplies." Society changes so fast, in other words, that Malthusian scenarios are useless. Given the level of productivity of our distant ancestors, in other words, we should already have run out of food. But we know more than they, and are more prosperous, despite our greater numbers.

Malthus and Condorcet fixed the two extremes of a quarrel that endures today. The language has changed, to be sure. Modern Cassandras speak of "ecology," a concept that did not exist in Malthus's day, and worry about exceeding the world's "carrying capacity," the ecological ceiling beyond which the land cannot support life. Having seen the abrupt collapses that occur when populations of squirrels, gypsy moths, or Lapland reindeer exceed local carrying capacities, they foresee the same fate awaiting another species: *Homo sapiens*. Pollyannas note that no such collapse has occurred in recorded history. Evoking the "demographic transition"—the observed propensity for families in prosperous societies to have fewer children—they say that continued economic growth can both feed the world's billions and enrich the world enough to end the population boom. No! the Cassandras cry. Growth is the *problem*. We're growing by 100 million people every year! We can't keep doing that forever!

True, Pollyannas concede. If present-day trends continue for centuries, the earth will turn into a massive ball of human flesh. A few millennia more, Ansley Coale, of Princeton, calculates, and that ball of flesh will be expanding outward at the speed of light. But he sees little point in the exercise of projecting lines on a graph out to their absurdly horrible conclusion. "If you had asked someone in 1890 about today's population," Coale explains, "he'd say, 'There's no way the United States can support two hundred and fifty million people. Where are they going to pasture all their horses?'"

Just as the doomsayers feared, the world's population has risen by more than half since Paul Ehrlich wrote *The Population Bomb*. Twenty-five years ago 3.4 billion people lived on earth. Now the United Nations estimates that 5.3 billion do—the biggest, fastest increase in history. But food production increased faster still. According to the Food and Agricultural Organization of the UN, not only did farmers keep pace but per capita global food production actually rose more than 10 percent from 1968 to 1990. The number of chronically malnourished people fell by more than 16 percent. (All figures on global agriculture and population in the 1990s, including those in this article, mix empirical data with projections, because not enough time has elapsed to get hard numbers.)

"Much of the world *is* better fed than it was in 1950," concedes Lester R. Brown, the president of the Worldwatch Institute, an environmental-research group in Washington, D.C. "But that period of improvement is ending rather abruptly." Since 1984, he says, world grain production per capita has fallen one percent a year. In 1990, eighty-six nations grew less food per head than they had a decade before. Improvements are unlikely, in Brown's view. Our past success has brought us alarmingly close to the ecological ceiling. "There's a growing sense in the scientific community that it will be difficult to restore the rapid rise in agricultural yields we saw between 1950 and 1984," he says. "In agriculturally advanced nations there just isn't much more that farmers can do." Meanwhile, the number of mouths keeps up its frantic rate of increase. "My sense," Brown says, "is that we're going to be in trouble on the food front before this decade is out."

Social scientists disagree. An FAO study published in 1982 concluded that by using modern agricultural methods the Third World could support more than 30 billion people. Other technophiles see genetic engineering as a route to growth that is almost without end. Biologists greet such pronouncements with loud scoffs. One widely touted analysis by Ehrlich and others maintains that humanity already uses, destroys, or "co-opts" almost 40 percent of the potential output from terrestrial photosynthesis. Doubling the world's population will reduce us to fighting with insects over the last scraps of grass.

Neither side seems willing to listen to the other; indeed, the two are barely on speaking terms. The economist Julian Simon, of the University of Maryland, asserts that there is no evidence that the increase in land use associated with rising population has led to any increase in extinction rates—despite hundreds of biological reports to the contrary. The biologist Edward O. Wilson, of Harvard University, argues that contemporary economics is "bankrupt" and does not accommodate environmental calculations—despite the existence of a literature on the subject dating back to the First World War. A National Academy of Sciences panel dominated by economists argues in 1986 that the problems of population growth have been exaggerated. Six years later the academy issues a statement, dominated by biologists, claiming that continued population growth will lead to a global environmental catastrophe that "science and technology may not be able to prevent." Told in an exchange of academic gossip that an eminent ecologist has had himself sterilized, an equally eminent demographer says, "That's the best news I've heard all week!" Asking himself what "deep insights" professional demographers have contributed, Garrett Hardin answers, "None."

The difference in the forecasts—prosperity or penury, boundless increase or zero-sum game, a triumphant world with 30 billion or a despairing one with 10—is so extreme that one is tempted to dismiss the whole contretemps as foolish. If the experts can't even discuss the matter civilly, why should the average citizen try to figure it out? Ignoring the fracas might be the right thing to do if it weren't about the future of the human race.

TWO NATIONS

Population questions are fuzzy. Even an apparently simple term like "overpopulation" is hard to define exactly. Part of the reason is that evaluating the consequences of rapid population growth falls in the odd academic space where ecology, economics, anthropology, and demography overlap. Another part of the reason is that attempts to isolate specific social or environmental consequences of rapid population growth tend to sink into ideological quicksand.

By way of example, consider two nations. One is about the size of Maryland and has a population of 7.2 million; the other is as big as Montana but has a population of 123.5 million. The first has a population density of 703 people per square mile, a lot by most standards; the second has a density of 860 per square mile, among the highest on the planet. Country No. 1 has tracts of untouched forest and reserves of gold, tin, tungsten, and natural gas. Country No. 2 has few natural resources and little arable land. Life there is so crowded that the subways hire special guards to mash people onto the trains. Is it, therefore, overpopulated?

Most economists would say no. Country No. 2 is Japan. Paul Demeny, a demographer at the Population Council in New York City, notes that Japan is where the Malthusian nightmare has come true. Population has long since overtaken agricultural capacity. "Japan would be in great trouble if it had to feed itself," Demeny says. "They can't eat VCRs. But they don't worry, because they can exchange them for food." Demeny is less sanguine about Country No. 1—Rwanda, the place with the highest fertility rate in the world. There, too, the production of food lags behind the production of people. But Rwanda, alas, has little to trade. "If something goes wrong," Demeny says, "they will have to beg."

Some economists might therefore attach to this crowded land the label "overpopulated." Others, though, might say that Rwanda has not yet reached the kind of critical mass necessary to develop its rich natural endowment. Fewer than 200,000 souls inhabit Kigali, its capital and biggest city, hardly enough to be the hub of a modern nation. In this case, a cure for having too many children to feed might be to have more children—the approach embraced by the Rwandan government until 1983.

Rwanda's leaders may well have been bowing to the popular will. By and large, people in the developing world have big families because they want them. "The notion that people desperately want to have fewer children but can't quite figure out how to do it is a bit simple," Demeny says. "If you picture an Indian who sees his children as capital because at the age of nine they can be sent to work in a carpet factory, his interest in family planning will not be keen." If the hypothetical impoverished Indian father does not today desperately need the money that his children can earn, he will need it in his dotage. Offspring are the Social Security of traditional cultures everywhere, a form of savings that few can afford to forgo. In such cases the costs of big families (mass illiteracy, crowded hiring halls, overused public services) are spread across society, whereas the benefits (income, old-age insurance) are felt at home. Economists call such phenomena "market failure." The outcome, entirely predictable, is a rapidly growing population.

Equally predictable is the proposed solution: bringing home the cost to those who experience the benefits. Enforcing child-labor and truancy laws, for example, drives up the price of raising children, and may improve their lives as well. Reducing price controls on grain raises farmers' incomes, allowing them to hire adults rather than put their children to work. Increasing opportunities for women lets them choose between earning income and having children. In the short term such modifications can hurt. In the long term, Demeny believes, they are "a piece of social engineering that any modern society should aspire to." Rwanda, like many poor countries, now has a population-control program. But pills and propaganda will be ineffective if having many children continues to be the rational choice of parents.

To ecologists, this seems like madness. Rational, indeed! More people in Rwanda would mean ransacking its remaining tropical forest—an abhorrent thought. The real problem is that Rwandans receive an insufficient share of the world's feast. The West should help them rise as they are, by forgiving their debts, investing in their industries, providing technology, increasing foreign aid—and insisting that they cut birth rates. As for the claim that Japan is not overpopulated, the Japanese are shipping out their polluting industries to neighboring countries—the same countries, environmentalists charge, that they are denuding with rapacious logging. "If all nations held the same number of people per square kilometer," Edward O. Wilson has written about Japan, "they would converge in quality of life to Bangladesh. . . ." To argue that Tokyo is a model of populousness with prosperity is, Wilson thinks, "sophistic."

Wait, one hears the economists cry, that's not predation, that's trade! Insisting on total self-sufficiency veers toward autarky. Japan logs other people's forests because its own abundant forests are too mountainous to sustain a full program of—*and wait a minute*, haven't we been here before? The competing statistics, the endless back-and-forth argument? Isn't there some better way to think about this?

GOOD NEWS, BAD NEWS

In 1968, when *The Population Bomb* was first published, the United Nations Population Division surveyed the world's demographic prospects. Its researchers projected future trends in the world's total fertility rate, a figure so common in demographic circles that it is often referred to, without definition, as the TFR. The TFR is the answer to the question "If women keep having babies at the present rate, how many will each have, on average, in her lifetime?" If a nation's women have two children apiece, exactly replacing themselves and the fathers of their children, the TFR will be 2.0 and the population will eventually stop growing. (Actually, replacement level is around 2.1, because some children die.) In the United States the present TFR is about 2.0, which means that, not counting immigration, the number of Americans will ultimately hit a plateau. (Immigration, of course, may alter this picture.) But the researchers in the division were not principally concerned with the United States. They were looking at poorer countries, and they didn't like what they saw.

As is customary, the division published three sets of population projections: high, medium, and low, reflecting different assumptions behind them. The medium projection, usually what the demographer regards as the most likely alternative, was that the TFR for developing nations would fall 15 percent from 1965–1970 to 1980–1985. At the time, Ronald Freedman recalls, this view was regarded as optimistic. "There was a lot of skepticism that anything could happen," he says. He was working on family-planning programs in Asia, and he received letters from colleagues telling him how hopeless the whole endeavor was.

Now a professor emeritus of sociology at the University of Michigan, Freedman is on the scientific advisory committee of Demographic and Health Surveys, a private organization in Columbia, Maryland, which is funded by the U.S. government to assess births and deaths in Third World nations. Its data, painstakingly gathered from surveys, are among the best available. From 1965–1970 to 1980–1985 fertility in poor countries dropped 30 percent, from a TFR of 6.0 to one of 4.2. In that period, Freedman and his colleague Ann K. Blanc have pointed out, the poor countries of the world moved almost halfway to a TFR of 2.1: replacement level. (By 1995, Blanc says, they might be two thirds of the way there.) If the decrease continues, it will surely be the most astonishing demographic shift in history. (The second most astonishing will be the rise that preceded it.) The world went halfway to replacement level in the twenty years from 1965 to 1985; arithmetic suggests that if this trend continues we will arrive at replacement level in the subsequent twenty years—that is, by 2005.

That's the good news. The bad news is that since the late 1960s, 1.9 billion more people have arrived on the planet than have left. Even if future rates of fertility are the lowest in history, as is likely, the children of today's children, and their children's children, will keep replacing themselves, and the population will increase vastly. Nothing will stop that increase, not even AIDS. Pessimists estimate that by the end of the decade another 100 million people will be infected by HIV. Almost ten times that number will have been born. Barring unprecedented catastrophe, the year 2100 will see 10 to 12 billion people on the planet.

Nobody will have to wait that long to feel the consequences. In a few years today's children will be clamoring to take their place in the adult world. Jobs, homes, cars, a few occasional treats—these are things they will want. And though economists are surely right when they say the lesson of history is that the great majority of these men and women will make their way, it is hard not to be awed by the magnitude of the task facing the global economy. A billion jobs. A billion homes. A billion cars. Billions and billions of occasional treats.

ASPECTS OF WRITING. Avoiding common errors; four sentence types.

Among the more common errors in writing are the comma splice, run-on sentence, and sentence fragment. These errors are easily avoided if you understand basic sentence structure.

Sentences are logical constructs and grammar enables us to describe them. It is helpful, therefore, if you know the appropriate terminology, so that you can better discuss this aspect of your writing with your professor. We'll look at four sentence types:

simple sentence	**complex sentence**
compound sentence	**compound-complex sentence**

> Independent clauses are also known as main clauses. Subordinate clauses are also known as dependent clauses.

In the following examples, the subject is underlined; the rest of the sentence or clause is the predicate.

Simple sentences consist of one independent clause. Note that the subject may have more than one part, and the predicate may have more than one verb.

a. The world is a crowded place.
b. Bangladesh and India have rapid population growth. [compound subject]
c. India is crowded and has rapid population growth. [only one clause, but two verbs]

Compound sentences consist of more than one independent clause. There are three ways of separating these clauses.

a. China has more than one billion people, but India may one day have the larger population. [clauses separated by comma, followed by an appropriate coordinating conjunction]
b. China . . . people; India may . . . [clauses separated by semicolon]
c. China. . . . India. . . . [Make separate sentences. When you do this, you create two simple sentences, not a compound sentence.]

Complex sentences consist of an independent clause and at least one subordinate clause.

a. Although China has the world's largest population, India's population growth rate is higher.

[The independent clause is the second one; the first clause cannot stand alone as a sentence and so is not an independent clause. Words such as "Although," "When," and "While" often introduce clauses; because they turn independent clauses into subordinate clauses, they are known as **subordinators.**]

b. China's population still grows by more than one million per year, even though they have a low population growth rate.

[The subordinate phrase does not have to come first]

> You may be used to identifying only a single word as the subject of a sentence, but it is often more helpful to identify a phrase; the logic of the above sentences is clear if you read "India's population growth rate" and "China's population" as the subjects.

Compound-complex sentences have at least two independent clauses and at least one dependent clause.

a. Because their economic growth cannot keep up with their population growth, many poor countries are getting poorer, but the opposite is true in the rich countries.

> ***Comma splices*** *and* ***run-on sentences*** *are simply punctuation errors in compound sentences:*
>
> **Canada is rich India is poor.** [WRONG: run-on sentence. No comma or conjunction.]
>
> **Canada is rich, India is poor.** [WRONG: comma splice. No conjunction after the comma.]
>
> **Canada is rich, but India is poor.** [OK]
>
> **Canada is rich; India is poor.** [OK]
>
> **Canada is rich. India is poor.** [OK]
>
> ***Sentence fragments*** *are incomplete sentences. One type occurs when subordinate clauses are [incorrectly] written as sentences:*
>
> **China and Sri Lanka are poor. Although the quality of life is quite good for most people.** [The second "sentence" is only a subordinate clause and should be combined with the independent clause.]

RESEARCH WRITING: Answer one of the following questions.

When using numbers in your writing, it is conventional to spell out any that require only one or two words but to use figures for any that require three or more words; however, *when using statistics, such as those in this unit, only figures should be used.* Similarly, when referring to dollar amounts, percentages, or similar numerical information, only figures should be used.

1. Optimists say that the world can support a larger population than the present 5.6 billion, but pessimists claim that we are heading for catastrophe unless world population growth is controlled. This debate is sometimes couched in terms of the economists' view (optimistic) and the biologists' view (pessimistic). Using the sources in this unit, describe this debate, making sure that you make reference to the numerical evidence as well as the written arguments.

Mann refers to several important sources in his article, include Malthus, Paul and Anne Ehrlich, Lester Brown, Edward Wilson, and Nathan Keyfitz [some of these names appear in the full text of Mann's article but not in the above extract]. These names can help you get started in your library search for further reading. Keyfitz's article, "Demographic Discord" (*The Sciences,* September/October 1994: 21–27), written in anticipation of the Cairo conference on world population in 1994, is an excellent source from a widely respected expert.

2. From your readings in this unit, select a topic that interests you. Here are some suggestions, but you may develop your own; class discussion may also help to generate ideas:

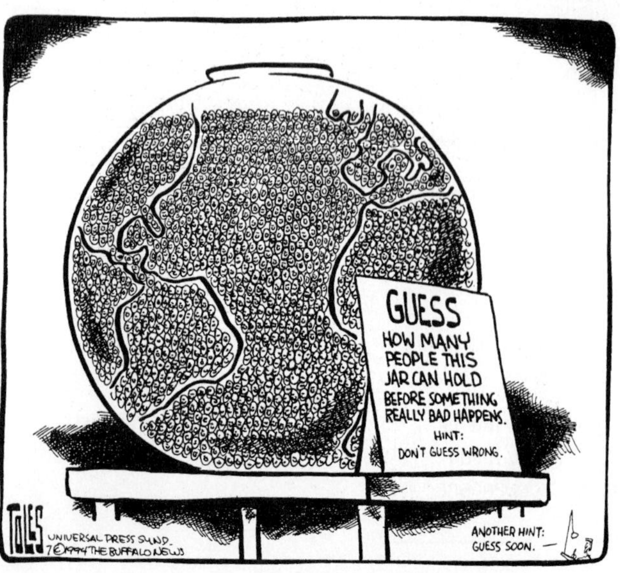

Numerical data and expert writings enable us to generalize about economic and social realities in high-income, middle-income, and low-income countries. What generalizations of this sort can you make?

What picture emerges from the data and discussion in this unit—and further reading, if you so choose—of the status of women in the world?

What picture of the world emerges from reading the numerical data provided by the World Bank and UNDP and the articles provided in this unit?

OPTION TWO

TALKING ABOUT LANGUAGE: English and other international languages.

When people from different cultures meet, the need arises for a **lingua franca**—a common language. In the course of history various languages have played this role, including Sanskrit, Greek, Latin, Arabic, Spanish, Russian, French, Swahili, and English. A few attempts have also been made to create an artificial world language; the best known of these is Esperanto. Trade languages also have been developed to facilitate commerce between people of different cultures. These *pidgin* languages combine elements from two languages; for example, indigenous grammar and English or French vocabulary merge in Melanesia and West Africa to produce new languages, some of which have official status. In Papua New Guinea, for example, many publications are written in *tok pisin* (literally "talk pidgin"), and the language has official status. In the United States a form of pidgin is widely used in Hawaii, as suggested in the accompanying cartoon. The word *haole* is commonly used in Hawaii to refer to white people.

No language in history, however, has achieved the global currency enjoyed today by English (for a brief history of English, see Unit Three, Option Two). It is the first language of over 400 million people in Britain, the United States, Canada, the Caribbean, Australia, New Zealand, and South Africa, and it is spoken as a second language by more than 400 million others, not only in the former British colonies in the Indian subcontinent, Africa, Asia, and the Pacific, but increasingly elsewhere in the world, especially in Europe. English is the most-studied foreign language, having more than 100 million students in China alone. It is the official world language for air traffic control and international maritime use as well as the predominant language of computer software. Furthermore, despite the fact that many local varieties of English are not easy for people from elsewhere to understand, the written form is standard and can be understood around the world. Apart from local words and references, English-language newspapers, scientific journals, and other publications are easily understood by English users all over the world. The same is true for other major international languages, including, in an extreme form, Mandarin Chinese, the written form of which is readable by speakers of different languages throughout China, even though the spoken words that the characters represent are different in different languages. Throughout China, therefore, people reading the same characters—with the same meaning—use different words.

FOR, FO' (FOAH) To.
Haole: "I was only trying to get to know you."
Pidgin: "Ah was on'y tryeen fo' touch yo' body."
FOR WHAT?/FOR WHY? Why?
"Fo' what you came ovah heah, turkey?"
FOR DAYS (fo' DAZE) Plenty, a lot.
Haole: "He certainly has long hair."
Pidgin: "He get hair fo' DAYS!"

(Reprinted by permission from Pidgin to da Max. *Copyright © 1986 Peppovision, Inc.)*

As English and the other international languages have become increasingly important, some other languages have been lost. In North and South America, for example, many indigenous languages have disappeared. Any language that has no written form is endangered as the population of native speakers dwindles. Some estimates claim that as many as 20% of the world's 2,000 languages are endangered. More optimistically, however, it can be said that the trend is not so much toward the elimination of languages but toward **bilingualism.** Hundreds of millions of people in the developing world speak fluent English or French as a second language, these being the languages of their schools and often the lingua francas of their multilingual countries.

In a world that is ever more closely interdependent, and where trade, communication, and mobility are all increasingly global in character, the international languages are likely to become more and more important. In the European Union all students are expected to study two foreign languages; in many countries Japanese is becoming a familiar language in schools; in the United States, Spanish is becoming a second language for many people. For employment, trade, vacations, international relations, politics, and many other areas of life, language skills are of great and increasing significance.

Esperanto is designed to be as logical as possible, and it is a highly inflected language, meaning that different word endings tell the user how that word functions in a sentence. Latin and German are examples of other inflected languages, but English is not; it generally uses word order to achieve the same thing. For example, if we see a headline reading:

Dog Bites Man

we know which one did the biting, just as we do if we read:

Man Bites Dog

The words are the same, but the *word order* makes the meaning clear. In inflected languages the reverse is true. Word order makes no difference; it is the words themselves that tell you what is happening. The rules of Esperanto include the following: all nouns (and *only* nouns) end in *-o,* but they add an *-n* when they are used as direct objects; all adjectives end in *-a;* and all present-tense verb forms end in *-as.* Thus, in Esperanto, we would read:

Hundo mordas viron. (Dog bites man)
Viron hundo mordas. (Dog bites man)
Viro mordas hundon. (Man bites dog)
Hundon viro mordas. (Man bites dog).

There is an international association of speakers of Esperanto, but, despite its predictable, phonetic pronunciation and its carefully constructed grammar, it seems unlikely that it will be able to supplant the existing international languages.

ASPECTS OF WRITING: Punctuation—reinforcing sentence structure.

THINK ON PAPER

What punctuation would you use in each of the following situations? If the grammatical terminology is not familiar to you, review the *Aspects of writing* section in Option One of this unit.

- Between sentences·
- Between independent clauses
- Between items in a list
- Between items in a list that already includes commas
- Between a subordinate clause and an independent clause
- After an independent clause but before a list

Many punctuation problems involve *commas* ***and*** apostrophes.

Problems with commas often occur when a word, phrase, or clause is embedded within an independent clause. In the following examples the independent clause (the basic sentence) is underlined; notice that a **two-comma pattern** is required:

The train, which was carrying two hundred passengers, passed through spectacular scenery.
My sister, Mary, was on board.

There is also a **one-comma pattern,** used after an introductory element in a sentence, before an independent clause:

First, let me welcome you all.
When everyone was aboard, the train left.

To read and play a musical score in the manner intended by the composer, musicians need more than the notes; they also need dynamic markings that indicate how to play the notes. A whole vocabulary of musical terms and symbols serve this function, including *forte, piano, crescendo, diminuendo,* and many more. In writing, punctuation is used in a similar way. The words themselves are not enough, as you can see in the following example, taken from a later part of Charles Mann's essay in Option One of this unit:

> I was driving around the Hudson Valley partly because I was looking for a house in the country my method of looking insofar as one could call it a method was to hunt in the counties with the lowest populations figuring that they would be the least spoiled I was trying to get away from people and from the unpleasantness I associated with urban life the more crowded an area I thought the more degraded its environment I wanted natural beauty and that meant "uninhabited."

Although not impossible to decipher, this simple paragraph is much harder to read without punctuation.

The basic purpose of punctuation, therefore, is to reinforce the sentence structure used by the writer. In speech, we do the same thing through intonation; we pause at the end of sentences or for interruptions within a sentence; we use a rising intonation at the end of questions, and so on, but in writing we have to put it all down on the page.

Apostrophes indicate possession or contraction; *they do not indicate plurality:*

The cats are hungry. (plurality, no apostrophe)
The cat's food is ready. (one cat, possessive)
The cats' food is ready. (more than one cat, possessive)
The cats aren't hungry. (contraction)

No apostrophes are used with possessive pronouns: yours; its, hers, his, ours, theirs.

The most common problem involves **its** and **it's;** *it's* ***always means*** it is (It's my cat) or **it has** (it's been a long week). The latter is usually only used in speech.

Quick Quiz

A. Answer the following questions.

1. What are these organizations?
   a. the World Bank
   b. the IMF
   c. WHO
   d. UNDP
2. Which country has the largest population in Africa?
3. What is GNP per capita?
4. What are the poorest and richest countries in the world, as measured by GNP per capita?
5. What is the current population of
   a. the United States?
   b. the world?
6. What are the five most populous countries?
7. Where is most of the world's population growth occurring?
8. Why is economics sometimes known as "the dismal science"?
9. Who was Malthus?
10. Why would some countries rank higher in social development than GNP per capita, and others higher in GNP per capita than social development?

B. Punctuate the following statements.

1. Although I did a lot of research I never found Smiths book on 20th-century art.
2. I wanted to buy several things a Braque a Picasso and a Dali.
3. I wanted to buy a Braque a Picasso and a Dali.
4. Their daughter who wants to be a brain surgeon and a concert pianist is now in college.
5. The arts don't just require talent they also require self-discipline.
6. Each instrument has its own character.
7. Its a matter of personal preference.
8. I like the piano but love the bagpipes.
9. Others who think they know better prefer the piano and the violin.
10. To annoy your neighbors however theres nothing quite like an electric guitar trumpet or drums.

C. Charles Mann refers to **Cassandras** and **Pollyannas;** what do these words mean, and what is their source?

SECTION ONE

PRIOR KNOWLEDGE: The industrial revolution, people, and Nature.

Only a few decades after the beginning of the industrial revolution, in mid-18th-century Britain, there arose a movement in literature, music, and the visual arts that was based in part on an appreciation of the natural world in its unspoiled state. This was **Romanticism,** and it was in part a reaction against the celebration of the human mind and its scientific and esthetic triumph over untamed Nature that was characteristic of the Age of Reason in the 18th century. One of the earliest voices of this type, a precursor of the movement that was to follow, was that of the poet and engraver William Blake, who encapsulated the view that industrialization was despoiling the natural world in his famous phrase: "dark Satanic mills."

Today, 200 years later, the industrial revolution has changed the face of the world—a world that is increasingly affected by human population growth, depletion of natural resources, pollution in its many forms, and urbanization.

Of course, the picture is not entirely bleak. Over several decades, more and more people worldwide have recognized a common interest in taking care of the environment, and this has even led to the formation of environmentally oriented political parties—the "Greens"—that have won influence in many countries, notably Germany. Greenpeace, Friends of the Earth, the Wilderness Society, the Sierra Club, National Arbor Day Foundation, the World Wildlife Fund, and the Audubon Society have become household words, and international conferences

The **Age of Reason,** sometimes known as the Augustan Age, was typified by the poet Alexander Pope, who said that "The proper study of Mankind is Man." It was an age of scientific and technological revolution, led by giants such as Isaac Newton and James Watt, the developer of the steam engine. It was also the age of "Capability" Brown, the most famous of landscape gardeners, who typified the idea that Nature could be improved. The gardens of stately homes and castles in Europe reflect this philosophy, with their manicured lawns and carefully laid out beds of flowers and shrubs. One wit remarked that he hoped he died before Capability Brown, because he wanted to see Heaven before it was "improved."

Blake's phrase, "dark Satanic mills," appears in a poem in the Preface to his "Milton"; this poem is best known today as a song, "Jerusalem," that also provides the title of a movie: *Chariots of Fire.*

The late-18th early-19th century was a period of political, economic, and social revolution, massive relocation of people from the rural to the urban areas, and unemployment on the farms as technological and other changes made laboring jobs redundant. Some of these themes are just as familiar today.

have been held at which governments from all over the world have expressed their concern over environmental issues. In some countries, major efforts to clean up the rivers and air have paid off; London is no longer the foggy (smoggy) town of old songs, and many rivers in industrial parts of the United States and Europe now support fish that have not been seen there for perhaps a hundred years.

Clear-cutting of forests is not just a tropical problem. Greenpeace reported in 1994 that the Scandinavian countries, Canada, the United States, and Russia export four times as much lumber as the tropical countries and that some regions, including Alaska and Siberia, are at great risk from the consequences of deforestation.

Despite the successes, however, environmental issues remain difficult. What right have rich countries like the United States or Germany to tell Brazil and other equatorial and tropical countries to stop cutting their forests and developing their wilderness areas? Didn't Western countries do the same thing in an earlier stage of their development? How are we to balance the need for continued economic development and improved living conditions against the need for environmental protection?

Such issues have often aroused controversy. Economic development projects in Brazil, funded by the World Bank, caused such an outcry that the World Bank now pays much more heed to the environmental impact of projects it has under consideration. In the United States, meanwhile, with its extensive legislation for the protection of habitat and species, developers and other commercial interests continue to do battle with environmentalists.

Deforestation is linked by environmentalists to some of the other major concerns in the world today, including the "hole on the ozone layer," climate change, soil erosion, loss of species diversity, and destruction of indigenous peoples.

In the essay that follows, the focus is on one of the best-known environmental issues of our day—the cutting of the Amazon rainforest—which has come to symbolize the complex issues and interwoven repercussions of large-scale human impact on the environment.

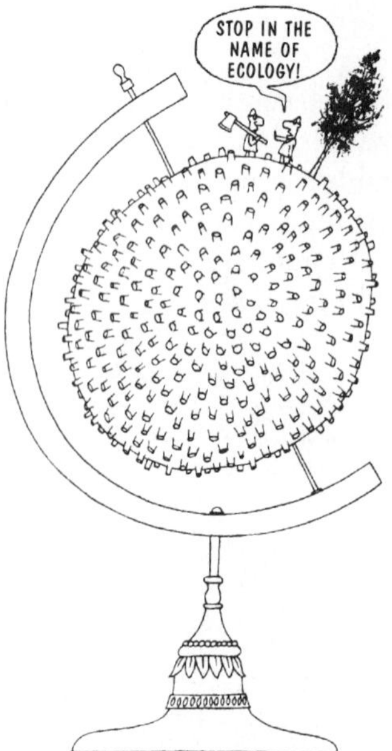

(Naranjo/El Universal/Mexico City)

ANNOTATED READING: Kenneth Maxwell. "The Tragedy of the Amazon." *The New York Review of Books* 7 March 1991: 24–29.

The Tragedy of the Amazon

If 1989 was the year of revolution in Eastern Europe, 1988 was the year of drought and fire in the Americas. It was a year of growing public concern about global warming, with dire projections of melting ice caps and ozone depletion. It was a year of dramatic images of the charred remnants of once majestic forests from the Rockies to the Amazon basin. For the first time the destruction of the tropical rain-forest of Brazil became a major issue for North Americans and for people concerned about the danger to the environment throughout the world. But how did this vast ecological disaster occur? What can be done to deal with its effects?

Some answers to these questions are provided by the books under review, each of which deals with some aspect of the tragedy of the Amazon. Another kind of answer is provided by the controversy over the murder in December 1988 of Francisco "Chico" Mendes, the ecologically minded leader of the Brazilian rubber tappers union whose two convicted killers, a father and son, were sentenced in December to nineteen years in prison. This article will examine the crisis in the Amazon and its causes. A second article will be devoted to the extraordinary story of Chico Mendes, and to potential remedies for the Amazon crisis, among them the idea of "extractive forest reserves," a concept Mendes helped to promote. By doing so, he brought on his assassination.

Gold miners at the Serra Pelada mine in the state of Pará, Brazil, 1986 *(UPI/Corbis-Bettman)*

This author is reviewing nine books on the Amazon. His article is a synthesis of information from these sources, mixed in with his own commentary on the books, their authors, and the situation under discussion. Note the detailed background he presents in his introduction before he even gets to the books under review. Typically, journals and newspapers ask experts in the appropriate field to review books; this introduction helps establish Maxwell's authority as the reviewer.

1.

The Amazon is a vast region; not all of it is rainforest, nor is all of it Brazilian. As it was legally defined in 1953, the Amazon region within Brazil incorporates about 60 percent of Brazil and includes savannah grasslands, wetlands, and shrublands, as well as humid rainforests, all connected with the Amazon river system, which contains one fifth of the earth's fresh water supply. The river rises 17,000 feet in the Andes and flows some 4,000 miles until it reaches the Atlantic, yet as one follows it 3,000 miles inland from the sea it rises only to 300 feet. The river's mouth is 200 miles wide, and for 1,000 miles upstream it remains seven miles wide; ocean-going liners can travel 2,000 miles up the river from the sea. The river and the rainforest cover the heart of the subcontinent and encompass nine South American countries. Seventeen of the Amazon's tributaries are more than 1,000 miles long, each longer than the Rhine.

Brazil's Amazonian forest is the largest remaining tropical forest on earth, and its natural life is the richest and most diverse in the world, containing 20 percent of all higher plant life, the same proportion of bird species, and 10 percent of the world's mammals. The tall trees produce a dense overhead canopy, which keeps out all but a fraction of the sunlight. Within the semidarkness thousands of species thrive, only a tiny number of which are known or recorded by scientists. Each tree can support as many as four hundred insect species. The rainy season's floods deposit alluvium along the river banks to form flood plains (*varzeas*), rich in palms, fruits, turtles, fish, and aquatic birds. Naturalists have found five hundred different plant species in one forest patch of the flooded plains. To the south and east are forests filled with mahogany, tropical cypress, and cherry wood trees. The westernmost tributary, the Araguaia, flows through swampy grasslands and forests of mahogany, Brazil nut, and rubber forests.

A marvelously comprehensive introduction to the rainforest can be found in the thoughtful and readable *The Last Rain Forests: A World Conservation Atlas* edited by Mark Collins. It provides maps of the present distribution of forest worldwide and helps to place the Amazon in a global context, while one can study some of the extraordinary fauna of the region in the beautifully produced and illustrated *Neotropical Rainforest Mammals: A Field Guide*, the first such broad regional guide ever produced.

The paradox of this "rich realm of nature," as the early Portuguese adventurers called it, is that while the soils of much of the Amazon region are extremely impoverished, they can still sustain more than 250 metric tons of living material per acre. For many years no one could explain how they did so. As Alexander Cockburn and Susanna Hecht point out in *The Fate of the Forest*, a survey of the region and its

The Last Rain Forests: A World Conservation Atlas edited by Mark Collins, foreword by David Attenborough. Oxford University Press, 200 pp., $29.95

Neotropical Rainforest Mammals: A Field Guide by Louise H. Emmons, illustrated by François Feer. University of Chicago Press, 281 pp., $45.00; $19.95 (paper)

The Fate of the Forest: Developers, Destroyers and Defenders of the Amazon by Susanna Hecht and Alexander Cockburn. Verso, 266 pp., $24.95

World Resources, 1990–1991: A Guide to the Global Environment a Report by the World Resources Institute. Oxford University Press, 383 pp., $17.95 (paper)

Government Policies and Deforestation in Brazil's Amazon Region by Dennis J. Mahar. The World Bank, 56 pp., $5.95 (paper)

Developing Amazonia: Deforestation and Social Conflict in Brazil's Carajás Programme by Anthony L. Hall. Manchester University Press, 295 pp., $45.00

The Decade of Destruction: The Crusade to Save the Amazon Rain Forest by Adrian Cowell. Holt, 215 pp., $19.95

Anatomy of the Amazon Gold Rush by David Cleary. University of Iowa Press, 245 pp., $17.95 (paper)

Alternatives to Deforestation: Steps Toward Sustainable Use of the Amazon Rain Forest edited by Anthony B. Anderson. Columbia University Press, 281 pp., $65.00

crisis, the beginning of an answer came in 1960, thanks to the cold war, when the US Atomic Energy Commission sought to find out what would happen to forests in the event of a nuclear war, stimulating the first interdisciplinary study of the tropical forest.

Students discovered that whereas forests in the temperate zone draw nutrients up from the soil, in tropical forests the nutrients derive from an exchange within the living forest and are held in the tissues of living organisms. The leathery leaves characteristic of the Amazon plant life conserve nutrients as well as high levels of secondary chemicals, which make tropical leaves tough or poisonous to eat, deterring predators and also making them a rich source of drugs. Latex, a substance that acts as a defensive membrane for the Brazilian rubber tree, *Hevea brasiliensis*, is just such an adaptation. The wild germ plasm of the forest includes cacao, palm hearts, *guarana*, Brazil nuts, rubber, chicle, babassu oil, fish, manioc, cashews, and coca. As Hecht and Cockburn observe, the global annual value of the Amazonian natural products may exceed one hundred billion dollars a year.[1]

2.

The assault on the tropical forests has a long history, and so does the

In discussing the Amazon's woes, Maxwell demonstrates his ability to tie together history, biography, botany, politics, and other relevant fields. This interdisciplinary competence helps the reader to develop a broad understanding of a complex situation.

[1]These figures were disputed by Roger Stone in a review of the Hecht and Cockburn book, "The Politics of Deforestation," *Issues in Science and Technology* (Spring 1990), pp. 77–78. He says, "The total value of Brazilian exports, including manufactured goods, amounted to less than $34 billion in 1988." Hecht and Cockburn's figure, however, included coca, the main product exported (albeit clandestinely) from the western Amazon basin.

history of human habitation in the forest. The year 2000 will mark the fifth century since the landfall on the Brazilian coast by the India-bound fleet of the Portuguese explorer Pedro Alvares Cabral. It was a land "with great groves of trees," according to the fleet's notary, Pero Vaz de Caminha, who described it in a letter to the king of Portugal on May 1, 1500.[2] Of the lush Atlantic coastal forest that so impressed the Europeans in 1500—a narrow belt of rainforest some one hundred miles deep, which then ran along virtually the whole coast of Brazil—no more than 4 percent remains today. From among its flora, ironically, Brazil took its name from the pau-brasil tree, which yielded a purple dye much in demand among sixteenth-century European textile manufacturers, and which can scarcely be found in the wild today. The Portuguese had called their new territory in South America the "Land of the True Cross," but this was soon forgotten and the more prosaic name stuck—resonant as it was of the forest and of business.

Like the coastal forest, the Amazon rainforest before the arrival of the Europeans sustained a large population—it is virtually impossible to estimate how large.[3] In two brilliant books, John Hemming, who is director and secretary of the Royal Geographical Society of London, has heroically tried to reconstruct from thousands of pages of travel accounts, official reports, diaries, and archaeological and anthropological research the lost history of the annihilated peoples of South America. He calculates that the native population of the Amazon basin alone could have been about 3.5 million in 1500.[4] It is, at most,

---

[2]Full text in W. B. Greenlee, ed., *The Voyage of Pedro Alvares Cabral to Brazil and India from Contemporary Narratives*, Hakluyt Series, No. 81 (1838), pp. 3–33. Caminha's letter is reproduced in facsimile in the New York Public Library exhibition catalog. *Brazil-Portugal: The Age of Atlantic Discovery* (Editora Bertrand and Franco Maria Ricci, 1990).

---

[3]All the early accounts spoke of large populations. See Sir C. R. Markham ed., *Expeditions into the Valley of the Amazon*: 1539, 1540, 1639, Hakluyt Series, No. 24 (1859), pp. 61, 79, passim.

---

[4]John Hemming, *Red Gold: The Conquest of the Brazilian Indians* (Harvard University Press, 1978), and *Amazon Frontier: The Defeat of the Brazilian Indians* (Harvard University Press, 1987). Hemming is also author of "How Brazil Acquired Roraima," *Hispanic American Historical Review*, Vol. 70, No. 2 (May 1990), pp. 295–325. Unfortunately, Hemming and other scholars rarely use the extraordinary riches of the Portuguese archives to study these questions. They are particularly valuable for any work on the Amazon, including scientific work. For an introduction to the extensive scientific mission of Alexander Rodrigues Ferreira in the late eighteenth century, for example, there is a good book by William Joel Simon, *Scientific Expeditions in the Portuguese Overseas Territories* (1783–1808) *and the Role of Lisbon in the Intellectual-Scientific Community of the Late Eighteenth Century* (Lisbon: Instituto de Investigação Cientifica Tropical, 1983). There is also an excellent, but regrettably unpublished and largely ignored, Yale Ph.D. dissertation by David Davidson, "The Madeira Route and the Incorporation of the Brazilian Far West, 1737–1808."

200,000 today. The lost population of Indians did not live in an untroubled paradise but they lived in harmony with the forest, and they did not destroy it.

Hecht and Cockburn tell us that the degree of human intervention in the forest ecosystem is much greater than we have realized. Scholars have learned from demographic reconstructions of the catastrophic and precipitate population decline in the Caribbean and in Mexico after the Spanish conquest that we should be very cautious before we dismiss the early accounts of large indigenous population as hyperbole.[5] As with the first reactions in our own century to the Holocaust in Europe, it has been difficult for many people to accept the vast scale of extermination.

Both greed and good intentions caused the destruction of the native population. By the 1570s, the rich forests of the coastal region, especially those of the flood plains around the great natural harbors of Rio de Janeiro and Bahia, as well as further north at Recife in Pernambuco, had been cleared and the land converted to sugar cane production. The sugar mills required huge quantities of firewood to heat the cauldrons that processed sugar and the coastal forests were increasingly depleted. Forced into slave labor, and lacking immunity to European and African diseases, the Indian population died by the tens of thousands. Enslaved Africans were imported to replace them, permanently transforming the ethnic composition of the Portuguese coastal enclaves on the edge of the continent.[6]

> The destruction of Indian populations in Brazil has a long history, as does slavery there. As elsewhere in the world, the discovery of gold, and the greed this evoked, played a big part in a sad history.

As the Indian populations of the coastlands died out, Portuguese missionaries who had arrived to proselytize the native population moved inland to gain new converts. The Franciscans established Belém (Bethlehem) at the mouth of the Amazon river in 1616, and after 1649, Jesuits, Carmelites, and Mercedarians divided up the main tributaries of the river between them. Throughout the colonial period royal governors, merchants, and Portuguese colonists regularly sent up river heavily armed flotillas of canoes in search of slaves.

> The disastrous impact of outsiders, who often thought of themselves as superior to the indigenes in different parts of the world, is also mentioned by James Goldsmith in Section Three of this unit.

The religious orders, especially the Jesuits, sought to protect the Indian population from enslavement by organizing new communities of would-be peasant farmers. Although these concentrations initially

---

[5]Sherborne F. Cook and Woodrow Borah, *Essays in Population History*, 3 vols. (University of California Press, 1971, 1974, 1979).

---

[6]The African component in the formation of Brazilian society of course parallels the story of the destruction of the Indians and is essential to any understanding of Brazil. There is an excellent new book by Joseph Miller, *A Way of Death: Merchant Capitalism and the Angolan Slave Trade, 1730–1830* (University of Wisconsin Press, 1988), which provides a good introduction to this story.

led to an even more rapid spread of disease, the Jesuits in time were able to establish a network of protected villages throughout the lower Amazon to complement the great missions they organized on the plains along the Uruguay and Paraguay Rivers to the south. The struggle between the Jesuits and others who sought to protect the Indians, and the colonists who argued that they should be integrated with the European communities, albeit as lowly workers, is a long one in Amazonian history, and the arguments on both sides were often well intentioned. The Marquis de Pombal, King Joseph's chief minister between 1750 and 1777, who expelled the Jesuits from Brazil, justified his actions in the language of the Enlightenment. (He ended African slavery in Portugal itself.) The writings in defense of the Indians by the Jesuit polymath António Vieira are among the most eloquent works in the Portuguese language.[7]

The Enlightenment was an 18th-century philosophical movement that espoused rationalism and questioned existing beliefs. The 18th century is sometimes known as the Age of Reason.

As Hemming shows, the missions were eventually suppressed by jealous officials of the monarchy abetted by the colonists' avarice. In the late seventeenth century gold was discovered and prospectors flooded into the interior. The colonial government, suspicious of the loyalty of the Jesuit missions that were strategically placed along the river systems, sent teams of surveyors, soldiers, and administrators to establish Portugal's authority over the land and establish frontiers. By the mid-eighteenth century they thus had laid claim to tens of thousands of square miles of unexplored territory. When Brazil gained its independence from Portugal in the 1820s, the new nation inherited this "hollow frontier," containing within it many unknown Indian communities.

During the nineteenth and twentieth centuries these hidden peoples would slowly be "discovered." Natural scientists arrived to study the teeming life of the forest. European anthropologists were sent to study living societies but, more often than not, and certainly unintentionally, their contacts with unknown groups of Indians helped to bring about their rapid disintegration. The Indians were proselytized by Protestant fundamentalist missionaries who brought with them values regarded as simplistic and ignorant by many in the societies they themselves came from. The Indians were victimized by free-lance miners, adventurers, and trappers, who were seeking gold, booty, or natural forest products, such as Brazil nuts and rubber. These pioneers were both fearful of the native forest dwellers and all too willing to exploit or kill them.

[7]The life of Vieira, one of the most remarkable figures of the seventeenth century, is currently the subject of a major biography by Gregory Rabassa.

John Hemming has very little use for either the Christian missionaries or the slavers, or for their modern counterparts. Amid the relentless destruction of the indigenous population, his heroes are those Indians who were uncompromising in their opposition to the white man. In fact, he sometimes implies that the only good white man is a dead white man. There is a special poignancy and irony to this view. During an expedition out of Cachimbo near the geographical center of Brazil in 1961, then a crude airstrip in the forest, members of Kreen-Akrore tribe had ambushed and killed Richard Mason, a young Englishman, among whose companions was John Hemming.

But the killing of whites, when it occurred, never did the Indians any good. The whites always had more guns and more resources—an inexhaustible supply. They also brought the invisible influenza and other viruses that could cause mass destruction of the Indians. The fatal power of such infection was something that the closed Indian societies never comprehended when they came into contact with Europeans. Along the river banks throughout Amazonia the Indian population was in large part decimated, and often replaced by what Hemming calls "a growing proletariat of semi-acculturated and discontented free Indians and mixed races (*caboclos*)."

In 1835, this population exploded in the most violent and revolutionary of all nineteenth-century Brazilian rebellions, the Cabanagem revolt, named after the migrants' cabana huts on the flood plains near Belém. Led by priests, rubber workers, and mutinous soldiers, the revolt was a mass popular uprising of the *caboclos* and large numbers of Indians against property owners and government officials. The rebellion was put down with great ferocity. Some thirty thousand lives were lost, a fifth of the population of the region. The rise in world demand for rubber brought new settlers and new international attention at the end of the century. The rubber tappers pushed far up into the tributaries of the Amazon and toward the border territory of Acre, which was also claimed by Bolivia and Peru. In 1903, after a series of revolts and plots, and much international intrigue, Acre became part of Brazil.

The struggle of the Indians and traditional rubber tappers for rights continues today, as political and commercial interests seek to develop the region.

But Brazilian rubber could not compete with the new plantations in Asia, and the region once more sank back into relative obscurity, though not before more wild schemes and ambitions had been consumed by the jungle, including the infamous and corruption-ridden construction of the Madeira Mamoré railroad in the early part of the century, the failed attempts at industrialized plantation agriculture by Henry Ford in the 1930s and the billionaire Daniel K. Ludwig in the 1960s, all well-known tales of greed, naiveté, and ecological ignorance, which are described with verve by Hecht and Cockburn and others in what is sure to be a new wave of travelers' tales of horror and disaster provoked by the growing interest in the Amazon.[8] A more realistic perspective was provided in the 1920s by Kenneth Grubb, a missionary who wrote, in a sad reflection of the destruction of Indian communities, that it was possible to travel from Belém to Peru

> without seeing a distinctly tribal Indian. These rivers are silent today, except for the lap of the waters along some deserted beach, the hoarse cry of the parrots or the call of the inambu. The past has gone, with its peoples, in central Amazonia, leaving only that bitter sense of impotence, as of being present before a consuming conflagration and at the same time being powerless to assist.[9]

3.

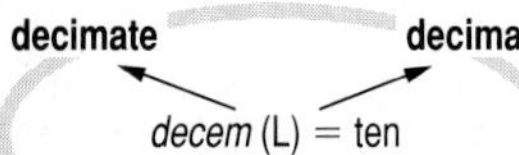

This unexpected connection between **decimate** (to kill or destroy a large part of a population of some kind) and the common mathematical term **decimal** comes from the Roman military, which sometimes killed one person in every ten as a punishment.

The decimation of the Amazonian Indians, leaving a population of no more than 200,000 today, is only part of the story of the destruction of the rainforest. Just as destruction of the forest itself brings with it the destruction of millions of unrecorded plants and creatures, so the destruction of the Amazon Indians destroys knowledge of the forest acquired over millennia. What is new since the 1980s is the scale of encroachment in the last redoubt of the Amazon's native people.

World Resources, 1990–1991: *A Guide to the Global Environment*, a marvelously comprehensive, well-produced handbook, cautiously estimates the yearly loss of tropical rainforest in Brazil to be somewhere between 1.7 and 8 million hectares The disparity between the figures demonstrates how tentative most calculations remain and how urgent is the need for more research. The World Resources experts believe that some 7 percent of the forested area has already been lost. Dennis J. Mahar, in his World Bank study, *Government Policies and Deforestation in Brazil's Amazon Region*, estimates on the basis of Landsat satellite images that the figure is as high as 12 percent. Both would agree, however, that, if the present rate of clearing continues, 15 percent of all plant life in the Latin American rainforest will become extinct by the end of the century. While accurate figures are difficult to come by, Mahar argues that "because pasture has clearly been the predominant form of agricultural land use in the region, cattle ranching would appear to be the leading proximate cause of deforestation." Small farming activity has also increased, but farm plots are often sold or abandoned after only a few years of use. These areas are then con-

---

[8]The best book on these topics, much mined though rarely acknowledged, is that by Warren Dean, *Brazil and the Struggle for Rubber: A Study in Environmental History* (Cambridge University Press, 1987). For a discussion of the new, or rather the revived, genre of Amazonian tales see Stephen Milk's review in the *TLS*, December 7–13, 1990, which examines Anthony Smith's *Explorers of the Amazon* (Viking, 1990), Dennison Berwick's *Amazon* (Hutchinson, 1990) and Stephan Nugent's *Big Mouth* (Fourth Estate, 1990).

---

[9]Cited by John Hemming in *Amazon Frontier*, p. 246.

verted to pasture or quickly invaded by secondary growth. Logging has also contributed to deforestation.

Cockburn and Hecht blame the generals who ran Brazil between 1964 and 1985 for the destruction of the rainforest. The generals must be held responsible for what occurred during these two decades, but like virtually all political explanations based on a single cause, this one is too simple and it may seem to imply that the solutions are simple as well, which, unfortunately, is not the case. In fact, the great push to the interior was under way well before the military coup of 1964; and, not surprisingly, it continued unabated after the military retreated to the barracks in 1985. The building of the new capital, Brasília, in 1960, and the coincidental opening of two arterial roads into the forest—the two-thousand-mile dirt highway moving north between the new capital and Belém at the mouth of the Amazon and the beginning of the Brasília-Pôrto Velho road moving west—were the events that in many respects set the contemporary disaster in motion. Both enterprises were part of a government policy of opening up the resources of the backlands to development—a policy broadly supported at the time by most of the different groups that make up Brazilian society. The idea of building a capital in the interior and of developing the Amazon goes back at least as far as the eighteenth century. Cockburn and Hecht don't make it sufficiently plain that the building of Brasília and the Brasília-Belém highway marked the high point of the boom under President Juscelino Kubitschek, a good democrat in his own fashion, and a politician who epitomized the expansionism, optimism, as well as the pervasive corruption of the Fifties.

As in any **critique,** the author is free to criticize, correct, or comment on the work(s) under discussion as well as praise them. Here, Maxwell notes that blaming Brazil's military government of 1964–1985 for the destruction of the forests is "too simple." Brazilian political history has seen many military coups and occasional interludes of more democratic, civilian rule, as at present. Brazil's wish to develop Amazonia has created worldwide controversy.

Brasilia was designed and built as the new capital of Brazil, replacing Rio de Janeiro. In part, this was intended to lead the way in developing the interior. Other cities designed from scratch to be their country's capital include Washington, D.C., Canberra (Australia), Islamabad (Pakistan), and Ajuba (Nigeria).

The approach of Kubitschek to development during the mid-1950s had very grave consequences that the books under review fail to assess, partly because they are excessively concerned to establish continuity with the exploitative Portuguese past. But Kubitschek and the military geostrategists who took power after 1964, such as the *éminence grise* of the military regime, General Golbery do Couto e Silva, did something radically new; they pressed for a network of roads linking the northeast to the center and south of the country to the Amazon basin. The credits and the special favors granted to southern businessmen were intended at first to encourage them to invest in a region in which they saw few prospects for profit. But the roads to the south undermined the assumption that had dominated all previous thinking about the Amazon—the central importance of the rivers. Now land routes were to have preference over riverine communication, forest clearance over forest extraction, and water was to be considered a source of energy and not of life.

The dirt road to Belém was soon paved, and between 1960 and 1970 some 300,000 migrants went to seek their fortune along the

The road-building project to open up **Rondônia** became an international symbol of environmental disaster that forced the World Bank to give added weight to the environmental impact of projects it funds. For a pictorial essay on this, see *National Geographic* 174 (December 1988): 772–799.

highway. The Transamazonian highway, intended to link the northeast and Amazonia, followed, as did the Cuiabá-Pôrto Velho highway in the states of Mato Grosso and Rondônia. The most severe deforestation has been concentrated along these roads and the many roads that feed into them, a process which is shown dramatically in the Oxford *Conservation Atlas*. The population of Rondônia grew by over 21 percent per annum between 1970 and 1978. In Rondônia and Mato Grosso over one fourth of the forest has disappeared during the past decade.

As the huge road-building programs opened up the region, government-sponsored projects to build new settlements attracted migrants from Brazil's poverty-stricken northeast as well as from its southern states, where extensive mechanization of agriculture and the spread of cash crops such as soya were displacing thousands of smallholders. The military regime encouraged cattle raising by providing special fiscal incentives, as well as easy and subsidized credit to would-be ranchers, and extensive benefits to businesses that invested in the region, exempting them from excise duties and from corporate income taxes for ten to fifteen years. Many of the ranch owners who received some $700 million in tax credits were never seriously interested in producing beef—they acquired property only to take advantage of the economic benefits. Once they received the tax credits they sold or abandoned the projects the credits were supposed to stimulate, but not before these speculative enterprises caused extensive damage to the environment.

Businessmen from the south of Brazil, especially the São Paulo-based association of Amazon businessmen, lobbied the central government in Brasília to subsidize cattle-ranching ventures, and in 1974 the government set up the extensive Polamazonia program to encourage selective investment in production intended for export such as beef, timber, and minerals. Subsidized rural credit was extended on very favorable terms (twenty-year investment credit was made available at a nominal annual rate of 12 percent to ranchers, for example). Because a land title was required to qualify for a subsidy, Amazonia's sharecroppers, tenants, and squatters were, in effect, denied access to this capital, which served to further concentrate wealth and land ownership throughout the region. A destructive sequence was established in the early 1970s which was to repeat itself throughout the Amazon basin. Forest was cleared and opened up through the sweated labor of poor migrants whose lands were later appropriated by large estates. The forests cut down and burned for conversion to pasture during the dry season were planted with African forage grains, which seldom provided more than two to three years of good fodder. Phosphorous levels in the soil thereafter fell dramatically, and the grasses were soon overtaken by shrubs and weeds.

Overstocked, compacted, leached, and degraded, these lands will require at least one hundred years to recover. Since government credits had been used by the proprietors to offset their expenses elsewhere in Brazil, the absentee landowners were not greatly concerned by the waste of the land. The small farmers in the meanwhile were forced to push on toward new frontiers to the west—first to Rondônia, then in the 1980s to Acre and Roraima. The pattern was one of settlement and then of the settlements' failure, of land grabbing and violent protest against it, of the concentration of ownership and ecological devastation.

All of this is described in absorbing detail by Anthony Hall in his splendid book, *Developing Amazonia*. Hall convincingly demonstrates that

> the notion of Amazonia as a vast, fertile empty space ready to permanently absorb the land-hungry masses from northeastern and southern Brazil is a myth.

In his more journalistic book, Adrian Cowell, who in the early 1980s was filming the onslaught of settlers, job-seekers, entrepreneurs, and speculators in Rondônia for a British TV documentary unit, describes how he became increasingly appalled by the scale and senselessness of this new phase of Amazonian development:

> The history of Amazonia may have been littered with visionaries like Ford and Ludwig who fruitlessly tried to impose some dream or vision on the forest. But here was a government and a whole society marching into the forest with the manic zest of a lemming migration, hypnotised by an obsession which was even more difficult than the lemmings' to understand. We seemed to have arrived at one of the frontier's dead-ends, where the forest mirrored the absurdity of the society confronting it.

4.

The Amazon frontier soon reproduced the large landowning (*latifundia*) pattern of the northeast and south of Brazil. In 1985, 30 percent of rural properties in Brazil were less than ten hectares, yet they occupied only 0.1 percent of farmland; 1.9 percent of properties of over a thousand hectares occupied 57 percent of the agricultural land. The largest 152 Amazonian estates occupied 40 million hectares, equal to the total area of cultivated land in Brazil. These estates, moreover, do not create many jobs, since lumbering and cattle ranching require few employees.

> The discussion of land ownership is very significant because it says much about the distribution of wealth in Brazil, which is often used to exemplify an unegalitarian pattern in which most of the country's wealth is in very few hands. As is noted in this article, the opening of the Amazon is, in part, an attempt to provide land for the impoverished people of Northeast Brazil while avoiding the need for large-scale redistribution, which is strongly opposed by wealthy landowners.

At the same time the exploration of the Amazon lands created a vast army of landless, temporary wage laborers who migrate to the urban centers, and take jobs as seasonal workers or try to make a living as independent prospectors for gold (*garimpeiros*). Small farmers still produce 80 percent of the basic food crops and provide 82 percent of jobs in the eastern Amazon, but the concentration of landownership between 1985 and 1988 has caused the output of such basic staples as beans and cassava to fall by 8 percent and 14 percent respectively.

In the eastern Amazon, and especially in the Araguaia-Tocantins region, the expansion of settlement and ranching followed the highway, and was accompanied by violent struggles over land. Until the 1950s, the economy was based on the harvest of Brazil nuts (*castanhas*) and other forest products, and controlled by a few powerful families, who shipped the nuts north to Belém. Between 1969 and 1975 the Maoist offshoot of the Brazilian Communist party established a guerrilla campaign in the region which fought sporadically with the Brazilian army. The guerrillas were eventually suppressed by thousands of troops.

Two other major factors came into play here, each no less dangerous to the ecology—one set in motion by mining for iron ore and the other by gold. These processes of mineral extraction and their ecological and social consequences are the subject of Anthony Hall's *Developing Amazonia*, which examines the vast complex for mining iron ore and other minerals called the Carajás project, and of David Cleary in his *Anatomy of the Amazon Gold Rush*. Both books, like Adrian Cowell's *Decade of Destruction*, have the great advantage of avoiding the hyperbole that characterizes so much writing about Brazil. Cowell has chosen, as he did in his television documentaries, to follow the lives of ordinary people in the hope that these case histories will help to explain the larger story. The three books taken together recreate the fascinating history of the struggle in the Amazon as it affects people in their everyday lives.

Rhetorical note: Maxwell's review of some literature on the Amazon is pulled together in a **synthesis** in which he describes and discusses the history of the region. He provides a good model for a research paper in which various sources are referred to but in which the author's voice is clearly and strongly heard. It is clearly *his* essay, not just a collection of quotes or paraphrases from other people's writing. The essay differs from most of your research papers, however, in not providing in-text citations.

Amazonian iron and gold could hardly have produced two more different kinds of organizations. Carajás is a huge state enterprise, regional in scope, mainly concerned with producing iron for export. To carry on the mining it has been provided with dams, hydroelectric power, railroads, and port facilities, and it has the benefit of large capital infusions from national and international investors. Prospecting for gold, by contrast, is generally an independent and uncontrolled activity, called *garimpagem* in Brazil, which is carried on by small entrepreneurs and adventurers. The large mining companies are implacable enemies of free-lance prospectors, who are continually penetrating company-held territory to set up their clandestine mining operations.

Only a small portion of the gold is sold to the state, and accurate production figures, as always in the Amazon, are impossible to come by. Cleary estimates that there are hundreds of thousands of *garimpeiros*. The gold they produce was estimated in the late 1980s to be worth over one billion dollars annually. Gold mining technology is cheap, and it is easy to run, the most complex machinery needed being a small internal combustion engine. According to Cleary, in 1987 mining professionals estimated that the *garimpos* were producing around 120 metric tons of gold annually—which would place Brazil third among world gold producers, behind only South Africa and the Soviet Union—an amount equal to the great nineteenth-century gold rushes. The most dramatic *garimpo* was the one found in 1979 at Serra Pelada, about 90 kilometers from the city of Marabá in the south of Pará. At its peak in 1983, Serra Pelada produced one metric ton of gold a year and had some 100,000 *garimpeiros* and traders who removed entire hills with pickaxes and shovels.

The gold prospectors do not cut down large [tracts] of forest or take up large stretches of land as the ranchers do, but the ecological impact of their activities can be devastating. The most insidious and lasting damage comes from mercury, which is used to separate the gold from the ore, and poisons both the environment and the *garimpeiros*. If the *garimpeiros* were, as Cleary suggests, producing over a hundred metric tons of gold per annum in the Brazilian Amazon during the 1980s, an equivalent amount of mercury escaped into the atmosphere in the form of vapor as it was burned off during the amalgamation process.

In addition, mercury is often spilled into the ground and rivers near the *garimpo*. Testing in the Madeira River found mercury levels in fish several times higher than World Health Organization safety levels. Cleary takes a relatively benign view of the *garimpeiros*, rightly saying that they are among the few groups of poor rural Brazilians who have a chance to rise in the world. But the invasion of 45,000 *garimpeiros* into the lands of the Yanomami in the far north of Brazil is wreaking havoc among the indigenous population.[10] Lucio Flavio Pinto, a courageous Amazonian journalist whose paper, *Jornal Pessoal* (regrettably now defunct), was almost alone in reporting in depth on Amazonian politics and corruption, points out that small-scale mining is sometimes carried on by extremely well-financed operators. Pinto estimates that there were 1,200 clandestine airstrips and at least 800 small airplanes to get the gold out, while the gold business has allowed some local bosses to exercise almost medieval feudal domination over the districts.[11]

[10]"*A morte ronda os indios na floresta*," *Veja*, September 19, 1990, pp. 70–77.

The Carajás iron project started as recently as 1967, when a helicopter with engine trouble landed in a bare patch in the forest southwest of Marabá. It was carrying several geologists who were astonished to find that they were standing on the top of a hill made up of billions of tons of highgrade iron ore, bauxite, manganese, copper, nickel, and cassiterite. The Brazilian government quickly took over the site and assigned the state-owned mining company CVRD (Companhia do Vale do Rio Doce) to develop it. The Greater Carajás Project, as it became known, was granted control of a region of some 900,000 square kilometers—the size of France and Britain combined—and started an enormous concentrated effort to build roads, a railway, dams, and a hydroelectric power plant.

The Carajás program has four major components: the iron ore mine, a highly mechanized open pit mine that began operation in 1986; two aluminum plants, one in Belém, the other in São Luis, the capital of the state of Maranhão; the Tucuruí hydroelectric complex on the Tocantins River; and a nine hundred kilometer railroad inaugurated in 1985 to link Carajás and São Luis, where a deep water port was opened a year later. Japanese corporations are the single biggest group of investors, through cheap loans of $500 billion to the Brazilian government. The EEC invested $600 million. The World Bank provided $304 million, and $250 million came from US commercial banks. Even the USSR provided $60 million. The CVRD contracts to supply iron to Japanese and European steel producers were tied to the loans. The CVRD is immensely profitable. Although only 294 in the Fortune Global 500, it is first in the world in profits as a percentage of sales (65 percent) and of assets (45 percent).[12]

Although within the CVRD enclave itself environmental deterioration has been carefully monitored and controlled, the company's own territory looks increasingly like a Potemkin village, surrounded everywhere by devastation. The Carajás program acted as a strong population magnet, attracting thousands of construction workers, gold panners, small farmers, and speculators into the region which until very recently had been tropical forest. The insatiable demands for the charcoal used to smelt the iron ore will eventually destroy over 70,000 acres of forest every year, and has already led to destruction of the surrounding forest in a manner recalling the insatiable demands of the sugar mills that consumed the coastal forests four centuries before. The Tucuruí hydropower complex, for which 35,000 people were displaced, has the largest dam in any of the world's tropical forests and it caused the flooding of 2,500 square kilometers of

[11]"*Belém Para*," *Jornal Pessoal*, Vol. 11, No. 64, July 1990.

[12]*Fortune*, July 30, 1990.

uncleared forest. The hydropower complex is central to the entire scheme—supplying electricity at subsidized prices to the iron mine, the aluminum plants, and the industries along the Carajás-São Luis Railroad.

The profitability of the Carajás project depends heavily on these huge state investments and on the cheap energy they will produce. Electronorte, the state monopoly electricity company in the Amazon, has grandiose plans for sixty-three new reservoirs in the Amazon basin, twenty-seven for the Tocantins-Araguaia region alone.[13] Road and dam building is immensely profitable, and all the major Brazilian public works and construction companies, such as Camargo Correa, Andrade Gutierrez, and Mendes Junior, are involved in the projects, which absorb vast sums of government resources. Lucio Flavio Pinto estimated that those expenditures represent some 15 percent of Brazil's foreign debt.[14]

The riches of the Amazon are both **environmental** and **economic.** As pointed out earlier in this essay, the natural products of the forest have tremendous economic potential as well—so protecting the environment and having economic development are by no means mutually exclusive—but the temptation to tap the mineral reserves and dam the rivers in pursuit of more traditional large-scale economic development is very great. The United States faces a similar dilemma in the Arctic Natural Wildlife Refuge, which has oil reserves, but Brazil is a much poorer country.

Many of the schemes for dams and reservoirs are particularly ill-considered. The recently completed Balbina reservoir near Manaus, capital of the state of Amazonas, covered an area of dense tropical forests and is, like almost all other Amazonian basin reservoirs, extremely shallow; it therefore produces a low level of energy per square kilometer flooded. Since no environmental impact studies or land surveys were made before the flooding, no one really knows what potential mineral resources were submerged in the process. No programs for saving animals have been set up, nor has provision been made for fish ladders at any of the dams. The deterioration of the quality of the impounded water through decomposition and absorption of organic matter can lead to a lack of oxygen in the water, cause corrosion of the hydroelectric turbines, create a buildup of sulfuric acid, and help in the proliferation of mosquitos and the spread of intestinal diseases. Not surprisingly, an epidemic of malaria has broken out in the Amazon region, rising from a reported 51,000 cases in 1970 to more than one million in 1990.

Nowhere, moreover, have small projects been developed to provide electricity to the rural populations. All the electrical power generated has been for urban and industrial use, which only serves to increase migration and to make more acute the crisis in producing food, which is largely grown by the poor and vulnerable Amazon peasants. As the small farmers and land-hungry migrants have faced the rapid concen-

[13]Wolfgang J. Junk and J. A. S. Nunes de Mello, "*Impactos ecológicos das represas hidrelétricas na bacia amazônica brasileira,*" *Estudos Avançados*, Vol. 4, No. 8 (January–April 1990), pp. 126–143.

[14]"*Belém Para,*" *Jornal Pessoal*, Vol. 11, No. 64, July 1990, p. 10.

tration of land into large holdings, society and the environment have been subject to damage that Hall claims to be "unprecedented in Brazilian history."

5.

The ending of military rule in 1985, if anything, speeded the process of ecological depletion in the Amazon and intensified the growing confrontation between large and small landowners. In 1986 it was estimated that 64 percent of all conflicts over land in Brazil occurred in the Amazon. The Amazon frontier also showed the highest incidence of murders involving more than two victims.

After 1985 the conflict in the Amazon changed. Powerful landed interests became politically more aggressive, as the military, which had protected them, retreated and the political system became more liberal. The Cruzado Plan of 1985–1986 which temporarily reduced speculative profits in the money markets shifted investments to land and property. The new civilian government also set up a ministry of agrarian reform and a program of land reform was announced.

The proposed reform threatened to expropriate land that was not in use and immediately caused more evictions and burning of forests as landowners avidly began to open more pastures in order to prove the land was being farmed. Peasants, too, occupied unused land on estates in the hope of acquiring titles to it. Increasingly active workers' movements emerged during the 1980s, organized by unions from the south and by the Church. They began to articulate peasant demands for land reform, while their members harassed and in some cases killed landowners. At the same time a powerful organization of landowners and ranchers, the Rural Democratic Union (UDR), was formed to oppose even the mild proposals for land reform that were put forward by the administration of President José Sarney. The UDR's lobbying in Brasilia was highly successful, and the constitutional assembly in 1988 voted down a proposal that would have allowed state expropriation of very large land holdings as part of a reform plan.

Many saw the hand of the UDR behind the increasing sophistication and violence of the ranchers' response to the rural workers' organizations, as well as the rising number of assassinations of union leaders, church men and women, and labor lawyers. Amnesty International's *Brazil: Authorized Violence in Rural Areas*, a report first published in September 1988, tells the story in grisly and horrifying detail. A steady increase in reported killings of peasants in rural areas had occurred throughout Brazil, more than one thousand between 1980 and 1986. Many of these killings were connected with disputes over land, and were carried out by hired gunmen (*pistoleiros*) employed by

As in many parts of the world, the indigenous population of the Amazon region has suffered from the massive intrusion of outsiders, bringing death by disease and violence. Other victims are the peasants who travel to the region in search of land and jobs and who often find themselves in a struggle with more powerful interests, as described here. The peasants have, however, attracted the sympathetic attention of Brazilian churchmen, unions, and lawyers, as well as international human-rights organizations such as Amnesty International.

landowners; but there was also increasing participation by state policemen.

The failure to pursue serious investigations of these crimes was tantamount to complicity in them, and Amnesty concluded that the pattern of assassinations of workers' leaders was "so persistent that it facilitates fresh killings and may amount to deliberate permissiveness toward them." Amnesty could find only two cases in which hired gunmen were convicted and sentenced for politically motivated killings and not a single case in which those accused of commissioning the killings were brought to justice.

The entire Amazon region was, in the words of Anthony Anderson, "increasingly out of the control of the public sector." Whereas government incentives and investment had once been a sine qua non for private activity, now ranchers, farmers, miners, loggers, and charcoal producers were working on their own. Ranchers were opening their own roads. Private gold mines were polluting the rivers. Settlements of new colonies were spreading along the southern flank of the region and overwhelming the frontier communities already in place.

By 1987, in the Cachimbo region near the center of Brazil where the Kreen-Akrore Indians had killed John Hemming's fellow explorer in 1961 and where in 1968 Adrian Cowell had filmed his *The Tribe that Hides from Man*, not a single Kreen-Akrore remained. Nor did most of the forest. During the 1970s two roads had joined up at Cachimbo, and hordes of prospectors had found gold in the Peixoto Azevedo River. The Kreen-Akrore had been forced from their forest redoubt by an epidemic of flu and were starving to death. With the tribe facing extinction, a handful of survivors were flown to the relative protection of the Xingú National Park in Mato Grosso. The region where the vast forest had stood was now populated by the cattle of ranchers and land speculators, some living in colonists' towns close to the river. Cachimbo itself is a large military base, used to test rocket technology that was later sold to Saddam Hussein, and . . . in 1990 . . . a deep pit for the underground testing of nuclear weapons [was revealed].

Maxwell explains the **process** by which the cutting and burning of the rainforest contributes to "the ultimate environmental threat"—global warming.

The 1995 United Nations climate conference in Berlin focused attention once again on **global warming.** For various discussions of the conference, see *World Press Review*, July 1995. Although the topic is in some ways still controversial, one German newspaper, *Der Spiegel*, noted "some clear evidence," including the disappearance of glaciers around the world and an 8-inch rise in sea level over the last 100 years. The article also notes the alarm of insurance companies as climate change appears to be influencing the frequency and severity of natural disasters.

The burning season, whether for clearing farmland, ranch land, or charcoal burning or for mining operations was now affecting a great arc from Acre and Rondônia along the western, southern, and eastern fringes of the Amazon rain forest. The global impact of this transformation in the Amazon and the effects of burning became dramatically evident in the mid-1980s, when satellite imaging revealed to scientists for the first time the monumental scale of the fires. In 1987 the dry season was unusually long, and as a result the forest fires in Amazonia were exceptionally intense and widespread. On August 24, 1987, Brazil's Institute for Space Research (INPE) detected 6,800 fires just in the states of Mato Grosso and a small portion of southern Pará and eastern Rondônia. Smoke from the Amazon fires lasted until December and forced the closing of most of the region's airports.

The fires in the Amazon are entirely manmade; they are not to be compared, for example, with the raging fires that strike in the American West. For trees to burn in the wet tropical forest they need to be felled and left for two or three months to dry. They are then ignited usually by people who want to clear the land, sometimes simply in the hope of selling it. That fire does not spread naturally in this region is central to the surveillance efforts of the Brazilian space institute, which began using meteorological satellites to provide four images each day of the Amazon region. Using high-resolution satellite imagery one can obtain a good map of areas burned, pinpointing particular properties.[15]

At the peak of the burning season, from the end of August until early September, this space imaging revealed as many as eight thousand separate fires in a single day throughout the region. Since at least half the rainfall in the Amazon basin comes from water that is condensed from within the forest atmosphere itself, the scale of deforestation threatened to heavily reduce the region's rainfall. But it was the scale of the burning forest revealed by the satellites that brought home to scientists that what was occurring in Brazil was no longer only a Brazilian disaster, it was a real threat to the global climate.

The reason for this threat lay in the vital link in the carbon cycle between climate and forest. Carbon dioxide, water, and sunlight make wood and release oxygen in a process of photosynthesis. In the opposite reaction, wood decomposes or burns, producing energy and carbon dioxide. What is important is the change in carbon dioxide levels in the atmosphere. Since carbon dioxide acts as a heat-trapping gas, it keeps the earth warmer than it would normally be. The burning of the Brazilian forest dramatically shifts the balance, changing from a situation where much carbon, perhaps 150 tons, is retained in the total mass of living organisms or "biomass," to a system where only a small amount of carbon, around fifteen tons, is retained in grassland or pasture. It is because of this process, in which the forest is transformed into grassland or pasture, that Brazil becomes dangerous globally for its release of carbon dioxide.[16]

How dangerous? José Goldemberg, a renowned Brazilian physicist

[15]Alberto Setzer, *Camões Center Quarterly*, Vol. 2, Nos. 1 & 2 (Spring and Summer 1990), pp. 22–24. Also in *Veja*, July 5, 1989, p. 104.

and former president of the University of São Paulo, estimated that the Amazon fires approximated the level of the carbon dioxide emissions from all of North America and was greater than that contributed by all of Western Europe.[17] Moist tropical forests contain approximately 35 percent of the world's living terrestrial carbon pool, according to Anthony B. Anderson in his introduction to the useful collection of essays by experts, *Alternatives to Deforestation*. The cautious estimate by *World Resources* is that deforestation is second only to fossil fuels as a human source of atmospheric carbon dioxide, almost all of which comes from the tropics and overwhelmingly from Brazil.

The report, *Environmental Damage and Climatic Change*, by the Ditchley Foundation, a body not exactly famous for its extremism, states without hesitation that "global warming is . . . the ultimate environmental threat." New global measures of the surface temperature of the oceans, according to the Ditchley report, show a rise of 0.1 degree centigrade per year for the last eight years. This is a rate of 1.0 degrees centigrade per decade. An average global warming of 1.5 degrees centigrade would alter the climate beyond anything experienced by the planet in the past 10,000 years.[18]

There is a crude irony in this tragedy. The Brazilian politicians and military strategists who planned and promoted the march to the west did so in large part out of the desire to see Brazil make its mark on the world. They succeeded in ways they never could have imagined. Brazil was indeed being taken note of, but for causing a global environmental disaster. Out of the vortex of fire, violence, and social and political conflict in the Amazon a powerful human voice briefly but memorably emerged, that of Chico Mendes. The consequences of his assassination in December 1988, and the possible responses to the ecological crisis in the Amazon basin, will be the subject of a second article.

Chico Mendes led the rubber tappers' union and became a symbol of the struggle for the rights of the poor and dispossessed in the Amazon. He was murdered at the direction of wealthy planters, but he was already a well-known spokesman for human rights, and his death caused a worldwide outcry.

[16]Foster Brown in "The Burning of Brazil: A Discussion with Foster Brown and Alberto Setzer," *Camões Center Quarterly*, Vol. 2, Nos. 1 & 2 (Spring and Summer 1990), p. 20.

[17]José Goldemberg, "A *Amazônia e seu futuro*," *Folha de São Paulo*, January 29, 1989, p. A3. Goldemberg, however, in a letter to the *New York Times* (July 28, 1990) gave much lower figures—since last year he has become secretary of state for science and technology in the Collar administration. The latest figures do show a fall-off in burning since 1988, a topic which will be discussed in part II.

[18]Pearce Wright, *Environmental Damage and Climatic Change* (Ditchley Foundation Report Number D88/4).

ASPECTS OF WRITING: Describing a process.

Ecology concerns the relationship between organisms and the environment, a concept popularized in the idea that "everything depends on everything else." This notion has awakened a realization in many people that damage done to habitats and organisms can have unforeseen consequences. Cutting trees removes the root systems that hold the soil in place; thus deforestation causes soil erosion. Draining of wetlands, similarly, can affect water quality, because these areas act as filters, removing pollutants and sediments. Destruction of wetlands can also lead to flooding, for the flow of water is regulated by the spongelike characteristics of marshes and bogs; when such areas are filled and covered with concrete—to build shopping malls and otherwise expand urban sprawl, for example—the result can be devastating floods, as occurred in northern Italy and northern Europe in the early 1990s.

Environmental topics, therefore, are ideally suited to cause-and-effect and process essays, as illustrated in the accompanying example, but such essays usually require the gathering of a certain amount of technical information—a little chemistry, in the case of acid rain. This may require some research, but many environmental themes are widely reported and described in the popular press as well as the technical literature. **Make sure that you find articles at an appropriate level of technicality.** The article reproduced here is moderately technical, and some readers may wish to find other articles to improve their sense of how acid rain is formed. For example, what kind of smokestacks are referred to in the second paragraph, and what is the formula for H_2SO_4 production? [$SO_2 + H_2O + O = H_2SO_4$.]

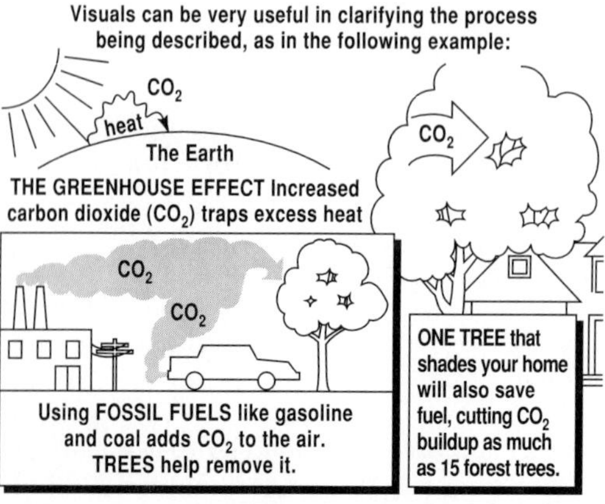

(Illustration courtesy of National Arbor Day foundation)

From Emission to Acidification: An Acid Rain Primer

Sulfur and nitrogen bound up in fossil fuels are the precipitating factors in acidification and environmental damage. How does it all come about?

Most of the sulfur leaves smokestacks in gaseous form as sulfur dioxide (SO_2). Sooner or later it is absorbed at the surface of water and land and by vegetation. This process is referred to as dry deposition because the deposition occurs in gaseous form or as small particles. Wet deposition is the result of an additional chemical change. Some of the sulfur dioxide is oxidized by atmospheric oxygen to sulfuric acid (H_2SO_4). This substance cannot exist in gaseous form; it occurs either on small particles or in solution in cloud and rain droplets. In due course the acid comes down along with precipitation—it literally rains acid.

Nitrogen is emitted as gaseous oxides (NO_2) from smokestacks and automobile exhaust pipes. Like sulfur dioxide, these oxides can be dry deposited. They may also become converted into nitric acid (HNO_3) and be wet deposited.

When sulfuric acid is dissolved in water, it appears largely in the form of sulfate ions (SO_4^{2-}) and hydrogen ions (H^+). Dissolved nitric acid consists of nitrate ions (NO_3^-) and hydrogen ions. In the last analysis, acidification is a matter of how many hydrogen ions get into circulation. (A hydrogen ion is a hydrogen atom that has lost its only election and become positively charged—a cation. In contrast, negatively charged nitrate and sulfate ions are called anions.) The concentration of hydrogen ions in a solution is a measure of its acidity. This acidity is stated as a pH value.

Acidified soil and water systems have undergone processes in which the hydrogen ion concentration in the soil water (the moisture in the soil) and surface water (lakes and waterways) or in groundwater has progressively increased. This hydrogen ion excess touches off chemical and biological processes that affect ions of other substances. Metals that are important plant nutrients—like potassium (K^+), magnesium (Mg^{2+}), and calcium (Ca^{2+})—are leached out of the ground, or "kicked out" by the hydrogen ions, and are thus lost to trees and field plants. Heavy metals such as cadmium and mercury and the metal aluminum begin to move, accumulating with time in excessively large and injurious quantities in water, soil, and living organisms (among them, human beings).

—Adapted from the Swedish Ministry of Agriculture, Acidification: A Boundless Threat to Our Environment *(Solna: National Swedish Environment Protection Board, 1983).*

Environment, Vol. 29, No. 9: 35.

WRITING EXERCISES: Answer one of the following.

Introductions should provide a general orientation to your topic and give it a specific focus. For example, you might begin by pointing out that environmental issues have received a great deal of publicity in recent years and that there is a growing perception that a global response is needed to counter global warming and other phenomena. You could then introduce your particular topic: "One of the most widely discussed of these crises is ___________." Your reader is led quickly and smoothly into a consideration of your theme.

1. Attitudes towards the environment vary considerably, especially when put into the context of choosing between the value of environmental conservation and the value of business profits, land rights, and so on. Discuss your view of such matters, making sure that you narrow your discussion immediately to give it a clear focus.
2. Describe an environmental controversy in your own region of the country, or one with which you are familiar. Describe the situation as objectively as possible, including the process that leads to environmental damage, and describe and discuss the competing views of this situation. Conclude with any appropriate observations on the controversy, on its resolution, on the conduct of the disputants, or on any important implications of the dispute.
3. Describe the principal causes of the environmental crisis in the Amazon—and the processes involved—as described in Maxwell's essay. When you quote or paraphrase Maxwell, or others cited in his essay, make sure that you identify the source and quote accurately.

(Wikborg/Berlingske Tidende/Copenhagen)

SECTION TWO

PRIOR KNOWLEDGE: Damaging the Earth.

Many people lament the environmental degradation that has been so well publicized over the past several decades. Such criticisms, as noted in Section One, have a history going back at least as far as the beginning of the Industrial Revolution. Resistance continues, however, in some areas to the idea that governments, representing the public interest, have a duty to protect the natural world and its species. The reason for this resistance is usually economic or commercial in nature. It raises fundamental questions, which can be asked in different ways, as in the following example:

Ecology has become a popular field in recent decades. The word uses a Greek root—*oikos*—meaning "house," which is often used to suggest a kind of domestic context:

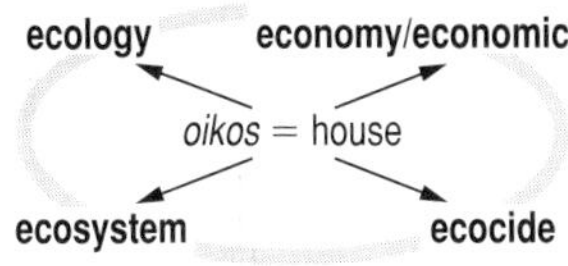

a. Does the government have a duty to protect the public interest by controlling or banning ecologically unsound development of private property?

b. Do private property owners have the right to destroy habitat and threaten the survival of species even when such actions are against the public interest?

c. More crudely, some would ask what right the government has to tell people what they can and cannot do with their own property.

Similarly, the question arises of jurisdiction over environmental issues. Can individual states or nations be left to decide for themselves what kind of regulations are needed, or does this require a regional or even global response? The world's governments have in recent years accepted that problems such as global warming and ozone depletion require a worldwide collaborative effort.

Sandra Postel's essay, which follows, provides an assessment of what needs to be done if the Earth is to avoid irreparable harm. Her assumptions are pessimistic; she sees the Earth facing catastrophe. Against this background she asks what can be done. Her solutions are challenging, even for fellow environmentalists, involving "a fundamental restructuring of many elements of society." Most dramatically, she argues that our whole notion of economic growth is the basic problem, and that "it calls for a rethinking of our basic values and vision of progress." The challenges entailed are described in the essay, in which she sees our current patterns of behavior as an addiction, which she compares to the addiction of an alcoholic.

THINK ON PAPER
Before you read Postel's essay, how would you answer the questions opposite? One key, which may usefully be discussed in class, is the meaning of the phrase "the public interest."

Viewed in such comprehensive terms, the global problems Postel describes must be met on many levels simultaneously. She talks about reducing world population growth, being much more generous in how we in the North help countries in the South, ending our addiction to massive consumption, and being much more creative and determined, in ways great and small, in developing more sustainable and less wasteful ways of living and working.

The relationship between people and Nature is different in different cultures and changes over time. Everyone is familiar with the dramatic contrast, for example, between the attitudes of Native Americans and European settlers in the 19th century toward land ownership. In the former Soviet Union, private ownership of land was not allowed. Western countries have increasingly embraced the idea that land development is subject to oversight and supervision on both ecological and aesthetic grounds.

Since Postel's essay was written, we have learned more about environmental devastation in the former USSR and Eastern Europe. Efforts are now underway to stop and reverse many of these situations. On the other hand, we may also observe the dramatic economic development of China and the aspirations of people there to join the consumer society. Half a billion new cars and the roads to drive them on may seem like heaven to those who manufacture and sell automobiles, asphalt, and concrete, but it sounds like the world's next nightmare to environmentalists, who see massive loss of critical arable land, increased consumption of scarce commodities, and disastrous pollution.

Thinking about environmental problems and their solutions has become the trademark of the Worldwatch Institution, in Washington, DC, for whom Sandra Postel writes. Worldwatch publishes an influential annual report called *State of the World,* which is a great source of information on all sorts of environmental issues. The president of Worldwatch is Lester Brown, who discusses the problems raised by the economic development of China in his article, "Nature's Limits," in the 1995 *State of the World.*

ANNOTATED READING: Sandra Postel. "Denial in the Decisive Decade." *State of the World 1992—A Worldwatch Institute Report on Progress Toward a Sustainable Society.* New York: Norton, 1992: 3–8.

The subtitle of the Worldwatch report is the same every year and alludes to the goal of **"sustainable development."** This is a key phrase among ecologists, environmentalists, and some experts in international development and infers that our past and present behavior is not sustainable. That is to say, with an ever-increasing world population to support, and if current trends continue, the Earth will eventually (perhaps soon) be unable to meet the demand for food, land, water, and other necessities. Postel's essay clearly reflects this view.

Denial in the Decisive Decade

Before August 1991, few people imagined that change so monumental could happen virtually overnight. In a remarkable series of events, the Soviet brand of communism crumbled irreparably, relegating the cold war to history. As striking and swift as these changes were, the remainder of this decade must give rise to transformations even more profound and pervasive if we are to hold on to realistic hopes for a better world. At issue is humanity's badly damaged relationship with its earthly home, and the urgency of repairing it before more lasting and tragic harm is done.

For better or worse, the nineties will be a decisive decade for the planet and its inhabitants. A glimpse at the environmental trends under way:

The protective ozone shield in heavily populated latitudes of the northern hemisphere is thinning twice as fast as scientists thought just a few years ago.

A minimum of 140 plant and animal species are condemned to extinction each day.

Atmospheric levels of heat-trapping carbon dioxide are now 26 percent higher than the preindustrial concentration, and continue to climb.

The earth's surface was warmer in 1990 than in any year since recordkeeping began in the mid-nineteenth century; six of the seven warmest years on record have occurred since 1980.

Forests are vanishing at a rate of some 17 million hectares per year, an area about half the size of Finland.

The numbers on extinctions are controversial. Critics argue that because we don't know how many species exist on Earth—or in the rainforests, for example—it isn't really possible to state with certainty how many become extinct when the habitat is destroyed. However, Postel and others believe that we are creating a **mass extinction** comparable, perhaps, to that of 64 million years ago, the most famous victims of which were the dinosaurs. Recent research has confirmed that the rain forests are uniquely rich in species diversity.

A **hectare** is a "metric acre":

1 **acre** = 100 sq. meters

100 acre = 1 **hectare** (= 2.471 acres)

Metric measurements are almost always used in international and scientific publications. The United States is the only significant non-metric country.

World population is growing by 92 million people annually, roughly equal to adding another Mexico *each year; of this total,* 88 *million are being added in the developing world.*

Eliminating these threats to our future requires a fundamental restructuring of many elements of society—a shift from fossil fuels to efficient, solar-based energy systems, new transportation networks and city designs that lessen automobile use, redistribution of land and wealth, equality between the sexes in all cultures, and a rapid transition to smaller families. It demands reduced consumption of resources by the rich to make room for higher living standards for the poor. And with current notions of economic growth at the root of so much of the earth's ecological deterioration, it calls for a rethinking of our basic values and vision of progress.

The key to Postel's essay lies here, in her assertion that what is needed is nothing less than **"a rethinking of our basic values and vision of progress."**

Many essays have a **thesis,** such as Postel's above, which suggests the main idea and, sometimes, the basic structure of the essay. This can help in note taking. As you read on, take note of all the ways in which Postel suggests that we should rethink our values and definitions.

Faced with this degree of change, we are tempted to deny the severity of environmental threats, and to assume we can get by with minor adjustments to business-as-usual. We elect politicians who validate our belief that the workings of the world are basically in order. And we tune out words like those spoken by José Lutzenberger, Brazil's Secretary of State for Environment, at a ceremony in Washington, D.C.: "It is impossible to give the whole planet the kind of lifestyle you have here, that the Germans have, that the Dutch have . . . and we must face this reality."

THINK ON PAPER
Making inferences from Postel's discussion so far, why does she apparently endorse Lutzenberger's view that the world's capacity to support a Western-style standard of living is limited?

Psychology as much as science will thus determine the planet's fate, because action depends on overcoming denial, among the most paralyzing of human responses. While it affects most of us to varying degrees, denial often runs particularly deep among those with heavy stakes in the status quo, including the political and business leaders with power to shape the global agenda.

THINK ON PAPER
An **analogy** often involves a comparison between an unfamiliar concept and a familiar one. What, exactly, is Postel's "denial" analogy? This is important—note the essay's title.

This kind of denial can be as dangerous to society and the natural environment as an alcoholic's denial is to his or her own health and family. Because they fail to see their addiction as the principal threat to their well-being, alcoholics often end up destroying their lives. Rather than face the truth, denial's victims choose slow suicide. In a similar way, by pursuing life-styles and economic goals that ravage the environment, we sacrifice long-term health and well-being for immediate gratification—a trade-off that cannot yield a happy ending.

There is a practice in the treatment of alcoholism called intervention, in which family members and friends, aided by a counselor, attempt to shake the alcoholic out of denial. In a supportive but candid manner, they help the person grasp the gravity of the disease, the harm it is causing at home and at work, and the need for fundamental change if life for them all is to improve. A successful intervention results in the alcoholic finally acknowledging the problem, and deciding to embark upon the challenging path back to health.

A similar kind of "intervention" is needed to arrest the global disease of environmental degradation, and a uniquely suitable forum is already planned. For the first time in 20 years, people around the world—including heads of state, scientists, and activists—will gather in June 1992 to focus on environment and development. This U.N. Conference in Rio de Janeiro offers a historic opportunity to shake up our senses, to admit—individually as earth citizens, and collectively as a community of nations—that dramatic course corrections are required.

If you were to research a related topic, this reference to the **Rio conference** would be valuable. Newspapers and journals of June 1992 and following weeks would offer a lot of discussion. Global warming—and what to do about it—was one of the major topics at this conference.

Building an environmentally secure world—one in which human needs and wants are met without destroying natural systems—requires a wholly new economic order, one grounded in the recognition that high levels of consumption, population growth, and poverty are driving the earth's environmental decline. Today, 85 percent of the world's income goes to 23 percent of its people—the affluent consumers. By contrast, more than 1 billion people, the absolute poor, survive on less than $1 a day.

In Unit Five, reference was made to the **distribution of income** within individual countries; here, Postel notes the hugely unequal distribution of income (and, concomitantly, consumption and poverty) on a worldwide basis.

The rundown of environmental threats is thus matched by an equally sobering list of unmet human needs:

One in three children is malnourished.

Some 1.2 billion people lack water safe to drink.

Nearly 3 million children die annually from diseases that could be averted by immunizations.

One million women die each year from preventable reproductive health problems.

About 1 billion adults cannot read or write.

More than 100 million children of primary school age are not in school.

Moreover, the developing world is dealing with these problems under greatly constrained conditions. Because of their staggering debt burdens, poor countries paid nearly as much to rich ones over the last decade as they received in new funds—including public and private loans, grants, and direct foreign investment. Besides sapping them of capital, large debt payments force developing countries to plunder forests, fisheries, and other natural resources to increase export earnings. Meanwhile, the international push for free trade may create competitive pressures for nations to adopt minimal environmental standards so as to attract investors.

Put simply, the global economy is rigged against both poverty alleviation and environmental protection. Treating the earth's ecological ills as separate from issues of debt, trade, inequality, and consumption is like trying to treat heart disease without addressing a patient's obesity and high-cholesterol diet: there is no chance of lasting success.

Thus far, global environmental politics has been characterized more by foot-dragging and denial of problems than by cooperation. Few rich countries have acknowledged that they have caused the preponderance of environmental damage, and therefore have the responsibility to underwrite most of the transition to global sustainability. The United States has stonewalled even modest efforts, such as setting targets to reduce carbon emissions as part of ongoing negotiations to protect the global climate. Developing countries, on the other hand, harbor suspicions that multilateral environmental deliberations are disguised attempts to keep them economically disadvantaged. A recipe for stalemate could not be more foolproof.

Applying old politics to new realities is a losing proposition for all. Just as a new set of relationships is taking shape between East and West, one that dismantles mutual threats and creates a climate of economic cooperation, so is there need for a new partnership between wealthier countries (the "North") and the developing world (the "South")—one that embraces the common goals of restoring the planet's health and promoting sustainable progress.

Postel calls for a "new partnership" between the North and the South with two broad goals: "restoring the planet's health and promoting sustainable progress." This would seem to necessitate a move away from nationalistic concerns and rivalries and toward a more global sensibility. Proponents would say, however, that these goals are not merely idealistic and utopian; the well-being of the planet is in the best interest of every nation, including the wealthy ones who would apparently have to share more with the rest of the world.

Few rich countries have acknowledged that they have caused the preponderance of environmental damage.

The ending of the cold war offers an auspicious opportunity to set new priorities and to reallocate resources. Bloated military budgets represent an enormous source of additional funds for investments in energy efficiency, forest protection, infant and maternal health, education, family planning, safe drinking water, and other development work. At roughly $980 billion in 1990, or $185 for every person on the planet, global military spending is way out of line with the diminishing magnitude of military threats. Efforts to ward off far more pervasive environmental and social hazards, meanwhile, are grossly underfunded. Worldwide spending on family planning, for instance, totals about $4.5 billion annually.

Estimates by the United Nations Development Programme (UNDP) suggest that additional investments equal to just over 2 percent of global military expenditures, or about $20 billion per year, would allow everyone in the world to receive primary education and health care, family planning services, safe drinking water, and adequate nutrition. Far larger shifts will be needed to deal with major environmental threats. Cleaning up nuclear weapons sites in the United States alone, for example, may cost upwards of $300 billion.

Military expenditures anywhere represent an unfortunate drain on productive resources, but they are strikingly wasteful in developing countries racked by poverty. Many Third World governments spend twice as much on the military as on health or education, and a few—including Angola, Iran, and Pakistan—expend twice as much as on both combined. While in the industrial world there are 3.3 soldiers for every doctor, in the developing world soldiers outnumber doctors by 8.4 to 1.

The political complexities are apparent here. Many countries—including the United States, Russia, France, and Britain—have big arms industries and aid money is often used to sweeten the deal in an attempt to win lucrative contracts. Some donor countries now tie at least some of their aid to projects that have a clear social and economic benefit to the people as a whole.

A successful global partnership would include sizable transfers of capital and technology from North to South on preferential terms.

To encourage shifts in public expenditures, Mahbub ul Haq, former Finance and Planning Minister of Pakistan and now an advisor to UNDP, advocates tying bilateral aid to reductions in military spending by recipient governments: "Unless external donors are willing to put a squeeze on powerful vested interests within the system, the squeeze will inevitably fall on the weakest and the most vulnerable groups in society. External assistance should be regarded as an alliance not with governments—which often change—but with people." Although developing countries often decry the imposition of conditions on bilateral aid, focusing on the people the funds are supposed to benefit puts the concept of development assistance in the proper perspective.

Efforts to curb consumption of energy and other resources would save money in most cases, yet some of the worst offenders are unwilling to commit to even a cost-effective efficiency path. The United States would have spent $160 billion more on energy in 1990 had it not improved energy efficiency beyond 1973 levels. But these savings are only a beginning: the California Energy Commission estimates that cost-effective investments could reduce total U.S. electricity demand by 40–75 percent while improving the quality of life through cleaner air and lower energy costs.

Nationwide installation of just one fixture—low-flow showerheads that conserve hot water—would save as much energy as oil drilling in Alaska's Arctic National Wildlife Refuge would be expected to produce, and at far lower economic and environmental cost. By insisting on drilling in the Arctic wilderness and other sensitive areas, the U.S. administration shows the degree to which its decisions are controlled by addiction to a destructive energy path and denial of the long-term

Postel sustains her "denial" analogy throughout the essay, as here, where she refers to the ongoing debate over oil drilling in the Arctic National Wildlife Refuge.

consequences—a dependency nourished by the power of special interests.

Along with an overhaul of domestic priorities within both industrial and developing societies, a successful global partnership would include sizable transfers of capital and technology from North to South on preferential terms. Ministers from 41 developing nations met in Beijing in June 1991 and called for the establishment of a new "Green Fund" to step up financial flows. The Beijing Declaration makes clear that for the developing world to sign on, a global bargain must include some such mechanism for the industrial countries to repay the ecological debt they incurred during decades of destructive economic practices.

One noteworthy move in this direction is the new Global Environment Facility managed by the World Bank (in collaboration with UNDP and the United Nations Environment Programme) and slated to invest some $1.5 billion over three years. Given the World Bank's poor environmental record, however, and the industrial countries' dominance of Bank lending practices, this pilot financing scheme has many obstacles to overcome if it is to promote both a new North-South partnership and conservation projects that meet local people's needs.

The reference to the World Bank's "poor environmental record" is not explained, but undoubtedly it is in part a reference to the World Bank's financing of projects in Amazonia, especially in Rondonia, as alluded to in Section One of this unit. The Bank has since made substantial efforts to improve its sensitivity to environmental concerns.

Additional financing could come from taxes on carbon emissions, the leading cause of global warming. Such levies would help bring the prices of fossil fuels into line with their true costs, including environmental damages, and thereby curb greenhouse gas emissions. The executive commission of the European Community (EC) has endorsed such a tax, and in mid-October 1991 the environment ministers of all 12 EC countries expressed support for it. Industrial countries could devote a share of the resulting revenues to energy efficiency improvements in poorer nations. An extra tax of $10 per ton of carbon emitted by the leading industrial nations, for instance, would initially generate some $30 billion per year for a global fund.

Rhetorical note: Postel's essay is a call to action. Her **argument** is supported by statistical evidence and is based in part on a central **analogy** (comparison) between the alcoholic's denial that he or she has a problem and the world's denial that we face urgent environmental problems.

Thus far, however, the United States and other key lenders remain opposed to the idea of greatly increasing investment aid to the developing world. Indeed, the foreign aid budgets of only a handful of countries—Denmark, the Netherlands, Norway, and Sweden—currently meet the internationally endorsed level of 0.7 percent of gross national product (GNP). The United States, near the bottom of the donors' list, gives 0.2 percent of its GNP in aid. And, as with many other countries' assistance, much U.S. aid serves strategic political purposes rather than development.

This target for foreign-aid donor countries (0.7% of GNP) is discussed in Unit Five. The U.S. figure declined to 0.1% of GNP in 1996, putting her at the bottom of the donors' list by this measurement. More than a quarter of American aid goes to two countries: Egypt and Israel.

At the heart of reshaping the global economy is the establishment of new goals centered on sustainability. "Economic growth," as measured by the GNP, continues to be our key indicator of "progress," even though it is steadily destroying the natural systems that are its foundation. Likewise, we persist in equating economic growth with "development," even when the poorest of the poor end up worse off. A revamping of economic rules and principles is essential to make them serve rather than subvert the fundamental aim of shaping a better future. National accounting that subtracts for the depletion or destruction of natural resources, decision-making techniques that value future costs and benefits more thoroughly, and investment criteria that stem the loss of natural capital are among the reforms vitally needed.

Here and there, creative approaches are helping to redefine progress. The Grameen Bank of Bangladesh, for instance, has boosted income among the poor by making more than 800,000 loans, averaging $67 each, to women possessing an entrepreneurial spirit but little or no capital. Local communities in the Brazilian Amazon are attempting to manage tropical forests sustainably for rubber, nuts, and other products, and have succeeded in getting the government to set aside 3 million hectares as "extractive reserves" for their use.

Postel makes several references in this essay to **"sustainability,"** and she notes some examples of projects that might offer models for others to follow. The **Grameen Bank** now operates internationally, making loans to people shunned by conventional lending institutions, and her other examples come from the developed as well as the developing world. Her essay, then, finishes on a more encouraging note, but the difficulties are not downplayed.

In the corporate world, Southern California Edison, an investor-owned energy utility with some 10 million ratepayers, plans to invest heavily enough in energy efficiency to reduce its carbon emissions by 19 percent over the next two decades. And among multilateral institutions, the U.N. International Fund for Agricultural Development has an impressive 14-year track record of more than 200 projects focused on helping poor people meet their needs as they perceive them. Working against the odds, initiatives like these advance the cause of global sustainability. But unless the odds are altered so as to favor such actions, they will remain too few in number and too small in scale.

We can choose to downplay the dangers of the trends now unfolding, and muddle through awhile longer. But where will denial get us in the end? As Sara Parkin, spokesperson for the U.K. Green Party, observes: "Our numbness, our silence, our lack of outrage, could mean we end up the only species to have minutely monitored our own extinction. What a measly epitaph that would make: 'they saw it coming but hadn't the wit to stop it happening.'"

Extraordinary change is possible when enough courageous people grasp the need for it and become willing to act. Five years ago, few envisaged that democratization could sweep so rapidly across so much of the world. Now the question is, who will lead an intervention against our collective denial of environmental threats? Who will be the Gorbachevs of the Environmental Revolution?

Building a sustainable world will ask a lot of ourselves and our leaders. But it is within our power, if we choose to take on the challenge. Once denial is stripped away, what other option do we have?

ASPECTS OF WRITING: Using examples to support an argument; anticipating objections.

In her appeal for a radical rethinking of what we mean by "economic development" and "progress," Sandra Postel takes us on a whirlwind tour of the world of international aid and development, and both developed and developing countries. Within three paragraphs, she talks about the bloated military budgets of many poor countries, improved energy efficiency in the United States, and installing low-flow showerheads. She makes reference to several international conferences and organizations, and she uses statistics by the dozen. All this in order to demonstrate the urgency of the environmental threat posed by our ingrained habits of wasteful consumption and environmental irresponsibility, and to indicate that apparently impossible change can be achieved, just like that which brought about the end of the Soviet Union and the establishment of new democracies there and in eastern Europe in the early 1990s.

By her examples, Postel demonstrates the urgency of the problem and the possibility of overcoming it. She opens with the idea that "monumental" changes can occur very suddenly; this is important, because she is proposing changes that many people would dismiss as impossible. Anticipating this at the outset, she notes that the sudden and virtually bloodless collapse of communism in Europe was "impossible," too, but it happened.

The **preemptive strike** is often a good tactic. If you can anticipate what an opponent would say, you can do what Postel does in her essay—rebut the objection at the outset—and then get on with your discussion.

Having made this comparison, Postel provides a litany of environmental and human crises in the world, providing lots of support for the proposition that present trends are unsustainable. Her essay is not simply a catalog of disaster, however; as is typical of Worldwatch writers, she describes the kind of change necessary if this revolution in thinking is to take place, and she gives specific examples of practical measures that countries, businesses, and individuals can take in order to eliminate wasteful levels of consumption.

Postel reinforces her main theme throughout the essay, often with topic sentences at the beginning of paragraphs:

> "Eliminating these threats to our future requires a fundamental restructuring of many elements of society."
>
> "Building an environmentally secure world . . . requires a wholly new economic order."
>
> "Put simply, the global economy is rigged against both poverty alleviation and environmental protection."

> "The ending of the cold war offers an auspicious opportunity to set new priorities and to reallocate resources."

These are just four examples, but each introduces an aspect of the discussion **which is then illustrated through statistical and real-life examples.** The examples drive home the particular point she is making at different moments in her essay.

Examples alone, of course, say little; it is the ability to generalize from and interpret the data that gives an essay its persuasive quality. The doomsday quality of some of Postel's examples is important because she is calling for a revolutionary change in the way we see ourselves, our fellow human beings, and the natural world.

WRITING EXERCISES: Answer one of the following.

In Unit One, Option One, we discussed various **fallacies** that should be avoided in writing; here are some more:

false analogy
A false comparison. For example, people often criticize the government for running a budget deficit and say, "I can't run my affairs that way, why should they?" This is a false analogy (even if you agree with the sentiment), because a government is in a very different position from an individual citizen. For example, a government can raise or lower taxes and can also print money! The premise of the analogy is also wrong: most individuals *do* run a deficit, which they pay back with interest every month, just like the government; in this way, then, perhaps the analogy is not false after all.

1. Explain Postel's analogy between the world's denial of an environmental problem and an alcoholic's denial of a drinking problem. Show how she uses this analogy in her essay.
2. Describe ways in which day-to-day life has changed and is changing in response to the kind of environmental challenges we face. Describe any further changes that you think are feasible and desirable.
3. Postel argues that we must change our thinking to focus on environmental protection and a more equitable distribution of resources (wealth) in the world. Do you agree, and which of these do you think would be easier to achieve?

overgeneralization
A statement based on insufficient or inadequate evidence. For example, if two countries in Africa are suffering from drought and scenes of starvation are shown on television, people might be tempted to draw the conclusion that "Africa is full of starving people." This would be a gross overgeneralization.

oversimplification
A statement that ignores significant evidence or details. For example, a statement that "the world is divided into rich and poor nations" ignores the countries in the middle, many of which are rapidly growing in economic strength. This, then, would be an oversimplification.

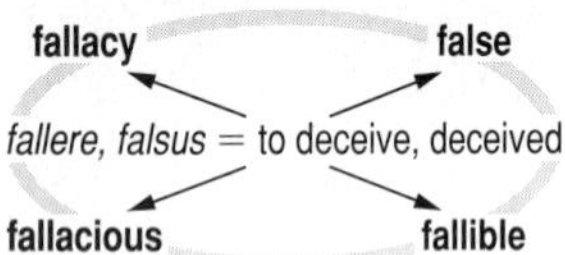

SECTION THREE

PRIOR KNOWLEDGE: Thinking about the environment.

Like many important issues, the environment arouses fierce passions, and people on both sides are often seen in stereotypical terms. The environmentalist becomes the "tree hugger"—someone removed from the realities of life—while the developer becomes the monstrous, rapacious capitalist, willing to destroy the natural world in the pursuit of profit. Like many stereotypes, these are easily recognizable but incomplete portraits.

The essay that follows is written by a business tycoon-turned-politician who, having become an extremely wealthy man, has also become a thoughtful voice in the politics of the European Union and the world at large. He thinks about the state of the world in ways both philosophical and practical. He alludes to the latest technologies and sees promise in their development and application, but he also sees the fundamental issue as being philosophical, with religious underpinnings related to the way we as humans see ourselves vis-à-vis the Earth itself. Like Sandra Postel, he sees the problem and the solution as being in large part attitudinal in nature.

The way people think about things is obviously important. Attitudes toward politicians determine how we vote; attitudes toward education and values help determine how we raise our children; attitudes toward the environment and business help shape how we behave as consumers and citizens. But where do our attitudes come from? The ideas that typify different periods of history are often the product of individual thinkers—philosophers, economists, theologians—who offer a new vision, a new way of seeing things. Some of these people are readily identifiable as being among the groundbreakers in creating an awareness of the dangers posed to the environment by modern industrial and agricultural practices, overpopulation, and other factors. Rachel Carson, for example, overcame fierce opposition and criticism from the chemical industry before seeing her book, *Silent Spring,*

James Goldsmith is not the only politician with a well-documented interest in the environment. Al Gore, Vice President in the Clinton Administration, has also written extensively on the subject. In a 1989 article, then-Senator Gore writes:

> Our complacency stems in part from a standard of living dependent on rapid consumption of the earth's resources. Our generation has inherited the idea that we have the right to appropriate for ourselves the earth's accumulated treasures as quickly as we can consume them. We reach back through millions of years for the deposits that fuel our industrial civilization.
>
> Just as a drug addict needs increasing doses to produce the same effect, our global appetite for the earth's abundance grows each year. We transform the resources of the past into the pollution of the future, telescoping time for self-indulgence in the present.

New York Times, March 19, 1989

Rachel Carson (1907–1964) is most widely associated with the documentation of the disastrous environmental impact of DDT (dichlorodiphenyltrichloroethane), an insecticide that, although highly effective against mosquitoes and other insects, and very widely used for both agricultural and domestic purposes, was found by her to be highly toxic to humans, birds, and other animals. DDT has been banned in the United States and many other countries, but it is still used in some countries for anti-malarial mosquito control and other functions. The title of Carson's most famous book, *Silent Spring,* evoked the grim possibility of a spring without birdsong.

change the way we think about the use of pesticides and other chemical agents.

It's not an exaggeration to say that Carson and others like her have effected a change in Western culture over the last 50 years; we think and behave differently from our predecessors. Sandra Postel's essay in Section Two suggests, however, that we have a long way to go, and Sir James Goldsmith, in the following article, seems to agree, although his tone is more philosophical. To what extent do we see ourselves as stewards, rather than exploiters, of the Earth? Goldsmith wants to influence the debate, and, as a well-known public figure, he is in a good position to do so.

Goldsmith brings to his essay a wealth of reference and allusion—to technology, religion, Marxist-Leninism, the United States, culture, the Greens, and the environment—and his essay (originally a speech) is a good example of how such a multiplicity of detail can enrich a discussion on a single theme. Environmental policy touches everyone, from the business executive to the householder separating his or her trash for recycling, but the public debate on whether we are willing to fundamentally change our attitudes—and even our way of life—in the interest of the environmental well-being of our planet has barely begun. Goldsmith, Postel, and others are helping to get that debate started.

ANNOTATED READING: James Goldsmith. "The Environment—Three Options." *Vital Speeches of the Day* 15 Jan. 1990: 221–224.

The Environment

Three Options

As the occasion is the bicentenary of the death of Adam Smith, I have an excuse to meander through thoughts which, rightly or wrongly, I consider to be of greater significance. My excuse is that *The Wealth of Nations* represented only one section of Adam Smith's works. It was part of a comprehensive system of moral or social philosophy. So, tonight, I will attempt to situate man's economic skills within the broader picture, as I see it.

Goldsmith is speaking at a meeting on the 200th anniversary of the death of **Adam Smith,** someone of whom it can certainly be said that he helped change the way people think. Smith (1723–1790) was a Scottish political economist and philosopher and author of *The Wealth of Nations,* which helped define and describe the modern capitalist economies.

When Adam Smith died, world population was under 900 million. Today, it has swollen to 5 billion. This vast crowd using technology principally invented since the 19th century industrial revolution has severely damaged our planet.

Now, our task is to reverse that damage whilst, at the same time, allowing the development of a diversity of stable societies in which free men and women can live according to their own cultures and traditions and in harmony with their environment.

Rhetorical note: In a model introduction, Goldsmith sets out the context of his speech. He promises not to deliver the usual litany of environmental disasters. Instead, he describes three types of response to the environmental problems we face: an impossible return to a preindustrial society; a nightmare in which Nature takes her revenge on we humans; and a more optimistic, rational future in which the people of the world "move forward with greater wisdom." This third approach is the focus of the speech, and he hopes to **persuade** people to think about the environment in this way.

It is not my purpose this evening to catalogue yet again the environmental dangers. Suffice it to say that we have reached the point where the quality of the most fundamental elements is threatened: air, water, food, soil, forests, oceans and climate.

Faced with this awesome challenge, solutions are proposed which tend to fall into three broad categories.

The first is based on the idea that the principal cause of our problems is industrialisation. So it is suggested we should retreat from industry and return to traditional and preindustrial societies. This proposal is intellectually incomplete. Preindustrial systems are not capable of supporting a world population of 5 billion and growing fast. A vast and poverty stricken population does not have the luxury to engage in the strategic thought necessary to protect the long term. For them, the long term is survival tomorrow.

By James Goldsmith, *Publisher and International Financier. Delivered at the Queen Elizabeth II Conference Center, London, England, October 19, 1989*

Jean-Jacques Rousseau (1712–1778) was a French writer and philosopher best known for *The Social Contract* (1762) in which he described an ideal based on democratic equality (égalité). He admired Nature, distrusted Reason, and influenced the Romantics as well as French and other revolutionaries. He is widely associated with the phrase "the noble savage."

Like the utopian egalitarian dreams of Jean-Jacques Rousseau, this avenue could lead to a new totalitarian quasi religion [that] could inflict medication as horrible as the disease it is supposed to cure.

The second school of thought is more fatalistic. Roughly speaking, it believes that human population growth is a malignant tumescence and that humans cannot or will not find an answer. So it is nature which must react as she has so often in the past. The question that follows is whether nature's healing powers have been overwhelmed by man's assault or whether her immunity has remained intact. If so, she will reestablish an equilibrium through terrible plagues and other natural disasters. Humanity, if it survives, will have been reduced to an acceptable position.

The third scenario is positive. It is based on the premise that it is difficult to turn back the clock and that man is able, under the right circumstances, to move forward with greater wisdom and to act before it is too late.

Those who agree point to the new industrial revolution which is just beginning. Some call it the Quantum revolution. Undoubtedly, it is the most powerful technological change experienced by man and will have a fundamental effect on our future. Either for good or for evil. Like all powerful tools, its effects will depend on the wisdom of those who use it.

Whereas the 19th century industrial revolution was based on natural resources and cheap labour, the new industrial revolution is based on knowledge. Its origins are chronicled in George Gilder's recent book "Microcosm" and I will draw liberally from his work and words when describing it.

Some of the symptoms of this revolution can be found in cybernetics, superconductivity, genetic engineering, communications, robotics and the as yet unproven, cold fusion.

Goldsmith sees new technologies—microchips, fiber optics, superconductivity—dramatically reducing the need for raw materials. This would reduce the need for mining, smelting, and other activities often deleterious to the environment.

However, it is fair to ask whether such a vision could be realized worldwide. Most countries don't possess, and can't afford, advanced technologies. Would the rich countries be prepared to transfer their technology to poorer countries? If not, how would countries such as China (heavily dependent on coal) achieve this "clean" industrial development? The question of technology transfer is widely discussed in development circles; see, for example, Sandra Postel in Section Two of this unit.

Environmentally, it will have a rapid impact. It radically changes the role of raw materials. The use of coal, steel, oil, and other materials will be sharply reduced as a share of value added in the economy. This will transform the need for industry to exploit the environment for raw materials.

Consider the micro chip—a computer inscribed on a tiny piece of processed material. It combines millions of components operating in billionths of seconds on a space the size of a wing of a fly. By overcoming the constraints of material resources, the microchip will make obsolete large accumulations of physical equipment. Less than 2 percent of the cost of a silicon chip is for raw materials.

Look at other examples. A few pounds of optical glass fibre made of the same elements as sand will soon carry as much information as a ton of copper. Superconductive elements could increase by compounding factors of between 5 and 100 the efficiency of every wire, receiver transmitter, electric motor, solar collector, power generator and magnetic battery.

By allowing sharp reductions in the weight of a wide array of mechanical systems, this technology could further accelerate the decline in the use of raw materials.

New knowledge could replace dangerous and dirty sources of energy. The use of coal and oil would be radically altered. The existing nuclear energy industry which is centralised, uneconomic and unsafe would be recognised as obsolete.

The effects of this revolution will not be confined to the transformation of the use of raw materials and therefore to the exploitation of the environment. It can do more. In this new age, the inventive inputs of man can launch a spiral of economic growth and productivity at steadily declining cost in each material domain: energy, natural resources and pollution.

As capital intensive accumulations of equipment become less necessary to industry, it will encourage decentralisation at every level of society and decentralisation will grow as the powers of bureaucracies and of the State are weakened. Centralised states can dig iron, pump oil, mobilise manpower, manipulate currencies, tax and spend. As George Gilder so eloquently says, and I quote, "the State can expropriate the means of production. But when it does it will find mostly sand. The entrepreneurs will run for the daylight of liberty and can take their minds elsewhere. Today the ascendant nations and corporations are masters not of land and material resources but of ideas and technologies. Wealth comes not to the rulers of slave labour but to the liberators of creativity, not to the conquerors of land but to the emancipators of mind."

George Gilder is right. The Quantum revolution offers the opportunity to create the conditions which could help us to heal the wounds that man has inflicted on the planet. But it also supplies man with the power to destroy more thoroughly and perhaps terminally.

In my opening remarks, I suggested that our objective should be to allow the development of a diversity of stable societies in which free men and women can live according to their own cultures and traditions. And do so in harmony with their environment.

Thus the question is how to use the immense new powers of the Quantum revolution to help us to attain that objective.

Cultural diversity allows each society to develop its own evolving model from which others can learn. Mistakes can be limited to one culture at a time and do not overwhelm everything, as would be the case with a global monoculture. The bedrock of diversity is mutual respect. And that means accepting that the beliefs of others, which may seem bizarre, might contain some wisdoms we are unable to perceive.

Goldsmith moves here from the technological to the cultural side of development. He begins with the humane but obvious assumption that technology is only valuable if it serves humanity rather than destroys it. Less predictably, he goes on to the interesting notion that each country should be free to use the new technologies in ways that enrich, rather than destroy, its own culture and sense of identity.

From here, Goldsmith leads us to consider two important terms, both of which represent trends that he considers profoundly undesirable: **"global monoculture"** and **"cultural imperialism."** He argues that when we try to make other cultures more like ourselves, we inevitably destroy their cultural integrity. This is relevant to the environmental theme of the essay, because a demoralized society loses its sense of responsibility for the Earth.

It has always been my conviction that cultural imperialism is more deeply harmful than territorial expansion. The Conquistadores plundered, raped and returned to their homelands. They caused pain and injury. But the long term consequences of their actions cannot be compared to the damage caused by their successors—the proselytizers. Often, with the best of intentions, they robbed whole nations of their language, religion and identity. It should not be forgotten that one man's missionary is the other man's spy. When the Communists sent their proselytizers to the West to convert us to Communism, we called them spies or agents of influence. When we sent ours to Africa to convert Africans to our religions, we called them educators or missionaries.

Seldom do we recognise that when we intervene and change the cultures of others, we destabilise them because we tear them away from their traditions. Deracinated they tend to drift to urban slums and sink into a slum culture. Such people lose their capacity to live in harmony with the environment. Respect for the long term is characteristic of proud and stable communities, confident in their traditions and seeking continuity so as to pass on to their successors a form of life at least as good as the one they themselves inherited. People who lack such stability replace respect for the long term by immediate self gratification. They are unable to be concerned by the long term degradation of their environment.

Similar, or even identical, words can have different derivations:

radix (Latin) = root → **deracinate,** to pull up by the roots

razza (Old Italian) = race, generation → **race, racial**

ras (Old Norse) = race → **race** [as in 100-meter dash]

Goldsmith's use of *-ise* in "destabilised," "proselytise," etc., reflects British spelling. American spelling usually requires *-ize.*

Too often, the West has contributed to this process. Much of the institutional aid that we have distributed has destabilised the cultures of others. Often, it masks a desire to proselytise by fiscal means.

Let us take the U.S.A. as an example. Americans are a warm and generous people. They have demonstrated their hospitality to immigrants and refugees from around the world. Their Founding Fathers created a constitution based on individual freedom—freedom of worship, speech and enterprise. When necessary Americans fought for these principles. Today the United States is more than a nation, it is a free world in which peoples of different religion and race can live side by side and work to improve the positions of their families and communities. It is America's creative vigour which is mainly responsible for the great new opportunities offered by the Quantum revolution.

But it would be a great mistake to suggest that the U.S. has developed a culture so superior that it should be forcefully exported to the world. America has a dark side. Many of its major cities are suffering from social breakdown. Drugs, crime, suicide and social disorder of the worst kind are the obvious symptoms. America's enormous appetite for drugs has created a market so valuable that it has polluted its neighbours, converting them into drug suppliers dominated by drug barons. America's underclass is not just poor, it is alienated.

That such an underclass can exist in the world's richest nation demonstrates, once again, that money cannot heal fundamental social disease. Many communities with much smaller monetary income than that of the American underclass display no symptoms of such disease and that is because they have maintained their stability according to their own traditions. Pride, self respect, self reliance, patriotism, stability, concern for the long term, have to grow from healthy soil. They cannot be bought with subsidies and charity.

It would be blind arrogance for America to wish to impose her culture on others. The world witnessed an example when in 1984, the U.S. government ceased to give certain funds to certain nations which promoted family planning acceptable within their own cultures. Thus overpopulated nations were given the choice of accepting the ideas of a vocal U.S. religious minority or abandoning part of the aid accorded to them.

The U.S. must not come to believe that because she is materially competent, she is spiritually superior. She should forcefully intervene internationally only when her national security is in danger. She should build on her noble strengths, strive to heal her great wounds and be a model from which others can learn as free and independent peoples.

Europe's foreign aid programme should also be reassessed to establish whether we are helping or meddling; whether we are doing good or merely gratifying our own conscience; whether we are encouraging industrialisation in a way which will lead to further social deracination and urban slums. In other words, whether we are intervening to push others to copy us, as though we hold the key to the best and only way of life.

As we look at Africa today, racked by local wars, stricken by disease, agglomerating in shanty towns, suffering increasing poverty, can we honestly believe that our proselytism has been a success or that our financial assistance has been enriching?

Good intentions are not a valid excuse to do harm—they are only a mitigating factor.

Let me suggest an example of aid which could be useful without damaging others. It is now generally accepted that the survival of the tropical rain forests is of global importance. Such forests are located principally in the third world and the largest is, of course, the Amazonian forest. It forms part of the territories of Brazil, Colombia, Venezuela, Bolivia, Peru, Ecuador, Surinam, Guyana and French [Guiana]. These I will describe as the "host nations."

Many proposals have been put forward to halt the destruction of the forests. But to be satisfactory, a proposal needs to respect two principal conditions:

It is natural for Goldsmith to turn his attention to the United States, because it is still the most powerful country in the world, and it is the country most often accused today of **"cultural imperialism,"** or of imposing its own values on others. Critics argue that pop culture, crass but cheap television shows and movies, fast-food restaurants and so on are overwhelming smaller cultures and replacing them with something not very desirable. Even rich countries like France frequently argue the need to protect their own cultural institutions and creativity by limiting the amount of American programming on TV, for example.

Goldsmith reminds us that the rest of the world does not generally want to be just like us, and our belief that this is so—that everyone is basically the same, and we are the model—is a **delusion** and is destructive of the rich cultural diversity in the world.

—firstly, it should not be imperial. The developed world should not seek to impose a solution, which in any case would be resisted and become ineffective. It has not been forgotten by others that the developed countries largely sacrificed their own environment in the process of industrialisation. Many in the third world interpret an attempt to stop them from exploiting their natural resources as "pulling up the ladder" and stranding them in an inferior position.

—secondly, we should recognise that the host nations own the forest; that it is a natural and vital resource; that it is needed by all; that, rightly or wrongly, they believe that they are sacrificing economic opportunities by protecting this resource; and that they should be compensated for doing so.

Goldsmith's suggestion here—that the Western nations pay the poorer countries for preserving their rainforests—has been put into practice in some parts of the world. Other experiments include conserving ecosystems through participatory schemes that give responsibility and compensation to villagers who traditionally exploit the resources in these areas. Optimists believe that creative thinking can offer alternatives to massive degradation in the name of development.

If we accept these premises, then we should enter into a fair market contract whereby, in return for not cutting the tropical forests, the host nations are paid a rent by the remainder of the world. This is not unlike the payments made to farmers, in the U.S. and in Europe, for not harvesting certain items.

The rent would be payable annually following a normal monitoring process. Its amount would compensate the host nations for the cost of maintaining the forests and for the perceived loss of income from not exploiting them on an unsustainable basis.

Such a transaction is a normal market contract. The host nations own a natural resource which we all need, just like the oil producing nations own a natural resource which we all need. In both cases, we should pay a fair price for the benefit of the resource.

I will not go further into the financial details, except to say that the international debt issued by the host nations could form part of the currency; and that current international aid programmes should be reprioratised so that they be laserbeamed onto projects of this kind.

THINK ON PAPER
Would you be prepared to help pay—through taxation—for the preservation of forests around the world (and in your own country)?

Let me now turn to a subject more fundamental than man's position relative to other men. And that is man's position within the natural world. The use to which we apply our skills will depend largely on how we see man's role and responsibilities.

To understand where we are and where we might hope to go, we must look to our past.

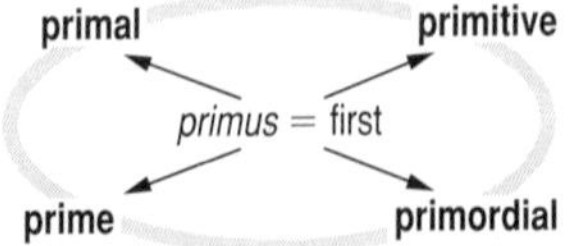

Primal religions, the most fundamental religious forms in the history of mankind, still account for the religious outlook of a significant proportion of the peoples of the world. They interpret man's role in a different way to that of the religions of modern Western man. Primal peoples cannot conceive of man as an individual existing by himself, unrelated to the animate or inanimate forces surrounding him. Whereas, in the Western tradition, the natural world is something to be investigated, explained and ultimately exploited, in the primal religious view the world is not alien to man. For them, the fundamental question is not "how" but "why." Men and women in primal societies must, therefore, approach the natural world with care and indeed with reverence. In the primal world, man's position vis-à-vis nature is not one of exploitation but of relationship.

vis-à-vis (French), in relation to (literally, "face to face")

The monotheistic religions have cast man in a different role. God transcends nature and man is made in the image of God. So man is set apart. The remainder of the world and all other animals therein are subordinated to him. So evolved an anthropocentric universe. There are those who argue that the emergence of a rigid and exclusive monotheism has led to a view of man and of his place in nature which threatens the primal sense of unity and reciprocity with nature. And that this could have contributed to that unbridled exploitation of nature that has created the ethical and ecological problems that confront us today.

The way we view our relationship with the Earth and its creatures is fundamental, and, according to Goldsmith, is cultural in nature. Fortunately, as he says, culture can change. Some of the changes may be more painful than some people are willing to accept, but the price of not changing, ecologists would argue, is likely to be even steeper.

Indeed Buddhists believe that the problem lies in the Western dichotomy of "man and nature." They consider that the radical separation of man from nature follows from the fundamental premises of the Judeo-Christian tradition and that within such a context, nature is there to be subjected to the will and aggressive instincts of man.

The great modern materialistic religion, Marxist-Leninism, rejected spiritual beliefs and placed its trust in science and technology. For them, the only moral criterion governing any action . . . [is] the service of man. Marxism feels free to exploit nature . . . in the service of man. The only brake on such exploitation will be the self interest of human society. So according to this philosophy man, or rather the society of men, is paramount.

It is not surprising that with such a background, Western man should have felt free to exploit nature and to attempt to dominate her. Nor that he felt protected from the consequences of his actions. After all, he had been brought up to believe that nature had been created expressly for this purpose.

If such a state of mind were to persist, then I believe that there would be little hope that man would reverse the damage already inflicted on the planet. Such hubris would inevitably lead to self-destruction, and the increased power provided by the new industrial revolution would merely speed the process.

Fortunately, there are some signs of change. Some concerned Christian theologians are reassessing their religious roots within the Hebraic tradition to assert man's stewardship of nature. As a steward, man has a responsibility for nature. This nonetheless leaves man apart from nature. There is also a Christian school of thought which considers that man is part of nature because, like the animals, he is created out of the dust of the earth (Genesis, 2:7 and 19). When God breathed into man the breath of life, it is said that he also breathed it into birds and animals. Yet man is also held to transcend other living beings in that he, and he alone, is created in the "image of God."

Graham Greene has died since Goldsmith wrote this essay. He was a leading British novelist, including many works set in the Caribbean *(Our Man in Havana, The Comedians)*, Africa *(The Heart of the Matter)*, and elsewhere around the world.

Graham Greene, who was described in an interview published in the Catholic magazine "The Tablet" as "perhaps the most famous Catholic layman alive," also recently talked about change. He stated that he was, I quote, "very uncomfortable with the Church's teaching on contraception. I think that contraception is vital for human life. . . . With over-population in Africa and all around the world I think that contraception and planned birth is a necessity." Greene went on to say, "It was quite clear that the majority of bishops under Paul VI were in favour of contraception, but he ignored it. . . ." "Don't you find," he continued, "that the Roman Curia reminds you a little bit of the Politburo? But even the Politburo is changing." It is difficult to disagree with Graham Greene when one remembers that, if present trends are maintained, world population is forecast to reach 11 billion at the end of the century.

The **Greens** are environmentally concerned political groups and parties. In parts of Europe, they have won a significant share of the votes in elections and have become politically important.

Of course, it is necessary to comment on the role of the environmentalists and the Greens. They have had a most salutary influence. They have drawn attention to an urgent and overwhelming problem. They are often attacked [as] being too extreme, but it is difficult not to be extreme when one can see man's activity infecting the world like some horrible, pervasive and progressive disease. So they should continue to militate and do so actively. But not by forming a political party nor by creating a quasi religion. Their concerns should transcend all political parties and religions. The global environment is not a partisan matter. By treating it as though it were and associating it with a party political programme containing a host of other items, environmentalists risk alienating many who are sympathetic to their concerns but reject their partisanship. The Greens should seek the best way of achieving their objectives and not just be tempted into an egocentric course. They should endorse politicians of whatever party who, in their view, are environmentally aware. They should condemn the others. They should participate in religious debates, each within their own different religious congregations, so as to encourage evolution from an anthropocentric doctrine to one which urges man to act responsibly and in harmony with nature.

Environmentalists come from every walk of life. They are brought together by an understanding of man's abuses. It is said that some among them, those who have formed the Green political parties, feel a kinship to socialism. If that is true, I find it hard to believe that it will be a lasting phenomenon.

Most of the members of the Green parties have grown up in relatively free and developed countries. It is in this context that they have witnessed the polluting side effects of industrialisation. They have reacted against what they experienced at first hand. But now that there is a greater freedom of information, we all know that the most heavily polluted nations of Europe are East Germany, Poland and Czechoslovakia. The most wilfully destructive of traditional communities is Rumania.

Only a few weeks ago, a Polish government economist, citing lack of sewage treatment, use of cheap coal and the death of rivers and lakes, lamented, and I quote, "we have the worst environmental problem in all of Europe."

In 1986, East Germany discharged some 5 billion tons of sulphur dioxide into the air. That is more than twice as much as West Germany, which has a population four times greater.

I do not say this to score a petty political point nor to make a qualitative judgment on individuals who believe in or live in different political and economic systems. My point is about power. Too much power is dangerous. Centralised systems have too much power. Even with the best intentions, they can do too much harm. That is why I am distrustful of centralising political systems, powerful bureaucracies and totalitarianism of whatever colour: red, blue or green.

Greens, more than anybody, understand the ideal of decentralisation. They were among the first to recognise the destructive power of the great international bureaucracies; the ecological damage caused by government sponsored monster projects; the horror of megacities in which the family unit has disaggregated. The Greens understood that the modern, soulless, high rise cities, scattered throughout the world, would become factories for alienating individuals who, pathetically, would try to replace their scattered families by grouping into gangs. Of course, one of the causes of these cities was the fashion created by the celebrated modern architects, like Le Corbusier and Oscar Niemeyer, who believed in and built for collectives and not for families. Collectivist architecture has not been a positive factor in building stable communities.

I feel confident that, in the fullness of time, environmentalists will reject socialism, that is unless socialism itself rejects the fundamental ideas on which it was founded. It is impossible for environmentalists to approve the most materialistic of philosophies, which, more than any other, places man and his artifacts above all else and regards nature as a thing to be exploited by him.

Let me finish with one last comment. No matter how brilliant the technological revolutions, no matter how useful the economic and political initiatives, there can only be hope if man can cast away his anthropocentric delusions and seek to find his place in nature, a place from which he can live in harmony with his universe.

ASPECTS OF WRITING: The writing process.

Brainstorming can be a group or individual activity; it involves simply thinking about a topic and coming up with any ideas at all that occur to you. All these ideas should be written down, even though it's likely that only a few will be used. At this stage you probably don't yet know exactly what the focus of your essay will be.
Organizing ideas can involve many different activities, but one good idea is **clustering.** This involves putting your brainstorming ideas into groups that seem to have a similar focus or character.
Identifying your audience means deciding who the intended reader is. This is easy to understand in the context of a speech; James Goldsmith knew that his audience was likely to be interested in and reasonably informed about economics, current affairs, and environmental issues. He could pitch his speech to an informed, educated audience. If he had been talking to children, his speech would have been different, even if his message were the same. You do the same thing when you write: think about your audience and pitch the language and content accordingly. For example, a discussion of acid rain written for *Scientific American* would probably be much more technical in language and content than one written for *Time* magazine. Of course, your audience is most likely to be your professor, who has read the same things you have for many assignments; your imaginary audience, however, might be educated and interested but not particularly well informed about the topic you are discussing. Concepts and background would, therefore, have to be explained.

Commentary on writing is dispersed throughout this text, because achieving and maintaining clarity, precision, and other attributes of "good writing" requires an ongoing effort; it isn't the product of a single exercise or unit. There are, however, broad guidelines that suggest a systematic approach to writing papers; taken together, these are often referred to as **"the writing process."**

In its basic form, the writing process describes a sequence of activities:

a. **prewriting** (brainstorming, organizing ideas, identifying your audience, developing a thesis or concept, creating an outline.
b. **writing a first draft**
c. **revising and editing the draft**
d. **rereading** (and further editing, as necessary)

Of course, not everyone meticulously follows this sequence, and in practice these activities are not necessarily sequential in the way described. For example, rereading and editing may be ongoing as you write. Some experts advocate not bothering with such things in the first-draft stage, believing that a freer flow of writing helps generate ideas and "gets things down on paper," but you may find that **reading-and-editing-as-you-write** helps you develop a better sense of what you are writing and thereby enhances the coherence and clarity of what you write. This is not to say that your first draft should be perfect—of course not—but that there are different ways to achieve the same ends. To use a cooking analogy, you may prefer to be like a chef who samples the food and sauces as s/he goes and makes adjustments as needed, not just at the end. There is nothing prescriptive here, except that the more you read your writing, the better chance you have of being satisfied with the end product, both in terms of mechanics (spelling, punctuation, word choice, sentence structure), organization, tone, and content.

WRITING EXERCISES: Answer one of the following questions.

The **thesis** provides the main idea in your paper and may also suggest its structure and tone. For more discussion, see Unit One, Section Two. The **concept** may be more general than the thesis, but it is very important. It answers the question, "What are you trying to do in this essay?" *This may or may not be explicitly stated in your paper, but you should know the answer to the question.*

Your **outline** enables you to map out the content and sequence of your paper. Some people resist doing formal outlines, but there are likely to be many occasions when the complexity of the subject you are writing about almost requires this preparatory step. For more on this, see Unit Two, Section Two.

1. James Goldsmith acknowledges the pessimistic view that overpopulation and environmental destruction will doom humanity to a miserable future, but he prefers to be more optimistic. His optimism is premised, however, on certain changes in our behavior and outlook. Describe the ways in which Goldsmith thinks we can save ourselves and other life on Earth.
2. Goldsmith talks about technological change and spiritual or cultural change. Explain and comment on what he says about either one of these **OR** explain and comment on the relationship between these two aspects.
3. Describe your perception of people's attitude toward the environment in the United States (or another country familiar to you) and discuss any changes you would like to see.

Here is an example of clustering, related to a discussion of Goldsmith's essay, perhaps usable for the first option in exercise 2:

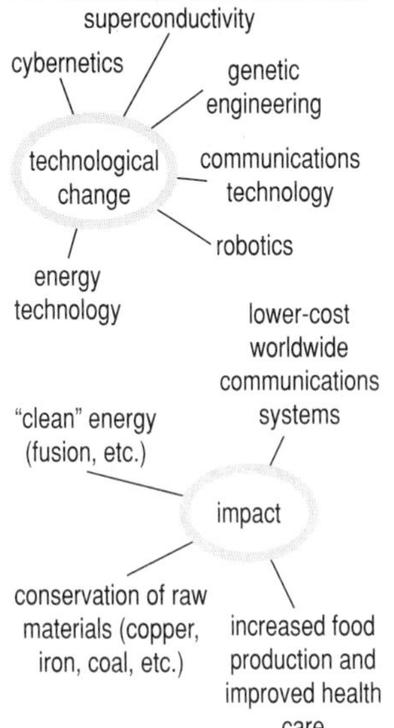

OPTION ONE

PRIOR KNOWLEDGE: A moral dimension.

In the essay that follows, Edward O. Wilson, one of the world's leading entomologists and a well-known contributor to discussion of many important issues, considers the ethics of species diversity. In other words, why should humans care about other species?

James Goldsmith addresses a similar topic in Section Three of this unit, when he considers the need to stop the destruction of the environment and develop a new (or old?) relationship in which we see ourselves as stewards of the Earth, not simply consumers and destroyers. Wilson focuses on the relationship between the human species and all the other species of life on Earth, most of which, he notes, are either unknown or little known to scientists and everyone else.

It is often said that we have a self-interest in preserving different species because different plants or animals may have medical, agricultural, or other value to humans. This is true, but it is a rather self-serving and anthropocentric formula, suggesting, perhaps, that other species would be dispensable if we could see no economic or scientific value in them.

Wilson suggests a more principled reason for valuing species diversity. He talks about "the human spirit" and "stewardship," just as Goldsmith does, and presents a compelling argument for enriching ourselves—our spiritual selves—by developing a reverence for life in all its diversity. This may mean not always putting people first, or it may mean changing what we mean when we talk of putting people first. The short-term interests of people are sometimes damaging in the long term. Perhaps the "bottom line" needs to have an environmental, as well as a financial, dimension to it. We all have an interest in, and a need for, the preservation of the natural world, even if it is mostly in parks and remote places. Why do millions of Americans go to the National Parks every year? Why do millions more, here and around the world, take such pleasure in wildlife films showing far-off places and unfamiliar animal behavior? Why is a walk in the woods, or along the beach or stream, so appealing? The obvious answer seems to be that the human imagination and spirit need these things; without them, or without the possibility of them, we would all be diminished.

Wilson speaks as a scientist who cares about the world, and his essay is philosophical in nature. It demonstrates the artificiality of borders between disciplines and the importance of putting all human activity within a moral context. Increasingly, as population growth and technology are irrevocably changing the Earth, we are being pressed by some thinkers to see ourselves as having a moral obligation to take care of the planet and all that it contains, and to think anew about the purpose of life. Wilson asks, "But what is fulfillment, and for what purpose did human potential evolve?" Such questions help us move beyond our immediate physical and economic needs—important though these are—to more profound territory. Writers like those in this unit—Maxwell, Postel, Goldsmith, and Wilson—seem to be saying that caring for the environment and the world's living things is both a moral imperative and a prerequisite for sustainable economic and social development.

READING: Edward O. Wilson. "Million-Year Histories—Species Diversity as an Ethical Goal." *Wilderness* 48 (165): 12–17 (Summer 1984).

Million-Year Histories

Species Diversity as an Ethical Goal

They are best seen not on foot or from outer space but through the window of an airplane: the newly cleared lands, the expanding web of roads and settlements, the inexplicable plumes of smoke, and the shrinking enclaves of natural habitat. In a glance we are reminded that the once mighty wilderness has shriveled into timber leases and threatened nature reserves. We measure it in hectares and count the species it contains, knowing that each day something vital is slipping another notch down the ratchet, a million-year history is fading from sight.

The loss of wilderness conforms to the original Greek concept of tragedy because it reveals in grave and somber manner the inexorable workings of the human condition. It presents us with a dilemma that the historian Leo Marx has called the machine in the garden. On the one hand the natural world is the refuge of the spirit, remote, static, richer even than human imagination. But on the other hand we cannot exist in this paradise without the machine that tears it apart. We are killing the thing we love, our Eden, progenitrix and sibyl.

Human beings are not natural creatures torn from a sylvan niche and imprisoned within a world of artifacts. The noble savage, a biological impossibility, never existed. The human relation to nature is vastly more subtle and irretrievably ambivalent, for what appears to be the following reason. Over thousands of generations the mind evolved within a ripening culture, creating itself out of symbols and tools, and genetic advantage accrued from planned modifications of the environment. The unique operations of the brain are the result of natural selection operating through the filter of culture. They have suspended us between the two antipodal ideals of nature and machine, forest and city, the natural and the artifactual, relentlessly seeking, in the words of the geographer Yi-Fu Tuan, an equilibrium not of this world.

Wilson alludes in this essay to people and ideas from many different fields, including **Yi-Fu Tuan,** whose essay on the nature of geography appears in Unit Two, Option One, of this text.

The impossible dilemma caused no problem for ancestral humans. For millions of years human beings simply went at nature with everything they had, scrounging food and fighting off predators across a known world of but a few square miles. Life was short, fate terrifying, and reproduction an urgent priority: children, if freely conceived, could just about replace the family members who seemed to be dying all the time. The population flickered around equilibrium, and sometimes whole bands became extinct. Nature was something out there—nameless, unconfined, and limitless, a force to beat against, cajole, and exploit.

If the machine gave no quarter, then it was also too weak to break the wilderness. But no matter: the ambiguity of the opposing ideals was a superb strategy for survival, so long as the people who used it stayed sufficiently ignorant. It enhanced the genetic evolution of the brain and generated more and better culture. The world began to yield, first to the agriculturists and then to technicians, merchants, and circumnavigators. Humanity accelerated toward the machine antipode, heedless of the natural desire of the mind to keep the opposite as well. Now we are near the end. The inner voice murmurs *you went too far* and disturbed the world and gave away too much for your control of nature. Perhaps Hobbes' definition is correct and this will be the hell we earned for realizing truth too late.

But it is not too late: the actors have not yet left the stage of this particular tragedy. The course of the future can be changed with sufficient knowledge and a strong enough commitment shared by enough people. Like many scientists concerned with the problem, I have emphasized two aspects I consider vital to the development of a better conservation ethic: the appreciation of the vastness of the species diversity that is endangered by the loss of wilderness and the lesser natural reserves, and a fuller understanding of the dependence people feel on other forms of life. Let us begin with the first.

Think of scooping up a handful of soil and leaf litter and spreading it out on a white ground cloth, in the manner of the field biologist, for close examination. This unprepossessing lump contains more order and richness of structure, and particularity of history, than the entire surface of all the other planets combined. It is a miniature wilderness that can take almost forever to explore.

Tease apart the adhesive grains with the aid of forceps, and you will expose the tangled rootlets of a flowering plant, curling around the rotting veins of humus, and perhaps some larger object such as the boat-shaped husk of a seed. Almost certainly among them will be a scattering of creatures that measure the world in millimeters and treat this soil sample as traversable: ants, spiders, springtails, armored oribatid mites, enchytraeid worms, millipedes. With the aid of a dissecting microscope now proceed on down the size scale to the roundworms, a world of scavengers and fanged predators feeding on them.

In the hand-held microcosm all of these creatures are still giants in a relative sense. The organisms of greatest diversity and numbers are invisible or nearly so. When the soil-and-litter clump is progressively magnified, first with a compound light microscope and then with scanning electron micrographs, specks of dead leaf expand into mountain ranges and canyons, and soil particles become heaps of boulders. A droplet of moisture trapped between root hairs grows into an underground lake, surrounded by a three-dimensional swamp of moistened humus. The niches are defined by both topography and nuances in chemistry, light, and temperature shifting across fractions of a millimeter. Organisms for which the soil sample is a complete world, now come into view. In certain places are found the fungi: cellular slime molds, the one-celled chitin-producing chytrids, minute gonapodyaceous and oomycete soils specialists, Kickxellales, Eccrinales, Endomycetales, and Zoopagales. Contrary to their popular reputation, the fungi are not formless blobs, but exquisitely structured organisms with elaborate life cycles worthy of their exotic titles.

Still smaller than the parasitic fungi are the bacteria, including colony-forming polyangiaceous species, specialized predators that consume other bacteria. All around them live rich mixtures of rods, cocci, coryneforms, and slime azotobacteria. Together these microorganisms metabolize the entire spectrum of live and dead tissue. At the moment of discovery some are actively growing and fissioning, while others lie dormant in wait for the right combination of nutrient chemicals. Each species is kept at equilibrium by the harshness of the environment. Any one, if allowed to expand without restriction for a few weeks, would multiply exponentially, faster and faster, until it weighed more than the entire earth. But in reality the individual organism simply dissolves and assimilates whatever appropriate fragments of plant and animal that come to rest near it. If the new-found meal is large enough, it may succeed in growing and reproducing briefly before receding back into the more normal state of physiological quiescence.

In other words, biologists have begun a reconnaissance into a land of magical names. In exploring life they have commenced a pioneering adventure with no imaginable end. The abundance of organisms increases downward by level, like layers in a pyramid. The handful of soil and litter is home for hundreds of insects, nematode worms, and other larger creatures, about 1 million fungi, and 10 billion bacteria. Each of the species of these organisms has a distinct life cycle fitted to the portion of the microenvironment in which it thrives and reproduces. The particularity is due to the fact that it is programmed by an exact sequence of nucleotides, the ultimate molecular unit.

The amount of information in the sequence can be measured in bits in the following way. One bit is the information required to determine which of two equally likely alternatives is chosen, such as heads or tails in a coin toss. The English language averages two bits per letter. A single bacterium possesses about 10 million bits of genetic information, a fungus 1 billion, and an insect from 1 to 10 billion bits according to species. If the information in just one insect—say an ant or beetle—were to be translated into a code of English words and printed in letters of standard size, the string would stretch over 1,000 miles. The lump of earth contains information that would fill all fifteen editions of the *Encyclopedia Britannica*.

I invite you now to try to visualize the loss in biological diversity due to the reduction of natural habitats. If so much complexity of information can be held in the cupped hands, think of how much more exists in an entire habitat. Consider the loss, mostly invisible to us today but destined to be painfully obvious to our descendants, that occurs when an entire wilderness area is degraded or destroyed.

It is an issue that turns otherwise cautious scientists into outspoken activists. On a worldwide basis, extinction is accelerating and could reach ruinous proportions during the next twenty years. Not just birds and mammals are vanishing but such smaller forms as mosses, insects, and minnows. A conservative estimate of the current extinction rate is 1,000 species a year, mostly because of the destruction of forests and other key habitats in the tropics. By the 1990s, the figure is expected to rise past 10,000 species a year (one species per hour). During the next thirty years, fully 1 million species could be erased.

Whatever the exact figure—and the primitive state of evolutionary biology permits us only to set broad limits—the current rate is at least the greatest in recent geological history. It is also much higher than the rate of production of new species by ongoing evolutionary processes, so that the net result is a steep decline in global biological diversity. Whole categories of organisms that emerged over the past 10 million years, among them the familiar condors, rhinoceros, manatees, and gorillas, are close to the end. For most of their species, the last individuals to exist in the wild state could well be those living there today. It is a grave error to dismiss the hemorrhaging as a "Darwinian" process, in which species autonomously come and go and humans are just the latest burden on the environment. Human destructiveness is something new under the sun. Perhaps it is matched by the giant meteorites thought to smash into the earth and darken the atmosphere every 100 million years or so (the last one apparently arrived 65 million years ago and contributed to the extinction of the dinosaurs). But even that interval is 10,000 times longer than the entire history of civilization. In our own brief lifetime humanity will suffer an incomparable loss in aesthetic value, practical benefits from biological research, and worldwide biological stability. Deep mines of biological diversity will have been dug out and carelessly discarded in the course of environmental exploitation, without our even knowing fully what they contained.

These calculations lend great importance to the National Wilderness Preservation System in our own country and underscore the need to both enlarge and strengthen it. The 1964 Wilderness Act that created the program is sound in philosophy, but its implementation thus far falls grievously short of protecting the American heritage of living diversity. Of the 233 distinct ecosystems recognized by the Forest Service in the United States and Puerto Rico, only 81 are represented in the National Wilderness Preservation System. Another 102 ecosystems could be set aside within the domain of federally owned undeveloped lands.

In the end, the problem of wilderness preservation is a moral issue, for us and for our descendants. It is a curious fact that when very little is known about a subject, the important questions people raise are ethical. Then as knowledge grows, they become more concerned with information than with morality, in other words more narrowly intellectual. Finally, as understanding becomes sufficiently complete, the questions turn ethical again. Environmentalism is now passing from the first to the second phase, and there is reason to hope that it will proceed directly on to the third.

The future of the conservation movement depends on such an advance in moral reasoning. Its maturation is linked to that of biology and a new hybrid field, bioethics, that deals with the many technological advances recently made possible by biology. Philosophers and scientists are applying a more formal analysis to such complex and difficult problems as the allocations of scarce organ transplants, heroic but extremely expensive efforts to prolong life, and the possible use of genetic engineering to alter human heredity. They have only begun to consider the relationships between human beings and organisms with the same rigor. It is clear that the key to precision lies in the understanding of motivation, the ultimate reasons why people care about one thing but not another—why, for example, they prefer a city with a park to a city alone. The goal is to join emotion with the rational analysis of emotion in order to create a deeper and more enduring conservation ethic.

Aldo Leopold, the pioneer ecologist and author of *A Sand County Almanac*, defined an ethic as a set of rules invented to meet circumstances so new or intricate, or else encompassing responses so far in the future, that the average person cannot foresee the final outcome. What is good for you and me at this moment might easily sour within ten years, and what seems ideal for the next few decades could ruin future generations. That is why any ethic worthy of the name has to encompass the distant future. The relationships of ecology and the human mind are too intricate to be understood entirely by unaided intuition, by common sense—that overrated capacity defined by Einstein as the set of prejudices we acquire by the age of eighteen.

An enduring code of ethics is not created whole from absolute premises but inductively, in the manner of common law, with the aid of case histories, by feeling and consensus, through an expansion of knowledge and experience, influenced by an understanding of human needs and mental development, during which well-meaning and responsible people sift the opportunities and come to agree upon norms and directions.

Why then should the human race protect biological diversity? Let me count the ways. The first is that we are part of life on earth, share its history, and hence should hesitate before degrading and destroying it. The acceptance of this principle does not diminish humanity but raises the status of nonhuman creatures. We should at least pause and give reason before treating them as disposable matter. Peter Singer, a philosopher and animal liberationist, has gone so far as to propose that the circle of altruism be expanded beyond the limits of our own species to animals with the capacity to feel and suffer, just as we have extended the label of brotherhood steadily until most people now feel comfortable with an all-inclusive phrase, the family of man. Christopher D. Stone, in *Should Trees Have Standing?*, has examined the legal implications of this enlarged generosity. He points out that until recently women, children, aliens, and members of minority groups had few or no legal rights in many societies. Although the policy was once accepted casually and thought congenial to the prevailing ethic, it now seems hopelessly barbaric. Stone asks, why should we not extend similar protection to other species and to the environment as a whole? People still come first—humanism has not been abandoned—but the rights of the owners should not be the exclusive yardstick of justice. If procedures and precedents existed to permit legal action to be taken on behalf of certain agreed upon parts of the environment, the argument continues, humanity as a whole would benefit. I am not sure I agree with this concept, but at the very least it deserves more serious debate than it has received. Human beings are a contractual species. The working principles of ownership and privilege are arrived at by long-term mutual consent, and legal theorists are a long way from having explored their ultimate limits.

If nobility is defined as reasoned generosity beyond expedience, animal liberation would be the ultimate ennobling act. Yet to force the argument entirely within the flat framework of kinship and legal rights is to trivialize the case favoring conservation, to justify one set of ethical beliefs (conservation, animal rights) on the basis of another (kinship, human rights). It is also very risky. Human beings, for all their professed righteousness and brotherhood, easily discriminate against strangers and are content to kill them during wars declared for relatively frivolous causes. How much easier it is to find an excuse to exterminate another species. A stiffer dose of biological realism appears to be in order. We need to apply the first law of human altruism, ably put by Garrett Hardin: never ask people to do anything they consider contrary to their own best interests. The only way to make a conservation ethic work is to ground it in ultimately selfish reasoning—but the premises must be of a new and more potent kind.

An essential component of this formula is the principle that people will conserve land and species fiercely if they foresee a material gain for themselves, their kin, and their tribe. By this economic measure alone the diversity of species is one of the earth's most important resources. It is also the least utilized. We have come to depend completely on less than 1 percent of living species for our existence, with the remainder waiting untested and fallow. In the course of history, according to estimates recently made by Norman Myers, people have utilized about 7,000 kinds of plants for food, with emphasis on wheat, rye, maize, and about a dozen other highly domesticated species. Yet at least 75,000 exist that are edible, and many of these have traits superior to those of the crop plants in use. The strongest of all arguments from surface ethics is a logical conclusion about this unrealized potential: the more the living world is explored and utilized, the greater will be the efficiency and reliability of the particular species chosen for economic use. Among the potential star species are the following:

The winged bean (*Psophocarpus tetragonolobus*) of New Guinea has been called a one-species supermarket. It contains more protein than cassava and potato and possesses an overall nutritional value equivalent to that of soybean. It is among the most rapidly growing of all plants, reaching a height of fifteen feet within a few weeks. The entire plant can be eaten, tubers, seeds, leaves, flowers, stems, and all, in both the raw state and when ground into flour. A coffee-like beverage can be made from the liquefied extract. The species has already been used to improve the diet in fifty tropical countries, and a special institute has been set up in Sri Lanka to study and promote it more thoroughly.

The wax gourd (*Benincasa hispida*) of tropical Asia grows an inch every three hours over the course of four days, permitting multiple crops to be raised each year. The fruit attains a size of up to one by six feet and a weight of eighty pounds. Its crisp white flesh can be eaten at any stage, as a cooked vegetable, base for soup, or dessert when mixed with syrup.

The Babassu palm (*Orbignya martiana*) is a wild tree of the Amazon rain forest known locally as the "vegetable cow." The individual fruits, which resemble small coconuts, occur in bunches of up to 600 with a collective weight of 200 pounds. A colorless oil makes up 60 to 70 percent of the kernel mass and can be used for margarine, shortening, fatty acids, toilet soap, and detergents. A stand of 500 trees on one hectare (2.5 acres) can produce 125 barrels of oil per year. After the oil has been extracted, the remaining seedcake, which is about one-fourth protein, serves as an excellent animal fodder.

Even with limited programs of research, biologists have compiled an impressive list of such candidate organisms in the technical literature. The vast majority of wild plants and animals are not known well enough (almost certainly many have not even been discovered) even to guess at those with the greatest economic potential. Nor is it possible to imagine all the uses to which each species can be put. Consider the case of the natural food sweeteners. Several species of plants have been identified whose chemical products can replace conventional sugar with negligible calories and no known side effects. The katemfe (*Thaumatococcus danielli*) of the West African forests contains two proteins that are 1,600 times sweeter than sucrose and are now widely marketed in Great Britain and Japan. It is outstripped by the well-named serendipity berry (*Dioscoreophyllum cumminsii*), another West African native whose fruit produces a substance 3,000 times sweeter than sucrose.

Natural products have been called the sleeping giants of the pharmaceutical industry. One in every ten plant species contains compounds with some anticancer activity. Among the leading successes from the screening conducted thus far is the rosy periwinkle, a native of the West Indies. It is the very paradigm of a previously minor species, with pretty five-petaled blossoms but otherwise rather ordinary in appearance, a roadside casual, the kind of inconspicuous flowering plant that might otherwise have been unknowingly consigned to extinction by the growth of sugarcane plantations and parking lots. But it also happens to produce two alkaloids, vincristine and vinblastine, that achieve 80 percent remission from Hodgkins' disease, a cancer of the lymphatic system, as well as 99 percent remission from acute lymphocytic leukemia. Annual sales of the two drugs reached $100 million in 1980.

A second wild species responsible for a medical breakthrough is the Indian serpentine root (*Rauwolfia serpentina*). It produces reserpine, a principal source of tranquilizers used to relieve schizophrenia as well as hypertension, the generalized condition predisposing patients toward stroke, heart malfunction, and kidney failure.

Usable wildness: meadow foam, *left,* currently under study as a hydrocarbon substitute, *(Jo-Ann Ordano/Photo/Nats);* spotted coral root, *right,* an Indian sedative, wormer, and remedy for pneumonia, *(Larry Kimball/Photo/Nats).*

The natural products of plants and animals are a select group in a literal sense. They represent the defense mechanisms and growth regulators produced by evolution during uncounted generations, in which only the organisms with the most potent chemicals survived to the present time. Placebos and cheap substitutes were eliminated at an early stage. Nature has done much of our work for us, making it far more efficient for the medical researcher to experiment with extracts of living tissue than to pull chemicals at random off the laboratory shelf. Very few pharmaceuticals have been invented solely from a knowledge of the principles of chemistry and medicine. Most have their origin in the study of wild species and were discovered by the rapid screening of large numbers of natural products.

Natural products also have been utilized in achieving many industrial and agricultural technological advances. Among the most important have been the development of phytoleum, new plant fuels to replace petroleum; waxes and oils produced from indefinitely renewing sources at more economical rates than previously thought possible; novel kinds of fibers for paper manufacture; fast-growing siliceous plants, such as bamboo and elephant grass, for economical dwellings; superior methods of nitrogen fixation and soil reclamation; and "magic bullet" techniques of pest control, by which microorganisms and parasites are set loose to find and attack target species without danger to the remainder of the ecosystem. Even the most conservative extrapolation indicates that many more discoveries will result from just a modest continuation of such research efforts.

Furthermore, the direct harvesting of free-living species is only a beginning. The favored organisms can be bred over about ten to one hundred generations to increase the quality and yield of their desired product. It is possible to create new strains that do well in new climates and the special environments required for mass production. The genetic material comprising them is an additional future resource; it can be taken apart gene by gene and distributed to other species. Thomas Eisner, one of the pioneers of chemical ecology, has used a striking analogy to explain these two levels of utilization of wild organisms. Each of the millions of species can be visualized as a book in a library. No matter where it originates, it can be transferred and put to use elsewhere. No matter how rare in its original state, it can be copied many times over and disseminated to become indefinitely abundant. An orchid down to the last hundred individuals in a remote valley of the Peruvian Andes, which also happens to be the source of a medicinal alkaloid, can be saved, cultured, and converted into an important crop in gardens and greenhouses around the world. But there is much more to the species than the alkaloid or some other useful material that it happens to package. It is not really a conventional book; it is more like a looseleaf notebook in which the genes are the equivalent of detachable pages. With new techniques of genetic engineering, biologists will soon be able to lift out desirable genes from one species or strain and transfer them to another. A valuable food plant, for example, can be given DNA from wild species conferring biochemical resistance to its most destructive disease. It can be altered by parallel procedures to grow in desert soil or through longer seasons.

A notable case in point is the primitive form of maize, *Zea diploperennis*, recently discovered in a mountain forest of southwestern Mexico. It survives only in three small areas totaling a mere ten acres (at any time a bulldozer might easily have extinguished the entire species within hours). *Zea diploperennis* possesses genes for perennial growth, making it unique among all other known varieties of corn. It is thus the potential source of a hereditary trait that could reduce growing time and labor costs, making cultivation more feasible in ecologically marginal areas.

Finally, beyond such practical concerns and far more difficult to put into words, is what biological diversity means to the human spirit. This is what can be called the deep ethic as opposed to the surface ethic of conservation. It is ultimately more convincing and durable and takes approximately the following form. We are human in good

More usable wildness: Indian pipe, *left,* used by the Indians for convulsions, epilepsy, and eye ailments *(Hal H. Harrison/Grant Heilman);* birthroot-trillium ovarum, *right,* a specific remedy to ease childbirth *(Bruce Matheson/Photo/Nats).*

part because of the particular way we affiliate with organisms. They are the matrix in which the human mind originated and is permanently rooted, and they offer the virtually endless challenge and freedom innately sought. The scientist is perhaps for the moment more aware than most of the opportunities for discovery and the unending sense of wonder that the living world offers—bear in mind the 1,000 miles of mostly new information in each handful of soil. To the extent that each person can feel as a naturalist, the old excitement of the untrammeled world will be regained. I offer this then as a formula of reenchantment to reinforce poetry and myth: mysterious and little known organisms still live within reach of where you sit. Splendor awaits in minute proportions.

The counterargument to a conservation ethic of any kind is that people come first. After their problems have been solved we can enjoy the natural environment as a luxury. If that is indeed the answer, the wrong question was asked. The question of importance concerns purpose. Solving practical problems is the means, not the purpose. Let us assume that human genius has the power to thread the needles of technology and politics. Let us imagine that we can avert nuclear war, feed a stabilized population, and generate a permanent supply of energy—what then? The answer is the same all around the world: individuals will strive toward personal fulfillment and at least realize their potential. But what is fulfillment, and for what purpose did human potential evolve?

The truth is that we never conquered the world, we never understood it; we only thought we had taken control. We do not even know why we respond in a certain way to other organisms and need them in diverse ways so deeply. The prevailing myths concerning our predatory actions toward each other and the environment are obsolete, unreliable, and destructive. The more the mind is fathomed in its own right, as an organ of survival, the greater will be the reverence for life for purely rational reasons.

Science and natural philosophy have brought into clear relief the following paradox of human existence. The drive toward perpetual expansion—or if you prefer, personal freedom—is basic to the human spirit. But to sustain it we need the most delicate, knowing stewardship of the living world that can be devised. Expansion and stewardship may appear at first to be conflicting goals, but they are not. The depth of the conservation ethic will be measured by the extent to which each of the two approaches to nature is used to reshape and reinforce the other. The paradox can be resolved by changing its premises into forms more suited to ultimate survival, by which I mean protection of the human spirit.

EDWARD O. WILSON, Baird Professor of Science at Harvard and curator of entomology at the university's Museum of Comparative Zoology, was one of the first scientists to perceive a relationship between population biology and the social structure of all organisms, including human beings. He is the author or coauthor of numerous books, including *Sociobiology: The New Synthesis* (1975) and *On Human Nature*, which won the 1979 Pulitzer Prize for general nonfiction. His article is based upon portions of his book, *Biophilia*. Cambridge: Harvard University Press, 1984.

ASPECTS OF WRITING: Overlapping subject areas; using and avoiding emotional terms.

Edward O. Wilson's classic essay in this unit is admirable in many ways; it is elegant, humane, rigorous, and philosophical. It is also rich in allusion, as in the second paragraph, which includes references to "the original Greek concept of tragedy" and to the historian, Leo Marx, citing his image of "the machine in the garden"; he also produces some lovely (and chilling) phrases, with evocative biblical and other references:

> We are killing the thing we love, our Eden, progenitrix and sibyl.

In these terms he introduces the central concept of his essay, to which he returns in the final paragraph, where he suggests a resolution of the tension between the human impulses to "perpetual expansion" and "stewardship."

In his essay, Wilson writes, "Why then should the human race protect biological diversity? Let me count the ways." This is an allusion to a well-known Elizabeth Barrett Browning poem:

> How do I love thee? Let me count the ways.
> I love thee to the depth and breadth and height
> My soul can reach. . . .

Wilson's breadth of reference enables him to see situations in different contexts. Ecology is about the survival of habitat and species, but it is also about the way we see ourselves as humans, the way we see our planet, and the values we embrace. Postel links economics and the environment; Maxwell links social justice and world climatic change to the environment; Goldsmith links our treatment of the natural world to our religious and cultural anthropocentrism; Wilson links the natural world with the needs of the human spirit. All of these linkages are made by people whose knowledge and vision goes beyond their narrow specialization. The principal objections of antienvironmentalists are economic and emotional in nature: why should people lose jobs, or natural resources not be exploited, in order to preserve a certain plant, animal, or habitat? In order to answer such objections, environmentalists sometimes resort to equally emotional outbursts. Wilson and other writers demonstrate, however, that there are philosophical, economic, social, and other reasons for fundamentally realigning our behavior in favor of long-term, sustainable development and protection of the natural world. In each case—especially in Postel's, Goldsmith's, and Wilson's essays—the writer offers a resolution that avoids mutually exclusive choices. Economic development such as we have now, says Postel, is unsustainable, but economic development based on good environmental principles is not only good for the planet, it's good for people, too—there is no conflict between economic growth and the environment when the argument is put in these terms. Wilson makes a similar point at the end of his essay.

There is nothing wrong with feeling strongly about an issue—we all feel emotionally involved in different situations—but *an overdependence on emotional terms can weaken, rather than strengthen, your discussion or argument.* In her essay in this unit, Sandra Postel reveals a high level of concern for the fate of the Earth, but much of the information is conveyed in **statistical** form, giving an objective quality to her discussion. Wilson achieves a similar end by suggesting moral aspects of the debate over the preservation of species; his essay is **thoughtful,** not rancorous. Telling people that they are stupid is not usually very effective as a means of argument; marshaling facts and figures, or putting the discussion into a more philosophical context, is likely to be more persuasive.

WRITING AND RESEARCH: Answer one of the following questions.

1. Choose one of the environmental topics from the following list (or substitute a similar example) and describe the process that is believed to be responsible for the problem. The list consists of some items that are the effects of problems and some that are the causes of problems.

   acid rain

   soil erosion

   global warming (the greenhouse effect)

   atmospheric ozone depletion

   deforestation

   loss of wetlands

2. What is "sustainable development"? Why do environmentalists and others consider this so important a concept?
3. Discuss two or more of the essays in this section in the form of a review. As in Maxwell's multiple book review in Section One of this unit, your own perception of the environmental situation in the world will be clearly in evidence, but you should make substantial reference to the essays. You may refer to other sources as well, for further discussion in support of or in opposition to the essays you choose.

The essays in this section are good sources, and they provide many references to other works and authors that may be useful for research into environmental topics. The *State of the World* annual reports of the Worldwatch Institute are a rich source for information on the environment and sustainable development.

Think about the **tone** of your discussion. All of the writers in this section have strong feelings about the environment and other matters, and their essays are not all identical in tone, but they are all couched in rational terms. Most college essays are probably fairly **formal** in tone, with a factual orientation. Essays of a more personal nature can be very effective, but they often fail because too much attention is drawn to the character of the writer rather than the ideas under discussion. People are more likely to be persuaded by evidence than by personal statements of belief.

Formal or **informal tones**—and all the gray areas in between—are achieved by different kinds of writing. Different **word choices** can affect the tone, as can the **sentence structure.** Consider the tone of these examples, and what kind of essay you would expect to follow:

Is the world in trouble? No! [very informal]

The idea that the world is experiencing an environmental collapse is exaggerated. [formal; could work as a thesis]

Environmentalists are tree-hugging idiots. [very informal, insulting, ineffective]

Environmental considerations are gradually changing the way we think about "progress." [formal, interesting]

OPTION TWO

TALKING ABOUT LANGUAGE: Language, Beauty, Truth, and Nature. Figurative and literal meanings.

Language comes naturally to us, and it has many practical uses. We use it when we shop, when we work, when we interact with other people (or even with our pets and plants). But there is also an esthetic side to language. We note that something was "beautifully said," or that someone's words were "moving" or "eloquent." The obverse is also true; speeches can be boring as well as interesting, awkward and incoherent as well as compelling; illogical as well as logical.

Aristotle believed that great poetry was a reflection of Nature; that its beauty was moral. John Keats captured something of this spirit in his "Ode on a Grecian Urn":

> "Beauty is truth, truth Beauty," —that is all
> Ye know on earth, and all ye need to know.

Bertrand Russell, the mathematician and philosopher, wrote that "The search for something permanent is one of the deepest of the instincts leading men to philosophy." Russell saw this as one key to the power of religion, which offered permanence—in a dangerous and ever-changing world—in the forms of God and immortality.

There appears to be common ground among these very different people, living in very different times. The language of the poet, the philosopher, the scientist, and the artist expresses a search for truth, in all its forms, and language is at its most powerful when it expresses ideas in terms that are clear and precise. In mathematics, just like poetry, the most elegant formulation is preferred because it is more likely to be true. Good writing is good, then, because of what it says *and* how it is said; both **content** and **style** are important.

Truth, of course, is not always stated directly. In ordinary speech, as well as writing, we tap a tremendous reservoir of figurative language, as illustrated in this sentence. This **figurative** use of language gives some readers trouble, because they expect the words on the page to mean exactly what they say; that is, they expect **literal** meanings.

The difference between the figurative and the literal can easily be demonstrated. Consider the saying,

> "I jumped out of my skin."

Literally, this would be difficult to do, but figuratively it merely means that I was taken by surprise.

Some people are very careless with the word "literally," saying things such as

> "When the team scored, the crowd literally exploded."

Literally, this is nonsense, for it means that people actually blew up, but figuratively it makes sense, meaning that the crowd was suddenly excited, or galvanized—another metaphor.

The most common images are **similes** and **metaphors,** and literature has innumerable famous examples. The difference between the two is simply that in the simile a direct comparison is made, usually using the words "like" or "as" ("As crazy as a coot"), whereas in a metaphor the comparison is implied; "like" or "as" are not used ("They were the cream of the crop").

If you cannot understand my argument, and declare "It's Greek to me," you are quoting Shakespeare; if you claim to be more sinned against than sinning, you are quoting Shakespeare; if you recall your salad days, you are quoting Shakespeare; if you act more in sorrow than in anger, if your wish is father to the thought, if your lost property has vanished into thin air, you are quoting Shakespeare; if you have ever refused to budge an inch or suffered from green-eyed jealousy, if you have played fast and loose, if you have been tongue-tied, a tower of strength, hoodwinked or in a pickle, if you have knitted your brows, made a virtue of necessity, insisted on fair play, slept not one wink, stood on ceremony, danced attendance (on your lord and master), laughed yourself into stitches, had short shrift, cold comfort or too much of a good thing, if you have seen better days or lived in a fool's paradise—why, be that as it may, the more fool you, for it is a foregone conclusion that you are (as luck would have it) quoting Shakespeare; if you think it is early days and clear out bag and baggage, if you think it is high time and that that is the long and short of it, if you believe that the game is up and that truth will out even if it involves your own flesh and blood, if you lie low till the crack of doom because you suspect foul play, if you have your teeth set on edge (at one fell swoop) without rhyme or reason, then—to give the devil his due—if truth were known (for surely you have a tongue in your head) you are quoting Shakespeare; even if you bid me good riddance and send me packing, if you wish I was dead as a doornail, if you think I am an eyesore, a laughing stock, the devil incarnate, a stony-hearted villain, bloody-minded or a blinking idiot, then—by Jove! O Lord! Tut, tut! for goodness' sake! what the dickens! but me no buts—it is all one to me, for you are quoting Shakespeare.

Levin, in McCrum, Cran, and MacNeil: 99–100

ASPECTS OF LANGUAGE: Creative language and Shakespeare.

Anyone can coin new words, phrases, and images—language is infinitely open to such creations—but the most successful coiner in English was Shakespeare. McCrum, Cran, and MacNeil list wellknown lines from just one play, *Hamlet,* to illustrate our debt to the Bard:

Frailty, thy name is woman!
More in sorrow than in anger
The primrose path of dalliance
Something is rotten in the state of Denmark
The time is out of joint
Brevity is the soul of wit
More matter with less art
Though this be madness, yet there is method in it
The play's the thing
To be or not to be: that is the question
A king of shreds and patches
I must be cruel, only to be kind
Alas poor Yorick
A hit, a very palpable hit
The rest is silence

The Story of English: 103

In another example, the authors of *The Story of English* quote Bernard Levin, an English journalist and television personality, who created the elaborate tribute to Shakespeare shown opposite.

Only humans are known to have language in its fullest sense—that is to say, language that is creative, not simply mimicry or genetically coded. All animals appear to communicate, some with an elaborate repertoire of gestures and noises, but claims that chimpanzees, for example, have humanlike capacity for sign language remain controversial, the most advanced individuals managing "only" the competence of young human children. Creatures as dissimilar as bees and whales show remarkable communicative behavior, but the flexibility and complexity of human speech seems unique. There is a lot of scientific interest in animal communication, and the topic could make a fascinating research paper.

Calvin and Hobbes **by Bill Watterson**

Quick Quiz

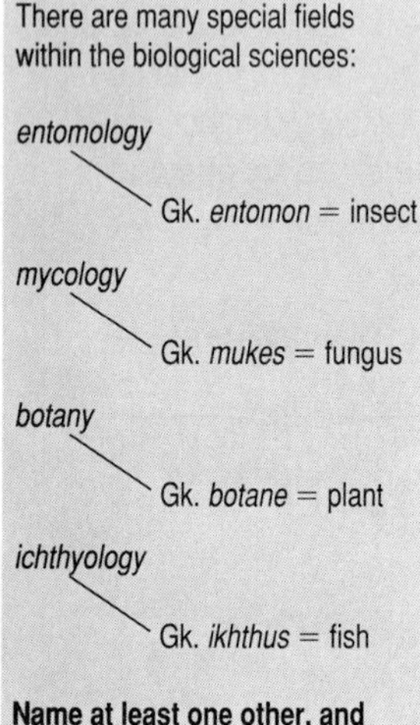

There are many special fields within the biological sciences:
entomology
Gk. entomon = insect
mycology
Gk. mukes = fungus
botany
Gk. botane = plant
ichthyology
Gk. ikhthus = fish

Name at least one other, and give its derivation

1. What is "sustainable development"?
2. Who are the "Greens"?
3. What is the capital of Brazil?
4. What is "the greenhouse effect"?
5. Why do some people argue that the West is hypocritical in its criticism of Brazil's development of the Amazon?
6. Who was Chico Mendes?
7. Why is rapid population growth a threat to the environment?
8. Why are environmental problems such as acid rain and deforestation of *global*, rather than simply *national*, significance?
9. Which gas is believed to be the biggest problem in global warming, and where does it come from?
10. Who was Rachel Carson?

One of America's best-known poets, Sylvia Plath, wrote works rich in imagery and reference to Nature. Here are two examples.

Frog Autumn

Summer grows old, cold-blooded mother.
The insects are scanty, skinny.
In these palustral homes we only
Croak and wither.

Mornings dissipate in somnolence.
The sun brightens tardily
Among the pithless reeds. Flies fail us.
The fen sickens.

Frost drops even the spider. Clearly
The genius of plenitude
Houses itself elsewhere. Our folk thin
Lamentably.

Metaphors

I'm a riddle in nine syllables
An elephant, a ponderous house,
A melon strolling on two tendrils.
O red fruit, ivory, fine timbers!
This loaf's big with its yeasty rising.
Money's new-minted in this fat purse.
I'm a means, a stage, a cow in calf.
I've eaten a bag of green apples,
Boarded a train there's no getting off.

SECTION ONE

PRIOR KNOWLEDGE: What do we value? Ideal and real culture; cultural relativism.

A 1989 survey of "the most important things in life," taken among people aged 15 to 25 in eight European countries, showed the result opposite. In-class surveys done informally by the author of this text have shown similar results over a number of years, except that the mostly American young people in my classes have, as a group, always given "family" the #1 ranking, and "money" hardly ever appears in the top five. Apart from the choices listed in the 1989 survey, others that have won some support include religion, country, and some personal qualities such as "honesty." A few students have even selected "education."

Most important things in life

	Items picked most often				
	First	*Second*	*Third*	*Fourth*	*Fifth*
Finland	Health	Love	Peace of mind	Happy family	Job security
France	Health	Success	Happy family	Love	Friends
Germay	Health	Friends	Happy family	Love	Free time
Greece	Health	Happy family	Job security	Love	Success
Italy	Health	Love	Happy family	Success	Money
Spain	Health	Happy family	Love	Friends	Success/ money
Sweden	Health	Love	Friends	Happy family	Fun
UK	Health	Happy family	Money	Friends	Success

The emphasis on family is hardly surprising; it's natural to love the family one is born into and to want a happy and successful family of one's own. Furthermore, the phrase "family values" has been part of the political debate in the United States for many years. If family is so highly rated, however, why do we hear so frequently that this core cultural unit is in disarray, that the number of dysfunctional families is ever-increasing, and that the "traditional" family is now a small percentage of the total number of households? If family is so important, why are child and spouse abuse so common, why is unwed motherhood so widespread, and why is divorce so prevalent? These are not just American problems; "Family Decay Global" was the headline for a *New York Times* discussion of *Families in Focus,* a 1995 report from the Population Council, which showed divorce and out-of-wedlock births increasing virtually everywhere, in poor and rich countries, with Japan being the most notable exception.

Apart from "family," the gap between **ideal** and **real culture** can perhaps be seen most clearly with regard to "money," which hardly ever appears among the most important things in the informal surveys mentioned, but for which many things seem to be sacrificed in real life.

Anthropologists sometimes talk about **"ideal"** culture and **"real"** culture, and this distinction can perhaps help explain the contrast between what people *say* they value and their actual behavior. The ideal culture is that description of ourselves which we nourish as an aspiration; it is what we tell ourselves we represent; it is the way we

COMPARE AND CONTRAST – FAMILY TIES: THE INTERNATIONAL TREND

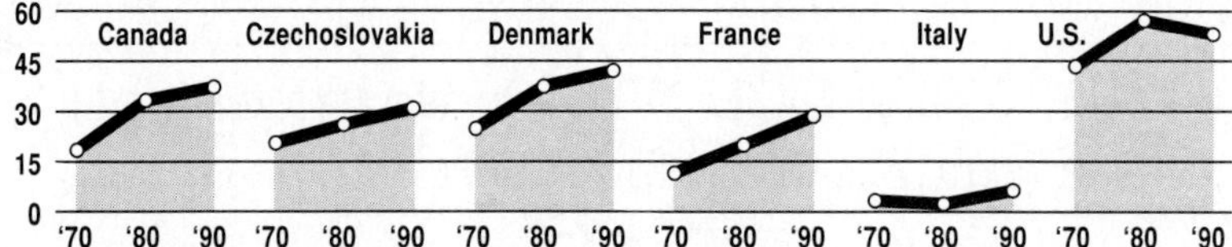

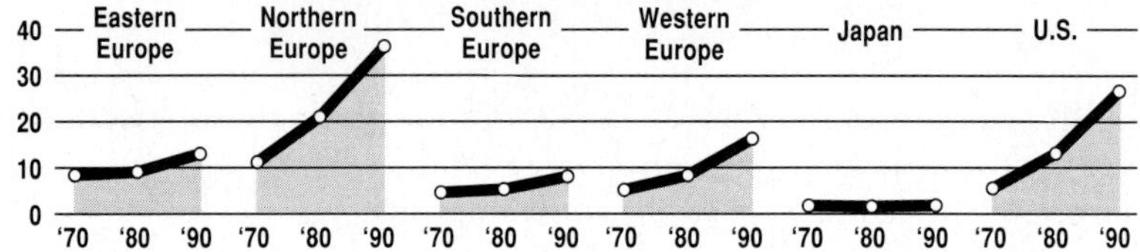

(*From: the* New York Times)

see our country, perhaps, on sentimental and patriotic occasions, or when we talk to foreigners. The real culture is what we experience in everyday life, what we read about in the newspapers, or hear on the radio, or see on the television news. In every culture there is a gap between the ideal and the real, and ours is no exception. Perhaps the value of the ideal is to give us a goal, an aspiration; as Robert Browning, in a famous line, wrote,

> Ah, but a man's reach should exceed his grasp,
> Or what's a heaven for?

Hatch paraphrases and quotes anthropologist Melville Herskovits in order to explain *the basic principle of **relativism.*** He notes the "indisputable fact . . . that peoples across the world have widely diverse value systems. Therefore, there are no absolute standards or fixed values. 'Evaluations are *relative* to the cultural background out of which they arise.'" (Hatch, *Culture and Morality:* 3.)

The evaluation and comparison of cultures can be a tricky business, as Elvin Hatch indicates in the following discussion of **cultural** (or **ethical**) **relativism.** His discussion has relevance beyond anthropology, for it touches on the way people see their own society (as superior?) and the way they see others (as inferior?). It also introduces a

Calvin and Hobbes **by Bill Watterson**

notion—relativism—that has gone from anthropology into other fields and into the general culture of our society. Critics might say that relativism of this sort is a rejection of standards, leading to a false equivalence between Bach and the latest rap group, or between Shakespeare and television soap operas. The more reluctant we are to say that one thing is *better* than something else, the more relativistic our position.

THINK ON PAPER
Some people take the relativist position that single-parent, divorced, same-sex, or other "new" family arrangements are just as good as the traditional two-parent family. What factors would you consider relevant to a discussion of this issue?

ANNOTATED READING: Elvin Hatch. "A Working Alternative." *Culture and Morality: The Relativity of Values in Anthropology.* New York: Columbia U.P., 1983: 133–144.

A *Working Alternative*

Hatch opens with the premise that **relativism** is "in . . . difficulty." This may be so in anthropology, but it is flourishing in some other contexts, as suggested earlier in this section. Relativism declined in anthropology in part because of the dubious morality of allowing cruelty to others to be excused as "OK within that culture." In a well-known essay by **Bagish,** cited by Hatch, the example of Nazism is used; was the Holocaust just an expression of Nazi culture? Such a concept is ethically untenable and does grave damage to any strong version of cultural or ethical relativism.

If relativism is in such difficulty as a moral philosophy, is there any role at all left for it to play in our thinking? I believe so, and one of my purposes in this chapter is to indicate what that is. There is another purpose: given that much of ethical relativism has been nudged aside by recent events, I want to advance a set of principles that will cover much of the ground that relativism has relinquished. These principles constitute a framework that we can use in evaluating cultures, including our own.

I will not try to give a satisfactory philosophical justification for the principles that follow. Such justification may be impossible to achieve, even by philosophers whose background in ethics is more secure than mine. This could lead some to conclude that the attempt to suggest general principles is misguided: would it not be better to accept a form of skepticism as a matter of necessity and to avoid cross-cultural value judgments? Yet skepticism here has moral consequences that are as unattractive as any that may follow from the principles I am about to suggest. If we hold that there truly are no valid principles that we may apply in assessing others, and that we should remain neutral in relation to them, then the tacit effect is to condone whatever takes place in foreign cultures. We are enjoined to look favorably on the brutalization of human beings by members of their own society, or upon the starvation of people whose subsistence system they themselves consider inadequate. Skepticism may be suitable for the philosopher who is interested in advancing the theoretical understanding of ethics, but in the context of interaction with foreign cultures, it is simply untenable. What follows is not to be taken as a contribution to the theoretical debate on normative ethics, a matter which would properly fall within the domain of philosophy. Rather, the purpose is to help clarify how we ought to react when we are confronted with behavior that is grounded in values different from our own, and also to help us define our own self-identity by indicating where we stand among human societies.

There are many **homophones** in English—words that sound the same, or almost the same, but are different in meaning and often in spelling and etymology. Some of these are widely confused:

principle—a basic truth, law, or assumption
principal—first, highest
compliment—praise, words of admiration
complement—something that completes, or enhances, or brings to perfection. (A full complement of recruits. The two workers had skills that complemented each other perfectly.)

Words that have abbreviated forms are also sometimes confused:

your—belonging to you
you're—you are
its—belonging to it
it's—it is (or, in speech, "it has," as in "It's been hot lately").

In saying that the following principles are not given full philosophical justification I do not mean that they have no justification at all, as will be evident as the discussion proceeds. These principles rest on a solid footing, in that a prima facie case can be made for them. Yet when a set of normative principles are accepted on prima facie grounds, deeper philosophical issues are left unresolved.

The first principle is that there is merit to the criticism that relativism has been accompanied by a conservative bias. What is at issue here is the relativist claim that all cultures or institutions are equally valid or fitting: anthropologists tended to assume that the mere presence of a cultural trait warrants our valuing it. Elizabeth Colson has put the case quite simply; she wrote, "Ethnographers have usually presented each social group they study as a success story. We have no reason to believe that this is true" (1976:264). A people may get by with inadequate solutions to their problems even judging by their own standards. For example, if the people are genuinely interested in ensuring the productivity of their gardens, they will find innovations like crop rotation and fertilization more effective than human sacrifice—although they will not have the statistical evidence to realize this (cf. Bagish 1981:12–20).

Hatch's essay is organized with commendable clarity. In the first paragraph he states his intention "to advance a set of principles." The **transitions** to each are standard, but no less effective for that; on the first page, we find two of the three:

"The first principle is. . . ."
"Second, a general principle. . . ."

Second, a general principle is at hand for judging the adequacy of institutions. It may be called the humanistic principle or standard, by which I mean that the well-being of people ought to be respected. The notion of well-being is a critical aspect of the humanistic principle, and three points can be made with respect to it. For one, I assume that human well-being is not a culture-bound idea. Starvation and violence, for example, are hardly products of Western thought or a function of Western thinking, although they may be conceived in a peculiarly Western idiom. Starvation and violence are phenomena that are recognized as such in the most diverse cultural traditions. Another is that the notion of human well-being is inherently value-laden, and concepts of harm and beneficence are inseparable from it: it seems impossible to imagine the idea of human well-being divorced from moral judgments of approval and disapproval. Whereas such notions as sky or earth may conceivably be held in purely neutral terms in a given culture, such ideas as hunger and torture cannot be. It is even reasonable to argue that the *point* of morality, as a philosophical if not a sociological issue, is to promote the well-being of others (Warnock 1971, esp. pp. 12–26). Finally, the notion of human well-being, when used as the central point of morality, serves to root moral questions in the physical, emotional, and intellectual constitution of people. It may be that any rigorous attempt to work out the content of morality will have to include an analysis of such notions as human wants, needs, interests, and happiness.

The humanistic principle can be divided into two parts. First is Redfield's point about humaneness, that it is good to treat people well, or that we should not do one another harm. We can judge that

Humanism is a term with different connotations for different people. The denotations, however, are quite clear.

human sacrifice, torture, and political repression are wrong, whether they occur in our society or some other. Similarly, it is wrong for a person, whatever society he or she may belong to, to be indifferent toward the suffering of others. The matter of coercion, discussed earlier, fits here, in that we may judge it to be wrong when some members of a society deliberately and forcefully interfere in the affairs of other people. Coercion works against the well-being of those toward whom it is directed. Second is the notion that people ought to enjoy a reasonable level of material existence: we may judge that poverty, malnutrition, material discomfort, human suffering, and the like are bad. These two ideas may be brought together to form one standard since both concern the physical well-being of the members of society, and the difference between them is that the former refers to the quality of interpersonal relations, and the latter to the material conditions under which people live.

An attitude or doctrine that emphasizes human needs, achievements, values, and civilization. Historically, humanists argued for emancipation from church dogma, which limited their intellectual and creative freedom. For this reason, the word "humanist," even today, has **connotations** for some people of a philosophy hostile to religion. For others, such as Hatch, however, the word has **positive connotations** associated with a concern for human dignity and freedom from suffering and abuse. Hatch includes "humaneness" in his definition of the humanistic principle.

The humanistic principle may be impossible to define very tightly; it may even be that the best we can do to give it shape is to illustrate it with examples as I have done here. And surely it is difficult to apply in actual situations. Yet these are not good reasons to avoid making judgments about the relative merit of institutions or about the desirability of change. Although we may do harm by expressing judgments across cultural boundaries, we may do as much or more harm by failing to do so.

The orthodox relativist would perhaps argue that there is no humanistic moral principle that we can use for this purpose, in that notions like harm and discomfort are quite variable from one culture to the next. Pain and personal injury may even be highly valued by some people. For example, the Plains Indian willingly engaged in a form of self-torture that a middle-class American could hardly tolerate. The Indians chopped off finger joints and had arrows skewered through their flesh; tied to the arrows were cords, by which the sufferer dragged buffalo skulls around the village. Some American Indians were also reported to have placed a very high value on bravery, and the captive who withstood torture without showing pain was highly regarded by the enemies who tormented him.

Yet cases like these do not make the point that notions of pain and suffering are widely variable. Following this same logic one could say that middle-class Americans value pain since they willingly consent to surgery, and the man or woman who bears up well is complimented

The ethical problems raised by discussion of **relativism** are difficult to resolve. In their colonial days, the British had a policy of "indirect rule" intended to minimize interference with local chiefs and culture. Certain behavior, however, was considered so objectionable that it had to be suppressed; this included suttee (widow burning) in India and cannibalism in Fiji. In a similar way, many people today find the practice of female circumcision in some countries, such as Sudan, to be cruel mutilation and argue that it should be suppressed. Many practitioners (and even some victims) defend this practice, however, on the grounds that it is a traditional female rite of passage. Advocates of strict relativism would approach such issues very differently from those who use Hatch's humanitarian principle.

Hatch doesn't avoid these problems; he acknowledges the difficulty of making moral judgments about other cultures but concludes that "we may do as much or more harm by failing to do so."

THINK ON PAPER
Sensitivity to cross-cultural ethical judgments goes both ways. Think of some examples of cultural practices in other countries that Americans generally criticize, and of practices in the United States that are often criticized by foreigners.

for his or her strength of character. The Indian who was tortured to death would surely have preferred a long and respectable life among his people to the honorable death that came to him. The Plains Indian who engaged in self-torture was trying to induce a vision (in our idiom, a hallucination) for the power and advantages it was believed such an experience would bring. The pain was a means to an end, and surely was not seen as a pleasurable indulgence to look forward to. The difference between middle-class Americans and Plains Indians on this point could be a difference in judgments of reality and not a difference in values—the American would not believe that the vision has the significance attributed to it by the Indian, so he or she would not submit to the pain. Similarly, the Plains warrior might not believe in the efficacy of surgery and might refuse to suffer the scalpel.

The widespread trend among non-Western peoples to want such material benefits as steel knives and other labor-saving devices is a clear indication that all is not relative when it comes to hard work, hunger, discomfort, and the like. Cultural values may be widely different in many ways, but in this sphere at least, human beings do seem to have certain preferences in common.

The Yanomamö are an instructive case, for here is a people who do not seem to share the humanistic value I am suggesting. The level of violence and treachery in this society suggests that their regard for pain and suffering is demonstrably different from what I am arguing is the norm among human beings. Yet this is not clearly the case either: individuals in Yanomamö society are more willing than middle-class Americans to inflict injury on others, yet they want to avoid injury to themselves. Why else would the wife flee in terror when her husband comes at her with a machete, and why else would a village seek refuge from enemies when it is outnumbered and weak? The Yanomamö seem rather to be a case in which we are warranted in making a value judgment across cultural boundaries: they do not exhibit as much regard for the well-being of other persons as they have for themselves, and this can be judged a moral error.

The **Yanomamö** are an Amazonian tribe. The plight of Indians in this region is discussed in Kenneth Maxwell's article in Unit Six, Section One, of this text. In response to Hatch's comments here, it might be worth remembering that many native people around the world have been called "savages." Such words have **negative connotations** to which cultural relativists (and many postrelativists) would object—but this brings the argument back to square one: is no moral condemnation to be allowed?

Does this point about the generality of the humanistic principle among human beings not make the same mistake that Herskovits, Benedict, and other relativists were accused of making, which is to derive an "ought" from an "is"? My argument is not quite that simple, for it has two parts. First is the generalization that the humanistic value seems to be widespread among human beings. Second, I am making the moral judgment (quite separately from the empirical generalization) that this is an estimable value to hold, or that it warrants acceptance—in contrast, say, to another widespread value, ethnocentrism, which is not meritorious even if it is universal.

When Hatch differentiates between "the moral judgment" and "the empirical generalization," he is making an important distinction for researchers. The "moral judgment" is subjective, but the "empirical generalization" is based on actual observation. Empiricists describe the world as they see it (in real life or experiments) and are not constrained by preconceived theories or ideologies; this approach to research is called the **empirical method.**

A third principle in the scheme that I propose is that a considerable portion of the cultural inventory of a people falls outside the scope of the humanistic standard mentioned above. In other words, once we have considered those cultural features that we can reasonably judge by this standard, a large portion remains, and it consists of those items which have little if anything to do with the strictly practical affairs of life and which then cannot be appraised by practical considerations. Included are sexual mores, marriage patterns, kinship relations, styles of leadership, forms of etiquette, attitudes toward work and personal advancement, dietary preferences, clothing styles, conceptions of deity, and others. Some of these nonappraisable features are closely linked to others that are, in that there are always nonessential cultural accouterments or trappings associated with institutions that are important on practical grounds. Western medicine provides a surfeit of examples. Health care clearly falls within the orbit of the humanistic principle, yet much of the medical system in the United States is hardly necessary for health's sake, including the rigid social hierarchy among doctors and nurses and the traditional division of labor between them. Successful health care systems can assume different forms from the one exhibited in this country. It is essential (but difficult) to keep in mind this division between what is essential and what is not in such matters as medicine, for otherwise civilization will tend to pack a good deal of unnecessary cultural baggage along with the genuinely useful features when it sets out to share its advantages with others.

Hatch is not rejecting relativism outright. He suggests that it "prevails" in most cultural areas—any, perhaps, except the most morally egregious situations, those that offend against "the humanistic principle." The opening lines in this chapter of Hatch's book ask whether there is any role left for relativism, and the author answers, "I believe so, and one of my purposes . . . is to indicate what that is."

Relativism prevails in relation to the institutions that fall outside the orbit of the humanistic principle, for here a genuine diversity of values is found and there are no suitable cross-cultural standards for evaluating them. The finest reasoning that we or anyone else can achieve will not point decisively to the superiority of Western marriage patterns, eating habits, legal institutions, and the like. We ought to show tolerance with respect to these institutions in other societies on the grounds that people ought to be free to live as they choose.

This leads to the fourth principle: is it possible to identify any areas of culture in which we may speak of improvement? Are there any criteria that will produce a hierarchical ordering of societies that we may say represents a pattern of advance? Or is the distinction between primitive and civilized societies but an expression of our cultural bias?

Some words of classical origin (Greek and Latin) don't use the standard [-s] ending. This is particularly common in scientific terminology:

criterion [Gk]—criteria
curriculum—curricula
medium—media
referendum—referenda
bacterium—bacteria
alumnus, alumna—alumni
amoeba—amoebae

For some of these words, however, the [-s] ending is now optional, as in "curriculums" and "mediums."

The first criterion that comes to mind is Redfield's and Kroeber's, according to which civilization has brought a more humane existence, a higher level of morality to mankind, inasmuch as people treat one another better in complex societies. This judgment is very difficult to accept today, however. Recent events have left most of us with considerable ambivalence about Western democracy, to cite one instance. Politicians seem too often to be both incompetent and dishonest, and to be willing to allow private economic interests to influence programs and policies at all levels. Similarly, there is a very strong distrust of the power and intentions of big business, which seems to set its policies chiefly by looking at its margin of profit. The risk of producing a dangerous product is calculated by assessing how much the company is liable to lose in lawsuits relative to its profits, and not by considering the real dangers to human life. Much of the difficulty of assessing moral advance is that this is a highly impressionistic matter. The ledger sheets on which we tote up the pluses and minuses for each culture are so complex that summary calculations of overall moral standing are nearly meaningless. Perhaps the most one can say about whether or not there has been moral advance is that it is impossible to tell—but that it is not very likely.

It is important to distinguish between this conclusion and Herskovits'. According to him, we cannot speak of progress in this sphere because any humanistic principle we might use will necessarily be culture-bound; we have no yardstick to measure with. My point is that we do have a suitable yardstick, but that there are so many measures to take in each culture that the sum total is too complicated to assess.

Another criterion for gauging improvement is the material well-being of people: disregarding whether or not the members of society behave well or ill toward one another, can we say that the material conditions of life have gotten better with civilization? In pursuing this question I need to digress somewhat. The issue of material improvement places the focus on economics and technology, and also on such technical knowledge as that which is provided by medical and agricultural research. So we need first to ask if it is possible to arrive at an objective and meaningful hierarchy of societies based on these features. Herskovits questioned that we can. To him, an ordering of societies according to our criterion of economic production and technological complexity will merely reflect our cultural perspective and not some fundamental principle of general significance to all peoples.

THINK ON PAPER
Hatch resists the inference that Western societies are better than others because "people treat one another better in complex societies"; he notes that "most of us . . . [have] considerable ambivalence about Western democracy." Explain this remark.

Herskovits' argument is off the mark. On one hand, the criterion of economic complexity and technological sophistication is objective in the sense that it is definable by reference to empirical features that are independent of our culture. For example, the intensity and scale of economic transactions have a physical aspect which is identifiable from other cultural perspectives than ours, and the same is true of such measures as the amount of food produced per farm worker.* What is more, the social hierarchy that results from the use of these criteria has historical significance: one would be astonished, say, to

*The World Bank and other organizations commonly use a number of objective measures in assessing such matters as poverty, physical quality of life, and economic and social development.

The "objective measures" referred to in Hatch's note will be familiar to readers of Unit Five of this text, in which the difficulty of comparing the **quality of life** in different countries is discussed.

discover evidence of complex forms of agricultural production in the Paleolithic. But on the other hand, and even more important, this is a meaningful hierarchy, in that the point of this ordering of societies would not be lost on people from other cultures: it would be meaningful to them because they see the value of increasing agricultural productivity, the use of bicycles (and automobiles), the availability of running water, and the like. It is surely the case that non-Western peoples all over the world are more interested in the products of Western industrial production than they are in the intricacies of Australian kinship, and are more likely to incorporate such Western innovations as fertilizers and matches into their cultures than they are the particulars of the Australian system of marriage and descent. This is an important message we get from the post-World War II drive for economic development among the newly independent nations.

There is a danger in using people's perceptions of the relative superiority of economic and technological systems as a test for the meaningfulness of this social hierarchy, because not all of the world's populations agree about what it is that is good about development and modernization. For example, Burma and Iran are highly selective in the changes they will accept, and at least some very simple societies (like the Andaman Islanders) want little if any change.

Hatch makes points here that are relevant to discussions in Units Five and Six of this text. Many poorer countries around the world want Western aid and technology to help with their economic development, but it is a mistake to assume that this means that they want to become Westerners—to adopt Western culture. Many governments—and the people they represent—strongly resist the idea that they should imitate Western social *mores.* When we see so much that is wrong with our own society, it's not surprising that people from elsewhere do too.

There is another way to establish the hierarchy without relying completely and directly on people's opinions. However another society may feel about what they do or do not want with regard to development, the economic and technological relationship between them and Western societies is asymmetrical. It is true that the fully developed nations rely on the less developed ones for natural resources like oil, but processed goods, and both economic and technological innovations, flow chiefly to and not away from the societies that are lower on the scale. To take an extreme case, there is little in the sphere of technology and economics that the Australian aborigines or Andaman Islanders can offer to the developed nations, whereas the reverse is not true. For example, some of the most isolated Andaman Islanders occasionally find empty gasoline drums washed upon their shore. They cut these in half and use them as enormous cooking pots (Cipriani 1966:52). It is unthinkable that this relationship could be reversed—that we would find some technological item from their cultural inventory to be especially useful in our everyday lives. It is true that we may value their pottery or other artifacts as examples of primitive art, but the use we have for such items is esthetic, not practical, and consequently such items are of a different order from the gasoline drums that the Andamanese find so useful.

In noting this asymmetry I do not mean that cultures which are lower in the hierarchy do not have a very sophisticated technical knowledge of their own (they must in order to survive) and in this sense "they have something to teach us," as Brokensha and Riley remark concerning the Mbeere of Kenya. "In fact," these writers continue, "Mbeere and other folk-belief systems contain much that is based on extremely accurate, detailed and thoughtful observations, made over many generations" (1980:115). It is easy to depreciate or ignore the cultural practices and ideas of another society, say, when assisting them in the process of development. In particular, it is tempting to want to replace their traditional practices with "modern" ones in wholesale fashion, instead of building on or incorporating the indigenous knowledge in helping to bring about change. Nevertheless, the presence of such useful knowledge in indigenous systems of thought does not negate the fundamental asymmetry that exists among societies or the hierarchy which the asymmetry suggests.

The pluralistic notion of development . . . has bearing on the way we should conceive this hierarchy. The idea that Third World countries should become more and more like Western industrial societies is subject to criticism, and it may be preferable to define development differently for each society according to the interests of the people concerned and the nature of their economic and ecological conditions. A people may have achieved as much development as they need and want without embarking on a trajectory of industrial "growth" in the Western sense. In other words, the hierarchy I am suggesting does not represent a set of stages through which all societies will necessarily want to pass. It is simply a ranking of cultural systems according to degrees of economic complexity, technological sophistication, and the like.

Yet this begs a crucial question. Is it not true that to suggest this hierarchy is to imply that the societies higher on the scale are preferable? Does the existence of the hierarchy not mean that the societies that fall below would be better off if only they could manage to come up to a higher level of economic complexity and technological sophistication?

The discussion now comes back to the issue that prompted this digression. Can we say that the social hierarchy we have arrived at represents improvement or advance? The response unfortunately is as indecisive as the one concerning moral progress, and for the same reason. On one hand, civilization has brought a lower infant mortality rate due to better diet, hygiene, and medical care; less vulnerability to infectious disease for the same reasons; greater economic security due to increased economic diversification; less danger from local famine due to improved systems of transportation and economic organization; greater material comfort due to improved housing, and the like. But on the other hand we have pollution, the horrors of modern warfare, and the boredom and alienation of factory work, to name a few. On one hand we have labor-saving devices like automatic dishwashers, but on the other we have to spend our lives on a treadmill to pay for them. The tally sheet is simply too complicated to make an overall judgment. It is not at all clear that other people should want to become like Western civilization.

What we can say about the hierarchy is that the nations that fall toward the upper end of the scale have greater resources than the others. They have better technical knowledge from which the entire world may benefit—knowledge about hygiene, diet, crop rotation, soils, and the like. They also have the physical capacity to undertake programs of assistance when other societies are interested. Yet the higher civilizations also have the capacity to do far greater harm. The industrial system has exploited the powerless, ravaged the environment, meddled in the affairs of other countries, and conducted war in ways that the simpler societies never dreamed of. Even when we set out altruistically to help others we often mismanage the effort or misunderstand what it is we should do. Just as it is not at all clear that industrial civilization provides a happier or more fulfilling life for its members, so it is not clear whether its overall influence on those below it in the hierarchy has been to their detriment or benefit. This is a pessimistic age, and at this point it is difficult to suppress a strong sense of despair on this score.

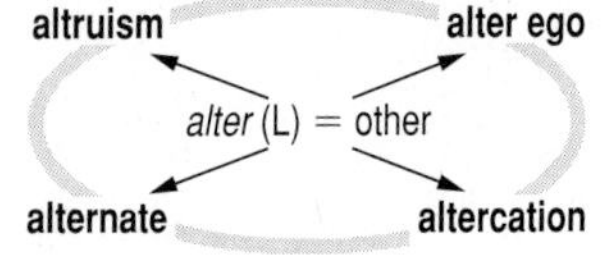

The place of Western civilization in the hierarchy of human societies is very different from what it was thought to be by Victorian anthropologists, who saw the differences among societies at bottom as a matter of intelligence: civilization is more thoughtful and shows greater sense than the lower societies, and it provides a happier and more benign mode of living; savages would embrace our way of life if they had the intelligence to understand it, for their institutions are but imperfect specimens of our own. Clearly this is inadequate. Many areas of life cannot be judged by standards that apply across cultural boundaries, for in many respects cultures are oriented in widely different directions. Still, all people desire material comfort and security, and in this sense Western civilization is distinguished from other cultures. The relationship among societies in this respect is one of asymmetry. Just as we may do far more harm to others than they can do to us, so we may do them more good, and we have the obligation to share the material advantages our civilization has to offer. Yet this asymmetry should not be confused with superiority. As a total way of life ours may not be preferable to others, and we need not try to turn them into copies of Western civilization.

THINK ON PAPER
What does Hatch mean when he says that the relationship between technologically advanced societies and others is "asymmetrical"?

An important implication follows from these conclusions: it is possible to arrive at a general principle for evaluating institutions without assuming that ours is a superior way of life. Herskovits for one seems to have believed that this could not be done, and that any general moral principle we might advance would express our own cultural bias and would tacitly make us appear to occupy a position superior to the rest. But this is not so. The matter of arriving at general moral principles and of how we measure up to these principles are two very separate issues.

The idea of ethical relativism in anthropology has had a complicated history. Through the 1930s the discipline expressed an overwhelming confidence in the notion, a confidence that was fortified by the empirical findings about the variability of moral values from culture to culture. And relativism was thought to be an idea of signal importance, for it could be used in world affairs and would contribute to peace and human understanding. But suddenly and with firm conviction, relativism was swept aside. It had all been a mistake.

Was relativism completely mistaken? After we have excised what is unacceptable, is there something left, a residuum of some kind, that still warrants approval? Certainly the relativists' call for tolerance contained an element that is hard to fault. This is the value of freedom: people ought to be free to live as they choose, to be free from the coercion of others more powerful than they. Equally fundamental, perhaps, is the message that relativism contained about the place of Western civilization among human societies. Rejected was the smug belief in Western superiority that dominated anthropological thinking during the 1800s. Just as the universe has not looked the same since the Copernican revolution, so the world and our place in it has not looked the same since ethical relativism appeared at about the turn of this century.

Rhetorical note: Hatch's essay is **expository**—it explains and informs—but it is also an **argument** concerning the status of relativism today and its place in the history of ideas.

ASPECTS OF WRITING: Tone and style.

In speech, we refer to "tone of voice" and recognize that **the way we say something** is sometimes even more important than what we say. This is a lesson children have to learn as they develop an adult competence in language. In writing, the same thing holds true; the tone of a piece may be light or heavy, comic or earnest, informal or formal, witty or dull, depending on the choice of words and way the words are put together. The following may serve as examples:

1. *I want to advance a set of principles that will cover much of the ground that relativism has relinquished. These principles constitute a framework that we can use in evaluating cultures, including our own.* Hatch, "The Evaluation of Culture."

   Comments: "I want to advance a set of principles"—The word **"advance"** is different in tone from other possibilities here. Hatch could have said, "I want to **state** . . . ," or "I want to **establish** . . . ," or "I want to **lay down** . . . ." "Advance" is more modest, suggesting that the writer is forwarding an idea for others to consider; he is not laying down the law or being dogmatic.

   "Relinquished" suggests giving up, or leaving behind; it has a nice suggestion of the outcome of an intellectual battle or struggle.

   "**I** want to advance . . . principles . . . **we** can use in evaluating cultures, including **our** own"—The use of the first person singular and plural forms establishes a personal relationship between the writer and the reader without distracting from the ideas presented. It draws the reader into the discussion as an equal; it is respectful and assumes that the reader has an interest in the subject similar to the author's.

   Summary: The language is **formal** and carefully chosen. It suggests a serious, civilized, interesting discussion without arrogance or combativeness.

2. *He would sell his London house. . . . He would set up as a mild eccentric, discursive, withdrawn, but possessing one or two lovable habits such as muttering to himself as he bumbled along pavements. Out of date, perhaps, but who wasn't these days? Out of date, but loyal to his own time. At a certain moment, after all, every man chooses: will he go forward, will he go back? There was nothing dishonourable in not being*

blown about by every little modern wind. Better to have worth, to entrench, to be an oak of one's own generation. John le Carré, *Tinker, Tailor, Soldier, Spy.*

Comments: ". . . **a mild eccentric, discursive, withdrawn** . . ."—the word "discursive" (wide-ranging, rambling, conversational) is unexpected and raises the level of the description to suit the actual character being described—the great, but unprepossessing, spy, George Smiley. The word captures Smiley's intellectual style without dwelling on it.

". . . muttering to himself as he **bumbled** along . . ."—The ordinariness of the scene and Smiley's dissatisfaction is captured in the colloquial "bumbled along"; in a crowd, no one would notice Smiley.

"Better to have worth, to entrench, **to be an oak of one's own generation.**"—To the humor of a grumpy, middle-aged man walking along a city street not knowing what to do with his life is added a wonderful image that is interesting, entertaining, and true—at least for Smiley.

Summary: Le Carré is introducing Smiley, and he does so with a lightness of touch that captures the physical ordinariness of the man while suggesting his intellectual quality. The language is **informal** and **educated** at the same time, with a touch of wry humor that is both particular and universal; it is recognizable to anyone who has ever felt left behind by the modern world. This is a work of fiction; the reader feels sympathetic to the character, interested in the story, and ready to take pleasure in the language and observation of the novelist.

WRITING EXERCISES: Answer one of the following questions.

The controversy over relativism has a long history, going back at least to the early part of the 20th century with anthropologists such as Franz Boas, Melville Herskovits, and Ruth Benedict, all of whom are discussed in Hatch's book. It is worth noting that truth is often elusive and attitudes toward truth may be at the mercy of prevalent cultural attitudes. Stephen Jay Gould's essay on scientific truth—in Unit One of this text—is relevant here. Hatch's essay suggests that what was once a strongly held principle of anthropology—and which was a kind of intellectual and methodological breakthrough in itself—is today in retreat. We may see some of these dynamics at work in the late 20th century in the realm of "political correctness." Does "P.C." get in the way of the truth, or does it suggest another kind of truth? What values are protected by "P.C." and what values are threatened? The questioning of "received wisdom" often makes interesting reading, and the ability to analyze and criticize (in either meaning of the word), as demonstrated by Hatch, helps free us from intellectual straitjackets.

1. **Either** define "relativism" and discuss its application in anthropology and/or in contemporary culture. Make reference to Hatch's essay. **Or** describe Hatch's comments on the legacy of relativism, which was an attempt to avoid ethnocentrism in the description and analysis of other cultures.
2. Defend **or** attack the idea that every judgment is subjective or "in the eye of the beholder." You may apply this to literature, music, science, ethics, or any other field.
3. Analyze the tone—and how it is achieved—in any two contrasting works, at least one of which should be from this text; the other may be a work of fiction. You may use the discussion on the previous page as a model, but you may wish to discuss your examples at greater length.

The tendency to put oneself, or one's culture or kind, at the center of things—to see oneself as the universal "norm"—has several manifestations, and invites original coinages, as suggested below.

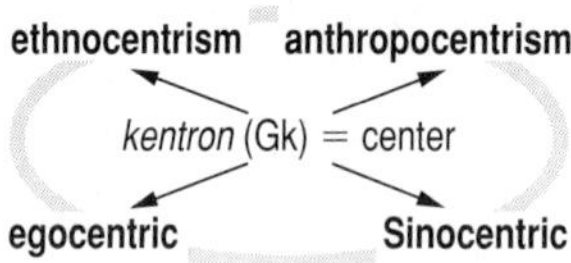

"Sinocentric" is a coinage suggesting China and things Chinese as the norm. A political analyst, for example, may adopt a Sinocentric view. Other nations, regions, and cultures also have useful prefix forms: **Franco-** = French, **Anglo-** = English or British, **Russo-** = Russian, **Euro-** = European, **Judeo-** = Jewish, **Afro-** = African, **Indo-** = Indian.

SECTION TWO

PRIOR KNOWLEDGE: Describing other cultures: How do foreigners view America?

In Section One of this unit, Elvin Hatch offers an academic discussion of the way in which different cultures can be described and compared, focusing in particular on cultural relativism. The focus of most such discussions in on the way we—Americans, that is—see other cultures, and it is perhaps salutary to turn this around and discuss how foreigners see *us.* This is what Janusz Mucha provides in the following essay.

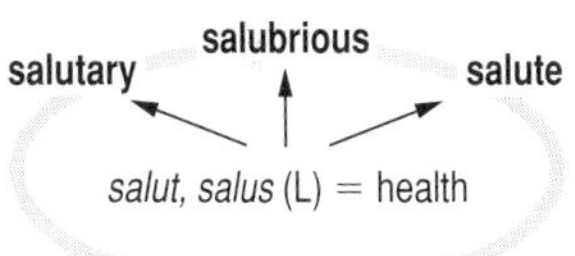

The most difficult thing about comparing cultures, their people, and their values may be that our own culture is, to us, so familiar that we consider it *normal.* This makes us see different customs and values outside our own culture as not just different but *abnormal.* Such ethnocentrism is common among people in all cultures, not just Americans, but Mucha contends that Americans are particularly susceptible to it. He claims, in fact, that "the American is generally more ethnocentric than the average European," and he describes in some detail why he thinks this is so.

It is often a shock to read other people's views of one's own country, and some people find themselves getting defensive over things that are said. It should be remembered that people in other cultures also often complain about the way they are described in the academic literature. A well-known example concerns Margaret Mead, the famous American anthropologist, whose book *Coming of Age in Samoa* (1928) was an influential and international best seller and continues to be widely read. In Samoa, however, Mead's account of the relaxed sex-

The sometimes profound differences between cultural values and assumptions is illustrated in the following discussion of notions of *efficiency:*

> In 1958 I lived with Bedouin tribes in the Sahara whose judgments of efficiency reflected their Muslim belief systems. An efficient way to work was one that gave them time to make Koranic prayers seven times daily, and that kept their expenditure of energy down during fasting periods. These tribes internalized religious values in their assessment of an efficient way to work. The efficient path was not to lead their flocks to pasture via the shortest route, . . . but one that allowed them to practice Koranic hospitality toward the poor along the way. Clearly, there are divergent criteria for defining efficiency in technological and other societies.
>
> Denis Goulet, "On the Ethics of Development Planning." Overseas Development Council, March 6, 1975

Rightly or wrongly, Freeman makes Mead's research in Samoa an example of a basic problem for anthropologists—namely, that the informants may tell you what they think you want to hear rather than the perhaps less interesting truth. Mead went to Samoa as a pioneering young woman doing fieldwork to establish whether the youth of this society exhibited the same problems and stresses associated with growing up that are apparent in Western societies. Franz Boas, her mentor, writes in the Preface to *Coming of Age in Samoa,*

> The results of her painstaking investigation confirm the suspicion long held by anthropologists, that much of what we ascribe to human nature is no more than a reaction to the restraints put upon us by our civilization.

This result, now strongly challenged by Freeman, among others, appeared to be decisive in the so-called **nature-nurture** debate. In other words, if some cultures produced young people free of the cares and anxieties that seemed to be an unavoidable part of growing up (nature), then these must in fact be cultural phenomena (nurture).

Many "borrowed" words and phrases in English have come unchanged from other languages. Some of these may still sound "foreign" even though they are well established in English, while others may not.

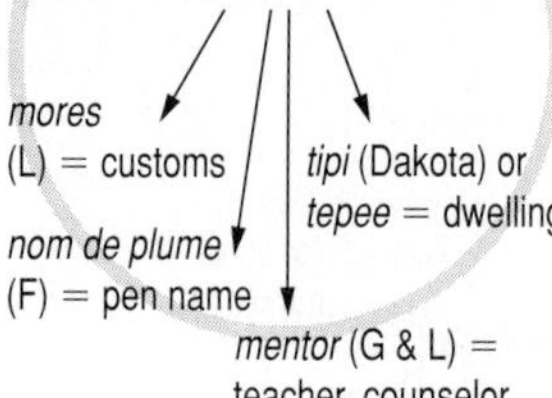

ual mores of the young people offended many of the Samoans themselves, and Margaret Mead was not very popular in some circles in the islands. Her research, moreover, has been strongly criticized by another anthropologist, Derek Freeman, in his *Margaret Mead and Samoa, the Making and Unmaking of an Anthropological Myth* (1983), which set in motion a vigorous debate over Mead's methodology, sources, and conclusions. The rights and wrongs of this dispute make interesting reading, but the point here is that many Samoans took offense at the way they were depicted because, presumably, they found the portrait of themselves to be as unflattering and embarrassing as some foreigners found it to be wonderful.

A similar response can be expected to essays like Mucha's which, although not especially critical of American life and culture, does clearly suggest the "strangeness" of things here to this Polish visitor and ways in which European life may be preferred. Much of the essay deals with simple things such as behavior relating to hospitality; he is bemused, for example, by the custom of guests taking home leftover food and drink that they bring to parties. Elsewhere, he discusses American parochialism and other larger issues in ways that may evoke strong responses. It should be remembered, however, that just because the people being described don't like the depiction does not make that depiction wrong.

Foreigners who have written about the United States include Alexis de Tocqueville and Charles Dickens; more recently, Francis Hsu, a Chinese anthropologist, and John Ogbu, a Nigerian sociologist, have added their insights.

Ogbu is perhaps best known for his discussions of *caste* as a feature of American life—a highly provocative idea.

ANNOTATED READING: Janusz L. Mucha. "An Outsider's View of American Culture." *Distant Mirrors—America as a Foreign Culture.* Philip R. DeVita and James D. Armstrong, eds. Belmont, CA: Wadsworth, 1993: 21–28.

An Outsider's View of American Culture

It is quite difficult to look at American culture with a fresh eye. One can easily become bewildered or upset, especially if one comes from a country where America has been treated as something special. And, in my case, having an education based on American sociology, cultural anthropology, and social psychology, having read all the classics of American literature, and having watched many movies, both classic and modern, directed by both foreigners and Americans, confusion about the culture persists. Further, this being my fifth time in the United States, having lived for months in big cities like Chicago and New York, in small towns like Stevens Point, Wisconsin, and South Bend, Indiana, I have had an opportunity to view, firsthand, the diversity of American culture.

Having the experience mentioned, liking America, and being rather flexible, I see how one can easily lose the sense of novelty of first contact and view this initial contact through later experiences. Ultimately,

Different perceptions of city life have led some observers to say—perhaps facetiously—that Americans have given up on their cities and now see the shopping mall as the central expression of their culture, whereas Europeans still see cities as essential to their cultural identity. This difference seems apparent in Mucha's view, but it might also be observed that some American cities are being renewed and reborn in ways of which Mucha might approve. One example is Pittsburgh, which bears little resemblance today to its grimy image from the steelworking past. Americans might also point to many smaller cities that have character and charm and that have a vibrant social and cultural function.

The nature of this essay makes the credentials of the author particularly significant; the following biographical notes are from *Distant Mirrors.*

A frequent visitor to America, Professor Mucha compares his European idea of the "city" to what he discovered in the United States. The immediate and informal cordiality of Americans is also discussed, as is urban anonymity, the profane naturalness of violence, patriotism, education, ethnocentrism, and the American potluck dinner.

Janusz L. Mucha is professor of Sociology at Nicolaus Copernicus University, in Torun, Poland. He received an M.A. in Sociology, an M.A. in Philosophy, a Ph.D. in Humanities, and a Habilitation Degree from the Jagiellonian University of Cracow, Poland. He also studied as a postdoctoral fellow at the Johns Hopkins University; the Bologna Center in Italy; the Taras Shevchenko University in Kiev, Ukraine; the University of Wisconsin; and the University of Chicago. His primary fields of interest are urban communities of Native Americans and Polish-Americans and the symbolic anthropology of Polish society.

one too easily begins to treat everything as normal; one attempts to understand everything, perceive the causes of everything that is going on, and frame one's observations and experiences into some structural and functional context.

Nothing bewilders or upsets me in America. After all these years I still see things that are different here than they are in both my native Poland and the many other countries that I have visited. Unfortunately, these observations are neither novel nor original: They are, or at least should be, obvious to many people, foreigners and Americans alike.

I love nature, but I am a city boy. I was born and raised and had lived for forty years in Cracow, a medieval university town of a half million inhabitants in southern Poland. An urban environment is very important to me. This is something I miss in America. The idea of the "city," as I conceive it, hardly exists in America. My idea of "city" can be found in parts of three American cities: San Francisco, New York, and New Orleans. There is a noticeable lack of an urban environment in America. I do not refer here to the fact of the deserted, burned-out, or depopulated parts of cities. I have noticed many empty, run-down apartment houses that would be put to good use in Poland. What I refer to is the physical and social structure of the towns and cities of America. It is the exception in America to have the excellent public transportation found in Vienna, Paris, London, and even Warsaw. In many American cities there are not even sidewalks: The people rarely walk, so why invest in sidewalks? If one jogs, one can use the street or roadway. American drivers understand the use of the roads for exercise and, unless a driver is drunk, there's not much risk.

Not only are there no sidewalks, there are no squares where people can safely gather, meet other people, talk, or buy flowers. There are no coffee shops like in Vienna, Rome, or Budapest. If you want coffee, you must drive to McDonald's or go to a restaurant. If you walk beyond the environs of "downtown," or the shopping mall, you will most likely be stopped by a police officer who will, if you are white, offer to assist you. But how can the officer be of assistance? Can he or she give you a ride to a real cafe? Can he or she return you to the "downtown" that, after dark, is most often both unsafe and deserted? There is no such thing as a real theater, and the movie theaters are back at the shopping mall, far removed from the empty downtowns of America.

THINK ON PAPER
Many foreign visitors have commented that Americans are friendly, open, and hospitable people, but Mucha suggests that this is largely superficial. Do you have any thoughts on this? Anyone in class who has lived in or visited another country might be able to provide comparative information.

Numerous sociologists and cultural anthropologists tend to identify American urban life with anonymity, the lack of primary groups and face-to-face contact, with only superficial and formal relationships. How do I see America? I have experienced a lot of friendliness and kindness in America. Everyone wants to help me, to thank me for calling or for stopping by. Everyone seems to care about me. When I make new acquaintances, including the dental hygienist, everyone addresses me by my first name, and I can be certain that he or she will make every effort to pronounce it as correctly as possible. Very soon, I discover that I am learning many intimate details of the personal lives of the people I have just met. I find myself a bit embarrassed, but I doubt that they are. They become my friends so quickly, and as quickly they begin to share their problems with me. There are, in the English language, the nouns *colleague*, and *acquaintance*, but I do not discover them to be in popular use. In America, when one meets someone, he or she immediately becomes a *friend*. Does this mean, for instance, that you can expect to be invited to his or her home for dinner or to just sit and talk? Absolutely not. I have often been invited to dinner, but perhaps I have been fortunate in meeting a different type of American. My brother, who teaches Russian and Polish at a Texas university, had not been invited to anyone's house for dinner during the entire academic year. My American friend, who teaches history in a New England college, had not been invited to anyone's home during her first year in the small college town. Therefore, I am forced to conclude that quality friendships in the sense of lasting, intimate, emotionally involving relationships are more difficult to develop.

You might infer from Mucha's discussion of the use of first names in America that people in other societies are more formal in their manner of address. This is certainly true of European societies, where even many neighbors and colleagues at work habitually address each other as Mr. ________ or Mrs./Ms ________.

Another linguistic item involves the use of *friend* in a way that includes what people in other cultures might call an *acquaintance*. The study of the way language is actually used in social contexts in different cultures is called *sociolinguistics*, or the *ethnography of communication*. Such things are also studied in courses on cross-cultural communication.

In reference to the anonymity of urban life, as I have mentioned earlier, urban "life" hardly exists. There are neighborhoods, however, and "urban villagers" reside therein. Is this anonymity a feature of these neighborhoods? I do know, at least by the faces, everyone who lives in my own neighborhood in South Bend. If I do not recognize someone, I can tell whether that person "belongs" to my neighborhood. If a nonresident is in the neighborhood, he or she will be singled out immediately. It is possible that a patrol car will stop and a police officer will kindly ask the stranger to produce identification. A black person obviously cannot rely on anonymity in a predominantly white neighborhood. Neighborhoods do not want anonymity. The neighbors, in this instance, want to know everyone, to be able to address everyone by his or her first name, to be able to say "hello," and to ask how one is doing. And, as I've learned, they prefer the answer to be brief and positive: "I am fine, thank you."

An obvious reason for this fear of urban anonymity is the problem of security. However, the lack of anonymity does not imply that the relationships are truly friendly in the deeper sense of the word. The neighbors know each other, but they do not visit each other's homes to sit and talk, to exchange recipes, to borrow household tools, or to help if the automobile is not running. In this age of telephones, neighbors do not ordinarily just stop by unexpectedly.

American society is famous for the brutality of social life. The high rate of violent crime is incomprehensible. Rapes, female battering, child abuse, and molestation are the lead stories for local television

Mucha says that "American society is famous for the brutality of social life," (perhaps he should have said "infamous"), but many Americans are unaware of how extraordinarily high their national crime rate is when compared with European countries—especially in the area of violent crime—and of the extent to which this damages the image of their country. This and other quality of life issues are discussed in Unit Five, Section Three, of this text, but here are some statistics that provide background to Mucha's discussion:

and the print media. This information about violence has many positive consequences. If we wish to fight something, if we want to prevent crime, we must be aware of it. However, the constant forced awareness—the information on why and how someone was killed or raped—accustoms Americans to violence. They treat it as something natural, as just another case of a person killing or being killed. Violent death or abuse belongs to the profane, ordinary world of America. There is nothing sacred about it, unless it is the residual fear that it can also happen to you. On the other hand, death of natural causes is almost completely removed from everyday lives. Old people die in nursing homes or hospitals, and even this type of death, in being generally ignored, does not belong to the sphere of the sacred.

The fact of violence in everyday American life has numerous social consequences. One consequence is the decline of urban life. Americans have now accepted the fact that downtown areas, after dark, belong to the criminals or misfits. Americans accept the fact that strangers may be dangerous. Americans, thus, try to avoid downtown areas and strangers, especially at night.

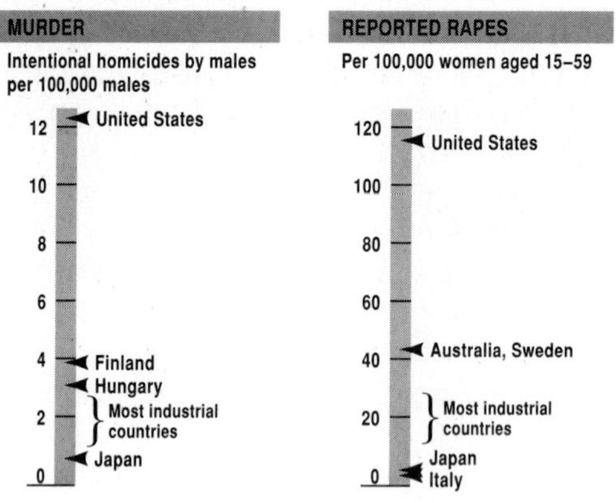

Profile of human distress in industrial countries. (Source: Human Development Report 1994.)

Mucha uses conventional **transitional sentences** and **questions** when he begins a new aspect of his discussion. This is well illustrated on this page where he uses the following:

> Patriotism is another feature of American life that appears to differ from many European countries. . . .
>
> Is there anything wrong with these public displays of patriotism? . . .
>
> What are the reasons for this general behavior and attitude? . . . .

Patriotism is another feature of American life that appears to differ from many European countries. I have been exposed to patriotism for the greatest part of my life. However, Polish patriotism, or nationalism, is different. Poland was, for forty-five years, under Communist rule, which was, to some extent, accepted, although the majority of Polish society treated it as alien domination. The Communists monopolized the use of national symbols. In the mid-1970s, the ruling party made it illegal to use these symbols without special permission by the state authorities. I can recall the unauthorized use of national symbols only within the religious context. I have never seen a Polish national flag in a private residence. Only once in my life did I see an eagle, the Polish national symbol, in a private residence. From my interpretation, the old national symbols became identified with a state that was not treated as the true embodiment of the national institutions. In America, state and nation are symbolically identified, and, moreover, nearly everyone feels the necessity to emphasize his or her identification with nation or state. I will not elaborate on the yellow ribbons in evidence during the Persian Gulf War, but it seems to me necessary to mention the presence of the American flag in most residences, offices, and clubs I have visited. Further, Lions Club lunches, university graduations, basketball games, and so on all begin with the singing of the national anthem.

Is there anything wrong with these public displays of patriotism? I do not believe so. However, the use of national symbols on an everyday basis has, in my opinion, two questionable consequences. First, the meanings of these symbols are shifting from the sacred to the profane, ordinary, everyday sphere of life. Second, the public display may indicate a strong degree of ethnocentrism. Excessive patriotism, pride in country and its achievements, may signify—and I am convinced that this is true in America—a very strong and blinding conviction that the American ways are much better than the ways of other countries and peoples. After all these years, after all these arrivals and departures, and after all these meetings with many Americans in Poland and in other countries of Europe, my impression is that American people, especially as visitors to foreign areas, are friendly but arrogant. They are arrogant in the sense that they do not understand non-American customs and habits, they do not even try to understand, and they are convinced that other customs "must" be much worse simply because they are not American. Americans are friendly in the sense that they would sympathize with other people; they would pity them and give them advice on how they should elevate themselves . . . to become more American.

What are the reasons for this general behavior and attitude? One reason is that the American educational system does not promote general knowledge about the United States and other countries. Personally, I am not of the opinion that education is the best solution to *all* social problems. Moreover, I believe that the significance of education is often exaggerated by politicians and mass media. However, American students at the grade school, middle school, and high school levels do know *much* less than students their ages outside of the United States. How can students learn more if no one demands that they learn more? I used to participate in monthly faculty meetings of the College of Liberal Arts and Sciences at a state university. Each month, a part of the agenda was a discussion of the admission policy. Should we accept candidates who cannot read, write, and calculate? Eventually, we continued to accept these deficient students . . . to a university! Their knowledge of their own country is minimal

THINK ON PAPER
Mucha's remarks on American public school education are scathing, but he is merely repeating what many experts in comparative education have said for years. As someone who is probably intimately familiar with the school system in the United States, would you agree with Mucha's assertion that Americans have "deep convictions that their ways are superior," but that this is based on knowing "little of their own country and less about other countries"? You might also review Ryan's remarks on education in Unit Four, Option One.

and inadequate. Their knowledge of other parts of the world is practically nonexistent. This may be the foundation for Americans' deep convictions that their ways are superior. They know little of their own country and less about other countries. What little they know is evidently the basis for their unquestioned views.

Another reason for the "friendly arrogance" of Americans may be their relative parochialism. The United States is so large and diverse that it is very difficult to learn much more than something of one's own state and, perhaps, neighboring states. Geographically and culturally (regions, ethnic groups), the United States is indeed so diverse that one can travel and study it for years, always learning something new and interesting. But, from my point of view of the whole of humankind, this big and diverse nation is only one relatively homogeneous spot on a map, a spot in which nearly everyone speaks the same language, can stay at the same type of hotel or motel, eat in the same type of restaurant, and shop at the same kind of supermarket. People living in Europe have a much better opportunity to appreciate the world's cultural diversity and to become much more relativistic than Americans. Europe remains a continent of natural cultural diversity, and the differences in the European educational system help in developing a relativistic attitude toward other peoples and customs. Naturally, not all Europeans take advantage of their educational opportunities, and they too often remain as rigidly ethnocentric as many educated Americans.

Notice the transitional phrase, "A third reason why the American is generally more ethnocentric than . . . ." The repetition of the theme here is a good device; it reminds the reader of the topic under discussion.

What are the other reasons referred to?

A third reason why the American is generally more ethnocentric than the average European is the nature of mass media. Reading American dailies (with perhaps the exception of the *New York Times*, *Chicago Tribune*, *Washington Post*, *USA Today*, and a few others), we get an impression that the entire world consists of some extension of the

Muchas's remarks about the parochial nature of the American media are borne out by the annual surveys of the *World Press Review.* Here are selections from their survey of the top ten stories around the world for 1994.

GEMINI NEWS SERVICE, LONDON
Daniel Nelson, Editor

1. Rwanda massacres.
2. Majority rule in South Africa.
3. China's booming economy.
4. Advances in human-gene research.
5. Yasser Arafat returns to Gaza.
6. Russia flounders and attacks Chechnya.
7. Rise of the U.S. right.
8. Uruguay round complete: World Trade Organization agreed on.
9. Violence in Algeria.
10. Soccer World Cup.

ASIAWEEK, HONG KONG
The Editors

1. Kim Il Sung's death; North Korea's nuclear accord with U.S.
2. Serbs beat the United Nations and NATO in Bosnia.
3. Global economic growth lifts interest rates, felling bond and stock markets.
4. Asia-Pacific Economic Cooperation summit sets tariff-reduction timetable for world's biggest trading area.
5. Western liberalism clashes with Asian values.
6. Unconditional renewal of China's MFN status marks a new U.S. pragmatism toward Asia.
7. Peace pact between Israel and Palestine Liberation Organization implemented.
8. South Africa elects Nelson Mandela as its first black president.
9. Genocide in Rwanda.
10. Association of Southeast Asian Nations accepts former enemy Vietnam as a member.

(Continued on next page.)

United States. In weekday editions, we rarely learn of the world beyond the Atlantic and Pacific Oceans, or even north and south of the nation's borders. In the case of an assassination of a public figure, a revolution, a minor war, or a significant natural catastrophe, we may learn something of the world beyond the borders. On a regular basis, we learn very little of other countries. I have discovered that educated people are not certain if Poles use the Latin or Cyrillic alphabet, if the Polish language is distinct from Russian, or if the Poles had their own army during the Communist regime. Even interested people are often of the opinion that Hungarians are Slavs and that Lithuanians and Latvians speak Polish or Russian. These facts are common knowledge to the people of Europe, but how could Americans know these things? Schools do not teach them, and the newspapers are more interested in a recent rape in Florida than in the economic, political, and cultural situations of their neighbors in Mexico or Canada.

American television does not help much. "Headline News" and "CNN" provide information about the rest of the world on a regular basis, but the major networks do not, unless, as we discover in the print media, there is news of a sensational nature. Local television stations inform mostly on local crimes or local economic and political happenings, such as the daily whereabouts of the president or governor. For local television, the world is further restricted, ending at the borders of the county.

Every teacher can provide many examples of the blatantly inadequate knowledge of many Americans about the world beyond the county. I offer two examples. An intelligent female student in a course, Principles of Sociology, was very active during the discussions and once volunteered to present a report based on a selection from Emile Durkheim. She came to me before the presentation and complained that it was too difficult. She had happened on a foreign word, *solidarity*. She was even unable to pronounce the word correctly. She did not understand and was curious to know why Durkheim had used the word, which was coined much later, somewhere in Eastern Europe, to describe a political movement. She could not recall the context in which she first learned of the word and, further, in her own town, there was no such thing as "solidarity."

A second example is about another intelligent female, a minority student enrolled in my course, Race and Ethnic Relations. After two weeks of the semester she came to me with a problem: How is it possible that some other students are able to answer some of my questions about racial and ethnic situations in the United States if these particular issues were not presented in the textbook? She was very sad because she knew everything about her town and actually believed that nothing was different than it was in her own social milieu.

La Nación, San José, Costa Rica
Eduardo Ulibarri, editor

1. Failure of world powers in the conflict between Bosnians and Serbs.
2. Elections and black-majority government in South Africa.
3. Uruguay round concluded in world trade talks.
4. Summit of the Americas; advances toward free trade.
5. End of Democratic Party majority in Congress.
6. Nationalist conflicts in the former Soviet Union.
7. International population conference in Cairo.
8. Advance of fundamentalists in North Africa.
9. Middle East peace process.
10. Chiapas conflict; assassination of candidate Luis Donaldo Colosio and elections in Mexico.

The Associated Press
U.S. editors/broadcast-news directors

1. O. J. Simpson.
2. U.S. elections.
3. Baseball and hockey labor troubles.
4. Susan Smith, who allegedly drowned her sons and claimed they were kidnapped.
5. Nancy Kerrigan-Tonya Harding.
6. Haiti.
7. Failed health-care reform.
8. Southern California earthquake.
9. Rwanda.
10. Palestinians replace Israeli occupiers in Gaza and Jericho.

Émile Durkheim (1858–1917) was an influential French sociologist who believed that common values hold society together. The loss of this common ground leads to social disorder and individual unhappiness. His best-known work is probably *Suicide: A Study in Sociology,* first published in 1897.

During my current visit to the United States, I have, in addition to teaching at the university, been studying a Polish community in a relatively small town. Both as a university professor and as a researcher, I participated in many parties of a more-or-less formal nature that were organized by individuals and various institutions. Nearly always, I went to these parties with my wife. Two things stand out from these gatherings. One was the way people greeted us. Sometimes we simply said hello, but most of the time we shook hands. But, by "we," I mean only myself and the host. Never that I recall, during the entire year, was my wife offered a hand in greeting or farewell. At the beginning, she was quite offended but then began to accept it as a local custom. I am certain that no one intended to offend her. Everyone was friendly to both of us. Why was she treated differently? Was it sexism? I inquired to learn if someone could explain and was told that this was a kind of custom. We do have different customs in Poland.

Another thing that surprised me was that private parties, but not formal dinner parties, were nearly always of the potluck character. The guests were expected to bring their own beverages and specialities. This does not happen in Poland. One may bring flowers (in the United States, women seemed to be deeply embarrassed when I brought them flowers) and/or a bottle of wine, vodka, or brandy. N*o one* brings food. The host would be offended. But in America, not only do people bring food but they can take the leftovers home. Many years ago, the first time I experienced this custom, I did not know what to say. I had brought a bottle of very good Polish vodka to an American friend, but it was too strong for the participants of the party. The people tasted it, perhaps out of courtesy. When I departed, the host gave me the bottle, nearly full, to take with me. For a long time I did not know if I was given a message that I had brought something bad or improper. The next time I brought a six-pack of beer and we drank all of it.

There was an additional surprise in store for me. My wife and I organized a potluck party for my departmental colleagues. One couple brought a homemade cake. Because they had to leave earlier than the other guests, they asked my wife to give them what remained of their cake. My wife was shocked. The fault was clearly mine. I forgot to tell her what to expect.

When I studied the Polish-American community, I participated in more formal dinners, as well. Some dinners were held by upper-middle-class associations of men and women. Sometimes, but rarely, these dinners were organized in restaurants. Mostly, however, dinners were served in large Polish-American clubs. Participants were dressed up: Men, mostly professionals or from the business community, were in suits; the women wore elegant dresses. The "equipment" was of a different nature. The tables were simple, the table cloths were of paper, and the plates were paper or plastic, as were the glasses. There were no separate plates for dessert. Dessert was thrown on next to the roast beef and potatoes. After dinner, the disposable plates and glasses were rolled into the table cloth and discarded. After dinner, coffee was drunk sitting at a formica table.

This is obviously an example of American efficiency and convenience. Paper table coverings and plastic plates, knives, forks, spoons, and glasses are always in evidence. Now, here in America, we have potluck lunches at work, and now my wife and I also use the products of American chemical expertise when we throw a party. The difference is that, for us, the use of the fake stuff is a problem, especially when the real stuff is so readily available. And, having noticed the dishwashing machines in most of the private houses, we are further confused.

I am led to wonder. American ingenuity, from all quarters addressed to labor-saving devices, serves to free its citizens from the tedious and time-consuming labors of everyday life. This provides free time, perhaps more free time than available in any complex, industrialized society. Why don't Americans devote a portion of this free time to learning something more about the world within and without their own provincial borders?

NOTE: *I would like to thank my wife, Maria Nawojczyk, and my brother, Waclaw Mucha, for their helpful comments with this paper.*

ASPECTS OF WRITING: Writer, reader, and text; knowing your audience.

Letters require an acute sense of audience. What you write to a boyfriend or girlfriend is likely to be quite different from what you write to your parents. This sense of audience is important in other kinds of writing, too. Some publications are known for their editorial liberalism, conservatism, or other, more specific, orientation, and writers know that their audience is likely to have certain sympathies. Statements and arguments that would be considered wildly extreme in other contexts might be guaranteed a sympathetic audience there. Readers of such publications know what they want to hear, and the writers usually give it to them.

In many situations, however, the writer does not know the audience very well and the level of the writing has to be carefully considered, taking into account a number of different factors, some of which overlap:

AGE—Does the audience consist of children, students, adults, working people, retired people?

This factor may influence word choice, sentence structure, length, complexity, and the scope of your essay. It will probably also affect your choice of allusions or references of all kinds, and the tone.

PRIOR KNOWLEDGE—What does the audience already know about my subject?

This factor will affect the level of technicality of essays where this may be relevant. It is not the job of a writer to leave his or her audience in the dust by using language and referring to information that the audience could not be expected to understand. On the other hand, explaining things that readers already know soon becomes tedious.

EXPECTATIONS—What does the audience expect?

Is the audience expecting to learn about something? To be entertained? Both? Are they interested in the topic, or in you personally? Are they expecting a serious discussion or something more lighthearted? The other side of this, of course, involves the writer's expectations. What do *you* want to achieve? Whether the expectations of the audience or the writer should take precedence depends on the circumstances, but, in college and work-related writing, the expectations of the audience may frequently have to take priority. At work, after all, the audience may well be your boss. Any surprises should be pleasant ones, where the quality—and sometimes even originality—of your work impresses the reader.

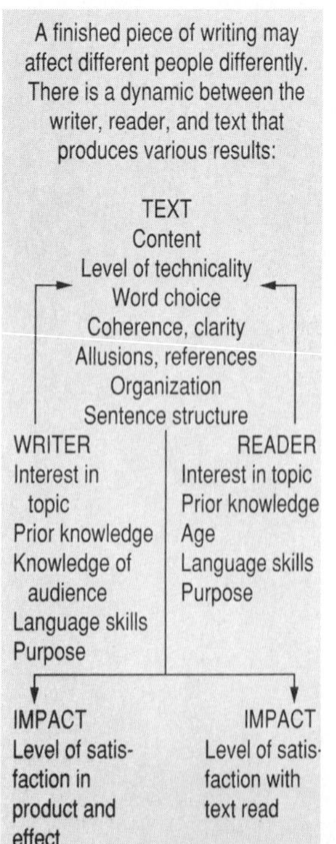

A finished piece of writing may affect different people differently. There is a dynamic between the writer, reader, and text that produces various results:
TEXT
Content
Level of technicality
Word choice
Coherence, clarity
Allusions, references
Organization
Sentence structure
WRITER
Interest in topic
Prior knowledge
Knowledge of audience
Language skills
Purpose
READER
Interest in topic
Prior knowledge
Age
Language skills
Purpose
IMPACT
Level of satisfaction in product and effect
IMPACT
Level of satisfaction with text read

WRITING EXERCISES: Answer one of the following questions.

1. Describe three of the charges Mucha makes against the American media, education, and society in general and then respond. You might, for example, include his charges that Americans are, on the whole, "parochial," "ethnocentric," and "arrogant."

> Think about the **tone** of Mucha's essay and about *the tone of your response.* What do you want to sound like?

2. Imagine that you are overseas, giving a speech to university students about American culture (or certain aspects of American culture). You may guess from Mucha's essay the kinds of things that your audience might be interested in hearing about. Write your speech, trying to be as systematic, interesting, and truthful as possible.

> A basic outline will be valuable for either of these essays. For question 1, you might respond to specific topics addressed by Mucha, such as city life, crime, patriotism, education, and the media. An outline based on such an approach might begin as follows:
>
> A. City Life
>   a. Mucha's view
>   i.
>   ii.
>   b. An American view
>   i.
>   ii.
> B. Crime
>   a. Mucha's view
>
> What kind of details would you include? The details would be important in either of the above essays.

Supporting your argument

Comparisons between cultures are often very subjective in nature, but an element of objectivity can be provided by **statistical information,** if you know where to find it. You may find the references in this text to be very useful in this regard. Your response to any of the questions on this page may benefit from reference to facts and figures of the sort provided in the annotations. When you use such information, however, make sure that you also provide information about the source.

Other kinds of support include **the detailed example** and **discussion** of the issue at hand. For example, you might comment on the widespread belief that America's rate of violent crime is connected to the availability of guns. On this subject Europeans are virtually unanimous in thinking that America's attitude is insane, but you might point out, among other things, that Americans are divided on the question of gun control and that the phrase "America's attitude" would have to be carefully defined. This might be an interesting element in a response to question 2, for you could confidently expect that your audience would be interested in this topic, and you could offer your own analysis of the situation.

SECTION THREE

PRIOR KNOWLEDGE: Different cultures and different values.

Most countries in the world have diverse populations. In Europe, immigration from former French and British colonies has created large African, Asian, and Caribbean communities, and "guest workers" from Turkey and other countries have long been settled in Germany and elsewhere. Australia and Canada receive immigrants from many parts of the world, and New Zealand has a growing population of Pacific Islanders. Malaysia has Chinese and Indian minorities, as do many other countries, such as Fiji and Trinidad. Russia and China also have large minority populations with different languages and customs. Even Japan, which is usually considered to be very homogeneous, has a growing non-Japanese population attracted by the prospect of employment in that wealthy country.

There are several references in this text, including those in Elvin Hatch's essay in this section, to the world's cultural diversity, and some of these have stressed the need to respect (within humane ethical limits, Hatch would add) the differences among us. This is hardly a new concept, especially for Americans, and yet it seems to need constant reinforcement on the domestic level, as racism and other forms of prejudice persist. Of course, prejudice and bigotry exist to some degree in all countries, and consideration of such matters should not be oversimplified into an "American" problem or a "black-white" problem. This is clear when one considers the grim examples of recent history in Bosnia, Rwanda, Sudan, and elsewhere. Wherever it exists, however, political, educational, judicial, and sometimes even military apparatus can be brought to bear in an effort to stop cruelty and ameliorate tensions between and among different cultural groups within countries.

This topic is important also in other ways, for it focuses attention on the nature of **cultural differences.** On a broad level, everyone has a lot in common. No matter who you are in the world, the fundamentals of life are much the same. The details may be different, but everyone is born, raised within a family group of some kind, acquires a language and culture within which s/he learns to operate reasonably effectively, eats, sleeps, dreams, learns, ages, and eventually dies. In the meantime, most people form families of their own, produce children, and perpetuate the cycle. Are all people, therefore, essentially the same?

Within the same and closely related cultures, this common experience of life gives a universal quality to the experience of being human and is the basis for the "universal themes" of great literature and art of all kinds. We can understand Shakespeare because his themes are utterly familiar—jealousy, foolishness, love, lust for power, and so on. It is also true, however, that cultural differences can affect the way literature is read. For an amusing example, see "Shakespeare in the Bush," which appears in Unit Nine of this text and in which the tribal elders interpret Hamlet according to their own cultural traditions and beliefs. Another example involves the great Indian epic, the *Ramayana;* many Westerners do not understand Rama's willingness to see his wife, Sita, burn on a pyre in order to prove her faithfulness during a period of captivity.

The answer is clearly "No," as is demonstrated in the following essay on India by Nemi Jain.

Jain talks about the **world view** of Hindu culture, and it is clear that this is shaped by religious and other cultural traditions that are often

Jain gives a useful definition of **"world view"**:

> . . . a set of interrelated assumptions and beliefs about the nature of reality, the organization of the universe, the purposes of human life, God, and other philosophical issues that are concerned with the concept of being.

The German word **"Weltanschauung"** (plural **Weltanschauungen**) is often used instead of the English "world view."

different from those in the Judeo-Christian West or the Islamic world. On a smaller scale, countries and cultures within any of these large groupings may have distinctive *Weltanschauungen.*

Jain's essay explains many Hindu concepts of which most Westerners have only a superficial understanding, including **reincarnation, dharma, karma,** and the **caste system.**

Beliefs such as these can shape people's world view, and this is true in the West as well as elsewhere. Consider, for example, the assertion by Edward Stewart, in his book *American Cultural Patterns: A Cross-Cultural Perspective,* that "rationality" is a central assumption of American culture; this means that everything can be explained—that there is a rational, rather than supernatural, explanation for events. This is a very different view from that which prevails in some cultures, in which it is believed that supernatural, forces influence events and human interference is futile. Stewart quotes an American aid worker in Cambodia:

> . . . people said if somebody was struck by a car, it was fate, and man had no business in interfering because the victim was being properly punished for past sins. We tried to explain . . . that auto accidents are different. They were not due to supernatural intervention, but rather to causes, to violations of laws. Now we do get policemen to give first aid.

Such stories tend to stress the difference between Western and Asian or other cultures, but we should remember that belief in fate and even astrology is not solely a foreign phenomenon.

Stewart's view that **rationality** is a core value of Americans may be challenged by polls that suggest widespread belief in **"fate"** and other supernatural influences. An informal poll in class may produce some interesting results.

THINK ON PAPER

While acknowledging that it is human to be inconsistent, it seems difficult to reconcile the widespread American belief in "fate" with the equally widespread belief in the efficacy of individual effort and hard work. Which of these do you think is the more powerful shaper of Americans' world view?

In many parts of the world cultural diversity seems threatened, even as most countries, paradoxically, become more diverse. The threat has two aspects: first, small indigenous groups in the Americas, Australasia, and elsewhere are under severe pressure, as described in Maxwell's essay on the Amazon (Unit Six, Section One). Linguists report a steep decline in the total number of languages spoken in the world. Second, some people worry that cultural diversity around the world will suffocate under the onslaught of Western commercialism and popular culture. James Goldsmith (Unit Six, Section Three) is one of several people who touch on this question in this text.

ANNOTATED READING: Nemi C. Jain. "World View and Cultural Patterns of India." *Intercultural Communication, A Reader.* 6th ed. Larry Samovar and Richard Porter, eds. Belmont, CA: Wadsworth, 1991: 78–86.

World View and Cultural Patterns of India

If I were asked under what sky the human mind . . . has most deeply pondered over the greatest problems of life, and has found solutions of some of them which well deserve the attention even of those who have studied Plato and Kant—I should point to India. And if I were to ask myself from what literature we . . . who have been nurtured almost exclusively on the thoughts of Greeks and Romans, and of one Semitic race, the Jewish, may draw the corrective which is most wanted in order to make our inner life more perfect, more comprehensive, more universal, in fact more truly human a life, not for this life only, but a transfigured and eternal life—again I should point to India.

—Max Muller[1]

For more than 3,000 years, the peoples of the Indian subcontinent have been seeking the deepest truths about the nature of reality and the self, exploring the depths of human consciousness. India's most brilliant thinkers have been preoccupied with the quest for perfection, for a way to transform this ordinary, limited, and imperfect human life into its potential greatness. Their insights and discoveries have shaped one of the world's richest and most long-lived cultures.[2]

Indian culture has a continuous history that extends over 5,000 years. Very early, India evolved a distinctive culture and religion, Hinduism, which was modified and adjusted as it came into contact with outside elements. In general, Hinduism is an amorphous body of beliefs, philosophies, worship practices, and codes of conduct. It is hard to define Hinduism or to say precisely whether it is a religion or not in the usual sense of the word. In its present form it embraces many beliefs and practices, as it did in the past, often opposed to and contradicting each other. Its essential spirit seems to be "live and let live." The very nature of Hinduism leads to a greater tolerance of other

As Jain notes, India has one of the world's most ancient civilizations, dating back over 5,000 years. Although this article is about **Hindu** traditions and beliefs, India also has a large **Moslem** population (about 80 million) and significant **Christian, Sikh,** and other religious minorities. **Buddhism** was founded in India by Gautama Buddha approximately 2,500 years ago and spread from there to other parts of Asia.

Professor Jain teaches in the Department of Communication and is a Research Fellow in the Center for Asian Studies at Arizona State University.

religions among its adherents, as they tend to believe that the highest divine powers complement each other for the well-being of humanity and the world. The qualities of resilience, absorption, and respect for alternative ways of reaching the same goals are perhaps the major characteristics that have generated vitality in Hinduism for millennia. In spirit, Indian culture has maintained the essential unity of the indigenous doctrines and ideas of Hinduism, which has enabled it to withstand many vicissitudes and to continue to mold the lives of millions of people in India and abroad.[3]

Like any other culture, the Indian culture is complex and consists of many interrelated beliefs, values, norms, social systems, and material cultural items. It has a world view comprising existential postulates that deal with the nature of reality, the organization of the universe, and the ends and purposes of human life. In spite of the multiethnic, multilingual, and highly stratified nature of contemporary Indian society, India is united by a set of cultural patterns that are widely shared among the Hindus, who comprise about 80 percent of India's population of over 850 million. The major aim of this article is to outline the Indian world view and some of the basic cultural patterns that have persisted over the thousands of years of Indian history, patterns that influence many aspects of Indian social institutions and affect the communication and thought patterns of millions of Hindus in India and abroad. More specifically, this article will describe briefly the following aspects of Indian culture: (1) world view, (2) reincarnation, (3) *dharma*, (4) stages of life, (5) the caste system, and (6) the spirit of tolerance.

Jain provides a brief but useful **orientation** to India and Hinduism before explicitly stating the writer's intention: "The major aim of this article is . . . ." The **statement of purpose** is equivalent to the **thesis;** it is most commonly used in technical writing but works well here.

Each of these cultural patterns includes several specific assumptions, beliefs, values, and norms that are closely interrelated and represents a continuum; within the same culture, variations of the pattern normally occur. Contradictions among cultural patterns are probably universal throughout societies, but, despite internal variations and contradictions, there is an overall integration to the patterns of Hindu Indian culture. It is possible to simplify its description by isolating the various cultural patterns and considering them one at a time.

Jain's point is important here—no cultural system is completely without paradox and contradiction; beliefs and behavior vary, but generalizations are usually possible.

WORLD VIEW

World view refers to a set of interrelated assumptions and beliefs about the nature of reality, the organization of the universe, the purposes of human life, God, and other philosophical issues that are concerned with the concept of being. In short, our world view helps us locate our place and rank in the universe.[4] A culture's world view includes both implicit and explicit assumptions underlying the values, norms, myths, and behavior of its people.

Indian world view is very complex. India's great sages and philosophers for the last several thousand years have sought to understand the deepest level of reality and to satisfy the deep human longing for spiritual fulfillment. They were impressed with our capacity for thought, feeling, imagination, and action, and with the ability to enter creatively into the shaping of our own humanness. They sought a link between the dynamic energy of reality in its deepest levels and the ground of human existence. This quest generated the basic Indian wisdom that the fundamental energizing power of the cosmos and the spiritual energy of human beings are one and the same.

At the deepest levels of our existence, we share in the very energies and powers that create and structure the universe itself. Because of our participation in the ultimate energy and power of reality, it is possible to transform our superficial, suffering, and limited existence into a free and boundless one in which life is experienced at its deepest and most profound level. This spiritual transformation has constituted the ultimate aim in life for most of the Indian people over the ages.[5]

The Indian world view has been shaped by this underlying belief of participation in the ultimate reality and the aim of spiritual transformation of human existence. We need to explore the origins and development of this world view in order to understand it fully and to understand its influence on other cultural patterns of India. Indian world view involves at least seven sets of assumptions, beliefs, and concepts: (1) undivided wholeness, (2) levels of reality, (3) the normative dimension of existence, (4) the boundlessness of ultimate reality, (5) the profundity of existence, (6) gods and goddesses as limited symbols of the ultimate reality, and (7) the limitations of ordinary means of knowledge.[6]

Undivided Wholeness

Jain continues the pattern here of telling the reader exactly what is coming. This is a common **pedagogic,** or **teaching,** device, and Jain is clearly teaching the reader about Hindu beliefs. Most writers indicate to the reader what is coming, but not necessarily quite so explicitly. For a discussion of the **thesis,** see Unit One, Section Two.

According to Hinduism, the world of distinct and separate objects and processes is a manifestation of a more fundamental reality that is undivided and unconditioned. This undivided wholeness constituting the ultimate level of reality is called by various names: *Brahman*, *Ātman*, *Puruṣa*, *Jīva*, Lord, and so on. What is especially important about this belief is that the ultimate reality is not seen as separate, apart from ordinary things and events, but as the inner being and ground of everyday existence. This belief, developed initially in the Vedas and Upaniṣads, became an integral part of Hinduism, Jainism, Buddhism, and Yoga systems.[7]

Levels of Reality

Within the undivided wholeness or the totality of existence, there are various levels of reality or orders of being. These range from nonexistence to empirical existence limited by space and time, to consciousness limited only by the conditions of awareness, to an indescribable level that is beyond all conditions and limits whatever. The deeper the level of reality, the more fully it participates in the truth of being and the greater its value.[8] One of the clearest examples of the tendency to distinguish between levels of reality occurs in the Taittirīya Upaniṣad, where five different levels of reality comprising the "Self" are identified:

> *At the lowest level the Self is material and is identified with food. At the next level the Self is identified with life: "Different from and within that which consists of the essence of food is the Self consisting of life." Identifying a still higher level of reality, the text goes on to say, "Different from and within that which consists of the essence of life is the Self which consists of mind (rudimentary forms of awareness that humans share with other animals)." Next, a fourth level of reality is recognized. Here is a still deeper source of consciousness and existence: the Self said to be of the nature of understanding* (vijnana). *Finally, Self is identified with joy as the fifth and ultimate level of reality. Joy* (ānanda) *or bliss is regarded as the root or source of all existence, the foundation of higher consciousness, lower consciousness, life, and matter.*[9]

The Normative Dimension of Existence

The deepest level of reality, which grounds all the other levels, is normative. It poses an "ought" for life that stems from the heart of existence. According to Hinduism, norms for right living are an integral part of the fabric of existence—they are not derived from human reason and are not imposed on life from the outside. The foundation of these norms is much deeper than reason; it emanates from the very nature and expression of reality at its deepest level. Human reason only interprets and applies the norms of true or right living. This is why in India it is generally recognized that a person who is true to the inner norms of existence has incredible power.

In the West, norms for human behavior are usually conceived as rationally derived to fulfill human needs and aspirations. In India, on the other hand, human existence is regarded as a manifestation and expression of a deeper reality, which constitutes its ground and measure. The fundamental norm of the universe (*rta*) is the orderly coursing of this deeper reality in its central being. Moral and social rules are partial expressions of this highest norm. The normative dimensions of the interconnected reality refer to the Hindu concept of *dharma* which will be discussed later in this article.[10]

The Boundlessness of Ultimate Reality

At the deepest level, existence is boundless. There are no limits and all possibilities may coexist without excluding or compromising each other. Time is endless, space is endless, the number of gods and goddesses is endless, and so on. Indian mythology especially celebrates the idea that opposites exist together, enriching each other, with all of their differences arising simultaneously in a totally unrestricted universe of infinite freedom and richness.[11]

The Profundity of Existence

The profundity of reality at the ultimate level is such that reason is incapable of apprehending it. Human reason is an effective faculty for guiding our investigations of the empirical world and for understanding the rules of our practical and theoretical activities. But since reason operates by differentiating and comparing, it is incapable of comprehending the deepest dimensions of reality that are beyond all divisions and differences. This sense of the profundity of reality underlies Indian mysticism and encourages the emphasis upon meditation and Yoga systems.[12]

Gods and Goddesses as Limited Symbols of the Ultimate Reality

Hinduism differs from Christianity, Judaism, and Islam in being **pantheistic** rather than **monotheistic.** Jain points out, however, that the many gods and goddesses of Hinduism can be seen as "symbols of the ultimate reality."

Indian gods and goddesses, from Vedic times to the present, are usually viewed as symbols of the ultimate reality rather than the ultimate reality itself. The ultimate level of reality is undivided; it has no form and no name. What can be given a name and form is not the ultimate. As symbols, gods and goddesses participate partially in the higher reality that they symbolize, pointing to the fullness of that reality. No number of symbols can exhaust the fullness of the ultimate, so there is no limit to the number of gods. This is why a Hindu can say in the same breath that there are millions of gods, only one god, and no gods, for the last two statements mean, respectively, that all gods symbolize the one ultimate reality and that this reality cannot be captured entirely by a symbol. But that a deity is not the ultimate reality does not mean that it is unreal. On the contrary, because the deity as symbol participates in the deeper levels of reality, its reality is greater than that of our ordinary existence. By identifying with the deity in love and through rituals, the power of this deeper level of reality becomes available for a spiritual transformation of life. It is this perspective of deity that underlies Hindu theism and devotionalism.[13]

The Limitations of Ordinary Means of Knowledge

Hindus believe that ordinary means of acquiring knowledge—human senses, human reason, and empirical methods—cannot penetrate the profound and undivided ultimate level of reality. For this reason they put great emphasis on developing extraordinary means. Through concentration and meditation, direct insight into the true nature of reality at its most profound level becomes possible. The limitations of knowledge mediated through sensory and conceptual filters are overcome in this direct and immediate knowledge through transempirical and transrational insight.[14]

REINCARNATION

In Hinduism, the Supreme Being is the impersonal *Brahman*, the ultimate level of reality, a philosophical absolute, serenely blissful, beyond all limitations either ethical or metaphysical. The basic Hindu view of God involves infinite being, infinite consciousness, and infinite bliss. *Brahman* is also conceived of as the Supreme Soul of the universe. Every living soul is a part, a particular manifestation, of the *Brahman*. These individual souls seem to change from generation to generation, but actually only the unimportant, outer details change—a body, a face, a name, a different condition or status in life. The *Brahman*, however, veiled behind these deceptive "realities," is continuous and indestructible. This hidden self or *ātman* is a reservoir of being that never dies, is never exhausted, and is without limit in awareness and bliss. *Ātman*, the ultimate level of reality at the individual level, is the infinite center of every life. Body, personality, and *ātman* together make up a human being.[15]

The old, pantheistic religions of the Europe, Egypt, and the Middle East faded during the Roman period, to be replaced by various religions with one God. The Emperor Constantine effectively made Christianity the official religion of the Roman Empire early in the fourth century. *The World Almanac* (a good source of reference information) notes that Judaism was "the only ancient religion west of India to survive."

The eternal *ātman* is usually buried under the almost impenetrable mass of distractions, false ideas, illusions, and self-regarding impulses that compose one's surface being. Life is ordinarily lived at a relatively superficial level, a level at which the ultimate reality is experienced only in fragmented and limited forms. These fragmented and partial forms of existence are actually forms of bondage, restricting access to the full power or energy of life flowing from the deepest level of reality. The aim of life is to cleanse the dross from one's being to the point where its infinite center, the eternal *ātman*, will be fully manifest.

The Hindu belief in reincarnation affirms that individual souls enter the world and pass through a sequence of bodies or life cycles. On the subhuman level, the passage is through a series of increasingly complex bodies until at last a human one is attained. Up to this point, the soul's growth is virtually automatic. With the soul's graduation into a human body, this automatic, escalator mode of ascent comes to an end. The soul's assignment to this exalted habitation is evidence that it has reached self-consciousness, and with this estate comes freedom, responsibility, and effort. Now the individual soul, as a human being, is fully responsible for its behavior through the doctrine of *karma*—the moral law of cause and effect. The present condition of each individual life is a product of what one did in the previous life; and one's present acts, thoughts, and decisions determine one's future states.[16]

Some people see a contrast between Hinduism and other religions in the emphasis of the former on **behavior** rather than **belief** or **faith.** As Jain notes, "one's present acts, thoughts, and decisions determine one's future states."

This concept of *karma* and the completely moral universe it implies carries two important psychological corollaries. First, it commits the Hindu who understands it to complete personal responsibility. Each individual is wholly responsible for his or her present condition and will have exactly the future he or she is now creating. Conversely, the idea of a moral universe closes the door to all appeals to chance or accident: In this world there is no chance or accident. *Karma* decrees that every decision must have its determinate consequences, but the decisions themselves are, in the last analysis, freely arrived at. Or, to approach the matter from the other direction, the consequences of a person's past decisions condition his or her present lot, as a card player is dealt a particular hand but is left free to play that hand in a number of ways. This means that the general conditions of life—rank, station, position—are predetermined by one's past *karma*. However, individual humans as carriers of a soul are free throughout their life span to make choices and to determine actions independently of the soul.[17]

According to Hinduism, the aim of life is to free oneself progressively from the exclusive identification with the lower levels of the self in order to realize the most profound level of existence. Since at this deepest level the self is identical with ultimate reality—the *Brahman*—once this identity has been realized there is nothing that can defeat or destroy the self. Thus, the soul puts an end to the process of reincarnation and merges with the *Brahman*, from whence it originated in the first place. This state for an individual soul is called *moksha* or *nirvana*.

"**Nirvana**" is a familiar word in English, but is most often associated with Buddhism. The word comes from **Sanskrit,** the classical language of ancient India. In the 18th century, Sir William Jones, a British judge in India, reported many similarities between Sanskrit and ancient Greek and Latin (for example, L. *pater, mater* = Skt. *pitar, matar* = English "father," "mother." Jones suggested that these ancient languages shared a common ancestor—**Indo-European.** Linguists now believe that about one-third of all languages are derived from this Indo-European source.

DHARMA

The concept of *dharma* is another unique feature of Hinduism and Indian culture. *Dharma* refers to a code of conduct that guides the life of a person both as an individual and as a member of society. It is the law of right living, the observance of which secures the double objectives of happiness on earth and salvation. The life of a Hindu is regulated in a very detailed manner by the laws of *dharma*. Personal habits, social and family ties, fasts and feasts, religious rituals, obligations of justice and morality, and even rules of personal hygiene and food preparation are all conditioned by it.

Dharma is the binding law that accounts for the cohesion in the Hindu society throughout the history of India. Since *dharma* is a social value with a strong sense of morality, harmony is achieved when everyone follows his or her *dharma*. It is not subjective in the sense that the conscience of the individual imposes it, nor external in the sense that the law enforces it. It is the system of conduct that the general opinion, conscience, or spirit of the people supports. *Dharma* does not force people into virtue but trains them for it. It is not a fixed code of mechanical rules but a living spirit that grows and moves in response to the development of the society.[18]

Dharma is only one of the four aims of human life, which according to the classical Indian philosophy, have constituted the basis for Indian values. The other three are wealth (*artha*), enjoyment (*kāma*), and liberation (*moksha*). The pursuit of wealth and enjoyment is regulated by *dharma*. Although much of the Western world regards Indians as having deliberately chosen poverty as a way of life, this is not true. The *Panctantra*, a popular collection of Indian wisdom, puts it this way: "The smell of wealth (*artha*) is quite enough to wake a creature's sterner stuff. And wealth's enjoyment even more. Wealth gives constant vigour, confidence and power. Poverty is a curse worse than death. Virtue without wealth is of no consequence. The lack of money is the root of all evil."[19]

THINK ON PAPER
Jain notes that good conduct, wealth, enjoyment, and liberation are basic Hindu values. What are the basic values in other religions familiar to you?

Hinduism also recognizes the importance of enjoyment or *kāma* in human life. The concept of *kāma* is used in two ways in the Indian literature. In the narrower sense, *kāma* is sexual desire or love, symbolized by Kāma, the love god. *Kāma Sutra*, along with a number of other texts, is devoted to *kāma* in this sense, providing instruction on how to obtain the greatest sexual pleasures. As a basic human aim, *kāma* goes beyond this narrower sense of sexual enjoyment to include all forms of enjoyment, including the enjoyment of fame, fortune, and power. Again, the common stereotype that presents the Indian people as so single-mindedly intent on pursuing religious salvation that there is no room for laughter, fun, or games gives us a false picture. Traditionally and currently, stories, games, festivals, and parties filled with music, laughter, and fun are highly prized by most of the people. As a recognized basic aim in life, *kāma* legitimizes the human need for enjoyment; it recognizes that not only are wealth and various goods necessary for life but they are to be enjoyed in life as a way of fulfilling human nature. As in the case of *artha* or wealth, however, only those activities aiming at *kāma* that are in accord with *dharma* are allowed. Enjoyment at the pain and expense of other creatures or persons is not allowed. Sexual activity is to be restricted to one's spouse; drugs and intoxicating beverages are regarded as wrong and sinful because of the injury they do.[20]

The fourth aim, that of *moksha* or liberation, has priority over the other three (*artha*, *kāma*, and *dharma*). It is the aim of *moksha* that guides one's efforts to realize identity with the ultimate reality. But *moksha* does not repudiate the other aims; indeed, it calls for fulfilling these aims as a preparation for achieving complete freedom and fulfillment. Even when the distinction between worldly and spiritual existence becomes prominent, there is a tendency to see the distinction in terms of higher and lower levels of the same reality rather than to postulate two different and opposed realities.[21]

D*harma* has two sides that are interdependent: the individual and the social. The conscience of the individual requires a guide, and one must be taught the way to realize one's aims of life and to live according to spirit and not sense. The interests of society require equal attention. D*harma*, on the social level, is that which holds together all living beings in a harmonious order. Virtue is conduct contributing to social welfare, and vice is the opposite. D*harma* is usually classified according to the requirements of one's position in society and stage in life, for these represent the main factors of time, place, and circumstance that determine one's own specific *dharma*. Thus, *varna dharma* refers to the duties attending one's caste or social class and position; for example, studying, teaching, and preaching are the primary duties of B*rahmins*. Ā*shrama dharma* refers to the duties attending one's particular stage in life. For example, the householder stage requires marriage, raising a family, producing the goods necessary for society according to one's occupation, giving to those in need, and serving the social and political needs of the community. For a fuller understanding of *dharma* appropriate for different stages of life, we need to examine the Indian concept of stages of life. Also, we need to understand the caste system, which influences *dharma* and other social norms.

Hinduism also recognizes a *universal dharma* that applies to a person regardless of caste, social class, or stage in life. For example, telling the truth, avoiding unnecessary injury to others, not cheating, and so on are common *dharmas* that all human beings share. There are some *dharmas* that are determined by particular circumstances and therefore cannot be identified in advance. But the rule for determining the specific requirements of action in unusual and unpredictable situations is that the higher dharmas and values should always prevail. Noninjury and compassion are basic moral principles in deciding cases of conflicting moral duties, and one must never engage in behavior that is detrimental to spiritual progress.[22]

STAGES OF LIFE [ASRAMAS]

The concept of *dharma* at the individual level recognizes four stages in each person's life: (1) *brahmacharya* or student stage, (2) *grahastha* or householder stage, (3) *vānaprastha* or retirement stage, and (4) *saimyās* or renunciation stage. In the first stage of *brahmacharya*, a child learns the requirements of *dharma* early in life and develops the appropriate attitudes and character that will allow him to consistently do his *dharma* for the rest of his life. At this student stage, the obligations of temperance, sobriety, chastity, and social service are firmly established in the minds of the young. All have to pass through this discipline, irrespective of caste, class, wealth, or poverty.

The second stage, beginning with marriage, is that of the householder or *grahastha*. At this stage, the individual normally undertakes the obligations of family life, becoming a member of a social body and accepting its rights and requirements. Self-support, thrift, and hospitality are enjoined, and the individual's energies and interests turn naturally outward. There are three fronts for fulfilling human aims—one's family, one's vocation, and the community to which one belongs—and normally the person will be interested in all three. This is the time for satisfying the first three human aims: wealth or *artha* through vocation, enjoyment or *kāma* primarily through the family, and *dharma* through one's responsibilities as a citizen.[23]

In the third stage of *vānaprastha* or retirement, the individual is required to control his or her attachment to worldly possessions. This stage begins when the duties of the householder stage have been fulfilled. At this stage, one needs to suppress all the conceits that entered through the accidents of the second stage (such as pride of birth or property, individual genius, wealth, fame, or good luck) and cultivate a spirit of renunciation. It is the time for working out a philosophy for oneself, the time of transcending the senses to find and dwell at one with the timeless reality that underlies the dream of life in this world.[24] This period of "retirement" from social life is one of asceticism aimed at achieving the self-control and spiritual strength needed to attain *moksha*. Honored and respected by nearly everyone, these "retired persons" or "forest dwellers" are sometimes sought out for their wise counsel, and therefore they constitute a vital part of the society.

The fourth stage, that of *sannyāsa* or renunciation, is one of complete renunciation of worldly objects and desires. At this stage, a person is a disinterested servant of humanity who finds peace in the strength of spirit. A *sannyāsin* lives identified with the eternal self and beholds nothing else. "He no more cares whether his body falls or remains, than does a cow what becomes of the garland that someone has hung around her neck; for the faculties of his mind are now at rest in the Holy Power, the essence of bliss."[25] At this final stage of life, one attempts to fulfill the ultimate aim of human life, *moksha* or liberation.

The concept of life stages (*āsramas*) and the basic human aims to be fulfilled at different stages embody the recognition that biological,

THINK ON PAPER
What **"stages of life"** are recognized in American culture?

economic, and social needs are legitimate and must be fulfilled in order to go beyond them. But it is also recognized in Indian philosophy that because of the deeper nature of human existence, the thirst for freedom and fulfillment cannot be satisfied by pursuing the lower needs of life. Their acquisition only increases the thirst for more and more of these material goods.

THE CASTE SYSTEM

As in many countries, there is a cultural gap between rural and urban India. Jain notes the weakening influence of **caste** in urban India today, partly as a result of antidiscrimination laws.

The caste system is a unique feature of Indian culture. No Indian social institution has attracted as much of the attention of foreign observers, nor has any other Indian institution been so grossly misunderstood, misrepresented, and maligned. Even the word *caste*, which is derived from the Portuguese *casta* (color), is a misnomer connoting some specious notion of color difference as the foundation of the system. It is a curious fact of intellectual history that caste has figured so prominently in Western thought.

The caste system began in India about 3,000 years ago. During the second millennium B.C., a host of Aryans possessing a different language and culture and different physical features (tall, fair-skinned, blue-eyed, straight-haired) migrated into India. The clash of differences that followed eventually established the caste system because the Aryans took for themselves the kinds of work thought to be most desirable: They became the rulers, the religious leaders, the teachers, and the traders. The other people were forced to become servants for the Aryans or to do less pleasing kinds of work. The outcome of this social classification and differentiation was a society clearly divided into four castes, hierarchically, from higher to lower:

Rhetorical note: Jain's essay is clearly **informative** in nature, and the organizational principle at work here is **division.** The Hindu world view is divided up into different categories and each, in turn, is **defined** and **described.**

1. *Brahmins*—seers or priests who perform such duties as teaching, preaching, assisting in the sacrificial processes, giving alms, and receiving gifts
2. *Kashtryās*—administrators and rulers responsible for protecting life and treasures
3. *Vaisyās*—traders, businesspeople, farmers, and herders
4. *Sūdras*—artisans such as carpenters, blacksmiths, and laborers.

In the course of time, a fifth group developed that was ranked so low as to be considered outside and beneath the caste system itself. The members of this fifth "casteless" group are variously referred to as "untouchables," "outcastes," "scheduled castes," or (by Mahatma Gandhi) *Harijans*—"children of God." People in this group inherit the kinds of work that in India are considered least desirable, such as scavenging, slaughtering animals, leather tanning, and sweeping the streets.[26]

The caste system began as a straightforward, functional division of Indian society. It was later misinterpreted by priests as permanent and immutable as the word of God. Accordingly, the caste system was justified in terms of the "immutable and inborn" qualities of individuals, the unchangeable result of "actions in previous incarnations," and the unalterable basis of Hindu religion.

The caste system applies only to the Hindu segment of the Indian society. The particular caste a person belongs to is determined by birth—one is born into the caste of his or her parents. Each caste has its appropriate status, rights, duties, and *dharma*. There are detailed rules about communication and contact among people of different castes. A caste has considerable influence on the way of life of its members; most important relationships of life, above all marriage, usually take place within the caste.

After India's independence in 1947, discrimination based on caste has been outlawed. In urban areas it is common for persons to cross caste lines in choosing their occupations, and intercaste marriages are also becoming quite popular. In rural areas, however, caste still is a major influence in one's life.

Gandhi was one of the principal leaders (with Jawaharlal **Nehru** and others) of the Indian independence movement. After qualifying as a lawyer in England, he worked for the rights of the Indian community in South Africa. Upon his return to India, he became famous as a spiritual and political leader and as an advocate and organizer of **nonviolent resistance,** a technique later imitated in the United States by **Martin Luther King, Jr.** Gandhi was assassinated by a Hindu fanatic in 1948.

THE SPIRIT OF TOLERANCE

An outstanding feature of Indian culture is its tradition of tolerance. According to Hinduism, the reality or existence at the deepest level is boundless. No description, formula, or symbol can adequately convey the entire truth about anything. Each perspective provides a partial glimpse of reality, but none provides a complete view. Different partial—even opposing—viewpoints are regarded as complementing each other, each contributing something to a fuller understanding of reality.

Traditionally, Indian thinkers have been willing to adopt new perspectives and new positions, without, however, abandoning old positions and perspectives. The new is simply added to the old, providing another dimension to one's knowledge. The new dimension may render the old less dominant or important, but it does not require the latter's rejection. The traditional storehouse of Indian ideas is like a four-thousand-year-old attic to which things were added every year but which were never once cleaned out.[27]

Indian culture believes in universal tolerance and accepts all religions as true. It is believed that the highest truth is too profound to allow anyone to get an exclusive grasp on it. When no beliefs can be said to be absolutely true, no beliefs can be declared absolutely false.

Indian culture is comprehensive and suits the needs of everyone, irrespective of caste, creed, color, or sex—it has universal appeal and makes room for all.

India's spirit of tolerance has been developed in the Jaina theory of *syādvāda*, the theory of "may be." According to this theory, no absolute affirmation or denial is possible. As all knowledge is probable and relative, the other person's point of view is as true as one's own. In other words, one must show restraint in making judgments—a very healthy principle. One must know that one's judgments are only partially true and can by no means be regarded as true in absolute terms. This understanding and spirit of tolerance have contributed to the advancement of Indian culture, helping to bring together the divergent groups with different languages and religious persuasions under a common culture.[28]

In summary, this article has discussed six basic cultural patterns of India: world view, reincarnation, *dharma*, stages of life, the caste system, and the spirit of tolerance. These are integral parts of Hinduism and Indian culture, and they have a significant influence on the personality, values, beliefs, attitudes, and communication behavior of Hindus in India and abroad. An understanding of Indian world view and cultural patterns, and of the influence of these cultural patterns on communication behavior, will improve the quality of intercultural communication between people of India and other cultures.

NOTES

1. Cited from Huston Smith. (1958). *The Religions of Man*. New York: Harper & Row, p. 13.
2. John M. Koller. *The Indian Way*. (1982). New York: Macmillan, p. v.
3. H. V. Sreenivasa Murthy and S. U. Kamath. (1973). *Studies in Indian Culture*. Bombay: Asia Publishing House, pp. 4–5.
4. Larry A. Samovar, Richard E. Porter, and Nemi C. Jain. (1981). *Understanding Intercultural Communication*. Belmont, Calif.: Wadsworth, p. 46.
5. Koller, p. 6.
6. Koller, p. 6. This entire description of Indian world view has drawn heavily on Koller's account.
7. Koller, p. 6.
8. Koller, p. 6 and pp. 101–102.
9. Cited from Koller, p. 101.
10. Koller, p. 7 and pp. 62–63.
11. Koller, p. 7.
12. Koller, p. 7.
13. Koller, pp. 7–8 and pp. 212–255.
14. Paul Hiebert. (1983). "Indian and American World Views: A Study in Contrasts," in

Giri Raj Gupta (Ed.) *Religion in Modern India*. New Delhi: Vikas Publishing House, pp. 399–414.

15. Smith, pp. 24–25.
16. Smith, pp. 67–68.
17. Smith, pp. 68–69.
18. S. Radhakrishnan. (1979). *Indian Religions*. New Delhi: Vision Books, pp. 61–62.
19. Koller, p. 65.
20. Koller, pp. 65–66.
21. Koller, pp. 66–69.
22. Koller, p. 62.
23. Smith, pp. 55–56.
24. Smith, pp. 57–58.
25. Smith, p. 59.
26. S. N. Chopra. (1977). *India: An Area Study*. New Delhi: Vikas Publishing House, pp. 27–29.
27. Koller, pp. 8–9.
28. Murthy and Kamath, p. 5.

ASPECTS OF WRITING: Responding to a text: generalizing and applying.

Reading on a sophisticated level involves being able to understand and think about the text on more than the literal level. Jain's essay is about the Indian (more specifically, the Hindu) world view and culture, but we should consider what else is suggested by the essay. If Indians have a describable world view, can the same be said about other people around the world? Is there an American world view, and, if so, what is it? Being able to generalize from a text and apply its ideas to different contexts enriches both your reading and your writing.

We don't usually think very much about our own culture. It's like the air around us, or the water around a fish; it's there but we (and the fish, presumably) are hardly ever conscious of it. It's all-pervasive and so "normal" to us that we don't even recognize its existence until we come into contact with people from other cultures or until something happens that forces us to think about ourselves as a nation or culture. It is difficult to be objective about one's own culture, but one attempt—Edward Stewart's—is summarized in the column opposite.

In *American Cultural Patterns: A Cross-Cultural Perspective*, published in 1972, Edward Stewart suggests that American culture emphasizes the following:

- Individual responsibility for one's actions and decisions
- Majority rule
- Rationality (everything is at least potentially explicable in a mechanistic world)
- Effort-optimism (hard work will eventually be rewarded)
- Future orientation
- Competition
- Measurable achievement (measure success by concrete achievements rather than—for example—personal relations)

We might generalize from Jain's essay by saying that **people within any given culture share, at least in general terms, a world view.** This world view reflects notions of (to borrow Jain's definition again) "the organization of the universe, the purposes of life, God, and other philosophical issues . . . concerned with the concept of being." Do we think of the universe in mechanistic terms, as something inherently comprehensible even if we don't yet have all the answers, or as something inherently mysterious and beyond human knowledge? Do we think of humans as having a special significance on Earth, or as one form of life among many? Do we believe that we have a responsibility to the Earth and other living things, or only to ourselves? Do we value only our personal happiness, or do we value the happiness of others, including the community as a whole? How does a world view change? The list goes on.

Jain's essay, then, is about India, but it opens up many other discussions about different cultures, including your own. One of the values of comparative studies is that they make us think more about what we believe, how we behave, and other aspects of our culture.

THINK ON PAPER

What are the implications for our notion of individuality if most of us share the same world view because we learned to think that way as we grew up in our culture?

WRITING EXERCISES: Answer one of the following questions.

1. Identify one or two aspects of Jain's account of Indian culture, describe them, and compare them with equivalent aspects of American culture (or another culture familiar to you). For example, you might choose stages of life, reincarnation, or caste.
2. Jain's account of the Hindu stages of life seems to present the "ideal" rather than the "real" culture, as discussed in Section One of this unit. Describe an aspect of American (or any other) culture in its "ideal" and "real" forms. You might begin by introducing the concepts involved and conclude with a brief, generalized comment on the value of having an ideal even if we don't usually live up to it.
3. Imagine yourself discussing American culture with a foreigner unfamiliar with American ways of thinking and behaving. In a systematic fashion, describe a few of what you consider to be the most significant and characteristic features of the culture.

Some people are used to writing very short essays in which one section = one paragraph. In more elaborate writing, each section may have several aspects, each requiring one or more paragraphs. Think about paragraphing and try to use effective transitions between paragraphs in order to provide something logical and coherent for your reader.

Each section of Jain's essay is given a **heading.** You will not usually do this, but each section should be **clearly focused** in this same way. This focus—or **unity**—is important at each level, as shown below:

UNITY OF ESSAY
controlled by thesis or statement of purpose

UNITY OF SECTION
controlled by introductory, transitional remarks

UNITY OF PARAGRAPH(S)
controlled by topic sentence

UNITY OF SECTION

UNITY OF PARAGRAPH(S)

With some variation, Jain's essay follows the pattern shown above, using different size fonts for each level of organization. *Even if you don't use headings and subheadings, your essay should be clearly and systematically organized.*

Title: World View and Cultural Patterns of India (followed by introductory remarks to orient the reader to the purpose and content of the essay in its entirety)
Section heading: WORLD VIEW
Subsection headings: Undivided Wholeness, Levels of Reality, etc. (each introducing one or more paragraphs)
Section heading: REINCARNATION (introducing several paragraphs)
Section heading: DHARMA [etc.]

OPTION ONE

PRIOR KNOWLEDGE: What are human rights? Who decides?

"Franchise" has many meanings, in business, politics, and the law, but the meaning used here is "the right to vote."
"Suffrage" comes from the Latin *suffragium,* to vote, giving us words and phrases such as "suffragette," "women's suffrage," and "universal suffrage."

It is clear that the rights people enjoy may be derived from, and protected by, the law of the land. When an 18-year-old woman says that she has "the right to vote," for example, the right referred to is enshrined in law, but if there were no law, or if the franchise were granted only to people over 21 years old, or only to men, could the young woman still claim a "right to vote"? Clearly, the change in context changes the meaning of "right."

The kind of right that is written into law is known as a **positive right,** and the second kind falls into the category once known as **natural rights** and now commonly called **human rights.** But what is a "human right"? Is being able to vote at 18 a human right? Is the franchise for women a human right? Are these ideas equal in weight? Are such rights "universal," or are they dependent on the cultural and political traditions of different societies? On what basis can we say that another country is breaching people's human rights if they don't allow women to vote? Questions of these kinds have become increasingly important in international affairs since the founding of the United Nations, and they have become a central concern of many governments and private organizations in recent years, particularly in the areas of state-sponsored terror, torture, imprisonment without trial, lack of free elections, and so on. In the United States, President Carter is often credited with making human rights issues more significant in the conduct of foreign affairs.

Albeit rather cynically, the following cartoon gives a Third-World view of human rights issues.

The Commoner/Katmandu, Nepal

If human rights are natural rights, then they must have a long history, for all people would have them as an automatic corollary of being human, but, of course, we know that securing "rights" has been a long and often painful struggle. The first country to enfranchise women was New Zealand, and that didn't happen until 1894; the women of most Western countries had to wait another 25–30 years to win the legal right to vote. Torture, death squad activity, and other abuses continue in many countries today.

The following essay shows how the idea of human rights has been shaped by philosophers and political thinkers over the centuries. The protection of human rights has been enshrined in the constitutions of many countries, including the United States, in the European Union, and in the United Nations, which, in 1945, issued the **Universal Declaration of Human Rights.** The signing of such declarations does not guarantee that rights will be protected, but the existence of such a document, to which most countries in the world are signatories, has great practical value as a standard against which all governments can be measured. The text of the declaration is provided on the accompanying pages.

The Universal Declaration of Human Rights (U.N. Document A/811) was adopted on 10 December, 1948, at the General Assembly of the United Nations. Forty-eight states voted for, none voted against, and eight abstained (Byelorussian S.S.R., Czechoslovakia, Poland, Saudi Arabia, Ukrainian S.S.R., U.S.S.R., Union of South Africa, and Yugoslavia). Byelorussia [Belarus] and Ukraine are now independent countries and no longer part of the Soviet Union; the Soviet Union no longer exists; Yugoslavia has broken up into its constituent parts, including Bosnia and Serbia; Poland is no longer dominated by the Soviet Union; and South Africa has transformed itself into a democracy where the majority rules.

The Declaration of Human Rights remains an important document, not least because different sections have been incorporated into international treaties and national constitutions that have the force of national and/or international law.

Universal Declaration of Human Rights, 1948

TEXT

Preamble

Whereas recognition of the inherent dignity and of the equal and inalienable rights of all members of the human family is the foundation of freedom, justice and peace in the world,

Whereas disregard and contempt for human rights have resulted in barbarous acts which have outraged the conscience of mankind, and the advent of a world in which human beings shall enjoy freedom of speech and belief and freedom from fear and want has been proclaimed as the highest aspiration of the common people,

Whereas it is essential, if man is not to be compelled to have recourse, as a last resort, to rebellion against tyranny and oppression, that human rights should be protected by the rule of law,

Whereas it is essential to promote the development of friendly relations between nations,

Whereas the peoples of the United Nations have in the Charter reaffirmed their faith in fundamental human rights, in the dignity and worth of the human person and in the equal rights of men and women and have determined to promote social progress and better standards of life in larger freedom,

Whereas Member States have pledged themselves to achieve, in cooperation with the United Nations, the promotion of universal respect for and observance of human rights and fundamental freedoms,

Whereas a common understanding of these rights and freedoms is of the greatest importance for the full realization of this pledge.

Now, Therefore,

The General Assembly

proclaims

This universal declaration of human rights as a common standard of achievement for all peoples and all nations, to the end that every individual and every organ of society, keeping this Declaration constantly in mind, shall strive by teaching and education to promote respect for these rights and freedoms and by progressive measures, national and international, to secure their universal and effective recognition and observance, both among the peoples of Member States themselves and among the peoples of territories under their jurisdiction.

Article 1

All human beings are born free and equal in dignity and rights. They are endowed with reason and conscience and should act towards one another in a spirit of brotherhood.

Article 2

Everyone is entitled to all the rights and freedoms set forth in this Declaration, without distinction of any kind, such as race, colour, sex, language, religion, political or other opinion, national or social origin, property, birth or other status.

Furthermore, no distinction shall be made on the basis of the political, jurisdictional or international status of the country or territory to which a person belongs, whether it be independent, trust, non-self-governing or under any other limitation of sovereignty.

Article 3

Everyone has the right to life, liberty and security of person.

Article 4

No one shall be held in slavery or servitude: slavery and the slave trade shall be prohibited in all their forms.

Article 5

No one shall be subjected to torture or cruel, inhuman or degrading treatment or punishment.

Article 6

Everyone has the right to recognition everywhere as a person before the law.

Article 7

All are equal before the law and are entitled without any discrimination to equal protection of the law. All are entitled to equal protection against any discrimination in violation of this Declaration and against any incitement to such discrimination.

Article 8
Everyone has the right to an effective remedy by the competent national tribunals for acts violating the fundamental rights granted him by the constitution or by law.

Article 9
No one shall be subjected to arbitrary arrest, detention or exile.

Article 10
Everyone is entitled in full equality to a fair and public hearing by an independent and impartial tribunal, in the determination of his rights and obligations and of any criminal charge against him.

Article 11
1. Everyone charged with a penal offence has the right to be presumed innocent until proved guilty according to law in a public trial at which he has had all the guarantees necessary for his defence.
2. No one shall be held guilty of any penal offence on account of any act or omission which did not constitute a penal offence, under national or international law, at the time when it was committed. Nor shall a heavier penalty be imposed than the one that was applicable at the time the penal offence was committed.

Article 12
No one shall be subjected to arbitrary interference with his privacy, family, home or correspondence, nor to attacks upon his honour and reputation. Everyone has the right to the protection of the law against such interference or attacks.

Article 13
1. Everyone has the right to freedom of movement and residence within the borders of each state.
2. Everyone has the right to leave any country, including his own, and to return to his country.

Article 14
1. Everyone has the right to seek and to enjoy in other countries asylum from persecution.
2. This right may not be invoked in the case of prosecutions genuinely arising from non-political crimes or from acts contrary to the purposes and principles of the United Nations.

Article 15
1. Everyone has the right to a nationality.
2. No one shall be arbitrarily deprived of his nationality nor denied the right to change his nationality.

Article 16
1. Men and women of full age, without any limitation due to race, nationality or religion, have the right to marry and to found a family. They are entitled to equal rights as to marriage, during marriage and at its dissolution.
2. Marriage shall be entered into only with the free and full consent of the intending spouses.
3. The family is the natural and fundamental group unit of society and is entitled to protection by society and the State.

Article 17
1. Everyone has the right to own property alone as well as in association with others.
2. No one shall be arbitrarily deprived of his property.

Article 18
Everyone has the right to freedom of thought, conscience and religion; this right includes freedom to change his religion or belief, and freedom, either alone or in community with others and in public or private, to manifest his religion or belief in teaching, practice, worship and observance.

Article 19
Everyone has the right to freedom of opinion and expression; this right includes freedom to hold opinions without interference and to seek, receive and impart information and ideas through any media and regardless of frontiers.

Article 20
1. Everyone has the right to freedom of peaceful assembly and association.
2. No one may be compelled to belong to an association.

Article 21
1. Everyone has the right to take part in the gov-

ernment of his country, directly or through freely chosen representatives.
2. Everyone has the right of equal access to public service in his country.
3. The will of the people shall be the basis of the authority of government; this will shall be expressed in periodic and genuine elections which shall be by universal and equal suffrage and shall be held by secret vote or by equivalent free voting procedures.

Article 22
Everyone, as a member of society, has the right to social security and is entitled to realization, through national effort and international cooperation and in accordance with the organization and resources of each State, of the economic, social and cultural rights indispensable for his dignity and the free development of his personality.

Article 23
1. Everyone has the right to work, to free choice of employment, to just and favourable conditions of work and to protection against unemployment.
2. Everyone, without any discrimination, has the right to equal pay for equal work.
3. Everyone who works has the right to just and favourable remuneration ensuring for himself and his family an existence worthy of human dignity, and supplemented, if necessary, by other means of social protection.
4. Everyone has the right to form and to join trade unions for the protection of his interests.

Article 24
Everyone has the right to rest and leisure, including reasonable limitation of working hours and periodic holidays with pay.

Article 25
1. Everyone has the right to a standard of living adequate for the health and well-being of himself and of his family, including food, clothing, housing and medical care and necessary social services, and the right to security in the event of unemployment, sickness, disability, widowhood, old age or other lack of livelihood in circumstances beyond his control.
2. Motherhood and childhood are entitled to special care and assistance. All children, whether born in or out of wedlock, shall enjoy the same social protection.

Article 26
1. Everyone has the right to education. Education shall be free, at least in the elementary and fundamental stages. Elementary education shall be compulsory. Technical and professional education shall be made generally available and higher education shall be equally accessible to all on the basis of merit.
2. Education shall be directed to the full development of the human personality and to the strengthening of respect for human rights and fundamental freedoms. It shall promote understanding, tolerance and friendship among all nations, racial or religious groups, and shall further the activities of the United Nations for the maintenance of peace.
3. Parents have a prior right to choose the kind of education that shall be given to their children.

Article 27
1. Everyone has the right freely to participate in the cultural life of the community, to enjoy the arts and to share in scientific advancement and its benefits.
2. Everyone has the right to the protection of the moral and material interests resulting from any scientific, literary or artistic production of which he is the author.

Article 28
Everyone is entitled to a social and international order in which the rights and freedoms set forth in this Declaration can be fully realized.

Article 29
1. Everyone has duties to the community in which alone the free and full development of his personality is possible.
2. In the exercise of his rights and freedoms, everyone shall be subject only to such limitations as are determined by law solely for the purpose of securing due recognition and respect

for the rights and freedoms of others and of meeting the just requirements of morality, public order and the general welfare in a democratic society.

3. These rights and freedoms may in no case be exercised contrary to the purposes and principles of the United Nations.

Article 30

Nothing in this Declaration may be interpreted as implying for any State, group or person any right to engage in any activity or to perform any act aimed at the destruction of any of the rights and freedoms set forth herein.

READING: Kenneth Minogue. "The History of the Idea of Human Rights." *The Human Rights Reader.* Walter Laqueur and Barry Rubin, eds. Markham, Ontario; Meridian, 1990: 3–17.

The History of the Idea of Human Rights

The idea of human rights is as modern as the internal combustion engine, and from one point of view, it is no less a technological device for achieving a common human purpose. The internal combustion engine moves us around swiftly, while human rights are protective devices designed to shield us from random violence and neglect. If the idea is widespread that men have a *right* to life, it may help to discourage careless aggression. Human beings badly need some sort of protection, since they are extremely vulnerable creatures. Snails have houses, chameleons can hide, and lions are strong and swift, but man is slow and soft. This point was made by political thinkers in the early modern period whenever the distinction between human and animal association was discussed. "Of all the animals with which this globe is peopled," wrote David Hume, "there is none towards whom nature seems, at first sight, to have exercised more cruelty than towards man, in the numberless wants and necessities with which she has loaded him, and in the slender means which she affords to the relieving of these necessities."[1]

Minogue puts the development of the idea of human rights into an historical context. His first reference is to David Hume (1711–1776), the Scottish philosopher, whose most famous work is the *Treatise of Human Nature* (1739–1740). Other references include John Locke (1632–1704), whose writings influenced the wording of the Declaration of Independence.

The solution to the problem Hume describes is society itself. Men can cooperate more effectively and intelligently than the animals. But society in its turn brings a new threat, for unlike most other species, men need protection also against other men. The protection can never be complete, but from early modern times the idea began to develop that, in addition to eyes and ears and all the other normal equipment, human beings also possess invisible things called "rights" that morally protect them from the aggression of their fellow men, and especially from the power of the governments under which they live. The idea grew very popular and prospered, in spite of the fact that it presents many intellectual difficulties. To say that each person ought not to be killed is an easily comprehensible moral statement,

KENNETH MINOGUE is Reader in Political Science at the London School of Economics, University of London.

however much it may in practice be violated. By contrast, the idea that each person has a "right" to life is, on the face of it, much more puzzling. The puzzling element has usually been concealed because of the fact that the idea usually comes to us accompanied by the beating of rhetorical drums, as in the Declaration of Independence of the United States in 1776: "We hold these truths to be self-evident, that all men are created equal, that they are endowed by their Creator with certain unalienable Rights, that among these are Life, Liberty and the Pursuit of Happiness." But is the idea of rights a "truth" at all? And in what sense can an idea developed so late in human history be described as "self-evident"? The idea of rights is indispensable to modern moral discussion, but it is also a thicket of problems. The history of the idea throws some light upon these problems.

THINK ON PAPER
Minogue notes that "the idea of rights is indispensable to modern moral discussion, but it is also a thicket of problems." In part, this is because different rights may conflict with each other, and people may disagree over their relative importance. Think of examples today in which different rights compete—and perhaps conflict—with each other.

The conceptual difficulties presented by the idea result from attributing rights to a universal class such as "man." For if a right means, as it always has, the legitimate powers that may be exercised by someone holding a special position, then it is as old as the institution of human society. Every officeholder has the rights belonging to his office. Kings and consuls in the ancient world enjoyed appropriate rights, and fathers in Rome possessed a bundle of rights described as *patria potestas*. Much of the political debate of the Middle Ages revolved around the question of just how extensive were the rights of pope, king, or baron. But the point of a "right" in this familiar sense was that it distinguished one person from his fellows.

The idea of a "right" that belonged to "man" as such is clearly a major extension of this idea. The status a man enjoyed—whether it was an officeholder or noble, as citizen or clerk—had previously been legal and customary, and its value resided in its exclusiveness. Everyone had some status or other, and those of low status enjoyed relatively less protection—though even slaves could seldom be killed with impunity. The new idea of natural rights involved appropriating ideas current in philosophy and religion in order to create, by philosophical fiat, a kind of universal status from which all other forms of status were thought ultimately to derive. The problem of doing so was to provide convincing arguments to show that a right was not merely a demand dogmatically asserted in moral language; the solution in the early modern period was to derive rights from a comprehensive idea of nature which had been philosophically current for many centuries. "Nature" described the proper ordering of the universe, and knowledge of its structure was believed to be accessible to all men by virtue of the faculty of reason they all possessed. A claim to a universal status couched in terms of "rights" by itself would have been vulnerable to the charge of dogmatism; but rights derived from a conception of nature could draw upon a long and splendid tradition of thought. Hence, the word "rights" has usually been partnered by an adjective that indicates the supposed source of the rights. In the early modern period, we find ourselves dealing with "natural" rights, and in more recent times it has become the practice to talk of "human" rights. The force of the word "human" here is to indicate that the rights in question are those we believe to be an essential part of a properly human life.

It is easy enough to give a date to inventions like the steam engine, but to say when an idea first became current is much more difficult. In trying to detect this moment, we must use the familiar distinction between the medieval and the modern world. It is an elastic distinction, but historians generally agree that the modern world superseded the medieval in the course of the sixteenth century. In the medieval world, men were regarded as dangerous brutes likely to do a great deal of damage unless they were carefully circumscribed within the roles appropriate to their station in life. The moral concept appropriate to this vivid sense of the sinfulness of man is that of duty. Duties set limits to the empire of desire, and it is extremely useful to know one's duty because such knowledge removes moral perplexities. A duty is something that must be performed; it is by definition morally obligatory, while a right may or may not be exercised, according as we choose. A common and useful way of describing the change from the medieval to the modern world is to say that the idea of *duty* gave way to the idea of *right*. It was certainly not the case, of course, that the idea of duty disappeared; it merely happened that instead of beginning with the structure of the creation and deducing the duties of man, thinkers took their initial bearings from man and derived the structure of the creation.

This reversal of philosophical priorities reflected far-reaching changes in the way the more active Europeans behaved. Kings grew restless under the tutelage of the Pope, and eventually rejected his authority—no less in Catholic than in Protestant lands. Ordinary men asserted the primacy of their consciences over the traditional authority of the church. Merchants broke free of the constraints forbidding usury. Society began to swarm with adventurers seeking to make their fortunes. Generation by generation, it often seemed as if the orderly conceptions of the Middle Ages had broken down, but in time it became clear that what was happening was the painful emergence of a new type of civilization.

One of the marks of this new civilization was the assertive vocabulary of rights. Kings claimed divine right in throwing off the shackles of the Pope, and they were led on to claim ever more grandiose powers over the subjects whom they now came to dominate. But the temper of the epoch was such that subjects as well as kings were growing more willful. In England, king and subjects fell out in 1642, and a long contest took place which was not finally settled until 1688, when James II (son of the Charles I, who had been executed in 1649) fled to

France, still babbling about divine right. And in that year it was clear that, so far as England was concerned, natural rights had defeated divine right. Philosophy in the form of John Locke legitimized the victory and carried the message to other lands.

The idea of natural rights found its base in England, but its victory there was doubly ironic. Although the idea had been a commonplace of political discussion during the civil war of the 1640s, most political discussion in England tended to be conducted in historical and legal terms rather than philosophical. Although the second of Locke's *Two Treatises on Civil Government* (published anonymously in 1690) became the most famous and influential of seventeenth-century Whig utterances, it was not typical in its time, nor did it set the tone for English political discussion in the century that followed. Edmund Burke, for example, was in many respects a good Lockean—he was certainly a defender of the Settlement of 1688—but he was profoundly hostile to the idea of natural rights. They were strictly a commodity for export, particularly to France, and to the American colonies.

The second irony is that such philosophical plausibility as the idea of natural rights could claim resulted from its association with the idea of natural law—yet that tradition had seldom found England a hospitable shore. Natural law had been first elaborated by the Stoics, who based their thinking upon Aristotelian ideas of nature. It had later been taken up by the Christian Scholastics and had found its classic expression in the *Summa Theologica* of St. Thomas Aquinas. In the sixteenth century, this tradition of thought had been particularly vital in Spain and Germany, though it also found an exponent in the Englishman Richard Hooker, whose *Laws of Ecclesiastical Polity*, first published in 1593, had strongly influenced John Locke. In the seventeenth century, this tradition had been invaded by the dominant intellectual current of rationalism, leading some of its exponents to dream that natural law might become an absolutely certain and deductive system of ethics, such that men faced with a moral or political problem would merely have to calculate in order to arrive at a solution. Such had been the dream of Leibniz, and even Locke had let drop some teasing remarks about the possibility of ethics becoming no less certain a science than mathematics. He did not follow them up.

No one familiar with the civil strife that ravaged Europe from the Reformation to the end of the Thirty Years War in 1648 could fail to sympathize with any intellectual project for bringing peace. Both natural law and natural rights had this character; the difficulty, however, was that any abstract body of ideas can function in diametrically opposite ways. It might be that such ideas represented the rational solution to all human conflict, the discovery at last of the proper basis of social and political life. In that case, all that competing and quarreling parties needed to do would be to consult a competent philosopher in order to discover the correct solution to their disputes. But, as Rousseau was later to observe, for all its supposed source in man's natural and unaided reason, the idea of nature was the subject of many learned disputes and disagreements among the philosophers. If it was self-evident, it was clearly not self-evident enough. It might thus be that the idea of nature, far from being the solution to civil strife, was in fact the problem itself. For one of its implications was that ordinary men might claim the right to pronounce upon the correct ordering of society; and since ordinary men did not agree in what they pronounced, they soon fell to killing each other.

Such was certainly the view of Thomas Hobbes, whose *Leviathan*, published in 1651, transposed the idea of natural law into individualist terms.

Hobbes was the first to produce a genuinely philosophical account of something called "natural right," but it was very different from the natural rights of later time. He was also the first philosopher (by contrast with the publicists of his time) to locate the source of political authority in the people below, rather than in God above. It is easy to misunderstand the character of this change. The medieval currency of the idea of *vox populi, vox dei* reminds us that something very like this idea has its roots in early medieval thought. But in the Middle Ages, the authority was unquestionably given by God, even though the end or *telos* of the authority was the good of the people; the famous slogan uniting the voice of the people with that of God amounted to an identification of the *source* of authority with the *end* for which authority was entrusted to rulers. The consent of the ruled was often thought necessary to authority, but it was not sufficient. In the Hobbesian argument, men who live in the perilous and insecure state of nature *authorize* a sovereign to declare and enforce the rules by which they will live. The authority thus given to the ruler is virtually without limit, and the subject's duty is to obey whatever laws the sovereign may make, for that is what justice *means*. No subject may appeal against the sovereign's decision to any natural rights he imagines to be declared by his faculty of reason. Hence, in a story full of twists and paradoxes, it is notable that Thomas Hobbes, generally regarded as a supporter of Stuart absolutism, should have produced the first full-dress philosophy of government by consent. It was partly because of this element of consent that his philosophy was not popular in Stuart circles, and some of his works were publicly burned in 1685 at the University of Oxford. Nevertheless, he must be counted as an ancestor of the idea of natural rights.

But he is certainly a somewhat remote ancestor. His right of nature is not some limited right to life, or property, or happiness. It is a right to everything, "even to one another's body." It is because men have this right in the state of nature that their situation is one of war and insecurity; the first thing a rational man does with this right of nature is to get rid of it. It is renounced in favor of the sovereign, who thereafter makes the laws and protects the persons of his subjects. The right of nature is nothing more than the moral capital with which men enter into civil society and invest its ruler with authority. And once in that civil society, men lose all right except that of self-defense. One of the strongest drives in Hobbes's thought is to destroy any possible plausibility that might attach to the idea that man may rationally appeal to an external standard of rights and thereby criticize the positive laws under which he lives. It is just this capacity to appeal to one's individual conscience that Hobbes thought had plunged his country into civil war. There can be no doubt that he was an inveterate foe of the idea that (as his contemporary, the pamphleteer Richard Overton, puts it) "To every Individuall in nature, is given an individual property by nature, not to be invaded or usurped by any [man]. . . ."[2] Yet Hobbes did shift the center of gravity in political philosophy by deriving civil authority, however remotely, from the consent of the subjects.

It was John Locke who pushed this movement very much further, and with whom we rightly associate the idea not only that the subjects authorize a government, but that they also require that it should be responsive to their wishes. Locke's *Second Treatise* has become a great classic of the liberal tradition, and any modern reader will find in it many familiar ideas. But the familiarity is in some ways misleading. The background of Locke's thought is profoundly theological: Men are God's property and may not dispose of each other, or even of themselves, entirely as they wish. The strong element of constitutionality in Locke's writings should be understood not in terms of the later practices of liberal and democratic states, but in terms of the medieval tradition from which it actually comes. And as we have seen, it is a gross error to imagine that the idea of government by consent is a modern invention. If anything, that idea was more strongly held in medieval times than it has been in modern. Nevertheless, Locke did take the existing materials of natural right and social contract and cast them in a form which later generations have found definitive. Just as the makers of the Settlement of 1688 in England were careful to conceal the novelty of their work beneath layers of traditional legalism, so also did Locke conceal the novelty and radical logic of his thought by placing it squarely in the natural law tradition represented by Richard Hooker. He did it all so plausibly as to conceal from later generations the main difficulty facing any doctrine of natural rights: namely, how to rescue it from hopeless dogmatism.

The real center of Locke's argument is in the last chapter of the *Second Treatise*, where he discusses the circumstances in which a people may legitimately overthrow a government that has breached its trust, but many later readers have looked with more attention to the arguments he presents for a natural right to property. The importance of property in Locke has provided a warrant for many interpreters[3] to see in Locke a spokesman for a class of people usually known in history textbooks as "the rising bourgeoisie." The main problem that actually concerned Locke, however, was theological rather than political. God had given the fruits of the earth in common to all men. How, then, could any particular man ever acquire the right of individual appropriation? This problem did not weigh so heavily upon medieval writers in the same tradition because they could interpret the holding of property as a trust: Those who own property have duties of charity toward the needier of their fellow men, and the property is given to them because only personal possession will impel men to keep property in good order. Such is the argument of Aquinas, living in times when property had a fixity and stability in comparison with which the men of each generation who passed over the earth looked like little more than (as Burke would say) the butterflies of a season. But Locke is concerned with individuals who own property and dispose of it at their pleasure, and he justifies their original title to property in terms of the labor they invest in developing it. This is the famous labor theory of value advanced in Chapter V of the *Second Treatise*. In the state of nature, men may pluck acorns from trees and take water from rivers for their own personal use, just so long as they only take what they need and do not prevent others from doing the like. The invention of money and the convenience of the division of labor justify the supersession of these somewhat quaint provisions, and the principle of equality is maintained by the suggestion that everyone has a property in his own person. Property and personhood are conceptually yoked together, and government is a trust whose duty it is to regulate and protect the enjoyment of these rights.

Locke's *Two Treatises of Government* was a Whig document designed to justify resistance to the pretensions of a divine-right monarchy threatening to abuse the prerogative powers attached to the English crown. And we may perhaps summarize the significance of the situation by saying that a claim to absolute right on the part of the sovereign had provoked a counterclaim to equally absolute rights on the part of the subjects. The ordinary business of government had been conspicuously incompatible with the idea of divine right under the Stuarts; it would no doubt have proved equally incompatible with a rigid doctrine of natural rights in later times. But England was saved from experiencing the latter kind of incompatibility because the idiom of natural rights did not take root in the center of British political thinking in the eighteenth century. Locke's writing was, compared with the flood of British political writing in his time, uncommonly abstract and philosophical; it justified a highly contingent historical settlement in terms of supremely abstract principles that, had they been taken seriously, might well have been extremely disruptive. As it happens, they were taken very seriously abroad, especially in France and in the American colonies, and they did in fact turn out to be highly disruptive.

That the idea of natural rights might be politically disruptive was clear, a century after Locke, to both Edmund Burke (whose *Reflections on the Revolution in France* of 1790 attacked the idea) and to Tom Paine (whose *Rights of Man*, written in reply to Burke, restated the idea and welcomed the element of disruption). But the explosive effect of the idea of natural rights was not merely a result of its logical implications becoming more evident. It was the result of a growing sense of the progress of the human race, in which progress the discovery of natural rights and the idea of government by consent played a major part. Educated men contemplated the Newtonian account of the cosmos with wonder and pride. They looked back with dismay at the sectarian passions of the earlier modern period. They often embraced a supposedly rational religion, Deism, in preference to many of the superstitious and archaic elements of Christianity to be found especially in the Old Testament. Science even came to be applied to the operations of the mind, as Locke's epistemology was converted by Frenchmen like Condillac into a reforming psychology. As has often been observed, the era of the Enlightenment was paradoxical in that, despising the very word "enthusiasm," it yet managed to become hopelessly intoxicated with its own brand of tolerance and moderation. The men of that time were irrationally rational, immoderately moderate, and very proud of themselves. "The age we live in is a busy age," as Bentham wrote in the preface to his *Fragment on Government*, "in which knowledge is rapidly advancing to perfection." It was the destiny of the doctrine of rights to take its place in the muted millenarianism of that optimistic period of European history. Natural rights emerged fully onto the grand stage of politics toward the end of the eighteenth century, and it was associated with two revolutions. In the end, logic triumphed over Locke's own cautious temperament. The apostle of order became the prophet of revolution itself.

It would be an exaggeration, though a pardonable one, to say that at the height of its vogue the idea of natural rights toppled two powerful governments—that of George III over the American colonies, and that of Louis XVI over France. Abstract ideas have no power to act alone. Nevertheless, the idea of natural rights was the vocabulary in which these revolutions were conducted, and the idea soon came to shine with all the luster of the events and the documents with which it was associated. The American Declaration of Independence and the French Declaration of the Rights of Man and Citizen have become statements of universal significance, testaments of the highest standards in politics to which, for example, colonial peoples might appeal against their European masters. At the very moment when Europeans were preparing to spread their domination all over the globe, their philosophers were devising the instrument of recoil. Indeed, it was sometimes the case, as in British India, that the very Europeans who came to rule were in the forefront of nationalist movements.

Natural rights were the cutting edge of the ax of rationalism that toppled many of the inherited medieval traditions of eighteenth-century Europe. They were part of that general aspiration toward bringing peace and order to the world that led Immanuel Kant to think that royal dynasties were the cause of war, and that a world of republics would bring a peaceful era to mankind. Tom Paine looked forward not only to peace but to a happy anarchy marked by little taxation and minimal government regulation of the lives of men.

Yet, although the idea of rights in one form or another has proved extremely durable, the heyday of natural rights was relatively short. By the end of the nineteenth century, the philosopher David Ritchie felt impelled to defend his criticism of the doctrine by denying that he was taking a sword to an already dead dragon. "Recent experience," he wrote, ". . . has convinced me that the theory is still, in a sense, alive, or at least capable of mischief."[4] Ritchie's argument was that the doctrine was excessively abstract and thus impeded mankind's capacity to learn from the experience of the human race. This criticism merely elaborated, in terms of evolutionary thought, much that had been said about the idea by Bentham and by Burke.

The more influential attack on the idea of natural rights, however, was voiced by Karl Marx. His interest for us is twofold. Firstly, he was a powerful critic of the received opinions on the subject; secondly, he represented a new direction of those millenarian strivings that had appeared in the course of the eighteenth-century Enlightenment.

Marx's criticism of the doctrine of natural rights was to issue in an altogether different conception of a right. The point can perhaps best be made if we say that having a right is like having an admission ticket to a club, or like having a supply of gambling chips. There is no guarantee that the club will be entertaining, or that the gambler will win anything. The slave has no right to property, though he may possibly enjoy the use of his owner's property. A free man, on the other hand, has a right to property, though he may possess little or nothing at all. Natural rights, then, are entirely formal, and all they describe is a status.

Now the actual world in which these rights were asserted was one in which some people were rich and powerful, and others were poor and powerless. Since this is a very common condition of things, it would be perilous to conclude that the doctrine of natural rights had actually brought this situation about. But opponents of the idea could, with rather more plausibility, suggest that the doctrine was designed to legitimize the inequalities that were universal in modern societies. Marx thought that the *meaning* of natural rights could be discovered if one looked to what he thought were their *consequences*. The whole idea seemed to him to be an ideological statement of the conditions necessary for the accumulation of wealth by the people who had done well out of modern industry, people whom he called "the bourgeoisie."

Marx himself thought of membership of a human community not in terms of formal rights, but in terms of what was actually enjoyed by the citizens. He thought, for example, that the right to a paid employment meant something more than merely that no man should be barred from taking employment by virtue of some irrelevant circumstance such as race or sex, and that the holder of such a right could (unlike a slave) change his employer if it should suit him. Marx considered that a right to employment meant that a job should actually be available to any bearer of the right. It is easy to see why he thought that a right to property was a meaningless mockery to the propertyless industrial workers of Europe; it is also easy to see that such an opinion quite transforms the meaning of the idea of a right. A right, construed in these terms, becomes a straightforward demand, rather than the assertion of a rule in terms of which something else might be demanded. For a natural (i.e., formal) right to work merely means that I may demand a specific job (if circumstances should make such a thing available) against any attempt to bar my claim in terms of characteristics which the right assumes to be irrelevant. Similarly, my right to property is not in itself a demand, though it may become the basis of a demand if some other citizen, or the government under which I live, should try to take my property away in some illegitimate manner. It was, of course, this right to private property which Marx thought to reveal most clearly the bourgeois provenance of the whole idea of natural rights, and he might seem to gain some support from Locke's deliberately dramatic juxtaposition of the rights of life and property: ". . . the Sergeant," Locke tells us, "that could command a Soldier to march up to the mouth of a Cannon, or stand in a Breach, where he is almost sure to perish, [cannot] command that Soldier to give him one penny of his Money. . . ."[5] This does not mean, of course, that Locke values money more than life; it merely means that the end or purpose of entering a State and the end or purpose of running an army require different things.

Marx criticizes the idea of natural rights on a variety of grounds which have since become the familiar currency of the discussion. He agrees with Burke that they are abstract and unhistorical. He regards the idea as expressing what the bourgeoisie thinks is the essence of human nature. ". . . man as he actually is," Marx tells us, "is only recognized in the form of the egoistic individual, and the true man only in the form of the abstract citizen." This particular point may confidently be regarded as a mistake. We have already observed that the modern world came into existence when individualist modes of action came to replace the communal sense of the Middle Ages, and everyone is familiar with the moral distinction between egoism and altruism. Like many other writers, Marx simply identified individualism with egoism, and a tendency to think in communal terms with altruism. An individualist, however, may well be altruistic to the point of self-abnegation; he merely wishes to choose his own way of acting. Similarly, egoism and selfishness can appear in the most communally minded people. That I should claim the right to own property might mean that I am greedy and wish to do in my fellow men; but it might also mean many other things—such as that I enjoy taking risks, investing, saving money, and so on. And if I should acquire a great deal of property, I may spend it on my own pleasure, or I may set up charitable foundations for art and science, or even (as some millionaires have done) spend it financing socialist revolutions, because such is my pleasure. There is, in other words, no logical relationship whatever between a right on the one hand, and a motive (such as egoism) on the other.

The crux of Marx's criticism appears when he writes:

> But the right of man to liberty is based not on the association of man with man, but on the separation of man from man. It is the *right* of this separation, the right of the *restricted* individual, withdrawn into himself.[6]

Superficially considered, this statement falsely describes modern life, since modern men and women associate together in a great variety of ways, in families, churches, conferences, unions, and all the rest. But it is certainly true that all of these communal activities are voluntary, and that the idea of natural rights operates to prevent the invasion of one man's right by another man, or by such institutions as government. This is the element of individuality in modern life; it is also the basis of the fundamental political distinction between the private and the public spheres of life. Such an idea is fundamental to the modern state. But Marx, it is well known, believed that the modern state should, and would, wither away. It would be replaced by a form of society in which men's communal qualities, supposedly frustrated by the alienation of capitalist life, would flow freely into a rich and superior common life. Whether such a condition of things would be preferable is perhaps a matter of choice; but it would certainly be very different from anything we know now. It would also be a good deal less plural than the modern world. For one thing, the variety of religious beliefs would have disappeared, discarded as incomplete stages in man's realization of his full social being.[7] For another, men would be understood as producers, and as satisfiers of needs, and these are the respects in which men are least differentiated one from another. Men would be equal, and equally satisfied.

A society conceived in this way has no place for the idea of rights in the strict sense; hence, it is a tribute to the strength of the idea that the ideological tradition to which Marx belonged did choose to appropriate—indeed to extend—at least the rhetoric, if not the reality, of rights. In this way, the tradition of rights has spread to new areas, at the price of becoming much more diffuse. The social and economic rights that have been added to the traditional canon of rights are in effect statements of desirable conditions of life for every human being. In the U.N. *Universal Declaration of Human Rights*, for example, the provision of appropriate holidays with pay is included as a right, and this is admitted to be something entirely dependent upon the level of industrial development a country has reached. It would certainly be entirely meaningless in the case, for example, of the nomadic tribes of sub-Saharan Africa. In this minimal sense, at least, the new rights are undeniably historical, if by the word "historical" is meant the fact that they cannot be asserted abstractly of the entity "man," but must be related to the economic development of the country in which particular men live.

Further, we now tend to talk of "human" rather than of "natural" rights, and this is because their derivation has changed. Rights are no longer derived from the operations of natural reason, but rather from our ideas of what it is to be human. We think that a person who is malnourished, tortured, wrongly imprisoned, illiterate, and perhaps lacking in regular paid holidays is not living in a manner appropriate to a human being. Again, natural rights, being abstract and eternal, were in principle available to any thoughtful caveman who considered the matter, but we tend today to regard the idea of rights as one that evolves from generation to generation. Marx talked sarcastically of the French and North Americans as being the people who "*discovered*" natural rights, but it is not uncommon these days to believe that modern society concerned itself over the centuries with political, then with social, and then with economic rights in turn. It is in this sense that, for example, Sir Leslie Scarman, a Lord Chief Justice of Appeal, talked of "the great strides that have been made by mankind generally in the identification of rights since 1948.[8] Human rights of this kind require much more positive action on the part of whoever is charged with the running of society. The natural rights to life, liberty, and property required little more of governments and other citizens than forebearance, but the right to be provided with an actual job requires that governments shall manage the economy, and it may also require that governments shall manage the lives of their citizens in very considerable detail. To have the right to be provided with an actual job is in some ways a great practical advance upon the old natural right to work, but it has an obverse side. It is the right—which may also become a duty—to do a socially necessary job. But such a job may not at all be the kind of job the bearer of the right had in mind. The evolution of the idea of rights to a point where they may become oppressive duties is a fascinating object lesson on the relation between rhetoric and reality.

Meanwhile, however, the rhetoric of rights, as it became increasingly sundered from any very sophisticated view of reason and the nature of man, spread in two directions. One of these is the elaboration of the rights of those who were thought to have been wrongly denied the full status of "man." This class of person includes racial minorities, homosexuals, children, and, above all, women.[9] In 1792, Mary Wollstonecraft published her *Vindication of the Rights of Women*. In her dedication to Talleyrand (who had until recently been Bishop of Autun), she wrote: "If the abstract rights of man will bear discussion and explanation, those of woman, by a parity of reasoning, will not shrink from the same test. . . . [I]f women are not permitted to enjoy legitimate rights, they will render both men and themselves vicious to obtain illicit privileges."[10] Here, then, is the idea of rights setting off on a new adventure as the argument of those seeking equal treatment. In such remarks is also to be found the classic, if slightly disingenuous, argument that the inequality is fundamentally as harmful to those who appear to benefit from it as it is to those who feel themselves oppressed. Both men and women will benefit from a liberation, Mary Wollstonecraft explains, since the time that women "choose to spend at their glass . . . is only an instinct of nature to enable them to obtain indirectly a little of that power of which they are unjustly denied a share. . . ."[11] And women's liberation has been partnered by a variety of other demands for liberation, down to and including the British National Council for Civil Liberties' call for "the right of children to determine their personal appearance."[12]

The other direction in which the idea of rights began to extend its sway was the expression of communal claims. When the individualism of the seventeenth and eighteenth centuries came to seem abstract and unhistorical, many Europeans believed that social reality was to be found in cultural groups, such as nations. Some of these people asserted that each nation should be a self-governing unity, and this political idea was advanced in the form of a "right to self-determination." In this form, it was no less disruptive of established patterns of rule than natural rights had been a few generations earlier, and in the Revolution of 1848, Europe was filled with the sounds of a new kind of turbulence. Nationalism was, by and large, hostile to the rationalism of the Enlightenment, and the basis of the right was a theory to the effect that a nation could not properly be a nation unless it was free to govern itself. National rights and human rights thus rest alike upon the abstract idea found in the adjective that partners the word "rights." In 1919, the map of Europe was redrawn in accordance with this theory, and since 1945 the modern world has seen a series of "liberations" which has increased the number of United Nations from the original 51 to over 150. As with the earlier theory of natural rights, the fundamental belief was that a moral imbalance was causing the majority of human discontents, and that once this imbalance had been removed, human beings would be happy, or at least less aggressive.

Such is the story of the idea of rights from its beginnings to its resurgence in the latter half of the twentieth century. Under U.S. President Carter, the idea became an instrument of foreign policy, and pressure was brought to bear upon America's allies and dependents to discourage them from expedients like arbitrary arrest and the torture of political opponents. In the elaborate package of agreements negotiated between the United States and the Soviet Union collectively referred to as *détente*, human rights played a pivotal role, even though skeptics suggest that the Russian government barely understands what the idea means. A glance at any newspaper will reveal the great variety of ways in which both ordinary people and professional politicians talk of rights. Were the word to be striken from their vocabulary, they would be briefly dumb, though they would certainly find new words before long in which to state their moral convictions. And it is in that uneasy borderland between people's demands on the one hand and their moral convictions on the other that the idea of rights has always belonged.

NOTES

1. David Hume, *Treatise of Human Nature,* vol. III, Part 2, Chap. 2 (Dents, London, 1911 [1951]), p. 191.
2. *An Arrow Against All Tyrants* (London, 1646); (Exeter: The Rota Press, 1976), p. 1.
3. See, for example, C. B. MacPherson, *The Political Theory of Possessive Individualism* (Oxford: Oxford University Press, 1962).
4. *Natural Rights: A Criticism of Some Political and Ethical Conceptions* (London, 1894), p. ix.
5. *Second Treatise,* Section 139.
6. Karl Marx, "On the Jewish Question," Karl Marx and Friedrich Engels, *Collected Works,* vol. 3 (Moscow: International Publishers, 1974), pp. 162–163.
7. Marx regards a right to choose one's religious belief as incompatible with the very idea of the rights of man as it will be fully realized. ". . . the religious spirit cannot be *really* secularised, for what is it in itself but the non-secular form of a stage in the development of the human mind? . . . Not Christianity, but the *human praxis* of Christianity is the basis of this state." Ibid., pp. 158–9.
8. "Human Rights" (Centenary Celebrity Lecture delivered at Senate House, University of London, October 13th, 1976; Subsequently published in the *University Bulletin* 39, February 1977).

This article uses traditional endnotes rather than in-text citations. There are many different documentation styles, and you will probably be required to use several of them in different subjects during your college career. It's always worthwhile checking with your professor to see whether any particular style is preferred.

9. It could even be extended to include animals, on the ground that they can certainly suffer, and may perhaps be conscious.
10. *The Rights of Women,* Mary Wollstonecraft (Everyman Edition, Dents, London, 1929) pp. 11–12.
11. Ibid.
12. See the letter to the *London Times* of May 26th, 1972, from Mr. Tony Smythe.

ASPECTS OF WRITING: Narrowing a research idea, indexes, and notes.

"Human rights" is a big subject, and this presents a problem for anyone who wishes to use it as a research paper topic. It needs to be reduced to a more manageable size, and this process is called **"narrowing."**

Reading is the first stage. If you know little about your topic, a good general introduction can be obtained from encyclopedias, almanacs, and other reference books. These works will not figure prominently in your research paper (they probably won't even be cited), but they can serve some useful functions in terms of orienting you to the topic and introducing you to some of the major **figures, issues,** and **terminology** involved. This will help you go on to the more specific search you will have to undertake.

You should take note of any major names and titles provided in the reference books, so that you can look for them in your library. This will give you a good start in your reading but is unlikely to be enough; to find more, you will probably have to use **indexes,** some of which are printed and others of which come online. Different libraries have different resources, and you should familiarize yourself with what is available to you, especially if the computerized catalogs and other resources are new to you.

Some indexes are more specialized than others. The best-known general index in printed form is probably the *Reader's Guide to Periodical Literature,* but this may not be adequate for your particular project. More specialized indexes are published in many fields, including the social sciences, nursing, law, education, engineering, and so on. Some of these are listed here.

As you locate books and articles, you will start to recognize themes within the literature, and this is a crucial step in narrowing your topic. You may do this even as you browse through the indexes. When you find several writers who focus on the same question or discussion, then you may have found your topic.

With a narrower topic in mind, you can then select articles and books that appear to be relevant, and the more focused reading and note taking begins. You may still have to be selective in what you read; sometimes, books and articles with titles that appear relevant may in fact be too technical or may in other ways not be what you were anticipating. These should be set aside, and you should continue to search for sources you can use effectively.

Selected printed indexes

Reader's Guide to Periodical Literature
Humanities Index
General Science Index
Business Periodicals Index
Applied Science and Technology Index
New York Times Index
Public Affairs Information Service (P.A.I.S.)
Social Science Index

Selected on-line indexes

Infotrac—index and abstracts for periodical articles within the previous three years; no books
ERIC—articles from education journals
ABI—articles and abstracts from business journals
CIML—articles from nursing and health journals

Your library may not have all of these indexes, but it may have others. Ask your reference librarian about specialized indexes in your field.

As you read, you should take notes and be thinking about a possible thesis, if you haven't developed one already. *For a discussion of the thesis, see Unit One, Section Two.*

Taking notes is a crucial part of any research project, and you can save yourself a lot of time if you do it properly. "Doing it properly" does not imply that there is a single predetermined and correct way to take notes. Your professor may require you to use note cards, but, no matter how you organize your notes, you should make sure that you supply yourself with all the relevant information: title of book or article, author, publisher, and place and date of publication. Further, you must **distinguish in your notes between direct quotes and paraphrases** (and, if necessary, your own comments). Whenever you copy words directly from the text—even single words, if they are significant—use quotation marks. **Make sure, *for both quotations and paraphrases,* that you provide the page reference for what you write down;** this is vital, for it can be very time consuming to go back and try to find page references at a later date. Note also that many references to texts involve a mixture of quote and paraphrase; your notes must distinguish between the two.

The more elaborate your research paper, the more important it is to organize your materials effectively. It's a good thing to practice now, even if any research paper you write in this course may be relatively short.

Sample note cards
(the page references are to the original text)

lib. call no.
Minogue, Kenneth
"The History of the Idea of Human Rights." *The Human Rights Reader. Eds. Walter Laqueur and Barry Rubin. Markham, Ontario: Meridian/Penguin, 1990:3–17.*

Minogue
In ancient and medieval times rights belonged to individuals of different stations—"Much of the debate of the Middle Ages . . . [concerned] just how extensive were the rights of pope, king, or baron" (4). Idea of universal rights was "a major extension of this idea" (4), but philosophical problems arose over how to justify these universal rights. Looked to natural laws . . . "rights derived from a conception of nature could draw upon a long and splendid tradition of thought" (4). Hence "natural rights" and, later, "human rights" which "indicate that the rights in question are those we believe to be an essential part of a properly human life" (4–5).

Minogue—natural/human rights
Difference between modern world and medieval world—"the idea of a *duty* gave way to the idea of a *right*" (5).

The amount of detail in your notes will vary. The key thing is that your notes should be ***useful*** *to you several days after you write them down. They should be legible, complete, and comprehensible. Notes that leave too much to your memory, or that are too skimpy to be informative, are of little use.*

WRITING AND RESEARCH: Answer one of the following questions.

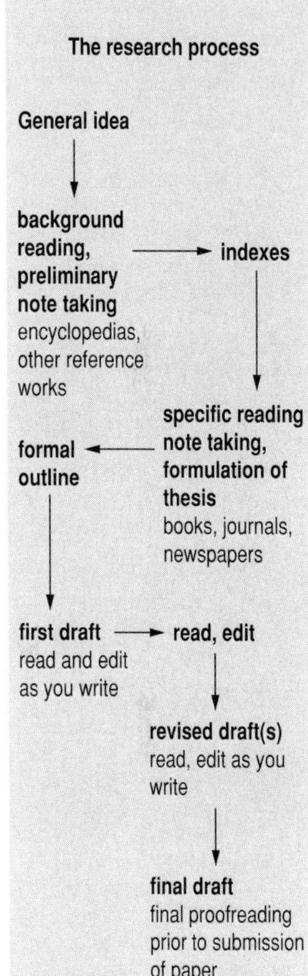

Note: This is a generic description of the research-paper process; not everyone works in exactly the same way. Some of these activities overlap. For example, you will probably continue to look for new articles etc. even after you begin writing, and you may formulate—and even revise—your thesis (or statement of purpose) at any stage. Late changes, however, can mean a lot more work. Forming a clear concept and outline is important—the earlier the better.

1. Choose a topic derived from the readings in this unit. Make reference to several writers in your discussion. You may wish to select the essay (or other discussion) which most interested you, look at it again, and identify a theme. Any references in the text to other writers may be useful, and you can use the process described in the *Aspects of writing* section above to find further sources. Possible topics include:

   Values in different cultures

   Cultural relativism

   Describing American values

   The concept of human rights

   The Universal Declaration of Human Rights

2. Discuss the idea that each culture has a "real" and an "ideal" form, and apply it to American or another culture. Stewart's essay, mentioned in Section Three of this unit, may be helpful here.
3. Some people deny that there is such a thing as "American culture." Discuss this, making at least some reference to the literature.

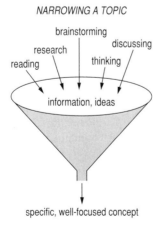

NARROWING A TOPIC

brainstorming
research
discussing
reading
thinking
information, ideas
specific, well-focused concept

OPTION TWO

TALKING ABOUT LANGUAGE: Language and values.

In the sense that we can talk about "American values," "Japanese values," and so on, values are a shared part of any given culture in the same way that language is—but what is the connection between the two? Does language reflect culture, or vice versa? Or both? Some linguists, most notably Edward Sapir and Benjamin Lee Whorf, have argued that our view of the world is shaped, more or less, by the language we acquire as children. Sapir, in *The Status of Linguistics as a Science,* published in 1929, observes the following:

> Language is a guide to "social reality." . . . [Language] powerfully conditions all our thinking about social problems and processes. Human beings do not live in the objective world alone, nor alone in the world of social activity as ordinarily understood, but are very much at the mercy of the particular language which has become the medium of expression in their society. . . . No two languages are ever sufficiently similar to be considered as representing the same social reality. The worlds in which different societies live are distinct worlds, not merely the same world with different labels attached.

Sapir's views remain controversial, for a "strong" interpretation of them would suggest that communication between speakers of different languages would be impossible, and that translation wouldn't help very much. Whorf offered a rather "weaker" version of what is now known as the **Sapir-Whorf hypothesis,** but he also affirmed the idea that our view of the world is conditioned by our language. It has been observed that Sapir and Whorf bring a new aspect to the discussion of relativity, for each person's view of the realities of the world would depend on the language they speak.

The Sapir-Whorf hypothesis has been criticized by many philosophers and linguists, but it remains a provocative idea, and one suspects that there must be at least an element of truth in what they say. Some examples are well known, like the fact that different languages classify colors differently, leading, perhaps, to different perceptions. Another example suggests that our political categories are shaped by our language, as follows:

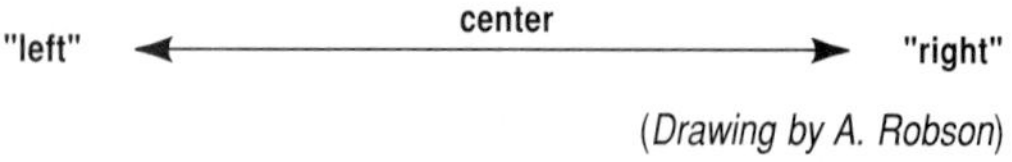

(*Drawing by A. Robson*)

Sapir's and Whorf's ideas came in part from their studies of Native American languages, including Hopi and Apache. Adam Schaff, in his *Language and Cognition* (1973), gives an interesting example from Whorf:

> According to Whorf, we perceive the world in a given way depending on how our language divides the stress of events into parts. [Most European] languages tend to analyze reality as a set of *things* and focus their attention mainly on human products, such as tables and chairs and so forth—objects artificially isolated from the rest of the world. The Hopi language implies a different analysis, it analyzes the world as a set of *events.* Here is an example of Whorf's reasoning.
>
>> We might isolate something in nature by saying "it is spring." Apache uses the verb *ga* to formulate the statement "be white (including clear, uncolored, and so on)." With a prefix *no-* the meaning of downward motion enters: "whiteness moves downward." Then *to,* meaning both "water" and "spring," is prefixed. The result corresponds to our "dripping spring," but synthetically it is "as water, or springs, whiteness moves downward." How utterly unlike our way of thinking!
>
> . . . In his paper on the model of the universe of the Hopi language, Whorf described the category of time in that language.
>
>> I find it gratuitous to assume that a Hopi who knows only the Hopi language and the cultural ideas of his own society has the same notions, often supposed to be intuitions, of time and space that we have, and

(Continued next page)

This categorization, with its historical roots in the seating of the French parliament at the time of the French Revolution (1789), has become so entrenched in our political thinking that it might be said to limit our capacity for understanding political realities. As an alternative, we might imagine a more circular configuration:

that are generally assumed to be universal. In particular, he has no general notion or intuition of *time* as a smooth flowing continuum in which everything in the universe proceeds at an equal rate, out of a future, through a present, into a past.

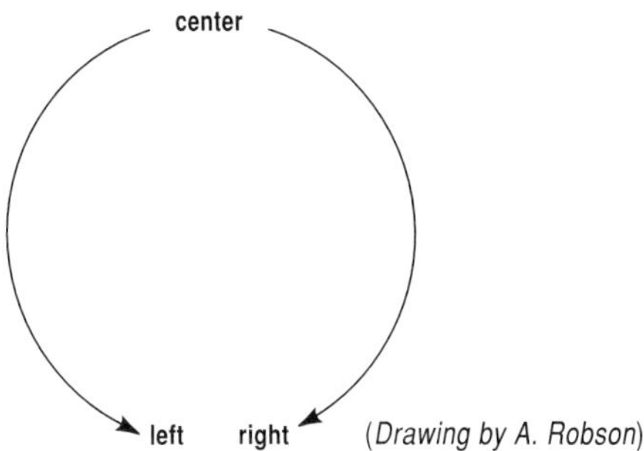

(*Drawing by A. Robson*)

The interesting reality suggested here is that the monsters of history—tyrants who murdered millions of people—stand together, whether they belong in the linear configuration to the extreme right (Hitler, for example) or the extreme left (Stalin, for example). This concept was used in the prosecution of Madame Mao after the Cultural Revolution in China, when she was accused of being so far left that she had become a fascist.

Another controversial notion involving the connection between language and thinking appears in a 1967 article by Robert Kaplan, "Cultural Thought Patterns in Inter-Cultural Communication." Kaplan analyzed essays written by people from different cultures and suggested that the organization of the essays followed certain patterns, which he depicted as follows:

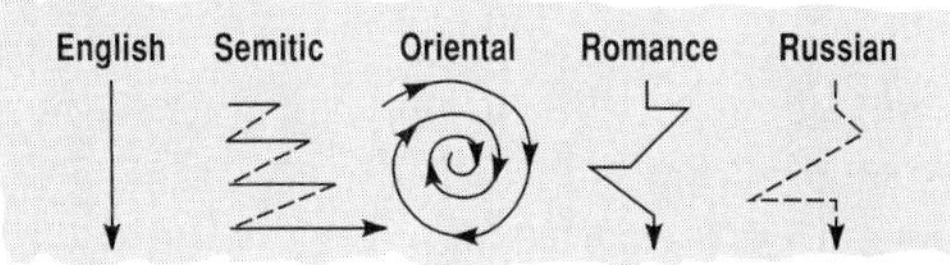

(*From* Language Learning *Vol. XVI, Nos. 1 & 2, 1967: 1-20*)

Kaplan argues that these patterns are well entrenched by adulthood, and that this poses problems for students and teachers from different cultures who work with each other in composition classrooms. Like Sapir and Whorf, Kaplan may overstate his case, but it remains an interesting example of the way language and culture intermingle and reflect each other.

The understanding of how people in different cultures regard time, space, and other basic categories of reality is important for successful **cross-cultural communication.**

THINK ON PAPER
Suggest other areas in which our language presupposes or imposes a certain view of the world. Some examples might be notions of time, intelligence, gender, and race Nemi Jain's essay in Section Two of this unit suggests ways in which Indian views of really are shaped by religious language and conventions, how does this apply to American culture.

ASPECTS OF WRITING: Unacceptable and acceptable words—and gestures.

In one sense, words are just words. They have meanings that can be described in dictionaries and, looked at objectively, they have no inherent moral dimension to them. Descriptive linguists emphasize this objective approach to words and try to avoid value judgments. In practice, however, everyone knows that words are characterized in ways that give them different levels of social acceptability. Dictionaries note when words are *slang, vulgar,* and *obscene,* and other categories also exist, including *racist, sexist, derogatory, rude, insulting,* and so on. Gestures are also an important part of communication, and sensitivity to the connotations of words and gestures is indicative of communicative competence within a culture.

Controversy over the use of words has a long history and has frequently led authors into court, as when D. H. Lawrence's *Lady Chatterley's Lover* or Henry Miller's *Tropic of Cancer* were banned by censors in Britain, the United States, and elsewhere. But what makes words correct, respectable, or otherwise? Certain principles apply here. Language is a living thing and changes over time, and the meaning and correctness of words is dependent on usage, which also changes over time. This relativism, however, should not lead one to conclude that it doesn't matter what one says or how one says it; it matters very much.

Notions such as "standard English" or "good English" may in a sense be arbitrary, but they are still important in many contexts. A company spokesperson who used "it ain't" as standard usage at a press conference would be lucky to hang on to his or her job, and educated people in general are expected to speak and write "correctly," especially at work and social gatherings, although they may switch to other codes in private or among friends. In *The American Heritage Dictionary,* Morris Bishop observes that the arbiters of correctness for that publication are mostly professional writers and others who have manifest expertise in the spoken and written language, and he includes a sample of their conclusions:

EXPRESSION	APPROVED BY	DISAPPROVED BY
ain't I? in writing		99%
between you and I in writing		99%

Expression	Approved by	Disapproved by
dropout used as a noun	97%	
thusly		97%
debut as a verb ("the company will debut its new models")		97%
slow as an adverb ("Drive Slow")	96%	
medias as a plural (instead of *media*)		95%
their own referring to the singular ("nobody thinks the criticism applies to their own work")		95%
but what ("There is no doubt but what he will try")		95%
myself instead of *me* in compound objects, in writing ("He invited Mary and myself to dinner")		95%
anxious in the sense of *eager*	94%	
type for *type of* ("that type shrub")		94%
rather unique; most unique		94%

Like words, gestures can also get one into trouble and/or lead to misunderstanding. The sideways shake of the head means "No" in many countries, but means "yes" in Greece, and a similar gesture also signals agreement in India. The slit-throat gesture means "stop" in Western cultures but "I love you" in Somalia. The hand gesture with fingers pointing downward that means "go away" in many cultures is almost identical with the gesture for "come here" in Samoa. The AOK sign, formed by touching the thumb and middle finger together, is obscene in much of Hispanic culture, and hitchhikers have to learn the appropriate gesture depending on where they are.

Quick Quiz

A. 1. What is "cultural relativism"?
2. What is "ethnocentrism"?
3. What does *Weltanschauung* mean?
4. What is the difference between the "real" and "ideal" culture?
5. What is the principal religion of India?
6. Which aspects of the Universal Declaration of Human Rights were Western inspired and which were Soviet inspired?
7. What is the basic idea behind the Sapir-Whorf hypothesis?
8. Is moral relativism struggling or flourishing in America today?

B. Commas are used before coordinating conjunctions linking two independent clauses. They are also used in one-comma or two-comma patterns. For example:

The moon, which had been shining brilliantly, was suddenly obscured. (Two commas acting in a parenthetical way, separating an embedded element from the main clause.)

Before I go, please tell me your name. (One comma separating an introductory element from the main clause.)

Put commas in the following paragraph.

When you're a student especially at this school you have to work hard. Among other things you'll probably have to work as well as study. The most difficult thing I think is to plan your time but some students even when they know that their lives are chaotic never learn to do this very effectively.

C. Indicate whether the following sentences contain standard or nonstandard usage. If in doubt, refer to your dictionary.

a. I've finished all ready!
b. Between you and I, I think that she made the right decision.
c. She gave a book each to Alex and me.
d. The judge was a disinterested observer.
e. She was disinterested in the movie.
f. I want to see her; on the contrary, I can't leave home today.
g. $200 or best offer. Runs good.
h. This is a very unique item.
i. The money was divided between the three children.
j. They should do it theirselves.
k. Go and lay down!
l. I have alot of time to study today.

SECTION ONE

PRIOR KNOWLEDGE: The universal language of the arts.

In the Western world, the discussion of beauty is often said to have begun with the Greek philosopher, Plato, who saw artistic creations as imitations of the realities we observe in the world around us, which, in turn, are imitations of archetypes that exist beyond human experience. This concept of art as an **imitation of life** persists to this day, although on different levels of sophistication. Some people, looking at an abstract or stylized painting, may say, "That doesn't look anything like a woman," or words to that effect, suggesting that only the *true* or "photographic" image may qualify as "art." In the arts, however, as in other areas of life, truth can be subtle and elusive, and the creative imagination often sees what others cannot or do not wish to see. Sometimes, the public can be won over; the granite wall of the Vietnam memorial in Washington, D.C.—an unconventional memorial—was very controversial when it was selected, but it evokes an overwhelming response in virtually everyone who visits it. The originality of the artist is not always vindicated in such a manner, however. Works that are universally admired by experts may be held in disdain by many members of the public, or at least may not be understood by them. This is as true in music, literature, and dance as it is in the visual arts.

The Greeks shaped the discussion of the purpose of the fine arts. Two competing ideas were proposed: first, that the arts had a **moral purpose** and that the poet or artist was, therefore, a teacher. The other view, characteristic of Aristotle, was that the arts should give **pleasure.**

THINK ON PAPER
How can the above observation be related to television today? Does the debate over some kinds of programming reflect this ancient dispute?

(Giraudon/Art Research, NY)

Guernica (1937), perhaps Picasso's most famous painting, depicts the aerial bombing (by German allies of General Franco) of the town of Guernica during the Spanish civil war. This event shocked the world, for it was the first such attack on civilian populations. Although Picasso was responding to this particular atrocity, *Guernica* came to be seen as a powerful protest against twentieth-century brutality in general. The painting, which is now displayed in the Centro d'Arte Reina Sofia, Madrid's modern art museum, is described by one art historian as follows:

> It does not represent the event itself; rather, with a series of powerful images, it evokes the agony of total war.
> Janson, *History of Art* 524

Music is less obviously an imitation of nature (although Aristotle and the Greeks thought it the *most* imitative), but it evokes responses of excitement, languor, sentimentality, happiness, and even national fervor, in much the same way through our aural sense as others do through the visual. Plato, who did not have anything even approaching the modern democratic spirit and who felt that the arts should teach rather than entertain, felt that some forms of music should be banned because they might seduce ordinary people into ill-considered behavior. A similar recognition of the power of music and other arts has provided ammunition for censors ever since.

The universality of human artistic activity is manifest in many ways. Prehistoric art dating back as far as 40,000 years suggests that our ancestors felt an urge to represent the world around them, possibly in association with ritualistic or religious ceremonies. Throughout history, all human societies have engaged in forms of artistic enterprise, be it the hand stencils in Australian aboriginal rock shelters, body decoration in virtually all cultures, or the painting of the Sistine Chapel.

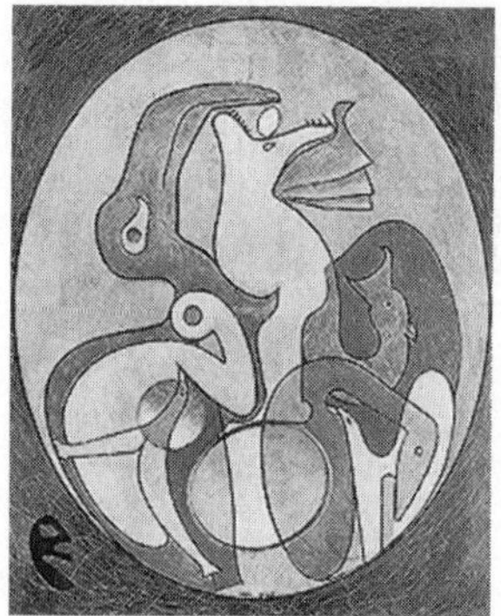

(Musée National d'Art Moderne, Centre National d'Art et de Culture Georges Pompidou, Paris)

(The British Museum)

Max Ernst (see left) seems to have been influenced by this Easter Island (Pacific) birdman motif (above). The modern work (right) is by Alberto Giacometti; the traditional figure (far right) is Tanzanian (West Africa). These illustrations are from *"Primitivism" in Twentieth Century Art*, Museum of Modern Art, 1984.

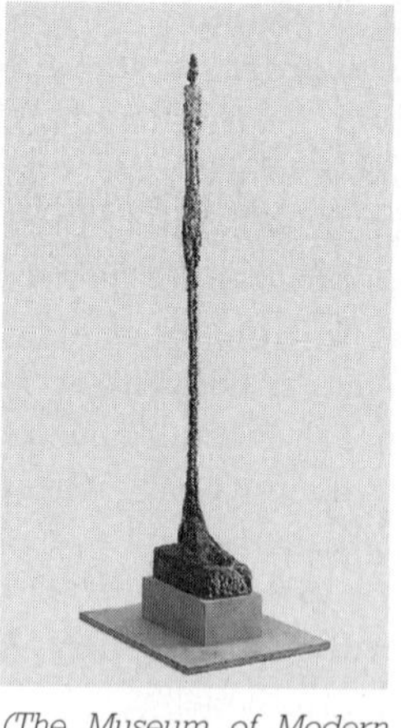

(The Museum of Modern Art, New York, James Thrall Soby Bequest. Photo © 1996 MOMA, NY)

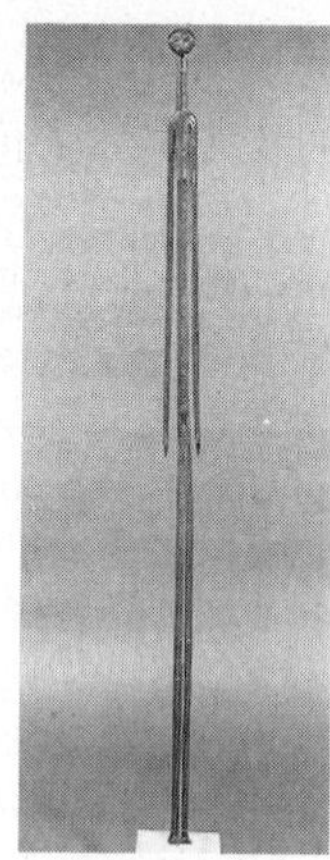

(Collection J.W. Mestach, Brussels)

Another type of universality involves the influence one tradition can have on another. Picasso, Braque, and others early in this century were strongly influenced by African and Oceanic art. Similarly, the influence of Asian artistic traditions is clearly apparent in late 19th-century design and music in the West, as for example, in the works of Debussy.

Western artistic style influenced by Chinese techniques is called *chinoiserie*, and the style influenced by Japanese works is called *japonisme*.

We encourage our children to paint, sing, write, and dance, and the arts in general entertain us and enrich our lives probably more than anything else—yet many people don't allow themselves to experience the most celebrated paintings, sculptures, music, theater, and literature and are even hostile to it. The following essay addresses this reality by discussing the question, What is art?

ANNOTATED READING: H. W. Janson. "The Artist and His Public." *History of Art.* New York: Prentice-Hall/Abrams: 1962:9–17 (extracts).

The Artist and His Public

"Why is this supposed to be art?" How often have we heard this question asked—or asked it ourselves, perhaps—in front of one of the strange, disquieting works that we are likely to find nowadays in museums or art exhibitions. There usually is an undertone of exasperation, for the question implies that *we* don't think we are looking at a work of art, but that the experts—the critics, museum curators, art historians—must suppose it to be one, why else would they put it on public display? Clearly, their standards are very different from ours; we are at a loss to understand them and we wish they'd give us a few simple, clear-cut rules to go by. Then maybe we would learn to like what we see, we would know "why it is art." But the experts do not post exact rules, and the layman is apt to fall back upon his final line of defense: "Well, I don't know anything about art but I know what I like."

Many societies and individuals have considered the arts to be so important to the quality of life, and even to the economy, that they have subsidized the work of individual artists and have founded and maintained museums, galleries, theaters, and concert halls for the display and performance of our artistic heritage and contemporary works. However, not many artists have rich patrons any more, as Mozart and others did, and so the state, or the government, typically plays this role. As public money is involved, it becomes more important that the citizenry understand more about the arts. The idea that the arts enrich the quality of life may be obvious to some, but it may be baffling to people unacquainted with such pleasures.

It is a formidable roadblock, this stock phrase, in the path of understanding between expert and layman. Until not so very long ago, there was no great need for the two to communicate with each other; the general public had little voice in matters of art and therefore could not challenge the judgment of the expert few. Today both sides are aware of the barrier between them (the barrier itself is nothing new, although it may be greater now than at certain times in the past) and of the need to level it. . . .

Defining art is about as troublesome as defining a human being. Plato, it is said, tried to solve the latter problem by calling man "a featherless biped," whereupon Diogenes introduced a plucked rooster as "Plato's Man." Generalizations about art are, on the whole, equally easy to disprove. Even the most elementary statements turn out to have their pitfalls. Let us test, for instance, the simple claim that a work of art must be made by man, rather than by nature. This definition at least eliminates the confusion of treating as works of art phenomena such as flowers, sea shells, or sunsets. It is a far from sufficient definition, to be sure, since man makes many things other than works of art. Still, it might serve as a starting point. Our difficulties begin as soon as we ask, "What do we mean by making?" If, in order to simplify our problem, we concentrate on the visual arts, we might say that a work of art must be a tangible thing shaped by human

Janson begins with definitional problems, and he jumps fearlessly into the fray with an example of exactly the kind of art that baffles many members of the public—Picasso's *Bull's Head.*

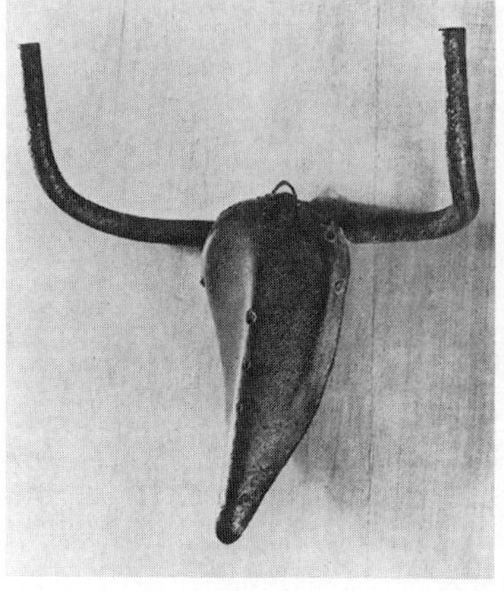

Pablo Picasso. *Bull's Head.* 1943. Handlebars and seat of a bicycle. *(Musée Picasso, Paris)*

Les demoiselles d'Avignon, Picasso, 1907. *(The Museum of Modern Art, NY. Acquired through the Lillie P. Bliss Bequest. Photo © 1996 MOMA, NY)*

Pablo Picasso (1881–1973) was a Spanish painter and sculptor. His name is virtually synonymous with "modern art," and he is generally acknowledged to be one of the twentieth century's greatest artists—perhaps *the* greatest. He settled in Paris in 1904. After his so-called Blue Period and Rose Period, he and the French painter, Georges Braque, developed a new way of looking at form that became known as **cubism.** Even today, nearly a hundred years later, many people see cubism as a baffling "modern" form.

hands. Now let us look at the striking *Bull's Head* by Picasso, which consists of nothing but the seat and handlebars of an old bicycle. How meaningful is our formula here? Of course the materials used by Picasso are man-made, but it would be absurd to insist that Picasso must share the credit with the manufacturer, since the seat and handlebars in themselves are not works of art. While we feel a certain jolt when we first recognize the ingredients of this visual pun, we also sense that it was a stroke of genius to put them together in this unique way, and we cannot very well deny that it is a work of art. Yet the handiwork—the mounting of the seat on the handlebars—is ridiculously simple. What is far from simple is the leap of the imagination by which Picasso recognized a bull's head in these unlikely objects; that, we feel, only he could have done. Clearly, then, we must be careful not to confuse the making of a work of art with manual skill or craftsmanship. Some works of art may demand a great deal of technical discipline; others do not. And even the most painstaking piece of craft does not deserve to be called a work of art unless it involves a leap of the imagination. But if this is true, are we not forced to conclude that the real making of the *Bull's Head* took place in the artist's mind? No, that is not so, either. Suppose that, instead of actually putting the two pieces together and showing them to us, Picasso merely told us, "You know, today I saw a bicycle seat and handlebars that looked just like a bull's head to me." Then there would be no work of art and his remark would not even strike us as an interesting bit of conversation. Moreover, Picasso himself would not feel the satisfaction of having created something on the basis of his leap of the imagination alone. Once he had conceived his visual pun, he could never be sure that it would really work unless he put it into effect.

Thus the artist's hands, however modest the task they may have to perform, play an essential part in the creative process. Our *Bull's Head* is, of course, an ideally simple case, involving only one leap of the imagination and a single manual act in response to it—once the seat had been properly placed on the handlebars, the job was done. Ordinarily, artists do not work with readymade parts but with materials that have little or no shape of their own; the creative process consists of a long series of leaps of the imagination and the artist's attempts to give them form by shaping the material accordingly. The hand tries to carry out the commands of the imagination and hopefully puts down a brush stroke, but the result may not be quite what had been expected, partly because all matter resists the human will, partly because the image in the artist's mind is constantly shifting and changing, so that the commands of the imagination cannot be very precise. In fact, the mental image begins to come into focus only as the artist "draws the line somewhere." That line then becomes part—the only fixed part—of the image; the rest of the image, as yet unborn, remains fluid. And each time the artist adds another line, a new leap of the imagination is needed to incorporate that line into his ever-growing mental image. If the line cannot be incorporated, he discards it and puts down a new one. In this way, by a constant flow of impulses back and forth between his mind and the partly shaped material before him, he gradually defines more and more of the image, until at last all of it has been given visible form. Needless to say, artistic creation is too subtle and intimate an experience to permit an exact step-by-step description; only the artist himself can observe it fully, but he is so absorbed by it that he has great difficulty explaining it to us. Still, our metaphor of birth comes closer to the truth than would a description of the process in terms of a transfer or projection of the image from the artist's mind, for the making of a work of art is both joyous and painful, replete with surprises, and in no sense mechanical. We have, moreover, ample testimony that the artist himself tends to look upon his creation as a living thing. Thus, Michelangelo, who has described the anguish and glory of the artist's experience more eloquently than anyone else, speaks of his "liberating the figure from the marble that imprisons it." We may translate this, I think, to mean that he started the process of carving a statue by trying to visualize a figure in the rough, rectilinear block as it came to him from the quarry. (At times he may even have done so while the marble was still part of the living rock; we know that he liked to go to the quarries and pick out his material on the spot.) It seems fair to assume that at first he did not see the figure any more clearly than one can see an unborn child inside the womb, but we may believe he

Michelangelo (1475–1564) was one of the most influential artists in history. A painter, sculptor, architect, and poet, he was a dominant figure in the High Renaissance in Italy. He painted the frescoes on the ceiling of the Sistine Chapel, in the Vatican, and among his other most famous works is the statue of *David,* on display in Florence, and the *Pietà,* in St. Peter's Basilica, in Rome, which portrays a serene Mary, the mother of Jesus, sitting, and holding Jesus, dead, across her lap.

could see isolated "signs of life" within the marble—a knee or an elbow pressing against the surface. In order to get a firmer grip on this dimly felt, fluid image, he was in the habit of making numerous drawings, and sometimes small models in wax or clay, before he dared to assault the "marble prison" itself, for that, he knew, was the final contest between him and his material. Once he started carving, every stroke of the chisel would commit him more and more to a specific conception of the figure hidden in the block, and the marble would permit him to free the figure whole only if his guess as to its shape was correct. Sometimes he did not guess well enough—the stone refused to give up some essential part of its prisoner, and Michelangelo, defeated, left the work unfinished, as he did with his *St. Matthew,* whose every gesture seems to record the vain struggle for liberation. Looking at the side view of the block, we may get some inkling of Michelangelo's difficulties here. But could he not have finished the statue in *some* fashion? Surely there is enough material left for that. Well, he probably could have, but perhaps not in the way he wanted, and in that case the defeat would have been even more stinging.

Michelangelo. *St. Matthew.* 1506. Marble, height 8′11″. Academy, Florence *(Alinari/Art Resource, NY)*

Clearly, then, the making of a work of art has little in common with what we ordinarily mean by "making." It is a strange and risky business in which the maker never quite knows what he is making until he has actually made it; or, to put it another way, it is a game of find-and-seek in which the seeker is not sure what he is looking for until he has found it. (In the *Bull's Head*, it is the bold "finding" that impresses us most, in the St. *Matthew*, the strenuous "seeking.") To the non-artist, it seems hard to believe that this uncertainty, this need-to-take-a-chance, should be the essence of the artist's work. For we all tend to think of "making" in terms of the craftsman or manufacturer who knows exactly what he wants to produce from the very outset, picks the tools best fitted to his task, and is sure of what he is doing at every step. Such "making" is a two-phase affair: first the craftsman makes a plan, then he acts on it. And because he—or his customer—has made all the important decisions in advance, he has to worry only about means, rather than ends, while he carries out his plan. There is thus little risk, but also little adventure, in his handiwork, which as a consequence tends to become routine. It may even be replaced by the mechanical labor of a machine. No machine, on the other hand, can replace the artist, for with him conception and execution go hand in hand and are so completely interdependent that he cannot separate the one from the other. Whereas the craftsman only attempts what he knows to be possible, the artist is always driven to attempt the impossible—or at least the improbable or unimaginable. Who, after all, would have imagined that a bull's head was hidden in the seat and handlebars of a bicycle until Picasso discovered it for us; did he not, almost literally, "make a silk purse out of a sow's ear"? No wonder the artist's way of working is so resistant to any set rules, while the craftsman's encourages standardization and regularity. We acknowledge this difference when we speak of the artist as *creating* instead of merely *making* something, although the word is being done to death by overuse nowadays, when every child and every lipstick manufacturer is labeled "creative."

Janson notes that the artist takes risks and never quite knows how his or her work will turn out. This is just as true of writing. The novelist often finds that the characters develop their own logic and start to dictate the action, and the story may go in unexpected directions.

THINK ON PAPER
What distinction is Janson making between the craftsman and the artist?

Needless to say, there have always been many more craftsmen than artists among us, since our need for the familiar and expected far exceeds our capacity to absorb the original but often deeply unsettling experiences we get from works of art. The urge to penetrate unknown realms, to achieve something original, may be felt by every one of us now and then; to that extent, we can all fancy ourselves potential artists—mute inglorious Miltons. What sets the real artist apart is not so much the desire to *seek*, but that mysterious ability to *find* which we call talent. We also speak of it as a "gift," implying that it is a sort of present from some higher power; or as "genius," a term which originally meant that a higher power—a kind of "good demon"—inhabits the artist's body and acts through him. All we can

The allusion to "mute inglorious Miltons" is a reference to Thomas Gray's "Elegy in a Country Churchyard," which is mentioned again in Section Two of this unit. Gray laments the undiscovered and undeveloped powers and talents of the uneducated and the impoverished. Perhaps among the dead in the churchyard is someone who could have become a great poet. His poem, written in 1751, has continuing relevance today. John Milton is one of the greatest names in English poetry. His most famous work is *Paradise Lost* (1667).

genius (L)—deity of generation and birth

The Moslem use of this word comes from the word *jinni* or *genie*, a spirit with supernatural abilities to influence humans.

Janson is not the only one to use the word carefully. Modestly disclaiming the application of the word to himself, the famous French flutist, Jean-Pierre Rampal, once said that the real genius is the creator, the composer.

really say about talent is that it must not be confused with aptitude. Aptitude is what the craftsman needs; it means a better-than-average knack for doing something that any ordinary person can do. An aptitude is fairly constant and specific; it can be measured with some success by means of tests which permit us to predict future performance. Creative talent, on the other hand, seems utterly unpredictable; we can spot it only on the basis of *past* performance. And even past performance is not enough to assure us that a given artist will continue to produce on the same level: some artists reach a creative peak quite early in their careers and then "go dry," while others, after a slow and unpromising start, may achieve astonishingly original work in middle age or even later.

Originality, then, is what distinguishes art from craft. We may say, therefore, that it is the yardstick of artistic greatness or importance. Unfortunately, it is also very hard to define; the usual synonyms—uniqueness, novelty, freshness—do not help us very much, and the dictionaries tell us only that an original work must not be a copy, reproduction, imitation or translation. What they fail to point out is that originality is always relative: there is no such thing as a completely original work of art. Thus, if we want to rate works of art on an "originality scale," our problem does not lie in deciding whether or not a given work is original (the obvious copies and reproductions are for the most part easy enough to eliminate) but in establishing just exactly *how* original it is. To do that is not impossible. However, the difficulties besetting our task are so great that we cannot hope for more than tentative and incomplete answers. Which does not mean, of course, that we should not try; quite the contrary. For whatever the outcome of our labors in any particular case, we shall certainly learn a great deal about works of art in the process.

Thorn Puller (Spinario). Bronze, height 28 3/4″. Capitoline Museums, Rome *(Alinari/Art Resource, NY)*

Let us look at a few of the baffling questions that come up when we investigate the problem of originality. The *Thorn Puller*, or *Spinario*, has long been one of the most renowned pieces of ancient bronze sculpture and enjoys considerable fame as a work of art even today—except among classical archaeologists who have studied it with care. They will point out that the head, which is cast separately and is of slightly different metal, does not match the rest: the planes of the face are far more severe than the soft, swelling forms of the body; and the hair, instead of falling forward, behaves as if the head were held upright. The head, therefore, must have been designed for another figure, probably a standing one, of the fifth century B.C., but the body could not have been conceived until more than a hundred years later. As soon as we become aware of this, our attitude toward the *Spinario* changes sharply; we no longer see it as a single, harmonious unit but as a somewhat incongruous combination of two ready-made pieces. And since the pieces are separate—though fragmentary—works of art in their own right (unlike the separate pieces, which are not works of art in themselves, in Picasso's *Bull's Head*), they cannot grow together into a new whole that is more than the sum of its parts. Obviously, this graft is not much of a creative achievement. Hence we find it hard to believe that the very able artist who modeled the body should have been willing to countenance such a "marriage of convenience." The combination must be of a later date, presumably Roman rather than Greek. Perhaps the present head was substituted when the original head was damaged by accident? But are the head and body really authentic Greek fragments of the fifth and fourth century B.C., or could they be Roman copies or adaptations of such pieces? These questions may be settled eventually by comparison with other ancient bronzes of less uncertain origin, but even then the degree of artistic originality of the *Spinario* is likely to remain a highly problematic matter.

A straightforward copy can usually be recognized as such on internal evidence alone. If the copyist is merely a conscientious craftsman, rather than an artist, he will produce a work of craft; the execution will strike us as pedestrian and thus out of tune with the conception of the work. There are also likely to be small slip-ups and mistakes that can be spotted in much the same way as misprints in a text. But what if one great artist copies another? . . . Edouard Manet's famous painting, *Luncheon on the Grass*, seemed so revolutionary a work when first exhibited almost a century ago that it caused a scandal, in part because the artist had dared to show an undressed young woman

The shocked response to Manet's painting reminds us that what is controversial in one period may be readily accepted in another. This is as true in music as it is in the visual arts. Janson also reminds us that artists sometimes *intend* to shock their audience, perhaps to wake them up.

Edouard Manet. *Luncheon on the Grass (Le Déjeuner sur l'Herbe).* 1863. Oil on canvas, 7′ × 8′10″. The Louvre, Paris *(Art Resource, NY)*

River Gods (detail of a Roman sarcophagus). 3rd century, Villa Medici, Rome *(Art Resource, NY)*

Marcantonio Raimondi, after Raphael. *The Judgment of Paris* (detail). c. 1520. Engraving *(Giraudon/Art Resource, NY)*

next to two fashionably clothed men. In real life such a party might indeed get raided by the police, and people assumed that Manet had intended to represent an actual event. Not until many years later did an art historian discover the source of these figures: a group of classical deities from an engraving after Raphael. The relationship, so striking once it has been pointed out to us, had escaped attention, for Manet did not *copy* or *represent* the Raphael composition—he merely *borrowed* its main outlines while translating the figures into modern terms. Had his contemporaries known of this, the *Luncheon* would have seemed a rather less disreputable kind of outing to them, since now the hallowed shade of Raphael could be seen to hover nearby as a sort of chaperon. (Perhaps the artist meant to tease the conservative public, hoping that after the initial shock had passed, somebody would recognize the well-hidden quotation behind his "scandalous" group.) For us, the main effect of the comparison is to make the cool, formal quality of Manet's figures even more conspicuous. But does it decrease our respect for his originality? True, he is "indebted" to Raphael; yet his way of bringing the forgotten old composition back to life is in itself so original and creative that he may be said to have more than repaid his debt. As a matter of fact, Raphael's figures are just as "derivative" as Manet's; they stem from still older sources which lead us back to ancient Roman art and beyond (compare the relief of *River Gods*).

Thus, Manet, Raphael, and the Roman river gods form three links in a chain of relationships that arises somewhere out of the dim and distant past and continues into the future—for the *Luncheon on the Grass* has in turn served as a source of more recent works of art. Nor is this an exceptional case. All works of art anywhere—yes, even such works as Picasso's *Bull's Head*—are part of similar chains that link them to their predecessors. If it is true that "no man is an island," the same can be said of works of art. The sum total of these chains makes a web in which every work of art occupies its own specific place, and which we call *tradition*. Without tradition—the word means "that which has been handed down to us"—no originality would be possible; it provides, as it were, the firm platform from which the artist makes his leap of the imagination. The place where he lands will then become part of the web and serve as a point of departure for further leaps. And for us, too, the web of tradition is equally essential. Whether we are aware of it or not, tradition is the framework within which we inevitably form our opinions of works of art and assess their degree of originality. Let us not forget, however, that such assessments must always remain incomplete and subject to revision. For in order to arrive at a definitive view, we should not only need to know *all* the different chains of relationships that pass through a given work of art, we should be able to survey the entire length of every chain. And that we can never hope to achieve.

Another poetic allusion:

> No man is an island entire of itself; every
> man is a part of a continent, a part of the main.
> (John Donne, *Devotions XVII)*

If originality is what distinguishes art from craft, tradition serves as the common meeting ground of the two. Every budding artist starts out on the level of craft, by imitating other works of art. In this way, he gradually absorbs the artistic tradition of his time and place until he has gained a firm footing in it. But only the truly gifted ever leave that stage of traditional competence and become creators in their own right. No one, after all, can be taught how to create; he can only be taught how to go through the motions of creating. If he has talent, he will eventually achieve the real thing. What the apprentice or art student learns are skills and techniques—established ways of drawing, painting, carving, designing; established ways of *seeing*. And if he senses that his gifts are too modest for painting, sculpture, or architecture, he is likely to turn to one of the countless special fields known collectively as "applied art." There he can be fruitfully active on a more limited scale; he may become an illustrator, typographer, or interior decorator; he may design textile patterns, chinaware, furniture, clothing, or advertisements. All these pursuits stand somewhere between "pure" art and "mere" craft. They provide some scope for originality to their more ambitious practitioners, but the flow of creative endeavor is hemmed in by such factors as the cost and availability of materials or manufacturing processes, accepted notions of what is useful, fitting, or desirable; for the applied arts are more deeply enmeshed in our everyday lives and thus cater to a far wider public than do painting and sculpture. Their purpose, as the name suggests, is to beautify the useful—an important and honorable one, no doubt, but of a lesser order than that of art pure-and-simple. Nevertheless, we often find it difficult to maintain this distinction. Medieval painting, for instance, is to a large extent "applied," in the sense that it

Janson's discussion of **tradition** is important. Great artists draw on those who have come before, and the most original of them may start off in a new direction from where the older masters left off. Even Shakespeare used old stories as the basis for many of his plays. His genius lay in what he did with the raw material.

embellishes surfaces which serve another, practical purpose as well—walls, book pages, windows, furniture. The same may be said of much ancient and medieval sculpture. Greek vases, although technically pottery, are sometimes decorated by artists of very impressive ability. And in architecture the distinction breaks down altogether, since the design of every building, from country cottage to cathedral, reflects external limitations imposed upon it by the site, by cost factors, materials, technique, and by the practical purpose of the structure. (The only "pure" architecture is imaginary architecture.) Thus architecture is, almost by definition, an applied art, but it is also a major art (as against the others, which are often called the "minor arts").

It is now time to return to our troubled layman and his assumptions about art. He may be willing to grant, on the basis of our discussion so far, that art is indeed a complex and in many ways mysterious human activity about which even the experts can hope to offer only tentative and partial conclusions; but he is also likely to take this as confirming his own belief that "I don't know anything about art." Are there really people who know nothing about art? If we except small children and the victims of severe mental illness or deficiency, our answer must be no, for we cannot help knowing *something* about it, just as we all know something about politics and economics no matter how indifferent we may be to the issues of the day. Art is so much a part of the fabric of human living that we encounter it all the time, even if our contacts with it are limited to magazine covers, advertising posters, war memorials, and the buildings where we live, work, and worship. Much of this art, to be sure, is pretty shoddy—art at third- and fourth-hand, worn out by endless repetition, representing the lowest common denominator of popular taste. Still, it is art of a sort; and since it is the only art most people ever experience, it molds their ideas on art in general. When they say, "I know what I like," they really mean, "I like what I know (and I reject whatever fails to match the things I am familiar with)"; such likes are not in truth theirs at all, for they have been imposed upon them by habit and circumstance, without any personal choice. To like what we know and to distrust what we do not know is an age-old human trait. We always tend to think of the past as "the good old days," while the future seems fraught with danger. But why should so many of us cherish the illusion of having made a personal choice in art when in actual fact we have not? I suspect there is another unspoken assumption here, which goes something like this: "Since art is such an 'unruly' subject that even the experts keep disagreeing with each other, my opinion is as good as theirs—it's all a matter of subjective preference. In fact, my opinion may be *better* than theirs, because as a layman I react to art in a direct, straightforward fashion, without having my view obstructed by a lot of compli-

With nice symmetry, Janson returns to his original focus on the ordinary person who thinks he or she knows nothing about art but "knows what s/he likes." He points out that everyone has much more exposure to art than they might realize: "They are . . . experts, people whose authority rests on experience rather than theoretical knowledge." He appeals for "an open mind and a capacity to absorb new experiences," and on this rests his hope that more people will become willing to explore the world of the arts and discover the beauty, the pleasure, and the challenges that await them there.

cated theories. There must be something wrong with a work of art if it takes an expert to appreciate it."

A similar point may also be made about writing. If you are a native speaker of English, or have equivalent fluency, you are an expert in the language, even if you don't know how to talk about the grammar and other elements. This is a solid basis on which to build real expertise, but you must be willing to explore and learn.

Behind these mistaken conclusions we find a true and important premise—that works of art exist in order to be liked rather than to be debated. The artist does not create merely for his own satisfaction, but wants his work approved by others. In fact, the hope for approval is what makes him want to create in the first place, and the creative process is not completed until the work has found an audience. . . .

The audience whose approval looms so large in the artist's mind is a limited and special one, not the general public: the merits of the artist's work can never be determined by a popularity contest. The size and composition of this primary audience vary a good deal with time and circumstance; its members may be other artists as well as patrons, friends, critics, and interested bystanders. The one qualification they all have in common is an informed love of works of art—an attitude at once discriminating and enthusiastic that lends particular weight to their judgments. They are, in a word, *experts*, people whose authority rests on experience rather than theoretical knowledge. And because experience, even within a limited field, varies from one individual to the other, it is only natural that they should at times disagree among themselves. Such disagreement often stimulates new insights; far from invalidating the experts' role, it shows, rather, how passionately they care about their subject, whether this be the art of their own time or of the past.

The active minority which we have termed the artist's primary audience draws its recruits from a much larger and more passive secondary audience, whose contact with works of art is less direct and continuous. This group, in turn, shades over into the vast numbers of those who believe they "don't know anything about art," the laymen pure-and-simple. What distinguishes the layman, as we have seen before, is not that he actually *is* pure and simple but that he likes to think of himself as being so. In reality, there is no sharp break, no difference in kind, between him and the expert, only a difference in degree. The road to expertness invites anyone with an open mind and a capacity to absorb new experiences. As we travel on it, as our understanding grows, we shall find ourselves liking a great many more things than we had thought possible at the start, yet at the same time we shall gradually acquire the courage of our own convictions, until—if we travel far enough—we know how to make a meaningful individual choice among works of art. By then, we shall have joined the active minority that participates directly in shaping the course of art in our time. And we shall be able to say, with some justice, that we know what we like.

ASPECTS OF WRITING: Improving style.

The Basque lying against my legs was tanned the color of saddle-leather. He wore a black smock like all the rest. There were wrinkles in his tanned neck. He turned around and offered his wine-bag to Bill. Bill handed him one of our bottles. The Basque wagged a forefinger at him and handed the bottle back, slapping in the cork with the palm of his hand. He shoved the wine-bag up.

"Arriba! Arriba!" he said. "Lift it up."

Hemingway, *The Sun Also Rises*

[Short, unadorned sentences are very characteristic of Hemingway's style.]

1664 West 54th Place was a dried-out brown house with a dried-out brown lawn in front of it. There was a large bare patch around a tough-looking palm tree. On the porch stood one lonely wooden rocker, and the afternoon breeze made the unpruned shoots of last year's poinsettias tap-tap against the cracked stucco wall. A line of stiff yellowish half-washed clothes jittered on a rusty wire in the side yard. . . .

The bell didn't work so I rapped on the wooden margin of the screen door. Slow steps shuffled and the door opened and I was looking into dimness at a blowsy woman who was blowing her nose as she opened the door. Her face was gray and puffy. She had weedy hair of that vague color which is neither brown nor blond, that hasn't enough life in it to be ginger, and isn't clean enough to be gray.

Chandler, *Farewell, My Lovely*

[Chandler uses many more adjectives and adverbs than Hemingway, and his prose suggests a keen observation and a wry sense of humor.]

There are several levels on which the quality of writing can be assessed, including **mechanical correctness, accuracy and interest of content,** and **style.** Of these, the last is probably the most elusive to diagnose and the most difficult to fix. Fortunately, if you are primarily concerned with matters of style, it suggests that the lower-level mechanical problems have largely been eliminated, and your ability to read and manipulate information is also satisfactory.

The first thing to think about is the nature of *good style.* What is it? This, of course, is not an easy question to answer, and it becomes impossible if you are looking for a single model that illustrates what is definitively "the best" in writing. Different styles can be equally effective, equally beautiful; some are spare and stark, some are full of detail and observation. The examples opposite, from Ernest Hemingway and Raymond Chandler, illustrate this.

Just because there are many good styles does not mean, however, that the evaluation of style is simply relative or a matter of personal opinion. We can look for clarity, coherence, and precision (see Section One, Unit One); we can expect a logical progression of ideas or events; and we can hope for a certain elegance in the language. This last quality is achieved, perhaps, by finding *le mot juste*—the right word—and by achieving a blend of sentence structure that avoids the dully repetitive and achieves a dynamic variety, similar to that found in music. Not every sentence or paragraph will be beautiful, but all should be carefully crafted. The message, *combined with* the language, will determine which passages the reader finds memorable.

WRITING EXERCISES: Answer one of the following questions.

Many questions seem more difficult than they really are. Analyzing the question can help, as illustrated below.

1. Janson asks the question, "What is art?" Describe and discuss his answer, with specific reference to his essay.
2. Describe ways in which the arts and crafts enrich people's lives. You might consider what life would be like without any literature, films, theater, dance, music, or painting and sculpture. You might also analyze what it means, exactly, to say that such things "enrich people's lives." This could be a personal essay, in which you discuss the place of the arts in your life, or a more general essay, discussing such issues in terms of society in general.
3. Janson describes what he calls the layman's "final line of defense: 'Well, I don't know anything about art but I know what I like.'" With this line in mind, describe a recent visit to an art gallery, play, or other performance (a good idea would be to go to something you haven't seen before, so that you can describe a very new experience). Write about the performance (or exhibition), your reaction, and the reaction of others around you. You may wish to take advantage of the humorous possibilities in this assignment.

If you choose **question 1,** you might start by noting that it asks for a discussion of *Janson's* answer to the question, "What is art?" This should lead you back to Janson's essay, looking specifically for comments on this question. This **focused reading** will quickly produce results—even on the first page of Janson's essay. The list you generate will give you a rough outline of your paper and will provide you with significant remarks that you might quote or paraphrase. Note that his discussion involves ascertaining what *isn't* art as well as what *is.* You might begin by observing that "art" is not easy to define.

If you attempt **question 2,** you might begin by noting that the question refers to "the arts" and to "people's lives." Each of these phrases covers a wide range of possibilities that could be explored in your paper. Approached in this way, your paper will probably reveal that the arts, broadly defined, are important in most people's lives.

SECTION TWO

PRIOR KNOWLEDGE: Why do people read literature?

"**Suspension of disbelief**" means that, even though we know that what we are seeing or reading is fiction and (in a play) that the people on stage are actors, we accept the story as being real. This is essential if we are to enter the imaginary world created by the author. The phrase comes from the poet Coleridge's *Biographia Literaria.*

There are many different kinds of novels:

- Historical novel
- Romance
- Science fiction
- Philosophical novel
- Novel of manners
- Stream-of-consciousness novel
- Gothic novel

and many more. Novels are fictional narratives dealing with aspects of life, character, and experience, although some include historical characters or thinly disguised but identifiable people from real life; in this latter case, the work is called a *roman à clef*—a novel with a key. Traditionally, they are discussed in terms of the quality of the writing and various formal aspects, including **plot, theme, characterization,** and **setting.** Popular novels are intended as entertainments; more serious works often have themes that address issues of social, intellectual, and moral interest.

The idea that art is an imitation of life is readily applicable to literature. The characters in many popular novels appeal to the reader because he or she can identify with the main character, perhaps, or because the human situation portrayed, even though fictional—and even though "writ large," with characters who may be more than commonly wealthy, arrogant, beautiful, and so on—is *true to life.* When reading a novel we like, we "suspend our disbelief" and enter into the world of the story, in much the same way that audiences do in the theater or in front of their televisions.

"Truth," however, can mean more than a representation of ordinary lives. The writer may have a particular purpose, or several purposes, in writing a novel or a play. Charles Dickens, for example, was hugely popular, and public readings of his stories were big events, with people sometimes crying *en masse* at sentimental or tragic scenes, but he also described the terrible conditions under which so many people in his day had to live and work. He was a social reformer, and his novels helped to move opinion and political action in a more humane direction.

Other writers have other themes, but great writers often have themes that are **universal** in nature. Shakespeare is perhaps the ultimate example of this, for his plays are not only about individuals in a certain context of time and place but are about jealousy, love, self-deception, foolishness, pride, power, cruelty, and so on. Theme is not the only element of interest, however. The plot should be compelling, the characters should be interesting and credible, the setting should be appropriate, and the language should resonate.

The beauty of the language is also a factor, but how can we assess this? As is the case with any of the arts, we have to be receptive, both emotionally and intellectually, in order to take pleasure in the beauty of literature. Emotionally, we can appreciate Keats' lines from the "Ode on a Grecian Urn," in which he addresses both the frustration of the lovers painted on the urn and the appealing idea that their love and beauty will never die:

Heard melodies are sweet, but those unheard
Are sweeter; therefore, ye soft pipes, play on;
Not to the sensual ear, but, more endeared
Pipe to the spirit ditties of no tone:

Fair youth, beneath the trees, thou canst not leave
Thy song, nor ever can those trees be bare;
Bold lover, never, never canst thou kiss,
Though winning near the goal—yet do not grieve;
She cannot fade, though thou hast not thy bliss,
For ever wilt thou love, and she be fair!

or Yeats's highly evocative lines from "The Second Coming":

Turning and turning in the widening gyre
The falcon cannot hear the falconer;
Things fall apart; the center cannot hold;
Mere anarchy is loosed upon the world,
The blood-dimmed tide is loosed, and everywhere
The ceremony of innocence is drowned;
The best lack all conviction, while the worst
Are full of passionate intensity.

On an intellectual level, we may further appreciate the technical features of the writing, and we may see the "truth" in the lines. The last two lines quoted from Yeats are a good example of how the writer can articulate what in others may be felt but inchoate.

Two essays follow. The first, by the author of one of the most admired American novels, discusses the appeal of fiction. The second describes Larkin's "Church Going" as one of the great poems in English this century.

THINK ON PAPER
What do you like most (an image or phrase, perhaps) in either or both the stanzas from Keats and Yeats provided above?

Titles of novels sometimes come from poems. Yeats inspired the title of Chinua Achebe's *Things Fall Apart.*

Nowhere is the power of the artist to influence others more readily acknowledged than in authoritarian and totalitarian societies. Writers are frequently among the first to be threatened, exiled, imprisoned, or even worse. Socrates is perhaps the most famous example from the ancient world, but many modern writers have also been victimized. The following, sad to say, is only a sampling.

Alexander Solzhenitsyn (b. 1918): Russian novelist. Imprisoned in the Soviet prison camp system that he later described and exposed in his *Gulag Archipelago* and other writings. Banished from the Soviet Union, he returned to Russia following the collapse of the communist government.

Vaclav Havel (b. 1936): Czech playwright and statesman; imprisoned by the former communist government, he became the first president of the post-communist Czechoslovakia and then the Czech Republic.

Wole Soyinka (b. 1934): Nigerian writer, winner of the Nobel Prize for Literature, 1986. Imprisoned during the Nigerian Civil War and harassed by the military government in 1994, when he escaped into exile.

Dennis Brutus (b. 1924): Zimbabwe/South African poet, imprisoned and banned by the former apartheid government in South Africa, then went into exile.

Salman Rushdie (b. 1947): Indian/British writer, sentenced to death by the Ayatollah Khomeini of Iran for "blasphemy" in his novel *Satanic Verses.* Lives in hiding, under police protection.

ANNOTATED READING 1: Robert Penn Warren. "On Reading Fiction." From *Robert Penn Warren: New and Selected Essays.* New York: Random House, 1989. Printed *in memoriam* in *The Chronicle of Higher Education.* 4 Oct. 1989: B64.

Robert Penn Warren, circa 1947 *(The Granger Collection)*

The conflict of which Penn Warren speaks may, of course, be of many kinds, but conflict in literature is usually seen as being either *external* or *internal.* A conflict between families or individual characters is external; a conflict within a person over his or her duty, or sense of self, or world view, or over some kind of divided loyalty is internal.

The standard sequences of a play were first described by Aristotle, in his *Poetics.* More recently, they have been applied to narrative fiction, as seen below in **Freytag's pyramid**, beginning with the exposition, or setting of the scene:

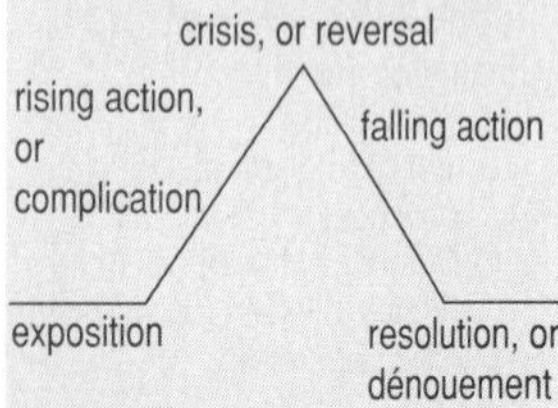

There are many possible variations on this pattern, but, as Penn Warren notes, they all promise conflict that is eventually resolved–for better or worse. Perhaps this is one part of the appeal of fiction, for the conflicts of ordinary life are sometimes never resolved.

On Reading Fiction

Why do we read fiction? The answer is simple. We read it because we like it. And we like it because fiction, as an image of life, stimulates and gratifies our interest in life. But whatever interests may be appealed to by fiction, the special and immediate interest that takes us to fiction is always our interest in a story.

A story is not merely an image of life, but life in motion—specifically, the presentation of individual characters moving through their particular experiences to some end that we may accept as meaningful. And the experience that is characteristically presented in a story is that of facing a problem, a conflict. To put it bluntly: no conflict, no story.

It is no wonder that conflict should be at the center of fiction, for conflict is at the center of life. But why should we, who have the constant and often painful experience of conflict in life and who yearn for inner peace and harmonious relation with the outer world, turn to fiction, which is the image of conflict? The fact is that our attitude toward conflict is ambivalent. If we do find a totally satisfactory adjustment in life, we tend to sink into the drowse of the accustomed. Only when our surroundings—or we ourselves—become problematic again do we wake up and feel that surge of energy which is life. And life more abundantly lived is what we seek.

So we, at the same time that we yearn for peace, yearn for the problematic. The adventurer, the sportsman, the gambler, the child playing hide-and-seek, the teen-age boys choosing up sides for a game of sandlot baseball, the old grad cheering in the stadium—we all, in fact, seek out or create problematic situations of greater or lesser intensity. Such situations give us a sense of heightened energy, of life. And fiction, too, gives us the fresh, uninhibited opportunity to vent the rich emotional charge—tears, laughter, tenderness, sympathy, hate, love, and irony—that is stored up in us and short-circuited in the drowse of the accustomed. Furthermore, this heightened awareness can be more fully relished now, because what in actuality would be the threat of the problematic is here tamed to mere imagination, and because some kind of resolution of the problem is, owing to the very nature of fiction, promised.

The story promises us a resolution, and we wait in suspense to learn how things will come out. We are in suspense to learn how things will come out. We are in suspense, not only about what will happen, but even more about what the event will mean. We are in suspense about the story in fiction because we are in suspense about another story far closer and more important to us—the story of our own life as we live it. We do not know how that story of our own life is going to come out. We do not know what it will mean. So, in that deepest suspense of life, which will be shadowed in the suspense we feel about the story in fiction, we turn to fiction for some slight hint about the story in the life we live. The relation of our life to the fictional life is what, in a fundamental sense, takes us to fiction.

Even when we read, as we say, to "escape," we seek to escape not *from* life but *to* life, to a life more satisfying than our own drab version. Fiction gives us an image of life—sometimes of a life we actually have and like to dwell on, but often and poignantly of one we have had and do not have now, or one we have never had and can never have.

There are many wonderful passages in Penn Warren's *All the King's Men,* and the following is one of them. It is the Deep South in 1922, and the narrator, at this time a reporter for a small town newspaper, is in Mason City on a story. He decides that the place to start is outside the harness shop—just as today, in many small towns, the coffee shop or similar local institution is a gathering place for the old folk.

> I went out into the street, where the dogs lay on the shady side under the corrugated iron awnings, and walked down the block till I came to the harness shop. There was one vacant seat out front, so I said howdy-do, and joined the club. I was the junior member by forty years, but I thought I was going to have liver spots on my swollen old hands crooked on the end of the hickory stick like the rest of them before anybody was going to say anything. In a town like Mason City the bench in front of the harness shop is—or was twenty years ago before the concrete slab got laid down—the place where Time gets tangled in its own feet and lies down like an old hound and gives up the struggle. It is a place where you sit down and wait for night to come and arteriosclerosis. It is the place the local undertaker looks at with confidence and thinks he is not going to starve as that much work is cut out for him. But if you are sitting on the bench in the middle of the afternoon in late August with the old ones, it does not seem that anything will ever come, not even your own funeral, and the sun beats down and the shadows don't move across the bright dust, which, if you stare at it long enough, seems to be full of glittering specks like quartz. The old ones sit there with their liver-spotted hands crooked on the hickory sticks, and they emit a kind of metaphysical effluvium by virtue of which your categories are altered. Time and motion cease to be. It is like sniffing ether, and everything is sweet and sad and far away. You sit there among the elder gods, disturbed by no sound except the slight *râle* of the one who has asthma, and wait for them to lean from the Olympian and sunlit detachment and comment, with their unenvious and foreknowing irony, on the goings-on of the folks who are still snared in the toils of mortal compulsions. *I seen Sim Saunders done built him a new barn.* Then, *Yeah, some folks thinks they is made of money.* And, *Yeah.*
>
> So I sat there and waited.

Before too long, they start talking, and the narrator, Jack Burden, learns what he needs to know.

ROBERT PENN WARREN, poet, novelist, critic, essayist, dramatist, and teacher, died September 15, 1989. Warren, the winner of three Pulitzer Prizes, retired as Professor of English at Yale University in 1973.

A Reader's Delight is a compilation of short essays on some of Perrin's favorite books. The author reminds us that there are many uncelebrated jewels in the world of literature.

ANNOTATED READING 2. Noel Perrin. "Philip Larkin's Greatest Poem." From *A Reader's Delight.* Hanover and London: UP of New England, 1988: 136–140.

Perrin alludes to several famous lines here:

This is the way the world ends
Not with a bang but a whimper.
T. S. Eliot, "The Hollow Men"

And what rough beast, its hour come round at last,
Slouches towards Bethlehem to be born?
W. B. Yeats, "The Second Coming"

Good fences make good neighbors.
Robert Frost, "Mending Wall"

Perrin warns that "fundamentalists of all sects should probably avoid [this poem]," but the end of the poem is a powerful testament to the universal yearning of even the most skeptical people for something "more serious," that is to say (probably) more *spiritual.* The poem addresses through one person the loss of faith in organized religion that is so characteristic of the twentieth-century experience, yet it articulates also the gaping hole this loss has created in the psyche and sensibility of individual human beings. The narrator of the poem is not a believer in any conventional sense, but he is not merely a tourist either; he visits churches because they acknowledge and represent the universal human quest to understand the purpose of life and to give our lives a dimension that is beyond the mundane and the material. Perrin's warning, therefore, may not be necessary.

Philip Larkin's Greatest Poem

Which are the great poems of the twentieth century? In English, that is. Some of Frost's, certainly. Some of T. S. Eliot's. Several by Yeats, several by Auden. One also by the English poet Philip Larkin.

Larkin is hardly an unknown poet. His is one of the names that have general though minor currency. Like William Carlos Williams, or Richard Wilbur, or Marianne Moore, he holds a sure place in the anthologies, and in the reference books, too.

But there is no line of his you can count on people to recognize—no world ending with a whimper, no rough beast slouching along, no fences making good neighbors. There is no book of his everybody has read. Surprisingly few people realize that Larkin has written one of the great poems of our time.

That poem is called "Church Going." Fundamentalists of all sects should probably avoid it, because its sensibility is so alien to their own. Most other people will find it profoundly moving. That's especially true for people who don't even believe in profundity (or in being moved). They will be hit hardest of all.

The poem is written in the anti-heroic style that is Larkin's specialty, and also the hallmark of our time. Fervor and lofty emotion are conspicuously lacking. As the poem begins, Larkin is on a bicycle tour and has stopped in some little English village to look at the parish church. His pause has nothing to do with piety, still less with wanting a chance to say a prayer. He's popping in tourist-style to check out the architecture.

Once I am sure there's nothing going on
I step inside, letting the door thud shut.
Another church: matting, seats, and stone.
And little books; sprawlings of flowers, cut
For Sunday, brownish now; some brass and stuff
Up at the holy end; the small neat organ;
And a tense, musty unignorable silence,
Brewed God knows how long.

The first line gives a strong clue to how the poem works. On the surface, it merely says the poet, like any prudent tourist, makes sure there's no service occurring in this nameless church before he strolls in. But underneath, "nothing going on" has another implication: that the church no longer has any significance.

Once inside, he looks around with a secular, almost a derisive eye. "Little books," as if he didn't know they were Church of England prayer books and hymnals. "Brass and stuff"—he is emotionally distant from the very concept of sacred objects. "The holy end" is downright mocking.

But already a counterpoint has begun. That silence may be musty, but there is a power in it. Enough to change the poet's mood? It's hard to tell.

Counterpoint is usually a musical term, denoting the combining of two or more melodies in a piece of music, so that one is played off against the other, as in a Bach fugue. Here it takes on a similar meaning; the narrator of the poem is skeptical but is also moved by the "unignorable silence" of the church. These feelings overlap and intertwine. Going into an ancient church is very different from going into a shopping mall.

Hatless, I take off
My cycle-clips in awkward reverence,
Move forward, run my hand around the font.

Here is what could be taken as a genuflection but is really just a bicyclist bending down to remove the ankle clips that keep his trousers from getting caught in the chain. And then we get our answer. The poet begins to make free with the empty church. The silence does *not* awe him—not yet, anyway. In fact, he casually dispels it.

reflection ← **inflection** ↑ → **deflection**
genuflection = *genu* (L), knee + *flectere* (L), bend

Mounting the lectern, I peruse a few
Hectoring large-scale verses, and pronounce
'Here endeth' much more loudly than I'd meant.
The echoes snigger briefly. Back at the door
I sign the book, donate an Irish sixpence,
Reflect the place was not worth stopping for.

Again there's a double meaning. On the surface, the poet is just imitating an Episcopal minister. Twice during the service of morning prayer, the minister goes to the lectern and reads a lesson from the Bible, one each from the Old Testament and the New. When he's done, he says, "Here endeth the lesson"—or at least he did until recently, when the Episcopal Church underwent its own little *aggiornamento*. Underneath, of course, the passage suggests that here endeth Christianity.

The rest of the poem is a meditation on that ending. The poet begins to wonder what will happen to little churches like this as faith dies out. Will they be abandoned, as the great abbeys were in Henry VIII's time? Will a few be kept as museums, and the rest degenerate into places of superstition? Yes, he thinks, they will. Old crones will come to touch a particular stone, and children will fear ghosts among the old graves outside.

Even that won't last, however.

It is conventional to put foreign words in italics, as here with *aggiornamento,* which means "modernization." Perrin is probably referring to the Church's switch to modern English rather than the language of the King James Bible of 1611; readings from the Bible, which are a part of every service, no longer close with the words, "Here endeth the lesson." An additional comment on the language of the Bible appears on the following page; it may be of interest to note that the language of the King James Bible is also the language of Shakespeare (1564–1616).

Sometimes known as the "Authorized Version," the King James Bible is renowned for **the beauty of its language,** and some people regret its replacement by modern translations. Compare, for example, two translations of the 23rd Psalm:

1. The LORD is my shepherd; I shall not want.
2. He maketh me to lie down in green pastures; he leadeth me beside the still waters.
3. He restoreth my soul: he leadeth me in the paths of righteousness for his name's sake.
4. Yea, though I walk through the valley of the shadow of death, I will fear no evil; for thou *art* with me; thy rod and thy staff they comfort me.
5. Thou preparest a table before me in the presence of mine enemies: thou anointest my head with oil; my cup runneth over.
6. Surely, goodness and mercy shall follow me all the days of my life: and I will dwell in the house of the LORD for ever.

(Authorized Version, 1611)

1. The LORD is my shepherd; I lack for nothing.
2. He makes me lie down in green pastures, he leads me to water where I may rest;
3. he revives my spirit; for his name's sake he guides me in the right paths.
4. Even were I to walk through a valley of deepest darkness I should fear no harm, for you are with me; your shepherd's staff and crook afford me comfort.
5. You spread a table for me in the presence of my enemies; you have richly anointed my head with oil, and my cup brims over.
6. Goodness and love unfailing will follow me all the days of my life, and I shall dwell in the house of the LORD throughout the years to come.

(The Oxford Study Bible, 1992)

But superstition, like belief, must die,
And what remains when disbelief has gone?
Grass, weedy pavement, brambles, buttress, sky.

This is the low point of the poem. The church has been drained of all value whatsoever; there is nothing left but a heap of meaningless stone, over which the briars grow. And then with seeming casualness Larkin starts to reintroduce meaning. He idly wonders who will be the very last visitor to stand where he is standing now, knowing that here was a church. He imagines several possibilities. It might be a "ruin-bibber, randy for antique." It might be a scholar, taking notes on the old building for an article. If the last visit occurs sooner than that, before services have completely ceased, it might be the sort of Christian-by-habit of which the Church of England is currently full, as American churches are, too. That is, someone who comes once or twice a year, usually with his or her family, for one of the great festival services. In that case, it would be what Larkin calls a "Christmas-addict, counting on a whiff/Of gown-and-bands and organ-pipes and myrrh."

And then there is a fourth possibility. The last visitor might be someone like Larkin himself. Here the poem soars. It becomes so splendid that the only sensible thing is to quote the whole two-stanzas-and-a-line with which it ends.

Or will he be my representative,

Bored, uninformed, knowing the ghostly silt
Dispersed, yet tending to this cross of ground
Through suburb scrub because it held unspilt
So long and equably what since is found
Only in separation—marriage, and birth,
And death, and thoughts of these—for which was built
This special shell? For, though I've no idea
What this accoutered frowsty barn is worth,
It pleases me to stand in silence here;

A serious house on serious earth it is,
In whose blent air all our compulsions meet,
Are recognized, and robed as destinies.
And that much never can be obsolete,
Since someone will forever be surprising
A hunger in himself to be more serious,
And gravitating with it to this ground,
Which, he once heard, was proper to grow wise in,
If only that so many dead lie round.

Here, I think, are the best lines Philip Larkin has ever written, and among the best done in this century. Here is an elegy written in a country church, and it is profounder than the one Gray wrote outside in the churchyard. The elegy is for Christianity itself, that great force, which could take ordinary human drives and robe them as destinies. The irreverent tourist has recognized the power of the brooding silence, and he has given it such an accolade as no mere believer possibly could.

THINK ON PAPER
Which of the above do you prefer? Why? Note: There are no "right" or "wrong" answers to this.

When writing about literature, or any text, it is good practice to make plenty of **reference to the original.** Perrin does this with a mixture of direct quote, paraphrase, explication, and discussion, **with the quotes well integrated into his discussion.** He provides a good model for a systematic critique.

Even though this is an appreciation of a favorite poem, Perrin avoids the **first person** until the very end. Instead of referring to himself, *he keeps the focus on the poem and Larkin by making* ***them*** *the subject of most of his sentences.* At the end, however, he passes his personal judgment on the poem, especially the final two stanzas, and his use of the first person is perfectly appropriate.

The allusion in the last paragraph is to Thomas Gray's famous poem, "Elegy Written in a Country Churchyard" (1751). Earlier, mention was made of poems inspiring titles for novels, and Gray's poem is the source of Thomas Hardy's title (and more recently a movie) *Far From the Madding Crowd:*

Far from the madding crowd's ignoble strife
Their sober wishes never learned to stray

Gray's "Elegy" is also the source of a famous **aphorism:**

The paths of glory lead but to the grave.

"Church Going."
Philip Larkin. 1955.

Many errors in usage involve misstating or misspelling common words, idioms, and phrases. The teacher and writer Richard Lederer has collected such errors in his amusing book, *Anguished English* (Dell, 1987) from which the following examples are taken. Lederer's examples are real but are published in a spirit of good humor. While you laugh, may also try to figure out what the poor student was trying to say.

Julius Caesar extinguished himself on the battlefields of Gaul. The Ides of March murdered him because they thought he was going to be made king. Dying, he gasped out the words, "Tee, hee, Brutus." Nero was a cruel tyranny who would torture his poor subjects by playing the fiddle to them.

The Renaissance was an age in which more individuals felt the value of their human being. Martin Luther was nailed to the church door at Wittenberg for selling indulgences. He died a horrible death, being excommunicated by a bull. It was the painter Donatello's interest in the female nude that made him the father of the Renaissance.

Writing at the same time as Shakespeare was Miguel Cervantes. He wrote *Donkey Hote.* The next great author was John Milton. Milton wrote *Paradise Lost.* Then his wife died and he wrote *Paradise Regained.*

George Washington married Martha Curtis and in due time became the Father of Our Country. His farewell address was Mount Vernon.

Abraham Lincoln became America's greatest Precedent. Lincoln's mother died in infancy, and he was born in a log cabin which he built with his own hands.

Bach was the most famous composer in the world, and so was Handel. Handel was half German, half Italian, and half English. He was very large.

(Lederer, *Anguished English*)

ASPECTS OF WRITING: Idiomatic language.

English is a highly **idiomatic** language, meaning that it contains innumerable words and phrases, often highly colorful, that have set forms and specific meanings that may have little to do with the literal meaning of the words. Such expressions are particularly difficult for speakers of English as a second language—although native speakers often make mistakes with idioms, too—but they are also an interesting and even amusing aspect of the language. Here are some common idioms, organized by prepositions; perhaps you can add to the lists.

in, into ←

- **in a state, in a funk** (upset)
- **getting into it** (getting enthusiastically involved in something
- **in a good/bad mood** (feeling happy/grumpy)
- **in the swing of** something (well-adjusted to a situation)

up →

- **up the creek [without a paddle]** (in trouble)
- **up and at 'em** (energetically starting the day's work)
- **give up** (surrender, abandon a project, admit defeat)
- **the run up to** something (the preliminary stages of an event or situation)

down ←

- **down and out** (impoverished, suffering hard times)
- **look down on** someone (feel superior to someone)
- **down at the heel** (impoverished)
- **getting down to work** (starting work)

over →

- **over the hill** (too old, ineffective)
- **to go overboard** (to be excessively enthusiastic)
- **a sleep over** (a party at which children sleep at a friend's house)

WRITING EXERCISES: Answer one of the following.

Aphorisms are pithy and memorable sayings. The best are witty and true—or at least have enough truth in them to make us laugh and recognize the point being made. Some writers have contributed richly to our store of such sayings:

Dr. Johnson (1709–1784): Patriotism is the last refuge of a scoundrel.

Will Rogers (1879–1935): The income tax has made more liars out of the American people than golf has.

Mark Twain (1835–1910): If you pick up a starving dog and make him prosperous, he will not bite you. This is the principal difference between a dog and a man.

Oscar Wilde (1854–1900): Life imitates art far more than art imitates life.

George Bernard Shaw (1856–1950): Do not unto others as you would they should do unto you. Their tastes may not be the same.

1. Choose a favorite work of literature and critique it in the manner illustrated by Perrin in the above reading. It would probably be helpful to reread Perrin's essay and the annotations before starting this. Make it clear what it is that you admire or enjoy about the work you choose.
2. Robert Penn Warren writes: *"Even as we read, as we say, to 'escape,' we seek to escape not* **from** *life but* **to** *life, to a life more satisfying than our own drab version."* Discuss the place of *escapism* in modern life—or your life. The tone of this essay may be serious or humorous, as you wish.
3. How do you respond to Penn Warren's essay on the reading of fiction? If the reading of fiction is an important part of your life, you will probably be able to endorse and add to his sentiments, but if you are not a reader of fiction you may have a very different reaction. Discuss Penn Warren's essay—and the reading of fiction—from your personal point of view.

SECTION THREE

PRIOR KNOWLEDGE: The creative struggle.

A good example of the artistic stereotype being manifest in real life is the French composer **Erik Satie** (1866–1923). Upon his death, Satie's apartment in Paris was found to contain hundreds of umbrellas and unopened mail from innumerable famous admirers. He also wrote some delightful piano music to which he gave odd titles such as *Piece in the form of a pear.* Satie quit the Paris Conservatory to work as a café musician. His eccentricity, revolutionary political tendencies, and bohemian nature were legendary, and his music, usually deceptively simple and short, influenced the likes of Debussy and Ravel. His best-known pieces are probably the lovely *Gymnopédies.*

Artists of many kinds are famously odd and/or difficult, but only opera has given us a phrase which describes one kind of personality—the *prima donna.* Literally, this means the "first lady" in an opera company, the *diva,* the goddess, but it has also come to mean a temperamental and self-centered person. Anyone familiar with opera can name great stars who fit this description, but it is all part of the tempestuous world of theater and the arts, and the singing is divine.

Artists seem different from other people, and this difference has led to stereotypes such as the "writer in the garret," the "bohemian," and the unpredictable and difficult "artistic temperament." It is an image that is sustained by the behavior of some famous artists and perpetuated by the media and the movies.

Given that many artists actually live perfectly ordinary lives, the origin of this stereotype may be worthy of exploration. The artist seems to be the antithesis of the executive, the secretary, the industrial worker, or the bureaucrat, but most people have little idea about an artist's life. Does he or she punch a clock or work at a desk? Dress in a suit and have a "normal" family life? The answer, of course, is different for different people; many artists support themselves and their families with jobs in teaching or other professions and devote their spare time to their own creative work. Some have positions designed to accommodate their creative work, like artists-in-residence at some universities. Some are employed by giant companies to create works for mass audiences, as in the movie and television industries. Some struggle along on their own, hoping to get a break one day.

No matter what the circumstances, however, all artists—be they painters, sculptors, writers, dancers, musicians, or actors—share one reality: what they do is hard work, in both senses of the word: it is exhausting and it is difficult. This will seem obvious to those familiar with the creative and interpretative arts, but will probably be incomprehensible to others. Why is such work so hard? What makes artists different from other people?

The following essay, by the great 19th-century novelist, Joseph Conrad, offers some insight into this mystery. He was a writer, but he makes reference to the other arts and he makes it clear that **the cre-**

Joseph Conrad (1857–1924) was Polish by birth, orphaned as a young boy, and a sailor by the age of 16. He worked on French and then British ships, eventually becoming a master mariner. He had many adventures, and some of his stories are set in Malaya and the Congo, places he knew firsthand. Eventually, he gave up the sea to devote himself to literature, and he became a celebrated stylist in English, which was his fourth language, after Polish, Russian, and French. His works are still widely read, including the novels *Lord Jim* and *Nostromo,* and his famous short story, "Heart of Darkness." In more recent times, *Lord Jim* was made into a successful movie, and "Heart of Darkness" inspired a Vietnam-era movie called *Apocalypse Now.*

ative struggle is what they all have in common, and Conrad describes it vividly as involving a "[descent] within himself, . . . [to] that lonely region of stress and strife." Conrad describes the goal of the artist and suggests the frustrations and the rewards. The artist is pursuing something abstract, something that appeals to the senses and to the emotions as well as to the intellect. In a phrase that recalls the ancient Greek philosophers' view, he calls music "the art of arts," perhaps in part because it is, in his view, the most purely and powerfully sensuous form.

The creative struggle involved in each of the arts is apparent in every performance. For a musician, it is not enough merely to play the right notes; he or she must capture the dynamics, the emotional force, of a piece. This is the hardest part, and it has its equivalent in every art, for what is being communicated is not just notes, not just paint, not just dance steps, but something that will make people listen, look, and feel in new ways. This is also suggested by Janson in Section One of this unit in the context of the visual arts, but his focus is on the audience and the audience's understanding of the nature of art; Conrad's focus is on the artist and the elusiveness of what he or she is trying to express. This struggle to communicate, to evoke the range of human emotions and experience, is what binds together all artists. It is the link between Beethoven and the blues, primitive cave paintings and Picasso, Emily Brontë and Anne Tyler.

One of the greatest 18th-century poets, Alexander Pope, observed in *An Essay on Criticism* that

True ease in writing comes from art, not chance,
As those move easiest who have learned to dance.

Pope is saying that artistic performances look easy only because of the years of dedication performers give to the perfection of their technique. The discipline of practice, often alone, sustained even when nothing seems to be achieved, day after day, year after year, is what makes it all look or sound so easy.

Conrad's novel, to which this essay is the preface, centers on a black sailor who, in real life, voyaged with the author. Because of the obvious sensitivity modern readers will have to Conrad's title, it might be worthwhile to note some remarks that precede the preface, in a section addressed "To My Readers In America." Here, Conrad describes the sailor, James Wait:

> I had much to do with him. He was on my watch. A negro in a British forecastle is a lonely being. He has no chums. Yet James Wait, afraid of death and making her his accomplice was an impostor of some character—mastering our compassion, scornful of our sentimentalism, triumphing over our suspicions. . . . [He] remains very precious to me. For the book written round him is not the sort of thing that can be attempted more than once in a life-time. . . . Its pages are the tribute of my unalterable and profound affection for the ships, the seamen, the winds and the great sea—the moulders of my youth, the companions of the best years of my life.

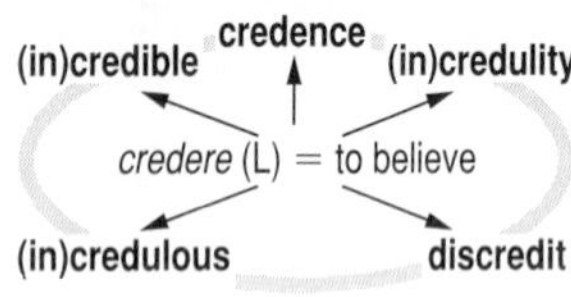

This beautiful passage, beginning on the previous page, is stylistically interesting for its *balance*, its *parallel structure*, and its use of *repetition*, as well as for its uplifting evocation of humanity's higher nature:

ANNOTATED READING: Joseph Conrad. "Preface" to the novel *The Nigger of the "Narcissus."* London, 1897.

Preface

A work that aspires, however humbly, to the condition of art should carry its justification in every line. And art itself may be defined as a single-minded attempt to render the highest kind of justice to the visible universe, by bringing to light the truth, manifold and one, underlying its every aspect. It is an attempt to find in its forms, in its colours, in its light, in its shadows, in the aspects of matter and in the facts of life what of each is fundamental, what is enduring and essential—their one illuminating and convincing quality—the very truth of their existence. The artist, then, like the thinker or the scientist, seeks the truth and makes his appeal. Impressed by the aspect of the world the thinker plunges into ideas, the scientist into facts—whence, presently, emerging they make their appeal to those qualities of our being that fit us best for the hazardous enterprise of living. They speak authoritatively to our common-sense, to our intelligence, to our desire of peace or to our desire of unrest; not seldom to our prejudices, sometimes to our fears, often to our egoism—but always to our credulity. And their words are heard with reverence, for their concern is with weighty matters: with the cultivation of our minds and the proper care of our bodies, with the attainment of our ambitions, with the perfection of the means and the glorification of our precious aims.

It is otherwise with the artist.

Confronted by the same enigmatical spectacle the artist descends within himself, and in that lonely region of stress and strife, if he be deserving and fortunate, he finds the terms of his appeal. His appeal is made to our less obvious capacities: to that part of our nature which, because of the warlike conditions of existence, is necessarily kept out of sight within the more resisting and hard qualities—like the vulnerable body within a steel armour. His appeal is less loud, more profound, less distinct, more stirring—and sooner forgotten. Yet its effect endures forever. The changing wisdom of successive generations discards ideas, questions facts, demolishes theories. But the artist appeals to that part of our being which is not dependent on wisdom: to that in us which is a gift and not an acquisition—and, therefore, more permanently enduring. He speaks to our capacity for delight and wonder, to the sense of mystery surrounding our lives; to our sense of pity, and beauty, and pain; to the latent feeling of fellowship with all creation—and to the subtle but invincible conviction of solidarity that knits together the loneliness of innumerable hearts, to the solidarity in dreams, in joy, in sorrow, in aspirations, in illusions, in hope, in fear, which binds men to each other, which binds together all humanity—the dead to the living and the living to the unborn.

It is only some such train of thought, or rather of feeling, that can in a measure explain the aim of the attempt, made in the tale which follows, to present an unrestful episode in the obscure lives of a few individuals out of all the disregarded multitude of the bewildered, the simple and the voiceless. For, if any part of truth dwells in the belief confessed above, it becomes evident that there is not a place of splendour or a dark corner of the earth that does not deserve, if only a passing glance of wonder and pity. The motive, then, may be held to justify the matter of the work; but this preface, which is simply an avowal of endeavour, cannot end here—for the avowal is not yet complete.

Fiction—if it at all aspires to be art—appeals to temperament. And in truth it must be, like painting, like music, like all art, the appeal of one temperament to all the other innumerable temperaments whose subtle and resistless power endows passing events with their true meaning, and creates the moral, the emotional atmosphere of the place and time. Such an appeal to be effective must be an impression conveyed through the senses; and, in fact, it cannot be made in any other way, because temperament, whether individual or collective, is not amenable to persuasion. All art, therefore, appeals primarily to the senses, and the artistic aim when expressing itself in written words must also make its appeal through the senses, if its high desire is to reach the secret spring of responsive emotions. It must strenuously aspire to the plasticity of sculpture, to the colour of painting, and to the magic suggestiveness of music—which is the art of arts. And it is only through complete, unswerving devotion to the perfect blending of form and substance; it is only through an unremitting never-discouraged care for the shape and ring of sentences that an approach can be made to plasticity, to colour, and that the light of magic suggestiveness may be brought to play for an evanescent instant over the commonplace surface of words: of the old, old words, worn thin, defaced by ages of careless usage.

The sincere endeavour to accomplish that creative task, to go as far on that road as his strength will carry him, to go undeterred by faltering, weariness or reproach, is the only valid justification for the worker in prose. And if his conscience is clear, his answer to those who in the fulness of a wisdom which looks for immediate profit, demand specifically to be edified, consoled, amused; who demand to be promptly improved, or encouraged, or frightened, or shocked, or charmed, must

But the artist appeals **to that part of our being which is** not dependent on wisdom: **to that in us which is** a gift and not an acquisition—and, therefore, more permanently enduring. He speaks **to our capacity** for delight and wonder, **to the sense of mystery** surrounding our lives; **to our sense** of pity, and beauty, and pain; **to the latent feeling** of fellowship with all creation—**and to the subtle** but invincible conviction of solidarity that knits together the loneliness of innumerable hearts, **to the solidarity in** dreams, **in** joy, **in** sorrow, **in** aspirations, **in** illusions, **in** hope, **in** fear, **which binds** men to each other, **which binds** together all humanity—**the dead to the living** and **the living to the unborn.**

The ultimate goal of the true artist is not money or amusement. It is something much harder and much more important. Conrad's fervor is apparent when he writes,

> **My task . . . is, by the power of the written word to make you hear, to make you feel—it is, before all, to make you see. *That—and no more, and it is everything.***

In this, Conrad may be seen as a spokesman for all the arts.

THINK ON PAPER

Describe any work of art, in any form, that has moved you, inspired you, opened your mind to a new way of thinking, or has in some way—as Conrad says—made you hear, made you feel, made you *see.*

There is a certain modern ring to Conrad's vision of a world in which we are all bound to each other "and all mankind to the visible world." His years at sea, and his familiarity with people from all parts of the globe, may have given him this humane vision. His novels are about the human condition, as in *Lord Jim,* in which a man spends much of his life trying to make up for an act of cowardice during a shipwreck in the Far East.

run thus:—My task which I am trying to achieve is, by the power of the written word to make you hear, to make you feel—it is, before all, to make you *see.* That—and no more, and it is everything. If I succeed, you shall find there according to your deserts: encouragement, consolation, fear, charm—all you demand—and, perhaps, also that glimpse of truth for which you have forgotten to ask.

To snatch in a moment of courage, from the remorseless rush of time, a passing phase of life, is only the beginning of the task. The task approached in tenderness and faith is to hold up unquestioningly, without choice and without fear, the rescued fragment before all eyes in the light of a sincere mood. It is to show its vibration, its colour, its form; and through its movement, its form, and its colour, reveal the substance of its truth—disclose its inspiring secret: the stress and passion within the core of each convincing moment. In a single-minded attempt of that kind, if one be deserving and fortunate, one may perchance attain to such clearness of sincerity that at last the presented vision of regret or pity, of terror or mirth, shall awaken in the hearts of the beholders that feeling of unavoidable solidarity; of the solidarity in mysterious origin, in toil, in joy, in hope, in uncertain fate, which binds men to each other and all mankind to the visible world.

It is evident that he who, rightly or wrongly, holds by the convictions expressed above cannot be faithful to any one of the temporary formulas of his craft. The enduring part of them—the truth which each only imperfectly veils—should abide with him as the most precious of his possessions, but they all: Realism, Romanticism, Naturalism, even the unofficial sentimentalism (which like the poor, is exceedingly difficult to get rid of,) all these gods must, after a short period of fellowship, abandon him—even on the very threshold of the temple—to the stammerings of his conscience and to the outspoken consciousness of the difficulties of his work. In that uneasy solitude the supreme cry of Art for Art itself, loses the exciting ring of its apparent immorality. It sounds far off. It has ceased to be a cry, and is heard only as a whisper, often incomprehensible, but at times and faintly encouraging.

Sometimes, stretched at ease in the shade of a roadside tree, we watch the motions of a labourer in a distant field, and after a time, begin to wonder languidly as to what the fellow may be at. We watch the movements of his body, the waving of his arms, we see him bend down, stand up, hesitate, begin again. It may add to the charm of an idle hour to be told the purpose of his exertions. If we know he is trying to lift a stone, to dig a ditch, to uproot a stump, we look with a more real interest at his efforts; we are disposed to condone the jar of his agitation upon the restfulness of the landscape; and even, if in a brotherly frame of mind, we may bring ourselves to forgive his failure. We understood his object, and, after all, the fellow has tried, and perhaps he had not the strength—and perhaps he had not the knowledge. We forgive, go on our way—and forget.

And so it is with the workman of art. Art is long and life is short, and success is very far off. And thus, doubtful of strength to travel so far, we talk a little about the aim—the aim of art, which, like life itself, is inspiring, difficult—obscured by mists. It is not in the clear logic of a triumphant conclusion; it is not in the unveiling of one of those heartless secrets which are called the Laws of Nature. It is not less great, but only more difficult.

To arrest, for the space of a breath, the hands busy about the work of the earth, and compel men entranced by the sight of distant goals to glance for a moment at the surrounding vision of form and colour, of sunshine and shadows; to make them pause for a look, for a sigh, for a smile—such is the aim, difficult and evanescent, and reserved only for a very few to achieve. But sometimes, by the deserving and the fortunate, even that task is accomplished. And when it is accomplished—behold!—all the truth of life is there: a moment of vision, a sigh, a smile—and the return to an eternal rest.

1897. J. C.

ASPECTS OF WRITING: Improving style.

Parallel structure often requires that you know the different forms of words. It is helpful here if you know the PARTS OF SPEECH: **noun, verb, pronoun, adjective, adverb, article, conjunction, preposition,** and **interjection.** Incidentally, not all lists of parts of speech are the same; linguists have competing ways of describing the language.

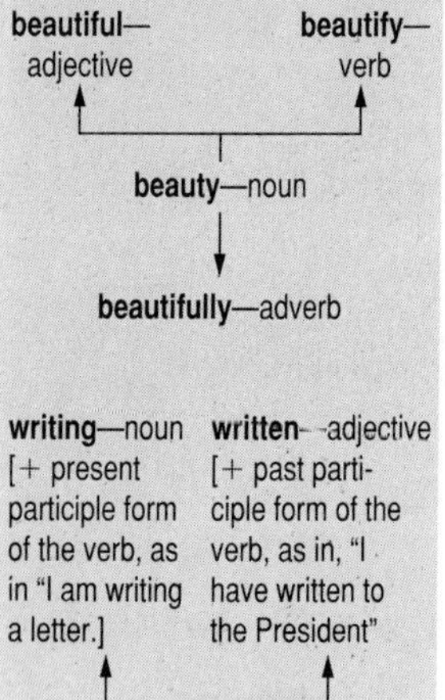

People have personal writing styles and sometimes respond to criticism by saying, "That's how I write." In most cases, however, this response is unhelpful. The purpose of writing is communication, and if "the way I write" impedes that goal, then some changes are clearly called for.

Some writing problems are stylistic in nature. A loss of clarity can be caused by a **convoluted sentence structure** and **vagueness:**

CONVOLUTED AND VAGUE: My sister loves to sail, being very committed to her self-image of courage and expertise, the romance of the seven seas.

COHERENT AND CLEAR: My sister loves to sail; she has courage and expertise, and she delights in the romance of the seven seas.

Another stylistic problem can be a lack of **variety in sentence structure.** Short sentences can be very effective, but too many together can be boring and may suggest an inability to see the relationships between ideas. Elaboration of ideas may also help create variety and interest:

CHOPPY AND UNCOORDINATED: The sea is beautiful. It can be dangerous. It is deceptive.

COORDINATED: The sea is beautiful, but it is also dangerous; its beauty can be deceptive.

ELABORATED: The sea is beautiful, but this beauty can be deceptive and dangerous. The unwary swimmer, lulled by the sun and surf, may be swept away by invisible currents.

A third problem may be a lack of **parallel structure,** which requires that lists and other sequences that have the same function in a sentence should be expressed in a structurally consistent (or "parallel") manner:

LACKS PARALLEL STRUCTURE: The sailor's life can be very challenging; it involves braving the elements, you are with the same people for weeks on end, separate from your family, and hard, physical work.

DEMONSTRATES PARALLEL STRUCTURE: The sailor's life can be very challenging; it involves **braving** the elements, **getting** along with the same people for weeks on end, **accepting** separation from family, and **doing** hard, physical work.

WRITING EXERCISES: Answer one of the following questions.

1. Conrad writes as a creative artist—a novelist. If you are (or have aspirations to be) a musician, a dancer, or in any way involved in the arts, describe the difficulties, challenges, and rewards that you experience. You may write this in a purely personal way, or you may refer to Conrad's essay, agreeing with or commenting on what he says there, based on your own experience.
2. The funding of the arts is sometimes controversial. When governments at different levels need to reduce spending, they often reduce support for orchestras, theater groups, museums, and so on, and when school budgets are being cut, the arts are often the first to suffer. Discuss this phenomenon from the point of view of a supporter of the arts. You might, for example, think about the discipline and pleasure that the arts provide and their lifelong significance to both performers and audiences.
3. Describe the appeal of the artistic forms (painting, music, literature, theater, film, dance, etc.) that you most enjoy—as a performer and/or as a member of the audience. To what extent does this appeal reflect the success of the artist in making you "think," "feel," and "see," to use Conrad's terms?

Here's a self-check exercise (or an oral, in-class exercise) on **parts of speech,** based in part on the examples on the previous page. If you don't get these right, you need to review this topic. Identify the part of speech of each underlined word:

a. His <u>writing</u> is <u>illegible</u>.
b. The <u>written</u> word <u>has</u> great power to persuade.
c. The children <u>are beautifying</u> <u>their</u> classroom for the open house.
d. <u>The</u> famous <u>virtuoso</u> was <u>enthusiastically</u> received, <u>but</u> the critics were not impressed.
e. The audience burst into <u>tumultuous</u> applause as the performance ended.

OPTION ONE

PRIOR KNOWLEDGE: Beauty in science, broadening the mind, and the two cultures.

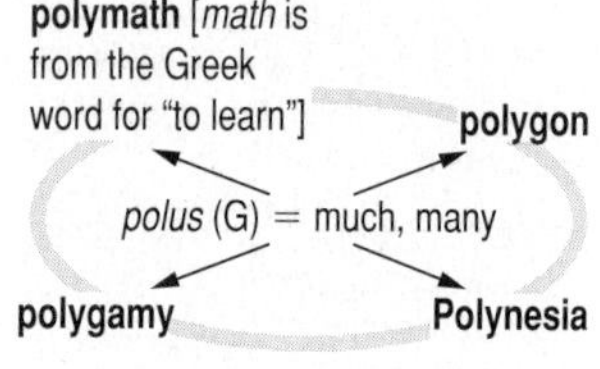

One of the most interesting aspects of intellectual inquiry is the discovery of connections between different disciplines—entirely unexpected relevancies. A closely related pleasure is the discovery of writers whose breadth of knowledge gives them a seemingly endless source of reference, allusion, and anecdote. We call such people **polymaths,** or sometimes Renaissance men or women. It is especially welcome to find individuals who can speak the language of both the sciences and the arts.

A distinguished Canadian novelist, the late Robertson Davies, was fond of polymaths, and included them in his stories. In so doing, he created characters whose lives and conversation take his readers into worlds that most have never explored—from Jungian psychoanalysis to the circus and the opera. An example is provided in the annotations on this page.

Among scientists, Stephen Jay Gould and E. O. Wilson—both already represented in this text—similarly draw on a wide range of knowledge from many fields. Stephen Jay Gould, with his references to literature, baseball, and many other aspects of life, enlivens and elucidates many discussions of evolution and thc history of science. In *Wonderful Life* he uses a Robert Frost poem to help explain and discuss the apparent randomness of evolution in its particularities, and the title of his book—a serious work on the lessons to be derived from the study of ancient fossils in the Burgess Shales in Western Canada—is an allusion to a popular and sentimental movie, often shown on television at Christmas. The bizarre beauty of many of the fossils does not go unnoticed either.

The novels of **Robertson Davies** (1913–1995) are full of interesting characters, ideas, situations, and information. Here is a sample from *Fifth Business* (1970), the first part of his Deptford trilogy:

> "Who are you? Where do you fit into poetry and myth? Do you know who I think you are, Ramsey? I think you are Fifth Business.
>
> "You don't know what this is? Well, in opera in a permanent company of the kind we keep in Europe you must have a prima donna—always a soprano, always the heroine, often a fool; and a tenor who always plays the lover to her; and then you must have a contralto, who is a rival to the soprano, or a sorceress or something; and a basso, who is the villain or the rival or whatever threatens the tenor.
>
> "So far, so good. But you cannot make a plot work without another man, and he is usually a baritone, and he is called in the profession Fifth Business, because he is the odd man out, the person who has no opposite of the other sex. And you must have Fifth Business because he is the one who knows the secret of the hero's birth, or comes to the assistance of the heroine when she thinks all is lost, or keeps the hermitess in her cell, or may even be the cause of somebody's death if that is part of the plot. The prima donna and the tenor, the contralto and the basso, get all the best music and do all the spectacular things, but you cannot manage the plot without Fifth Business! It is not spectacular, but it is a good line of work, I can tell you, and those who play it sometimes have a career that outlasts the golden voices. Are you Fifth Business? You had better find out."
>
> (*Fifth Business:* 227. Penguin)

Beauty and elegance are important concepts among mathematicians and scientists as well as among artists, and their work also has an esthetic (and moral) dimension. This ability to see connections among apparently different fields and phenomena encourages the reader to broaden his or her mind and to explore unfamiliar territory when opportunities arise.

In a celebrated 1959 lecture in Britain, C. P. Snow lamented and decried the scientists' lack of knowledge of the arts, and the artists' lack of knowledge of the sciences. He argued that most were unfamiliar with even the most basic information outside their own field. Most people in the arts and humanities, Snow asserts, could not describe Newton's second law of thermodynamics, and he suggests that most scientists would not do any better if asked about one of Shakespeare's plays.

Snow regrets this mutual ignorance for many reasons. It leads to estrangement rather than intimacy; it leads to barrenness rather than cross-pollination; and it limits everyone's imaginative and intellectual life.

Snow's essay remains relevant as a call for people in all fields to know at least something about the world outside their own specialty, and the following reading offers a good example of how a sense of beauty and a wealth of interdisciplinary reference can help give focus to matters that are important in the philosophy of science. Right from the start, Hoffmann alludes to the worlds of art and ancient philosophy. If you are not a chemist, don't be put off by the illustrations; the text is less intimidating than you might expect; in fact, it's a delight to read.

Snow's Rede Lecture was published under the title *The Two Cultures* (1959), and it stirred a great debate about the nature of education in Britain, where students begin to specialize in a few academic areas while still in high school. Snow noted that the gulf between the two cultures (the Arts and the Sciences) was more easily crossed in the United States. In this country too, however, his lecture became popular reading.

The debate over *Two Cultures* was in some ways similar to the more recent American debate sparked off by **E. D. Hirsch's** book *Cultural Literacy* (1987). Both books take aim at the education system in their respective countries, both lament a general lack of knowledge (and a lack of general knowledge), and both aroused a lively controversy. In Britain, a famous literary critic, F. R. Leavis, published a scathing and mocking attack on Snow (*Two Cultures? The Significance of C. P. Snow,* 1962), whom he accused of being "intellectually as undistinguished as it is possible to be." Hirsch, similarly, was roundly criticized by some for suggesting specific lists of facts which every educated person should know, the argument being that such lists revealed a class bias. Despite the critics, however, both Snow and Hirsch stimulated important debates, and the titles of their respective books have become established phrases in the language.

READING: Roald Hoffmann. "How Should Chemists Think?" *Scientific American* Feb. 1993: 66–73.

How Should Chemists Think?

Chemists can create natural molecules by unnatural means. Or they can make beautiful structures never seen before. Which should be their grail?

Plato and Aristotle in a detail of Raphael's fresco *The School of Athens* are depicted in a way that symbolizes their approach to knowledge. Aristotle gestures toward the earth; Plato points his finger to the heavens. Aristotle looked to nature for answers; Plato searched for the ideal. Should chemists follow the hand sign of Aristotle or that of Plato? *(Scala/Art Resource, NY)*

The Vatican holds a fresco by Raphael entitled *The School of Athens*. Plato and Aristotle stride toward us. Plato's hand points to the heavens, Aristotle's outward, along the plane of the earth. The message is consistent with their philosophies—whereas Plato had a geometric prototheory of the chemistry of matter, Aristotle described in reliable detail how Tyrian purple (now known to be a precursor of indigo) was extracted from rock murex snails. Plato searched for the ideal; Aristotle looked to nature.

Remarkably, modern chemistry faces the quandary that Raphael's fresco epitomized. Should it follow the hand sign of Aristotle or that of Plato? Is nature as fertile a source for new materials as some assert it to be? Can we, for example, hope to make better composites by mimicking the microstructure of a feather or of a strand of spider's silk? Are chemists better advised to seek their inspiration in ideal mathematical forms. In icosahedra and in soccer balls? Or should we hazard chance?

To some, the division between natural and unnatural is arbitrary; they would argue that man and woman are patently natural, and so

ROALD HOFFMANN shared the 1981 Nobel Prize in Chemistry with Kenichi Fukui. He was born in 1937 in Zloczow, Poland. Having survived the war, he came to the U.S. in 1949. He studied chemistry at Columbia University and received his Ph.D. from Harvard University. In 1965 he joined the faculty at Cornell University and is now the John A. Newman Professor of Physical Science. Hoffmann describes his contribution to science as "applied theoretical chemistry"—a particular blend of computations stimulated by experiment and the construction of generalized models. He writes essays and has published two poetry collections, *The Metamict State* and *Gaps and Verges*.

are all their transformations. Such a view is understandable and has a venerable history, but it does away with a distinction that troubles ordinary and thoughtful people. So I will not adopt it and instead will distinguish between the actions, mostly intended, of human beings and those of animals, plants and the inanimate world around us. A sunset is natural; a sulfuric acid factory is not. The 1.3 billion head of cattle in this world pose an interesting problem for any definition. Most of them are both natural and unnatural—the product of breeding controlled by humans.

The molecules that exist naturally on the earth emerged over billions of years as rocks cooled, oceans formed, gases escaped and life evolved. The number of natural molecules is immense; perhaps a few hundred thousand have been separated, purified and identified. The vast majority of the compounds that fit into the unnatural category were created during the past three centuries. Chemists have added some 15 million well-characterized molecules to nature's bounty.

To every thing of this world, be it living or not, there is structure. Deep down are molecules, persistent groupings of atoms associated with other atoms. There is water in the distilled form in the laboratory, in slightly dirty and acid snow, in the waters associated with our protein molecules. All are H_2O. When chemistry was groping for understanding, there was a reasonable reluctance to merge the animate and inanimate worlds. Friedrich Wöhler convinced many people that the worlds were not separate by synthesizing, in 1828, organic urea from inorganic silver cyanate and ammonium chloride.

How are molecules made in nature—penicillin in a mold or a precursor of indigo in a rock murex snail? How are they made in glass-glittery laboratories—those acres of food wrap, those billion pills of aspirin? By a common process—synthesis.

Chemistry is the science of molecules and their transformations. Be it natural or human-steered, the outcome of transformation, $A \rightarrow B$, is a new substance. Chemical synthesis, the making of the new, is patently a creative act. It is as much an affirmation of humanity as a new poem by A. R. Ammons or the construction of democracy in Russia. Yet creation is always risky. A new sedative may be effective, but it also may induce fetal malformation. A Heberto Padilla poem may be "counterrevolutionary" to a Cuban apparatchik. Some people in Russia still don't like democracy.

Wöhler mixed together two substances, heated them and obtained an unexpected result. Much has happened since 1828. To convey what the making of molecules is like today and to relate how the natural intermingles with the unnatural in this creative activity, let me tell you about the synthesis of two substances: Primaxin and the ferric wheel.

Primaxin is one of the most effective antibiotics on the market, a prime money-maker for Merck & Co. The pharmaceutical is not a single molecule but a designed mixture of two compounds, imipenem and cilastin [*see box*]. These are their "trivial" names. The "systematic" names are a bit longer; for instance, Imipenem is

[5R-[5α, 6α(R*)]]-6-(1-hydroxyethyl)-3-[[2-[(iminomethyl)amino] ethyl]thio]-7-oxo-1-azabicyclo[3.2.0]hept-2-ene-2-carboxylic acid.

Primaxin was created by a bit of unnatural tinkering, emulating the natural tinkering of evolution. Imipenem by itself is a fine antibiotic. But it is degraded rapidly in the kidney by an enzyme. This would give the drug limited use for urinary tract infections. The Merck chemists found in their sample collection a promising compound, synthesized in the 1940s, that inhibited that orney enzyme. Modified for greater activity, this became cilastatin. It was obvious to try the combination of the antibiotic and the enzyme inhibitor, and the mix worked.

Imipenem derives from a natural product; cilastatin does not. Both are made synthetically in the commercial process. I will return to this after tracing further the history of one of the components.

Imipenem was developed in the 1970s by a team of Merck chemists led by Burton G. Christensen. It is a slightly modified form of another antibiotic, thienamycin. That, in turn, was discovered while screening soil samples from New Jersey. It is produced by a mold, *Streptomyces cattleya*, so named because its lavender color resembles that of the cattleya orchid. The mold is a veritable drug factory, producing thienamycin and several other varieties of antibiotics.

Unfortunately, thienamycin was not chemically stable at high concentrations. And, to quote one of the Merck crew, "The lovely orchid-colored organism was too stingy." The usual fermentation processes, perfected by the pharmaceutical industry over the past 50 years, did not produce enough of the molecule. So the workers decided to produce greater quantities of thienamycin in the laboratory.

The production of thienamycin required 21 major steps, each involving several physical operations: dissolution, heating, filtration, crystallization. Between the starting material—a common amino acid, L-aspartic acid—and the desired product—thienamycin—20 other molecules were isolated and purified. Of these, only eight are shown in the condensed "reaction scheme."

The first impression that one gets is of complexity. That intricacy is essential, a laboratory counterpoint to the biochemical complexity of bacteria and us. We would like there to be "magic bullets" of abiding simplicity. The real world is complicated and beautiful. We had better come to terms with that richness.

To get a feeling for the sweat, if not the blood and tears, of the process, we need to turn to the experimental section of the paper reporting the synthesis. Here is an excerpt of that experimental pro-

The Making of an Antibiotic

The antibiotic Primaxin is a mixture of two compounds known as Imipenem *(ball-and-stick model at right)* and cilastatin *(model at left).* Imipenem is a slightly modified form of thienamycin, which is produced naturally by a mold. Chemists developed a procedure (summarized below) that produces thienamycin more efficiently than any known natural process. The stick figures shown are the chemist's typical notation; not all atoms are identified. Those vertices that do not have atomic labels represent carbon atoms. Most of the hydrogen atoms have been left out. It is possible to deduce the location of the missing hydrogen atoms because every carbon atom should form four bonds. An arrow represents each chemical transformation in the process. The percent figure near each arrow is the experimental yield. . . . Wedges indicate details of geometry, atoms above or below the plane.

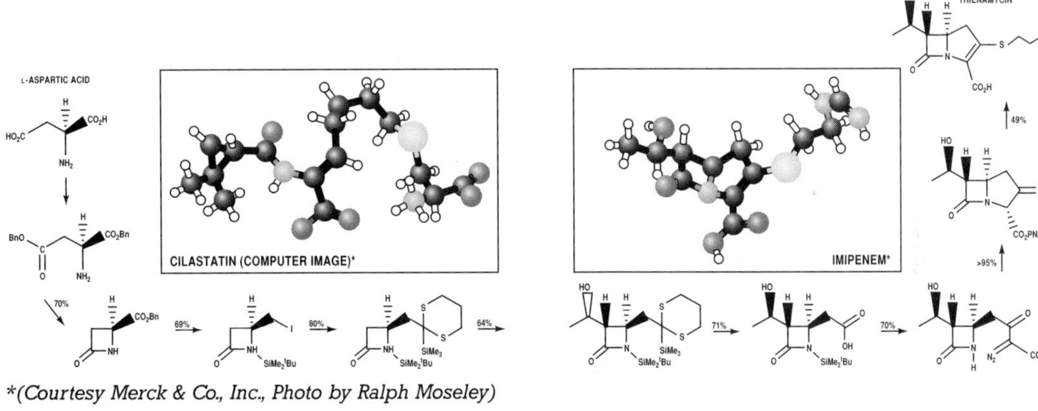

*(Courtesy Merck & Co., Inc., Photo by Ralph Moseley)

tocol, describing a critical, inventive step in the synthesis—the transformation from compound 8 to 9:

> A suspension of diazo keto ester 8 (3.98 g, 10.58 mmol) and rhodium(II) acetate dimer (0.04 g, 0.09 mmol) in anhydrous toluene (250 mL) was thoroughly purged with nitrogen, and then heated with stirring in an oil bath maintained at 80°C. After heating for two hours, the reaction mixture was removed from the bath and filtered while warm through a pad of anhydrous magnesium sulfate. The filtrate was evaporated under vacuum to afford the bicyclic keto ester 9 (3.27 g, 89%) as an off-white solid. . . .

You can be sure that this jargon-laden account of an experimental procedure is a sanitized, too linear narrative; it is the way things were at the end: neat, optimized. Not the way it first happened. Putting that aside, you feel work, a sequence of operations that take time and effort. Sometimes, just as in our romantic notions of words springing from the brow of inspired poets, we forget the sheer labor of creation. Even the Creator rested on the seventh day.

You might be interested to see the way these experimental procedures change when the very same process is scaled up. You can't make hundreds of millions of dollars' worth of thienamycin the same way you make a few grams in the laboratory. Here is the description of the industrial synthesis, for the very same step:

> The solids containing 200 kg of 8 are dropped into 476 gallons of $MeCl_2$ in tank TA-1432. Meanwhile, the reactor ST-1510 is cleaned out by a 200-gallon $MeCl_2$ boilout. The slurry is transferred to ST-1510, followed by a 50-gallon $MeCl_2$ line flush. An additional 400 gallons of dry $MeCl_2$ are added to ST-1510, and hot water (65°C) is applied to the jackets to concentrate the batch to 545 gallons where the slurry KF (Karl Fischer) is approximately 0.5 g/l H_2O. Distillates are condensed and collected in another tank.

Making veal stroganoff for a thousand people is not the same as cooking at home for four.

The synthesis of thienamycin is a building process, proceeding from simple pieces to the complex goal. It shares many features with architecture. For instance, a necessary intermediate structure may be more complicated than either the beginning or end; think of scaffolding. Chemical synthesis is a local defeat of entropy, just as our buildings and cities are. The analogy to architecture is so strong that one forgets how different, how marvelous, this kind of construction is. In a flask there may be 10^{23} molecules, moving rapidly, colliding often. Hands off, following only the strong dictates of thermodynamics, they proceed to shuffle their electrons, break and make bonds, do our bidding. If we're lucky, 99 percent of them do.

Chemists can easily calculate, given a certain number of grams of starting material, how much product one should get. That is the theoretical yield. The actual amount obtained is the experimental yield. There is no way to get something out of nothing but many ways to get less than you theoretically could. One way to achieve a 50-percent yield is to spill half the solution on the floor. This will impress no one. But even if you perform each transfer as neatly as possible, nature may not give you what you desire but instead transform 70 percent into black gunk. This is also not impressive, for it does not demonstrate control of mind over matter. Experimental yields are criteria not only of efficiency, essential to the industrial enterprise, but also of elegance and control.

There is more, much more, to say about the planned organic synthesis. But let me go on to my second case study: the ferric wheel.

Stephen J. Lippard and Kingsley L. Taft of the Massachusetts Institute of Technology synthesized the ferric wheel, also known as $[Fe(OCH_3)_2(O_2CCH_2Cl)]_{10}$. They discovered this exquisite molecule while studying model molecules for inorganic reactions that occur in biological systems. For instance, a cluster of iron and oxygen atoms is at the core of several important proteins, such as hemerythrin, ribonucleotide reductase, methane monooxygenase and ferritin (not household words these, but essential to life).

In the course of their broad attack on such compounds, Lippard and Taft performed a deceptively simple reaction. Just how simple it seems may be seen from their experimental section, reproduced in its entirety:

> Compound 1 was prepared by allowing the monochloroacetate analogue of basic iron acetate, $[Fe_3O(O_2CCH_2Cl)_6(H_2O)_3](NO_3)$ (0.315 g, 0.366 mmol), to react with 3 equiv of $Fe(NO_3)_3{\cdot}9H_2O$ (0.444 g, 1.10 mmol) in 65 mL of methanol. Diffusion of ether into the green-brown solution gave a yellow solution, from which both gold-brown crystals of 1 and a yellow precipitate deposited after several days.

Using x-ray diffraction on the gold-brown crystals, Lippard and Taft determined the arrangement of atoms in the molecule. The structure consists of 10 ferric ions (iron in oxidation state three) in a near circular array. Each iron atom is joined to its neighbors by methoxide

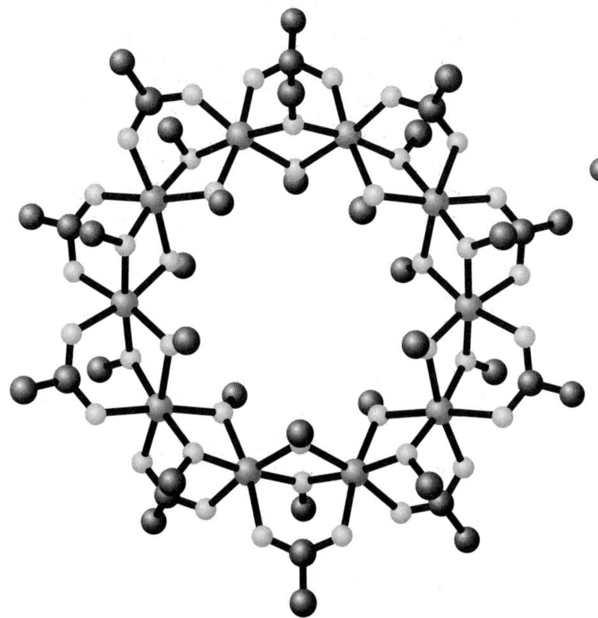

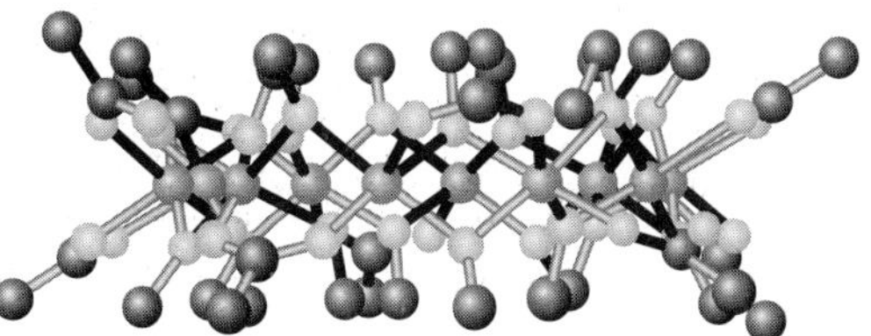

Ferric wheel, $[Fe(OCH_3)_2(O_2CCH_2Cl)]_{10}$ (as formally known), exemplifies the ideal in chemistry. The molecule consists of iron, oxygen, and carbon. To highlight the symmetry, the chlorine and hydrogen atoms are not shown.

and carboxylate bridges, "forming a molecular ferric wheel," to quote its makers.

No one will deny the visual beauty of this molecule. It does not have the annual sales of Primaxin, estimated to be $500 million. On the contrary, it probably cost the U.S. taxpayer several thousand dollars to make it. But I do not know a single curmudgeonly chemist who would not respond positively to this lovely creation. Perhaps some day the ferric wheel will find a use; perhaps it will form a link in explaining the function of iron-containing proteins. I do not really care—for me, this molecule provides a spiritual high akin to hearing a Haydn piano trio I like.

Why is this molecule beautiful? Because its symmetry reaches directly into the soul. It plays a note on a Platonic ideal. Perhaps I should have compared it to Judy Collins singing "Amazing Grace" rather than the Haydn trio. The melodic lines of the trio indeed sing, but the piece works its effect through counterpoint, the tools of complexity. The ferric wheel is pure melody.

Were we to write out the synthesis of the ferric wheel, there would be but a single arrow, from the iron chloroacetate and ferric nitrate to the product. This is a very different type of synthesis—the product essentially self-assembles to its final glory. When I see such a process, much more typical of inorganic systems than organic ones, I immediately wonder what I'm missing. The Swedish chemist Sture Forsén has aptly expressed the frustration in not being able to observe the intermediate stages of a reaction:

> The problem facing the scientist has been compared with that of a spectator of a drastically shortened version of a classical drama—"Hamlet," say—where he or she is only shown the opening scenes of the first act and the last scene of the finale. The main characters are introduced, then the curtain falls for change of scenery, and as it rises again we see on the scene floor a considerable number of "dead" bodies and a few survivors. Not an easy task for the inexperienced to unravel what actually took place in between.

Wheels, ferric or ferris, don't really self-assemble in one fell swoop. It remains for us to learn in the future how those bridges and irons come together.

Some chemists, especially those who practice the mentally demanding, intellectually exhilarating many-step, planned synthesis of the thienamycin type look askance at one-step self-assembly. Such one-fell-swoop syntheses are especially common in solid-state chemistry, in the formation of materials extended infinitely in one, two or three dimensions. The high-temperature superconductors are a good example of molecules made just this way. Their synthesis does not appear to show control of mind over matter. It looks like magic.

I exaggerate, but this is one strand of thought in the community. If I could corner my straw-man scoffer at self-assembly, typically an organic chemist, and engage him or her in a Socratic dialogue, I would begin with the question "When have you made any diamond for me lately?" Diamond is a beautifully simple three-dimensional structure (natural!). It contains in it six-membered rings, the bread-and-butter of organic chemistry. Such rings of carbon atoms are easy to make in a discrete molecule. But diamond can be made only by techniques organic chemists find unsporting, by discharges forming a plasma in methane or by pressing graphite.

Organic chemists are masterful at exercising control in zero dimensions. To one piece of carbon, perhaps asymmetric, they add another piece. Slowly, painstakingly, a complex edifice emerges. (Thienamycin is pretty simple compared to what you can do today.) One subculture of organic chemists has learned to exercise control in one dimension. These are polymer chemists, the chain builders. Although they may not have as much honor in organic chemistry as they should, they do earn a good bit of money.

But in two or three dimensions, it's a synthetic wasteland. The methodology for exercising control so that one can make unstable but persistent extended structures on demand is nearly absent. Or to put it in a positive way—this is a certain growth point of the chemistry of the future.

Syntheses, like human beings, do not lend themselves to typology. Each one is different; each has virtues and shortcomings. From each we learn. I will stop, however reluctantly, with primaxin and the ferric wheel and turn to some general questions they pose, especially about the natural and the unnatural.

Two paradoxes are hidden in the art of synthesis. The first is that the act of synthesis is explicitly human and therefore unnatural, even if one is trying to make a product of nature. The second is that in the synthesis of ideal molecules, where doing what comes unnaturally might seem just the thing, one sometimes has to give in to nature. Let me explain in the context of the two syntheses I have just discussed.

Imipenem, one component of the successful Merck antibiotic, is made from thienamycin. The thienamycin is natural, to be sure, but an economic and chemical decision dictated that in its commercial production thienamycin be made synthetically.

There is no doubt in this case that the natural molecule served as an inspiration for the synthetic chemists. But, of course, they did not make thienamycin in the laboratory the way it is made by the mold. The organism has its own intricate chemical factories, enzymes shaped by evolution. Only recently have we learned to use genetic engineering to harness those factories, even whole organisms, for our own purposes.

We have grown proficient at simpler, laboratory chemistries than those evolved by biological organisms. There is no way that Christensen and his team would set out to mimic a mold enzyme in detail. They did have confidence that they could carry out a very limited piece of what the lowly mold does, to make thienamycin, by doing it differently in the laboratory. Their goal was natural, but their process was not.

To make thienamycin, Christensen and his co-workers used a multitude of natural and synthetic reagents. For instance, one of their transformations—the synthesis of compound 3 [*see box*]—uses a magnesium compound, $(CH_3)_3CMgCl$, known as a Grignard reagent. Magnesium compounds are abundant in nature (witness Epsom salt and chlorophyll). But the reagent in question, a ubiquitous tool of the synthetic chemist, was concocted by Victor Grignard some time around the turn of the century. The creation of compound 3 also requires treatment with hydrochloric acid and ammonium chloride, both natural products. (Your stomach has a marginally lower concentration of hydrochloric acid than that used in this reaction, and ammonium chloride is the alchemist's sal ammoniac.) But even though these molecules occur in nature, they are far easier to make in a chemical plant.

Because everything in the end does come from the earth, air or water, every unnatural reagent used in the synthesis ultimately derives from natural organic or inorganic precursors. The very starting material in the synthesis of imipenem is an amino acid, aspartic acid.

Now consider the most unnatural and beautiful ferric wheel. It was made simply by reacting two synthetic molecules, the iron monochloroacetate and ferric nitrate, in methanol, a natural solvent. The methanol was probably made synthetically; the two iron-containing reagents derive from reactions of iron metal, which in turn is extracted from iron ores. And the final wrinkle is the method of assembly: the pieces of the molecule seem to just fall into place (self-assembly). What could be more natural than letting things happen spontaneously, giving in to the strong dictates of entropy?

It is clear that in the unnatural making of a natural molecule (thienamycin) or of an unnatural one (the ferric wheel), natural and synthetic reagents and solvents are used in a complex, intertwined theater of letting things be and of helping them along. About the only constant is change, transformation.

We may still wonder about the psychology of chemical creation. Which molecules should we expend our energies in making? Isn't there something inherently better in trying to make the absolutely new?

Four beautiful polyhedra of carbon have piqued the interest of synthetic organic chemists during the past 40 years: tetrahedrane (C_4H_4), cubane (C_8H_8), dodecahedrane ($C_{20}H_{20}$) and buckminsterfullerene (C_{60}). Cubane is quite unstable because of the strain imposed at each carbon. (In cubane the angle between any three carbon atoms is 90 degrees, but each carbon would "prefer" to form angles of 109.5 degrees with its neighbors.) C_{60} is also somewhat strained because of both its nonplanarity and its five-membered rings. Tetrahedrane is particularly unstable. One has to create special conditions of temperature and solvent to see it; even then, the parent molecule has not yet been made, only a "substituted derivative," in which hydrogen is replaced by a bulky organic group.

As far as we know, tetrahedrane, cubane and dodecahedrane do not exist naturally on the earth. C_{60} has been found in old soot and a carbon-rich ancient rock, shungite. It may turn up elsewhere. Be that as it may, all four molecules were recognized as synthetic targets at least 20 years, in some cases 50 years, before they were made. Some of the best chemists in the world tried to make them and failed. The syntheses of cubane and especially dodecahedrane were monumental achievements in unnatural product chemistry.

C_{60} was different. The pleasing polyhedral shape was first noted by some theoreticians. Their calculations indicated some stability; such

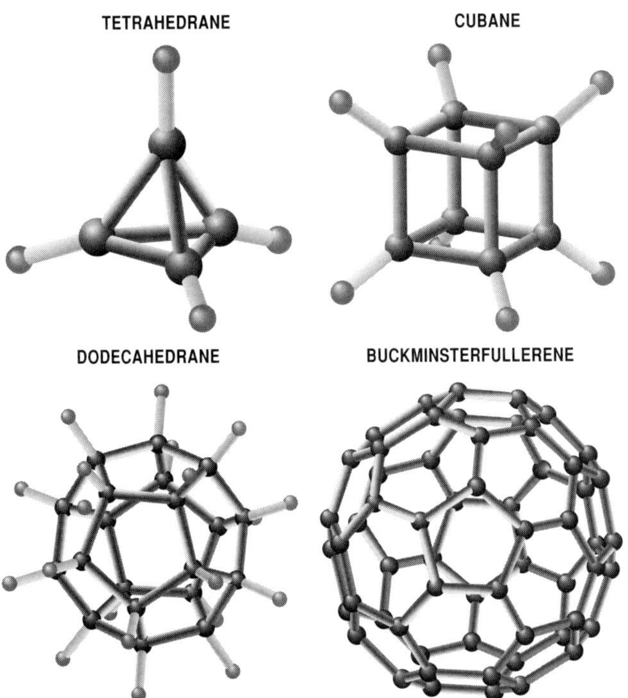

Four polyhedra based on carbon were recognized decades ago as targets for chemists to synthesize. Buckminsterfullerenes were discovered in 1985 and were then found to occur naturally on the earth. Tetrahedrane, the simplest of the structures, has not yet been synthesized. Tetrahedrane, cubane and dodecahedrane consist of carbon atoms and hydrogen atoms. Buchminsterfullerenes are made solely from carbon.

indications as the theoreticians had at their command were sometimes unreliable. These theoreticians' dreams were ignored by the experimentalists and by other theoreticians. It is sometimes difficult to see the shoulders of the giants we stand on when we are looking so intently ahead. I myself have suggested a still unsynthesized metallic modification of carbon, different from diamond or graphite, and even though I have substantially more visibility among chemists than the proposers of buckminsterfullerene, no one has paid much attention to my pipe dream either, probably for good reason. We see what we want to see.

One organic chemist I know, a very good one, Orville L. Chapman of the University of California at Los Angeles, independently thought up the structure and devoted much time to the planned, systematic making of C_{60}. After all, this was a "simple" molecule, not an extended material like the repeating lattice of carbon atoms that make up a diamond. So it should be possible to make it. Despite persistent efforts over a 10-year period, Chapman and his students failed in their effort.

The first evidence, indirect but definitive, for C_{60} was obtained from a very different branch of our science, physical chemistry. The credit for the discovery belongs properly to Richard E. Smalley and Robert F. Curl of Rice University and Harold W. Kroto of the University of Sussex. They obtained hard evidence for tiny amounts of C_{60} in the gas phase, assigned the molecule its name and, more important, deduced its structure. Did they make it? Absolutely. It did not matter to me or to other believers in their evidence that they had made "just" 10^{10} molecules instead of the 10^{20} we need to see in a tiny crystal. But there were doubters, many I suspect, in the organic community. One wanted to see the stuff.

Grams of buckminsterfullerene were provided by a synthesis by Donald R. Huffman of the University of Arizona and Wolfgang Krätschmer and Konstantinos Fostiropoulos of the Max Planck Institute for Nuclear Physics in Heidelberg. Striking a carbon arc in a helium atmosphere (which is what they did) is about as unsporting as firing a laser at graphite (the Smalley-Kroto-Curl synthesis). But it certainly makes plenty of C_{60}, enough of the molecule to determine its structure by typical organic methods, enough to convince any chemist that it has the soccer-ball structure ["Fullerenes," by Robert F. Curl and Richard E. Smalley; SCIENTIFIC AMERICAN, October 1991].

I think many chemists wished C_{60} had been made in a planned, unnatural way. I am happy that—just to make the world slightly less rational than we would like it to be—it was made in a serendipitous way.

Serendipity—a word invented by Horace Walpole—has come to mean "a discovery by chance." Yet whether it is a chemical synthesis or a Japanese master potter piling organic matter around the ceramic objects in his Bizen kiln, chance favors the prepared mind. You need to have the knowledge (some call it intuition) to vary the conditions of striking the arc or the arrangement of the leaves in the kiln just so. You need to have the instruments and intuition to deduce structure from a few fuzzy lines in a spectrum and to reject false leads. And you need to have the courage to shatter a vase that didn't come out right and to learn from one firing what to do in the next.

Many chemical syntheses, even if part of a grand design, proceed by steps that are serendipitous. One wants to link up a bond here, but it doesn't work. So one follows a hunch, anything but the codified scientific method. One knows that if a reaction works, one can construct a rationalization for it—an argument spiffy clean enough to make an impression on one's colleagues. Eventually one can make the damned reaction work if it is a necessary step in the design.

Because chance also operates to foil every design, it is almost certain that in the course of any planned synthesis there will be a step that will not work by any known process. So a new one will be invented, adding to the store of the chemists, aiding others around the world facing the same problem. Some synthetic chemists—for instance, E. J. Corey of Harvard University, a grand master of the art—have a special talent for not only making interesting molecules but also using the opportunity of the synthesis to introduce a brilliant, unprecedented methodology, applicable to other syntheses.

When the synthesis is planned, be its aim a natural or unnatural molecule, we suppress the aleatory nature of the enterprise. We want to project an image of mind over matter, of total control. When the molecule made is unanticipated, as the ferric wheel was, we find it very difficult to hide the workings of chance. But hazard—to use the meaning that is dominant in the French root of our word, and secondary in ours—plays an unrecognized and enlivening role in all synthesis.

Let us return to nature and our struggles to emulate it. Or surpass it. Can we make substances that have properties superior to those found in nature? I say "yes" while recognizing that the phrase "superior to nature" is patently value laden and anthropocentric and should immediately evoke ecological concerns.

There is nylon instead of cotton in fishing nets, nylon instead of silk in women's stockings. No one, least of all Third World fishermen, will go back to the old nets. Some people may go back to silk stockings, but they will only be the rich, out to impress. There are new chemical materials and new combinations of old materials for dental restorations. They make a world of difference to older people in this world, and their benefit cannot be dismissed.

Yet the thought that we can do better than nature is provocatively arrogant. As we have attempted to improve on nature (while failing to control the most natural thing about us, our drive to procreate), we have introduced so many transformations and in such measure that we have fouled our nest and intruded into the great cycles of this planet. We must face the reality that natural evolution proceeds far too slowly to cope with our changes. This is a concern that, just as much as utility, should guide the industrial-scale syntheses of the future.

I want to touch on another kind of human arrogance implicit in the intellectual drama of synthesis. A French chemist, Alain Sevin, has put it well:

> The incredible richness and fantasy of Nature is an act of defiance to Man, as if he had to do better in any domain. Flying faster than birds, diving deeper than whales. . . . We are Promethean characters in an endless play which now is in its molecular act.

We are driven to transform. We have learned to do it very well. But this play is not a comedy.

Were chemical synthesis in search of a single icon, the outstretched hand of Prometheus bringing fire to humanity would serve well. Prometheus, a name meaning "forethought," represents the element of design, the process of fruitfully taking advantage of chance creation. Fire is appropriate because it drives transformation. The hand of Prometheus is the symbol of creation—the hand of God reaching to Adam in Michelangelo's fresco, the hands in contentious debate in Dürer's *Christ among the Doctors*, the infinite variety of hands that Rodin sculpted. Hands bless, caress and hide, but most of all, they shape.

The sculptor's art itself mimics the complexity of motion of a chemist across the interface between natural and unnatural. Rodin, in his human act of creation, sketches, then shapes by hand (with tools) an out-of-scale yet "realistic" artifact, a sculpture of a hand, out of materials that are synthetic (bronze) but that have natural origins (copper and tin ores). He uses a building process (maquettes, a cast) that is complex in its intermediate stages. The sculptor creates something very real, whose virtue may reside in calling to our minds the ideal.

Margaret Drabble has written that Prometheus is "firmly rooted in the real world of effort, danger and pain." Without chemical synthesis, there would be no aspirin, no cortisone, no birth-control pills, no anesthetics, no dynamite. The achievements of chemical synthesis are firmly bound to our attempt to break the shackles of disease and poverty. In search of an ideal, making real things, the mind and hands engage.

Further Reading

Synthesis. R. B. Woodward in *Perspectives in Organic Chemistry.* Edited by A. R. Todd. Interscience, 1956.

A Stereocontrolled, Enantiomerically Specific Total Synthesis Of Thienamycin. T. N. Salzmann, R. W. Ratcliffe, F. A. Bouffard and B. G. Christensen in *Philosophical Transactions of the Royal Society of London,* Series B, Vol. 289, No. 1036, pages 191–195; May 16, 1980.

Molecules. Peter W. Atkins. Scientific American Library, 1987.

The Logic of Chemical Synthesis. E. J. Corey and Xue-Min Cheng. John Wiley and Sons, 1989.

Synthesis and Structure of $[Fe(OMe)_2\ (O_2CCH_2Cl)]_{10}$, A Molecular Ferric Wheel. Kingsley L. Taft and Stephen J. Lippard in *Journal of the American Chemical Society,* Vol. 112, pages 9629–9630; December 19, 1990.

The Organic Chemistry of Drug Design and Drug Action. Richard B. Silverman, Academic Press, 1992.

The key concept in documentation involves the relationship between what appears in your text and the **Works Cited** or **References** at the end.

MLA One scientist notes that chemistry faces the same dilemma illustrated in a Raphael fresco; should we pursue "the ideal" or should we pursue "nature"? (Hoffmann 66). [No name in text; put name in parenthetical reference]

or Hoffmann notes that chemistry faces the same dilemma illustrated in a Raphael fresco; should we pursue "the ideal" or should we pursue "nature" (66). [Name appears in text; not needed in parenthetical reference.]

Within your text, what goes in the parentheses is determined by whether you have already provided the name of the author you are citing; if you have, then this name does not appear in the parenthetical reference. In either case, the **page number** on which the quote or paraphrase originally appears is given. Also, in both instances the name of the author is provided and this refers the reader to the Works Cited, where Hoffmann's name must appear:

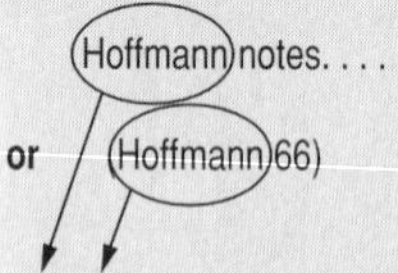

Hoffmann, Roald. "What Should Chemists Think? *Scientific American*, February 1993:66–73.

For more discussion and an example of APA documentaion, see Unit Two, Option One. Summaries of MLA and APA styles can be found in the following **Writing and research** section.

ASPECTS OF WRITING: MLA and APA documentation styles.

All documentation styles attempt to do the same thing: they provide the reader (and the writer, of course) with a record of the sources cited and, sometimes, with a record of other relevant works that may have been consulted or may be of interest.

When you write for publication, you should first check the documentation style required by the journal to which you are submitting your paper. When you write a document for a company, you will probably also have to follow the in-house documentation guidelines. Similarly, in college or university you should first check whether your professor requires a particular documentation style or not. No matter which system you are required to use, the mastery of one easily transfers to others.

The most widely used documentation styles in the United States are those of the Modern Language Association and the American Psychological Association—although other styles work just as well—and these will be outlined here. Both use in-text citations (also known as parenthetical references) and virtually dispense with footnotes.

The major differences between MLA and APA may be summarized as follows:

APA includes date of publication in the parenthetical reference and the References list; MLA puts this in the Works Cited only.

APA capitalizes only the first word in a title; MLA capitalizes each main word.

APA does not require a page reference for a paraphrase or summary of part of the text; MLA requires a page reference for all citations, including paraphrases and summaries.

APA uses the author's last name and first initial in the References list; MLA uses last name and first names, if known, in Works Cited.

APA uses **p.** before page numbers (p. 66); MLA uses only the number (66).

WRITING AND RESEARCH: Answer one of the following questions. Make sure that your essay is correctly documented.

MLA format for Works Cited and in-text citations

The basic rules include the following:

- List only those titles actually cited in your paper
- List entries alphabetically by last name of author
- If author is not known, alphabetize by title of article or book (excluding *The, A,* or *An*)
- Indent second and subsequent lines five spaces or one-half inch
- Double space between lines and between entries
- Underline or italicize titles of books and names of journals and articles
- Put titles of articles in quotation marks
- Use abbreviated forms of the publisher's name (Random, not Random House, Inc.)
- Capitalize all major words in titles
- Give citations (including page numbers) for paraphrases as well as direct quotes

1. Describe and discuss the controversy over the issues raised in E. D. Hirsch's *Cultural Literacy.* Newspapers and periodicals are likely to be your best sources of information, together with Hirsch's book, of course.
2. Essays in this unit have suggested the struggle of the audience to understand some kinds of art; the creative struggle of the painter, the writer, and other artists; and the creation and appreciation of beauty in science. Discuss one of these themes, making reference to any of these essays—and others, should you wish.
3. Use your library to find articles and books in which a particular work of art or literature (a favorite poem or novel, for example) is discussed. Write an essay about this work, making reference to at least two different critical discussions. Make your essay more than just a summary of the critics' views. Provide some background and describe the work in your own words, as well as discussing what you have read about it.

A book by one author

Boorstin, Daniel J. *The Discoverers.* New York: Random, 1983.

Take careful note of punctuation and other aspects of the format in this and the following examples.
In-text: . . . (Boorstin 38).

Two or more books by same author

Boorstin, Daniel J. *The Creators.* New York: Random, 1992.
______. *The Discoverers.* New York: Random, 1983.

Present in alphabetical order by title (ignoring *A, An,* or *The*)
In-text: . . . (Boorstin, *Discoverers* 26).

A book by two or three authors

Rosenblum, Mort, and Doug Williamson. *Squandering Eden: Africa at the Edge.* San Diego: Harcourt, 1987.

Note presentation of names—last name first for first author, first name first for second author.
If three authors, present as follows: Smith, Jane, Don Brown, and Tina Chavez.
In-text: . . . (Rosenblum and Williamson 67).

A book by more than three authors

Brown, Lester, et al. *The State of the World 1995.* New York: Norton, 1995.

et al. = "and others."
Use first name listed among authors (not necessarily the first alphabetically).
In-text: . . . (Brown et al. 186–187).

in-text: . . . (FAO 2).

A book by a corporate author

FAO. *Forest Product Yearbook 1992.* Rome: FAO, 1994.

Cite author of the article to which you are referring (not the editor, or other possibilities).
In-text: . . . (Weber 45).

A work in an anthology

Weber, Peter. "Safeguarding Oceans." *State of the World 1994.* Lester Brown et al. New York: Norton, 1994. 41–60.

Use ed. *for one editor,* eds. *for more than one.*
In-text: Cite editors, if using their text, or individual authors (as in an anthology), if using their texts.

A book with an editor

Ashcroft, Bill, Gareth Griffiths, and Helen Tiffin, eds. *The Post-Colonial Studies Reader.* New York: Routledge, 1995.

In-text: . . . (Silverman, Hughes, and Wienbroer 28).

A book other than a first edition

Silverman, Jay, Elaine Hughes, and Diana Roberts Wienbroer. *Rules of Thumb. A Guide for Writers.* 2nd ed. New York: McGraw, 1990.

In-text: . . . (Gatland 11)

A signed article in a reference book

Gatland, Kenneth. "The Space Pioneers." *The Illustrated Encyclopedia of Space Technology* 1981.

No page numbers necessary.
In-text: . . . ("Chemistry" 76)—the page reference in the parenthetical reference would be a courtesy to your reader if citing a long entry in the reference book.

An unsigned article in a reference book

"Vietnam." *The World Almanac and Book of Facts 1994.*

Government documents can be complicated to document. Provide all the information available.
In-text: . . . (United States 12–17). Remember to specify particular department or publication if citing more than one U.S. government publication.

A government document

United States. Office of Technology Assessment. *Defense Conversion: Redirecting R & D.* Washington: GPO, 1993.

If known, always cite the author, never the name of the newspaper or journal. Use + when article is not on continuous pages.
In-text: . . . (Kakatani 1).

A signed article in a daily newspaper

Kakatani, Michiko. "The Word Police." *New York Times* 31 Jan. 1993, sec. 9:1+.

If no author is identified, always cite by title of article, never by name of newspaper or journal. Title may be shortened, as illustrated here
In-text: . . . ("Ben Bows Out" 13).

An unsigned article in a daily newspaper

"Ben Bows Out in Fine Style." *New York Times* 16 Feb, 1994: B13.

Notice the punctuation—and lack of it—in periodical listings.

An article from a weekly magazine

Lane, Charles. "Let's Abolish the Third World." *Newsweek* 27 Apr. 1992: 43.

An article in a monthly magazine

Beatty, Jack. "Along the Western Front." *Atlantic Monthly* Nov. 1986: 29–38.

In-text: . . . (Beatty 33).

An article in a journal with continuous pagination

Nilsen, Alleen Pace. "In Defense of Humor." *College English* 56 (1994): 929–933.

"Continuous pagination" means issues in any given year start page numbers where the previous issue ended.

An article in a journal numbering pages separately in each issue

Mukherjee, Arun P. "Whose Post-colonialism and Whose Post-modernism?" *World Literature Written in English* 30.2 (1990): 1–9.

In-text: . . . (Mukherjee 7–8).

Online database

"Wetlands." *Academic American Encyclopedia.* Online. Compuserve. 10 Aug. 1993.

In-text: . . . ("Wetlands").

CD-Rom

Jones, Jane. "Building Collapses in Bronx." *New York Times* 12 Apr. 1993: C1. *New York Times Ondisc.* CD-ROM. UNI-Pro-quest. Oct. 1993.

CD-ROM sources may be documented as follows: Author. Printed source information, if any. Title of database. Publication medium. Vendor. Electronic publication date.
When information is not available, use what is given.

Interview

Charles, Jane. Personal interview. 10 Jan. 1990.

In-text: . . . (Charles, interview).

Lecture

Gotwald, William. "Army Ants." Borders. Syracuse, N.Y., 12 Dec. 1995.

In-text: . . . (Gotwald, lecture).

Sample abbreviations for publishers (MLA)

Allyn and Bacon, Inc.	Allyn
Basic Books	Basic
Congressional Record	Cong. Rec.
Doubleday and Co., Inc.	Doubleday
Government Printing Office	GPO
Harcourt Brace	Harcourt
Harvard University Press	Harvard UP
Holt, Rinehart, and Winston, Inc.	Holt
Houghton Mifflin, Co.	Houghton
McGraw-Hill, Inc.	McGraw
Oxford University Press	Oxford UP
Charles Scribner's Sons	Scribner's
Simon and Schuster, Inc.	Simon
University of Chicago Press	U of Chicago P

Don't forget that in-text citations come in two basic forms, and that direct quotes *and* paraphrases must be cited. The following examples make reference to Daniel Boorstin's *The Discoverers:*

1. It has been observed that, in his day, Captain Cook won "signal recognition . . . not from his navigating exploits but from what he did to improve the health and save the lives of men at sea" (Boorstin 288).
2. Boorstin has noted that, in his day, Captain Cook won "signal recognition . . . not from his navigating exploits but from what he did to improve the health and save the lives of men at sea" (288).
3. It has been said that Cook was more famous in his day for looking after the health and safety of his crew—especially in saving them from scurvy—than he was for his great feats of navigation (Boorstin 288).
4. Boorstin observes that Cook was more famous in his day for his enlightened and innovative ways of looking after his crew than he was for his great feats of navigation (288).

Notes on APA Documentation

Basic Rules—Highlighted where different from MLA

Bibliography is called ***References***
Double-space between lines and between entries
Identify author by last name and **initials**
List in alphabetical order by author's last name
When citing more than one work by the same author, **list name each time and place the earliest one first**
List last name first for all authors (even co-authors)
If more than one author, **use the ampersand (&) before last one**
Don't use **et al.** in Reference list; name all co-authors. In text, use **et al.** only when there are more than six co-authors or when referring to three or more authors more than once
Put date of publication in parentheses after author's name
Capitalize only the first letter of book titles and subtitles
Don't use quotation marks around article titles
Use p. or pp. for page numbers in parenthetical references and for newspaper and magazine articles in References
Indent first line of each entry
Don't give page references for paraphrases
Indent first line of each entry
Publishers' names not abbreviated

Examples

A book by one author

Boorstin, D. (1983). *The discoverers.* New York: Random House.

Two or more books by same author

Boorstin, D. (1983). *The discoverers.* New York: Random House.

Boorstin, D. (1992). *The creators.* New York: Random House.

A book by more than one author

Rosenblum, M. & Williamson, D. (1987). *Squandering Eden: Africa at the edge.* San Diego: Harcourt, Brace, Jovanovich.

A book by more than six authors

Brown, L., et al. (1995). *The state of the world 1995.* New York: Norton.

A book by a corporate author

FAO. (1994). *Forest product yearbook 1992.* Rome: U.N. Food and Agriculture Organization.

A work in an anthology

Weber, P. (1994). Safeguarding oceans. In L. Brown et al., *State of the world 1994.* New York: Norton.

A signed article in a daily newspaper

Kakatani, M. (1993, January 31). The word police. *New York Times,* p. 9:1.

An unsigned article in a daily newspaper

Ben bows out in fine style (1994, February 16). *New York Times,* p. B13.

An article from a weekly magazine

Lane, C. (1992, April 27). Let's abolish the third world. *Newsweek,* p. 43.

An article in a journal with continuous pagination

Nilsen, A. P. (1994). In defense of humor. *College English, 56,* 929–933.

CD-ROM

Chapman, R. (1993). Acupuncture. *Grolier's Multimedia Encyclopedia.* (CD-ROM).

Interview

Charles, Jane (1990, January 10). Personal interview.

APA In-text Citations

APA requires in-text page references only for direct quotes:

1. It has been observed that Captain Cook was most famous in his day for "what he did to improve the health and save the lives of men at sea" (Boorstin, 1983, p. 288).
2. Boorstin (1983) has remarked that Captain Cook was most famous in his day for saving his men from the effects of scurvy.

For complete information on the MLA and APA documentation styles, see the style manuals for each. You should be able to find one in your library, writing center, or similar facilities.

OPTION TWO

TALKING ABOUT LANGUAGE: Language and beauty—sound and sense.

The fact that beauty in any form is not easily achieved has already been noted in this unit. Alexander Pope, it may be recalled, states that

> True ease in writing comes from art, not chance,
> As those move easiest who have learned to dance.

This poem continues,

> 'Tis not enough no harshness gives offence,
> The sound must seem an echo to the sense.
> *"An Essay on Criticism," Part 2*

The key line here is the last, with its suggestion that whatever is being described in the poem should also be captured or reflected in the rhythm or meter and sound of the lines.

In poetry, this is manifest in many famous lines, as in Browning's poem about riders bringing news of battle:

> I sprang to the stirrup and Joris and he;
> I galloped, Dirck galloped, we galloped all three;
> *"How They Brought the Good News from Ghent to Aix"*

> [galloping meter that is perfectly complementary to the sense of the lines]

Other examples are given in Pope's "Essay on Criticism," already cited:

> Soft is the strain when Zephyr gently blows,
> And the smooth stream in smoother numbers flows;

> [gentle, smooth sounds imitating the light wind and placid stream]

> But when loud surges lash the sounding shore,
> The hoarse, rough verse should like the torrent roar;

> [louder, more robust and clashing sounds, imitating the rough waves in a storm]

In World War I, Wilfred Owen, himself fighting in the trenches, where he died just a few days before the armistice, described exhausted soldiers staggering back to their trenches at the end of the day:

Bent double, like old beggars under sacks,
Knock-kneed, coughing like hags, we cursed through sludge,

[The weariness and anger of the soldiers is reflected in the stumbling, lurching phrases]

Technically, it might be observed that both these lines by Owen begin with two stressed syllables. This pattern, called a **spondee,** is hard to read in a light and smooth way; it slows you down and has a deliberately ponderous effect, imitating the movements of the soldiers.

There are many other poetic devices that are used to create particular effects. Among them are **onomatopoeia,** in which the poet's words imitate actual sounds in nature ("plop" and "fizz" are onomatopoeic words). There is a wonderful example in Keats, when he describes one of the sounds of summer:

The murmurous haunt of flies on summer eves.
"Ode to a Nightingale"

[The two sounds made by flies—the droning mmmmm and the buzzing zzzzz—are both apparent in this line if you read it out loud]

These and other effects are, of course, not only the preserve of the poets. Other writers and orators make good use of them too, as in this famous example from Britain's World War II leader, Winston Churchill, as he rallied the nation, standing alone against Hitler's Germany:

Even though large tracts of Europe and many old and famous States have fallen or may fall into the grip of the Gestapo and all the odious apparatus of the Nazi rule, we shall not flag nor fail. We shall go on to the end. We shall fight in France, we shall fight in the seas and oceans, we shall fight with growing confidence and growing strength in the air; we shall defend our island whatever the cost may be.

We shall fight on the beaches, we shall fight on the landing grounds, we shall fight in the fields and in the streets, we shall fight in the hills; we shall never surrender; and even if, which I do not for a moment believe, this island or a large part of it were subjugated and starving, then our Empire beyond the seas, armed and guarded by the British Fleet, would carry on the struggle until, in God's good time, the New World, with all its power and might, steps forth to the rescue and the liberation of the Old. [House of Commons, June 4, 1940]

Quick Quiz

A.
1. What is *Guernica?*
2. Who painted the Sistine Chapel?
3. What artistic movement was begun by Georges Braque and Pablo Picasso around 1904?
4. What is Freytag's pyramid?
5. Who were the Greek philosophers most commonly associated with analysis of the nature and purpose of the arts?
6. What are the "two cultures" described by C. P. Snow?
7. What is meant by "cultural literacy," and who popularized the term?
8. What does Alexander Pope mean when he writes, "The sound must seem an echo to the sense"?
9. Who are Alexander Solzhenitsyn, Vaclav Havel, and Wole Soyinka, and what do they have in common?
10. What does Conrad mean when he writes that the purpose of the artist is to make the audience *see?*

B. Analyze and correct the following sentences:
1. I am in the mists of choosing colleges.
2. Every morning my father takes exercises to strengthen his abominable muscles.
3. Two cycles belonging to girls that had been left leaning against lamp posts were badly damaged.
4. On the floor above him lived a redhead instructor in physical education, whose muscular calves he admired when they nodded to each other by the mailbox.
5. Our menu is guaranteed to wet your appetite.
6. This book belongs to the anals of English literature.
7. Wanted: Man to take care of cow that does not smoke or drink.
8. Don't sit there like a sore thumb.
9. Milwaukee is the golden egg that the rest of the state wants to milk.

(From Lederer, *Anguished English*)

SECTION ONE

PRIOR KNOWLEDGE: The nature and purpose of comedy.

Explaining jokes is a notoriously good way to kill them, but comedy, like beauty, has been a subject of discussion at least since the days of Plato (427?–347 B.C.) and Aristotle (384–322 B.C.).

In a discussion of Aristotle's *Poetics,* S. H. Butcher observes the status of comedy in the philosopher's mind:

> Though Aristotle did not assign to the different kinds of art their respective ranks, or expressly say that the pleasure of tragedy is superior to that of comedy, the distinction he draws between various forms of music may be taken as indicating the criterion by which he would judge of other arts. Music, apart from its other functions, may serve as an amusement for children, it is a toy which takes the place of the infant's rattle; or, again, it may afford a noble and rational enjoyment and become an element of the highest happiness to an audience that is capable of enjoying it. Again, Aristotle asserts that the ludicrous in general is inferior to the serious, and counts as a pastime that fits men for serious work. We may probably infer that the same principle holds in literature as in life; that comedy is merely a form of sportive activity; the pleasure derived from it is of corresponding quality; it ranks with the other pleasures of sport or recreation.
>
> *Aristotle's Theory of Poetry and Fine Art.* Translated and with Critical Notes by S. H. Butcher. New York: Dover, 1951.

The comedy of Ancient Greece often has a decidedly modern ring, as in Aristophanes' *Lysistrata,* in which male foolishness and warmongering (the war between Athens and Sparta) are brought to a halt by a female boycott of sex with their husbands. The bawdiness of the play, with its mixture of satire and farce, and a theme that suggests the empowerment of women, both seem strikingly contemporary.

Everybody likes a kidder, but nobody lends him money.
Arthur Miller, *Death of a Salesman*

My way of joking is to tell the truth.
George Bernard Shaw, *John Bull's Other Island*

It seems undoubtedly true that, in general, we also consider comedy to be lighter and less substantial than tragedy, but it must also be said that not all comic works are frivolous. Satire may make us laugh, but it is barbed and may have a potent message. Jonathan Swift's "A

A light tone and a happy ending are two distinguishing features of most comedies.

Swift (1667–1745) remains one of the most famous satirists in the English language. He is the author of *Gulliver's Travels.* One part of *Gulliver* involves the hero's travels to Lilliput, and this is often thought of as a children's story, but *Gulliver's Travels* has four parts and is a biting political and human satire. Swift is sometimes referred to as Dean Swift; he was the Dean of St. Patrick's Cathedral (Anglican) in Dublin, where his epitaph reads: "Here lies the body of Jonathan Swift, D.D., dean of this cathedral, where burning indignation can no longer lacerate his heart. Go, traveler, and imitate if you can a man who was an undaunted champion of liberty."

Modest Proposal," for example, is a savage attack on the indifference of English absentee landlords to the suffering of their tenants in Ireland. His essay attacks their greed and indifference in a classic satirical mode by suggesting that the landlords could purchase the babies of the Irish poor and eat them, thereby solving the problem of overpopulation, giving the parents a bit of money, and supplying a new dish for the gentry. Satire pushes human weaknesses and vices to their extreme, to the *reductio ad absurdum,* and the "Modest Proposal" is a devastating example.

Humor can be cruel as well as funny—sometimes simultaneously—and it can reveal something about the comedian or joke teller as well as about the butt of the joke. The fact that humor is taken seriously in contemporary culture is manifest in the sensitivity of people to jokes that are considered to be in "bad taste"; sexist and racist jokes, for example, are usually frowned upon. Clearly, as in most other areas, social conventions and rules govern humor.

The following essay discusses what people find funny, and it includes discussion of jokes directed at other cultural groups. Why do some people laugh and some not when they hear the same joke? Berger and Wildavsky suggest that it depends in part on what kind of culture we represent, and they link different cultural types to different types of humor.

There are many types of comedy between the extremes of vulgar **low comedy** and more subtle **high comedy.** It has been said that some high comedy is closer in spirit and seriousness to tragedy than it is to low comedy. Berger and Wildavsky mention many types of humor, but some commentators divide the genre into four broad types: satire, humor, farce, and irony. One critic comments on these as follows:

> The distinctions among these four elements of comedy may be briefly clarified by noting the manner in which each handles folly. Traditional satire excoriates folly, finding it ridiculous but also corrigible. Humor seeks, not to expunge folly, but to condone and even bless it, for humor views folly as endearing, humanizing, indispensable. Farce also accepts folly as indispensable, but only because folly promises delightful annihilation of restraint. Finally, irony sees folly as an emblem of eternal irrationality, to be coolly anatomized and toyed with.
>
> Morton Gurewitch. *Comedy—The Irrational Vision.* Ithaca: Cornell, 1975

Calvin and Hobbes **by Bill Watterson**

ANNOTATED READING: Arthur Asa Berger and Aaron Wildavsky. "Who Laughs at What?" *Society* Sept./Oct. 1994: 82–86.

Who Laughs at What?

Humor has remained an enigma throughout the ages. Many of the greatest thinkers, among them Aristotle (who is supposed to have written a book on the subject, now lost), Plato, Hobbes, Kant, Schopenhauer, Bergson, and Freud, have speculated about what humor is, how it works, and why people laugh. Humor still remains a subject of considerable controversy, even though in recent years we have begun to recognize its numerous powers and the role it plays in our lives.

An "enigma" is something that is obscure or puzzling. A person who is "hard to read" or whose motives and inner life are mysterious, may be described as "enigmatic." The derivation of the word, however, is surprising:

> [Latin *aenigma,* from Greek *ainigma,* from *ainissesthai,* to speak in riddles, hint, from *ainos,* tale, story.]

There are any number of theories about why people laugh. Four major theories will be considered here. The currently dominant theory suggests that humor is based on incongruity—on the difference between what people expect and what they get. In a joke, for example, the punch line generates humor by being unexpected and unanticipated, and its incongruity creates laughter—in good jokes, that is. (Humor can be found in many other forms and places: cartoons, comic strips, plays, films, graffiti, and so on.) Incongruity in more specific terms of culture theory also suggests a difference between what is normative and what is not.

THINK ON PAPER
Identify other words—besides "enigma"—that take **-atic** or **-atical** endings in their adjectival forms.

A second important theory argues that humor involves a sense of superiority that those who laugh feel about those (people, animals, objects) they laugh at. A person slips on a banana peel and we laugh—because, for a moment, we, who have not lost our balance, feel superior to him. A classic statement of the superiority theory of humor comes from Thomas Hobbes' work *Leviathan*. In it Hobbes proposes that humor involves a "sudden glory arising from some sudden conception of some eminence in ourselves; by comparison with the infirmity of others, or with our own formerly." From a cultural theory perspective, Hobbes' notion can be extended to a sense of eminence not only in our person but in our political culture by comparison with other political cultures.

Hobbes' *Leviathan* is best known for the author's observation that life in its natural state—that is, without civilized government—is "solitary, poor, nasty, brutish, and short."

Freud's psychoanalytic theory of humor argues that humor is tied to psychic economies and to aggression, often of a sexual nature, and it is usually masked. His book *Jokes and their Relation to the Unconscious* contains a number of wonderful Jewish jokes. No people, Freud points out, makes more fun of itself than the Jews, a remark that has been distorted to suggest he believed Jewish humor was masochistic.

Finally, there is a theory of humor that ties it to cognitive abilities and the way information is processed. This theory is connected to semiotic theories, which deal with how people find meaning in texts and to theories of how the mind resolves puzzles such as paradoxes and play frames. Paradox and the moving in and out of play frames generates the kind of humor that depends, in many instances, on the listener recognizing that the humorist is just kidding or playing around and does not mean what he says. Humor is part of play and play involves finding ways to let others know when one is playing with them, that "this is play." Insult is a common technique of humorists, but insults are humorous only in a play frame.

The semioticians would take their cue from the French thinker Ferdinand de Saussure, who declared that concepts have no meaning in themselves, the only meaning they have is differential. For a joke to have meaning, there must be differences, which usually take the form of polar opposites that can be elicited from the joke. There are numerous books by proponents of each of these four positions and some in which two or more are combined. None of these theories, however, deals with specific jokes or other humorous texts, except in very broad terms. Their generalizations cover all socio-economic backgrounds and all cultures.

Consider, for example, the following joke: A prestigious Talmudic scholar reaches retirement and a fête is held in his honor in the course of which he is praised from morning till night. As he leaves, late at night, a young man approaches the revered rabbi and says, "Great rabbi, your praises have been sung from morning until night. Is it enough?" The rabbi replies, "It is enough. But of my modesty, they said nothing."

Why is this joke funny? Let us consider this joke in terms of the four dominant theories of why people find things funny.

For the incongruity theorists, the difference between what the rabbi says at first—"It is enough"—and what he says in the punchline—"but

Some words are derived from people's names

sadism—from Comte Donatien de Sade, a French nobleman and writer, associated with the condition of deriving pleasure from the infliction of pain on others.

masochism—from Leopold von Sacher-Masoch (1836–1895), an Austrian novelist, who described the condition of deriving pleasure from being subjected to pain.

hedonism, however, is derived from the Greek *hedone*, pleasure. It is the pursuit of pleasure and the avoidance of pain.

Berger and Wildavsky provide an excellent model for introducing a paper of this kind, summarizing "four major theories" about the nature of humor, focusing on **incongruity, superiority, psychology,** and **semiotics,** respectively.

The Talmud consists of two collections of ancient scholarly writings on scripture: the Mishnah and the Gemara. It is of profound importance in traditional Judaism.

THINK ON PAPER

Notice the important transitional observation at the end of the second full paragraph on this page: "None of these theories, however, deals with specific jokes or other humorous texts, except in very broad terms. Their generalizations cover all socioeconomic backgrounds and all cultures." What does this suggest you might expect in the rest of the essay?

of my modesty they said nothing" (revealing his ego)—is what generates the humor. For the superiority theorists, we laugh because we feel superior to the rabbi, who reveals he really has a great ego. A psychoanalytic theorist would say that we laugh at this joke because of the aggression it contains. As the great rabbi is attacked, he is revealed to have an ego that is not satisfied by being praised from morning to night. And the cognitive/semiotic theorists would say that the opposition between egotism and modesty is at the heart of the joke.

semiotics = **semantics**
the study of meaning in language; the relationship between signs or symbols and meaning

sema (G) = sign

semaphore **sematic**

The cultural theory of humor narrows the field and ties specific jokes and humorous texts to smaller groupings—people who belong to one of four basic cultural groups: elitists, egalitarians, individualists, and fatalists. This is a step in the right direction in that it moves from glittering generalities about humanity to smaller cultural groupings. Another question suggests itself. Is it possible that people, regardless of their cultural group, respond to humor because of the techniques used in these texts to generate humor?

An elaborate content analysis of joke books, comic books, cartoons, plays, and any other examples from many different cultures was used to set up a typology of forty-five techniques, found generally in combination, that show what it is that makes people laugh. This is a "what makes people laugh" pragmatic typology and does not attempt to deal with why people laugh or how their cultural biases affect their response to humor. Some of the more important of these techniques are allusion, exaggeration, insult, mistake, misunderstanding, and parody.

> *The cultural theory of humor ties specific jokes and humorous texts to smaller groupings.*

Here the authors introduce their fifth theory of humor—the **cultural theory.** This, then, becomes the principal focus of the essay.

This assumes that people of all socio-economic classes, nationalities, and cultural groups respond immediately, and perhaps even automatically since laughter is a reflex, to the various techniques of humor. These techniques, it is implied, are psychological or more primary than "cultural." The basic technique of humor in the rabbi joke is revelation—the punchline reveals the true nature of the rabbi, namely that he is somewhat of an egotist. There is also an element of reversal, as the rabbi says yes, the praises he received were adequate, but why did nobody mention his great modesty, reversing himself.

The **cultural groupings** or ways of life suggested here may be surprising to the reader. Only four types are suggested, but they are very suggestive of different world views, as discussed in Jain's essay in Unit Seven, Section Three.

Another approach is a cultural theory of humor, which provides important insights into humor and its role in society. Cultural theory, as elaborated by Mary Douglas and others, deals with how cultural biases (shared values and beliefs) and social relations (patterns of interpersonal relations) affect our beliefs and behavior, and, by implication, can be applied to our response to humor. An elaboration of Douglas's original "grid" and "group" notion takes into consideration group boundaries on a horizontal plane and rules and prescriptions that guide individuals on a vertical plane. This perspective on cultures cuts across class structure and allows individuals to change as their perceptions of themselves and their possibilities are modified by experience. Individuals move between cultural groups, depending on such factors as chance, bad luck, bad decisions, a lack of payoff, and the like.

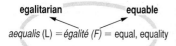

egalitarian **equable**
aequalis (L) = *égalité (F)* = equal, equality

From this perspective, only four ways of life are possible: fatalist, individualist, elitist (hierarchical), and egalitarian. Each culture differs in values and "collective moral consciousness about man and his place in the universe." Though they are different, they all need one another. In principle, members of each cultural group should respond positively to humorous texts that reflect their values and beliefs and negatively to texts that attack them. But this assumes a response to the contents of texts and not to the techniques that generate the humor in them.

From the cultural theory perspective, jokes may be conceived of as involving one culture puffing itself up or putting another culture down. From this viewpoint, the joke about the Talmudic scholar is not about an isolated or fatalistic person, nor is it about hierarchy building up its authority. On the contrary, it is a put-down of authority showing that one of its leading members believes one thing but claims another. From the context, however, we cannot tell whether this is an egalitarian or an individualist put-down. We cannot tell whether the rabbi is simply greedy for praise, as an individualist might be, or whether he thinks himself more worthy of praise than others, like a good hierarchical elitist. This brings out another possible classification of jokes, namely by cultural dimensions.

Berger and Wildavsky's technique is similar to that employed by other writers in this course, such as Janson in Unit Eight, who illustrate their general points with specific examples. In Janson's case, his discussion of the nature of art is illustrated with reference to individual works; here, the authors illustrate their discussion of humor with reference to particular jokes.

Providing examples is a very good way to make essays more meaningful and therefore more interesting.

Jokes often contain a great deal of masked aggression.

There are several problems with regard to relating cultural theory to humorous texts. For one thing, even seemingly simple humorous texts, like jokes, are frequently quite complex and often use several humorous techniques in combination to achieve their effects. An interesting question arises: Do people respond primarily to the content of humorous texts or primarily to the techniques that generate the humor—or do they respond to some combination of both?

Consider the following joke: A traveling salesman is doing business in Montana. One evening he goes to a bar and has a few drinks.

A bit inebriated he yells out, "Nixon is a horse's ass!"

A tough looking cowboy sidles over to the salesman, "You'd better watch what you say," he says.

"Oh, I'm sorry. I didn't realize I was in Nixon territory."

"You aren't," says the cowboy. "You're in horse territory."

The basic techniques of this joke are insult ("Nixon is a horse's ass"), comparison (Nixon and the horse's ass), and reversal ("You're not in Nixon territory but in horse territory.") But to which cultural group does the joke appeal and which cultural group is ridiculed by it? The joke suggests that Nixon is not nearly as good as a horse's ass. Being about a Republican president, this joke would appeal to Democrats.

In terms of cultural theory, the joke would appeal to egalitarians, who are critics of hierarchy and thus of Nixon, who was president, or hierarchists, who saw him as an immoral and rather gross individualist. Fatalists may respond to insult and aggression, but from a cultural theory perspective, they are not significant since they see life is as unfair and tied to luck and chance and thus would not feel envious about Nixon. In principle, however, fatalists are the polar opposites of individualists, who are strivers and who believe in the efficacy of personal effort and initiative.

An interesting question suggest itself here: Are certain of the forty-five techniques tied to one or another of the four cultures? Is there an element of cultural bias in some of the humorous techniques? Some possible connections are: 1) hierarchical—ridicule dialect; 2) individualist—exaggeration, before (poor) and after (rich), imitation, eccentricity; 3) egalitarian—repartee, reversal, exposure, allusions, unmasking, insults, satire; 4) fatalist—absurdity, disappointment, mistakes, ignorance, accident, coincidence. These techniques tend to reflect, or are often connected to, the cultural biases of a group, though not every situation containing absurdity is fatalistic nor is every joke that involves unmasking egalitarian in nature.

Do individuals from a particular culture, such as egalitarians, only laugh at jokes that reflect their cultural biases, or do they laugh at jokes because some elements in a given joke reflect them? Might people from all four cultures laugh at different parts of a particular joke? Or, do people only laugh at certain jokes that are essentially congruent with their cultural biases? Or those which attack other cultural groups?

The effective **use of questions** in essay writing is illustrated here. *Questions should not take the place of discussion;* they are one means—though not the only means—of introducing a particular idea or a new direction in the essay. Berger and Wildavsky ask questions here, but they use them to launch a new aspect of their discussion.

People search for texts that reinforce their values and beliefs and try to avoid texts that attack their values and beliefs and create cognitive dissonance. Is it possible, however, that in some cases people laugh at jokes for the wrong reasons—as far as cultural theory is concerned? Might an egalitarian, for example, laugh at a joke that reflects hierarchical values? Quite possibly, but we can assume that egalitarians laugh more heartily at jokes that reflect egalitarian beliefs and values or attack hierarchical ones.

Do people in a given culture find jokes that support and reaffirm their cultural biases funnier and more appealing than jokes that attack other cultures? If the psychoanalytic humor theorists are correct, there is often a great deal of masked aggression in jokes. A joke that "attacks" another cultural group tells whom we do not like, but it does not necessarily tell which group is benefitting from the "attack" by having its values reaffirmed. Neither does it tell whether there are cultural groups that get a psychic pay-off from a given joke or humorous text.

The following joke shows how the cultural perspective is useful for understanding jokes and other humorous texts. The scene is the world's richest synagogue and the protagonists are the world's best rabbi and the world's finest cantor, as well as the shammas, the non-Jew who looks after the synagogue. After a glorious Yom Kippur service the three gather in the rabbi's office. The rabbi in the world's richest synagogue says to the world's best cantor that he has sung the Kol Nidre better than it has ever been sung before. In all modesty, the great cantor in the world says that his singing was not bad, but when he thinks of the great cantors of the past, he is really nothing. Then the cantor turns to the rabbi and says, "But rabbi, your sermon was the best that has been delivered anywhere at any time." In all due modesty, the world's greatest rabbi in the world's richest synagogue says that the sermon was not bad, but when he thinks of the great rabbis and great sermons of the past, he is really nothing.

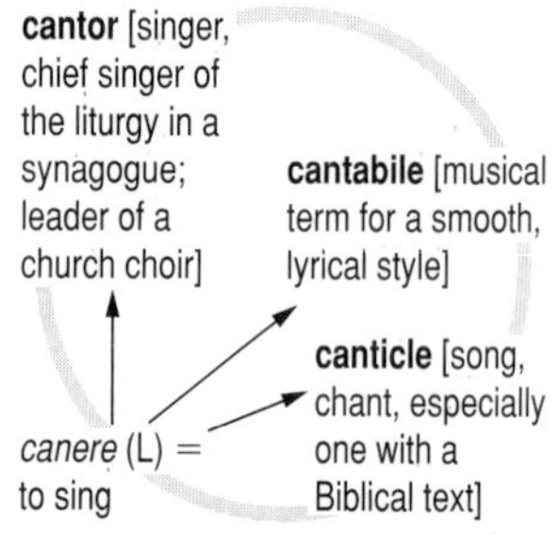

By this time the shammas thinks he understands how these Jews talk to each other and is determined not to be outdone. So when the rabbi and the cantor praise the shammas for having prepared the synagogue for the High Holidays better than it has ever been prepared before, the shammas replies, "The synagogue was prepared all right, but when I think of the great shammases of the past, I'm really nothing." The world's greatest rabbi and the world's greatest cantor in the world's richest synagogue turn to each other and say in unison, "Look who says he's nothing!"

An **arriviste** (from the French *arriver*, to arrive) is an upstart, or a social climber. In other words the literal meaning is one who has arrived, but, as you can tell by the joke, he is really someone who only *thinks* he has arrived and been accepted.

Clearly, this arriviste is being put down for aspiring to a status to which he is not entitled. This is not an egalitarian joke because it is the lowest person in the social order who is being put down. It is not an individualist joke because the shammas, by his own abilities, is not able to rise in status, however good his work. It is not a fatalistic joke because the shammas tries. It is a hierarchical joke in which those, whether individualist or egalitarian, who try to climb the ladder of status by aping the manners of those above them, cannot succeed.

The fact that the synagogue is the world's richest synagogue and that the cantor is the world's greatest cantor and the rabbi is the world's best rabbi are clues that we are dealing with hierarchy and the joke appeals to hierarchical elitists. And the punchline—"Look who says he's nothing!"—reinforces the point. The rabbi and cantor can say they are nothing because they know they are the world's greatest, but the shammas is not entitled to this false modesty.

There are several humorous techniques in this joke. First, we have the exaggeration, as we are told about the heroes of the joke: the world's richest synagogue, the world's greatest rabbi and the world's best cantor. Then we have imitation, as the shammas learns from the rabbi and cantor and says that he, too (like them) is "nothing." There may be an element of misunderstanding on the part of the shammas, who hears the rabbi and cantor claim they are nothing and who might believe they actually mean it.

Hierarchists and individualists make up the "establishment" in a given society and are natural allies.

The joke also involves unmasking and revelation, as it shows that the rabbi and cantor are really vain and only pretending to be modest, as was the Talmudic scholar in the other Jewish joke. Finally, there is the element of ridicule, as the rabbi and cantor attack the shammas for claiming, like them, to be a "nothing," since, unlike the rabbi and the cantor, he is not the greatest in the world. The joke is a put-down of an individualist, the shammas, who aspires to a status to which he is not entitled. While hierarchical elitists and egalitarians are logical opposites, the hierarchists also face the problem of dealing with individualists who make claims to status.

The detailed manner in which the authors analyze the joke is a good model. Even when you think there is nothing to say, or that what you have already said speaks for itself, there are usually opportunities for discussion.

Some insight may be gained on which groups laugh and benefit from jokes and why by suggesting that there are natural allies and natural enemies amongst all four cultural groups. Individualists (weak group, few rules), who believe in taking risks for private gain and in personal responsibility, are at the opposite end of the spectrum from fatalists (weak group, many rules), who think luck is basic and who are led by external forces. Egalitarians (strong group, few rules), who argue that equality of power relationships are basic and who stress certain common needs and downplay differences among people, are polar opposites of hierarchists (strong group, many rules), who believe in stratification and blame difficulties on deviants, not, as egalitarians do, on "the system."

There are also natural allies. The egalitarians ally themselves with and strive to "lift up" the fatalists, who are the primary object of their concern in this regard (but not vice versa: fatalists do not ally themselves with egalitarians). In the same light, the hierarchists and individualists make up "the establishment" in a given society and are natural allies, though as the great rabbi joke shows, they often are in conflict as individualists try to make claims to status that hierarchical groups do not believe are merited or do not wish to recognize. Though the groups are often in opposition, as cultural theorists continually point out, all the groups need each other. If there were no fatalists, the egalitarians would have no one to criticize and the hierarchical elitists and hierarchists would have no group to "lord over."

Since individuals move from one cultural group to another, a joke can reflect several different things. A joke ridiculing hierarchists can reflect the values and beliefs of a group, such as the individualists, that a person is connected with, or it could be an indicator of a potential movement by that person from his original group to a different one, such as the egalitarians.

Probably the best approach to the enigmatic nature of humor is through the principle of selectivity. While members of each group may laugh at all kinds of different jokes, certain jokes—those speaking most directly to the cultural biases of each group—would be seen as particularly funny and resonant. These jokes achieve their resonance by reaffirming the group's values and by attacking the values of other groups. It is quite likely, furthermore, that members of each of the four cultural groups seek out humorists who reflect their values.

Thus, comedians and comediennes who support egalitarian beliefs and attack the establishment and ridicule politicians, business people, and celebrities as part of it, and if the performers are sympathetic to fatalists, so much the better. In humor, the ridiculer of my enemy is my ally.

A wasp is walking along the Nile when it meets a frog.

"I've got to get over to the other side and need someone to take me. Will you do it?" asks the wasp.

"No," says the frog. "I'm afraid that when we're in the middle of the Nile you'll sting me and I'll die."

"But that would be crazy," says the wasp, "because I'd die as well."

"Okay," says the frog.

The wasp hops on the frog's back and the frog starts swimming towards the other bank. When they are halfway there the wasp stings the frog.

"How could you sting me like this when you'll die as well as me?" asks the frog.

"You forget," says the wasp. "This is the Middle East."

From a cultural theory perspective, this reflects a fatalistic position. In the Middle East, it suggests, hatreds are so strong, destroying enemies is so important that individuals feel compelled to kill their enemies, even if it means their self-destruction at the same time. The techniques used in the joke are rigidity (the wasp must kill frogs) and stereotyping ("this is the Middle East").

Mary Douglas has suggested in her article on "Jokes" in *Implicit Meanings* that "a joke is seen and allowed when it offers a symbolic pattern of a social pattern occurring at the same time." All jokes are expressive of the social situations in which they occur. This comment places humorous texts, in general, and jokes, in particular, in a new light. They are not just trivial amusements and entertainments but are related, in complicated ways, to society and to the four cultures found in any society.

Since jokes are complex matters, we must assume that individuals respond to the content of a given joke based on their identification with one of the cultural groups—a response based on reinforcing the values of the individuals' cultural group or on attacking those of other cultural groups. And they respond to the techniques generating humor in a given joke more or less automatically. Most people are not aware of the various techniques found in humor, but have a great deal of experience reacting to texts based on them, since these techniques are widespread, if not universal.

There are different ways of concluding a piece of writing (see Unit Three, Section One for more on this). This essay ends effectively and usefully with a summary of the conclusions drawn from the discussion of the cultural theory of humor.

ARTHUR ASA BERGER *is professor of broadcast communication arts at* San Francisco State University. *He has written widely on popular culture. Among his books are* Agit-Pop: Political Culture and Communication Theory; Reading Matter: Multidisciplinary Perspectives on Material Culture; Political Culture and Public Opinion; *and* An Anatomy of Humor; *all published by* Transaction.

AARON WILDAVSKY *was professor of political science and public policy and a member of the Survey Research Center at the University of California, Berkeley. Among his many books are* The Beleaguered Presidency; Craftways: On the Organization of Scholary Work; Assimilation Versus Separation: Joseph the Administrator and the Politics of Religion in Biblical Israel; *and (with Richard Ellis)* Dilemmas of Presidential leadership: From Washington through Lincoln; *all published by Transaction.*

ASPECTS OF WRITING: Paragraphs.

Paragraphs are logical units, and mention has been made earlier in this text of the need for paragraph **unity** (see Unit Seven, Section Three). Sometimes a lack of unity is apparent when the focus of discussion shifts within a paragraph, and sometimes it is apparent in a different way when ideas are broken up, unnecessarily, into separate paragraphs. Simply stated, the first type of problem can lead to paragraphs that contain incompatible material, while the second type can lead to a string of short paragraphs that could be combined. Deciding what to do may, however, require a judgment call on the writer's part. Here is an example from the essay in this section.

In their second paragraph, Berger and Wildavsky write,

> There are any number of theories about why people laugh. Four major theories will be considered here. . . .

The second sentence could be a type of topic sentence in which the purpose of the paragraph is stated, or it could be an introduction to a more elaborate discussion. If the former, the authors might have continued something like this:

> . . . considered here. The first is based on incongruity, the idea that a joke is funny when there is a difference between what people expect and what they get. The second is based on superiority, the idea that people find jokes or situations funny when they are left feeling superior to the butt of the joke. The third type of humor is based on psychoanalysis, which ties humor to aggression, and the fourth involves semiotics and explains that humor involves the recognition that many jokes are funny only within a recognized playful context.

In this paragraph, all four theories are briefly explained, and the author may or may not intend to elaborate further on them, depending on the purpose of the essay.

Alternatively, like Berger and Wildavsky, the writer may devote a paragraph to each of the four theories, explaining them fairly briefly but in more detail than is appropriate for the one paragraph model above. Thus, they write four separate paragraphs, linked together by standard transitions:

> . . . The currently dominant theory suggests that humor is based on incongruity. . . .
>
> A second important theory argues that. . . .

> Freud's psychoanalytic theory of humor argues that. . . .
>
> Finally, there is a theory of humor that ties. . . .

The authors then proceed to discuss these theories in the context of particular examples before moving on to the main discussion, which they introduce as follows:

> Another approach is a cultural theory of humor. . . .

The possibility of adding a fifth theory has already been suggested when the authors noted that the first four theories failed to explain specific jokes and texts: "Their generalizations cover all socio-economic backgrounds and all cultures."

The organization of your essay into paragraphs should reflect the logic of your paper. It may, for example be relevant to mention different theories if the purpose of your paragraph is to give brief analyses of a particular joke. If you are discussing these analyses in detail, however, each theory should be treated separately and may, indeed, require several paragraphs.

A conventional **thesis-oriented essay** may have required a different introduction, along these lines:

> Among the major theories purporting to explain why things are funny are the incongruity theory, the superiority theory, Freud's psychoanalytic theory, and a number of cognitive/semiotic theories. These all offer interesting generalizations about humor, but a fifth theory, the cultural theory, helps explain why specific jokes and other humorous texts are funny.

WRITING EXERCISES: Answer one of the following.

Wit suggests a quickness and cleverness with words. It sometimes has a certain acidity. Some famous examples include Dorothy Parker's cruel but funny response on being told that President Coolidge had died: "How can you tell?" George Bernard Shaw commented that "Democracy substitutes election by the incompetent many for appointment by the corrupt few." Will Rogers noted, "You can't say civilization don't advance . . . in every war they kill you in a new way."

1. Summarize Berger and Wildavsky's account of five theories of humor and apply each to jokes familiar to you. Use their essay as a model for integrating the jokes into your essay.
2. Discuss the jokes that Berger and Wildavsky use in their essay and comment, from your personal point of view, on their analysis of why they are funny.
3. Plays, movies, and everyday situations can be comic. Using your own examples, analyze why some people find such things funny but others do not. Make reference to the theories of humor in the Berger and Wildavsky essay.

SECTION TWO

PRIOR KNOWLEDGE: Finding humor in situations.

Over the centuries, many writers have commented on the human condition. Horace Walpole, an 18th-century man of letters, observed that "The world is a comedy to those that think, a tragedy to those that feel." The poet John Gay, in a two-line poem called "My Own Epitaph" (1720), wrote:

Life is a jest; and all things show it.
I thought so once; but now I know it.

Elbert Hubbard wrote, "Life is just one damn thing after another," to which the 20th-century poet and playwright Edna St. Vincent Millay responded, "It's not true that life is one damn thing after another—it is one damn thing over and over." Shakespeare often describes life as a stage:

All the world's a stage,
And all the men and women merely players.
(*As You Like It,* II, vii)

When we are born, we cry that we are come
To this great stage of fools.
(*King Lear,* IV, vi)

Life's but a walking shadow, a poor player
That struts and frets his hour upon the stage
And then is heard no more. It is a tale
Told by an idiot, full of sound and fury,
Signifying nothing.
(*Macbeth,* V, v)

Seeing the humor in life's situations, even some of the painful ones, and being able to laugh at oneself, are great gifts. The following incident, recounted by a former Peace Corps volunteer to Nigeria, suggests an ability to see both the serious and humorous—even farcical—side of life in the same incident.

> While leafing through a magazine recently, I became transfixed by a sportswear ad showing a man running. The picture did not show where he came from or where he was going; he was simply running. And for a strange moment I was with him, not loping through a glossy layout in color-coordinated athletic shoes and warmup suit, but in the tiny,

remote village in Nigeria where I served as a Peace Corps volunteer some years ago.

In a flash I saw the one-lane bush road outside my cinder-block house, a road that ambled through jungle and scrubland to the nearest electricity and running water—a three-hour bike ride away. And I remembered how the adventure of the first few months gave way, through lazy afternoons and candlelit nights, to long daydreams about the sandlot ball games of my childhood. For some time I puzzled over what, if any, sport I could play at my unlikely outpost. At last it occurred to me that right there on the narrow bush road, under ancient layers of naturally crushed terra cotta, lay a perfect jogging path. I had never jogged before in my life. But, being 6,000 miles from the nearest sandlot ball game, I was willing to expand my sporting horizon.

Later that same afternoon, as the equatorial sun dipped below the palm trees, I laced up my old US Keds and, stretching my arms exultantly, set out on the road. I had guessed right; its firm but resilient surface was perfect under foot. Overhead, giant banana leaves seemed to wave me on to the cheers of a host of birds invisible in the jungle forest.

Just as I was about to hit my stride, I heard the distinct rattle and whirr of the oft-repaired local bicycles. In seconds I was joined on either side by two cassava farmers, pedaling their way home from the fields after a long day's work in the sun. Managing my best American Peace Corps smile, I turned each way and nodded to them without breaking stride. To my surprise, they did not pass. Holding even with me, they stared.

"You got trouble?" one asked, his voice grave.

"Oh . . . (puff) . . . no," I said, holding my pace. Again, I smiled to each side.

"You need help?" the other farmer urged.

"Uh . . . no . . . (puff) thank you," I wheezed. "No help. Everything OK (puff). Thank you (puff)."

The soft, chipped clay crunched beneath my feet as the two bicycles rattled along beside. Ahead was a chuckhole the size of a basketball; the bicycles swerved, I leaped it and continued. The two drew back beside me.

"You run," one noted.

"Yes (puff), I run (puff)."

"You run," the other repeated, hesitating: "Where?"

With some discomfort, I shifted my stride, I was out of shape, and had expected the running to get difficult, but carrying on a conversation at the same time was beginning to tax my patience. "Up the road!" I snapped.

"You run up road," the two echoed. Rattling and whirring together, they looked ahead and, seeing only the same road and forest that they had seen for years, they turned back to me with blank expressions. For a brief second their mutual bewilderment slowed their pedaling, and I strode ahead. Catching themselves, they pulled even with me again.

"No trouble. You run. Up road." The one farmer spoke studiously, as if writing out the problem before himself on a blackboard, the more clearly to grasp its components.

"Why you run up road?!" the two burst out at once.

It was no use. I did what is forbidden to all joggers. There, beneath the waving banana leaves and cheering birds, I stopped. We all stopped. Panting, sweating in the humid dusk, frustrated at being interrupted on my first jog, I struggled to remain calm: "You want to know why I am running up the road . . . right?" I offered.

Standing patiently beside their bicycles, they nodded.

"Right," I repeated, stalling as a feeling of being oddly out of place crept over me. Drawing a deep breath, I simply said, "I am running to get exercise."

"Exercise?" one echoed. "What is ex-ercise?"

I stood there for a long second, my mouth open, beginning to sense the scene's absurdity: Two thin, overworked cassava farmers sitting astride broken-down bicycles that represented a measure of their success; an overcaloried white man in canvas shoes running nowhere to get something that no one here had ever heard of. Words failed me. Where we stood, farmers have for centuries harvested barely enough calories to continue toiling in the fields. We were an arm's length apart, but a hopeless cultural gulf yawned between us.

I spread my hands, palms upward, and shook my head. At last, clumsily, I reached out and shook each man's hand. "Thank you . . . for stopping to check on me," I said, faltering. "You are good friends."

And then, wiping my brow quickly, turned and ran back to my house.

Gordon Dalbey, "A Jogger Fails to Cross the Culture Gap."
RPCVoice

ANNOTATED READING: Laura Bohannan. "Shakespeare in the Bush." *Natural History* Aug./Sept. 1966: 28–33.

Shakespeare in the Bush

An American anthropologist set out to study the Tiv of West Africa and was taught the true meaning of Hamlet.

Laura Bohannan was studying at Oxford University, England, when she went to southern Nigeria to live among the **Tiv.** This well-known essay was presented on BBC radio and has been widely read since its first publication in *Natural History.* It's funny, and it is also interesting from a cross-cultural point of view.

The idea that "human nature is pretty much the same the whole world over" is widely held, perhaps because we find it difficult to imagine sensible people being very different from ourselves. Clearly, Bohannan's story is going to challenge this notion.

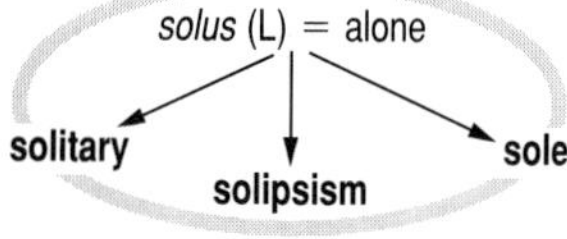

Just before I left Oxford for the Tiv in West Africa, conversation turned to the season at Stratford. "You Americans," said a friend, "often have difficulty with Shakespeare. He was, after all, a very English poet, and one can easily misinterpret the universal by misunderstanding the particular."

I protested that human nature is pretty much the same the whole world over; at least the general plot and motivation of the greater tragedies would always be clear—everywhere—although some details of custom might have to be explained and difficulties of translation might produce other slight changes. To end an argument we could not conclude, my friend gave me a copy of *Hamlet* to study in the African bush: it would, he hoped, lift my mind above its primitive surroundings, and possibly I might, by prolonged meditation, achieve the grace of correct interpretation.

It was my second field trip to that African tribe, and I thought myself ready to live in one of its remote sections—an area difficult to cross even on foot. I eventually settled on the hillock of a very knowledgeable old man, the head of a homestead of some hundred and forty people, all of whom were either his close relatives or their wives and children. Like the other elders of the vicinity, the old man spent most of his time performing ceremonies seldom seen these days in the more accessible parts of the tribe. I was delighted. Soon there would be three months of enforced isolation and leisure, between the harvest that takes place just before the rising of the swamps and the clearing of new farms when the water goes down. Then, I thought, they would have even more time to perform ceremonies and explain them to me.

I was quite mistaken. Most of the ceremonies demanded the presence of elders from several homesteads. As the swamps rose, the old men found it too difficult to walk from one homestead to the next, and the ceremonies gradually ceased. As the swamps rose even higher, all activities but one came to an end. The women brewed beer from maize and millet. Men, women, and children sat on their hillocks and drank it.

People began to drink at dawn. By midmorning the whole homestead was singing, dancing, and drumming. When it rained, people had to sit inside their huts: there they drank and sang or they drank and told stories. In any case, by noon or before, I either had to join the party or retire to my own hut and my books. "One does not discuss serious matters when there is beer. Come, drink with us." Since I lacked their capacity for the thick native beer, I spent more and more time with *Hamlet*. Before the end of the second month, grace descended on me. I was quite sure that *Hamlet* had only one possible interpretation, and that one universally obvious.

Early every morning, in the hope of having some serious talk before the beer party, I used to call on the old man at his reception hut—a circle of posts supporting a thatched roof above a low mud wall to keep out wind and rain. One day I crawled through the low doorway and found most of the men of the homestead sitting huddled in their ragged clothes on stools, low plank beds, and reclining chairs, warming themselves against the chill of the rain around a smoky fire. In the center were three pots of beer. The party had started.

The old man greeted me cordially. "Sit down and drink." I accepted a large calabash full of beer, poured some into a small drinking gourd, and tossed it down. Then I poured some more into the same gourd for the man second in seniority to my host before I handed my calabash over to a young man for further distribution. Important people shouldn't ladle beer themselves.

"It is better like this," the old man said, looking at me approvingly and plucking at the thatch that had caught in my hair. "You should sit and drink with us more often. Your servants tell me that when you are not with us, you sit inside your hut looking at a paper."

Bohannan's story assumes some familiarity with Shakespeare's *Hamlet.* If you don't know the play, you are encouraged to see it on stage if you have an opportunity, or see one of the movie versions, or, of course, read it. Meanwhile, here is a brief summary.

Soon after the death of his father, (the King), Hamlet, Prince of Denmark, is mortified by the remarriage of his mother, Queen Gertrude, to his uncle, Claudius, who takes the throne. Hamlet learns from his father's ghost that Claudius had killed the King, and the ghost tells him to "Revenge his foul and most unnatural murder." To prove that this was true, Hamlet invites some actors to put on a performance depicting the murder of a king and imitating other aspects of Claudius's plot. The performance enrages the King, and, afterward, Gertrude calls her son to her room to see her. Polonius, the Lord Chamberlain, hides behind the arras, or curtain. The Queen, feeling threatened by her son, calls out, and Polonius cries out for help. Hamlet, thinking that it may be the King, stabs through the arras, killing Polonius, whose daughter, Ophelia, loves and is loved by Hamlet. Polonius, however, has discouraged Ophelia from receiving Hamlet, causing the prince to fall into a morose state, perhaps even madness. In her distress over the loss of her father and over her failed friendship with Hamlet, Ophelia drowns herself, leaving her brother, Laertes, swearing revenge. In a tempestuous conclusion, Hamlet and Laertes engage in swordplay; Laertes, using a poisoned rapier, stabs Hamlet, but, in a scuffle, the rapiers are exchanged and Laertes is stabbed also. Gertrude drinks a poisoned cup of wine, intended for Hamlet, and dies. Laertes, dying, tells Hamlet that the King has poisoned the blade and the wine, and Hamlet turns on Claudius and kills him. Laertes then dies, closely followed by Hamlet.

Minor characters in the play include Rosencrantz and Guildenstern, who also die, having been betrayed by their friend, Hamlet. These characters are the stars of a witty modern play (and movie) by Tom Stoppard, *Rosencrantz and Guildenstern Are Dead*, which tells the story of *Hamlet* from their point of view.

The old man was acquainted with four kinds of "papers": tax receipts, bride price receipts, court fee receipts, and letters. The messenger who brought him letters from the chief used them mainly as a badge of office, for he always knew what was in them and told the old man. Personal letters for the few who had relatives in the government or mission stations were kept until someone went to a large market where there was a letter writer and reader. Since my arrival, letters were brought to me to be read. A few men also brought me bride price receipts, privately, with requests to change the figures to a higher sum. I found moral arguments were of no avail, since in-laws are fair game, and the technical hazards of forgery difficult to explain to an illiterate people. I did not wish them to think me silly enough to look at any such papers for days on end, and I hastily explained that my "paper" was one of the "things of long ago" of my country.

"Ah," said the old man. "Tell us."

I protested that I was not a storyteller. Storytelling is a skilled art among them; their standards are high, and the audiences critical—and vocal in their criticism. I protested in vain. This morning they wanted to hear a story while they drank. They threatened to tell me no more stories until I told them one of mine. Finally, the old man promised that no one would criticize my style "for we know you are struggling with our language." "But," put in one of the elders, "you must explain what we do not understand, as we do when we tell you our stories." Realizing that here was my chance to prove *Hamlet* universally intelligible, I agreed.

The old man handed me some more beer to help me on with my storytelling. Men filled their long wooden pipes and knocked coals from the fire to place in the pipe bowls; then, puffing contentedly, they sat back to listen. I began in the proper style, "Not yesterday, not yesterday, but long ago, a thing occurred. One night three men were keeping watch outside the homestead of the great chief, when suddenly they saw the former chief approach them."

In the play, the ghost appears first to Hamlet's friend, Horatio, and two officers, Marcellus and Bernardo. Horatio tells Hamlet, who then waits to see the ghost for himself.

"Why was he no longer their chief?"

"He was dead," I explained. "That is why they were troubled and afraid when they saw him."

"Impossible," began one of the elders, handing his pipe on to his neighbor, who interrupted, "Of course it wasn't the dead chief. It was an omen sent by a witch. Go on."

Slightly shaken, I continued. "One of these three was a man who knew things"—the closest translation for scholar, but unfortunately it also meant witch. The second elder looked triumphantly at the first. "So he spoke to the dead chief saying, 'Tell us what we must do so you may rest in your grave,' but the dead chief did not answer. He vanished, and they could see him no more. Then the man who knew things—his name was Horatio—said this event was the affair of the dead chief's son, Hamlet."

There was a general shaking of heads round the circle. "Had the dead chief no living brothers? Or was this son the chief?"

"No," I replied. "That is, he had one living brother who became the chief when the elder brother died."

The old men muttered: such omens were matters for chiefs and elders, not for youngsters; no good could come of going behind a chief's back; clearly Horatio was not a man who knew things.

"Yes, he was," I insisted, shooing a chicken away from my beer. "In our country the son is next to the father. The dead chief's younger brother had become the great chief. He had also married his elder brother's widow only about a month after the funeral."

"He did well," the old man beamed and announced to the others, "I told you that if we knew more about Europeans, we would find they really were very like us. In our country also," he added to me, "the younger brother marries the elder brother's widow and becomes the father of his children. Now, if your uncle, who married your widowed mother, is your father's full brother, then he will be a real father to you. Did Hamlet's father and uncle have one mother?"

In approving of Claudius' marriage to Gertrude, his dead brother's wife, the old men undercut one of Hamlet's principal grievances. In many cultures, however, it is considered normal for a widow to marry her husband's brother, and thereby come under his protection. This, of course, is more easily done in polygamous societies.

The old man makes the same assumption as Bohannan. He is sure that if his friends knew more about Europeans, they would find them to be "very like us."

His question barely penetrated my mind; I was too upset and thrown too far off balance by having one of the most important elements of *Hamlet* knocked straight out of the picture. Rather uncertainly I said that I thought they had the same mother, but I wasn't sure—the story didn't say. The old man told me severely that these genealogical details made all the difference and that when I got home I must ask the elders about it. He shouted out the door to one of his younger wives to bring his goatskin bag.

Many people in the West are interested in **genealogy,** but this interest is mainly personal—we want to know more about our roots. In many cultures, however, genealogy can determine rank and status and is important on a practical level. In Samoa, in the South Pacific, where the people of entire villages sometimes visit each, orators ("talking chiefs") greet their guests with a long account of the visitors' history and make reference to all the important titles in that village in order of rank. This is a great feat of memory, but it is also a great strain, for mistakes can give offense and bring "shame" on the orator and his village.

Determined to save what I could of the mother motif, I took a deep breath and began again. "The son Hamlet was very sad because his mother had married again so quickly. There was no need for her to do so, and it is our custom for a widow not to go to her next husband until she has mourned for two years."

"Two years is too long," objected the wife, who had appeared with the old man's battered goatskin bag. "Who will hoe your farms for you while you have no husband?"

"Hamlet," I retorted without thinking, "was old enough to hoe his mother's farms himself. There was no need for her to remarry." No one looked convinced. I gave up. "His mother and the great chief told Hamlet not to be sad, for the great chief himself would be a father to Hamlet. Furthermore, Hamlet would be the next chief: therefore he must stay to learn the things of a chief. Hamlet agreed to remain, and all the rest went off to drink beer."

While I paused, perplexed at how to render Hamlet's disgusted soliloquy to an audience convinced that Claudius and Gertrude had behaved in the best possible manner, one of the younger men asked me who had married the other wives of the dead chief.

"He had no other wives," I told him.

"But a chief must have many wives! How else can he brew beer and prepare food for all his guests?"

I said firmly that in our country even chiefs had only one wife, that they had servants to do their work, and that they paid them from tax money.

It was better, they returned, for a chief to have many wives and sons who would help him hoe his farms and feed his people; then everyone loved the chief who gave much and took nothing—taxes were a bad thing.

I agreed with the last comment, but for the rest fell back on their favorite way of fobbing off my questions: "That is the way it is done, so that is how we do it."

I decided to skip the soliloquy. Even if Claudius was here thought quite right to marry his brother's widow, there remained the poison motif, and I knew they would disapprove of fratricide. More hopefully I resumed. "That night Hamlet kept watch with the three who had seen his dead father. The dead chief again appeared, and although the others were afraid, Hamlet followed his dead father off to one side. When they were alone, Hamlet's dead father spoke."

"Omens can't talk!" The old man was emphatic.

"Hamlet's dead father wasn't an omen. Seeing him might have been an omen, but he was not." My audience looked as confused as I sounded. "It *was* Hamlet's dead father. It was a thing we call a 'ghost,'" I had to use the English word, for unlike many of the neighboring tribes, these people didn't believe in the survival after death of any individuating part of the personality.

The word **"ghost"** is one of the oldest words in English, having an Old English derivation (see Unit Three, Option Two, for a brief history of English).

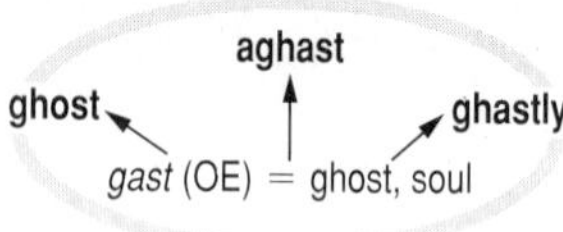

"What is a 'ghost?' An omen?"

"No, a 'ghost' is someone who is dead but who walks around and can talk, and people can hear him and see him but not touch him."

They objected. "One can touch zombis."

"No, no! It was not a dead body the witches had animated to sacrifice and eat. No one else made Hamlet's dead father walk. He did it himself."

"Dead men can't walk," protested my audience as one man.

I was quite willing to compromise. "A 'ghost' is the dead man's shadow."

The word **"zombie"** is usually associated with voodooism. It is derived from Kongo, a central African language, in which it means "fetish." The word has entered English via Haiti and parts of the United States. Its most common usage is to describe the "living dead"—someone who has died but who has come back to life.

But again they objected. "Dead men cast no shadows."

"They do in my country," I snapped.

The old man quelled the babble of disbelief that arose immediately and told me with that insincere, but courteous, agreement one extends to the fancies of the young, ignorant, and superstitious, "No doubt in your country the dead can also walk without being zombis." From the depths of his bag he produced a withered fragment of kola nut, bit off one end to show it wasn't poisoned, and handed me the rest as a peace offering.

"Anyhow," I resumed, "Hamlet's dead father said that his own brother, the one who became chief, had poisoned him. He wanted Hamlet to avenge him. Hamlet believed this in his heart, for he did not like his father's brother." I took another swallow of beer. "In the country of the great chief, living in the same homestead, for it was a very large one, was an important elder who was often with the chief to advise and help him. His name was Polonius. Hamlet was courting his daughter, but her father and her brother . . . [I cast hastily about for some tribal analogy] warned her not to let Hamlet visit her when she was alone on her farm, for he would be a great chief and so could not marry her."

"Why not?" asked the wife, who had settled down on the edge of the old man's chair. He frowned at her for asking stupid questions and growled, "They lived in the same homestead."

"That was not the reason," I informed them. "Polonius was a stranger who lived in the homestead because he helped the chief, not because he was a relative."

"Then why couldn't Hamlet marry her?"

"He could have," I explained, "but Polonius didn't think he would. After all, Hamlet was a man of great importance who ought to marry a chief's daughter, for in his country a man could have only one wife. Polonius was afraid that if Hamlet made love to his daughter, then no one else would give a high price for her."

"That might be true," remarked one of the shrewder elders, "but a chief's son would give his mistress's father enough presents and patronage to more than make up the difference. Polonius sounds like a fool to me."

"Many people think he was," I agreed. "Meanwhile Polonius sent his son Laertes off to Paris to learn the things of that country, for it was the homestead of a very great chief indeed. Because he was afraid that Laertes might waste a lot of money on beer and women and gambling, or get into trouble by fighting, he sent one of his servants to Paris secretly, to spy out what Laertes was doing. One day Hamlet came upon Polonius's daughter Ophelia. He behaved so oddly he frightened her. Indeed"—I was fumbling for words to express the dubious quality of Hamlet's madness—"the chief and many others had also noticed that when Hamlet talked one could understand the words but not what they meant. Many people thought that he had become mad." My audience suddenly became much more attentive. "The great chief wanted to know what was wrong with Hamlet, so he sent for two of Hamlet's age mates [school friends would have taken long explanation] to talk to Hamlet and find out what troubled his

Bohannan's story reminds us how our reading of *Hamlet* (and any text) is dependent to a large extent on our assumptions about human relationships, (especially within a family), ghosts, death, madness, spells, and so on. Sharing common assumptions allows people within a culture to see and understand the world—and literature—in pretty much the same way.

THINK ON PAPER
Think of situations in which people from different cultures make assumptions or have beliefs that give them a completely different view of the world from your own.

heart. Hamlet, seeing that they had been bribed by the chief to betray him, told them nothing. Polonius, however, insisted that Hamlet was mad because he had been forbidden to see Ophelia, whom he loved."

"Why," inquired a bewildered voice, "should anyone bewitch Hamlet on that account?"

"Bewitch him?"

"Yes, only witchcraft can make anyone mad, unless, of course, one sees the beings that lurk in the forest."

I stopped being a storyteller, took out my notebook and demanded to be told more about these two causes of madness. Even while they spoke and I jotted notes, I tried to calculate the effect of this new factor on the plot. Hamlet had not been exposed to the beings that lurk in the forests. Only his relatives in the male line could bewitch him. Barring relatives not mentioned by Shakespeare, it had to be Claudius who was attempting to harm him. And, of course, it was.

For the moment I staved off questions by saying that the great chief also refused to believe that Hamlet was mad for the love of Ophelia and nothing else. "He was sure that something much more important was troubling Hamlet's heart."

"Now Hamlet's age mates," I continued, "had brought with them a famous storyteller. Hamlet decided to have this man tell the chief and all his homestead a story about a man who had poisoned his brother because he desired his brother's wife and wished to be chief himself. Hamlet was sure the great chief could not hear the story without making a sign if he was indeed guilty, and then he would discover whether his dead father had told him the truth."

The old man interrupted, with deep cunning, "Why should a father lie to his son?" he asked.

I hedged: "Hamlet wasn't sure that it really was his dead father." It was impossible to say anything, in that language, about devil-inspired visions.

"You mean," he said, "it actually was an omen, and he knew witches sometimes send false ones. Hamlet was a fool not to go to one skilled in reading omens and divining the truth in the first place. A man-who-sees-the-truth could have told him how his father died, if he really had been poisoned, and if there was witchcraft in it; then Hamlet could have called the elders to settle the matter."

The shrewd elder ventured to disagree. "Because his father's brother was a great chief, one-who-sees-the-truth might therefore have been afraid to tell it. I think it was for that reason that a friend of Hamlet's father—a witch and an elder—sent an omen so his friend's son would know. Was the omen true?"

"Yes," I said, abandoning ghosts and the devil; a witch-sent omen it would have to be. "It was true, for when the storyteller was telling his tale before all the homestead, the great chief rose in fear. Afraid that Hamlet knew his secret he planned to have him killed."

The stage set of the next bit presented some difficulties of translation. I began cautiously. "The great chief told Hamlet's mother to find out from her son what he knew. But because a woman's children are always first in her heart, he had the important elder Polonius hide behind a cloth that hung against the wall of Hamlet's mother's sleeping hut. Hamlet started to scold his mother for what she had done."

There was a shocked murmur from everyone. A man should never scold his mother.

"She called out in fear, and Polonius moved behind the cloth. Shouting, 'A rat!' Hamlet took his machete and slashed through the cloth." I paused for dramatic effect. "He had killed Polonius!"

The old men looked at each other in supreme disgust. "That Polonius truly was a fool and a man who knew nothing! What child would not know enough to shout, 'It's me!'" With a pang, I remembered that these people are ardent hunters, always armed with bow, arrow, and machete; at the first rustle in the grass an arrow is aimed and ready, and the hunter shouts "Game!" If no human voice answers immediately, the arrow speeds on its way. Like a good hunter Hamlet had shouted, "A rat!"

I rushed in to save Polonius's reputation. "Polonius did speak. Hamlet heard him. But he thought it was the chief and wished to kill him to avenge his father. He had meant to kill him earlier that evening. . . ." I broke down, unable to describe to these pagans, who had no belief in individual afterlife, the difference between dying at one's prayers and dying "unhousell'd, disappointed, unaneled."

This time I had shocked my audience seriously. "For a man to raise his hand against his father's brother and the one who has become his father—that is a terrible thing. The elders ought to let such a man be bewitched."

I nibbled at my kola nut in some perplexity, then pointed out that after all the man had killed Hamlet's father.

"No," pronounced the old man, speaking less to me than to the young men sitting behind the elders. "If your father's brother has killed your father, you must appeal to your father's age mates; *they* may avenge him. No man may use violence against his senior relatives." Another thought struck him. "But if his father's brother had indeed been wicked enough to bewitch Hamlet and make him mad that would be a good story indeed, for it would be his fault that Hamlet, being mad, no longer had any sense and thus was ready to kill his father's brother."

There was a murmur of applause. *Hamlet* was again a good story to them, but it no longer seemed quite the same story to me. As I thought over the coming complications of plot and motive, I lost courage and decided to skim over dangerous ground quickly.

"The great chief," I went on, "was not sorry that Hamlet had killed Polonius. It gave him a reason to send Hamlet away, with his two treacherous age mates, with letters to a chief of a far country, saying that Hamlet should be killed. But Hamlet changed the writing on their papers, so that the chief killed his age mates instead." I encountered a reproachful glare from one of the men whom I had told undetectable forgery was not merely immoral but beyond human skill. I looked the other way.

"Before Hamlet could return, Laertes came back for his father's funeral. The great chief told him Hamlet had killed Polonius. Laertes swore to kill Hamlet because of this, and because his sister Ophelia, hearing her father had been killed by the man she loved, went mad and drowned in the river."

The belief that "Only witches can make people drown" makes it impossible for the men to see Ophelia's death as suicide; someone must have been responsible. By this time, Bohannan has lost control of the story, and her hosts have transformed it and made it into their own.

"Have you already forgotten what we told you?" The old man was reproachful. "One cannot take vengeance on a madman; Hamlet killed Polonius in his madness. As for the girl, she not only went mad, she was drowned. Only witches can make people drown. Water itself can't hurt anything. It is merely something one drinks and bathes in."

I began to get cross. "If you don't like the story, I'll stop."

The old man made soothing noises and himself poured me some more beer. "You tell the story well, and we are listening. But it is clear that the elders of your country have never told you what the story really means. No, don't interrupt! We believe you when you say your marriage customs are different, or your clothes and weapons. But people are the same everywhere; therefore, there are always witches and it is we, the elders, who know how witches work. We told you it was the great chief who wished to kill Hamlet, and now your own words have proved us right. Who were Ophelia's male relatives?"

"There were only her father and her brother." Hamlet was clearly out of my hands.

"There must have been many more; this also you must ask of your elders when you get back to your country. From what you tell us, since Polonius was dead, it must have been Laertes who killed Ophelia, although I do not see the reason for it."

We had emptied one pot of beer, and the old men argued the point with slightly tipsy interest. Finally one of them demanded of me. "What did the servant of Polonius say on his return?"

With difficulty I recollected Reynaldo and his mission. "I don't think he did return before Polonius was killed."

"Listen," said the elder, "and I will tell you how it was and how your story will go, then you may tell me if I am right. Polonius knew his son would get into trouble, and so he did. He had many fines to pay for fighting, and debts from gambling. But he had only two ways of getting money quickly. One was to marry off his sister at once, but it is difficult to find a man who will marry a woman desired by the son of a chief. For if the chief's heir commits adultery with your wife, what can you do? Only a fool calls a case against a man who will someday be his judge. Therefore Laertes had to take the second way: he killed his sister by witchcraft, drowning her so he could secretly sell her body to the witches."

I raised an objection. "They found her body and buried it. Indeed Laertes jumped into the grave to see his sister once more—so, you see, the body was truly there. Hamlet, who had just come back, jumped in after him."

"What did I tell you?" The elder appealed to the others. "Laertes was up to no good with his sister's body. Hamlet prevented him, because the chief's heir, like a chief, does not wish any other man to grow rich and powerful. Laertes would be angry, because he would have killed his sister without benefit to himself. In our country he would try to kill Hamlet for that reason. Is this not what happened?"

"More or less," I admitted. "When the great chief found Hamlet was still alive, he encouraged Laertes to try to kill Hamlet and arranged a fight with machetes between them. In the fight both the young men were wounded to death. Hamlet's mother drank the poisoned beer that the chief meant for Hamlet in case he won the fight. When he saw his mother die of poison, Hamlet, dying, managed to kill his father's brother with his machete."

"You see, I was right!" exclaimed the elder.

"That was a very good story," added the old man, "and you told it with very few mistakes. There was just one more error, at the very end. The poison Hamlet's mother drank was obviously meant for the survivor of the fight, whichever it was. If Laertes had won, the great chief would have poisoned him, for no one would know that he arranged Hamlet's death. Then, too, he need not fear Laertes' witchcraft; it takes a strong heart to kill one's only sister by witchcraft.

"Sometime," concluded the old man, gathering his ragged toga about him, "you must tell us some more stories of your country. We, who are elders, will instruct you in their true meaning, so that when you return to your own land your elders will see that you have not been sitting in the bush, but among those who know things and who have taught you wisdom."

ASPECTS OF WRITING: Improving spelling.

One reason for providing so many vocabulary webs in this text, with their focus on the derivation of words, is to promote an interest in words, trusting that this will enhance vocabulary, reading comprehension, and spelling. There are, however, other practical ways to eliminate spelling mistakes. It is important that this be achieved, because spelling errors are probably the most obvious of mistakes; they look bad in your writing, and you don't want your readers—your boss, your customers, or your colleagues—to raise their eyebrows at the way you write.

Here are several tips that may be useful:

1. *Have a dictionary available and use it.* Learn to love your dictionary and always check the derivation of words when you look them up. This will help prime and maintain your interest in words.
2. *Use other texts to check spelling.* Many people misspell names and other words that are right in front of them in what they have just been reading. For example, in the essay you write in this unit, there is no excuse for misspelling **Bohannan.**
3. *As you read, write down—or at least take note of—words that you often misspell or words whose spelling surprises you.* If you read carefully, you will notice such things, and you should take note of them. It's another manifestation of your interest in words.
4. *Pay attention to words that are often mispronounced or that are pronounced in a manner that doesn't wholly reflect their spelling.* For example, **athlete** (not athelete), **modern** (not modren), **surprise** (not suprise), **government** (not goverment), and **Arctic** (not Artic).
5. *Learn to distinguish between homophones—words that sound similar or the same.* The most common error in this category is probably the confusion of **its** (*This is its best feature*—talking of a computer, for example) and **it's** (*It's a nice day*—contraction of **it is**). Other examples include **accept** *(Thank you, I accept the Oscar)* and **except** *(I'd like everything except the anchovies, please)*; **conscience** *(I have a guilty conscience)* and **conscious** *(With the local anesthetic, I was fully conscious but could feel no pain)*; **proceed** *(The road is clear; you may proceed)*, and **precede** *(The article must always precede the noun);*

and **affects** *(The weather affects my mood)* and **effects** *(The effects of the storm were disastrous).*

6. *Remember the rules,* such as "'i' before 'e' except after 'c.'" Examples include *relieve, receive, deceive,* and *believe.* There are exceptions, however, as in *seize, feign, feisty.* Another rule is to double the final consonant before a suffix, as in *occur, occurrence, occurred; begin, beginning.*
7. *Learn irregular or unusual plurals.* Among commonly misspelled words of this sort are some surprising examples, including *woman, women.* Others include *analysis, analyses;* and *criterion, criteria.*

WRITING EXERCISES: Answer one of the following questions.

One clue to the success of Bohannan's essay is her good-natured readiness to reveal her own errors and confusion. She sets herself up by alluding to her belief in the fundamentally universal quality of human nature and then proceeds to show how mistaken she was. It is, then, an essentially modest and self-deprecating essay, told with verve and humor.

From Lederer's *Anguished English,* here are some literary sentences as an exercise in spelling. Correct the following:

a. Defoe wrote simply and sometimes crudly.
b. Thomas Gray wrote the Alergy in a Country Churchyard.
c. Poe was kicked out of West Point for gamboling.
d. Whitman wrote much illiteration and compacked verse. He often wrote long and rumbling lines.

And here are some bloopers from the author's collection of spelling and other errors. Correct the following:

a. The Catholic church frowns on premartial sex.
b. Both abortion and the use of contraceptives are condomed by the Catholics.
c. The tourist expressed herself through her dress and was arrested for it.
d. In the twelve commandments, it states, "I shall not kill thy neighbor."
e. Preppies conform right down to their gargoyle socks.
f. At this college women outweigh the men by a ratio of 2:1.
g. I will always have the ability to swim under my belt.
h. The skill of swimming is another mountain I have climbed.
i. Every American has the right to bare arms.

1. Analyze Laura Bohannan's story and explain the cultural assumptions on both sides that led to such different interpretations of *Hamlet.* It may be appropriate to adopt a relatively light tone in this essay, as Bohannan herself does.
2. Experiences like Bohannan's and Dalbey's, in which cultural differences and contexts present barriers to mutual understanding, can be comic (sometimes more so in retrospect than at the time), but they also tell us something about our own culture as well as the other person's. Such situations can also occur when there are differences between people within the same culture. Describe an example from your own experience (intercultural or intracultural).
3. Are Bohannan and Dalbey laughing at themselves, at others, or at both in their accounts? Explain why the attitude of the storyteller is significant, and give examples to illustrate your point.

SECTION THREE

PRIOR KNOWLEDGE: The butt of the joke and political correctness.

The butt of a joke is the one laughed at, and it is understandable that people sometimes resent this status. On the other hand, Catholics continue to tell Pope jokes, Jews and Arabs continue to tell Jew and Arab jokes (see Berger and Wildavsky's essay in Section One of this unit), African-Americans continue to tell black jokes, and so on. Have we reached the stage where only in-groups can tell such jokes and get a laugh?

In the following essay, Alleen Pace Nilsen finds it necessary to come to the defense of humor. This remarkable situation is, of course, the consequence of a sensitivity to perceived insult and innuendo that has spawned so-called "political correctness." Does "being p.c." mean that we can no longer tell jokes with any ethnic, sex (whoops! I mean *gender*), or other references that might conceivably give offense? This seems to be what Nilsen is saying, and she regrets this situation.

Many humorists and cartoonists take jabs at people very different from themselves, and this often reveals interesting attitudes. In the first cartoon opposite, a prostitute, representing the vulgarity and sexual irresponsibility of parts of Western culture, is seen soliciting donations for the campaign to fight AIDS. What significance should we give to the fact that the cartoon comes from India? Is it a slur on Western society? Should Westerners be offended? The cartoon certainly exaggerates the responsibility of the West for the AIDS catastrophe, but it also suggests the hypocrisy (or at least the paradox) of telling people in non-Western countries to behave in ways that are the opposite of much that is purveyed on television, in popular music, and in sexually oriented magazines that make millions of dollars for Western companies around the world and that give a certain luster to the very

Puri/The Statesman/New Delhi

De Angelis/Il Popolo/Rome

behavior that causes such diseases to spread. For the Westerner, then, the cartoon may be oversimplified, but the germ of truth in it may cause discomfort and the message may be acknowledged.

The second cartoon is from the West—in this case, Italy—and shows a Sikh snake charmer conjuring up a cobra from a basket, except that the cobra is actually a fuse, and the basket presumably contains a bomb. This is a reference to separatist terrorism in the Kashmir in Northern India. It uses an old stereotype—the snake charmer—for contemporary purposes, to suggest the contrast between what is normally a street entertainment and the bloody reality of the political struggle.

ANNOTATED READING: Alleen Pace Nilsen. "In Defense of Humor." *College English* 56.8 (1994): 929–933.

In Defense of Humor

What's happened to American humor lately would be funny if it weren't so serious. Potshots have been fired at it from the highest levels of government and academe; it's been unjustly accused, mangled beyond recognition, and in some cases outlawed. A recent potshot came from Harvey I. Saferstein, the president of the California Bar Association, after a gunman opened fire in the offices of a law firm, killing eight people before shooting himself—and leaving a letter that railed against lawyers and others involved in a failed real estate deal. In response, Saferstein called a news conference to denounce lawyer jokes. "Mean-spirited jokes about lawyers could lead to more violence like the massacre," he warned, according to an Associated Press story dated July 6, 1993; such jokes could be "the straw that breaks the camel's back" for a "fringe person"; Americans should "stop the lawyer-bashing . . . that sometimes can incite violence and aggression toward lawyers."

Saferstein's plea was undoubtedly well intentioned, and he joins a long line of protesters who are tired of being the butt of jokes. However, the point he missed is that humor flourishes only when there's a moderate level of tension between groups. If the tension becomes too high, then humor won't suffice, which is what Cicero observed two thousand years ago when he said that people want criminals attacked with more forceful weapons than ridicule. The man who shot up the law offices was feeling a much greater level of tension than that felt by people who tell lawyer jokes. And although it's risky to guess about someone else's innermost thoughts, one could conceivably argue that if, over the years since the man's business dealings went awry, he had been able to relieve his tensions through laughter—even laughter at his lawyers' expense—he might not have resorted to violence.

The use of jokes to relieve tension is clearly an important function, and Nilsen seems to suggest that self-censorship can lead to intolerable tensions. When everyone is walking on eggshells, it's impossible to cultivate satisfactory relationships.

One of the few things that humor scholars agree on is that for something to be funny there has to be an element of surprise. But in these days of political correctness, when speakers are so fearful of making a mistake that they run every witticism through internal censors, spontaneity disappears. And even if we serve as our own best censors, there's no guarantee of staying out of trouble. At a humor workshop on our campus, a woman told how her parents had taught her never to laugh at ethnic jokes. When she arrived at college as a freshman, her assigned roommate happened to be Jewish. While the two of them were getting acquainted, some of the roommate's friends from high school dropped in and told the latest Jewish jokes. The woman was proud that she didn't laugh, but the next day she was called in by the head resident and told that her roommate didn't feel comfortable and wanted a change. The roommate had concluded that the woman was anti-Semitic and hadn't laughed because she accepted the caricatures in the jokes as accurate and therefore not funny. Thanks to the head resident's help, what was a communication problem rather than an instance of ill will had a happy ending.

A **caricature** is usually a cartoon in which a person's distinguishing features are exaggerated. The "cartoonist's eye" is able to identify this feature and make the caricature immediately recognizable.

Sensitivity to the feelings of others is fine, but we also need to consider some of the benefits of humor. Remember how former First Lady Barbara Bush used humor to salvage the awful situation in Japan when President Bush grew ill and vomited on Japanese Prime Minister Kiichi Miyazawa? After the President was escorted from the room, Mrs. Bush stood up and bravely placed the blame on the American ambassador. As could be seen from the security camera TV tape, her accusation stiffened the audience and increased the already high tension, but then as she explained with a twinkle in her eye that the Ambassador and the President had been badly beaten that afternoon in tennis by the Emperor Akihito and Crown Prince Naruhito and that "We Bushes aren't used to losing," relief washed over the room.

The laughter was all the sweeter because it followed such high tension. Her quick thinking made it possible for the dinner to continue and for the world to relax; compare President Reagan's famous quip made while he was on the operating table after he had been shot—he hoped the doctors treating his wounds were Republicans.

The success of both of these jokes illustrates the point that humor is a release from a moderate level of tension. The world relaxed upon hearing Reagan's joke because it let us know that he did not consider himself to be in imminent danger. Similarly, in Japan, members of the audience, although from two very different cultures, instinctively recognized that if Barbara Bush had thought that her husband had been poisoned or suffered a heart attack she would not have made a joke. But on the other hand, neither would she have been inspired to make the joke if there hadn't been discomfort in the situation.

The vocabulary that we use in talking about jokes shows that at least subconsciously we recognize that humor carries with it a degree of pain. For example, a joke with a good *punchline strikes* us as funny and most people would rather hear a *barbed* than a *pointless* joke. And we enjoy a *biting satire* from a *sharp-tongued wit*, especially if it's *aimed* toward a *target* other than ourselves. We even get a certain satisfaction from *sick* and *gallows* humor. In the preface to his 1941 *Subtreasury of American Humor*, E. B. White compared humor to playing with fire,

Politics is one of the great arenas for cartoonists and comedians. Sometimes the individual is the target—as in these merciless views of Russia's President Yeltsin with one foot in the political grave and Zambia's former President Kaunda emerging from the same place—and sometimes a political situation is caricatured, as in this view of Sino-American relations being soured by the issue of Taiwan coming between them.

Riber/Svenska Dagbladet/Stockholm

Gado/Daily Nation/Nairobi

Heng/Lianhe ZaoBao/Singapore

while in the preface to his 1969 *Encyclopedia of Jewish Humor* Henry D. Spaulding wrote that his people have a fondness for "honey-coated barbs . . . a kiss with salt on the lips, but a kiss nevertheless."

The discomfort that is an integral part of humor is what has caused people to overgeneralize and to make such statements as "There's no place on a university campus for sexist or ethnic humor." This was the conclusion of a videotape shown as part of a cultural diversity workshop we recently attended. The audience nodded in solemn agreement as they walked from the meeting room to lunch. But by the time they had eaten and were settled back in their chairs to listen to the after-lunch speaker, they had apparently forgotten about the videotape, because when the speaker, a popular black professor of sociology, did an imitation of whites excusing blacks for poor academic performance, they responded with uncomfortable smiles of recognition followed by genuine laughter and amusement. Later that afternoon, they laughed with the Chinese American professor from the School of Social Work who confessed that he started college as a computer major because he had fallen for the stereotype of Asians-as-high-tech-coolies. A Hispanic professor got an equally big laugh when he rushed in late to join a panel presentation and explained that it wasn't his cultural background but the university that had made him late: he had been teaching a class.

Each of these speakers used humor to challenge the audience's assumptions. They surprised listeners by making them bump up against some of their own prejudices, and because these lessons came with a smile rather than a scolding the audience was more receptive.

With humorous incidents or jokes, there are at least four characteristics that need to be looked at:

1. the subject,
2. the tone,
3. the intent, and
4. the situation, including the teller and the audience.

People who overgeneralize and want to censor all ethnic and gender based humor are looking at only the subject, that is, the one-fourth of the picture that is the most concrete and the easiest to identify.

The tone and the intent of a joke are so interrelated to its situation that once a joke is removed from a particular situation it's sometimes impossible to understand what was intended. Of course there are jokes so hostile and insulting that when they are repeated in a news story, a hearing, or a court case the tellers' claims of "only kidding" or of being "quoted out of context" and thereby misunderstood lack credibility. We are not defending such obviously hostile humor. We are looking instead at the much larger body of humor whose creators deal with sensitive subjects in a way that requires some thinking, the kind of humor that William Davis, an editor of *Punch*, once described as humor that will make people laugh for five seconds and think for ten minutes.

Punch, published in London, was famous for its political and social humor and satire for over a hundred years until its recent demise.

In the early 1970s Senator Margaret Chase Smith from Maine was being discussed as a possible candidate for President. This elegant and highly accomplished woman garnered headlines when a reporter asked her what she would do if she should wake up one morning and find herself in the White House. Without a moment's hesitation, she responded, "I would go to the President's wife, apologize, and then leave at once."

In the anti-humor mood of today, Smith's comment probably wouldn't amuse as many people as it did two decades ago. But the question to ask is whether Smith was perpetuating an offensive stereotype or making fun of it. We can ask the same thing about today's domestic humor, à la Judith Viorst and Erma Bombeck. Feminist critics have complained that these women are contributing to the stereotype that women's interests are confined to home and hearth, but if we look a little deeper we may see that they are actually challenging old ideas about women being judged solely on the basis of their housework. Humor at its best is excellent for challenging the status quo, and we need to make sure that we're not getting in its way.

Crucial to a consideration of the situation is who is telling the joke and who is in the audience. An ethnic or gender-based joke is quite different when told by an insider than an outsider. Back in the 1920s, Henri Bergson wrote that humor is the great corrective for social deviance. Most sophisticated jokes are not about physical differences; they're about personal characteristics and attitudes. The creators and tellers are teaching lessons.

For example, a cartoon drawn by Calvin Grondahl which appeared several years ago in the Brigham Young University student newspaper showed a bloodied and battered student arising from a pile of stones. As the campus policeman walks up, the student explains, "All I said was 'Let he who is without sin cast the first stone.'" Told by an outsider, this joke about Mormon self-righteousness would have been offensive, but told by an insider it teaches the same lesson that Mormons have been teaching their children for years through a story about St. Peter cautioning people in Heaven to tiptoe past the room where the Mormons are because "They think they're the only ones here."

When insiders tell such jokes, the jokes are tiny revolutions in chiding friends about the frailties to which human beings are prone. The insider is trying to expand the possibilities for group attitudes and behavior. But when outsiders tell the jokes, the effect is quite the opposite. Outsiders tend to focus on the group's most obvious characteristics and to imply that these characteristics belong to everyone in the group. As outsiders, they have little power to bring internal change, so the effect is to stereotype the group, thereby shrinking the options for thought and action. The insider expands the boundaries, while the outsider telling the same or a similar joke tightens the noose.

One of the reasons for humor's recent bad rap is that new technology has blurred the lines between insiders and outsiders. Someone puts a joke on a computer bulletin board and forgets that the twinkle in his eyes and the teasing of his voice won't be electronically reproduced and that more people will read the bulletin board than the two

THINK ON PAPER

Do you agree with Nilsen's basic idea that there is an "anti-humor mood" on college campuses and in the country at large today? Are we still able to laugh at ourselves and our problems, or not?

Nilsen's distinction between "perpetuating an offensive stereotype [and] making fun of it" is important. Television shows that portray racism, ignorance and bigotry à la Archie Bunker (for anyone who can remember *All in the Family*) can be very funny because it is clear that we are laughing *at* these things. It is both a recognition that such things exist in this world and a kind of **catharsis** in which we put them in their place.

The word **catharsis** comes from the Greek *kathairein*, meaning to purge or purify. This is an important word in Aristotle, who sees the release of certain emotions—pity and fear—(within the safe confines of the theater) as being one of the purposes of tragedy. Perhaps a similar catharsis occurs when we are able to laugh at things that cause grievous social tension.

or three friends he can count on to understand his intentions. In a similar way, police dispatchers trying to liven up long, lonely nights forget their messages are being listened in on and recorded, and political candidates forget that those people they've been traveling with and talking to for weeks are not personal friends but reporters looking for news stories.

The English language makes many distinctions between different kinds of humor, including **satire, irony, sarcasm, innuendo, burlesque, slapstick, farce, parody, lampoon, spoof, takeoff,** and **caricature.**

The simplistic solution is to do what Mr. Saferstein did in calling for a ban on the offending jokes. Censorship appeals to people's desire to control others. It also feeds into wishful thinking about easy solutions to difficult problems. Speaking out against ethnic humor or giving an icy stare when someone tells a joke is an easy and satisfying way to express moral superiority. But it's also a good way to cut off communication and to drive particular kinds of humor underground.

Incidents where humor offends someone need to be discussed because that's where learning will occur and where tensions will be released. On the other hand, we don't want to go overboard and promise more than humor can deliver. It's not a panacea or cure-all. In a *New York Times* interview (June 6, 1993), Dick Gregory said that he doesn't like it when people tell him that his humor has done a lot for race relations, but then he added the almost contradictory, "I never thought comedy did anything but make uncomfortable people feel comfortable."

In an observation clearly relevant to Nilsen's essay, **William Hazlitt** (1778–1830), an English essayist, commented that comedy "exposes the follies and weaknesses of mankind to ridicule."

Increasing comfort levels between groups may not change the power structure, but it can go a long way toward increasing understanding, which is a crucial first step for any groups to take if they want to get along with each other. For example, those who believe that jokes have the potential of decreasing tensions because they make people feel more knowledgeable and therefore more comfortable point to a correlation over the last decade between an increased level of joking about handicaps and access by the disabled to public facilities, education, and employment. Twenty years ago the jokes that the public heard about handicaps were truly tasteless because most people of good will censored themselves and their friends so that only those without a social conscience dared to tell "sick" jokes. Today we have several stand-up comedians making audiences laugh about the daily complications caused by their various disabilities. John Callahan, perhaps the world's best "sit-down comedian," is a paraplegic cartoonist living in Seattle. He delights in shining an illuminating light on a wide range of topics that others shy away from. People are often offended at his humor until they find out where he's coming from.

In a recent *60 Minutes* interview broadcast on CBS, Callahan compared himself to Cinderella: during the day he's out and about in his wheelchair, taking taxis and going wherever he wants in Seattle, but at night an attendant puts him to bed and leaves him imprisoned until morning, when another attendant comes and works with him for the two hours it takes to get out of bed and prepare for the day. Viewing this one aspect of a paraplegic's life through his own humorous comparison goes a long way toward increasing empathy and understanding in a way that is neither schmaltzy or pitying. What more could we ask?

ALLEEN PACE NILSEN is a professor of English at Arizona State University where, with Don L. F. Nilsen, she was instrumental in founding the International Society for Humor Studies.

ASPECTS OF WRITING: Politically correct language.

The idea of "political correctness" elicits paradoxical responses in people. On the one hand, the concept is powerful; *words matter,* and what we say and how we say it can both betray and influence attitudes towards important social and political realities. On the other hand, the excesses of "p.c." seem absurd and amply deserving of scorn.

George Orwell, the author of *Animal Farm, 1984,* and other works (including "Politics and the English Language," an essay found in Option Two of this unit), is often mentioned in this context because of his invention of "Newspeak," a language in which ideological correctness is everything. Orwell is mentioned in the following article, which looks at the current obsession with politically correct speech.

Michiko Kakutani. "The Word Police." *The New York Times* Sunday 31 Jan. 1993: Sec. 9:1+.

This month's inaugural festivities, with their celebration, in Maya Angelou's words, of "humankind"—"the Asian, the Hispanic, the Jew/ The African, the Native American, the Sioux,/ The Catholic, the Muslim, the French, the Greek/ The Irish, the Rabbi, the Priest, the Sheik,/ The Gay, the Straight, the Preacher,/ The privileged, the homeless, the Teacher"—constituted a kind of official embrace of multiculturalism and a new politics of inclusion.

The mood of political correctness, however, has already made firm inroads into popular culture. Washington boasts a store called Politically Correct that sells pro-whale, anti-meat, ban-the-bomb T-shirts, bumper stickers and buttons, as well as a local cable television show called "Politically Correct Cooking" that features interviews in the kitchen with representatives from groups like People for the Ethical Treatment of Animals.

The Coppertone suntan lotion people are planning to give their longtime cover girl, Little Miss (Ms?) Coppertone, a male equivalent, Little Mr. Coppertone. And even Superman (Superperson?) is rumored to be returning this spring, reincarnated as four ethnically diverse clones: an African-American, an Asian, a Caucasian and a Latino.

Nowhere is this P.C. mood more striking than in the increasingly noisy debate over language that has moved from university campuses to the country at large—a development that both underscores Americans' puritannical zeal for reform and their unwavering faith in the talismanic power of words.

Certainly no decent person can quarrel with the underlying impulse behind political correctness: a vision of a more just, inclusive society in which racism, sexism and prejudice of all sorts have been erased. But the methods and fervor of the self-appointed language police can lead to a rigid orthodoxy—and unintentional self-parody—opening the movement to the scorn of conservative opponents and the mockery of cartoonists and late-night television hosts.

It's hard to imagine women earning points for political correctness by saying "ovarimony" instead of "testimony"—as one participant at the recent Modern Language Association convention was overheard to suggest. It's equally hard to imagine people wanting to flaunt their lack of prejudice by giving up such words and phrases as "bull market," "kaiser roll," "Lazy Susan," and "charley horse."

Several books on bias-free language have already appeared, and the 1991 edition of the Random House Webster's College Dictionary boasts an appendix titled "Avoiding Sexist Language." The dictionary also includes such linguistic mutations as "womyn" (women, "used as an alternative spelling to avoid the suggestion of sexism perceived in the sequence m-e-n") and "waitron" (a gender-blind term for waiter or waitress).

Many of these dictionaries and guides not only warn the reader against offensive racial and sexual slurs, but also try to establish and enforce a whole new set of usage rules. Take, for instance, "The Bias-Free Word Finder, a Dictionary of Nondiscriminatory Language" by Rosalie Maggio (Beacon Press)—a volume often indistinguishable, in its meticulous solemnity, from the tongue-in-cheek "Official Politically Correct Dictionary and Handbook" put out last year by Henry Beard and Christopher Cerf (Villard Books). Ms. Maggio's book supplies the reader intent on using kinder, gentler language with writing guidelines as well as a detailed listing of more than 5,000 "biased words and phrases."

Whom are these guidelines for? Somehow one has a tough time picturing them replacing "Fowler's Modern English Usage" in the classroom, or being adopted by the average man (sorry, individual) in the street.

The "pseudogeneric 'he,'" we learn from Ms. Maggio, is to be avoided like the plague, as is the use of the word "man" to refer to humanity. "Fellow," "king," "lord" and "master" are bad because they're "male-oriented words," and "king," "lord" and "master" are especially bad because they're also "hierarchical, dominator society terms." The politically correct lion becomes the "monarch of the jungle," new-age

Say What? Bias-Free Substitutions

ABOMINABLE SNOWMAN: yeti.
BULL MARKET: rising, improving, escalating, buy or favorable market.
DON JUAN: sexually aggressive/sexually active person.
DUTCH TREAT: separate checks or say, "I insist on paying for myself."
GLOOMY GUS: spoilsport.
JAVA MAN: early human found in Java.
MAN IN THE MOON: face in the moon.
MAN'S BEST FRIEND: use the devoted dog, our faithful canine friends.
MASTER BEDROOM: main, owner's principal or largest bedroom.
NO-MAN'S-LAND: limbo, wasteland, no-wheresville.
NOT A FIT NIGHT FOR MAN OR BEAST: "not a fit night to be out" and "for two-legged creatures nor four-legged ones either."
QUEEN BEE: big wheel.
WAITRESS: waitron, waitperson.

Adapted from "The Bias-Free Word Finder" by Rosemary Maggio (Beacon Press, 1992).

children play "someone on the top of the heap," and the "Mona Lisa" goes down in history as Leonardo's "acme of perfection."

As for the word "black," Ms. Maggio says it should be excised from terms with a negative spin: she recommends substituting words like "mouse" for "black eye," "ostracize" for "blackball," "payola" for "blackmail" and "outcast" for "black sheep." Clearly, some of these substitutions work better than others: somehow the "sinister humor" of Kurt Vonnegut or "Saturday Night Live" doesn't quite make it; nor does the "denouncing" of the Hollywood 10.

For the dedicated user of politically correct language, all these rules can make for some messy moral dilemmas. Whereas "battered wife" is a gender-biased term, the gender-free term "battered spouse," Ms. Maggio notes, incorrectly implies "that men and women are equally battered."

On one hand, say Francine Wattman Frank and Paula A. Treichler in their book "Language, Gender, and Professional Writing" (Modern Language Association), "he or she" is an appropriate construction for talking about an individual (like a jockey, say) who belongs to a profession that's predominantly male—it's a way of emphasizing "that such occupations are not barred to women or that women's concerns need to be kept in mind." On the other hand, they add, using masculine pronouns rhetorically can underscore ongoing male dominance in those fields, implying the need for change.

And what about the speech codes adopted by some universities in recent years? Although they were designed to prohibit students from uttering sexist and racist slurs, they would extend, by logic, to blacks who want to use the word "nigger" to strip the term of its racist connotations, or homosexuals who want to use the word "queer" to reclaim it from bigots.

In her book, Ms. Maggio recommends applying bias-free usage retroactively: she suggests paraphrasing politically incorrect quotations, or replacing "the sexist words or phrases with ellipsis dots and/or bracketed substitutes," or using "sic" "to show that the sexist words come from the original quotation and to call attention to the fact that they are incorrect."

Which leads the skeptical reader of "The Bias-Free Word Finder" to wonder whether "All the King's Men" should be retitled "All the Ruler's People"; "Pet Semetary," "Animal Companion Graves"; "Birdman of Alcatraz," "Birdperson of Alcatraz," and "The Iceman Cometh," "The Ice Route Driver Cometh"?

Should 'All the King's Men' be retitled 'All the Ruler's People'?

Will making such changes remove the prejudice in people's minds? Should we really spend time trying to come up with non-male-based alternatives to "Midas touch," "Achilles' heel," and "Montezuma's revenge"? Will tossing out Santa Claus—whom Ms. Maggio accuses of reinforcing "the cultural male-as-norm system"—in favor of Belfana, his Italian female alter ego, truly help banish sexism? Can the avoidance of "violent expressions and metaphors" like "kill two birds with one stone," "sock it to 'em" or "kick an idea around" actually promote a more harmonious world?

The point isn't that the excesses of the word police are comical. The point is that their intolerance (in the name of tolerance) has disturbing implications. In the first place, getting upset by phrases like "bullish on America" or "the City of Brotherly Love" tends to distract attention from the real problems of prejudice and injustice that exist in society at large, turning them into mere questions of semantics. Indeed, the emphasis currently put on politically correct usage has uncanny parallels with the academic movement of deconstruction—a method of textual analysis that focuses on language and linguistic pyrotechnics—which has become firmly established on university campuses.

In both cases, attention is focused on surfaces, on words and metaphors; in both cases, signs and symbols are accorded more importance than content. Hence, the attempt by some radical advocates to remove "The Adventures of Huckleberry Finn" from curriculums on the grounds that Twain's use of the word "nigger" makes the book a racist text—never mind the fact that this American classic (written in 1884) depicts the spiritual kinship achieved between a white boy and a runaway slave, never mind the fact that the "nigger" Jim emerges as the novel's most honorable, decent character.

Ironically enough, the P.C. movement's obsession with language is accompanied by a strange Orwellian willingness to warp the meaning of words by placing them under a high-powered ideological lens. For instance, the "Dictionary of Cautionary Words and Phrases"—a pamphlet issued by the University of Missouri's Multicultural Management Program to help turn "today's journalists into tomorrow's multicultural newsroom managers"—warns that using the word "articulate" to describe members of a minority group can suggest the opposite, "that 'those people' are not considered well educated, articulate and the like."

The pamphlet patronizes minority groups, by cautioning the reader against using the words "lazy" and "burly" to describe any member of such groups; and it issues a similar warning against using words like "gorgeous" and "petite" to describe women.

As euphemism proliferates with the rise of political correctness, there is a spread of the sort of sloppy, abstract language that Orwell said is "designed to make lies sound truthful and murder respectable, and to give an appearance of solidity to pure wind." "Fat" becomes "big boned" or "differently sized"; "stupid" becomes "exceptional"; "stoned" becomes "chemically inconvenienced."

Wait a minute here! Aren't such phrases eerily reminiscient of the euphemisms coined by the Government during Vietnam and Watergate? Remember how the military used to speak of "pacification," or how President Richard M. Nixon's press secretary, Ronald L. Ziegler, tried to get away with calling a lie an "inoperative statement"?

Calling the homeless "the underhoused" doesn't give them a place to live; calling the poor "the economically marginalized" doesn't help them pay the bills. Rather, by playing down their plight, such language might even make it easier to shrug off the seriousness of their situation.

Instead of allowing free discussion and debate to occur, many gung-ho advocates of politically correct language seem to think that simple suppression of a word or concept will magically make the problem disappear. In the "Bias-Free Word Finder," Ms. Maggio entreats the reader not to perpetuate the negative stereotype of Eve. "Be extremely cautious in referring to the biblical Eve," she writes; "this story has profoundly contributed to negative attitudes toward women throughout history, largely because of misogynistic and patriarchal interpretations that labeled her evil, inferior, and seductive."

The story of Bluebeard, the rake (whoops!—the libertine) who killed his seven wives, she says, is also to be avoided, as is the biblical story of Jezebel. Of Jesus Christ, Ms. Maggio writes: "There have been few individuals in history as completely androgynous as Christ, and it does his message a disservice to overinsist on his maleness." She doesn't give the reader any hints on how this might be accomplished; presumably, one is supposed to avoid describing him as the Son of God.

Of course the P.C. police aren't the only ones who want to proscribe what people should say or give them guidelines for how they may use an idea; Jesse Helms and his supporters are up to exactly the same thing when they propose to patrol the boundaries of the permissible in art. In each case, the would-be censor aspires to suppress what he or she finds distasteful—all, of course, in the name of the public good.

In the case of the politically correct, the prohibition of certain words, phrases and ideas is advanced in the cause of building a brave new world free of racism and hate, but this vision of harmony clashes with the very ideals of diversity and inclusion that the multi-cultural movement holds dear, and it's purchased at the cost of freedom of expression and freedom of speech.

In fact, the utopian world envisioned by the language police would be bought at the expense of the ideals of individualism and democracy articulated in the "The Gettysburg Address": "Fourscore and seven years ago our fathers brought forth on this continent a new nation, conceived in liberty and dedicated to the proposition that all men are created equal."

Of course, the P.C. police have already found Lincoln's words hopelessly "phallocentric." No doubt they would rewrite the passage: "Fourscore and seven years ago our foremothers and forefathers brought forth on this continent a new nation, formulated with liberty, and dedicated to the proposition that all humankind is created equal."

WRITING EXERCISES: Answer one of the following questions.

Jokes and implied criticisms of the excesses of political correctness should not take away from the core truth that deliberately offensive statements and words are normally considered socially unacceptable and should be avoided.

1. Nilsen entitles her essay, "In Defense of Humor." Explain why such a defense is necessary. Why is humor important and why is it under threat, according to Nilsen?
2. Discuss the paradox suggested by Michiko Kakutani and Alleen Nilsen that "political correctness," a well-intentioned attempt to make people more sensitive to what they say, can also be seen as producing unhealthy self-censorship and an absurd mangling of the English language.
3. The P.C. story on the next page is a spoof of a well-known fairy tale. Like satire, it takes a kind of human weakness or foolishness (in this case, the sensitivity to political correctness) and pushes it to an extreme. Write a similar rendition of another fairy tale.

James Finn Garner. "Little Red Riding Hood." From *Politically Correct Bedtime Stories.* New York: Macmillan, 1994: 1–4.

Little Red Riding Hood

There once was a young person named Red Riding Hood who lived with her mother on the edge of a large wood. One day her mother asked her to take a basket of fresh fruit and mineral water to her grandmother's house—not because this was womyn's work, mind you, but because the deed was generous and helped engender a feeling of community. Furthermore, her grandmother was *not* sick, but rather was in full physical and mental health and was fully capable of taking care of herself as a mature adult.

So Red Riding Hood set off with her basket through the woods. Many people believed that the forest was a foreboding and dangerous place and never set foot in it. Red Riding Hood, however, was confident enough in her own budding sexuality that such obvious Freudian imagery did not intimidate her.

On the way to Grandma's house, Red Riding Hood was accosted by a wolf, who asked her what was in her basket. She replied, "Some healthful snacks for my grandmother, who is certainly capable of taking care of herself as a mature adult."

The wolf said, "You know, my dear, it isn't safe for a little girl to walk through these woods alone."

Red Riding Hood said, "I find your sexist remark offensive in the extreme, but I will ignore it because of your traditional status as an outcast from society, the stress of which has caused you to develop your own, entirely valid, worldview. Now, if you'll excuse me, I must be on my way."

Red Riding Hood walked on along the main path. But, because his status outside society had freed him from slavish adherence to linear, Western-style thought, the wolf knew a quicker route to Grandma's house. He burst into the house and ate Grandma, an entirely valid course of action for a carnivore such as himself. Then, unhampered by rigid, traditionalist notions of what was masculine or feminine, he put on Grandma's nightclothes and crawled into bed.

Red Riding Hood entered the cottage and said, "Grandma, I have brought you some fat-free, sodium-free snacks to salute you in your role of a wise and nurturing matriarch."

From the bed, the wolf said softly, "Come closer, child, so that I might see you."

Red Riding Hood said, "Oh, I forgot you are as optically challenged as a bat. Grandma, what big eyes you have!"

"They have seen much, and forgiven much, my dear."

"Grandma, what a big nose you have—only relatively, of course, and certainly attractive in its own way."

"It has smelled much, and forgiven much, my dear."

"Grandma, what big teeth you have!"

The wolf said, "I am happy with *who* I am and *what* I am," and leaped out of bed. He grabbed Red Riding Hood in his claws, intent on devouring her. Red Riding Hood screamed, not out of alarm at the wolf's apparent tendency toward cross-dressing, but because of his willful invasion of her personal space.

Her screams were heard by a passing woodchopper-person (or log-fuel technician, as he preferred to be called). When he burst into the cottage, he saw the melee and tried to intervene. But as he raised his ax, Red Riding Hood and the wolf both stopped.

"And just what do you think you're doing?" asked Red Riding Hood.

The woodchopper-person blinked and tried to answer, but no words came to him.

"Bursting in here like a Neanderthal, trusting your weapon to do your thinking for you!" she exclaimed. "Sexist! Speciesist! How dare you assume that womyn and wolves can't solve their own problems without a man's help!"

When she heard Red Riding Hood's impassioned speech, Grandma jumped out of the wolf's mouth, seized the woodchopper-person's ax, and cut his head off. After this ordeal, Red Riding Hood, Grandma, and the wolf felt a certain commonality of purpose. They decided to set up an alternative household based on mutual respect and cooperation, and they lived together in the woods happily ever after.

OPTION ONE

PRIOR KNOWLEDGE: Local color; humor in literature and essays.

A **sense of place** is important to many writers, even to some who no longer live in the place they most often write about. James Baldwin lived in France, as did James Joyce, but they wrote about Harlem and Dublin, respectively. India's R. K. Narayan has created a fictional town, Malgudi, in which to set many of his novels. Other writers with a strong sense of place include Anne Tyler, whose novels are set in Baltimore, and Carson McCullers, William Faulkner, and Eudora Welty, whose fiction is mostly set in the South.

Not all writers, however, are associated with a particular place. V. S. Naipaul has written fiction and nonfiction set in Trinidad, India, England, parts of Africa, and elsewhere, and Graham Greene, W. Somerset Maugham, Paul Theroux, Anthony Burgess, and many others have set stories in the countries in which they have traveled. India is the setting for much of Salman Rushdie's work, but he also captures the excitement, confusion, tension, and humor of the world's kaleidoscopic and cosmopolitan cities in his phantasmagorical novels.

No matter where a story is set, it is essentially a human tale, and its "truth" and the manner of its telling are what can set it apart. Many of the above writers have comic voices, including Tyler, Rushdie, Naipaul, Greene, and Joyce.

Setting has significance in most literature, but in comedy and humor it often has a special place. When writers are writing about their own region, their own town, their own people, many things are permitted that might not be open to outsiders. The insider can be affectionate, intimate, and critical all at the same. It's based on knowledge, and on a sense of identity. Whether it's Woody Allen writing about New York City, Molly Ivens writing about Texas, or Garrison Keillor writing about Minnesota, even the reader from elsewhere senses the ring of truth in what is written. It's reality, albeit seen with a comic eye.

Molly Ivens has written about politics and other aspects of life for many magazines, including the *New York Times* (who were too squeamish for her brand of humor and eventually fired her), and the *Texas Observer.* As a native Texan, her irreverent and scathing wit might make some people squirm, but it will probably make them laugh as well.

Garrison Keillor is a native Minnesotan well known for his weekly Public Radio show, *A Prairie Home Companion,* the centerpiece of which is his story giving "The News from Lake Wobegon." His accounts of Midwestern people, stolid Lutherans, the Catholics of "Our Lady of Perpetual Responsibility," the Norwegian bachelor farmers, and so on, suggest a way of life, a culture, very different from that in Ivens's Texas, but just as real and just as interesting to the humorist and the storyteller.

Humorists remind us how interesting we can be to each other, how our frailty and predictability can be funny, and our sadness can be poignant.

READING: Molly Ivens. "Texas Women: True Grit and All the Rest." From *Molly Ivens Can't Say That, Can She?* New York: Vintage, 1992: 165–170.

Texas Women: True Grit and All the Rest

Writing a humor column for Ms. magazine always sounded like the punchline of a joke to me. That estimable publication tends toward the sober. There's something awfully daunting about having a box that says "Humor" on what you write, a set-up for people to say, "*This* is supposed to be *funny*?" Still, being female is often a comical proposition in this world, and being a Texas feminist is a particularly oxymoronic vocation.

Writing for and about women in various publications over the years has given me the opportunity to write more personal pieces than political reporting allows, and I am grateful.

They used to say that Texas was hell on women and horses—I don't know why they stopped. Surely not because much of the citizenry has had its consciousness raised, as they say in the jargon of the women's movement, on the issue of sexism. Just a few months ago one of our state representatives felt moved to compare women and horses—it was the similarity he wanted to emphasize. Of course some Texas legislator can be found to say any fool thing, but this guy's comments met with general agreement from his colleagues. One can always dismiss the entire Legislature as a particularly deplorable set of Texans, but as Sen. Carl Parker observes, if you took all the fools out of the Lege, it wouldn't be a representative body anymore.

I should confess that I've always been more of an observer than a participant in Texas Womanhood: the spirit was willing but I was declared ineligible on grounds of size early. You can't be six feet tall and cute, both. I think I was first named captain of the basketball team when I was four and that's what I've been ever since. I spent my girlhood as a Clydesdale among thoroughbreds. I clopped along amongst them cheerfully, admiring their grace, but the strange training rituals they went through left me secretly relieved that no one would ever expect me to step on a racetrack. I think it is quite possible to grow up in Texas as an utter failure in flirting, gentility, cheerleading, sexpottery, and manipulation and still be without any permanent scars. Except one. We'd all rather be blonde.

An **oxymoron** is an apparently self-contradictory combination of words. Here are some examples:

She is *ridiculously brilliant.*
I feel *awfully well.* (Chiefly British)
The story is *bittersweet.*

Shakespeare employs a spectacular string of oxymorons in *Romeo and Juliet.*

Here's much to do with hate, but more with love:—
Why, then, O brawling love! O loving hate!
O anything, of nothing first create!
O heavy lightness! serious vanity!
Misshapen chaos of well-seeming forms!
Feather of lead, bright smoke, cold fire, sick health!
Still-waking sleep, that is not what it is!—
This love feel I, that feel no love in this.
Dost thou not laugh?
(Romeo, Act I, Scene I)

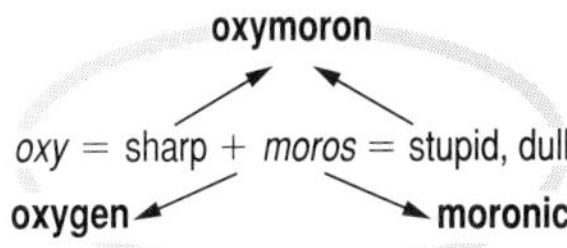

THINK ON PAPER
As you read this, you might consider the importance (or otherwise) of the fact that the author is a woman—and a Texan. Does it make any difference?

Please understand I'm not whining when I point out that Texas sexism is of an especially rank and noxious variety—this is more a Texas brag. It is my belief that it is the virulence of Texas sexism that accounts for the strength of Texas women. It's what we have to overcome that makes us formidable survivors, say I with some complacency.

As has been noted elsewhere, there are several strains of Texan culture: They are all rotten for women. There is the Southern belle nonsense of our Confederate heritage, that little-woman-on-a-pedestal, flirtatious, "you're so cute when you're mad," Scarlett O'Hara myth that leads, quite naturally, to the equally pernicious legend of the Iron Magnolia. Then there's the machismo of our Latin heritage, which affects not only our Chicana sisters, but has been integrated into Texas culture quite as thoroughly as barbecue, rodeo, and Tex-Mex food.

Next up is the pervasive good-ol'-boyism of the *Redneckus texensis*, that remarkable tribe that has made the pickup truck with the gun rack across the back window and the beer cans flying out the window a synonym for Texans worldwide. Country music is a good place to investigate and find reflected the attitudes of kickers toward women (never ask what a kicker kicks). It's your basic, familiar virgin/whore dichotomy—either your "Good-Hearted Woman" or "Your Cheatin' Heart," with the emphasis on the honky-tonk angels. Nor is the jock idolatry that permeates the state helpful to our gender: Football is not a game here, it's a matter of blood and death. Woman's role in the state's national game is limited, significantly, to cheerleading. In this regard, I can say with great confidence that Texas changeth not—the hopelessly intense, heartbreaking longing with which most Texas girls still want to be cheerleader can be observed at every high school, every September.*

Last but not least in the litany of cultures that help make the lives of Texas women so challenging is the legacy of the frontier—not the frontier that Texas women lived on, but the one John Wayne lived on. Anyone who knows the real history of the frontier knows it is a saga of the strength of women. They worked as hard as men, they fought as hard as men, they suffered as much as men. But in the cowboy movies that most contemporary Texans grew up on, the big, strong man always protects "the little lady" or "the gals" from whatever peril threatens. Such nonsense. Mary Ann Goodnight was often left alone at the JA Ranch near the Palo Duro Canyon. One day in 1877, a cowboy rode into her camp with three chickens in a sack as a present for her. He naturally expected her to cook and eat the fowl, but Goodnight kept them as pets. She wrote in her diary, "No one can ever know how

*In February 1991, a woman in Channelview, Texas, was indicted for plotting the murder of the mother of her own daughter's chief rival for the cheerleading squad.

much company they were." Life for farm and ranch wives didn't improve much over the next 100 years. Ruth White raised nine children on a farm near High, Texas, in the 1920s and thirties. She used to say, "Everything on this farm is either hungry or heavy."

All of these strains lead to a form of sexism so deeply ingrained in the culture that it's often difficult to distinguish the disgusting from the outrageous or the offensive from the amusing. One not infrequently sees cars or trucks sporting the bumper sticker HAVE FUN—BEAT THE HELL OUT OF SOMEONE YOU LOVE. Another is: IF YOU LOVE SOMETHING, SET IT FREE. IF IT DOESN'T COME BACK, TRACK IT DOWN AND KILL IT. I once heard a legislator order a lobbyist, "Get me two sweathogs for tonight." At a benefit "roast" for the battered women's shelter in El Paso early in 1985, a couple of the male politicians told rape jokes to amuse the crowd. Most Texas sexism is not intended to be offensive—it's entirely unconscious. A colleague of mine was touring the new death chamber in Huntsville last year with a group of other reporters. Their guide called to warn those inside they were coming through, saying, "I'm coming over with eight reporters and one woman." Stuff like that happens to you four or five times a day for long enough, it will wear you down some.

Other forms of the phenomenon are, of course, less delightsome. Women everywhere are victims of violence with depressing regularity. Texas is a more violent place than most of the rest of America, for reasons having to do with guns, machismo, frontier traditions, and the heterogeneous population. While the law theoretically applies to male and female alike, by unspoken convention, a man who offs his wife or girlfriend is seldom charged with murder one: we wind up filed under the misnomer manslaughter.

That's the bad news for Texas women—the good news is that all this adversity has certainly made us a bodacious bunch of overcomers. And rather pleasant as a group, I always think, since having a sense of humor about men is not a luxury here; it's a necessity. The feminists often carry on about the importance of role models and how little girls need positive role models. When I was a kid, my choice of Texas role models went from Ma Ferguson to the Kilgore Rangerettes. Of course I wanted to be a Rangerette: Ever seen a picture of Ma? Not that we haven't got real women heroes, of course, just that we were never taught anything about them. You used to have to take Texas history two or three times in order to get a high school diploma in this state: The Yellow Rose of Texas and Belle Starr were the only women in our history books. Kaye Northcott notes that all the big cities in the state have men's last names—Houston, Austin, Dallas. All women got was some small towns called after their front names: Alice, Electra, Marfa. This is probably because, as Eleanor Brackenridge of San Antonio (1837–1924) so elegantly put it, "Foolish modesty lags behind while brazen impudence goes forth and eats the pudding." Brackenridge did her part to correct the lag by founding the Texas Woman Suffrage Association in 1913.

It is astonishing how recently Texas women have achieved equal legal rights. I guess you could say we made steady progress even before we could vote—the state did raise the age of consent for a woman from 7 to 10 in 1890—but it went a little smoother after we got some say in it. Until June 26, 1918, all Texans could vote except "idiots, imbeciles, aliens, the insane and women." The battle over woman's suffrage in Texas was long and fierce. Contempt and ridicule were the favored weapons against women. Women earned the right to vote through years of struggle; the precious victory was not something handed to us by generous men. From that struggle emerged a generation of Texas women whose political skills and leadership abilities have affected Texas politics for decades. Even so, Texas women were not permitted to serve on juries until 1954. As late as 1969, married women did not have full property rights. And until 1972, under Article 1220 of the Texas Penal Code, a man could murder his wife and her lover if he found them "in a compromising position" and get away with it as "justifiable homicide." Women, you understand, did not have equal shooting rights. Although Texas was one of the first states to ratify the Equal Rights Amendment, which has been part of the Texas Constitution since 1972, we continue to work for fairer laws concerning problems such as divorce, rape, child custody, and access to credit.

Texas women are just as divided by race, class, age, and educational level as are other varieties of human beings. There's a pat description of "what every Texas woman wants" that varies a bit from city to city, but the formula that Dallas females have been labeled with goes something like this: "Be a Pi Phi at Texas or SMU, marry a man who'll buy you a house in Highland Park, hold the wedding at Highland Park Methodist (flowers by Kendall Bailey), join the Junior League, send the kids to St. Mark's and Hockaday in the winter and Camps Longhorn and Waldemar in the summer, plus cotillion lessons at the Dallas Country Club, have an unlimited charge account at Neiman's as a birthright but buy almost all your clothes at Highland Park Village from Harold's or the Polo Shop, get your hair done at Paul Neinast's or Lou's and drive a Jeep Wagoneer for carpooling and a Mercedes for fun." There is a kicker equivalent of this scenario that starts, "Every Texas girl's dream is a double-wide in a Lubbock trailer park. . . ." But I personally believe it is unwise ever to be funny at the expense of kicker women. I once met a kicker lady who was wearing a blouse of such a vivid pink you could close your eyes and still see the color; this confection was perked up with some big rhinestone buttons and a lot of ruffles across an impressive bosom. "My," said I, "where did you get that blouse?" She gave me a level look and drawled. "Honey, it come from mah coutouri-ay, Jay Cee Penn-ay." And if that ain't class, you *can* kiss my grits.

To my partisan eye, it seems that Texas women are more animated and friendly than those from, say, Nebraska. I suspect this comes from early training: Girls in Texas high schools are expected to walk through the halls smiling and saying "Hi" to everyone they meet. Being enthusiastic is bred into us, as is a certain amount of obligatory social hypocrisy stemming from the Southern tradition of manners, which does rather tend to emphasize pleasantness more than honesty in social situations. Many Texas women have an odd greeting call—when they haven't seen a good friend for a long time, the first glimpse will provoke the cry, "Oooooooo—honey, how good to see yew again!" It sounds sort of like the "Soooooey, pig" call.

Mostly Texas women are tough in some very fundamental ways. Not unfeminine, nor necessarily unladylike, just tough. It may be possible for a little girl to grow to womanhood in this state entirely sheltered from the rampant sexism all around her—but it's damned difficult. The result is that Texas women tend to know how to cope. We can cope with put-downs and come-ons, with preachers and hustlers, with drunks and cowboys. And when it's all over, if we stick together and work, we'll come out better than the sister who's buried in a grave near Marble Falls under a stone that says, "Rudolph Richter, 1822–1915, and Wife."

Texas Celebrates, 1986

ASPECTS OF WRITING: Storytelling.

It is a cliché to say that you should write about what you know, but it is also true. The effectiveness of Molly Ivens's essay lies in part in the fact that she is a Texan woman herself; she *feels* what she writes. This does not mean, however, that writers should only write about people just like themselves. Most people's experience brings them into contact with many different kinds of people, and, if we are interested and observant, we can learn about them—how they speak and act, what they say and do, and something of their personal histories, perhaps. All such observations help shape our own view of the world and of ourselves and are part of "what we know." Because so much or what we know about the world is shared information—common knowledge—it becomes potentially useful for comedy and storytelling of all kinds. The reader often enjoy stories the best when there is a shock of recognition, a sense that what is being said is true in the reader's experience or frame of reference. A joke or story beyond the experience or frame of reference of the reader is not likely to be found funny or to be understood.

Garrison Keillor's Lake Wobegon stories have a very particular setting, but many of the situations described are within virtually everyone's experience, as in the following extract taken from a story called "School." Writing about a particular place does not necessarily make the story less universal in significance or interest. The skill of the storyteller lies in his ability to convey how children think and what they think is funny. The humor is in the details and in the capturing of the divide between the child's view of the world and the teacher's.

> On the way home, we sang with special enthusiasm,
>
> On top of old Smoky, two thousand feet tall,
> I shot my old teacher with a big booger ball.
> I shot her with glory, I shot her with pride.
> How could I miss her? She's thirty feet wide.
>
> I liked Mrs. Meiers a lot, though, She was a plump lady with bags of fat on her arms that danced when she wrote on the board: we named them Hoppy and Bob. That gave her a good mark for friendliness in my book, whereas Miss Conway of fourth grade struck me as suspiciously thin. What was her problem? Nerves, I suppose. She bit her lips and squinted and snaked her skinny hand into her dress to shore up a strap, and she was easily startled by loud noises. Two or three times a day, Paul or Jim or Lance would let go with a book, dropping it flat for max-

imum whack, and yell, "Sorry, Miss Conway!" as the poor woman jerked like a fish on the line. It could be done by slamming a door or dropping the window, too, or even scraping a chair, and once a loud slam made *her* drop a stack of books, which gave us a double jerk. It worked better if we were very quiet before the noise. Often, the class would be so quiet, our little heads bent over our work, that she would look up and congratulate us on our excellent behavior, and when she looked back down at her book, *wham!* and she did the best jerk we had ever seen. There were five classes of spasms: The Jerk, The Jump, The High Jump, The Pants Jump, and The Loopdeloop, and we knew when she was prime for a big one. It was after we had put her through a hard morning workout, including several good jumps, and a noisy lunch period, and she had lectured us in her thin weepy voice, then we knew she was all wound up for the Loopdeloop. All it required was an extra effort: *throwing* a dictionary flat at the floor or dropping the globe, which sounded like a car crash.

We thought about possibly driving Miss Conway to a nervous breakdown, an event we were curious about because our mothers spoke of it often. "You're driving me to a nervous breakdown!" they'd yell, but then, to prevent one, they'd grab us and shake us silly. Miss Conway seemed a better candidate. We speculated about what a breakdown might include—some good jumps for sure, maybe a couple hundred, and talking gibberish with spit running down her chin.

Miss Conway's nervous breakdown was prevented by Mrs. Meiers, who got wind of it from one of the girls—Darla, I think. Mrs. Meiers sat us boys down after lunch period and said that if she heard any more loud noises from Room 4, she would keep us after school for a half hour. "Why not the girls?" Lance asked. "Because I know that you boys can accept responsibility," Mrs. Meiers said. And that was the end of the jumps, except for one accidental jump when a leg gave way under the table that held Mr. Bugs the rabbit in his big cage. Miss Conway screamed and left the room, Mrs. Meiers stalked in, and we boys sat in Room 3 from 3:00 to 3:45 with our hands folded on our desks, and remembered that last Loopdeloop, how satisfying it was, and also how sad it was, being the last. Miss Conway had made some great jumps.

From Garrison Keillor, *Lake Wobegon Days.*
New York: Viking, 1985: 173–174.

WRITING AND RESEARCH: Answer one of the following questions. Make sure that your essay is properly documented.

As discussed in Unit Four, Option One, **synthesis** involves the pulling together of disparate sources to create a coherent discussion. *Certain patterns of in-text citation suggest whether or not this has been achieved:* if each paragraph contains a single in-text citation, appearing at the end, this is not a good sign, because it suggests a "cut-and-paste" kind of summary. On the other hand, if each paragraph (or, more realistically, at least the occasional paragraph) contains more than one in-text citation, and from different sources, this is a good sign, because it suggests that you have found common ground between two or more of your sources and have been able to bring them into your discussion. **A true synthesis draws on sources whenever they are relevant to *your* discussion; it does not merely paraphrase successive people's views.**

1. Many books and movies are reviewed in the newspapers and critiqued in academic publications. Find reviews and critiques of a comedy or humorous work familiar to you, and describe what two or three critics say about this work. Try to make this a synthesis rather than just a series of summaries. (See opposite.)
2. Discuss what Molly Ivens says about women in Texas (and about Texas), consider aspects of her account that could be generalized to the national level, and introduce other authors of your choice who also comment on the position of women within American culture. You may use these other writers to support any position you wish to take vis-à-vis Ivens.
3. Describe and discuss the form of three types of humor that you enjoy, making sure that you refer to some literature on the subject. Include definitions and examples.

OPTION TWO

TALKING ABOUT LANGUAGE.

Among the most famous essays on the use and abuse of English is George Orwell's "Politics and the English Language" (1946), which is reproduced below. It contains some excellent advice to writers. Orwell (1903–1950) is the author of *Animal Farm, 1984, Burmese Days, The Road to Wigan Pier,* and more. This essay comes from *In Front of Your Nose 1945–1950. The Collected Essays, Journalism and Letters of George Orwell, Vol. IV.* Eds. Sonia Orwell and Ian Angus. New York: Harcourt, Brace & World, 1968: 127–140.

Politics and the English Language

Most people who bother with the matter at all would admit that the English language is in a bad way, but it is generally assumed that we cannot by conscious action do anything about it. Our civilisation is decadent, and our language—so the argument runs—must inevitably share in the general collapse. It follows that any struggle against the abuse of language is a sentimental archaism, like preferring candles to electric light or hansom cabs to aeroplanes. Underneath this lies the half-conscious belief that language is a natural growth and not an instrument which we shape for our own purposes.

Now, it is clear that the decline of a language must ultimately have political and economic causes: it is not due simply to the bad influence of this or that individual writer. But an effect can become a cause, reinforcing the original cause and producing the same effect in an intensified form, and so on indefinitely. A man may take to drink because he feels himself to be a failure, and then fail all the more completely because he drinks. It is rather the same thing that is happening to the English language. It becomes ugly and inaccurate because our thoughts are foolish, but the slovenliness of our language makes it easier for us to have foolish thoughts. The point is that the process is reversible. Modern English, especially written English, is full of bad habits which spread by imitation and which can be avoided if one is willing to take the necessary trouble. If one gets rid of these habits one can think more clearly, and to think clearly is a necessary first step towards political regeneration: so that the fight against bad English is not frivolous and is not the exclusive concern of professional writers. I will come back to this presently, and I hope that by that time the meaning of what I have said here will have become clearer. Meanwhile, here are five specimens of the English language as it is now habitually written.

These five passages have not been picked out because they are especially bad—I could have quoted far worse if I had chosen—but because they illustrate various of the mental vices from which we now suffer. They are a little below the average, but are fairly representative samples. I number them so that I can refer back to them when necessary:

> 1. I am not, indeed, sure whether it is not true to say that the Milton who once seemed not unlike a seventeenth-century Shelley had not become, out of an experience ever more bitter in each year, more alien (sic) to the founder of that Jesuit sect which nothing could induce him to tolerate.
>
> Professor Harold Laski (Essay in *Freedom of Expression*).
>
> 2. Above all, we cannot play ducks and drakes with a native battery of idioms which prescribes such egregious collocations of vocables as the Basic *put up with* for *tolerate* or *put at a loss* for *bewilder.*
>
> Professor Lancelot Hogben *(Interglossa).*
>
> 3. On the one side we have the free personality: by definition it is not neurotic, for it has neither conflict nor dream. Its desires, such as they are, are transparent, for they are just what institutional approval keeps in the forefront of consciousness; another institutional pattern would alter their number and intensity; there is little in them that is natural, irreducible, or culturally dangerous. But *on the other side,* the social bond itself is nothing but the mutual reflection of these self-secure integrities. Recall the definition of love. Is not this the very picture of a small academic? Where is there a place in this hall of mirrors for either personality or fraternity?
>
> Essay on psychology in *Politics* (New York).
>
> 4. All the "best people" from the gentlemen's clubs, and all the frantic Fascist captains, united in common hatred of Socialism and bestial horror of the rising tide of the mass revolutionary movement, have turned to acts of provocation, to foul incendiarism, to medieval legends of poisoned wells, to legalise their own destruction to proletarian organisations, and rouse the agitated petty-bourgeoisie to chauvinistic fervour on behalf of the fight against the revolutionary way out of the crisis.
>
> Communist pamphlet.
>
> 5. If a new spirit *is* to be infused into this old country, there is one thorny and contentious reform which must be tackled, and that is the humanisation and galvanisation of the BBC. Timidity here will bespeak canker and atrophy of the soul. The heart of Britain may be sound and of strong beat, for instance, but the British lion's roar at present is like

> that of Bottom in Shakespeare's *Midsummer Night's Dream*—as gentle as any sucking dove. A virile new Britain cannot continue indefinitely to be traduced in the eyes, or rather ears, of the world by the effete languors of Langham Place, brazenly masquerading as "standard English". When the Voice of Britain is heard at nine o'clock, better far and infinitely less ludicrous to hear aitches honestly dropped than the present priggish, inflated, inhibited, school-ma'amish arch braying of blameless bashful mewing maidens!
>
> Letter in *Tribune*.

Each of these passages has faults of its own, but, quite apart from avoidable ugliness, two qualities are common to all of them. The first is staleness of imagery: the other is lack of precision. The writer either has a meaning and cannot express it, or he inadvertently says something else, or he is almost indifferent as to whether his words mean anything or not. This mixture of vagueness and sheer incompetence is the most marked characteristic of modern English prose, and especially of any kind of political writing. As soon as certain topics are raised, the concrete melts into the abstract and no one seems able to think of turns of speech that are not hackneyed: prose consists less and less of *words* chosen for the sake of their meaning, and more of *phrases* tacked together like the sections of a prefabricated hen-house. I list below, with notes and examples, various of the tricks by means of which the work of prose construction is habitually dodged:

Dying metaphors. A newly invented metaphor assists thought by evoking a visual image, while on the other hand a metaphor which is technically "dead" (e.g. *iron resolution*) has in effect reverted to being an ordinary word and can generally be used without loss of vividness. But in between these two classes there is a huge dump of worn-out metaphors which have lost all evocative power and are merely used because they save people the trouble of inventing phrases for themselves. Examples are: *Ring the changes on, take up the cudgels for, toe the line, ride roughshod over, stand shoulder to shoulder with, play into the hands of, no axe to grind, grist to the mill, fishing in troubled waters, rift within the lute, on the order of the day, Achilles' heel, swan song, hotbed*. Many of these are used without knowledge of their meaning (what is a "rift", for instance?), and incompatible metaphors are frequently mixed, a sure sign that the writer is not interested in what he is saying. Some metaphors now current have been twisted out of their original meaning without those who use them even being aware of the fact. For example, *toe the line* is sometimes written *tow the line*. Another example is *the hammer and the anvil*, now always used with the implication that the anvil gets the worst of it. In real life it is always the anvil that breaks the hammer, never the other way about: a writer who stopped to think what he was saying would be aware of this, and would avoid perverting the original phrase.

Operators, or verbal false limbs. These save the trouble of picking out appropriate verbs and nouns, and at the same time pad each sentence with extra syllables which give it an appearance of symmetry. Characteristic phrases are: *render inoperative, militate against, prove unacceptable, make contact with, be subjected to, give rise to, give grounds for, have the effect of, play a leading part (rôle) in, make itself felt, take effect, exhibit a tendency to, serve the purpose of,* etc etc. The keynote is the elimination of simple verbs. Instead of being a single word, such as *break, stop, spoil, mend, kill,* a verb becomes a *phrase,* made up of a noun or adjective tacked on to some general-purposes verb such as *prove, serve, form, play, render.* In addition, the passive voice is wherever possible used in preference to the active, and noun constructions are used instead of gerunds (*by examination of* instead of *by examining*). The range of verbs is further cut down by means of the *-ise* and *de-* formations, and banal statements are given an appearance of profundity by means of the *not un-* formation. Simple conjunctions and prepositions are replaced by such phrases as *with respect to, having regard to, the fact that, by dint of, in view of, in the interests of, on the hypothesis that;* and the ends of sentences are saved from anticlimax by such resounding commonplaces as *greatly to be desired, cannot be left out of account, a development to be expected in the near future, deserving of serious consideration, brought to a satisfactory conclusion,* and so on and so forth.

Pretentious diction. Words like *phenomenon, element, individual* (as noun), *objective, categorical, effective, virtual, basic, primary, promote, constitute, exhibit, exploit, utilise, eliminate, liquidate,* are used to dress up simple statements and give an air of scientific impartiality to biassed judgements. Adjectives like *epoch-making, epic, historic, unforgettable, triumphant, age-old, inevitable, inexorable, veritable,* are used to dignify the sordid processes of international politics, while writing that aims at glorifying war usually takes on an archaic colour, its characteristic words being: *realm, throne, chariot, mailed fist, trident, sword, shield, buckler, banner, jackboot, clarion.* Foreign words and expressions such as *cul de sac, ancien régime, deus ex machina, mutatis mutandis, status quo, Gleichschaltung, Weltanschauung,* are used to give an air of culture and elegance. Except for the useful abbreviations *i.e., e.g.,* and *etc,* there is no real need for any of the hundreds of foreign phrases now current in English. Bad writers, and especially scientific, political and sociological writers, are nearly always haunted by the notion that Latin or Greek words are grander than Saxon ones, and unnecessary words like *expedite, ameliorate, predict, extraneous, deracinated, clandestine, sub-aqueous* and hundreds of others régime claim that it is a democracy, and fear that they might have to stop using the word if it were tied down to any one meaning. Words of this kind are often used in a consciously dishonest way. That is, the person who uses them has his own private definition, but allows his hearer to think he means something quite different. Statements like *Marshal Pétain was a true patriot*, *The Soviet press is the freest in the world*, *The Catholic Church is opposed to persecution*, are almost always made with intent to deceive. Other words used in variable meanings, in most cases more or less dishonestly, are: *class, totalitarian, science, progressive, reactionary, bourgeois, equality*.

Now that I have made this catalogue of swindles and perversions, let me give another example of the kind of writing that they lead to. This time it must of its nature be an imaginary one. I am going to translate a passage of good English into modern English of the worst sort. Here is a well-known verse from *Ecclesiastes*:

> I returned, and saw under the sun, that the race is not to the swift, nor the battle to the strong, neither yet bread to the wise, nor yet riches to men of understanding, nor yet favour to men of skill; but time and chance happeneth to them all.

Here it is in modern English:

> Objective consideration of contemporary phenomena compels the conclusion that success or failure in competitive activities exhibits no tendency to be commensurate with innate capacity, but that a considerable element of the unpredictable must invariably be taken into account.

This is a parody, but not a very gross one. Exhibit 3, above, for instance, contains several patches of the same kind of English. It will be seen that I have not made a full translation. The beginning and ending of the sentence follow the original meaning fairly closely, but in the middle the concrete illustrations—race, battle, bread—dissolve into the vague phrase "success or failure in competitive activities". This had to be so, because no modern writer of the kind I am discussing—no one capable of using phrases like "objective consideration of contemporary phenomena"—would ever tabulate his thoughts in that precise and detailed way. The whole tendency of modern prose is away from concreteness. Now analyse these two sentences a little more closely. The first contains 49 words but only 60 syllables, and all its words are those of everyday life. The second contains 38 words of 90 syllables: 18 of its words are from Latin roots, and one from Greek. The first sentence contains six vivid images, and only one phrase ("time and chance") that could be called vague. The second contains not a single fresh, arresting phrase, and in spite of its 90 syllables it gives only a shortened version of the meaning contained in the first. Yet without a doubt it is the second kind of sentence that is gaining constantly gain ground from their Anglo-Saxon opposite numbers.[1] The jargon peculiar to Marxist writing (*hyena, hangman, cannibal, petty bourgeois, these gentry, lacquey, flunkey, mad dog,* White *Guard,* etc) consists largely of words and phrases translated from Russian, German or French; but the normal way of coining a new word is to use a Latin or Greek root with the appropriate affix and, where necessary, the *-ise* formation. It is often easier to make up words of this kind (*deregionalise, impermissible, extramarital, non-fragmentatory* and so forth) than to think up the English words that will cover one's meaning. The result, in general, is an increase in slovenliness and vagueness.

Meaningless words. In certain kinds of writing, particularly in art criticism and literary criticism, it is normal to come across long passages which are almost completely lacking in meaning.[2] Words like *romantic, plastic, values, human, dead, sentimental, natural, vitality,* as used in art criticism, are strictly meaningless, in the sense that they not only do not point to any discoverable object, but are hardly even expected to do so by the reader. When one critic writes, "The outstanding features of Mr X's work is its living quality", while another writes, "The immediately striking thing about Mr X's work is its peculiar deadness", the reader accepts this as a simple difference of opinion. If words like *black* and *white* were involved, instead of the jargon words *dead* and *living,* he would see at once that language was being used in an improper way. Many political words are similarly abused. The word F*ascism* has now no meaning except in so far as it signifies "something not desirable". The words *democracy, socialism, freedom, patriotic, realistic, justice,* have each of them several different meanings which cannot be reconciled with one another. In the case of a word like *democracy,* not only is there no agreed definition, but the attempt to make one is resisted from all sides. It is almost universally felt that when we call a country democratic we are praising it: consequently the defenders of every kind of

[1]An interesting illustration of this is the way in which the English flower nar which were in use till very recently are being ousted by Greek ones, *snapd* becoming *antirrhinum, forget-me-not* becoming *myosotis,* etc. It is hard to see any cal reason for this change of fashion: it is probably due to an instinctive away from the more homely word and a vague feeling that the Greek wor tific. [Author's footnote.]

[2]Example: "Comfort's catholicity of perception and image, strangely range, almost the exact opposite in aesthetic compulsion, cont trembling atmospheric accumulative hinting at a cruel, an inexc ness . . . Wrey Gardiner scores by aiming at simple bullseyes are not so simple, and through this contented sadness runs ter-sweet of resignation." (*Poetry Quarterly.*) [Author's footnote.]

régime claim that it is a democracy, and fear that they might have to stop using the word if it were tied down to any one meaning. Words of this kind are often used in a consciously dishonest way. That is, the person who uses them has his own private definition, but allows his hearer to think he means something quite different. Statements like *Marshal Pétain was a true patriot, The Soviet press is the freest in the world, The Catholic Church is opposed to persecution*, are almost always made with intent to deceive. Other words used in variable meanings, in most cases more or less dishonestly, are: *class, totalitarian, science, progressive, reactionary, bourgeois, equality*.

Now that I have made this catalogue of swindles and perversions, let me give another example of the kind of writing that they lead to. This time it must of its nature be an imaginary one. I am going to translate a passage of good English into modern English of the worst sort. Here is a well-known verse from *Ecclesiastes*:

> I returned, and saw under the sun, that the race is not to the swift, nor the battle to the strong, neither yet bread to the wise, nor yet riches to men of understanding, nor yet favour to men of skill; but time and chance happeneth to them all.

Here it is in modern English:

> Objective consideration of contemporary phenomena compels the conclusion that success or failure in competitive activities exhibits no tendency to be commensurate with innate capacity, but that a considerable element of the unpredictable must invariably be taken into account.

This is a parody, but not a very gross one. Exhibit 3, above, for instance, contains several patches of the same kind of English. It will be seen that I have not made a full translation. The beginning and ending of the sentence follow the original meaning fairly closely, but in the middle the concrete illustrations—race, battle, bread—dissolve into the vague phrase "success or failure in competitive activities". This had to be so, because no modern writer of the kind I am discussing—no one capable of using phrases like "objective consideration of contemporary phenomena"—would ever tabulate his thoughts in that precise and detailed way. The whole tendency of modern prose is away from concreteness. Now analyse these two sentences a little more closely. The first contains 49 words but only 60 syllables, and all its words are those of everyday life. The second contains 38 words of 90 syllables: 18 of its words are from Latin roots, and one from Greek. The first sentence contains six vivid images, and only one phrase ("time and chance") that could be called vague. The second contains not a single fresh, arresting phrase, and in spite of its 90 syllables it gives only a shortened version of the meaning contained in the first. Yet without a doubt it is the second kind of sentence that is gaining constantly gain ground from their Anglo-Saxon opposite numbers.[1] The jargon peculiar to Marxist writing (*hyena, hangman, cannibal, petty bourgeois, these gentry, lacquey, flunkey, mad dog, White Guard,* etc) consists largely of words and phrases translated from Russian, German or French; but the normal way of coining a new word is to use a Latin or Greek root with the appropriate affix and, where necessary, the *-ise* formation. It is often easier to make up words of this kind (*deregionalise, impermissible, extramarital, non-fragmentatory* and so forth) than to think up the English words that will cover one's meaning. The result, in general, is an increase in slovenliness and vagueness.

Meaningless words. In certain kinds of writing, particularly in art criticism and literary criticism, it is normal to come across long passages which are almost completely lacking in meaning.[2] Words like *romantic, plastic, values, human, dead, sentimental, natural, vitality,* as used in art criticism, are strictly meaningless, in the sense that they not only do not point to any discoverable object, but are hardly even expected to do so by the reader. When one critic writes, "The outstanding features of Mr X's work is its living quality", while another writes, "The immediately striking thing about Mr X's work is its peculiar deadness", the reader accepts this as a simple difference of opinion. If words like *black* and *white* were involved, instead of the jargon words *dead* and *living,* he would see at once that language was being used in an improper way. Many political words are similarly abused. The word *Fascism* has now no meaning except in so far as it signifies "something not desirable". The words *democracy, socialism, freedom, patriotic, realistic, justice,* have each of them several different meanings which cannot be reconciled with one another. In the case of a word like *democracy,* not only is there no agreed definition, but the attempt to make one is resisted from all sides. It is almost universally felt that when we call a country democratic we are praising it: consequently the defenders of every kind of

[1]An interesting illustration of this is the way in which the English flower names which were in use till very recently are being ousted by Greek ones, *snapdragon* becoming *antirrhinum, forget-me-not* becoming *myosotis,* etc. It is hard to see any practical reason for this change of fashion: it is probably due to an instinctive turning-away from the more homely word and a vague feeling that the Greek word is scientific. [Author's footnote.]

[2]Example: "Comfort's catholicity of perception and image, strangely Whitmanesque in range, almost the exact opposite in aesthetic compulsion, continues to evoke that trembling atmospheric accumulative hinting at a cruel, an inexorably serene timelessness . . . Wrey Gardiner scores by aiming at simple bullseyes with precision. Only they are not so simple, and through this contented sadness runs more than the surface bitter-sweet of resignation." (*Poetry Quarterly.*) [Author's footnote.]

ground in modern English. I do not want to exaggerate. This kind of writing is not yet universal, and outcrops of simplicity will occur here and there in the worst-written page. Still, if you or I were told to write a few lines on the uncertainty of human fortunes, we should probably come much nearer to my imaginary sentence than to the one from *Ecclesiastes*.

As I have tried to show, modern writing at its worst does not consist in picking out words for the sake of their meaning and inventing images in order to make the meaning clearer. It consists in gumming together long strips of words which have already been set in order by someone else, and making the results presentable by sheer humbug. The attraction of this way of writing is that it is easy. It is easier—even quicker, once you have the habit—to say *In my opinion it is a not unjustifiable assumption that* than to say *I think*. If you use ready-made phrases, you not only don't have to hunt about for words; you also don't have to bother with the rhythms of your sentences, since these phrases are generally so arranged as to be more or less euphonious. When you are composing in a hurry—when you are dictating to a stenographer, for instance, or making a public speech—it is natural to fall into a pretentious, latinised style. Tags like *a consideration which we should do well to bear in mind* or *a conclusion to which all of us would readily assent* will save many a sentence from coming down with a bump. By using stale metaphors, similes and idioms, you save much mental effort, at the cost of leaving your meaning vague, not only for your reader but for yourself. This is the significance of mixed metaphors. The sole aim of a metaphor is to call up a visual image. When these images clash—as in *The Fascist octopus has sung its swan song, the jackboot is thrown into the melting-pot*—it can be taken as certain that the writer is not seeing a mental image of the objects he is naming; in other words he is not really thinking. Look again at the examples I gave at the beginning of this essay. Professor Laski (1) uses five negatives in 53 words. One of these is superfluous, making nonsense of the whole passage, and in addition there is the slip *alien* for akin, making further nonsense, and several avoidable pieces of clumsiness which increase the general vagueness. Professor Hogben (2) plays ducks and drakes with a battery which is able to write prescriptions, and, while disapproving of the everyday phrase *put up with*, is unwilling to look *egregious* up in the dictionary and see what it means. (3), if one takes an uncharitable attitude towards it, is simply meaningless: probably one could work out its intended meaning by reading the whole of the article in which it occurs. In (4) the writer knows more or less what he wants to say, but an accumulation of stale phrases chokes him like tea-leaves blocking a sink. In (5) words and meaning have almost parted company. People who write in this manner usually have a general emotional meaning—they dislike one thing and want to express solidarity with another—

but they are not interested in the detail of what they are saying. A scrupulous writer, in every sentence that he writes, will ask himself at least four questions, thus: What am I trying to say? What words will express it? What image or idiom will make it clearer? Is this image fresh enough to have an effect? And he will probably ask himself two more: Could I put it more shortly? Have I said anything that is avoidably ugly? But you are not obliged to go to all this trouble. You can shirk it by simply throwing your mind open and letting the ready-made phrases come crowding in. They will construct your sentences for you—even think your thoughts for you, to a certain extent—and at need they will perform the important service of partially concealing your meaning even from yourself. It is at this point that the special connection between politics and the debasement of language becomes clear.

In our time it is broadly true that political writing is bad writing. Where it is not true, it will generally be found that the writer is some kind of rebel, expressing his private opinions, and not a "party line". Orthodoxy, of whatever colour, seems to demand a lifeless, imitative style. The political dialects to be found in pamphlets, leading articles, manifestos, White Papers and the speeches of Under-Secretaries do, of course, vary from party to party, but they are all alike in that one almost never finds in them a fresh, vivid, home-made turn of speech. When one watches some tired hack on the platform mechanically repeating the familiar phrases—*bestial atrocities, iron heel, blood-stained tyranny, free peoples of the world, stand shoulder to shoulder*—one often has a curious feeling that one is not watching a live human being but some kind of dummy: a feeling which suddenly becomes stronger at moments when the light catches the speaker's spectacles and turns them into blank discs which seem to have no eyes behind them. And this is not altogether fanciful. A speaker who uses that kind of phraseology has gone some distance towards turning himself into a machine. The appropriate noises are coming out of his larynx, but his brain is not involved as it would be if he were choosing his words for himself. If the speech he is making is one that he is accustomed to make over and over again, he may be almost unconscious of what he is saying, as one is when one utters the responses in church. And this reduced state of consciousness, if not indispensable, is at any rate favourable to political conformity.

In our time, political speech and writing are largely the defence of the indefensible. Things like the continuance of British rule in India, the Russian purges and deportations, the dropping of the atom bombs on Japan, can indeed be defended, but only by arguments which are too brutal for most people to face, and which do not square with the professed aims of political parties. Thus political language has to consist largely of euphemism, question-begging and sheer cloudy vagueness. Defenceless villages are bombarded from the air, the inhabitants driven out into the countryside, the cattle machine-gunned, the huts set on fire with incendiary bullets: this is called *pacification*. Millions of peasants are robbed of their farms and sent trudging along the roads with no more than they can carry: this is called *transfer of population* or *rectification of frontiers*. People are imprisoned for years without trial, or shot in the back of the neck or sent to die of scurvy in Arctic lumber camps: this is called *elimination of unreliable elements*. Such phraseology is needed if one wants to name things without calling up mental pictures of them. Consider for instance some comfortable English professor defending Russian totalitarianism. He cannot say outright, "I believe in killing off your opponents when you can get good results by doing so". Probably, therefore, he will say something like this:

> While freely conceding that the Soviet régime exhibits certain features which the humanitarian may be inclined to deplore, we must, I think, agree that a certain curtailment of the right to political opposition is an unavoidable concomitant of transitional periods, and that the rigours which the Russian people have been called upon to undergo have been amply justified in the sphere of concrete achievement.

The inflated style is itself a kind of euphemism. A mass of Latin words falls upon the facts like soft snow, blurring the outlines and covering up all the details. The great enemy of clear language is insincerity. When there is a gap between one's real and one's declared aims, one turns as it were instinctively to long words and exhausted idioms, like a cuttlefish squirting out ink. In our age there is no such thing as "keeping out of politics". All issues are political issues, and politics itself is a mass of lies, evasions, folly, hatred and schizophrenia. When the general atmosphere is bad, language must suffer. I should expect to find—this is a guess which I have not sufficient knowledge to verify—that the German, Russian and Italian languages have all deteriorated in the last ten or fifteen years, as a result of dictatorship.

But if thought corrupts language, language can also corrupt thought. A bad usage can spread by tradition and imitation, even among people who should and do know better. The debased language that I have been discussing is in some ways very convenient. Phrases like *a not unjustifiable assumption, leaves much to be desired, would serve no good purpose, a consideration which we should do well to bear in mind*, are a continuous temptation, a packet of aspirins always at one's elbow. Look back through this essay, and for certain you will find that I have again and again committed the very faults I am protesting against. By this morning's post I have received a pamphlet dealing with conditions in Germany. The author tells me that he "felt impelled" to write it. I open it at random, and here is almost the first sentence that I see: "(The Allies) have an opportunity not only of achieving a radical transformation of Germany's social and political structure in such a way as to avoid a nationalistic reaction in Germany itself, but at the same time of laying the foundations of a co-operative and unified Europe." You see, he "feels impelled" to write—feels, presumably, that he has something new to say—and yet his words, like cavalry horses answering the bugle, group themselves automatically into the familiar dreary pattern. This invasion of one's mind by ready-made phrases (*lay the foundations, achieve a radical transformation*) can only be prevented if one is constantly on guard against them, and every such phrase anaesthetises a portion of one's brain.

I said earlier that the decadence of our language is probably curable. Those who deny this would argue, if they produced an argument at all, that language merely reflects existing social conditions, and that we cannot influence its development by any direct tinkering with words and constructions. So far as the general tone or spirit of a language goes, this may be true, but it is not true in detail. Silly words and expressions have often disappeared, not through any evolutionary process but owing to the conscious action of a minority. Two recent examples were *explore every avenue* and *leave no stone unturned*, which were killed by the jeers of a few journalists. There is a long list of fly-blown metaphors which could similarly be got rid of if enough people would interest themselves in the job; and it should also be possible to laugh the *not un-* formation out of existence,[1] to reduce the amount of Latin and Greek in the average sentence, to drive out foreign phrases and strayed scientific words, and, in general, to make pretentiousness unfashionable. But all these are minor points. The defence of the English language implies more than this, and perhaps it is best to start by saying what it does *not* imply.

To begin with, it has nothing to do with archaism, with the salvaging of obsolete words and turns of speech, or with the setting-up of a "standard English" which must never be departed from. On the contrary, it is especially concerned with the scrapping of every word or idiom which has outworn its usefulness. It has nothing to do with correct grammar and syntax, which are of no importance so long as one makes one's meaning clear, or with the avoidance of Americanisms, or with having what is called a "good prose style". On the other hand it is not concerned with fake simplicity and the attempt to make written English colloquial. Nor does it even imply in every case preferring the Saxon word to the Latin one, though it does imply using the fewest and shortest words that will cover one's meaning. What is above all

[1]One can cure oneself of the *not un-* formation by memorising this sentence: A *not unblack dog was chasing a not unsmall rabbit across a not ungreen field*. [Author's footnote.]

needed is to let the meaning choose the word, and not the other way about. In prose, the worst thing one can do with words is to surrender to them. When you think of a concrete object, you think wordlessly, and then, if you want to describe the thing you have been visualising, you probably hunt about till you find the exact words that seem to fit it. When you think of something abstract you are more inclined to use words from the start, and unless you make a conscious effort to prevent it, the existing dialect will come rushing in and do the job for you, at the expense of blurring or even changing your meaning. Probably it is better to put off using words as long as possible and get one's meaning as clear as one can through pictures or sensations. Afterwards one can choose—not simply *accept*—the phrases that will best cover the meaning, and then switch round and decide what impression one's words are likely to make on another person. This last effort of the mind cuts out all stale or mixed images, all prefabricated phrases, needless repetitions, and humbug and vagueness generally. But one can often be in doubt about the effect of a word or a phrase, and one needs rules that one can rely on when instinct fails. I think the following rules will cover most cases:

i. Never use a metaphor, simile or other figure of speech which you are used to seeing in print.

ii. Never use a long word where a short one will do.

iii. If it is possible to cut a word out, always cut it out.

iv. Never use the passive where you can use the active.

v. Never use a foreign phrase, a scientific word or a jargon word if you can think of an everyday English equivalent.

vi. Break any of these rules sooner than say anything outright barbarous.

These rules sound elementary, and so they are, but they demand a deep change of attitude in anyone who has grown used to writing in the style now fashionable. One could keep all of them and still write bad English, but one could not write the kind of stuff that I quoted in those five specimens at the beginning of this article.

I have not here been considering the literary use of language, but merely language as an instrument for expressing and not for concealing or preventing thought. Stuart Chase and others have come near to claiming that all abstract words are meaningless, and have used this as a pretext for advocating a kind of political quietism. Since you don't know what Fascism is, how can you struggle against Fascism? One need not swallow such absurdities as this, but one ought to recognise that the present political chaos is connected with the decay of language, and that one can probably bring about some improvement by starting at the verbal end. If you simplify your English, you are freed from the worst follies of orthodoxy. You cannot speak any of the necessary dialects, and when you make a stupid remark its stupidity will be obvious, even to yourself. Political language—and with variations this is true of all political parties, from Conservatives to Anarchists—is designed to make lies sound truthful and murder respectable, and to give an appearance of solidity to pure wind. One cannot change this all in a moment, but one can at least change one's own habits, and from time to time one can even, if one jeers loudly enough, send some worn-out and useless phrase—some *jackboot, Achilles' heel, hotbed, melting pot, acid test, veritable inferno* or other lump of verbal refuse—into the dustbin where it belongs.

Horizon, April 1946; *Modern British Writing*, ed. Denys Val Baker, 1947; SE; OR; CE

Quick Quiz

Instead of the usual questions, you might enjoy and analyze the following cartoons, which come from or allude to various disciplines.

The word **"comedy"** is derived from the Greek—via Latin, Old French, and Middle English. It comes from *komoidos*, "a singer in the revels."

Calvin and Hobbes **by Bill Watterson**

THE FAR SIDE By GARY LARSON

"**Anthropologists! Anthropologists!**"

Rivero/Clarín/Buenos Aires

Roger L. Welsch, "The Stand-Up Chemist." *Natural History,* November 1994: 34.

Hi O SILVER
Ag is the symbol for silver.

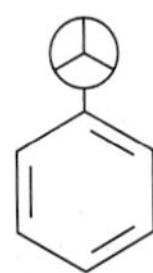

MERCEDES BENZENE
A hexagon with the dashes as shown represents a benzene (C_6H_6) molecule.

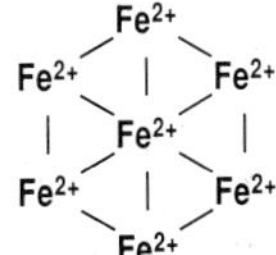

FERRIS WHEEL
Ferrous is the name of Iron in many of its compounds, and Fe^{2+} is the symbol for ferrous iron.

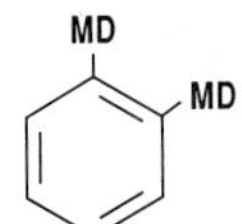

ORTHODOX
Adjacent positions on a benzene ring are said to be "ortho" to each other, and MD is a doctor

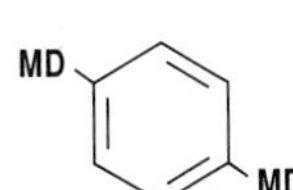

PARADOX
Opposite positions on a benzene ring are said to be "para" to each other.

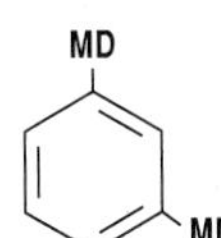

METAPHYSICIANS
Positions that are neither opposite nor adjacent are said to be "meta" to each other.

ACKNOWLEDGMENTS

p. 3 Trefil, James S. From *Space Time Infinity, The Smithsonian Views the Universe* by James S. Trefil, Smithsonian Books. Copyright © 1985 Smithsonian Institution. Used with permission.
p. 8 Hagar the Horrible. Reprinted with special permission of King Features Syndicate.
p. 12 Allman, William F. "The origins of modern humans: Who we were" by William F. Allman in *U.S. News and World Report,* September 16, 1991. Copyright © Sept. 16, 1991, U.S. News & World Report.
p. 19 The Lockhorns. Reprinted with special permission of King Features Syndicate.
p. 24 Boorstin, Daniel J. "The Temptations of the Moon" from *The Discoverers* by Daniel J. Boorstin. Copyright © 1983 by Daniel J. Boorstin. Reprinted by permission of Random House, Inc.
p. 37 Gould, Stephen Jay. "Evolution as Fact and Theory" from *Hen's Teeth and Horse's Toes: Further Reflections in Natural History* by Stephen Jay Gould. Copyright © 1983 by Stephen Jay Gould. Reprinted by permission of W. W. Norton & Company, Inc.
p. 43 World Bank. From *The Development Data Book, Teaching Guide,* 1984. Reprinted by permission of the World Bank.
p. 48 Calvin and Hobbes. Copyright © 1994 Watterson. Dist. by Universal Press Syndicate. Reprinted with permission. All rights reserved.
p. 50 Maps from *Earth's Dynamic Crust.* Copyright © National Geographic Society. Reprinted by permission.
p. 51 Davis, Kenneth C. From *Don't Know Much About Geography* by Kenneth C. Davis. Copyright © 1992 by Kenneth C. Davis. By permission of William Morrow & Company, Inc.
p. 57 New York Times. Excerpt and Map from "Weather Highlight" in the *New York Times,* February 16, 1994. Copyright © 1994 by the New York Times Company. Reprinted by permission.
p. 63 World Bank. "Global manufacturing: The component network for the Ford Escort (Europe)" in *World Development Report 1987.* Used with permission of the World Bank.
p. 64 Makower, Joel. From *The Map Catalog* by Joel Makower. Copyright © 1986 by Joel Makower. Reprinted by permission of Vintage Books, a division of a Random House, Inc.
p. 74 Paringaux, Roland-Pierre. "A Day in the Life of Catherine Bana" by Roland-Pierre Paringaux in *Guardian Weekly (Le Monde Section),* August 20, 1989. Reprinted by permission of Le Monde.
p. 82 Norris, Darrell A. From "Global Interdependence: Learning from Personal Effects" by Darrell A. Norris in *Social Education,* October 1991. Copyright © National Council for the Social Studies. Reprinted by permission.
p. 83 Tuan, Yi-Fu. "A View of Geography" by Yi-Fu Tuan in *The Geographical Review,* Vol. 81, No. 1, January 1991. Reprinted by permission of the American Geographical Society.
p. 98 World Bank. Map from *The Development Databook Teaching Guide, 1995.* Used with permission of the World Bank.
p. 101 Frankel, Glenn. "How Europeans Carved up Africa" by Glenn Frankel, *Guardian Weekly* (Washington Post Section), January 27, 1985. Copyright © 1996, the Washington Post. Reprinted with permission.
p. 109 Associated Press. "Europe's geography and two world wars." Reprinted by permission.
p. 110 Gray, Paul. "The Astonishing 20th Century" by Paul Gray in *Time* (Special Issue) "Beyond the Year 2000," Fall 1992. Copyright © 1992 Time Inc. Reprinted by permission.
p. 119 Kennedy, Paul. From *The Rise and Fall of the Great Powers* by Paul Kennedy. Copyright © 1987 by Paul Kennedy. Reprinted by permission of Random House, Inc.
p. 131 Beatty, Jack. "Along The Western Front" by Jack Beatty. Copyright © 1986 Jack Beatty as first published in the November 1986 issue of the *Atlantic Monthly.* Reprinted by permission.
p. 152 Beetle Bailey. Reprinted with special permission of King Features Syndicate.
p. 155 Lane, Charles. "Let's Abolish the Third World" by Charles Lane in *Newsweek,* April 27, 1992. Copyright © 1992, Newsweek, Inc. All rights reserved. Reprinted by permission.
p. 163 Ollapally, Deepa. "The South Looks North: The Third World in the New World Order" by Deepa Ollapally. Reprinted with permission from *Current History* magazine, April 1993. Copyright © 1993, Current History, Inc.
p. 170 Cartoon. Chappatte/La Tribune de Geneve/Geneva
p. 173 Attenborough, David. From *The Living Planet* by David Attenborough. Copyright © 1979 by David Attenborough Productions Ltd. By permission of Little, Brown and Company and HarperCollins Publishers Ltd.

p. 187 Ryan, Alan. "Twenty-First Century Limited" by Alan Ryan. Reprinted with permission from *The New York Review of Books,* November 19, 1992. Copyright © 1992 Nyrev, Inc.
p. 209 *World Development Report, 1990.* New York: Oxford University Press, 1990.
p. 214 *World Development Report 1994.* New York: Oxford University Press, 1994.
p. 230 Rosenblum, Mort, and Doug Williamson. "Women and Children First" and excerpts from *Squandering Eden, Africa at the Edge.* Copyright © 1987 by Mort Rosenblum and Doug Williamson. Reprinted by permission of Harcourt Brace & Company.
p. 244 *Human Development Report 1993.* New York: Oxford University Press, 1993.
p. 265 Mann, Charles C. "How Many is Too Many?" by Charles C. Mann in *Atlantic Monthly,* February 1993.
p. 278 TOLES. Copyright © the Buffalo News. Reprinted with permission of Universal Press Syndicate. All rights reserved.
p. 280 Cartoon. Illustration reprinted by permission from *Pidgin to da Max.* Copyright © 1986 Peppovision, Inc.
p. 281 Mother Goose and Grimm. Reprinted by permission: Tribune Media Services.
p. 286 Naranjo/El Universal/ Cartoonists & Writers Syndicate. Reprinted by permission.
p. 287 Maxwell, Kenneth. "The Tragedy of the Amazon" by Kenneth Maxwell. Reprinted with permission from *The New York Review of Books,* March 3, 1991. Copyright © 1991 Nyrev, Inc.
p. 306 Illustration. Reprinted by permission of the National Arbor Day Foundation.
p. 307 Adapted from the Swedish Ministry of Agriculture. Acidification: A Boundless Threat to Our Environment (Solna: National Swedish Environment Protection Board, 1983). As appeared in *Environment,* Vol. 29, No. 9:35.
p. 308 Cartoon. Wikborg/Berlingske Tidende.
p. 311 Postel, Sandra. "Denial in the Decisive Decade" by Sandra Postel, from *State of the World 1992: A Worldwatch Institute Report on Progress Toward a Sustainable Society* by Lester R. Brown, et al. Copyright © 1992 by Worldwatch Institute. Reprinted by permission of W. W. Norton & Company, Inc.
p. 323 Goldsmith, James, "The Environment" by James Goldsmith in *Vital Speeches of the Day,* January 15, 1990. Reprinted by permission.
p. 336 Wilson, Edward O. "Million-Year Histories—Species Diversity as an Ethical Goal" by Edward O. Wilson in *Wilderness,* Summer 1984. Based on portions of *Biophilia* by Edward O. Wilson. Reprinted by permission of the publishers from Biophilia by Edward O. Wilson. Cambridge Mass.: Harvard University Press. Copyright © 1984 by the President and Fellows of Harvard College.
p. 353 Calvin and Hobbes. Copyright © 1996 Watterson. Dist. by Universal Press Syndicate. Reprinted with permission. All rights reserved.
p. 354 Plath, Sylvia, "Frog Autumns" from *The Collected Poems of Sylvia Plath,* edited by Ted Hughes. Copyright © 1960, 1965, 1971, 1981 by the Estate of Sylvia Plath. Editorial material copyright © 1981 by Ted Hughes. Reprinted by permission of HarperCollins Publishers, Inc. and Faber and Faber Ltd.
p. 354 Plath, Sylvia. All lines from "Metaphors" from *Crossing the Water* by Sylvia Plath. Copyright © 1960 by Ted Hughes. Copyright Renewed. Reprinted by permission of HarperCollins Publishers, Inc. and Faber and Faber Ltd.
p. 356 New York Times. Graphic, "Family Ties: The International Trend" in the *New York Times,* May 30, 1995. Copyright © 1995 by the New York Times Company. Reprinted by permission.
p. 356 Calvin and Hobbes. Copyright © 1995 Watterson. Dist. by Universal Press Syndicate. Reprinted with permission. All rights reserved.
p. 358 Hatch, Elvin. "A Working Alternative" from *Culture and Morality* by Elvin Hatch. Copyright © 1982 by Columbia University Press. Reprinted with permission of the publisher.
p. 373 Mucha, Janusz L. "An Outsider's View of American Culture" by Janusz L. Mucha as appeared in *Distant Mirrors—America as a Foreign Culture,* edited by Philip R. DeVita and James D. Armstrong, 1993. Reprinted by permission.
p. 386 Jain, Nemi C. "World View and Cultural Patterns of India" by Nemi C. Jain in *Intercultural Comunications: A Reader,* 6e, edited by Larry Samover and Richard Porter. Copyright © 1991 by Nemi C. Jain. Reprinted by permission of the author.
p. 402 Ninan/The Commoner/ Cartoonists & Writers Syndicate. Reprinted by permission.
p. 408 Minogue, Kenneth. "The History of the Idea of Human Rights" by Kenneth Minogue from *The Human Rights Reader,* edited by Walter Laqueur and Barry Rubin. Reprinted by permission of Kenneth Minogue.
p. 427 Kaplan, Robert. From "Cultural Thought Patterns in Inter-Cultural Communication" in *Language Learning,* Vol. XVI, Nos. 1 and 2, 1967. Reprinted by permission.
p. 428 Copyright © 1981 by Houghton Mifflin Company. Reproduced by permission from the *American Heritage Dictionary of the English Language.*
p. 433 Janson, H. W. From "The Artist and His Public" in *History of Art* by H. W. Janson. Englewood Cliffs, N.J.: Prentice-Hall, 1962.
p. 447 Yeats, William Butler. From "The Second Coming." Reprinted with the permission of Simon & Schuster from *The Poems of W. B. Yeats: A New Edition,* edited by

Richard J. Finneran. Copyright © 1924 by Macmillan Publishing Company. Renewed 1952 by Bertha Georgie Yeats.
p. 448 Warren, Robert Penn. "On Reading Fiction" from *New and Selected Essays* by Robert Penn Warren. Copyright © 1989 by Robert Penn Warren. Reprinted by permission of Random House, Inc.
p. 450 Perrin Noel, "Philip Larkin's Greatest Poem" by Noel Perrin. Copyright © 1988 by permission of University Press of New England.
p. 450 Yeats, William Butler. From "The Second Coming." Reprinted with the permission of Simon & Schuster from *The Poems of W. B. Yeats: A New Edition,* edited by Richard J. Finneran. Copyright © 1924 by Macmillan Publishing Company. Renewed 1952 by Bertha Georgie Yeats.
p. 450 Eliot, T. S. Excerpt from "The Hollow Men" in *Collected Poems 1909–1962* by T. S. Eliot, copyright 1936 by Harcourt Brace & Company. Copyright © 1964, 1963 by T. S. Eliot, reprinted by permission of Harcourt Brace & Company and Faber and Faber Ltd.
p. 452 *The Oxford Study Bible.* New York: Oxford University Press, 1992.
p. 452 Larkin, Philip. "Church Going" by Philip Larkin is reprinted from *The Less Deceived* by permission of the Marvell Press, England and Australia.
p. 466 Hoffmann, Roald. "How Should Chemists Think?" by Roald Hoffmann in *Scientific American,* February 1993. Reprinted with permission. Copyright © 1993 by Scientific American, Inc. All rights reserved.
p. 490 Calvin and Hobbes. Copyright © 1995 Watterson. Dist. by Universal Press Syndicate. Reprinted with permission. All rights reserved.
p. 491 Berger, Arthur Asa and Aaron Wildavsky. "Who Laughs at What?" by Arthur Asa Berger and Aaron Wildavsky in *Society,* September/October 1994. Reprinted by permission of Transaction Publishers; all rights reserved.
p. 503 Dalbey, Gordon. "A Jogger Fails to Cross the Culture Gap" by Gordon Dalbey in *Los Angeles Times,* June 4, 1981. Copyright © 1981 Gordon Dalbey. Reprinted by permission of the author.
p. 506 Bohannan, Laura. "Shakespeare in the Bush" by Laura Bohannan in *Natural History,* August/September 1966. Reprinted by permission of the author.
p. 519 Puri/The Statesman/ Cartoonists & Writers Syndicate. Reprinted by permission.
p. 520 De Angelis/II Popolo/ Cartoonists & Writers Syndicate. Reprinted by permission.
p. 521 Nilsen, Alleen Pace. "In Defense of Humor" by Alleen Pace Nilsen in *College English,* December 1994. Copyright 1994 by the National Council of Teachers of English. Reprinted with permission.
p. 523 Cartoon. Reprinted with permission from The Daily Nation of Kenya.
p. 523 Riber/Svenska Dagbladet/ Cartoonists & Writers Syndicate. Reprinted by permission.
p. 523 Heng Kim Song/Singapore.
p. 529 Kakutani, Michiko. "The Word Police" by Michiko Kakutani in the *New York Times,* January 31, 1993. Copyright © 1993 by the New York Times Company. Reprinted by permission.
p. 530 Maggio, Rosalie. From *The Bias-Free Word Finder* by Rosalie Maggio. Copyright © 1991 by Rosalie Maggio. Reprinted by permission of Beacon Press, Boston.
p. 536 Garner, James Finn. "Little Red Riding Hood" is reprinted with permission of Macmillan General Reference USA, a Division of Simon & Schuster, from *Politically Correct Bedtime Stories* by James Finn Garner. Copyright © 1994 by James Finn Garner.
p. 539 Ivins, Molly. "Texas Women: True Grit and All the Rest" from *Molly Ivins Can't Say That, Can She?* by Molly Ivins. Copyright © 1991 by Molly Ivins. Reprinted by permission of Random House, Inc.
p. 544 Keillor, Garrison. From *Lake Wobegon Days* by Garrison Keillor. Copyright © 1985 by Garrison Keillor. Used by permission of Viking Penguin, a division of Penguin Books USA Inc.
p. 547 Orwell, George. "Politics and the English Language" by George Orwell, copyright 1946 by Sonia Brownell Orwell and renewed 1974 by Sonia Orwell, reprinted from his volume *Shooting an Elephant and Other Essays* by permission of Harcourt Brace & Company and the estate of the late Sonia Brownell Orwell and Martin Secker and Warburg Ltd.
p. 559 Calvin and Hobbes. Copyright © 1995 Watterson. Dist. by Universal Press Syndicate. Reprinted with permission. All rights reserved.
p. 559 Larson, Gary. The Far Side cartoon by Gary Larson is reprinted by permission of Chronicle Features, San Francisco, Calif. All rights reserved.
p. 559 With permission from *Natural History,* November 1994. Copyright the American Museum of Natural History 1994.
p. 559 Rivero/Clarin/Buenos Aires.

INDEX

Page numbers followed by *f* indicate figures; by *t* indicate tables; and by *m* indicate marginal notes.